The World Bank

The World Bank
Development, Poverty, Hegemony

Edited by David Moore

UNIVERSITY OF KWAZULU-NATAL PRESS

Published in 2007 by University of KwaZulu-Natal Press
Private Bag X01, Scottsville, 3209
South Africa
Email: books@ukzn.ac.za
Website: www.ukznpress.co.za

© 2007 University of KwaZulu-Natal

All rights reserved. No part of this publication may be reproduced or transmitted in any form or by any means, electronic or mechanical, including photocopying, recording, or any information storage and retrieval system, without prior permission in writing from University of KwaZulu-Natal Press.

ISBN 13: 978-1-86914-100-4

Editors: Mike Kirkwood and Andrea Nattrass
Cover designer: Sebastien Quevauvilliers, Flying Ant Designs
Typesetter: RockBottom Designs
Indexer: Brenda Williams-Wynn

Printed and bound by CTP Book Printers, Cape

Contents

Preface viii
Acknowledgements x
Abbreviations xi

INTRODUCTION
The World Bank and its (Sheepish) Wolves
David Moore 1

CHAPTER ONE
The World Bank and the Gramsci Effect:
Towards a Transnational State and Global Hegemony?
David Moore 27

CHAPTER TWO
Plenty of Poverty or the Poverty of Plenty? The World
Bank at the Turn of the Millennium
Scott MacWilliam 63

CHAPTER THREE
Constructing the Economic Space: The World Bank
and the Making of *Homo Oeconomicus*
David Williams 95

CHAPTER FOUR
The Developmental State is Dead: Long Live Social Capital?
Ben Fine 121

CHAPTER FIVE
The Bank's 'Greenspeak', the Power of Knowledge and
'Sustaindevelopment'
Thomas Wanner 145

CHAPTER SIX
Governing through Participation? The World Bank's New Approach to the Poor
Susanne Schech and Sanjugta vas Dev 171

CHAPTER SEVEN
The World Bank and the Liberal Project
David Williams and Tom Young 203

CHAPTER EIGHT
Sail on Ship of State: Neoliberalism, Globalisation and the Governance of Africa
David Moore 227

CHAPTER NINE
Japan, the World Bank, and the Art of Paradigm Maintenance: *The East Asian Miracle* in Political Perspective
Robert Wade 267

CHAPTER TEN
Miracles of Modernisation and Crises of Capitalism: The World Bank, East Asian Development and Liberal Hegemony
Mark T. Berger and Mark Beeson 317

CHAPTER ELEVEN
Structural Adjustment and African Agriculture: A Retrospect
Henry Bernstein 343

CHAPTER TWELVE
The World Bank and the Construction of Governance States in Africa
Graham Harrison 369

CHAPTER THIRTEEN
Levelling the Playing Fields and Embedding Illusions: 'Post-conflict' Discourse and Neoliberal 'Development' in War-torn Africa
David Moore 387

CHAPTER FOURTEEN
Producing the Poor: The World Bank's New Discourse of Domination
Richard Pithouse 413

CHAPTER FIFTEEN
The King is Dead (Long Live the King?): From Wolfensohn to Wolfowitz at the World Bank
Marcus Taylor and Susanne Soederberg 453

CHAPTER SIXTEEN
Civil Society and Wolfowitz's World Bank: Reform or Rejection?
Patrick Bond 479

Contributors 507
Select Bibliography 513
Index 569

Preface

As the World Bank goes through its sixth decade and opponents continue with the slogan '(however many) years are enough', it is time to gather together the last decade and a half's radical analytical assessments of the world's most visible development institution. They must be assessed and reassessed, and new critiques must be built on the shoulders of the old. This is the intention of this book. Some of the contributions that must be considered classical are reproduced in this volume in their original state, other classics have been revisited by their authors, more are refinements of the trails blazed by the 'originals' in the field, and several are new entrants taking the field of what could be labelled 'World Bank studies' into uncharted territory.

All of the chapters in this volume confront major World Bank documents or intellectual turning points marking significant attempts for the Bank to break new ground in development discourse – to make new efforts to alter the hegemonic contours of the intelligentsia and political actors working on the terrain of the 'Third World's' uneven capitalist transformations, but without challenging the essentials of its project. To the original critical accounts of the trials and tribulations of the Bank, built on historical materialist foundations, more ideational, post-structural, and even philosophical studies have been added – just as the Bank itself has moved from being an institution based in 'economics' to one grabbing on to every other social sector and its 'science'. To make it easy for readers to know whether the chapters are 'original and unchanged', revisited by their authors in the light of this project, or specially commissioned for this book, each chapter is identified within these categories. Hopefully the whole makes up more than the sum of its parts, and a consistent and rigorous intellectual challenge to the Bank's assumptions emerges by the last page.

It will be up to readers to decide whether or not my attempt at a Gramscian understanding of the Bank (see Chapter One) is enough to bring together the old, the new and the revisited, but certainly anyone who took seriously past-President James Wolfensohn's efforts to bring all the institution's critics onside to a friendly neoliberal project could not have failed to see efforts at hegemony – attempts to co-opt and persuade opponents that they could be incorporated into a moral and material project (Mallaby 2005, Goldman 2005). Conversely, Paul Wolfowitz's subsequent attempts to move with a contradictory blend of neoliberal and neo-conservative ideologies along his peers' lines will show whether the Bank has a deeply engrained momentum of its own (see Chapter Fifteen) or will move in radically different, if as yet unclear, directions (see Chapter Sixteen). The consequences of Wolfowitz being caught with his pants down and his hands in the till regarding his award of a huge pay-raise to his girlfriend may or may not affect the Bank's prospects seriously – but less than reduced investment in its bonds or fewer loans due to increased commodity prices or the rise of the Chinese economy. These will, of course, condition the strategies of those critical of the Bank. Be they reformers who might have been half-heartedly cooperative with the Wolfensohnian tenor of reform and restructuring, or those who see Wolfie I and Wolfie II (as Wolfensohn and Wolfowitz are respectively known) as sharing essentially the same skin – and maybe, secretly, glad to see the second more willing to expose it – their efforts of criticism and alternatives will have to change with the new regime and the new 'world order' it represents.

These chapters will possibly constitute at least part of a foundation for these new constructions. As William Robinson (2005: 14) has written recently, 'sound theoretical understandings are crucial if we hope to intervene effectively' as resolutions emerge in response to the structural and hegemonic crises in which our emergent global society is immersed. The World Bank is a key structural and ideological component of an unevenly developing 'transnational state' tasked to ameliorate the contradictions of a global political economy fraught with more tensions than in any other period since the end of the Cold War. If these chapters help at all to gain a 'more nuanced theoretical [and empirical] understanding of emergent global social structures' and the beliefs of those who are in charge of them, then it just might be that 'the power of collective agencies to influence history' at such 'time of crisis' (Robinson 2005: 14) will be augmented to some extent.

Durban, South Africa
November 2006

Acknowledgements

Many people are owed much gratitude for the appearance of this book. Glenn Cowley, the publisher at the University of KwaZulu-Natal Press, and editors Sally Hines, Mike Kirkwood and especially Andrea Nattrass have been very tolerant and helpful stalwarts deserving grateful appreciation. Norma Hatcher and Deborah Bobbett at the University of KwaZulu-Natal assisted in standardising editorial styles and the initial stages of getting the Select Bibliography all in one place. Most of all, though, the contributors – many of whom kept me going on this when I was flagging – are to be thanked profusely for the display of their critical talents, and their patience. For those whose works are appearing here for the second time, their original publishers are thanked for their permission for the use of material held in copyright – some freely given, some charged at 'free-market' rates.

Abbreviations

ACP	African, Caribbean and Pacific (countries)
ADB	Asian Development Bank
AGM	annual general meeting
ANC	African National Congress
ASEAN	Association of South-East Asian Nations
BWI	Bretton Woods Institutions
CAFOD	Catholic Action For Overseas Development
CARP	Comprehensive Agrarian Reform Programme
CDF	Comprehensive Development Framework
CDR	Centre for Development Research
CG	Consultative Group
COSATU	Congress of South African Trade Unions
CPE	complex political emergencies
CSO	civil society organisation
DfID	Department for International Development (UK)
DRC	Democratic Republic of Congo
DSF	Durban Social Forum
ED	executive director
EDF	Electronic Discussion Forum
EDI	Economic Development Institute
EIR	Extractive Industry Review
EU	European Union
FDI	Foreign Direct Investment
FfD	Financing for Development
f.o.b.	free on board
FGR	First Generation Reform
GDP	gross domestic product
GEAR	Growth, Employment and Redistribution
GNI	gross national income
GNP	gross national product

HIPC	Heavily Indebted Poor Countries (initiative)
HPAE	High Performing Asian Economy
IBRD	International Bank for Reconstruction and Development (World Bank)
IDA	International Development Association
IDS	Institute for Development Studies (Sussex University)
IEA	Institutional Environmental Assessment
IFC	International Finance Corporation
IFI	international financial institution
IMF	International Monetary Fund
IPRs	intellectual property rights
IR	International Relations
JDB	Japan Development Bank
LDC	less-developed country
MCA	Millennium Challenge Account
MCC	Millennium Challenge Corporation
MDAs	ministries, departments and agencies
MGJ	Mobilisation for Global Justice
MITI	ministry of international trade and industry (Japan)
MOF	ministry of finance (Japan)
NATO	North Atlantic Treaty Organisation
NGO	non-governmental organisation
NIC	newly industrialising country
NIE	newly industrialising economy
ODA	official development assistance
OECD	Organization for Economic Cooperation and Development
OECF	Overseas Economic Cooperation Fund (Japan)
OED	Operations Evaluation Department
PCF	Prototype Carbon Fund
PCU	Post-Conflict Unit
PPA	Participatory Poverty Assessment
PRA	Participatory Rural Appraisal
PRSPs	Poverty Reduction Strategy Papers/Programmes

SAL	Structural Adjustment Loan
SAP	structural adjustment programme
SAPRI	Structural Adjustment Participatory Review Initiative
SECAL	Sectoral Adjustment Loan
SGR	Second Generation Reform
SII	Structural Impediments Initiative
SSA	sub-Saharan Africa
SWAP	Sector-wide Approach
UDW	University of Durban-Westville
UK	United Kingdom
UN	United Nations
UNCTAD	United Nations Conference on Trade and Development
UNDP	United Nations Development Programme
UNHCR	United Nations High Commissioner for Refugees
UNICEF	United Nations Children's Emergency Fund
UPE	universal primary education
US	United States
USA	United States of America
USAID	United States Agency for International Development
WCD	World Commission on Dams
WTO	World Trade Organization

Introduction

The World Bank and its (Sheepish) Wolves

David Moore

Writers and literary scholars often argue against social scientists that novels best explain societies' contours. A book on the World Bank is not the place to engage such debates,[1] yet when the subject of the following pages joins portrayals of confused colonial subjects, angst-ridden civil servants, and quiet Americans (Achebe 1958, 1969, 1987, Greene 1955) in novels from and about the Third World, it is a sign that this most august of global development institutions has joined a plane of contemplation uniting artists and economists. If Michael Holman's *Last Orders at Harrods* (2005) is indicative, the World Bank, its presidents, and all those who work in or for it, are fair targets for novelists as well as academics. This suggests it is a cultural as well as an economic institution. Attempts to chart the cultures and ideologies of social formations at the periphery of global capitalism can ignore the World Bank no more than their presidents, their chiefs, their bar-owners or their street kids.

Last Orders at Harrods introduces us to World Bank president Hardwick Hardwicke and his spindoctor Jim 'Fingers' Adams, 'one of the best jugglers of the code-word vocabulary of the aid and development business . . . a master of the ambiguous word or phrase, a wizard of the weasel-word vocabulary of development' (Holman 2005: 49, 104) as they visit the fictional state of Kuwisha, and its even wilier president. Hardwicke and Adams are surrounded by an array of characters who seem to have been plucked in bizarre simultaneity from

Graham Greene's (1948) and Ngugi wa Thiong'o's (2006) worlds – the latter now including 'The Global Bank' in the ruling class's projects.

Reading *Last Orders at Harrods* is one way of understanding the World Bank's latest 'wolves' – immediate past president James Wolfensohn and his replacement, Paul Wolfowitz.

Antonio Gramsci's studies of hegemony (explored further in Chapter One) help, too, in unsheathing the constant interplay between strategies of consent and coercion as the world's most important 'development' institution vacillates between façades while it attempts to create consensus around capitalism's mission in the Third World. On the one hand, there is the meek, mild and munificent façade – Wolfensohn as the sheep, crying when a Christian Aid video portrays him unkindly. And, on the other hand, there is the cruel wolf revealed beneath the sheep's soft and woolly guises – Wolfowitz striding to his new position at the World Bank, fresh from the planning and execution of the invasion of Iraq, only to be stalled by his own crude corruption.

The World Bank's partners and critics know that it cannot be a sheep without turning out to be a wolf, but it certainly pretends hard to be the meeker animal. This book attempts to unravel the efforts taken by the World Bank to make capitalist economic transformation in the Third World seem 'natural'. Michael Holman's insights, as his fictitious World Bank president arrives at a Nairobiesque city, help us to achieve this unravelling in the 'real' world.

As Hardwicke and his entourage enter Kuwisha's capital city, Kareba, 'Fingers' recalls the first speech he drafted for the new president, eager to convince the 'new generation' of African leadership of the commercial banking world's verities as represented by their latest envoy. Holman's comical weaving of the banking world's manipulation of the discourse of 'relationships' into Fingers' public relations efforts to renew trust among participants in the aid and development business illustrates the delicate dialectic of mutual deception at play in such transactions:

> 'The relationship between the Bank, the donors and most of the African governments is akin to a bad marriage . . . The two parties have known each other intimately, but no longer can

the one surprise, inspire, delight or engage the other. Indeed, the relationship is dominated by expectation of failure or disappointment, which in turn helps shape response. The Bank is not a marriage guidance agency. But I believe we can act as an honest broker, and help restore an excitement that has been lost, and help recover some of the magic that all couples need, but which has faded' (Holman 2005: 50).

Even such a consummate practitioner of confidence trickery, however, has his doubts. Fingers is sure that the Bank's principles and policies are praiseworthy:

African ownership of development blueprints, transparency and good governance, the involvement of civil society, the critical importance of locally trained management, the need to encourage the private sector, all those words and phrases and concepts that were essential to the aid lexicon could be found in every subsequent speech . . . But did his boss really understand the reason for this strange, damaging intimacy between the World Bank and its African clients?

Or was he like a victim of Nigeria's financial scams . . . known as '419s'? (2005: 50).

After explaining the nature of Nigeria's notorious banking scams, Holman proffers the view that the World Bank itself may be the victim of such an elaborate hoax. He elucidates claims by 'some critics' that, just as the hoodwinked keep trying to recover their initial outlay,

[i]n much the same way . . . the Bank poured good money after bad, desperately believing that a development bonanza – Africa's recovery – was just around the corner. A few hundred million dollars here, a low interest loan there, coupled with frank talking and appropriate reforms, and that elusive target of self-sustained growth would be reached. But twenty-five years after the Bank had first rung alarm bells, reporting a deepening economic crisis

on what was then a war-torn continent, recovery remained a remote prospect (2005: 51).

Holman suggests that some of the Bank's own staff share such worries, but the iconic figures at its head go their own way. Even Fingers cautions that 'dangling a carrot in front of a donkey' might not get the animal to move in the desired direction. The beast might be a carnivore, and a nasty one at that. 'Big carrot, small stick, was bad enough – but the man who dangled a carrot in front of a lion was likely to get eaten' (2005: 51).

Holman offers no dates in his novel, consigning his 'war-torn Africa' into the abyss of the continent's history, but he gives the reader the idea that the Bank, not its 'clients', is being fleeced. He acknowledges the infamous structural adjustment policies, starting in the early 1980s in much of Africa and claimed by many to be at the base of Africa's contemporary underdevelopment. But he also attributes much culpability to the leaders of the African states whose chicanery and corruption divert the World Bank's charitable inclinations. Could their lion even 'eat' the carrot-dangling World Bank?

It is, however, more appropriate to see the 'lion' as capitalism's brutal and 'primitive' accumulation processes as they 'devour' well-meaning (but too suave by half) bankers, grasping and groping politicians, and the many rather more likeable characters in novels such as this one reworking Dickensian themes in capitalism's 'new worlds'.

Of course, if we were living in England, and had read our Dickens – or, more appropriately for social scientists, Friedrich Engels's *The Condition of the Working Class in England* (1845) – we could put this process in a global historical context. Ensconced in the contemporary consumerist cornucopia (of which novel reading is a part), we might comfortably decide that Africa *will* develop; it's just a matter of time. As one philosopher at the University of KwaZulu-Natal put it recently, Africa's trials are 'growing pains'.

If we live in Africa, however, even if as members of the same global class as Northern readers, it is a bit harder to get the rationalisation right: 'Yes, twenty-five years is a short time. Those developmentalists always were a bit naive: maybe another couple of hundred years will do the trick.'

But even those who accept a long-term view wonder *how* long the process will take. If we go back to the first days of capitalism's genesis in Africa – by external or internal agency – the timeframe pre-dates the first days of colonialism. After all, Marx's primitive accumulation process includes the Atlantic slave trade (Marx 1867: 832). If the process and Africa's 'war-torn' state look never-ending, then the lions are simply eating each other and the long process of primary accumulation drops dead, without any hope of resuscitation.[2] The small cadre of Africa's ruling classes – 'new generation' or not – circle around the corpses, inviting their transnational counterparts every now and then to celebrate the birth of new development ideologies while the old remain stillborn.

To alter the metaphor, while the rich elephants in the global and local ruling classes fight over conditionalities on ever-renegotiated and relieved loans, the poor get trampled – with no chance to become either the bold and assertive proletariat prophesied by Marxist variants of a Western teleology or the quietly industrious middle class of the Weberians.

Hegemony, too, would get kicked out of such development ontology. Who wants to gain hegemony over a permanent 'semi-' or, worse, lumpen proletariat? Who even has to? The eternal subjects of flood, famine, corruption and war are of little concern to those whose only aim for Africa is to see it continually produce minerals, objects of charity and child-soldiers – or to the rulers for whom 'Africa works' (Chabal and Daloz 1999). As Holman's sympathetic portrayal of the parentless, unschooled, and unemployed youth bearing the brunt of these policies and the obfuscation of their failure suggests, these invisible 'pieces of nothing' (2005: 188) are clearly not the target of hegemonic construction – although when hegemony slides or slackens they are subjected to political plays and display considerable agency. But even when they are the subjects of hegemony's dislocation, more often than not a little force puts them in their place. The hope that they can find some entrepreneurial space in the cracks will be enough to rebuild the hegemony of capital and its administrators.

The gendarmes of local regimes usually mete out this 'order' – as long as the World Bank and its consorts trust them. The World Bank, punctilious about the sanctity of sovereignty, rarely deigns to dirty its hands with truncheons, teargas and tanks. Its job is to win the war of the words and symbols that lie behind economic 'structures' as it tries to move the world to market motivation. Indeed, its task is to move the world until the contours of capitalism do not even need the moral and ethical justification the Bank preaches now: in its nirvana, the 'market' is so natural that it does not even warrant comment. Its dull compulsions – perhaps even its pleasant pursuit – will eventually transcend rationalisation and just 'be'.

Then, and only then, will the World Bank have outlived its *raison d'être*. Its job until that moment is simultaneously to push for *and* ease the strain of primitive accumulation on a global scale, avoiding being turned into Holman's ironic inversion in *Last Orders at Harrods* – or postponing the admission that capitalism has no chance at all.[3] In Holman's fictional account, ever since the riots on Kuwisha's Independence Day (now remembered as 'World Bank Day'), the institution meant to be synonymous with 'global (financial) order' and equitably distributed economic opportunities has been turned into the adjective for anything that does not work:

> Cars with flat batteries were 'World Bank', fridges that failed to chill the beer were 'World Bank', and traffic lights that did not operate were 'World Bank'. Indeed, some cynics went so far as to say that Kuwisha itself was 'World Bank' (2005: 243).

Away from Holman's world, until the World Bank's heaven emerges from its current purgatory, it is up to its organic intellectuals to save it from such a showing in popular culture.

Those who envision this utopia, and even include the street urchins in it, want more than the messy confluence of coercion and consent that comes to the fore with 'IMF riots', coups, and even, when regimes themselves get fed up with pretences and perform their own versions of market creation, operations to 'restore order' or 'clean up the trash'.[4] Their mission to create the market includes dreams of dynamic and innovative entrepreneurs and inventors, good governors and creative (even cantankerously contesting) citizens, regional reliability and global stability. They do not take the task of progress lightly. As Henry Bernstein puts it in Chapter Eleven of this book, those who take the construction of the 'mutually linked benefits of prosperity and order unique to bourgeois civilisation' seriously are steadfast in their goals, if somewhat cynical about the methods to which they have to resort. They see the World Bank as functionally equivalent to the Vaticans and London Missionary Societies of their proselytising predecessors: remember, they say they are doing 'God's work'. For them, conversations such as that among Hardwicke and his fellow travellers in Kareba would be common. As Holman's cast waits at a malfunctioning traffic light, the Kuwisha World Bank resident comments:

> 'Probably another power cut. Sooner they sign the loan agreement for the new power plant, the better.'
> 'I see that Nduka's [Kuwisha's president] over-spending on defence again. Time to clamp down,' said Hardwicke . . . 'What can we call the latest loan? I gather that the president insists in going through with that arms order. Says it's to put down the rebels. If we give him the benefit of the doubt we need to call it something respectable' (2005: 103).

Remembering that Nduka's order includes British helicopters with night vision, manufactured in a marginal constituency the ruling party needs to maintain, Fingers decides to develop a better justification:

> 'Let's call it "pre-humanitarian assistance".'
> The Bank president nodded. Fingers really did have a way with words . . .
> 'Have you got that statement ready?' Hardwicke asked.
> 'Five minutes, Hardwick. Five minutes' (2005: 103).

It is no easy task for World Bank diplomats and/or economists to maintain the geopolitical loyalty of fickle African politicians, while persuading them to adopt the precepts of bourgeois governance – transcendentally transparent, level with the law, and pre-eminently participatory – while many of their own masters are adept at stepping over these liberal hurdles and ignoring the dictates of university economics textbooks. When the pressure is on, however, global capital's organic intellectuals know how to secure a pivotal advantage:

> 'At a time when Kuwisha is fighting against the terrible impact of the floods that have left tens of thousands of people without homes or food, the World Bank is at your side . . . But there is a high price to pay at times like this for weak institutions and inadequate policies . . . Reform is vital – however hard it seems . . . Our message is strong and unequivocal [. . .]
>
> If Kuwisha and its leaders set their development agenda, and take the lead in implementing it, the World Bank will be a full partner in their efforts [. . .] If we work together, as partners, Kuwisha can at last realise its enormous potential' (Holman 2005: 106).

As Holman adds, to those in the know, the code behind such bland pronouncements is clear. Floods create problems, but government mismanagement creates more – and indeed creates the conditions in which floods' effects are worse because corrupt officials misspend money intended for dams or misdirect food aid. 'Market-friendly' policies will reduce the effects of floods because the spread of wealth will allow people to build houses away from the river banks as well as limit the temptation for corruption. The words 'as partners [we] can realise [Kuwisha's] enormous potential' can be decoded to mean that the Kuwishan state must follow the Bank's dictates: it was 'short of the kick in the pants that Kuwisha's critics wanted, but certainly not the endorsement sought by President Nduka' (Holman 2005: 106).[5]

At an even deeper level, however, the codes mean: 'Capitalists all over the world, we'll keep on trying to develop the mode of production you like best. We'll endeavour to bring you the raw materials and cheap labour you require, but simultaneously develop globally competitive national economies that also match the Human Development Index's holistic strictures and meet the NGO lobby's churchly chorus. We will constantly campaign for "free trade" but acquiesce in Europe and North America's agricultural subsidies.' In order for the institutions to continue to pursue such contradictory goals, hegemonic fudging accompanies every policy. Development's hegemonic organisers have to work hard.

New conjunctures, new presidents

At times of crises, hegemonic organisers work hardest. Perhaps it is at such a conjuncture that global institutions such as the World Bank now sit. The story of Iraq contains the nucleus of this new moment between 'empire' and an imperialism that might be fading.[6] It signifies that the neoliberal myth of magically emerging and merging markets is a lie: it takes military might to impose them, or at least to make them serve the interests of the world's largest imperial power, while alternative empires circle around its relative decline.[7] Meanwhile, trillions of dollars float around the world, but very few of them settle and build up the forces of production in the places the World Bank sees as its forte (aside from in China). As laissez-faire has disappeared and 'good governance' fails to arrive as the market facilitator and saviour, the neo-conservative model of 'state building' after wars appears to be a losing endeavour too – except, of course, for the corporations that make Suharto cronyism appear clever and peaceful (Harriman 2005).[8] Is rebuilding 'war-torn' societies – torn up by those who then rebuild them – now simply recognition of military Keynesianism's final stage?

While these questions are being asked, the World Bank has had a new president chosen for it by the political masters of the world's only superpower. With the appointment of Paul Wolfowitz (Wolfie II), is the world witnessing a transformation of the Bank into an institution now representing and furthering a 'unilateralist' global project led by a neo-conservative wing of the American Republican party? (Is it thus an extension of the 'imperialist' thrust of a strong and vibrant – or weakening but grasping – state?) Or, can the Bank remain part of a relatively new, slowly and unevenly developing 'transnational state' represented by the more flamboyant past president, James Wolfensohn (Wolfie I)?

One slicks his hair down; the other lets his white locks flow. Wolfie I dances with the African natives, while Wolfie II makes it clear that on his trip to the dark continent nobody asked him any questions about Iraq. One is a George W. Bush sidekick – conservative, repressed and repressive; the other is part of the previous, sexy saxophonist president's past. Their styles may indeed symbolise different forms of capitalism, and thus very significant differences in the way the world unfolds. As the 'Retort' collective writes about the meaning of the war in Iraq, the image of a new Bank president could signify new modes of global capitalist accumulation. They could be a new form of 'neoliberalism mutating from an epoch of "agreement" and austerity programmes to one of outright war', that is, 'military neoliberalism', or a renewed and rapacious version of primitive accumulation ('Retort' 2005: 74–75).

If the Wolfie II presidency of the World Bank can be paralleled with the invasion of Iraq, then it will represent 'a radical, punitive "extra economic" restructuring of the conditions necessary for expanded profitability... paving the way... for new rounds of American-led dispossession and capital accumulation' ('Retort' 2005: 72). To this way of thinking, Wolfie II epitomises the new world order, led by a US crazed either by the smell of total power or the fear of losing it. His appointment symbolises the end of the Clinton-Wolfensohn era, wherein there was confidence 'that the new world of capital penetration would come about essentially by means of agreement (between governments and corporations), "fiscal discipline", fine tuning of subsidy and bailout, and nonstop pressure from US creditors' ('Retort' 2005: 74).

This may have ended with the destruction of the Twin Towers. Yet even before that, American ruling circles were edging towards a very volatile combination of 'paleo'- and neo-conservatism (Lind 2004). The presumptions of post-Cold War, free-and-easy neoliberalism and libertarianism had frayed and a colder, conservative reaction – one that saw state intervention as a sin only if it had the word 'socialism' attached – had emerged to take its place. As a new and even more fundamentalist enemy stepped forward to replace the Communists, this group's think tanks worked busily on 'Projects for the American

Century'[9] – projects that were in themselves chilling recognition of the hubris of a waning superpower only partially conscious of its relative decline. Meanwhile, some parts of the periphery of global capitalism turned into a challenging 'semi-periphery'. In any case,

> cracks began to appear within the World Bank establishment. Stiglitz fought with Summers, Western Europe fought with the Washington consensus, and the South often refused to take its bitter medicine. The grotesqueries of Third World indebtedness and First World subsidies to corporate agriculture became an issue in polite society. The back-slapping and mutual congratulation of the Uruguay Round descended into the fiasco of Seattle – and the deeper fiascos of Doha and Cancun. At Cancun, what emerged was an in-house insurgency: a Group of Twenty steadfast in its refusal to endorse the massive US-EU subsidies to North Atlantic agriculture, and WTO rules crafted to prevent the South from protecting itself ('Retort' 2005: 74).

Some of those fissures were recognised, by those slightly to the left of the libertarians, as inherent to the economics of Third World transformation: one-time World Bank chief economist and instigator of the 'Post-Washington Consensus' Joseph Stiglitz, for example, recognised that 'whenever information is imperfect and markets incomplete, which is to say always, *and especially in developing countries*, then the invisible hand works most imperfectly' (Friedman 2002: 50). People such as Wolfensohn are said to have attempted to give them space – to no avail – against the dictates of the American Treasury office.[10]

The problem with interventionists such as Stiglitz, however, is that they tend to substitute the older liberals' confidence in an impartial and capable state for the neoliberals' faith in a neutral market. In the Third World, states are just as 'imperfect and incomplete' as markets. Thus the notion of 'good governance' was tacked on to the verities of market promotion, allowing the Bank and other development agencies to nudge Third World states to a position in which they could at least create and maintain private property rights. The neo-conservatives could take this insight all the way, and decide that Americans were the only ones who could impose the states – indeed, the American state – upon which markets could be erected. Of course, their states were just as corrupt as the Third World ones they wanted to replace, and their 'markets' were simply transplanted corporations, but their sheer weight would create a world in their image and the narcissism of their praise-singer would not allow their flaws to enter their consciousness.

The Iraqi-style development state, then, is not 'development', but transplantation and usurpation. Furthermore, if sovereignty becomes no more than a sideshow, all the fuss and bother of tariffs and protection versus free trade is unnecessary: if the world is one corporation, such nuisances disappear. With the market imposed turnkey-style, all the niceties of tariff negotiations and the like could be dispensed with: in one world market and one state, such remnants of sovereignty would be mere relics of the past.

These are the fantasies upon which the current conjuncture hangs. If they fall asunder in Iraq, the latest version of the American dream will be 'World Bank' in the Kuwishan sense. It will not be the image at which James Wolfensohn and Yoweri Museveni chuckled as they travelled towards the latter's country residence (in the film *The Bank, the President and the Pearl of Africa* [Lanning 1998]): the World Bank will not be seen as an automated teller in front of which Africans would like to queue. In the meantime, however, Iraq is not representative of the rest of the world. Africa, for example, has not quite so much oil or strategic minerals,[11] does not harbour any regimes roguish enough to rouse the American populace to legitimise an attack, and would be hard put to mount a credible threat of 'weapons of mass destruction'. There are undoubtedly human rights abuses, but we only have to be reminded of Western inaction vis-à-vis the Rwandan genocide to see the emptiness of that rhetoric (Melvern 2000, 2004; Dallaire 2003). As for 'democracy' plain and simple, it takes *Le Monde Diplomatique* to remind us that as the processions of political succession go on in *le tier monde*, when 'voices on all sides' proclaim the birth of new democratic dispensations, no one notices that the reality is much more akin to 'feudal succession'

(Gresh 2005: 1) – unless the democratic discourse can be fitted into the imperially ordained array of friends and enemies.

Regardless of the presence of a Wolfowitz or a Wolfensohn, then, it seems that much of the World Bank's work will remain the same as ever. It will plug away at trying to set the agenda for states and other agencies alike, tripping lightly between discourses of good governance and better markets, sustainability of the environment and debt repayments, and gender equality through affirmative action and merit. Behind its deft discursive skipping, however, it will chafe away at the intractability of tenure relations mired in pre-capitalist societies surrounding enclaves of globally integrated capitalist spaces. It will hope against hope that the whole project will not explode in its face as politicians holding perilously to the precarious power that only 'quasi-states' can produce mobilise their masses at something the Bank and its partners left out of their plan. Zimbabwe's 'fast-track' land reform, for example, which expropriated a few thousand white commercial farmers and replaced them with 130 000 ill-equipped 'new settlers' and a few hundred politicians and their relatives to save the ageing president from democratisation's threat, is a clear example of how easily the World Bank's sort of hegemony can tumble down around it.

How then do we measure the Bank's work in worlds far from Iraq, Washington and universities? Aside from roads, power lines and dams, how does it change societies?[12] What are the material impacts of its efforts to perform history's biggest task – the 'development' of capitalism, merging and transforming modes of production to aggrandise its dominant forms while creating clones that may well compete with these? Are its outcomes enjoyable and natural (at best), palatable and predictable (if possible), or simply horrible and immoveable? How do efforts to make capitalism hegemonic actually change that system? Is there a happy ending, if, as in *Last Orders at Harrods*, a wonderful collaboration for health clinics and roads can be made between a 'Worldfeed' NGO, the Bank, local entrepreneurs and the most venal of politicians, if only the phrase 'ownership' can be mouthed by all? Or must we look to see if the evolution of a classical, and very active, proletariat is emerging amidst processes of urbanisation and industrialisation? This would be a sign of both capitalist development and the foreshadowing of what socialists really want: a class that can push the development of the forces of production forward, challenge the rule of capital with a vigorous democracy rooted on the shopfloor, and simultaneously 'prepare the graves' of those pushing them for profit.

No matter the *intent* of the Bank and its partners, these are the signs we must look for. The difficult part of the calculation lies in unearthing the Bank's exact role in these processes, and whether or not its intellectuals' efforts to make it 'user-friendly' have appreciable effects on the subjects destined to take history forward. Even more difficult is the issue of whether or not the Bank colludes in a process of keeping the Third World 'underdeveloped' as a reservoir of cheap labour and raw materials to be exploited by the advanced part of the world (including, as some versions of 'dependency theory' allude, the Western working class). Or does it hasten capitalist transformation in the periphery and ameliorate some of its harsher consequences?

The few billion dollars a year the Bank circulates pale in the shadows of capital and commodity circulation, the booms and busts, the long waves and cycles, the ebb and flow of transitions to capitalism. The real role of the Bank – of its presidents, its 10 000 or more permanent employees, its temps, contractees and consultants – is to take in and modify the legitimating ideologies of a constantly changing capitalism so that they meet the needs and demands of their counterparts in capitalism's hinterlands. And they, in turn, mediate the struggling desires of their subjects while embarking on relatively autonomous accumulation paths of their own.

This complex concatenation of processes and strategies – not whether Wolfowitz is allied with Rumsfeld, or Wolfensohn with Powell – is the primary object of study for those who are interested in how the Bank affects the way capitalism grows in the Third World. To be sure, if the Washington alliances – globally and locally – affect whether or not the 'consensus' emerging is named after that city or the capital of China, then this is important. Unless development theory and practice is all ideological 'trickle down' from the West (and increasingly from the

East, which is now better described as an authoritarian capitalist region than anything democratic socialists would recognise as their own) then it is equally important to see how the Bank's ideologies and ideologues respond to the results of implementation at the periphery. If it can be shown that (1) there is increasing inequality between the South and the North, and (2) within countries in the South, and that (3) even if the inequality occurs within increasing but unevenly distributed *growth* it still leads to devastating impacts on human lives,[13] then it must also be shown how the Bank is working to change these conditions for the better – or worse. These are not easy questions to answer, not least because no one knows what would happen if the Bank were not present.

Those who condemn the Bank for its collusion with global capital and its agents in its substations must be as wary and objective in their analysis as its supporters. Warnings to those who involve themselves in the study of the powerful are plentiful enough. Terry Eagleton is as good an arbiter of these matters as anyone else. As he cautions, 'trying to be objective is an arduous, fatiguing business' and it takes 'patience, honesty, courage and persistence [to] delve through the dense layers of self-deception which prevent us from seeing the situation as it really is' (2003: 132). When those with power are trying to analyse themselves, however, their delusions tend to replicate themselves. Objective analysis is

> especially difficult for those who wield power – for power tends to breed fantasy, reducing the self to a state of querulous narcissism. For all its tough-minded pragmatism, it is riddled with delusion, assuming that the whole world centres subserviently upon itself. It dissolves reality into a mirror of its own desires. It is those whose material existence is pretty solid who tend to assume that the world is not. Power is naturally solipsistic, incapable of getting out of its own skin. Like sexuality, it is where we are most infantile (Eagleton 2003: 132).

These words put the process of reading World Bank reports, scanning press releases, and listening to policy pronouncements in a new light.

But at this point Eagleton avoids the issue of how the subaltern classes – or those purporting their representation – can avoid the same problems. He adds, reflexively, 'it is the powerless who are more likely to appreciate that the world does not exist to pander to our needs, and rolls on its own sweet way with scarcely a side-glance at us' (2003: 132). Consequently, they will be more objective. Whether or not this is so, those aspiring to the status of organic intellectuals to the poor and the powerless – that is, those on the way to a powerful role – must be wary of narcissism, infantilism, solipsism, and all the other delusions of power. While condemning the World Bank and its partners to their proper place of irrelevance, we must also work on the construction of alternatives less prone to the traps of command: the institutions of a 'people's power' must be prefigurative; the discourse of critique must be capable of resisting power in all its forms.

This book: New hegemonies in the making?

The chapters in this book are levelled against the power that is, in the hopes that the power that is coming will be at least more responsive to its subjects than the status quo, and at best formed from the struggles of those on the rocky road to true citizenry themselves (Mamdani 1996) – and that the critique of power they construct leads to these ends. Their common denominator is a concern to expose the deceptions, hubris, and plain 'bad sense' (as opposed to Gramsci's good – and even 'common' sense, given that the aim of hegemonic aspirants is to *create* 'common sense') of the World Bank's organic intellectuals. Not all of the chapters are inspired by Gramsci directly, but the one inspiring the book – Robert Wade's 1996 *New Left Review* article (see Chapter Nine) on the Bank's efforts to sanitise the state-centredness of the newly industrialising countries' climb up the development ladder – is clearly indebted to an understanding of how a certain form of hegemony within development economics is manufactured. Wade's chapter charts how the Japanese attempts to stamp their capitalist style on what might have been a new paradigm was air-brushed out of the final draft of the World Bank's special report. His analysis of the roles of various corps of intellectuals is intricate and precise, but perhaps his lack of direct theoretical engagement with Gramsci has hindered its being taken up as a 'template' for other studies of the Bank rather than simply as a description of a moment in the rise (or rise and fall?) of neoliberalism in the predominant development institution. That is why David Moore's contribution on 'the Gramsci effect' (see Chapter One) – the title is borrowed from one of Wade's book reviews – has been written: it will serve to set the contours of a Gramscian perspective on 'World Bank studies' for the rest of this book.

The chapters that follow are a combination of some of the classics in a field populated by World Bank critics, and newer additions to a subdiscipline of development studies. Henry Bernstein, Patrick Bond, Ben Fine, Susanne Soederberg, Marcus Taylor, Robert Wade, David Williams and Tom Young are well-seasoned thorns in the side of the Bank's efforts to make its label as 'the Knowledge Bank' stick. Mark Beeson, Mark T. Berger, Graham Harrison, Scott MacWilliam, David Moore, Richard Pithouse, Susanne Schech, Sanjugta vas Dev and Thomas Wanner are less well known at the craft, some within or just out of doctoral thesis writing, while others are known primarily for other closely related work. As such, the book's emphasis on ideology, politics and hegemony complements other works, such as *Development Policy in the Twenty-first Century: Beyond the Post-Washington Consensus* (Fine, Lapavitsas and Pincus 2003) and *Reinventing the World Bank* (Pincus and Winters 2002a), which are more concerned with economics and case studies, and Michael Goldman's impeccable analysis of the World Bank's relationship with NGOs (2005). Perhaps it will bridge these texts and the more popularly aimed *Masters of Illusion: The World Bank and the Poverty of Nations* (Caufield 1996) and Sebastian Mallaby's (2005) much less critical biography of James Wolfensohn. (Although Washington gossip says that Wolfensohn thought this book finished his career: if so, that is more than left-wing critics and anti-globalisation demonstrators have accomplished.)

As well as representing a range of scholars, this book is also wide in scope. There is no united front, or lowest common denominator, of critique here. Indeed, if the authors were to present their ideas at a round-table discussion, we could be assured of vigorous debate. Scott

MacWilliam's criticism of those condemning the Bank for perpetuating poverty by intent – blaming it instead for not getting labour attached to the forces of production – would undoubtedly be disputed by Patrick Bond, whose (arguably) 'dependency school' roots would allow him to see little hope in the development of such forces through capitalist means, publicly funded or not.[14] Similarly, Thomas Wanner's nearly deep ecology would run into contestation with many of the contributors, for whom the environment is more of a side issue. Susanne Schech and Sanjugta vas Dev's implicit advocacy of a much deeper participatory model of democracy might well be seen as beside the point by Robert Wade, and they might see him as a Keynesian economist who would happily endorse an authoritarian and bureaucratic North-East Asian state capitalism. Richard Pithouse's moral critique of the Bank might rub Henry Bernstein's deep empiricism the wrong way, while Williams and Young's theoretical stretch might see more of the liberal project in the Ugandan and Tanzanian state-society complexes[15] than Harrison's cases seem to detect. Bond would not agree with Soederberg and Taylor that Wolfowitz will not move the Bank too far from the direction in which it was heading under Wolfensohn.

What the pieces share, however, is the ability to illustrate a wide range of ways in which the Bank and its peers can be criticised. They are rooted in a healthy suspicion of the ability of either the market or the state – or civil society amalgams thereof – to change diverse societies into mirror images of themselves. Equally, there are few romantic invocations of pre-capitalist 'others' or permanently united multitudes, created by their own prophets in Spinozist fashion, against an equally monolithic oppressor (Nairn 2005).

Of course, hegemony is not won by 'ideas' alone. Indeed, it is gained through many methods and strategies, and in different 'regions' of the political and ideological map as well as the one with which cartographers try to make sense of the world. Thus the book is divided into themes that spread from the more or less 'intellectual' through to a focus on politics and the state to regional foci and finally to the realm of full critique: Patrick Bond's recommendation not to 'fix' the Bank, but to 'nix' it.

The first section on 'ideas and hegemony' starts with a focus on how Gramsci might have dealt with the World Bank as an instance of a global state-in-the-making. It continues with an idea that is counter-intuitive to most critiques of the bank, MacWilliam's contention that the Bank is not 'trying' to create poverty, but rather to create the conditions to 'attach labour to capital'. This section goes on to Fine's blistering deconstruction of the colonising discourse of 'social capital' and Wanner's discussion of how the Bank has hammered environmental discourse on its anvils, pushing out alternative ideas of the ecological-economic nexus. Central to this intellectual apparatus is David Williams's pathbreaking argument that all the energies of the Bank are directed at the construction of that 'man' at the core of capitalist modernity – *homo oeconomicus*.

Aside from the effects this meta-strategy has on those living in their own modes of social relations of production in the many peripheries of global capitalism, Williams's economic man is at the core of Western perceptions of what 'development' and 'progress' are all about. Thus this representation of the Bank's mission serves as its hegemonic foundation in its homelands: those members of the House of Representatives vote for the Bank, or not, depending on how they see it performing the 'white man's burden' as it has mutated into a relatively race- and gender-less formulation.

This brings to mind one of Edward Said's final renditions of how this mission merges with the larger ones of imperial thrust and empire: the real 'history' of peoples has to be wiped clean in order for the 'new' – but, in this formulation, always there and just waiting to be released from the bonds of tradition and obscurity – men and women to emerge. As Said wrote on the eve of his death, Iraq's experience of the most self-evident perversion of progress was a result of 'our leaders and their intellectual lackeys' [incapability] of understanding . . . that history cannot be swept clean like a blackboard, clean so that "we" might inscribe our own future there and impose our own forms of life for these lesser people to follow' (2003: xiii).

If the subjects of 'our leaders' cooperate and perpetuate this delusion actively – or even collude passively – it will continue. Similarly, the many 'compradors' buy into the idea with various levels of enthusiasm. Because they are 'relatively powerless' to resist the onslaught of *homo oeconomicus* and his military brothers and sisters, 'they turn their energies to repressing and keeping down their own populations, which results in resentment, anger and helpless imprecations that do nothing to open up societies where secular ideas about human history and development have been overtaken by failure and frustration' (Said 2003: xiii).

Focusing on the subject of 'orientalism', Said suggests that this has led to the reassertion of 'an Islamism built out of rote learning . . . and an inability to analyze and exchange ideas within the generally discordant world of modern discourse' (2003: xxi). When the intellectuals organic to this mode of understanding walk the streets, fly the jets, and take the subways in the centres of this discordant world, 'blowback' happens (Moore 2003a). The West becomes more fundamentalist than ever, too. As the project of creating *homo oeconomicus* in the Third World fails, it loses its reflexive side in the First World, too. The liberal project becomes more tentative than ever.

Perhaps in the mid-1990s there was a realisation that this liberal man could not be made by neoliberal means alone. Structural adjustment policies went too far towards laissez-faire and from the dreaded *dirigisme* with its rent-seeking propensities, so in the mid-1980s and early 1990s the Bank and its peers turned back slightly to politics and the state. The banking behemoth took on political discourses of democracy and 'good governance'. In the book's second section Schech and Vas Dev's intricate deconstruction of the Bank's well-intentioned efforts to link participatory politics with the eradication of poverty makes salutary reading in this respect, and their invocation of Foucauldian perspectives warn us that this project is just as much about the control of 'bio-power' as it is about creating the conditions to turn over better profit (although we could argue that the latter depends a lot on the former). Rethinking their 1994 *Political Studies* classic, the first academic effort to pull apart the political nature of the Bank's widening hubris, Young and Williams confirm the relevance of political theory to the deconstruction of the 'good governance' project. Moore's 1999 effort pushes this approach a bit further into the realms of political economy, emphasising that the Bank's surprise at the role of the state in paving the way for the universality of property rights is matched only by its distaste at the prospect of working with this untrustworthy ally.[16]

The third section approaches the Bank's efforts to implement its mission in Africa and Asia. Henry Bernstein's reconsideration of what is probably the first sustained attack on the Bank's 'crisis think' and its embeddedness in the contradiction of agricultural modernisation remains a sterling example of the meticulous application of Marxist method to the ambiguous unfolding of the intricate modalities of 'small commodity production' the World Bank tries to encourage and expand. Yet at the end of a nuanced analysis of a recent slew of studies, Bernstein's words are essentially political, too: what is most notable, and depressing, about the Bank – even as it espouses its propensities to 'listen' – is its 'lack of any accountability, and responsibility . . . to those on whom its policies are imposed'. The ultimate reasons for this lie in the 'conditions of contemporary imperialism and its institutional order' (see Chapter Eleven, page 363). Thus, the ultimate way to transform the Bank also lies here: until there are significant changes in that imperial order, we would be wise to follow Bernstein's modest advice on advice. He claims 'no competence to offer "alternative" policies' (see Chapter Eleven, Note 26, page 368), knowing they will come, for good or evil, from the new forms of imperialism on the agenda. Chinese agricultural relations of production and politics in Africa, anyone? Of course, those who offer alternative policies are actors on imperialism's – or empire's – ever-shifting stage, and as such the alternatives on offer become part of the shifts. Bernstein's principled abstentionism, however, is a result of intensive empirical study and the hope that those offering new worlds realise the complexity of the old. It could also be born of fear that those offering policy alternatives too often see monoliths, themselves mirroring that seeming omnipotence.

Moore's contribution on the Bank's post-conflict advice tries to unearth the roots of its efforts to intercede on the 'humanitarian' side of development practice, a side now so prevalent in parts of Africa as to be nearly permanent. This realm of intervention appears to take one step further than expected in its 1997 injunction that the best time to reshape 'the values and norms of the state and the state's relationship to the economy' is 'when the normal rules of the game are in flux' (World Bank 1997a: 155–56, 144). Perhaps if we add Afghanistan and Iraq to this chapter's focus on such African states as Sierra Leone and the Democratic Republic of Congo we see this logic's endpoint. If it was not *homo oeconomicus* who went into today's wars, the Bank (though it miscalculated the origins of these wars) certainly hopes to see him walking out of it (Cramer 2002: 1845–64, 2006; Cramer and Goodhand 2002: 885–909). As Harrison illustrated in one of the first assessments of the implementation of the Bank's injunctions on 'good governance' in Africa, the 'economic' men and women on that continent must become *homo good governus* too. Harrison's work on 'neo-statism' in Africa – further elaborated in his book (2004b) – puts much-needed flesh on some of the theoretical perspectives on states and politics in this book.

As already mentioned, Robert Wade's incisive 1996 analysis of the making of the World Bank's report on *The East Asian Miracle* (World Bank 1993a) is the template for the approach that this book advocates. The chapter chronicles 'the tired old technique of US and European leaders' within the Bank of beating 'the Japanese with a piece of two by four' (see Chapter Nine, page 275) as the latter tried to move Bank perspectives on development in East Asia towards its brand of state-assisted capitalism. Wade's contribution is a sophisticated combination of the politics of paradigm maintenance – or hegemony – as they play themselves out in state versus state conflict, the battle of ideas, and personalities (such as former Harvard president Lawrence Summers, then the Bank's chief economist and vice-president), and on down the line. Yet Wade's work also alerts us to the positive utopian thinking of every slightly left-of-centre policy adviser/critic immersed in an institution he or she does not like: incremental indications of the holes in neoliberalism's logic creep through such reports. Such 'attractor points' may be used by 'those wishing to put new questions on the agenda to claim legitimacy'. This, Wade suggests, may be the 'way that big organisations change their minds; sharp changes are rare' (see Chapter Nine, page 303).

They – and we – live in hope. In the meantime, a year or so after Wade's *magnum opus* was published, the 'Asian miracle' was in deep crisis.

Those wedded to market- or state-centred views fought to determine which mode of development was to blame. But as Berger and Beeson show in their historical picture of how the 'tigers' fit into the history of World Bank thought, the neoliberal way of 'legitimat[ing] authoritarianism and endeavour[ing] to accommodate the developmental state and ideas about Asian democracy and Asian values' gave way to its more natural association of all things Asian 'with cronyism, corruption and inefficiency', while the Bank moved slightly away from the IMF's hard line to Stiglitz's 'Post-Washington Consensus' (see Chapter Ten, page 337). Now, as indicated above, the Post-Post-Washington Consensus is neo-conservatism, that strange hybrid of gung-ho liberalism tied to the military state rather than the market. Its main contradiction may not be an incompatibility with authoritarianism, but with the cost of bombing and reconstructing.

In the end, all of this flitting about from one mode of hegemonic accommodation to another must be challenged at its core. This is the aim of the book's fourth section. Richard Pithouse's challenge comes from a deep philosophical discomfort with the way in which the Bank perceives 'the poor'. The contrasts between the Bank's constructing of *The Voices of the Poor* (Narayan, Patel et al. 2000), with Durban activist-scholar Ashwin Desai's *We are the Poors* (2002b) go far beyond differences between the singularity indicated in the Bank's formulation and Desai's plurality.

For Patrick Bond, this discomfort moves from philosophy to economic practice. His construction of a case for the Bank's elimination represents the reality of what has been incorrectly called the 'anti-globalisation movement', but is really the embodiment of the belief that 'another world is possible'. His assessment of the changes in the bank consequent on Wolfowitz's assumption of power are challenged somewhat by Marcus Taylor and Susanne Soederberg. They see the Bank's shifts emerging from a restructuring of the USA's relationship to the Bank, which is wider than a change in chief executives, but not too deep in the *longue durée*.

The contributors to this volume indicate by their work that they indeed believe another world to be possible. They may not agree on what that world will be, or what they would like it to be, but their contributions suggest that they know another world is unfolding and they hope to influence it positively to varying degrees. In that, they are at one with a history of 'global movements', based at the centre or at the periphery and dating from the anti-slavery movements and the campaigns against King Leopold's barbarous rule over the Congo (Cooper 2001; Hochschild 1998). They are also at one with, or embedded within, what Thomas Callaghy (2001) calls a 'triple helix' of 'the institutions of the international debt [and development] regime, the NGO debt [and development] networks, and the epistemic community' of scholars in their field. Whether or not the World Bank is the prototype of a new form of transnational ultra-imperialism or but a minor player in the battle of states while empires ebb and flow, it plays a key role in the hegemonies emerging from this helix's dynamics and how they play out on the stages of global political economies. Of course, the outcomes of these struggles cannot be determined at this point, but scholarly analysis and activism can condition them. These forms of intervention do affect the 'mad men' who, as Keynes says, when in power, mouth what they thought they had learned from their economics lecturers 25 years before (Keynes, in Cockett 1995: 112; and see Moore's Chapter Eight in this volume).

To invoke another literary parallel suggested by the serendipity of having successive World Bank presidents whose names begin with 'Wolf', all that can be hoped is that supporters and opponents of the Bank and its discursive practices do not cry 'wolf' about the development process *in general* too often. Without careful observation and assiduous critique at all turns, the wrong shepherds will take charge of the flock, remaining only to supervise a slaughter. To build and rebuild the herd, we need workable alternatives based on strategies of public accumulation. These must be constructed on modalities of participation that keep the herdboys and the masters to account whenever they stray from the task they purport to perform and the ideologies to which they declare adherence. These structures will only emerge, however, when powerful constituencies demand them. It is only then that hegemonic strategies develop to meet the demands of reform, and even revolution.

Notes

1. If it were to be tackled, Terry Eagleton's *After Theory* (2003) would be a good starting place.
2. Christopher Cramer (2006) offers a fine interpretation of the relationship between accumulation processes and war.
3. As Saul and Leys (1999) would claim, but Sender (1999) would dispute.
4. This refers to the Zimbabwean government's Operation *Murambatsvina* or 'Clean up the Trash', which during May–July 2005 bulldozed the homes and destroyed the livelihoods of at least 700 000 people soon after a strong electoral challenge from, and huge urban victories for, the ruling party's opposition. The UN report is a masterly example of the 'international community's' discursive tactics when faced with such coercion – behind every thundercloud lies the silver linings of private property rights and good governance: 'The humanitarian response provides a unique opportunity and entry point to link the provision of temporary shelter and other forms of humanitarian assistance with immediate security of tenure for all those affected and to prepare the ground for overcoming the failures and inherent weaknesses in governance' (United Nations 2005: 8).
5. See Holman (2005: 226) for more detailed policy document deconstruction.
6. 'Empire' is taken here to mean what Hardt and Negri's *Empire* (2000) theorises as a state-less global economy ruled by financial flows and bio-power, and what Robinson (2001a and b, 2005) would call the 'transnational state', while 'imperialism' refers to the power of the USA to rule the world the way its governing classes would like. See Cox (2005) and Rothschild (2004).
7. The best prognostic work in this tradition is Arrighi and Silver (2001), for whom the new empire may well be centred on China. In the interim lies much uncertainty.
8. For a relatively calm argument for 'state building' from a nearly neo-conservative perspective, see Fukuyama (2002, 2004). For his later rejection of neo-conservatism, see Fukuyama (2006).
9. For a defence, see Barry (2004).
10. See Chapter Nine for more on this. For Stiglitz's minimal ideas of democratic reform, see Stiglitz (2003).
11. They are not inconsequential, however.
12. And if production relations in the society onto which such infrastructural aids are grafted do not change, enabling them to add to rather than subtract from its accumulation processes, then dams, power lines and roads will simply add to its debt and have to be rebuilt by yet another Bechtel.
13. For example, increasing urbanisation in the context of better incomes for the cities' residents may be occurring while cholera is on the rise because of poor sanitation in the informal settlements and a bustling new bourgeoisie is building mansions in new suburbs.
14. See Brown (2002), arguing against the idea that the Bank 'creates' poverty, articulated by Cammack (2001a and b, 2002). It should be noted that Bond's deeply researched

work on Zimbabwe (1998), however, illustrates that the Rhodesian form of state capitalism 'worked' for a definitive period of time. Whether 'nixing' the World Bank would facilitate this project is another question.

15. The phrase 'state-society complex' is a key component of Robert Cox's theoretical apparatus. See Cox (1987, 1996).
16. This work foreshadows Moore (2004a).

Chapter One

The World Bank and the Gramsci Effect
Towards a Transnational State and Global Hegemony?

David Moore

THIS IS AN ORIGINAL CHAPTER FOR THIS BOOK.

This book is about how the World Bank attempts to perform what Robert Wade (1997) has called the 'Gramsci effect'.[1] How does it educate the present and potential policy-making intellectuals in Third World societies and those of the First World working alongside (or dominating) them? How does it persuade them to accept – indeed, embrace enthusiastically – the Bank's prescriptions for capitalist development? How does it meet challenges to its discourse and practice?

The chapters of this book explore some of the ways in which the Bank constructs hegemony. How does it manufacture moral and intellectual leadership within the development industry and on behalf of the protagonists of a global project – for an emerging transnational capitalist class and a state managing the contradictions in its wake?[2] Is the Bank an apparatus – a sort of Ministry of Development – within an unevenly developing world state and are its managers and employees organic intellectuals (Gramsci 1971: 5) constructing hegemony for a global bourgeoisie, emerging with the fits and starts of neoliberal globalisation? How does the Bank wield the weapon of ideological formation: one weapon of many by which ruling classes construct that ideal social, political and ideological condition – hegemony? How does it help the transnational and national bourgeoisie (including their organic intellectuals), who hitch their stars to it, to make most people believe, most of the time, that the class ruling them is doing so in their own best interests? (Or, at lesser and larger levels, that the institutions running their lives are doing a good job, while the social system as a whole appears to function as a happily integrative and reified whole?) At best, how does it craft the conditions in which the questions of who rules and how are never asked at all?

This chapter attempts to put the chapters that follow into global and theoretical context – or, as Henry Bernstein (2003b) might put it, to contextualise them in the 'world-historical' of what analysts are increasingly calling 'empire' (Hardt and Negri 2000). It asks: can concepts developed in the 1930s by an imprisoned Marxist revolutionary in an unevenly developed Italy on the verge of full-blown fascism have any relevance today? And, can contemporary theories of what may be an emerging transnational state be bolstered by an analysis of the World Bank's role in constructing hegemony for the classes that are behind this state-in-formation? Are Antonio Gramsci's words applicable to a *global* political economy extending far beyond the confines of his original purview? Can there be such a thing as 'global hegemony'? What is the role of the World Bank in its construction?

At moments such as March 2003, when bombs were dropping on Baghdad while millions of global citizens protested and scores of governments abstained from approval, it is difficult to give much credence to the notion that the leaders of empires rule through consent as much as coercion.[3] When hundreds of thousands of English-speaking troops invaded and encircled Iraq, it was even harder to think that a comparative handful of economists and 'Third World experts' – the World Bank employs approximately 10 500 people – speaking the same language, rank with all those troops in terms of their importance to the empire's construction. As the discourse and practice of 'post-conflict' reconstruction and democracy-talk hide the emperor's old clothes – when they are not being ripped open by Iraqi resistance – it is harder than ever to discern how Iraq's economic structures can be reformed to feed the oil-fired furnaces of the global factory. Moreover, as the George W. Bush government in the USA has adopted an increasingly selfish and short-sighted profile in the wake of 9/11, the concept of a stateless empire – one in which that nasty concept of imperialism has disappeared, replaced by images of free-flowing finance and the cyberspaced disciplines of self-regulating and reflexive bio-power[4] – has seemed increasingly and anachronistically premature. In global forums such as the World Trade Organization, too, multilateralism and economic opening seem to have been on the decline (Becker 2003).[5] Images of a unified transnational capitalist class, its global state, and transnational bureaucrats quietly transforming global space into one seamless market seem inadequate to the task of understanding a world dominated by a 'hegemon' more unilateralist than ever and inspiring those further down the hierarchy of global power to take the same stance.[6] Have the Bush II regime's overblown responses to Al Queda's attack, along with the early closing of the World Trade Organization's September 2003 Cancun meeting and the stalling of Doha in 2006 (triggered in part by too-evident hypocrisy regarding the basic principles of neoliberal ideology) signalled the beginning of the end of free-trade globalisation? Can the misnamed 'anti-globalisation' activists see light for a 'people's globalisation' at the end of the tunnel?[7] Or does the Iraqi invasion presage a new phase of globalisation announced in blood and bombs?

Moments of unilateralism, war, carnage and 'relief' are only the most violent and visible forms of the massive restructuring experienced by the world as its new hegemon, unshackled from the constraints of the Cold War and post-Cold War multilateralism, takes the imperial mission of capital to heights unparalleled since the end of the nineteenth century (Arrighi and Silver 2001; Silver and Arrighi 2003). Particular regimes and the ebbs and flows of consensus on free trade may only temporarily dislodge the process of globalisation – or even, in certain conjunctures, hasten it. Wars such as the one in Iraq only serve to remind us that socio-economic transformations inherent in a myriad of moves to a truly globalised capitalism are uneven and violent. Beneath them are the comparatively silent ways in which millions of people's relations to their material means of existence are transformed. These fundamental and multifaceted changes are no easier than 'regime change' at more 'political' levels. Indeed, their quotidian forms of violence – remember Marx's words about blood oozing from many pores as the process of primitive accumulation unfolds and a new mode of production emerges – often turn from quantity to quality. They add up to both the shock and awe of war directly driven from the core of the world system, such as the Iraqi episode, its less headlined versions in places such as the Democratic Republic of the Congo,[8] and the disruptions of millions of people leaving their land to join the unemployed urban masses, unworthy of news stories at all. Transnational capitalists and the global bureaucrats sometimes supporting and sometimes 'correcting' them – and both of their public relations experts – are involved at all levels of this global process of primitive accumulation.[9] Their vision goes far beyond that of those currently in charge of the American state (Monbiot 2003a).[10]

While buildings are bombed and soldiers – and civilians – slaughtered as exemplars of global power shifts, and as the everyday relations of production and reproduction are transformed in fields, factories and families, the contours of culture and ideology are reinvented and the structures of economic and political governance are reformed. Somewhere in between the warriors forcing global regime change and the soldier-kulaks despoiling their neighbours' commons are the people fashioning and refashioning the institutions and ideologies making these socio-economic alterations work, and crafting universality, normality and naturalness out of them. These are the organisers of new historic blocs – the organic intellectuals of restructured class formations and accompanying new forms of hegemony in which the old is forgotten and radical alternatives are stillborn. As Gramsci put it, these intellectuals are an 'élite' emerging along with 'fundamental groups . . . coming into existence on the original terrain of an essential function in the world of economic production' (1971: 5). These organic intellectuals give their class 'homogeneity and ... awareness of its own function not only in the economic but also in the social and political fields' (1971: 5). They 'must have the capacity to be ... organiser[s] of society in general, including all its complex of services, right up to the state organism' (1971: 5). They must make the new order appear 'natural' to most of the rest of society most of the time – or at least to the organic intellectuals of the subaltern classes a lot of the time. At times they must convince their class peers that such efforts require 'sacrifices of an economic-corporate kind' (1971: 161) so they can appear to be the 'motor force of a universal expansion, of a development of all the "national" energies' (1971: 182).[11] This intellectual elite tries to ensure that 'the dominant group is coordinated concretely with the general interests of the subordinate groups' and indeed does much of that work itself, all the while remembering that 'such sacrifices and such compromise cannot touch the essential' (1971: 182). They cannot go too far in their efforts to gain and maintain the high ground of 'ethico-political' hegemony: the consent they manufacture must not stretch the economic foundations of the 'decisive [economic] function exercised by the leading group in the decisive nucleus of economic activity' (1971: 182) to breaking point.

In this age of globalisation, hegemonic organisers work at local and global levels of the world's political economy, in positions within states, international organisations and the interstices of civil society. This is where the global economists come in, working for the World Bank and similar development institutions from Sierra Leone to Indonesia, and the Democratic Republic of Congo to Bolivia. They are the organic intellectuals of the transition from various non-capitalist modes of production – or state-capitalist and Stalinist interregna – to the utopia of totally 'free' markets and the reified and eternally self-interested *homo oeconomicus*.[12] They have to make it all seem inevitable and without alternative, and they have to make it work well enough so all its 'stakeholders' can share in its universal benefits – or hope to at some time in the future.

At times they are constrained in the universal task of spreading capitalism qua capitalism – especially in its 'free trade' ideological cloaks – around the world by the particular political gambits of empire's hegemon that are sometimes much more mercantile than the ideals of their universal (neo)liberalism. Such may be the case now, if the current leaders of the USA are not prepared to sacrifice some of their particular interests for the interests of those behind the more universal form of capitalism promised by the ideology of globalisation. Hypocrisy and fragmentation, hidden by bluster and militarism, do not make for good hegemony.

At other moments they struggle as the tenets of Hayekian doctrine are tested by the rise and fall of its relevance to their task. After crises and contradictions such as those sweeping Asia in 1997, mildly Keynesian challenges to the outlines of the Washington (or some other) Consensus make brief appearances – but as often as not their proponents go the same way as the starbursts of previous policy innovations.[13]

These are the tasks of those who manufacture and craft consent for capitalism's global project. This is a mode of production and illusion wherein all are formally entitled to property while in reality they are dispossessed; all are credited with the capacity to truck, barter and trade while actually they are bereft of all but their labour to sell – though there is often no 'labour market' demanding it; and all are geared to consume like Hollywood stars but most are lucky if they have the incomes of streetsellers. Its intellectuals face a gargantuan and probably impossible task. The busy clerks of the World Bank – most of them humble, if grossly overpaid; others more highly ranked accountants full of the hubris inspired by what they think is 'God's work'[14] – are building the foundations for a global hegemony absorbing most of the cadres (Van der Pijl 1998: 162) of the underdeveloped world as well as their core-centred peers. They could be labelled in a number of ways: as economists within the transnational capitalist class's intelligentsia; as financial, economic and developmental bureaucrats within an emerging transnational state; or simply as members of a transnational managerial class (Cox 1987: 359–60, 367–68)[15] floating in and out of global corporations, states and international organisations, but presently ensconced in multilateral financial institutions. However described, they are busy changing the most intimate details of the lives of billions of people not yet fully embraced by the market.

Even if it could be carried out – and there are many reasons why it may be impossible[16] – changing the world to an imagined capitalism is a fundamentally revolutionary project. Yet because the manufacturers of this dream are also concerned with maintaining order, it must be executed with the intricate finesse of a passive revolution that changes socio-economic structures without unbundling too much in the way of politics – that sphere of life that economists suppose to be hermetically sealed from their realm of expertise. The leading political manifestations of global order cannot afford too many Iraq invasions to impose a new world order, anyway: very few of their targets have Iraqi-like resources to pay the *ex post facto* bills, and the world's moral elasticity and democratic relativism can only stretch so far.

No wonder, in the age when their apolitical speciality was supposed to reign – when history qua ideology was supposed to have ended and the market could march where soldiers had feared to tread – there is malaise in the global economists' ranks (Denny 2000; Kahn 2001). As the World Bank's missions expand to cover the hegemonic fall-out from the proliferation of its primary one's contradictions, it finds itself performing state-like functions after it has hollowed out the local states in which it has been inserted. As the difficulties of maintaining hegemony compound, mission creep ensues (Einhorn 2001: 22–35). The contradictions multiply because its previous ideology and policies of structural adjustment have delegitimised states – and sometimes even catalysed their ruin, so it has had to develop a post-conflict unit to patch them together again (Reno 1998). In any case, most of the states with which it works do not have the capacity to supervise the 'mass dislocation and conflict [resulting] from a rapid programme of converting land and labour into commodities', as Colin Leys puts it so stringently (1994: 44–45).[17] Its ideology has swept states into the dustbin but it needs them more than ever: thus they become part of its position as a global state. In spite of their protestations to the contrary, economists pushing the market are statists par excellence. They stride on, denying their real role while cultivating allies within civil society and states where they can. They thus smother the development industry with 'comprehensive frameworks' when there is a counter-hegemonic challenge to co-opt and a cause to commandeer. All they really want to do is make the world into a place where property rights rule – but that is simultaneously far too (theoretically) simple and (practically) complex. Until the troops are mobilised for that task, environmental reviews, gender awareness, indigenous knowledge and anti-corruption workshops fill the dead space of overly educated wheels spinning in a vacuum. Meanwhile, they have to apologise meekly when the huge subsidies that Americans, Europeans and Japanese states give their agriculturalists – corporations and humble family farmers alike – make the headlines and contradict their textbook dictums about comparative and competitive advantage and the evils of state interference with the divine laws of invisible forces.

This book is not about the coercion and corruption that share the tripod of hegemonic construction with the manufacture of consent.[18] It does not concern the politics of the process by which ruling classes and bureaucrats all over the world are absorbed into a global historical bloc. Rather, these chapters consider the Bank's 'educative function' – the output of what is effectively its 'publishing house' (Gramsci 1996: 52) – in its attempts to fashion intellectual and moral leadership on the terrain of the economic restructuring making up the development agenda, and some of the results of these attempts.[19] Without falling prey to the common neo-Gramscian problem of excessive concern with ideology, they concentrate on development theories and policies that wind their ways through the array of institutions and material capabilities that Robert Cox considers to be, in partnership with ideas, the crucial components of changing world orders (1996: 98, 100). They focus on what Robert Wade has called the most visible of the World Bank's public relations functions, the publication of its annual development reports and other widely disseminated media initiatives

(Wade 2002: 224, Note 15).[20] If, as Ben Fine reminds us, the World Bank spends two to three times as much money on public relations as on research (Fine 2002b: 205), and if we see the annual development reports as public relations exercises as much as research, a focus on this discursive activity is appropriate. And if it is true that a World Bank consultant's post-conflict strategy for Eritrea had the name of another country inserted in the text every time the word 'Eritrea' was supposed to appear, then it is clear that the institution in question has its collective mind made up about its policy template (anonymous interviews conducted in 2002). Research is hardly necessary.[21] The only task left is to hammer established conclusions home. If 'home' is hubristically defined as 'the world' – true cosmopolitanism is global in reach – and it is where the heart is, then this task is to win the hearts and minds of all those sharing one's home. There is little doubt that this is a hegemonic project of some magnitude, requiring some hearty work.

When the mission of economics is to proselytise, however, these 'scientists' weaken. They have been weaned in the best schools of economics the Anglo-American world can provide, but their science is that of the self-revealing laws of nature. Thus they are shocked and ill-prepared when encountering resistance, be it from the deluded practitioners of other disciplines, antithetical members of global civil society, or peasants and petty bureaucrats in the Third World who fail to see the logic of a market that allows only some states to subsidise. Even though they are born and bred to rule, they are neither propagandists nor arms-bearing brigades. Having no guns, they must hide their contempt behind the reams and reams of words that will silence – if not bury – those of the more poetic dissenting environmentalists, democrats, activists and even other economists (if they are Keynesians, or something to the left of that). But the banality and the hypocrisy of their prose and propositions are too easily deconstructed by their critics, if the latter are not worn down by the practical demonstration of the proposition that if a lie is told often enough, it will become the truth. However, the critics can do little about the power that backs up the economists, except to mobilise counter-power. Critical incisiveness is but the first step in the breaking of hegemony. With it comes an awareness of the power – the coercion, the corruption and the co-option – backing up every consensual effort in the realm of political economy propaganda. Those who try to speak the truth to such power have to account for the arrogance of those who know that, in the last instance, force wins. In the meantime, it is worth investigating the extent to which a transnational state *is* emerging, and how the World Bank is playing its role within this new array of institutions.

The World Bank and a transnational state

The brief discussion of the force underlying the hegemony of neoliberal economics illustrates the pitfalls inherent in delineating a clear distinction between the concepts of *American* and *transnational* hegemony in the post-9/11 conjuncture. In dealing his final blow to William Robinson's (2001b) grand theoretical claims about the emergence of a transnational state, Fred Block notes that there is no 'effective monopoly on legitimate violence' at the global level, so there can be no global state (2001: 220). Such a claim appears to be supported by recent American unilateralism, indicating diminished supra-state globalisation. However, if what Robert Wade (2001b, 2002) condemns as 'American' hegemony is really confined to the American *Treasury* (as he also suggests) and the Treasury is partial to transnational more than to domestic capital, then the force the USA is expending globally may be as much in the interests of a transnational entity as in those of a state perceived in more traditional terms. That European states in earlier epochs did not enter into a 'coalition of the willing' does not mean that the forces invading Iraq were acting only in the interests of American capital.[22] American capital is the leading edge of globalisation. Even if the Treasury is acting in American qua American interests, and the World Bank and the IMF follow suit, this is not necessarily incompatible with the interests of global capital. Opening capital markets in Thailand is as good for pension funds in Luxembourg as in New York; likewise with stock markets in Nairobi. In both cases, the international financial institutions – or rather, the Global Ministry of Finance and the Transnational Department of Development – will follow to administer bail-outs in the case of openness gone wrong, and to empower local bureaucrats with the capacity to facilitate the flow of portfolio investments. In similar fashion, the breakdown of the World Trade Organization's meetings in Seattle in 1999 and Cancun in 2003 may not be a blow for neoliberal and core-centric globalisation if bilateral negotiations open up the Third World to transnational service corporations and only slightly loosen the West's protectionist barriers (Monbiot 2003b; Becker 2003). There is even a possibility that the economic blowback resulting from the Iraqi invasion might hasten the integration of global capital. Thus, the biggest military adventure for the biggest world power since the Vietnam War may have served the interests of a 'global' class and state in spite of the intentions of its protagonists. The mere presence of a unilateralist administration will not stop the forward march of globalisation. As Robinson puts it, 'the "US" is playing a leadership role *on behalf of* a transnational élite' (2001a: 227).

The accuracy of speculation about the ramifications of the George W. Bush regime can only be determined after the event. Nonetheless, those who raise the issue of a monopoly on violence have a valid point. If we were to cling to the claim of a transnational state, we would certainly have to say that its repressive apparatuses were underdeveloped. However, the presence of UN peacekeeping forces around the world, and the length of time the Americans devoted to trying to persuade the UN Security Council to legitimise its plans to invade Iraq, do indicate a somewhat more multilateral deployment of force than there was in the age of the Roman Empire. In any case, theorists of the emerging global state only claim to have seen its earliest and most tentative stages. There are, however, other, more interesting reasons to interrogate the notion.

Both advocates and critics of the theory of the transnational state share a propensity to have their state rule over a single mode of production and a one-dimensional cultural formation. William Robinson stakes his claim for a global state on the proposition that globalisation is 'the near culmination of a centuries-long process of the spread of capitalist production relations around the world and its displacement of all pre-capitalist production relations' so the main task for the transnational state is to manage the capital–labour nexus (2001b: 158). Although they may be linked with the global market, pre-capitalist production relations certainly have not disappeared in rural Africa, where more than 90 per cent of the land has no state-recognised (or formal) tenure, be it customary or capitalist. In peri-urban areas in Africa and Asia, between 40 and 50 per cent of residents have only informal land rights (Deininger 2003: xxi, xxiii, xxv). They have not passed through the many phases of primitive accumulation. Thus Philip McMichael can say that Robinson's claim for a single global mode of production is at best a 'provocative telos' that 'suspends the dialectic' as these 'residuals' resist transformation, suggesting this as reason enough to dismiss the theory (2001: 201–02). However, McMichael is too quick to jump to conclusions: cannot a transnational state preside over a primitive accumulation process? National states mediate a mix of cultures and modes of production, so Robinson's supposed teleological assumptions do not throw the baby out with the bathwater. Uneven articulations of culture and production relations are no reason to trash the idea of a global state, any more than they would rule out national ones. Analysis of social formations as far apart as Canada and South Africa would observe these states' attempts to mediate the struggles of language-groups-cum-nations. Their states govern ethnic formations historically shunted aside by capitalism's imperial spread and now on 'reserves' ruled by 'traditional' authorities empowered by a history of colonial state formation in a criss-crossing context of class structuration and primitive accumulation.[23]

In other respects, these two national states fail to meet the criteria of those who think states can only rule over a smooth national space, or something functionally equivalent at the global level. They download responsibility to provinces and cities, retaining a principle of subsidiarity – often without the resources to match.[24] Canada's provinces have egg and milk marketing boards to ease the production and marketing problems of their farmers and protect them from their compatriots in other provinces. Beer cannot be sold across provincial borders; thus people say that there is more free trade between Canada and the US than between Quebec and Ontario. In South Africa – home of the greatest income inequalities in the world – the disparities between cheek-by-jowl townships and financial centres illustrate what William Robinson notes is a global phenomenon:

> A simple loop by car through Third World . . . principal urban centres reveals the vast gap between social and cultural worlds within the very same city. Glittering malls replete with the latest the global economy has to offer, fast-food chains, beckoning recreational centres and well-guarded residential neighbourhoods that would be the envy of any First World centre stick out as lagoons of wealth and privilege surrounded by oceans of poverty and mass misery, often divided only, and literally, by the very best security systems that money can buy. One slips from 'development' into 'underdevelopment' without any geographic significance beyond urban geography. In an absolute sense the poor in the South are much more poor [*sic*] than the poor of the North. But the social dividing line is clearly not a national one (2002: 1066).

Both states must simultaneously mould their political economies within the constraints of larger and smaller neighbours and regional state apparatuses such as the North American Free Trade Agreement and the Southern African Development Community. Concurrently, they are constantly grooming themselves to be 'competitive states' (Porter 1990) hammering out policies to augment productivity and job creation that will not contradict the dictates of the World Trade Organization, yet another international organisation in which they try to wield influence. Depending on class and location within their nation-states Canadians and South Africans alike must negotiate with all sorts of *levels* of state organisation, from those with modified pre-capitalist roots to those regulating cyberspace. State-like structures at a transnational level are gaining increasing relevance to the people of these countries, as are the transnational classes forming and accumulating within them (Sklair 1997: 514–38). Yet in spite of their multilayered cultural formations, socio-economic disparities, mixed modes of production and globally tied political economies, no one challenges the 'stateness' of these social formations. It is clear, then, that the category of statehood does not require a unified and undifferentiated social formation, or totally free trade within its borders. There is no reason on those counts to exclude the possibility of a transnational state.[25] Neither Canada nor South Africa has been labelled a 'quasi-state', that is, one with juridical sovereignty granted with the fortunes of the decolonisation moment, but very little in the realm of empirical sovereignty (Jackson 1990). It is to these states that this chapter turns: for them, a transnational state is much more real, and begins to resemble the colonial states of not so long ago.

If words written from inside the quasi-states on the periphery of the global economy were read in its centre, a version of political theory might emerge allowing more plausibility to the idea of a transnational state. They might remind us, as did Karl Polanyi during colonial times, that neither metropolitan nor (neo)colonial states have been able to offer much protection against the 'ravaging international trade and imperialism ... destroy[ing] precapitalist communit[ies] of kinship, neighbourhood, profession and creed ... all forms of indigenous, organic society' (Polanyi in Burawoy 2003: 219; Polanyi in Silver and Arrighi 2003: 328). Close attention to the new and fragile states under construction since the days of decolonisation would lead to theories about states differing from those on offer in the bookshelves of the West. As wars and their lords crossed porous boundaries from Liberia to Sierra Leone and Rwanda and Uganda to the Democratic Republic of Congo, and swept across seas and skies as in the American invasion of Iraq, the fusion of state and nation and the legal monopoly of violence therein, would seem precarious indeed (Reno 2002; Clark 2001). As the mendicants of global empire arrive to 'reconstruct' with humanitarian and transformative largesse in the post-conflict moment, we might wonder, too, where the loci of the state's legitimation building and welfare functions lie.[26] From the point of view of those living in what Mark Duffield calls the world's 'borderlands' (2001b), the contradictorily coercive and consensual – and precarious – construction of class and state rule is rooted in local *and* global processes.[27] For the people living in post-conflict societies such as Kosovo and East Timor, the administrations ruling them

> constitute a new type of loosely bounded political system in which the policy makers are both international and national, and the exercise of policy depends on the cooperation and coordination of a range of military, political, administrative and non-governmental organisations. They borrow elements from the UN trusteeship system, from colonial administration and governance, and from post-Second World War reconstruction in Europe and Asia (Baskin 2003: 165).[28]

Why not consider the actions of the World Bank, the UN High Commission for Refugees and the UN Security Council as part of the functions of an emerging 'transnational state' – as busy handing out contracts to transnational construction companies to rebuild oilfields as it is subcontracting non-governmental organisations in global civil society to paste on band-aids and sending confused peacekeepers to carve out small 'zones of safety' in the mêlée of reconstruction gone wrong?[29] From Southern points of view, there are many manifestations of a global state, from structural adjustment programmes to humanitarian relief. Parts of their local states are incorporated into its apparatuses, as are their classes.

The question is: if this new state is emerging – and states do not emerge overnight – is a new form of hegemony being born along with it? The advantage of a *class* perspective on hegemony is that it enables us to see many classes, within many nation-state formations *and* social formations above and below them, battling for survival, domination and hegemony. During those struggles, their organic intellectuals will create state-like institutions and utilise already existing ones – at any level of the global economy. So too will ideologies develop. Even at the local level, they are intimately embedded. As noticed by the theorist on whom this chapter rests, we must:

> take into account the fact that international relations intertwine with those internal relations of nation-states, creating new, unique, and historically concrete combinations. A particular ideology, for instance, born in a highly developed country, is disseminated in less developed countries, impinging upon the local interplay of combinations (Gramsci 1971: 182).

What better way to highlight the imposition of neoliberalism, for example, in the Third World? How better to illustrate the organic intellectuals of a global class and transnational state encroaching on local social relations? Could there be a clearer method of interrogating the globalisation of hegemony, and the institutions for its propagation such as the World Bank?

Global hegemony and the World Bank
Gramsci's words, quoted above, are easy to apply to the Third World. He could have been writing about the transmission and reception of neoliberal ideology – 'born in a highly developed country' (after it has used many tried-and-true means of protectionism on its way to the top of the ladder, which it then kicks down [Chang 2003]) – and exported, along with many other goods and cultural forms from the West or the North, to the Third World. The task of making such an ideology hegemonic is the crucial one, however. If the 'local interplay of combinations' is to coalesce into a historical bloc that can truly mobilise national and global developmental energies, these ideologies must not be 'arbitrary, rationalistic, or "willed"' (Gramsci 1971: 376–77). Hegemonic organisers from the World Bank and institutions working with it – and even to some extent 'against' it in so far as they do not challenge its fundamental imperatives and serve to illustrate the pluralistic nature of the global development industry – must make

their discursive practices 'necessary to a given structure' (Gramsci 1971: 376–77). Even to construct a 'minimal hegemony' (Femia 1981: 47) that barely brings the 'junior officers' on the edge of the global economy into the larger hegemonic project, the ideology of the global ruling class must 'have a validity which is "psychological"' and capable of '"organising" human masses' (Gramsci 1971: 376–77).

To be successful, this new ideology – and the policies in its train, creating no small material benefits – must 'create the terrain on which men move, acquire consciousness of their position, struggle, etc.' Otherwise, only 'individual "movements", polemics and so on' will be created, 'even though these are not completely useless, since they function like an error which by contrasting with the truth, demonstrates it' (Gramsci 1971: 376–77). One wonders on reading this passage if neoliberalism is such an ideology – one whose error has not quite been demonstrated to the satisfaction of its progenitors. Or if it has, do they say, 'Sorry, we made some mistakes, and we will do better next time', but continue in the old ways? Saying sorry has become an integral part of global hegemonic strategies. Working out complicated Heavily Indebted Poor Country (HIPC) debt-relief programmes, renaming Structural Adjustment Programmes (SAPs) as Poverty Reduction Strategy Papers (PRSP), and starting up Structural Adjustment Participatory Review procedures makes it look like saying sorry *means* something, even though the results of such attempts have been disappointing to the participants the Bank is wooing so assiduously. However, if conjunctures such as the current one – wherein WTO meetings are unpacking the hypocrisy of the neoliberal agenda and the American economy itself unravels – are truly structural and do lead to a global hegemony comprising 'new architecture', there is little doubt that the hundreds of recipes for 'passive revolution' in circulation will be incorporated in a reborn World Bank.[30] Perhaps the workers in the research department of the Bank – those who stir up the Keynesian ideas for the 'Knowledge Bank' whilst the operations department goes on as usual (Pincus 2001) – will have the opportunity to gain hegemony in their institution as it struggles, Phoenix-like, to take over the development agenda in a world turned into ashes by the leadership of a hegemon *manqué*.

It may well be that, as Karl Polanyi is famous for noting, the utopia of fully free markets is just that (Silver and Arrighi 2003), and excessive moves in the direction of the mirage will lead to destruction unless the 'double movement' that comes about as a response to the over-marketisation of society goes in the direction of progressive embeddedness – that is, towards reciprocity and social welfare – instead of fascism. Seemingly oblivious to this possibility in spite of the rhetoric of those on the public relations side of the Knowledge Bank, most of the 'real' organisers of World Bank hegemony – those on the operations side as well as those closest to the US Treasury – are devoted to the embodiment of their dreams, even if they have to bend over backwards to incorporate their critics. There are many analyses of the shortcomings of efforts to meet the challenges of the most vociferous civil society organisations, ranging from HIPC relief packages to the establishment of inspection panels to investigate accusations of non-compliance with the Bank's own environmental and human rights policies, but they do not move far from the oxymoron of spontaneous neoliberalism (Beattie 2002; Fox 2002).[31] In the end, the efforts by the 'reformers' simply look more like meek justifications for World Bank intervention at any cost – or rants against the IMF making the World Bank look favourable in contrast – rather than coherent alternatives to neoliberalism.[32]

Yet still, those intent on seeing change to their liking in the Bank insist that if they read closely enough between the lines, evidence of important shifts in Bank 'thinking' can be discerned (Rodrik 2002).[33] This tendency could well have been set in motion by Robert Wade's essay on the 'art of paradigm maintenance' (reproduced as Chapter Nine in this book)[34] – ironically, perhaps, setting a paradigm on its own – in which the Bank's efforts to gloss over the counter-hegemonic implications of the East Asian 'miracle' could be perceived only after careful scraping away revealed the empirical truths of pragmatic industrialisation policies. Meticulous empiricism could thus wash away the ideological imperatives of self-interested but ephemeral politicians.

To be sure, such a perspective did not wish away the long-term implications of a march through the institutions, but can it too easily build castles of knowledge in the air on one hand, and too much concentration on battles over who is the Bank's chief economist on the other (Wade 2002)? It may also encourage too much focus on the relationship of the USA to the Bank, rather than concentrating on the evolution of its relationship within the ideological ramifications of shifts in the global political economy and development practice – not to speak of the question Patrick Bond (2001a and Chapter Sixteen of this book) consistently raises along with several social movements (including some of the populist right-wing mould in the USA): should the Bank be 'fixed' or 'nixed'? But even the question of fixing it or nixing it can sidestep the actual grounding of the World Bank as an institution that grows out of a global class and its embeddedness in a transformed world space of accumulation. In terms of this perspective, the true organic intellectuals of a transnational bourgeoisie will soon create a new institution – or a substantially modified one – which will do a better job of justifying the global spread of capitalism. If that new institution is simply a better Keynesian one than its predecessor, and simply more effective at a process of mission creep incorporating all special interest groups, this will mean that global capitalists have woken to realise that neoliberalism is not integrative enough to make capitalism look like it can operate beyond the corporate interests of its dominant members.

To be more precise, a new institution may only mean that global capital's organic intellectuals have awakened their more parochial peers to make some economic-corporate sacrifices in order to reconstruct the hegemony that neoliberalism caused to crumble. The degree of those changes could be measured by the extent to which a new global development institution decommodified many basic needs; how they would be supplied as a public good that would not destroy the other public good, a sustainable environment; how much it relied on private investment; who would be represented in its system of governance – and so on. Such measures would reflect much larger structural changes in the global political economy. To get to the nub of the Bank's hegemonic role it is necessary to address the question of how the Bank itself effects these larger changes. To reach that point, we must first examine the 'transnationalness' of this particular component of the transnational intelligentsia. Then, secondly, we must see how the Knowledge Bank is transforming global consciousness about development itself (or vice versa). If both of these features of the construction of historical blocs and hegemonic struggles are seen to be robust and well embedded, then capitalism's various ideologies may be 'necessary to a given structure' rather than 'arbitrary, rationalistic, or "willed"' (Gramsci 1971: 376–77).

The first question may be more easily addressed than the second. A quick look at the structure of employment at the Bank may indicate how transnational the institution is. Wade's 1996 *New Left Review* article suggested that the academic credentials of the Bank's economists are what counts: mostly they are trained in the Anglo-American economics departments and are more likely to be disciples of Smith than List or Marx. Nevertheless, the national composition of the Bank – like that of the UN of which it is a part – signifies how cosmopolitan its organic intellectuals are, and could suggest how widely and deeply a defence of liberal capitalist principles would go if the Bank were under ideological siege. To be sure, many of its high-level economists might well hold out for the sake of theological principles, but might the 'subalterns' in the Bank change ideological sides if some simmering nationalism came to the surface? Where would the team in the Distance Education Unit go in the event of a battle between the legions from Porto Alegre and the Wall Street–Treasury Complex? Where would lie the ultimate hegemonic allegiance of the Irish manager, the Canadian task manager, the American co-ordinator for planning and partnerships, the Russian information officer, the American consultant and telecourse producer-director, the Canadian instructional designer-consultant, the Indian information officer, the American broadcast and communications engineer, the Cameroonian education specialist, the Canadian instructional designer, the American instructional designer, the Argentinian studio manager, the American programme assistant, the American audio-visual assistant, the Guatemalan team assistant, the Peruvian production assistant, the Russian team assistant, the American team assistant, the Puerto Rican woman with no job description, the American project assistant, the American training technician, the Spanish audio-visual technician, the Korean visual information specialist, and the Hong Kong (or is that supposed to be Chinese?) education and technology specialist?[35] Would they give up their large salaries and pensions to join a (hypothetical) Global Social Forum project to teach community activists how to set up People's Budget committees? Could the Forum offer them enough in the way of material incentives to supplement the clear moral imperative of 'another world'? Would an 'opinion survey' reveal the true ideological propensities – a difficult task, given the predilection of the petite bourgeoisie to be a rather precarious ideological grouping in any case – of this small group within the Bank, or its approximately 9876 other employees? And how would it stack up – ideologically as well as numerically – with its class peers around the corner at the IMF, down the street at the White House, or further afield in states and corporations all over the world? Such issues cannot be decided in advance of the showdown – but it is clear that the people working for the Bank are representative of a globalised class. When (or if – this chapter makes no claim to the certainty of a revolution within and without the World Bank) the chips are down, the ideologies of such actors will be determined by neither nationalism nor cosmopolitanism, but by a combination of principles incorporating interpretations of universal rights and the role of nation-states and global bodies in their implementation, which in turn will be heavily influenced by the nature of the realignment of global 'historic blocs' in the wake of structural crises and their resolution.[36]

We could argue that if indeed a world movement had reached a stage at which the Bank was truly challenged, the proclivities of a mere 10 000 would not matter. There are many media technicians among the multitude[37] capable of running a distance education programme, and perhaps the energies of a global Zapatistan economic cadre would overcome its shortages of technocratic skills in the event of all neoclassical economists taking early retirement or being forced to become peasants. What matters are the ideological contours of the world at the moments of economic and political crisis. Gramsci was not at all convinced that such a crisis would automatically engender a socialist revolution: this is why, for him, a war of position was necessary. In the absence of a well-prepared counter-hegemony, fascism would win the day and all of its 'morbid symptoms' would pervade the interregnum between the dying of the old and the birth of the new (Gramsci 1971: 276). This is where the second question comes into play: what is the Bank doing to alter global consciousness?

The Bank's hegemonic battles are not all about capital controls and slightly modified financial architectures, or grooming postgraduates into its McNamara fellowships. As if taking the Gramscian injunction to heart, the Bank is preparing its own long-term war of position. In the Jesuit tradition of capturing the minds of children, it has websites full of questions and answers for inquiring youth. A brief look at an online Development Education Programme indicates that the answer to just about any question leads to the confirmation of 'market' over 'state' and all the permutations of that belief.[38] The site guides the user to choose to tackle social, health or economic issues – but no matter where he or she starts, the endpoint is pro-market economics. It would take a sophisticated discourse analyst and an expert in website construction to ascertain why and how the questions on the site lead to answers in which privatisation and foreign investment appear repeatedly as the solutions, but a quick description of some of the site's routes to predestined conclusions may suffice to illustrate its discursive closure.

On entering the site (in late 2003), the user is asked to solve a social or economic or environmental issue. Social issues lead to health, and the problem of river blindness. The viewer sees a photograph of a young person leading a blind person, and reads that in Africa, a programme 'involving private business, international organisations, and the governments of 30 countries' is spraying 'environmentally safe' pesticides over a space nearly three times the size of France, and that

Merck pharmaceutical corporation's supply of Ivermectin treated 21 million people in 1998. Why was this order of priority chosen? Did the transnational corporation play the key role?

Beneath the description of this health problem, and medium-sized hot-link icons to other sites dealing with social issues, there is a large 'balloon' with characters in big italicised fonts and lots of white space around it, advising the viewer to 'go to economic challenges'. When on this site, little balloons appear automatically. They tell the viewer that privatising state businesses strengthens 'economies through encouraging competition and efficiency . . . frees governments to focus on policies that strengthen both business and civil society . . . [and] helps companies attract investors'. Another link on the 'economic challenges' site takes the viewer to a cement factory in Kunda, Estonia. It tells the reader that at one time this factory emitted 15 per cent of its cement into the air as dust. However, with the winds of privatisation in the air, a partnership including the government, the International Finance Corporation (a division of the World Bank that loans money to private enterprises) and foreign investors reduced that dust by 98.5 per cent – because it was more profitable. That is the only motivation the World Bank's educator deemed worth suggesting. Is it just coincidental that the singular inspiration of 'profit' resulted in such a surfeit of benefits?

A site accessed via the 'environment' page brings the surfer to a section on Africa, which informs that 250 million people – 'almost ½ the population' (an error as Africa's population is slightly over 700 million) – are suffering due to war. Peace is praised because it lets us 'raise our families, run businesses and build communities'. The user is told that 'we [Are 'we' all Africans? Or do 'we' all work for the World Bank?] make peace last by strengthening civil society, setting up systems to resolve conflict and helping veterans re-enter civilian life'. We are not told that the profit motive will usher in peace, but running businesses is a good reason for (somehow) creating peace. The environmental portion of the website menu had some slight criticism for 'business', however: 'sometimes', the viewer would learn, 'it is hard to get companies to pay fines for pollution'. The criticism is short-lived, though: young scholars are informed that fines are not the solution. In Indonesia, the government persuaded the newspapers to publish 'which companies were meeting environmental standards and which weren't. Within a year, half of the companies on the list were polluting less.' The positive story does not reveal whether the half that polluted less were the ones who met standards or did not, but in any case the lesson is clear. All corporations need is a combination of positive support and public shaming, and they will keep the environment clean.

The site seems a never-ending source of teleological quests: it could take hours to get through its 'interactive learning experience'. It may only be a very small component of a large ideological armoury, but it suggests as well as any other discursive dissemination the single-minded nature of the Knowledge Bank. From dissenting economists to inquisitive ten-year-olds, the Bank has the answers. Get fired, or get to the market – or at least to a 'public-private partnership' – and neutralise as many buzzwords about democracy or sustainability as you can on the way. Only history will tell whether these answers will suffice to weather the storms 'global civil society' might wish upon it, or those that may be caused by the bumpy transfer of global power from the USA to China, or an economic crisis resulting from the USA's disastrous combination of war and debt. In the meantime, the simple fact of increasing global poverty and inequality and poor growth rates since the moment of neoliberalism should be enough to mobilise counter-hegemonic questions, at least. If those questions inspire more inquiries about the nature of the global economy and how institutions such as the World Bank attempt to mediate the contradictions of accumulation, dispossession and class formation on a world scale, that may be another step on the road towards a new hegemony. If this new hegemony takes seriously the *public* nature of the tentative yet brutal first steps of primitive accumulation,[39] and how those representatives of transnational classes and their state in apparatuses such as the Bank have the power to ameliorate *and* facilitate those steps, it may be worth fighting for.

This book and banking for hegemony

The chapters in this book, disparate as they are, have in common a desire to expose the precariousness underlying the World Bank's hegemonic pretension. This chutzpah is most evident when such dominant personalities as Robert McNamara and James Wolfensohn have taken the helm of the institution and presented the crusade of poverty reduction as their own moral campaign. The fact that neither has been able to hide the ravages resulting from primitive accumulation on a global scale illustrates for most serious academics little more than the contradictions of the process of uneven capitalist development, the unsavoury interests it inspires, and the futility of attempts to airbrush them away. Yet the Bank maintains a hold on the process. Even though the capital it transfers to the Third World does not count for much beside the global circuits of purely private investment,[40] it has considerable power in the countries where foreign investment does not freely flow, and it appears to have taken the 'Gramsci effect' to a global level. It works to convince the Third World elites that there are no alternatives to its models. Confusingly for the products of an institution premised on one menu for all, these may be neoliberal or mildly Keynesian; they may have all sorts of gender, poverty alleviation and apparently environmentally sensitive add-ons; but they all presume the bedrock of commodity capitalism, whether this is attributed to states, domestic capitalists or – their favourite class – global capitalists. But the Bank also seems to compete with the Oxfams, Save the Childrens, UNICEFs, Christian Aids, and World Wildlife Funds for the moral leadership of all the bemused but supposedly well-meaning citizens of the wealthy West who would like to think their mode of production and consumption is as good for the global poor as it is for them.[41] As Stiglitz notes in the Introduction to the memoirs of his time in the Bank and his battles against the nastier scions of globalisation in the IMF, sixteen-year-olds in American high schools now debate the merits of structural adjustment programmes imposed in the USA's backyard (Stiglitz 2002: 4). The Bank can take some credit for this element of an emerging global consciousness – and its website, referred to above, suggests that it takes the sixteen-year-olds seriously – but such a position necessarily subjects it to as much criticism as praise. It is doubtful, as some proponents of moderate re-invention suggest, that a concentration on public-sector-style development – instead of knowledge and good feelings – would take the Bank out of the spotlight and let it get on with a pared-down job (Pincus and Winters 2002a: 225). 'Development' has come to mean far too much in this 'world-historical' moment; as James Ferguson notes in his *Anti-politics Machine* (1990), it has become our equivalent of the nineteenth-century quest for 'civilisation' and thus a significant component of the hegemonic quest of an emerging transnational class, its organic intellectuals, and the state forms they create.

This book was inspired by reading, in the early and mid-1990s, a number of superb critiques of World Bank publications, including the Bank's annual *World Development Report* and key publications indicating what appeared at the time to be significant 'rethinking' of the Bank's development policy. Henry Bernstein's 1990 article 'Agricultural "modernisation" and the era of structural adjustment', a searing critique with an incisive materialist analysis of the World Bank's 1989 *Sub-Saharan Africa: From Crisis to Sustainable Growth* (upon which his chapter in this book is a 'retrospective') is the main inspiration for this effort. The theoretical interrogation of 'good governance' discourse by David Williams and Tom Young (1994) – also revitalised in this book (see Chapter Seven), with a review of a decade's efforts toward the realisation of liberal verities – was another crucial intervention, this time with the benefit of critical political science theory, in the increasingly searching academic examination of Bank practice. Robert Wade's now classical *New Left Review* article on the 'art of paradigm maintenance' (1996b) – reproduced here in full in Chapter Nine – was the final proof that the World Bank was a worthy subject of political and ideological critique, and that the arguments contributing to hegemonic construction in the realm of development in the post-Cold War era would revolve around the roles of the Third World state in areas such as industrial policy. My 1999 and 2000b essays highlighted the tensions in World Bank discourse on this Third World state. It is simultaneously seen as necessary but distrusted for the implementation of its liberal vision, because liberal states and economies are born out of and perhaps perpetually supplemented by very illiberal processes. Furthermore, the democratic politics growing out of liberalism can place demands on these states that capitalism cannot possibly meet: this is the Hayekian dilemma. In the last analysis these states are subject to the ultimate World Bank fantasy expressed in its post-conflict dreams: their destruction and reconstruction can be afforded only by 'post-conflict' scenarios.[42] In retrospect, it is from the work of William Robinson (2001a and b, 2005) and the 'cosmopolitanist' political theory growing out of globalisation, some of it encountered while I was working on a project on state formation and the humanitarian agenda (Moore 2000a), that the notion of the World Bank as a key institution in an emerging 'transnational state' took shape. David Williams's concept of *homo oeconomicus* (1999) confirmed the primacy of deep political theory within any searching interrogation of the Bank. In the same year, Ben Fine's blistering polemic on 'social capital' reinforced that obligation: theory must be important if the Bank and its economist allies make such gargantuan efforts to colonise it, confining and reducing it to the realms of neoclassical economics. That is why they are both reproduced here. Finally, the Berger and Beeson study in *Third World Quarterly* (published in late 1998, but discovered by me after reading Fine and Williams, and rewritten for this book) served to unite the empirical reality of the Asian crisis that so nearly destroyed those economies with an historically bound study of the eternal liberal verities that still stand hegemonic, in spite of near-annihilation in the crisis.

In sum, the chapters reproduced here are worthy of recirculation because they combine rigorous theoretical analysis and engagement with the contemporary outpourings of the Bank. Thus they will stand the test of time and serve as 'models' for further critical research. The 'rethought' essays reinforce this point: solid but reflexive conceptual frameworks can interrogate their past and throw stronger light on the present. They also illustrate the ongoing nature of the work at hand: as the Bank re-invents itself, so it is necessary to revisit the incarnations of the past. The academic subdiscipline of development studies is notoriously myopic and ahistorical. In such an environment the Bank can continuously pretend to remake itself while retreading tired old platitudes. These chapters show that historical memory is important, but also that such memory cannot remain in institutional showcases.

Last, but certainly not least, the chapters commissioned for this book, mostly from a newer generation of World Bank critics – many of them from Australia – illustrate how both new and more orthodox critical modes of analysis cast light on its myriad efforts. Scott MacWilliam (Chapter Two) raises critical questions about the Bank's ability to do what it really wants – to assist capital's transformative task of attaching 'freed' labour power to productive means, sometimes via smallholder production; not to maintain poverty, as some critics allege – but is restrained from so doing by neoliberal policies, the particular interests of the Bank's main shareholders, and the perverse forms of primitive accumulation practised by postcolonial elites. If the Bank's 'real' interest is to widen the process of capitalist transformation, it needs to follow 'intentional' development policies negated by today's dominant ideologies (and maybe by some of the less than dominant ones that it tries to co-opt). Neither populist nor laissez-faire proposals will do the trick.

MacWilliam might consider Susanne Schech, Sanjugta vas Dev and Thomas Wanner, also based in Australia, as populists concerned with direct poverty alleviation, real participation and ecological sensitivity rather than with the hard but necessary slog of capitalist development, but their intense and focused critiques of the Bank's hypocritical 'mission creep' illustrate the dangers of going into the uncharted and dangerous waters required by those who have to construct and maintain global hegemony.[43] As Wanner makes clear, the Bank's Orwellian discourse on the environment seems to be based on the principle that if you tell a lie over and over again, it will be believed. Perhaps the (partially postmaterialist) constituency devoted to environmental issues is not strong enough globally to call the Bank to task on such issues, but one would think that too much economy with the truth on the issue of democracy would be quite liable to create blowback. Schech and Vas Dev's careful dissection of how the Bank has managed the merger of poverty and participation, two key themes of legitimacy – in one concerted *fin de siècle* effort to convince both the rich and the poor that it is doing the right thing – is an excellent example of the use of some of the tools of postmodern and/or 'postdevelopment' thinking. Furthermore, such theory serves to take us somewhat beyond the economistic nature of most World Bank criticism: their focus on the Bank's attempts to forge legitimacy lends itself to a framework based on hegemony. Their findings about the limitations of even this 'softer' approach to rule through bio-power and discursive co-option – that is, that the efforts will probably fail in this realm as much as in the economic – bolster other more traditional modes of analysis.

Graham Harrison's chapter, commissioned for an International Political Science Association conference in Durban in July 2003 and this book on the basis of my reading of his 'Administering Market-Friendly Growth' (Harrison 2001a) and his research in eastern Africa, is the most empirically based of the chapters, but illustrates the practice of implementing minimal hegemony at the periphery, and thus buttresses just about everything in the book. If, in spite of continuing crisis-ridden political economies, the rulers of Uganda, Tanzania and Mozambique accept and benefit from 'second generation' governance regimes, those hoping to counter that hegemony will have to consider carefully the nature of these systems of rule. If rulers 'buy in' so easily, what will be the basis of a new hegemony in such 'gelatinous' societies (to borrow from Gramsci's somewhat binary distinction between civil society in East and West [1971: 238, 242–43])? Could it be on the *illiberality* of such regimes? Or on their inability to 'deliver' – a constant theme in Africa's southern powerhouse?

Richard Pithouse's philosophically trenchant contrast between Bank and South African scholar-activist modes of accounting for the participation of the poor – including an account of how even relatively mild voices of researchers on the periphery, trying to reflect their findings with accuracy, were silenced – simply serves to emphasise that the Bank's anodyne endeavours to straddle all sides of the hegemonic divide result in sterility at best and failure at worst. Finally, Susanne Soederberg and Marcus Taylor pursue the Bank's post-Wolfensohnian postures and see a strengthening of USA–World Bank intellectual and institutional synergies. They do not think the 'Wolfowitz moment' will change that process too much. Patrick Bond, however, pushes the contradictions of the current presidential conjuncture to face the 'fix it or nix it?' question directly, in favour of the latter.

Maybe it would not have to be nixed if, say, Amartya Sen became the next Bank president with Bond at his side as chief economist. Such a change at the helm would suggest it had gone some way towards repair: but it would still have to deal with the global state and the transnational bourgeoisie pushing it, regardless of whether 'hegemony' in the traditional international relations sense was passing from the USA to China, or going through more multilateral interregna. In the radical sense of 'hegemony', whoever is at the helm, the Bank or its alternative will be continuing to negotiate the contradictions of constant efforts to take 'economies' from being 'permanently at the mercy of rulers' (Dunn 2005: 135) and people not appreciated by the Bank's masters to a condition wherein private property is perceived to be eternal. As John Dunn (2005: 135) has put it, 'private property, the foundation on which a capitalist economy operates, is sustained or cancelled at political will'. Old or new versions of the Bank will have to traverse the teleology of the struggles over whether that contingency is maintained – and heightened – or annulled. Even if the footings of capitalism are solid and almost beyond politics, the permutations between the private and public 'development' of this mode of production will still be bones of contention. This is the political and ideological essence of 'uneven development'. Fixed or nixed, the global Ministry of Development has a huge task ahead of it. At the very least, more honesty about its agenda and its mistakes would help its hegemonic task. Hopefully this book, and many more like it, will encourage a bit more of that commodity than has been offered in the past.

Notes

1. Wade (1997) in a somewhat 'pro-World Bank' review of Caufield (1996).
2. See Sklair (1997); Robinson (2001a and b, 2005); and his vociferous critics of McMichael (2001); and Block (2001) thereafter.
3. The first words for this chapter were written over the period in mid-March 2003 when nearly 300 000 American and 43 500 British troops – with 2 000 Australians and a few Bulgarians, Czechs, Danes and other members of the 'coalition of the willing' in various capacities – began their invasion of Iraq.
4. These are some of the key notions developed in Hardt and Negri's best-selling *Empire* (2000). See D. Moore (2001, 2003a) for criticism.
5. See Monbiot (2003b) and Elliot and Denny (2003) for reports suggesting that Europe and the US were attempting to scuttle the World Trade Organization September 2003 Cancun meetings, given Third World pressure to reduce agricultural subsidies and tariffs on manufactured goods in the First World. Monbiot suggests that the Third World would have much less power in the one-on-one bargaining positions that unilateralism would impose. See also Battersby (2003) for discussion of the IBSA group – India, Brazil, and South Africa – and its role in the international arena in the context of global shifts since 9/11.
6. The notion of 'hegemon' in traditional international relations does not quite match the Gramscian perspective. The former is much closer to the Gramscian sense of a coercive power, dominant because of force and economic power more than consensus. Cox's use of Gramscian theory has brought a sense of global class alliances and the construction of ideological consensus to international political economy. For a useful perspective on the Third World in international organisations, written before Cox's engagement with Gramsci but foreshadowing it in many ways, see Cox (1979).
7. Most intellectuals within this movement assert that their aims are consistent with 'people's globalisation' rather than its corporate variety. A Gramscian perspective would suggest that these movements are proposing one or more counter-hegemonic views of world integration. Of course, it is open to question if the movements represent the emergence of a new cadre of organic intellectuals for a new 'fundamental class'.
8. On the Democratic Republic of Congo see Moore (2003b, 2004b). More generally see Jung (2003).
9. For a more detailed theoretical analysis of the global process of primitive accumulation see Moore (2004a).
10. It may be premature, however, to make clean distinctions between the supposedly 'national' and short-term interests of the Bush Jr. regime and a longer view of a transnational class. Given the predominant position of the US, its dominant class is also a 'transnational' class and thus many of the current state's apparently narrow-minded actions could actually be facilitating more 'globalisation'.

11. If we replace 'national' here with 'global', we can see how the current regime in the USA is failing the test for global hegemony. For how other powerful blocs are planning in the event of American financial implosion, see Greider (2002).
12. See Cramer (2002) for how neoclassical economists have turned even civil wars into individualist self-maximising enterprises.
13. Wade (2001a) remarks that since the Asian crisis, the IMF and the American Treasury have been relatively quiet on the issue of opening capital markets around the world, but he has 'little doubt that when the dust settles, the push for unrestricted capital flows will strengthen again'. The 'policy innovator' behind what may be a short-lived 'Post-Washington Consensus' was Joseph Stiglitz: on his sacking see Wade (2001b, 2002). For critical analysis of the Post-Washington Consensus, see Fine, Lapavitsas and Pincus (2003).
14. The former managing director of the IMF, Michel Camdessus, once claimed that the IMF's work was 'part of the building of the Kingdom of God', while World Bank President James Wolfensohn concluded an address to the 2000 UNCTAD conference pleading for delegates to unite with the Bank to 'complete the work of God'. See Bello (2000b).
15. Oddly, for a work that is considered the foundation of Gramscian international relations theory, the concept of 'organic intellectual' is not considered at length.
16. We could go on extensively as to why a universal global capitalism may not be possible. Perhaps not all people really want to be positioned within capitalist society, either for cultural (Gray 1998a) or even ethical reasons. Perhaps the globe's carrying capacity could not sustain much more American-style excess. Maybe Rosa Luxemburg is right: once the whole world is commoditised and there are no 'natural' economies to exploit, then capitalism's contradictions really become serious (2003 [1913]). But even if all of these caveats are little more than the whimpering of those who fear to go 'all the way', there is still a lot of history to come.
17. Leys's formulation captures Goran Therborn's (1996) celebration of Marxism's version of modernity. Therborn opens with the statement that Marxists are alone among modernists in combining a celebration of capitalism's destruction of the 'rural idiocy' and the various opiums associated with pre-capitalist social forms while criticising its contradictions, crises and conflict. On top of that it imagines a better modernism.
18. See Anderson (2002) on the oft-neglected role of corruption – the simple buying of allies, something often done by the international financial institutions – in Gramscian formulations on hegemony.
19. Graham Harrison's contribution to this book (Chapter Twelve) is an exception to the rule because it so cogently illustrates the hegemony of the 'good governance' agenda among some African ruling classes.
20. According to Wade (2002: 224, Note 15) the core budgets for the *World Development Reports* range from US$3.5 to US$5 million 'handsomely supplemented from trust

funds and foundations' (this in itself suggests the Bank's hegemonic power over such institutions). Their print runs range between 50 000 and 100 000 in English, with more in languages spanning Vietnamese to Spanish – and they are free in the Third World. UNCTAD's intervention-friendly report has a budget of under US$700 000 and runs 12 000 English copies and 7 000 to 8 000 in the other five languages used by the UN. The UNDP prints 100 000 copies in twelve languages and spends US$1.5 million in producing its welfarist *Human Development Report*.

21. There are always notable exceptions: Milanovic's (2002) paper is produced out of the World Bank Research Department and pours much cold water on the myth that globalisation leads to increasing equality. The paper is clearly labelled as not attributable to the Bank, and gets very little publicity.

22. It has been said that some of the reasons behind the American invasion of Iraq included stopping Middle Eastern oil producers from selling their oil for euros, and to gain control over oil destined, in the future, for China. These *are* 'unilateralist' reasons, but we can be sure that American-based oil corporations would soon learn to deal with euros, and their control over oil going to China would mean further involvement in the Chinese economy; see Klare (2003).

23. In South Africa the 'reserves' are, of course, formally disestablished, but they remain in the guise of trusts and are commonly labelled 'the former bantustans'. In Canada, reserves remain a formal as well as a material reality, although of course the population therein is much less than the millions in the poor rural areas of South Africa. See Mamdani (1996); Ntsebeza (2001); Kymlicka and Norman (2000); and Tully (1995).

24. In the days of welfare capitalism in Canada, the 'have' regions transferred resources through the central state to the 'have not' regions. These resource transfers have decreased recently. Cities have been given more responsibility for welfare recipients, but resources have decreased. Perhaps there are parallels here with 'global federalism'.

25. Canada and South Africa satisfy criteria of territorial integrity and democratic legitimacy, while global state-like institutions do not: this issue will be raised during the latter part of the section on quasi-states.

26. Humanitarian workers are designated 'mendicants of empire' in Hardt and Negri (2000: 35–37, 136).

27. Hoffman (1984) emphasises the inextricable intertwining of coercion and consent.

28. See also Moore (2000a).

29. See Ignatieff (1998) on the changing role of warriors – and humanitarians – in the new world order.

30. For example, Stiglitz (2003); and compare with Ladd (2003), prepared for the Southern African Regional Poverty Network, presumably in the hopes that South African Minister of Finance Trevor Manuel, chair of the World Bank's and the IMF's 'Expert Group' on the 'democratisation' of the institutions, would read it in

preparation for the meeting in Dubai in September 2003 at which he was supposed to report. For analysis of the World Bank's governance structures see Kapur (2002).

31. For a debate with a Hayekian political theorist – not an economist – on the lessons of East Asia as propounded to the Mont Pélerin Society see Moore and Kukathas (1999/2000).

32. See, for example, Stiglitz (1998c) for a clear statement of the social reconstruction through a liberal – be it prefixed by 'neo' or not – reform agenda. It is understandable why 'post-development' theorists, when reading such documents, see little point in debating the pros and cons of modernisation's various guises: for them development is simply about the destruction of non-capitalist societies and is nothing but a manifestation of the power of Western logo-centrism. It does not make much difference to them if modernisation is through Keynesian states or other neoliberal institutions.

33. A sceptic would see Sen's (1999, 2003) Herculean – or Sisyphean? – efforts to get the IFIs to think in welfarist terms in similar light. He does not necessarily interpret minuscule changes in World Bank documents as meaningful, but believes his proposals for change would be simultaneously small enough to implement without drastic changes to the IFIs and big enough to mean real change for the world's poor. A cynic would simply conclude that such global intellectuals would stick together in the end. On the limitations of Sen's democratic political theory see Hamilton (1999).

34. An interesting aspect of a retrospective analysis of Wade's 'paradigm' piece is that it preceded the East Asian financial crisis by only a few months. It was after that crisis that some elements in the Bank, notably Joseph Stiglitz, went public with a 'rethink' taking its tentative neo-statism in the 1997 *World Development Report* on 'the state' (on which see Chapter Eight in this volume) a step further with the trial balloons of the 'Post-Washington Consensus'. Two contending interpretations of the financial crisis ensued, consistent with neoliberal and interventionist hegemonic battles. The first said the crisis was a result of too much statism and crony capitalism while the second – for example, Wade and Veneroso (1998a) – blamed exuberant liberalisation. Others outside the pale – for example, Cumings (1998) – opined that the drastic shift in geopolitical structures after the end of the Cold War has made 'developmental states' such as those of South Korea a thing of the past.

35. This sample is taken from http://www.worldbank.org/distancelearning/About/team.htm, the website of the Bank's Distance Education Unit. Accessed 27 September 2003.

36. If the crisis led to a situation in which many societies had to be rebuilt, Cramer and Goodhand's words would be put to the test:

> Economists commonly project a fantasy of perfectly competitive markets onto the real world, where it becomes a benchmark against which actual market institutions and behaviour look distorted. Equally, political

scientists, political economists, and international financial institutions regularly project a fantasy of liberal states benignly providing basic services and public goods. Set against reality, this fantasy becomes a benchmark of 'good governance' and, in an extraordinary double-twist of self-deception, 'shared values' . . . these common fantasies show a remarkable lack of historical memory and contemporary understanding. And they are never more common than at the beginning of so-called post-conflict moments (2002: 885).

Hegemony would be put to the test by the templates for 'post-conflict' reconstruction.

37. 'The multitude' is Hardt and Negri's (2000) re-invention of the global proletariat.
38. To see the site 'where *you decide* where to start acting on social, economic and environmental challenges' through a process of interactive decisions, visit the Bank's Development Education Programme at http://www.worldbank.org/challenge/html/build_it.html (accessed 27 September 2003). Queries to the site's email address were not answered: perhaps a university address suggested to the site manager that the questions did not come from a primary school, which seemed to be the intended target.
39. Moore (2004a) attempts to explore this issue.
40. The Bank's over US$17 billion in loans in 2001 is a large part of the global development industry, which then averaged around US$50 billion per year. Moreover, the Bank's influence is great due to its ability to bring many other agencies on board with it in 'joint ventures' and its role in drafting many states' development strategies with policy conditionalities (or, as Graham Harrison suggests in Chapter Twelve, by making its ideas so hegemonic among ruling classes that they do the job almost voluntarily). Another factor is the volatility of private flows of capital: as Pincus and Winters (2002b: 20–21) point out, after the 1997 Asian crisis the low-income countries experienced a net outflow of US$3.4 billion in commercial bank lending. Thus the World Bank may represent a steady hand in the unpredictable world of finance.
41. The by now apocryphal story about the survey testing American public opinion on foreign aid illustrates this point. Question One asked: 'Do you think the American government spends too much on aid to Third World countries?' and got a vast majority of 'yes' answers. Question Two asked: 'What percentage of GDP does the American government spend on aid?' The average answer was '16 per cent'. According to Somberg (2005), American official development assistance in 2004 was 0.16 per cent of GDP, while Anup Shah (2006) counts 0.33 per cent in 2005, including US$19 billion of debt relief to Iraq and Nigeria (which is not supposed to be included in official aid) and US$2.2 billion for tsunami aid. Without these additions, the proportion is 0.22 per cent.
42. This point is made most effectively by Duffield (2001b, 2002).
43. Williams (2000) has discussed the issue of sovereignty and the World Bank, but as the tenor of the chapters in this book illustrates – in a world of quasi-states where a

transnational state is emerging to the detriment of peripheral ones – the concept of sovereignty is more a belief system than an empirical reality. Nevertheless, arguments can be made that the notion should be bolstered rather than jettisoned – see De Waal (1997). Certainly, if we argue that development of any sort is impossible without a domestic – or regional? – bourgeoisie made somewhat accountable by the development of democracy, the cultivation of strong states in peripheral capitalist social formations should be a 'public good' that would even be in the interests of a transnational state. As noted in Harrison (Chapter Twelve) and Moore (Chapter Thirteen) in this volume, the 'good governance' discourse is too vapid to make any but the most rhetorical impact on this phenomenon. See also Moore (2004a).

Chapter Two

Plenty of Poverty or the Poverty of Plenty?
The World Bank at the Turn of the Millennium

Scott MacWilliam[1]

THIS IS AN ORIGINAL CHAPTER FOR THIS BOOK.

In 1958, the assistant administrator for the colony of Papua and New Guinea drew a direct line between the ill health and undernourishment of the indigenous population and the central task of the Australian administration. The official said: 'the physical condition of the people . . . has to be improved so that their country may progress, for they are the only labour force available to achieve development' (MacWilliam 1988: 92). Over 40 years later, there is a major drive, not only in the independent nation-state of Papua New Guinea but globally to 'attack poverty' in order to raise the capacity to labour. The most senior officials of the World Bank see the institution at the centre of the drive and the annual *World Development Reports*, including that for 2000/1 (the *Report*) examined here, as expressions of that central position.[2]

In the words of the then Bank President James Wolfensohn, the *Report* expressed the twin objectives of 'expand(ing) the understanding of poverty and its causes' and 'set(ting) out actions to create a world free of poverty in all its dimensions' (World Bank 2000/1d). The manifestations of impoverishment, ill health, insufficient formal education and training, and the potential for disorder form a major current barrier to further growth. As with the Australian colonial official cited above, the Bank's policies are driven by a productionist objective, of extending the capacity to labour of the currently unemployed and underemployed on a global scale of reckoning. Health, nutrition, education and similar projects are specifically concerned to reduce important barriers against raising the capacity to labour.[3] For example, World Bank officials, when speaking of the success of a particular project such as the West African Onchoceriasis Control Programme, launched in 1974 against river blindness, emphasise that 'it has prevented an estimated 600 000 cases of blindness and added 5 million years of productive labour to the 11 countries' economies' (Goldin, Rogers and Stern 2002).

The *Report* therefore expresses far more than an 'affected concern for poverty' (Cammack 2001b) with an 'emancipatory tinge' (Cammack 2002). This World Bank document suggests a major international financial institution driven by a much deeper and wider purpose, that of providing a revitalised direction for development itself. That revitalisation is, necessarily, within the framework provided by capitalist commodity production, and can only accommodate the 'decommodification' rhetoric of anti-globalisation protests within that framework.

Nor can the World Bank's purpose be adequately described as enlarging the global space over which the hegemony of the USA is exercised (Soederberg 2001c; Wade 2001b). Indeed, Bank officials make no bones about the extent to which the development of capitalism in the 'developed world', including the USA, contains important barriers to extending accumulation and raising living standards globally (World Bank 2000/1a: Chapter 10). Since the publication of the *Report*, World Bank and other multilateral institutional reports have become even more pronounced in their opposition to directions being pursued by governments in 'developed countries' that include providing subsidies for local agricultural producers (see Badiane et al. 2002; Wolfensohn 2002; World Bank 2002d).

In attempting to construct a reformed direction for development, the IBRD/World Bank is forced not only to confront the national expressions of accumulation highlighted by the matter of subsidies and tariff barriers in the 'developed world'. The Bank also must deal with the opposition between forms of money capital that are represented by distinct institutions within the World Bank Group. The often-tense relationship between the World Bank and the International Finance Corporation, lender to private firms, often played out publicly as statism versus anti-statism, is testimony to the depth of this opposition (Caufield 1996: Chapter 16).

This tension within the Group, as well as that between the Bank and its major shareholders, including the USA, pales by comparison to the more serious obstacles to the international drive led by the Bank to attach labour to other means of production in order to reduce unemployment and underemployment. Perhaps the most important obstacle to the Bank's current direction comes from the growing ascendancy of local, mainly indigenous accumulators and their political allies in countries where poverty is especially widespread. The buccaneering activities of these accumulators, whether in 'clean' or 'dirty' arenas of commerce and industry (Bayart, Ellis and Hibou 1998) are important barriers to schemes to construct labour-extensive forms of production in rural and urban areas.

The power of local rentiers who feed off expanded production of rice in the Sourou Valley in Mali, made possible by the construction of a dam funded by the European Union in neighbouring Burkina Faso, necessarily limits the benefits which flow to smallholder growers (Woodhouse, Trench and Tessougue 2000: 49). In Mozambique, asset stripping when public enterprises are privatised to local entrepreneurs bolstered by internationally supplied funds secures little or no improvement in output or employment, whether processes are transparent or not (Alves 1999). No matter how or by how much real wages are slashed in Sierra Leone and Tanzania, the labour markets in these countries do not clear.

During development's 'golden age' after the Second World War, it was widely recognised that development required restraining particular forms of local capital (Cowen and Shenton 1996: Chapter 6) in order to secure households to rural smallholdings. Yet in country after country, post-independence political shifts (Swainson 1980: Part 3; Thompson and MacWilliam 1992: Chapter 3) and the 'freeing up the market' phase of 1980s and 1990s reform has unleashed trading and other capitals which have played an important part in undercutting previously constructed forms of household production. In these same countries, state power has been captured by the representatives of local, especially indigenous accumulators whose trajectory has come to limit the chances of replicating the post-war growth strategy.[4]

As the *Report* emphasises, following on from the drive for governance reforms and persistent attacks against corruption, the grip upon state power of local 'élites' is now an obstacle to turning national state institutions towards the 'needs of poor groups' (2000/1d: 39). One direct objective of 'popular empowerment' (Part 3), 'making state institutions more responsive to poor people' (Chapter 6), and 'removing social barriers and building social institutions' (Chapter 7), is to confine the now-rampant advance of the local, primarily indigenous class of capital.[5] Given this objective it is unsurprising that holders of state power in many countries often have a deep antipathy towards democratisation, branding it a form of foreign intrusion. In as much as local capital, the latest layer of capital in so many countries of the former colonial world, especially in Africa and the South Pacific, is engaged in primary or primitive accumulation of land and other natural resources, then the Bank's pro-poor direction aims to check these particular primary accumulators.[6]

This chapter proceeds initially by re-examining the distinction between absolute and relative poverty. It is emphasised that both must be given a historical rendering. Absolute poverty occurs at differing, relative levels of need. Relative poverty's most important expression is the accumulation of capital. While aiming to achieve an upward shift in levels of need for the poorest people, the *Report* and other development plans seek to do so by extending the relative impoverishment of all the world's working people. Their absolute poverty could conceivably be alleviated but they would be poorer relative to capital. However – and this is the next focus of the chapter – the form of development as employed in these plans as well as much official practice is now much more limited than in the 'golden age' of development after the Second World War. This chapter describes the difference between the present and the earlier phase as one of development, followed by non-development. Currently, attacking poverty tends to mean the dominance of the 'free market': spontaneous development without any substantial application of the development intent[7] to re-attach labour to other means of production through the agency of the state.

The chapter concludes by arguing that even if a major ideological shift towards intentional development occurred globally, there are now much more substantial barriers to the application of intent in the countries where poverty is most extreme than was the case after the Second World War. There has been a major change in class and state power with the growing ascendancy of a local class of accumulators, including the much-vaunted indigenous entrepreneurs. Holding state power, the class is now in a position to block moves comparable to the land and other reforms that opened space for expanded smallholding production in the post-war years. If popular empowerment is the rallying cry for attempts to mobilise domestic opposition to this class, respect for national sovereignty and local ownership are just as easily turned into weapons by the local, often indigenous, bourgeoisie for their asset-stripping, buccaneering activities.

Absolute and relative poverty
When Seebohm Rowntree included tea as an essential item in working-class consumption for his 1899 study of poverty in York, England, he contributed to arguments about absolute and relative poverty that continue to this day (Hartwell 1988; Alcock 1997). While the World Bank's concern is sometimes directed at a particular form of malnourishment – undernourishment expressed as shortages of food – as well as other dimensions of absolute poverty, its poverty reduction drive also is informed by recent changes in the idea of relative poverty.

Significantly, in the *Report* Bank President Wolfensohn emphasised that poverty now has a particularly distinct characteristic – its pervasiveness alongside great affluence (World Bank 2000/1d; MacWilliam 2003). That this is not, as it is so often portrayed, a concern about inter-country differences is made clear by Amartya Sen, Nobel-Prize-winning economist and Bank adviser. Sen notes that 'remarkable deprivation, destitution and oppression . . . can be observed, in the one form or another, in rich countries as well as poor ones' (1999: vi).[8] While the *Report* connects inequality and a plea for redistribution to a growth strategy, the coupling of plenty and poverty by the Bank president and numerous others is not a plea for the redistribution of wealth along social democratic lines, either domestically or internationally.[9] Nor does the connection form the basis for an objection to the enormous concentrations of wealth which have occurred in most countries over the last twenty to thirty years.

Instead, the principal significance of the increased wealth, for the compilers of the *Report*, is as an objective or goal towards which the living standards of those in poverty can be raised. That is, if plenty is most prominently the enormous concentrations of wealth in particular countries, it is also and more importantly the upward shift in the mass of necessary consumption for working people that has occurred across much of the globe since the Second World War. The *Report* captures both concentration and upward shift. It is concerned with absolute poverty in developing countries, including the so-called emerging market economies of Europe and Central Asia where there have been real and substantial declines in living standards for many people in recent years. But the *Report* is also informed by and driven to transform the poverty that separates so many people from others relatively advantaged by the post-war upward shift in levels of consumption. That is, the *Report* is concerned with the fact that absolute poverty is also relative to the levels of consumption attained by many working people across the globe. However, it is not concerned, indeed quite the opposite, that capitalism always means relative impoverishment of the class of labour in relation to the class of capital.

It is the former, limited sense of relative poverty, explained in more detail below, that is employed to describe a difference between levels of need in different countries and regions. Much popular concern is currently directed at the difference which exists between the bulk of the world's population, for whom there has been a major increase over the last 50 years, and people for whom no such rise has occurred or who have suffered absolute declines, particularly in the last two decades.[10] Hence the transformation of the idea of poverty central to the *Report*, beyond 'low income and consumption' to include 'low achievement in education, health, nutrition, and other areas of human development' (Wolfensohn 2000/1: v). That is, absolute poverty levels have shifted upwards. Poverty is now 'pronounced deprivation in well-being'. Following the 1990 *World Development Report, Poverty*, this encompasses 'not only material deprivation (measured by an appropriate concept of income or consumption) but also low achievements in education and health'. As a more recent World Bank 'case for aid' study stresses 'continued learning and knowledge are essential to scaling up the fight against poverty' (World Bank 2002b: 55).

Emphasising changes that have occurred in official development thought since 1990:

> This report also broadens the notion of poverty to include vulnerability and exposure to risk – and voicelessness and powerlessness. All these forms of deprivation severely restrict what Amartya Sen calls the 'capabilities that a person has, that is, the substantive freedoms he or she enjoys to lead the kind of life he or she values' (World Bank 2000/1d: 15, citing Sen 1999: 87).

It is important to recall two points made by Karl Marx about necessary consumption that assist in explaining the importance of the changing idea of poverty. The points also are important for ascribing more substantial meanings to the ideas of absolute and relative poverty than are commonly given. In *Capital*, Volume 1, Marx explains and emphasises that necessary consumption is (always and everywhere) socially determined.[11] Where capital reigns, the relation between labour, subsumed by and subject to capital, and other forms of nature, determines necessary consumption at distinct levels of need (distinct in part because of different levels of development of the productive forces in continents, countries and regions). As with all commodities, these satisfy human needs 'whether they arise ... from the stomach ... or the imagination' (Marx 1976: 125).

Absolute poverty occurs at different levels of need, and is not the a- or even anti-historical categorisation of deprivation that often appears in radical thought. As capitalism has raised the level of the productive forces, expanding capitalist commodity production into more and more areas of human life, levels of need have shifted upwards for a dramatically expanded population. The ability to grasp a potential for a better future is one effect of that shift, a point discussed briefly below and developed in more detail elsewhere (MacWilliam 2003). However, raising the commodity production of food or improving educational and health services, or building better housing – to use instances of changes which occurred for much of the increased population over the post-war 'long boom' period – did not end absolute poverty, even where the upward shifts were most pronounced. It is worth recalling that during the post-war long boom, when living standards rose for so many in the industrial countries, a Democratic president of the USA declared a 'war on poverty' in probably the most prosperous country, where levels of need had shifted upwards substantially during the post-war period. Nor can capitalism ever eliminate absolute poverty, in part because much of its dynamic depends upon 'promoting' ever-increasing levels of need, raising the level at which absolute poverty will occur. A shift upwards in the mass of necessary consumption changes the level at which absolute poverty is conceived. This comparative character of absolute poverty leads to one sense in which absolute poverty is also relative. As much as absolute poverty arises at a new higher level of need, that level is also relative to an earlier, lower level of need.

Marx's second point is that the slavery of the wage form exists not by virtue of some ahistorical description of absolute poverty and constant immiseration, but because of relative impoverishment, a second sense of relative poverty. The continuous revolutionising of the forces of production, one central pillar of capitalism's 'growth obsession' (Altvater 2001), requires a class of labour with a capacity to consume as well as to produce so that surplus value is realised (in production and consumption). As Marx emphasised in his rebuttal of Ferdinand Lassalle's so-called iron law of wages: '[T]he system of wage labour is consequently a system of slavery, increasing in severity commensurately with the development of the social productive forces of labour, *irrespective of whether the worker is then better or worse paid*' (Marx 1974: 352, emphasis added).

As greater wealth is produced socially, more and more is amassed in the hands of the class of capital and *relatively* less garnered by those who, acting upon other forms of nature, produce *all* the wealth. Even as living standards rise, as absolute poverty appears at new, often higher levels of need in which household consumption increases *absolutely*, labour is *relatively impoverished* in its relation with the bourgeoisie, the class of capital. This is the deepest sense of relative impoverishment, that the class which produces all material goods, must under capitalism always receive less than all that is produced. Simultaneously, more and more of social production is grasped by the class that produces nothing and engages in continuous parasitism, supervising the pathology of accumulation.

The importance of this deep sense of relative impoverishment should not be underestimated when so much misplaced criticism is directed at capitalism for producing different levels of need among working people. In its most vulgar form the criticism is expressed as 'guilt' about levels of First World consumption when Third World people are 'so poor'. An associated Marxist point related to the error in this criticism of the inequalities expressed as distinct levels of need is the proposition that people who subsist at lower levels of need are the most exploited, while highly paid skilled workers are less so. The reverse is the case, as what remains the clearest exposition of the point makes clear (Kay 1976). Contra the radical critics, that the expansion of capitalism requires and is well served by a low-wage, cheap labour economy (Chossudovsky 1997), dominated by shoe and fast-food companies, it is critical to recognise that as much as driving down wages and replacing living labour by dead are central to the competition between capitalists and therefore the behaviour of firms, such action also poses major threats to the process of accumulation. While in long downturns, the drive for lowering the value of labour power by sacking workers and cutting wages appears the norm, no upturn is possible as long as attacks against levels of working-class consumption remain predominant.

Unemployment and development intent

The representatives of capital, as well as sympathetic social reformers, therefore maintain a contradictory stance toward rising levels of absolute poverty, and increased levels of unemployment and underemployment. When Paul Cammack cites Marx, writing from the vantage point of the mid-nineteenth century, on the increase in the relative surplus population as a direct expression of the absolute general law of capitalist accumulation he does so accurately (Cammack 2001a: 194–98; Marx 1976: Chapter 25). However, at least two other matters are missing from Cammack's account, the second of them a particularly critical component of the modern idea of development. The first omission is Marx's rebuttal of Lassalle, cited above: the impoverishment of workers subsumed by capital is not necessarily absolute. Wage slavery, for those in continuous work and those who form the industrial reserve army of labour, exists 'irrespective of whether the worker is then better or worse paid'. Even for the relative surplus population, unemployment may occur at any one moment at a relatively higher level of absolute poverty than at another, earlier moment, through the availability of state and other 'poor relief' benefits.

Secondly, while unemployment and underemployment undoubtedly act to discipline labour and assist restraining wages, the inability to exercise labour's value-creating potential is also a barrier to accumulation. For the potential to be attained requires means, particularly intervention by the state, of joining production and consumption. (This was especially obvious for the form of rural household production that increased after the Second World War, as explained below.) We cannot predetermine or generalise the 'best', 'most suitable', or the optimum relationship for capital between unemployment as a disciplining force against wage and other demands by labour, and unemployment as a constraint on accumulation. The absence of a predetermined optimum level is most apparent at times, including the 1980s and 1990s, when the rate of increase in the rate of unemployment increase becomes especially pronounced.

Butter mountains, surplus rice stored in warehouses, motor vehicles unsold standing in factory lots and car yards as well as large numbers of unemployed and underemployed worldwide express the difficulty of achieving any optimum level of unemployment and underemployment. So too do rural households that have turned away from producing crops for international and even some domestic markets to forms of production and consumption that either do not yield surplus value or do so at stagnant or declining rates of profit (Cowen 1986: 355–84; MacWilliam 1996: 40–78). Consequently, and especially at particular moments, some of the representatives of capital, too, have a heightened interest in reducing unemployment and impoverishment.

This interest has been extended and enlarged in the modern idea of development, which was formulated to apply intent to deal with the negatives – unemployment and disorder – that were seen to accompany the spontaneous process of capital accumulation. The absolute general law referred to by Cammack (see above) of the tendency, noted by Marx a century and a half earlier, for a continuous increase in the relative surplus population is a characteristic of accumulation, one which in particular circumstances has been countered by the application of intent through state agency. One such set of circumstances arose immediately after the Second World War, when many international, national and colonial officials were imbued with development intent and enthusiasm for development doctrines.[12] By anticipating increases in the relative surplus population, intentional development was meant: 'to give order to a particular process of development, the development of capitalism, which, it was believed, embodied no developmental purpose and whose destructive dimension was poverty and the unemployment of the potential of productive power' (Cowen and Shenton 1996: ix).

What have the relative character of the impoverishment of labour and unemployment as a constraint on accumulation to do with the World Bank, poverty and development? With its expanded sense of poverty, enlarged even between 1990 and 2000/1, the Bank is signalling the need to raise production, and thus also levels of necessary consumption on a global scale. There is no necessary requirement for absolute poverty to increase on a global scale even if the Bank successfully acts as the leading multilateral representative of capital.[13] However, if the Bank's measures are successful, relative impoverishment for labour – relative, that is, to capital – will occur as unemployment declines and living standards rise.

Over the last quarter of a century, support for intentional development has become less widespread and powerful in an age of non-development. While unemployment and poverty are seen in most official circles as undesirable and underpinning the potential for disorder which lies within conditions of widespread impoverishment, there also remains a widespread scepticism towards and uncertainty about proposals for reform along the lines of earlier development doctrines. There is little official enthusiasm for the view that the spontaneous process of development, everywhere urged in such expressions as 'freeing up the market', carries a negative dimension which developmental purpose can anticipate.

Consequently there is little by way of reform which seeks through the agency of the state to re-attach labour to other means of production in order to increase productive force, historically the defining characteristic of intentional development. Instead, as with the European Union, attempts are now made by the World Bank and other development agencies to find a direction between market forces and the need for state action to provide social protection while emphasising individual and community responsibility (Cowen and Shenton 1999). The direction being advanced by the World Bank as well as civil society organisations (CSOs/NGOs), employs the contemporary language of empowerment and cultural identity (World Bank 2000/1d: Overview and Part 3). Yet these strategies are often simply a replay of positions adopted after the Second World War in metropolitan Britain by social work and in the colonies as community development. Such positions in turn have their precursors in the nineteenth century. As will be seen, the principal development vision of the World Bank, as evidenced by the *Report* examined here, but also in numerous other documents by Bank officers, goes no further (Collier and Dollar 2002).

Nevertheless, within this limited vision of development the attack upon poverty has become an urgent necessity. A protracted global increase of the relative surplus population unable to be subsumed by capital (as productive labour, labour producing surplus value), as well as the severe shake the 1997 'Asian crisis' gave to prevailing ideas about development, has inspired even greater urgency. The drive to raise the capacity to labour of the unemployed and underemployed has become a central objective for national as well as international institutions and officials. In turn, the haste behind the objective has brought about a heightened tussle over the scope of permissible state action (compare UNCTAD 1999, 2002; Rodrik 2001; Collier and Dollar 2002). After years of assaults on trade unions as rent-seeking, anti-competitive monopolists who distort price signals, there is even occasional support by prominent institutional officials for forms of collective action by workers. As the soon-to-depart senior economist of the World Bank stated in February 2000, '[w]orkers' rights should be a central focus of a development institution such as the World Bank' (Stiglitz 2000a).[14]

From development to non-development

Intentional development aimed to re-attach labour to other means of production in order to develop productive force without circumscribing the general principle that 'the external authority of development continues to be capital' (Cowen and Shenton 1996: xv). Unemployment and disorder, as existing or anticipated conditions, have in the past driven development intent. Whether as agrarian or manufacturing doctrine, state agency has been employed, harnessed as positive measures to deal with what spontaneous development necessarily creates as a relative surplus population.

The 1930s depression, a major war and the rush to decolonise produced a widespread international belief in development intent (Leys 1996a). It was believed that plans and practices could be informed by intent and forestall the worst consequences of spontaneous development, unemployment and disorder. As agrarian development doctrine, schemes were formulated and implemented to expand smallholder production of crops for immediate consumption, as well as for domestic and international markets. As manufacturing development doctrine, state-sponsored industrialisation captured pools of unemployed in towns and cities, for the production of exported as well as locally consumed products.[15] In each case, development doctrine joined agrarian and manufacturing forms of production to check rural as well as urban unemployment increases (Cowen and Shenton 1996: Chapters 6–7).

More recently, during what has become popularly known as the age of neoliberal ascendancy, development underwent another change along the lines of earlier cyclical movements. The previous widespread application of intentional development was checked and spontaneous development gained a renewed political-ideological force. Crudely, Reaganism, Thatcherism, neo-conservatism and neoliberalism have ruled. At the same time, a series of major ruptures has transformed the international political economy (Brenner 1998, 2000; *Historical Materialism* 2000; *Capital and Class* 1999). It is important here to re-emphasise that these ruptures followed upon, and were in part a consequence of, the very substantial expansion of accumulation and increase in living standards which occurred after the Second World War in most countries and for many people.[16] One reason for repetition is to stress that the current drive to reduce poverty globally does not represent an initial effort for 'the conversion of the world's poor into proletarians, stripped of alternative means of survival, and obliged to offer themselves to capitalists for work' (Cammack 2002: 127). In most countries, 'stripping' occurred much earlier, especially by the destructive force of trading capital in the late eighteenth and nineteenth centuries (Kay 1976; Davis 2001). That is, the World Bank is not engaged in completing a process of primitive or primary accumulation. Indeed, in an important respect, as noted above and discussed below, forms of primary accumulation form a barrier to the development envisaged by Bank officials.

The major increase of unemployed and underemployed of the 1980s and 1990s is an expression as well as a consequence of the end of the long-boom post-war period. During the earlier period, labour across the globe was subsumed by capital in new as well as old forms, resulting in enormous increases in production and productivity. The current impoverishment has followed the end of that expansion phase, in what is here described as the failure to reproduce the capitalisation that accelerated in the earlier period.

The upward shift of the 'golden age' of development

Two particular difficulties stand in the way of recognising that the current impoverishment follows upon an earlier generalised upward shift in living standards as a consequence of the expanded subsumption of labour to capital. The first is the simple denial that any such period existed, a denial which was so central first to dependency accounts and then to the anti-statist component of neo-conservatism and neoliberalism. Fortunately it is now clear and increasingly acknowledged[17] that for between two and three decades after the Second World War ended there was a major increase in production and consumption of manufactured goods as well as agricultural produce. Expanded smallholder production comprised and in some regions continues to comprise an important part of the increases (Kitching 1980; Thompson and MacWilliam 1992: Chapter 4; Badiane et al. 2002; Spoor 2002).

Secondly, and more contested, is the matter raised again by Cammack's phrase 'stripped of alternative means of survival'. For those who insist that proletarianisation requires a classic 'English' form of labour separated from ownership or even occupation of land, much of the post-war expansion is not seen as a form of proletarianisation. In particular it is claimed that households in occupation of smallholdings remained non-capitalist, simple or petty commodity producers. Such households are exploited by capital in a trading relation, but not subsumed by capital as productive labour.[18] The post-war expansion did involve the movement of peasant small farmers off the land into factories where manufacturing growth and an upward shift in the mass of necessary consumption took place, including in what was termed 'Third World countries' (Warren 1973: 3–44, 1980). Even for those who retain and require the classical defining characteristic of proletarianisation as labour removed from occupation of land, there was a major change after the Second World War in many countries. While seriously underestimating the continuing global significance of rural households, Eric Hobsbawm (1995: 289) points to the extent of the movement in claiming that: 'The most dramatic and far-reaching social change of the second half of this [the twentieth] century . . . is the death of the peasantry'. The impoverishment which now requires 'attacking' affects many urban households, including the 'urban peasants' who have been shifted off smallholdings into marginal wage positions and self-employment in burgeoning cities and towns during the post-war expansion phase.[19]

But what of circumstances where labour was not separated from the occupation of smallholdings but entrenched upon land through schemes of household production? That is, how should the form of labour be described which resulted in growth through expanded smallholder production? There is an argument, largely stemming from the work of Mike Cowen on smallholders in central Kenya,[20] that shows how the expansion occurred in a manner not amenable to the prevailing version, as an expression of 'underdevelopment', a stunted 'peasant society' (compare Leys 1971, 1975, 1978), or as simple commodity production.

The central tenet of Cowen's argument is that the smallholder increases occurred through advances of money capital directed and superintended by first the colonial and subsequently the postcolonial state. In this manner, households became a form of labour subsumed by capital *without* being separated from the occupation of smallholdings. Subsequently, following Cowen and in work on Papua New Guinea, I stressed again how this agricultural form involved both household production and consumption (Thompson and MacWilliam 1992: Chapter 4; MacWilliam 1988). As production and consumption were commercialised through labour's subsumption and in a period of global expansion, living standards for households rose.

An important component of state supervision, and intentional development, meant confining the advance of capitals that could have denuded household production. In certain conditions, barriers were constructed against the further expansion of large-holding agriculture. Blocking occurred through prohibiting land acquisition by the firms (including international firms) most likely to expand (MacWilliam 1987, 1988), and by land redistribution to smallholders as European settlers were excised from their holdings. Checking also meant constructing state marketing boards to purchase peasant crops, thus forestalling the encroachment of private trading firms whose actions might impoverish the growers.[21] But, more generally, the expansion of smallholders required constraining indigenous capital that would have centralised and concentrated agricultural production. Such an advance would push households off land and increase unemployment, which possibility the schemes of smallholder production were intended to anticipate and prevent in the first place.[22]

The age of non-development
For all the talk of trade and stock market booms, regional miracles and anticipated returns to growth through revitalised economies, the 1980s and 1990s have meant lengthened working hours, reduced employment security and declining real hourly wages for many of the working population in the most advanced industrial countries. Even where for a time exceptional growth occurred, as in the newly industrialising countries (NICs) and some of the former socialist countries, including China, unemployment and underemployment have again come to the

fore. In Vietnam, which underwent major reforms in the 1980s and early 1990s leading to growth, rural impoverishment has also been widespread (Consultative Group Meeting for Vietnam 1999). The Chinese government, too, is currently engaged in a massive poverty reduction drive.

With population increases still occurring on a global scale, despite whatever output growth occurred during the latter years of the last two decades, 'the number of people in poverty hardly changed'. Indeed:

> Between 1987 and 1998 the share of the population in developing and transition economies living on less than $1 a day fell from 28 per cent to 24 per cent . . . This decline is below the rate needed to meet the international development goal of reducing extreme income poverty by half by 2015 (World Bank 2000/1d: 21).

Since the *Report* was published, even this picture seems overly optimistic, especially in the poorest countries. UNCTAD, using 'new poverty estimates' based upon national-accounts-consistent estimates for 39 less-developed countries over the period 1965–99, describes an 'international poverty trap'. These estimates, 'suggest that the severity of poverty has been hitherto underestimated in the poorest countries, particularly in Africa', at the same time as concluding that the 'poverty-reducing effects of economic growth have equally been underestimated' (UNCTAD 2002: 11).

The 2000/1 *World Development Report* anticipates in one direction the subsequent UNCTAD emphasis upon deepening poverty, even as it considers the matter on a wider scale than the 'less-developed countries (LDCs)'. The *Report* notes how poverty reduction occurred between 1987–98, roughly the period covered by the UNCTAD study, in East Asia and the Middle East. 'But in all other regions the number of people living on less than $1 a day has risen' (World Bank 2000/1d: 22). Even where, as in South Asia, the proportions of poor fell, as measured by the minimalist US$1 a day in the purchasing-power-parity description of poverty, the numbers of poor increased. However:

Two regions fared particularly badly. In Europe and Central Asia the number in poverty soared from 1.1 million to 24 million. In sub-Saharan Africa the number of poor people increased from an already high 217 million to 291 million over the same period, leaving almost half the residents of that continent poor . . . These variations in regional performance are leading to the shift in the geographical distribution of poverty. In 1998 South Asia and sub-Saharan Africa accounted for around 70 per cent of the population living on less than $1 a day, up 10 percentage points from 1987 (World Bank 2000/1d: 23).

UNCTAD stresses two components of the poverty trap which are central for this examination of the *Report*. The components are examined at first by way of describing as 'grossly simplistic' (UNCTAD 2002: 101) claims made, sometimes by World Bank officials and in Bank policy statements, that the poorest countries are insufficiently 'integrated' into the global economy. The insufficiency allegedly is due in large measure to the failure to adopt open trade regimes.[23] UNCTAD instead notes the very high level of 'integration', as measured by the ratio of exports and imports of goods to gross domestic product (UNCTAD 2002: Chapter 3). On this measure, the LDCs have an average level of trade integration which is around the world average, is about the same as for what the World Bank terms 'the more globalised developing countries', and '*is actually higher than that of high-income OECD* [Organization for Economic Cooperation and Development] *countries*' (UNCTAD 2002: 103, emphasis added).

The 1990s also saw this index of integration increasing for LDCs, with a 'larger proportionate increase in the trade/GDP ratio than the world average', even if less than the increase in 'other developing countries and much less than that of the 'more globalised developing countries'. The latter had the lowest average level of trade integration in the early 1980s, or when the global downturn became most severe, but their position was transformed through the industrial expansion of the next decade (UNCTAD 2002: 103).

The deepening impoverishment, with its focus in some countries and primarily if not solely in rural areas, can be better understood once the relationship between imports and exports is examined further. Unprocessed primary commodities were the most important component of exports for the LDCs as a whole through to at least the late 1990s, amounting to 62 per cent of merchandise exports. Processed primary commodities accounted for a further 8 per cent and manufactured exports 30 per cent of merchandise exports, with considerable variation between LDCs (UNCTAD 2002: 107, Table 26). For all the LDCs, but in particular the non-oil-exporting countries, declining terms of trade between exports and imports, as well as a faster rate of growth of the latter compared to the former, have propelled increased national indebtedness.

Indebtedness has been dealt with by a rapid increase in public borrowings and (reducing) flows of international aid, amounting to unsustainable levels of external debt (UNCTAD 2002: Chapter 4). In turn, growing national debt gave rise from the late 1990s to the early 2000s to the Heavily Indebted Poor Countries (HIPC) initiative and a new form of conditionality. This conditionality requires the poorest countries to produce Poverty Reduction Strategy Papers/Programmes in return for more favourable treatment of their borrowings (World Bank 2000/1d: 201, Box 11.7).

Expanded production and consumption of commodities was central to the living conditions of smallholder producers, described above. But if this produced improved living standards in one period, why did the increased ratio of exports and imports to GDP not have the same result over the later years, instead of having as a corollary greater impoverishment? The decline in the ratio of the value of food exports to food imports suggests only part of the explanation (UNCTAD 2002: 111, Chart 29). Among the structural adjustment market reform conditionalities of the 1980s and 1990s were several which hit directly at the various schemes of expanded smallholder production begun in the 1950s and 1960s (Gibbon, Havnevik and Hermele 1993). As Spoor (2002) concludes for changes over three decades to the agricultural sector in Latin American and Caribbean countries, against the forecasts of structural adjustment programmes, growth was more substantial under the earlier import-substituting industrialisation phase. Privatisation of marketing authorities, and the removal of a brake initially installed to constrain private trading capital in the countryside, played some part in reducing support for smallholders, even where domestic opposition limited the effect of this drive.[24] Cuts in state expenditure reduced the capacity of agricultural and other officials to underpin household producers, although here too there have been institutions that acted against the trend, so that high-quality smallholder production expanded rather than declined.[25]

When coupled with great price volatility along a declining trend line of export prices, and the reduced capacity of national governments to maintain price supports, the distance between the rationality of household producers and national states became apparent. If governments needed expanded production of export crops to maintain national account surpluses, and keep borrowings down, smallholders acted according to a different logic. They switched from producing export crops and substituted produce for immediate and locally marketed consumption, when prices for the latter exceeded prices for an export crop such as coffee (Cowen 1986). This form of fungibility, the capacity to shift household labour from the production of export and nationally marketed produce, including milk, to production for immediate consumption or local markets was not the fungibility at the centre of Bank and other international institutional concerns (World Bank 2000/1d: 192–94). Instead of governments switching borrowings between expenditures to thwart demands of foreign donors, households moved out of export crop production and further exacerbated national balance of payments problems. In so doing, they responded to the price logic of individual households but against the capitalised form of production and consumption that had been central to the earlier increases in living standards.

The earlier form of household production of the post-war expansion phase had also provided a basis for what is generally and sometimes erroneously dubbed import-substituting industrialisation – erroneously because the order and thus basis of action is frequently misrepresented.

Local manufacturing production for household consumption was not always of goods whose importation preceded smallholder expansion and was subsequently cut off in favour of local producers. The agrarian doctrine of development that secured increases in household production provided space for local manufactures of goods that were inserted into household consumption as part of smallholder capitalisation.[26] Against this earlier tie between smallholder agriculture and local industry, the 1980s attacks against local manufactured production, allegedly because of its inefficiency and subsidised character, leading to the growing importation of food and other products for household consumption, further undercut national balances of payments.

Price volatility of export crops was exacerbated with the parallel reduction of support for international commodity marketing arrangements that previously had stabilised prices globally. Where smallholders had been encouraged to maintain output by national price support instrumentalities constructed in the 1960s and 1970s, extreme reductions in prices, as for coffee in the early 1990s, weakened stabilisation schemes. Scheme officials were forced to seek additional funds from governments. With national treasuries already under pressure from balance of payments problems, their capacity to assist price stabilisation measures was much reduced.

Even where the rhetoric of governments suggested a commitment to maintaining smallholders on the land, the limited support underpinning the proclamations meant that households were forced into an agrarian variant of 'working for the dole'. Even if civil war, ethnic cleansing and other forms of domestic conflict did not reduce production, smallholdings increasingly became plots of land that acted as sponges to soak up unemployed and underemployed rather than sites of expanded reproduction (of capital) (MacWilliam 1996).

Capital, the World Bank and development

To a considerable extent, capital's long-term prospects have come to depend upon attaching labour to other means of production, particularly land but also machinery. This is especially important in sub-Saharan Africa (SSA). As William van der Gheest and Rolph van der Hoeven note, while in 'other regions of the world labour supply growth rates are falling', in Africa they are rising. 'Over the thirty-year period 1995 to 2025 the total labour supply in SSA will increase at a rate above that for the previous thirty years' (Van der Gheest and Van der Hoeven 1999: 35). If the principal contemporary objective of reducing, or even eliminating poverty,[27] is the need to renew labour's subsumption to capital, then the *Report* is a major statement of what is to be done towards that end. It is, however, also an attempt to influence, to inform and to persuade, made with awareness of the World Bank's position as a comparatively small lender of total funds employed. Bank officials repeatedly stress that, even in the areas to which Bank lending is increasingly directed, weight of funds is not the principal source of their leverage.

With the proportion of GDP committed to aid having declined for most of the major donor countries, at the same time as domestic subsidies for production, including production by agribusinesses, has increased,[28] Bank loans comprise a very small proportion of public spending in key areas. While the World Bank is 'the world's largest external funder of education ... and of health programmes' (World Bank 2002b: 45), these loans, on whatever terms, give it more political-ideological than economic leverage. A Bank paper prepared for the Monterrey Conference noted that while development aid amounted to about US$54 billion in 2000, this was slightly less than one-third as much as foreign direct investment in developing countries, and an even smaller proportion of total investment of nearly US$1.5 trillion. While the Bank provides around US$2 billion annually in direct assistance for education, public spending in developing countries over the same period amounts to more than US$250 billion. So 'even if the World Bank were to greatly increase its lending in the (education) sector, its effectiveness would have to come primarily through catalysing institutional development and policy change in education, rather than through resource transfer alone' (World Bank 2002b: 53). As with education, so with health and other areas. Accordingly, given the primacy of domestic revenues for expenditures on the Bank's favoured areas, 'country ownership of the reform programme and development strategy is essential' (World Bank 2002b: 53). Or in the terms of the earlier 2000/2001 *World Development Report*: 'Both the strategic approach and the area of suggested action are only a guide. Actual priorities and actions need to be worked out in each country's economic, sociopolitical, structural, and cultural context – indeed, each community's' (World Bank 2000/1d: 37).

While the primacy given in the *Report* to the political-ideological role of the Bank's efforts, as catalyst for change, using limited funds to obtain maximum leverage, is acknowledged,[29] so too are the more important elements of the reformed strategy that directs these efforts. This reformed strategy aims to produce labour sufficiently skilled to meet contemporary levels of demand.

The *Report* stresses how the initial concern with poverty expressed in the 1990 *World Development Report* was defined by the difference between East Asia, 'where poverty had fallen sharply, and . . . Africa, Latin America and South Asia, where poverty had declined less or even risen'. On this experience, labour-intensive growth and a broad provision of social services had become the basis for a two-pronged approach to reduce poverty (World Bank 2000/1d: 31–32). But following the Asian crisis, it was recognised that technological change in the 1990s 'has been increasingly biased towards skills' so that 'in contrast to what was expected and needed, the pattern of growth in developing countries is not necessarily intensive in unskilled labour' (World Bank 2000/1d: 32).

With changes occurring in the direction followed by the UK government (UK Department for International Development 1997, 2000) and by the Asian Development Bank, the World Bank, too, recognised that the earlier strategy was insufficient to deal with deepening poverty. As the *Report* explained: 'The effects of market reforms are complex, deeply linked to institutions and to political and social structures. The experience of transition, especially in the countries of the former Soviet Union, vividly illustrates that market reforms in the absence of effective institutions can fail to deliver growth and poverty reduction' (World Bank 2000/1d: 32).

The regressiveness of much social services expenditure, even where this had not declined, linked with increasing inequality, had hindered growth and thus poverty reduction. It had even been recognised that as much as 'global forces of integration, communication, and technological advance' as well as increases in private capital flows had produced significant advances, the effects were not uniform between countries or people (World Bank 2000/1d: 32–33). The poverty definition as well as the strategy that flowed out of the earlier drive to reduce poverty needed reform and further revitalisation. It is in this context that the *Report's* emphasis upon increasing the capacity to labour of the unemployed and underemployed, especially in countries where literacy rates are lowest, where infant mortality rates are highest, and where vulnerability to economic and political 'shocks' is most severe, is an important shift.

The emphasis in the 1997 *World Development Report: The State in a Changing World* upon the importance of strengthening institutions (the state and civil society organisations/NGOs) is re-emphasised in the *Report* and subsequent Bank documents. But where the *Report* makes a shift, the full implications of which are perhaps not yet entirely clear, is in its increasing recognition of the need to mobilise popular support behind reform in places where impoverishment has been greatest. While the terms of this mobilisation are within the limits noted above, with the ideas of community, empowerment and personal responsibility little changed beyond earlier usages, nevertheless the increased urgency behind the Bank's concerns suggests that gaining domestic support constitutes a vital political imperative for reform efforts.

Driving that political imperative, as previously suggested, is the need to effect a major change to the balance of state power in the countries where poverty is deepest. Within the parameters set by the Bank's charter requiring it to avoid direct internal political involvement, and the global ascendancy of the idea of spontaneous development, forms of production are to be constructed and extended which will increase employment. If this is to occur, it is clearly insufficient to argue, as does the International Finance Corporation, the Bank's lender to private firms, for the centrality of entrepreneurs as 'pioneers of development' (Marsden 1990). Instead the IBRD/World Bank has framed a direction designed to give public institutions a greater role in promoting labour-intensive production. Hence the connections between equality and growth are stressed, as is the need to 'mak[e] markets do more for poor people' with 'public action to facilitate the accumulation of assets' (World Bank 2000/1d: Chapters 4–5).

To give this direction political weight *within* countries where poverty is greatest, and while emphasising the profitability of such activities,[30] the Bank needs to establish and strengthen domestic political opposition to more than corruption and 'bad' governance (compare MacWilliam 1986, 2002). The *Report* stresses from where it hopes the opposition to these buccaneering 'elites' will come, primarily by popular empowerment, the 'means of enhancing the capacity of poor people to influence the state institutions that affect their lives, by strengthening their participation in political processes and local decision-making' (World Bank 2000/1d: 39). But, as well, the poor require support from others exercising trusteeship, whose 'efforts are needed to make state and social institutions work in the interests of poor people – to make them pro-poor'. This alliance, or form of trusteeship, is the process of empowerment, of which 'formal democratic processes are part' (World Bank 2000/1d: 39).

Conclusion

If the strategy outlined in the *Report* succeeds in extending proletarianisation more widely across the globe, then this should be welcomed (compare Cammack 2001a, 2002). After all, spurring the formation of a class of labour with the potential to 'unite' globally is one of capitalism's progressive qualities. Further, in as much as an enlarged proletariat represents a potential capacity to abolish scarcity, then this too is commendable (Berman 1999; MacWilliam 2003). For the existence of scarcity is a major barrier to the development of human abilities to imagine a better future.

There are, however, good reasons to be sceptical about the potential of the World Bank's strategy. This scepticism is warranted even in terms of the limited vision of development portrayed in the 2000/1 *Report*, as well as subsequently. The vision remains one-sided, unable to rediscover the need for intentional development in the negatives of spontaneous, so-called 'free market' development. The enthusiasm for 'building institutions for markets' (World Bank 2001d), 'sustainable development in a dynamic world' (World Bank 2002f), or 'making services work for poor people' (World Bank 2002g) suggests that the earlier recognition of the need to anticipate development's negatives remains of little significance for Bank plans. Whether and under what circumstances this might change, short of a prolonged international downturn or a major war, is not immediately apparent.

While building popular support for pro-poor development might seem to represent an advance over 'elite capture' of national and local state institutions, this too is a particularly limited political direction with the (re)construction of national states as its principal focus. Once again, as after the Second World War, nation building is to be employed in order to turn attentions away from the internationality of capital, but this time on the even more limited ground of nation-states without development intent. The basis of World Bank and other international opposition is to a particular form of rule, that expressed by the 'elite' or local class of accumulators, over states where race, ethnicity, region and other particularisms hold sway, the so-called 'weak states' (Migdal 1988; Dauvergne 1998; Dinnen 2001). Local opposition to the class, sustained by flows of funds into NGOs/CSOs, seems unlikely to move much further than substituting one form of nationalism for another, populist nationalism opposing elite or bourgeois nationalism.

Most important of all objections to the Bank's strategy is that it seeks to refasten chains which have been loosened by another period of downturn and crises, preparing the way for further moments of expansion and contraction. Even if the terms of subsequent reform were to include another burst of intentional development, reducing the relative surplus population to a bare minimum and propelling another upward shift in living standards globally, the universal limit to the free development of each – that is, capitalism – would still remain.

Neither spontaneous nor intentional development as now conceived can produce a world in which needs are joined to capacities, for the free development of all. While exchanging plenty of poverty for the poverty of plenty is an important enlargement of human potential, capitalism's destructive need to re-impose scarcity at every opportunity and preclude a true age of abundance means that the main task still lies ahead.

Notes

1. I am indebted to David Moore, as editor, Rick Kuhn and Tony Smith for their comments and advice on an earlier draft of this chapter.
2. The World Bank Group comprises five institutions. These are the International Bank for Reconstruction and Development (IBRD, more commonly the World Bank); the International Development Association (IDA); the International Finance Corporation (IFC); the self-described private sector development arm of the Group, the Multilateral Investment Guarantee Agency (MIGA); and the International Centre for Settlement of Investment Disputes (ICSID). The annual *World Development Report* is a publication of the IBRD/World Bank. Other institutions of the Group have their own publications and reports, which invariably reflect the tensions within the Group's institutions flowing from the different relations of money capital these embody.
3. In mid-2002, the main page of the World Bank's website (http://www.worldbank.org) listed 'Ten Things You Never Knew About the World Bank'. The first three things proclaimed the Bank's importance as a lender for education, HIV/Aids programmes and health. As evidence of the Bank's changing priorities, the document announced: 'In 1980, investment in the power sector accounted for 21 per cent of Bank lending. Today that figure is down to 5 per cent. By contrast, lending for health, nutrition, education and social protection has grown from 5 per cent in 1980 to 25 per cent today.' The same document claims that the Bank is the world's largest external provider of funds for education, currently financing 153 projects in 79 countries.
4. For one location among many where the tussles between indigenous accumulation and smallholder production have become especially pronounced, see Southgate and Hulme (2000) on southern Kenya.
5. Compare Bayart (1993); Cowen and MacWilliam (1996); and MacWilliam (2002).
6. Compare Cowen and MacWilliam (1996); MacWilliam and Daveta (2000); MacWilliam (1999); MacWilliam (2002); and Cammack (2002: 126).
7. Cowen and Shenton (1996: viii) explain intent and doctrine in the following terms:

> The doctrine of development ... embodies the intent to develop ... to intend to develop does not necessarily mean that development will result from any particular action undertaken in the name of development. However, the existence of an intent to develop does mean that it is believed that it is possible to act in the name of development and that it is believed that development will follow from actions deemed desirable to realise an intention of development. An intention to develop becomes a doctrine of development when it is attached, or when it is pleaded that it be attached, to the agency of the state to become an expression of state policy.

8. The World Bank's Collier and Dollar (2002: 46–51) also note that between 1980 and 1995, during the period of 'third wave globalisation' there has been a substantial increase in household inequality in 'rich countries'.
9. Where redistribution, as with land reform, and welfare measures, as with public provision of education and health facilities, are advocated these are done so as to increase growth and reduce inequality, because the latter is regarded as an important impediment to further growth. See World Bank (2000/1d: Part II, Chapter 3).
10. Again, for one location and some children, see Verlet (2000).
11. This point includes the current emphasis on poor people's self-construction. See, for instance, Anderson and Broch-Due (1999); Narayan, Patel et al. (2000); Narayan, Chambers et al. (2000); Narayan and Petesch (2000).
12. See Note 7 for Cowen and Shenton's explanation of 'development intent'.
13. Compare Cammack (2002: 133), where it is unclear if expressions including 'extending poverty's dominion' mean enlarging absolute poverty.
14. See also World Bank (2000/1d: 73–74) on the importance of promoting core labour standards.
15. The significance of the so-called 'East Asian miracle' and the Asian developmental state lies in the success as well as the limits of the latter form of intentional development: compare Amsden (1989, 1990); World Bank (1993a, 1998b); McKibbin and Will (1999); and Stiglitz and Shahid (2001).
16. The World Bank (2000/1d: 58) acknowledges the changes, without really trying to explain the connection between the expansion phase and the break. Thus: 'One study estimated that had growth rates in the developing world (excluding China and India) been as high in the 1980s as they were in the 1960s and 1970s, 656,000 deaths could have been averted during the 1980s among children under five.'
17. While the World Bank (2000/1d) notes a connection between economic expansion and contraction, and changes in poverty, it tends to do so in a manner that ignores the cyclical character of the former emphasised here. Thus:

> Some countries in East Asia sustained per capita GDP growth rates of 4–5 per cent over four decades, with massive improvements in living standards and in health and education for poor people and everyone else. Other countries, mostly in Africa, registered negative or no growth at all over the same period, delivering no improvements even in average living standards (2000/1d: 35).

By comparison, UNCTAD (1999: 3), while downplaying the extent of production increases in many colonies and countries of the first twenty years after the war, speaks of a 'post-independence take-off' which was widespread although differing in its extent among countries on the continent. This expansion 'averaged an annual rate of 4.5 per cent or more than 1 per cent per capita' from the mid-1960s until the first oil shock of the early 1970s. Growth faltered in the 1970s: averaging over an entire period for 'other countries', as the World Bank does in the statement quoted above, provides little insight into the processes at work. For another take on the changes over the period, see Mosley (2002).

18. For references to this well-developed argument, see the subject index entry 'Simple Commodity Production' in the *Journal of Peasant Studies Index* 1994: 130; and also Leys (1987).
19. The urban character of poverty is receiving increasing attention from multilateral and bilateral institutions, as the World Bank (2002f, especially Chapter 6) emphasises.
20. For an extended list of references to this work, see Shenton (2000: especially 163–64).
21. On the general effect of trading capital, and particularly its tendency to take surplus value out of production, see Kay (1976).
22. For the case of Kenya, see Cowen and Shenton (1996: Chapter 6).
23. For World Bank claims, see UNCTAD (2002: 133, Chapter 3, Footnote 1).
24. See MacWilliam, Desaubin and Timms (1995: Chapter 2) for a relevant account of the Maize Produce Board in Kenya.
25. For the case of the Kenya Tea Development Authority, see Leonard (1991).
26. See Cowen and Shenton (1996: Chapter 6); Cowen and MacWilliam (1996: Chapter 5); and, for the particular instance of biscuit manufacturing in Kenya, see Manji (1995).
27. An Asian Development Bank Report (2001: 1) opens with the statement: 'Poverty is an unacceptable human condition. It is not immutable; public action can, and must, eliminate poverty. This is what development is all about.'
28. In a major speech given in March 2002, prior to the UN international conference on Financing for Development held at Monterrey, Mexico, which sought to stimulate greater support for increases in aid flows, the World Bank president, Wolfensohn (2002: 10–11), urged

> rich nations ... to take action to cut agricultural subsidies – subsidies that rob poor countries of markets for their products. Farm support goes mainly to a relatively small number of agribusinesses, many of them large corporations, and yet those subsidies of $300 billion a year are six times what the rich countries provide in foreign aid to a developing world of close to five billion people.

Wolfensohn called for a doubling of aid, requiring an additional US$40 to US$60 billion a year, if the Millennium Development Goals are to be reached, a doubling which would bring aid flows to 0.5 per cent of donor countries' GNP – 'still well below the 0.7 per cent target agreed to by global leaders years ago'.

29. Reports and statements regularly emphasise the connection between official development assistance and private investment, even in the poorest countries. 'Thus

The World Bank: Development, Poverty, Hegemony

[International Development Association, the Bank's concessional arm which lends to the poorest countries] aid draws in private investment, rather than crowding it out' (World Bank 2002b: 92).

30. The World Bank's 'The Role and Effectiveness of Development Assistance', prepared for the Monterrey conference, notes:

> Well-targeted aid has high overall economic payoffs. Because aid creates new economic possibilities, improving the investment climate and increasing investment, its economywide returns are far greater than even the direct poverty-reduction returns – with a rate of return as high as 40 percent in the case of IDA (World Bank 2002b: 92).

Chapter Three

Constructing the Economic Space
The World Bank and the Making of *Homo Oeconomicus*

David Williams[1]

THIS WAS ORIGINALLY PUBLISHED IN 1999 IN
MILLENNIUM 28 (1): 79–101.

This chapter aims to examine the discourses and practices surrounding the attempt to construct market-based economic systems in developing countries. The discourses that are currently popular all rely on a view that market-based economic arrangements are more or less natural. Even those arguments which accept that there remains an important role for the state in setting the 'right' economic policies, or providing an effective regulatory and institutional environment for the market, nonetheless rely on a view that, at bottom, market-based economic arrangements are natural because they are the product of an economic rationality inherent in all persons. This view is a vitally important part of the justification for the activities of those international organisations, such as the World Bank, that are attempting to spread and consolidate market-based economic systems around the world. When examining the actual practices of these organisations, however, the 'naturalness' of the economy is called into question because they actually attempt to construct the traits of economic rationality upon which the naturalness of the economy is supposed to rest. This chapter shows that in practice the economy seems to be constructed 'all the way down', and does not, and cannot rest upon any natural foundations.

This analysis has a number of implications. Firstly, it allows us to question many of the arguments surrounding the spread of market-based economic arrangements. This chapter is not concerned with a discussion of their desirability, but rather with showing that many of the current ways of thinking about, or arguing for, market-based economic arrangements are seriously incomplete. As these arguments have become so characteristic of much of the discussion surrounding economic development, such questioning has both political and academic importance. It opens up a space for political engagement by questioning the arguments that development agencies use to legitimise their actions. Moreover, this work allows us to bring together analysis of the attempt to spread market-based economic arrangements in developing countries with those analyses of the growth of capitalism in the now developed world which have recognised the important role played by the deliberate transformation of institutions and the habits, attitudes and mores of persons (compare McKendrick 1961; Neeson 1993). That is, it allows us to see how international organisations are replicating the patterns of transformation characteristic of Western economic history (Young 1995).

Secondly, the analysis presented here shows how international organisations are engaged in detailed and intrusive activities in many countries that are designed to construct the foundations of a market system. Much discussion of relations between international organisations and developing countries has failed to recognise the extent to which these organisations are attempting transformations at the most detailed level. The story of how this has become possible is beyond the scope of this chapter, but by illustrating that it is happening, the chapter tries to present a more accurate picture of what organisations such as the World Bank are engaged in.[2] Thirdly, the chapter aims to open up an area of debate by showing that we need not take economics' self-descriptions at face value. By elucidating a radical disjunction between the discourse of economics and the actual practices surrounding the expansion of market-based economic arrangements, we can start to question the cornerstone of modern economics and thus go some way to delegitimating its hegemonic claims.

The chapter begins by delineating some aspects of the conceptual structure of economics, and then outlines those arguments that market-based economic arrangements are natural, all of which have at some time or another been accepted within the World Bank. The chapter then turns to an examination of the work of Adam Smith as the first step in a critique of these views. This suggests that, contrary to many interpretations, Smith was deeply ambivalent about the naturalness of the market. What an examination of Smith's work seems to suggest is that in order for economic rationality to become a sociological reality, persons must be situated within highly disciplinary institutional arrangements and made to internalise certain habits such as self-monitoring and economic calculation.

Finally, the chapter turns to the activities of the World Bank and its attempts to construct *homo oeconomicus*, which mirror the arguments of Adam Smith. This is not to imply any straightforward link between Smith and contemporary development practice; the attempt to create *homo oeconomicus* does not emerge from a careful reading of *The Wealth of Nations*. Rather, we should see it as the practical manifestation of a clash between the mainstream view that the economy is fundamentally natural and the actual experience of the World Bank in its attempt to develop market-based economic arrangements. The World Bank has learned from its own experience that economic development requires detailed transformations in institutions and habits, attitudes and mores (Williams 1997). 'Institutional learning' is an important, albeit partial and complex, process within the Bank (Haas 1990).

As will be argued below, a crucial part of the justification for the Bank's activities is that economic relations are natural, hence aiding their development is not imposing its own conception of the good but rather assisting in what is a natural course of development. This is a powerful normative commitment that has a long theoretical and practical history bound up with notions of self-determination, tolerance, and neutrality.[3] What follows is an interpretation of the activities of the World Bank, designed to reveal the clash between what it says and what it does and make sense of this disjunction within the wider context of the discourse and practice of economic development.

Economic rationality
There has been an extensive debate within economics over what precisely 'economic rationality' consists of.[4] To classical economists such as Adam Smith it seems to have referred simply to the pursuit of self-interest. For neo-classical economists such as Alfred Marshall it referred to the maximisation of utility across a variety of goods given limited resources (1962: 78–81). Both of these views relied upon a substantive conception of human nature. Later economists such as John Hicks attempted to purge economics of any reliance on claims about human nature and argued that the discipline could rest simply on the assumption that individuals are able to rank their preferences in a consistent manner (Blaug 1992: 141–44). While this debate has a certain methodological importance within economics concerning whether or not it can be given a 'scientific' foundation, it has not been practically important for economists, who have tended to work with the view that economic rationality consists of the 'pursuance of self interest' (Vriend 1996). As one commentator has argued, 'preferences' is simply the modem economist's term for self-interest (Vriend 1996: 265). While this view of economic rationality is the cornerstone of most mainstream economics (Blaug 1992: 230–32),[5] there remains a debate within economic theory about whether this is an accurate description of how people actually are, or whether it is simply a necessary axiom in order to produce coherent economic models (in other words, whether it is empirically true or simply theoretically necessary).[6] For our purposes this debate is unimportant, because when it comes to advocating policy prescriptions most economists seem to have taken it to be an empirical concept, as is certainly the case with the World Bank.

In line with the procedure recommended by Michael Freeden (1996), it is possible to sketch out some of the concepts, categories and arguments that derive from and support this fundamental commitment. The practical understanding of economic rationality as natural performs a key legitimating function. Whatever else economists recommend the state do in terms of providing a framework for the market (the 'right' policies, 'good' regulatory institutions), it is seen, at bottom, to be a natural phenomenon. Any appeal to 'nature' to provide the foundation for economic arrangements is, of course, something we should be distinctly wary of, as Michel Foucault (1994), among others, reminds us. Nevertheless, this kind of appeal has a long tradition of providing a key justification for social and political arrangements.

The legitimacy of market-based economic arrangements is supported by two other associated concepts. The first is that of *universality/formal equality*. According to this claim, all persons everywhere exhibit the traits of economic rationality, and this universality theoretically strips away concepts such as culture, class or gender. In the work of Smith this was a potentially radical notion (Shapiro 1993). The second concept is that of the *social/good*. The pursuit of individual self-interest, in the right kind of policy or institutional environment, is compatible with, and even necessary for, the advancement of the general social good. This argument, foreshadowed in Mandeville, allowed economists to abandon the centuries-old argument that the pursuit of self-interest was socially destructive (Hirschman 1997; Mandeville 1970).

These two concepts support the view that the development of a market economy is desirable. Firstly, a market economy is thought to be the most efficient arrangement for persons who naturally seek to maximise their material well-being or pursue their preferences. Secondly, market-based economic arrangements are good for everyone, everywhere, because everyone, everywhere is essentially the same. Thirdly, market-based economics is underpinned by a general-rule utilitarian justification, which sees the market as providing the best institutional structure for the achievement of both individual and social material well-being, understood in terms of welfare or utility (Goodin 1995; Harsanyi 1983). These are not only arguments for the desirability of market-based economic arrangements, but also more specific justifications for attempts by international organisations such as the World Bank to construct them in developing countries.

Economic rationality is also tied theoretically in the literature to three other concepts: autonomy, reflexivity, and calculation. *Autonomy* is conceptually entailed by a commitment to economic rationality. As argued above, the idea of economic rationality strips away cultural and other social ties to leave a radically autonomous and internally (though not externally) self-sufficient individual. Individuals, in turn, possess a capacity for *reflexivity* and the ability to *calculate*. They are able to monitor their preferences and to calculate the best course for satisfying them within the constraints of limited resources. The work of Smith and the activities of the World Bank both suggest that autonomy, reflexivity, and economic calculation, however, are not natural and have to be made into sociological and psychological realities, and that persons do not possess these characteristics naturally.

Before elaborating this point, the next section briefly discusses three sets of arguments about economic development that rely on the view that economic rationality is natural. The major differences between these arguments concern the constraints that prevent economic rationality from producing socially beneficial outcomes. When 'liberated' from these constraints, then, economically rational agents will 'naturally' produce the desired outcomes.

Economy as natural order

Orthodox development economics accepts the naturalness of economic rationality, but stresses the need for injections of capital infrastructure, and 'human capital' development (education, health) to provide incentives to save and invest, safeguard the efficient working of the market, and ensure that all persons can contribute to and benefit from economic growth. Albert Hirschman, one of the pioneers of development economics, argued in 1958 that in 'underdeveloped' economies there is 'not only underutilised labour in agriculture, but unutilised ability to save [and] latent or misdirected entrepreneurship' (1958: 6). That is, persons were indeed economically rational, but conditions were such that this was only 'latent' or misdirected. One of the key concepts of orthodox development economics, the 'vicious circle of poverty', was founded on the idea that persons in developing countries were economically rational:

[T]he inducement to invest may be low because of the small buying power of the people, which is due to their small income, which ... is due to low productivity. The low level of productivity, however, is a result of the small amount of capital used in production, which in turn may be caused at least partly by the small inducement to invest (Nurkse 1953: 5).

The way to overcome these problems, according to these economists, was to provide 'inducements' to invest and save by stimulating the economy through injections of capital, and through a certain amount of government intervention to allocate that capital to those industries which would contribute most to economic growth.[7] In addition, investment would be targeted at increasing productivity through the transfer of technology and education. This view heavily influenced the World Bank during the l950s and 1960s (Black 1963; Mason and Asher 1973).

The neoclassical revival in economics of the late l970s and 1980s similarly asserts that economic relations are natural because persons exhibit the traits of economic rationality (Toye 1993). For example, in 1981 the World Bank argued that 'all the evidence points to the fact that smallholders are outstanding managers of their own resources ... [and] can be counted on to respond to changes in the profitability of different crops and of other farming activities' (World Bank 1981: 4). Similarly, Deepak Lal argued that there is a 'vast body of empirical evidence from different cultures and climates which shows that uneducated peasants act economically as producers and consumers. They respond to changes in relative prices much as neo-classical economics predicts' (1983: 105).[8]

According to this argument, however, economic rationality will produce mutually beneficial outcomes only when there is a concerted effort on the part of the state to construct the 'correct' policy environment, which became the rationale for the pursuit of 'structural adjustment' programmes by the World Bank and the IMF.

Finally, 'New Institutional Economics', an approach increasingly favoured among contemporary development economists, also starts with the naturalness of the economy (Heertje 1989; Harriss, Hunter and Lewis 1995). Here again, persons are assumed to exhibit the characteristics of economic rationality. Douglass North, Nobel Prize winner for economics, has argued that New Institutional Economics builds on the 'choice theoretic approach of neoclassical theory' (1990: 5). More emphasis is given in this view to the transaction costs involved in economic exchanges, such as the costs of collecting information and the costs involved in enforcing contractual agreements. If these costs become too high they act as a disincentive to engage in economic exchanges. Hence New Institutional Economics calls for effective regulatory and institutional structures to reduce these costs and so increase the incentives for economically rational agents to engage in economic activity. It has also underpinned the recent move by the World Bank and other development organisations to consider the institutional and governance environment of developing countries, which includes among other things reducing corruption, reforming legal systems and improving banking and financial institutions (World Bank 1991c: especially Chapter 7; World Bank 1997b).

The making of *homo oeconomicus*: Adam Smith

Some of the views outlined above can be seen in the work of Adam Smith. He argued that we all have within us the 'desire of bettering our condition, a desire which, though generally calm and dispassionate, comes with us from the womb, and never leaves us till we go to the grave' (Smith 1976a: 341). For Smith, this impulse produced mutually beneficial outcomes through the operation of the 'invisible hand' and certain universal laws concerning the natural movement of prices and wages) (1976a: 72–80). On this common reading of Smith it seems that the development of a market economy is the outcome of a natural propensity within people to 'truck, barter and exchange' in the pursuit of their material well-being (1976a: 30). This argument leads to the familiar set of claims about the role of the state in the economy. Apart from providing for defence, administering justice, ensuring the provision of public works and institutions necessary for facilitating commerce, and providing for some forms of public education, the state should stay out of the economy as much as possible (Smith 1976a: 689–816).

These seemingly straightforward and familiar arguments are called into question, however, by Smith's more 'sociological' observations about actually existing economic institutions and practices (Veblen 1948: 242–43). On closer examination it becomes clear that Smith had serious doubts that people did in fact naturally possess the traits necessary to produce a flourishing market economy. For Smith it was not enough that people be simply 'liberated' from constraints to the free expression of their economic rationality: economic rationality itself had to be constructed. Because Smith was committed to the market economy as a good, he could not simply describe these divergences from his philosophical arguments; he had to advocate eliminating them. This produces a wholly new vision of the role of the state in economic development. The state is no longer seen as at best facilitating the continued development of a flourishing market economy; rather, the state is to be a central agent in the construction of the economy and the traits that underpin it.[9]

There are a number of important examples in *The Wealth of Nations* that illustrate the divergence between Adam Smith's theoretical and sociological visions of the economy. For Smith the laws governing the apprentice system in England, Scotland, and France were 'absurd' (1976a: 151). They prevented the free movement of labour; they were a violation of the liberty which everyone has to dispose of their labour as they please; and, importantly, they had 'no tendency to form young people to industry', because an apprentice has no 'interest' in being anything other than idle. Thus, 'boys who are put out to apprentices . . . generally turn out very idle and worthless' (Smith 1976a: 139).[10] Smith was perfectly aware of the extent of apprenticeship in Europe, but he condemned it because it prevented the emergence of a specifically economic rationality. The whole apprentice system was regulated in detailed ways by local and national laws (such as the Statute of Apprenticeship) and rooted in traditional practices. It is clear, however, that only by exposing people to the discipline of the market do they acquire the 'habits of industry', and only by abolishing apprenticeship do people gain the autonomy necessary for the emergence of economic rationality:

> A young man would practice with much more diligence and attention, if from the beginning he wrought as a journeyman, being paid in proportion to the little work which he could execute, and paying in his turn for the materials which he might sometimes spoil through awkwardness and inexperience (Smith 1976a: 140; compare McKendrick 1961).

For Smith, the abolition of apprenticeship was not simply a matter of liberating people from 'oppressive' social institutions, but about placing them in new, highly disciplinary social arrangements within which they would learn through necessity the injunctions of economic rationality.

Another important example is Smith's discussion of land. Smith argued vehemently against the continued existence of large semi-feudal holdings that precluded the possibility of land being divided into smaller plots in the future. Smith argued that nothing could be 'more completely absurd than these laws', because they prevented the land from being 'improved'. It 'seldom happens . . . that a great proprietor is a great improver':

> To improve land, like all other commercial projects, requires an exact attention to small savings and small gains, of which a man born to a great fortune is seldom capable. The situation of such a person naturally disposes him to attend rather to ornament which pleases his fancy than to profit for which he has so little occasion (Smith 1976a: 385).

Smith suggested that if you compared the condition of these large estates with those of smaller possessions 'you will need no other argument to convince you how unfavourable such extensive property is to improvement' (1976a: 386). Smith's attack on these large estates was based on the twin notions of ownership and improvement (Vogel 1988:

102–22). While these estates were 'owned', the laws of inheritance prevented them from being broken into smaller landholdings and sold. Large landholdings were a barrier to improvement because landowners could have no real need or desire for more money and because they were incapable of the attention to small savings and gains necessary for improvement. Only when the plots are broken up and sold to smaller cultivators is there any incentive to improve the land.

Smith argued that the 'desire of bettering our condition' was a universal human characteristic (1976a: 341). It might be asserted that landowners were 'bettering' their condition by attending to ornament and fancy, and apprentices by being idle, but this is not the kind of behaviour that Smith had in mind when he argued the economy was natural because it accorded with human nature. Rather, Smith is clear that this kind of behaviour is a great barrier to the public good. Stated baldly as the pursuit of self-interest, economic rationality has no substantive content; it says nothing about what individuals will actually, or should, do (Vriend 1996).

Smith, thus, was theoretically caught: he realised that depending on the social and institutional context, and the habits, attitudes and mores of individuals, the pursuit of 'self-interest' could lead to socially undesirable outcomes. He wanted to argue that the economy was natural because it was the product of certain natural propensities, but in certain circumstance these natural propensities could lead to undesirable outcomes. This dilemma challenges the extent to which the economy can be seen as resting on any natural foundations.

Firstly, the pursuit of self-interest has to be located in a wider institutional and social environment in order for it to produce beneficial outcomes, in Smith's term 'improvement'. Nathan Rosenberg argues that the examples of apprenticeship and land ownership suggest that Smith sought arrangements which ensured the autonomy of individuals from masters and large landowners and placed these individuals 'under the right kind of psychic tension' (1960: 559). Individuals will apply themselves to improvement, and hence advance the general happiness of mankind, when the 'reward for effort is neither too low (apprentices) nor too great (large landowners)' (Rosenberg 1960: 559). This casts doubt on the economy as natural order, for it is clear that the necessary attitudes will emerge only under quite specific institutional conditions which Smith thought were not yet in place. It is also clear from this that, even for Smith, the release from 'oppressive' social institutions was not unambiguously a 'liberation', and it was certainly not an unalloyed individual good. As Smith says, in the abolition of apprenticeship the apprentice 'in the end perhaps . . . would be a loser': 'in a trade so easily learnt he would have more competitors, and his wages, when he came to be a compleat [sic] worker, would be much less than at present' (1976a: 140). The point of this release for Smith was that it relocated individuals in new disciplinary structures that would lead to the development of economic rationality, which would in turn benefit society as a whole (assuming the 'invisible hand' operated as Smith thought it did).

Secondly, Smith recognised that certain habits of industry such as self-monitoring and calculation had to be constructed.[11] The provision of the 'most essential parts of education', reading, writing, and accounting (basic numeracy) represents a duty of the sovereign, because there is 'scarce a trade which does not afford some opportunities' of applying them (Smith 1976a: 764). Smith goes so far as to suggest that the sovereign can impose upon,

> [a]lmost the entire body of the people the necessity of acquiring those most essential parts of education, by obliging every man to undergo an examination or probation in them before he can obtain the freedom in any corporation, or be allowed to set up any trade either in a village or town corporate (1976a: 786).

The specific attitudes necessary to produce a flourishing commercial society are for Smith far from natural, and there is a recognition that the state should go some way to constructing them, not only directly through educational practices, but also through institutional engineering. As Donald Winch has argued, Smith had a consistent concern 'to demonstrate how actual practices or outcomes in modern commercial societies require the attention of the legislator' (Winch 1983: 258–59).

Economic rationality conceptually entails an autonomous, reflexive and calculating individual. Smith clearly recognised these had to have a real, but constructed, sociological referent. In order for economic rationality to produce socially beneficial outcomes there had to be large-scale changes in the social and institutional context, and in the habits, attitudes and mores of individuals. This is not, as might be suggested, an exercise to assist people in properly prioritising their rational interests.[12] Rather, Smith's project is the creation of entirely new modes of reasoning within newly atomised persons (Bazerman 1993). Here is the radical disjunction between discourse and practice: the natural possession of economic rationality justifies the pursuit of market-based economic arrangements. But if the emergence of economic rationality requires locating individuals in new institutional arrangements and inculcating new habits, then individuals do not naturally possess economic rationality.

The making of *homo oeconomicus*: Contemporary practice

One obvious difference between contemporary practice and the arguments of Smith concerns the role of the state. For Smith, as we have seen, the state was charged with reforming institutional structures and with developing 'habits of industry' such as calculation and reflexivity. For organisations such as the World Bank, the state has come to be seen as a significant barrier to economic development. As the move towards considering issues such as 'governance' has shown, this concern with the state is not simply that its role in resource allocation has to be reduced, but rather that it is incapable of effecting the transformation in institutions, social structures and habits necessary for a flourishing market economy to emerge (Williams and Young 1994; Leftwich 1993; Robinson 1993). The contemporary attempt to make *homo oeconomicus*, then, has three parts: transforming institutional structures and creating autonomy; inculcating certain habits such as calculation and reflexivity; and developing the capacities of the state so that it can itself undertake these tasks.

Institutional reform and autonomy

The most obvious examples of large-scale institutional reform undertaken by the World Bank in the pursuit of market-based economic arrangements are structural and sectoral adjustment programmes. During the 1980s structural adjustment programmes had a large number of objectives, including removing import quotas; cutting tariffs; reducing interest rate controls; currency devaluation; eliminating state marketing boards; reducing bureaucratic controls on industry; privatising state-owned enterprises; and removing price controls on food, energy and agricultural inputs.[13] Sectoral adjustment programmes, which became increasingly used during the second half of the 1980s, attempted to promote the same objectives, but were targeted at specific sectors of the economy (Jayarajah and Branson 1995: 108–09).

Both kinds of programme were underpinned by the same rationale. Structural and sectoral adjustment programmes seek to put economic agents under the right kind of 'psychic tension'. They attempt to reduce the possibilities for rent seeking produced by currency and trade restrictions, thus to 'encourage' more directly productive economic activity.[14] They also represent attempts to reduce the reliance of economic agents on the state and to expose them to the discipline of the market. Agricultural producers would be freed from a reliance on state marketing boards which provided little incentive for increased production because the price that producers received was too low. State-owned enterprises would be freed from government control and exposed to competition that would, in theory, lead to increased output and productivity. There are clear parallels with the arguments of Smith here: the only way economic agents can be 'induced' to engage in economically productive activity is by ensuring their autonomy and constructing the right kind of institutional framework.

In addition to these 'macro-level' reforms, the World Bank has been engaged in more detailed micro-level institutional reforms with the aim of creating an autonomous individual who can be subjected to the 'discipline' of the market. One of the most striking of these is land reform. The World Bank, for example, has designed and funded a community development project in the Philippines to support the Comprehensive Agrarian Reform Programme (CARP) initiated by the Philippine government in 1988 (World Bank 1996a).[15] CARP envisioned a massive restructuring of agrarian tenure in an effort to boost agricultural productivity and reduce the high incidence of rural poverty. Once beneficiaries received land under CARP they would have to convert from being sharecroppers, landless farm workers, or illegal occupants of public lands, into 'farmer entrepreneurs', when they would have to make 'all farm management decisions . . . secure timely availability of inputs, and arrange for marketing their produce' (World Bank 1996a: 3–7).

The Bank is undertaking the Agrarian Reform Communities Development Project in approximately one hundred of the communities participating in CARP, with the aim of developing rural infrastructure and promoting farm production and other income-generating activities, through technical support, marketing assistance and credit provision. Under the project, infrastructure development includes the rehabilitation of roads and bridges, the construction of water supply schemes, and the construction of community, commercial, education and health facilities (World Bank 1996a: 73–77). Communities are provided with organisational development assistance through NGOs and government agencies. This assistance concentrates on credit and financial management training, familiarisation with 'commercial practices', improvement of accountancy skills, including the calculation of profit, and improvement of the understanding of formal credit. Running parallel to this is a programme of agricultural and enterprise development, designed to increase family incomes by providing economic support services, and building the capacity of families and communities to undertake income-generating activities. 'Income-generating activities', the Bank maintains, 'will be purposely market and private sector-oriented, with credit, farm inputs and technical services directed at improving productivity and ensuring ready access to viable outlets for the products of beneficiaries and their cooperatives' (World Bank 1996a: 13, 78–80).

Echoing Smith, this land reform project is distinctly double-edged, attempting to ensure 'improvement' by placing previously landless persons in a new institutional context that ensures their autonomy and exposes them to the discipline of the market. It is only in this way that they can be converted into 'farmer entrepreneurs'. The project explicitly invokes the necessity for calculation and reflexivity (making all farm management decisions, securing timely availability of inputs, marketing their produce). However, as with Smith, it is clear that these previously landless workers do not simply possess these attributes. Hence the training in 'commercial practices', accounting and calculations of profit and loss. In short, these persons have to be taught to be economically rational. As the next section tries to show, this is an important part of a number of other World Bank projects and initiatives.

Calculation and reflexivity

A recent World Bank report argues that 'numerous studies of accounting in sub-Saharan Africa have concluded that sustained economic growth cannot be maintained without a sound accounting infrastructure and an appropriately trained accounting profession', and that in many sub-Saharan African countries, 'accounting and auditing performance has been unsatisfactory in recent years' (Johnson 1996: 1). The recommendations of this report are unsurprising, but illustrative of this drive to create an autonomous, calculating self:

- [this education] must give students the necessary life skills for a career as an accountant;
- the accounting profession needs to review the way it examines students to test personal and problem-solving skills, as well as technical knowledge;
- accounting degree programmes need to change to focus on providing students with transferable skills;
- continuing professional education must be provided (Johnson 1996: 1).

The donor community can assist by funding the development of accounting education and examinations, while making sure that accounting education is providing 'the skills that the marketplace requires', and by conducting 'quality reviews' of training, education and examinations (Johnson 1996: 27–29). The drive to create a particular form of rational subjectivity is expressed here in the language of accountancy and management consulting, and these practices entail the ever-expanding use of techniques to discipline the self (Miller 1992: 61–86; Miller and Cleary 1987: 235–65). But it is not just in the World Bank's larger understanding of what is necessary for economic growth that we find this desire to recreate the self. It is above all visible in the details of its development projects.

In Ghana, for instance, the World Bank funded a 'Community Water and Sanitation Project' to upgrade and extend the provision of basic water and sanitation services, especially in rural areas (World Bank 1994b). A key element in the project was the provision of water and sanitation services to community groups who contributed towards the capital costs of the project (5 to 10 per cent), and the community management of these services, including paying all of the normal operations, maintenance and repair costs. This was designed to ensure 'commitment' to the project, to ensure that revenues were collected, and to help communities see 'a clear relationship between services rendered and tariffs charged' (World Bank 1994b: 8). According to the World Bank, community groups needed their 'capacity' enhanced through education to ensure the sustainability of the project (World Bank 1994b: 7). One indicator of sustainability was the groups' ability to 'effectively operate, maintain, repair, collect revenue, keep records and accounts, evaluate and resolve problems' (World Bank 1994b: 81). The project 'would adopt participatory techniques of modern adult education, which are much more effective at inducing behavioural change' (World Bank 1994b: 85).

Also in Ghana, the World Bank funded a 'Literacy and Functional Skills Project' (World Bank 1992b). According to the Bank, as many as two-thirds of the Ghanaian population is functionally illiterate, and of those who attended school, as many as 40 per cent have 'lapsed' into illiteracy due to a lack of 'appropriate' reading materials' (World Bank 1992b: 1). The aim of the project was to give people the 'necessary consciousness, attitudes, skills and knowledge so that their creativity can be applied to further national development'. Literacy is not an end in itself, but the 'first step towards the introduction of a more systematic approach to problem solving' (World Bank 1992b: i). The project's main objective was the provision of literacy and numeracy skills, and new knowledge and attitudes, including 'the discouragement of negative and dangerous social customs' (World Bank 1992b: 3). The basic literacy lesson topics included family planning, teenage pregnancy, community empowerment, income generation activities, management practices and drug abuse (World Bank 1992b: 35). As two World Bank staff members have said, there are a number of areas, such as family planning, savings and credit, income generation and new farm practices, which *'require changes in individual and family behaviour'* (Bhatnagar and Williams 1992: 4, emphasis added).

Micro-level attempts to create economic rationality are not only taken by the World Bank but also by some Western NGOs. While these NGOs have often been critical of the World Bank, and particularly its structural adjustment programmes (Oxfam 1995; Clark 1991: Chapter 12), this has not prevented them from attempting to create the very economic rationality which is a key justification for these programmes.[16] For example, the need to instil the traits of economic rationality has been recognised by Intermediate Technology. A recent evaluation of credit provision to small producers argues that 'there are unquestionably instances where the provision of credit on its own will release the binding constraint on certain types of small producers. However this cannot be assumed to be the case – and only in certain limited circumstances . . . is it likely to be true' (Dawson and Jeans 1997: 10).

The report goes on to argue that the response of small producers to the emerging opportunities provided by economic liberalisation has been 'generally weak' (Dawson and Jeans 1997: 13). This being the case, it is clear more has to be done than simply liberating people from financial constraints. What must be improved, according to Intermediate Technology, is the 'technological capacity' of these small producers, defined as: 'ability . . . to identify opportunities; to source, install and operate equipment; to apply skills and techniques to the production process; and to respond to changing market conditions' (Dawson and Jeans 1997: 11).

Training in basic capitalist economic skills is characteristic of much Western NGO activity. For example, a joint Oxfam/Intermediate Technology training manual outlines the skills a small business needs to master to be successful: the measurement of fixed and variable costs, the cost of labour, the basics of pricing and value in a market economy, calculations of profit and loss at various output levels, the basics of accounting, and the basics of credit and interest (Millard 1987). The training manual is, in effect, a brief course in standard micro-economics. An Oxfam pamphlet suggests 'credit . . . may be a foreign concept' in certain cultural environments; if this is so, 'beneficiaries should understand their obligations clearly and be trained in book-keeping'. This training fulfils the function of 'encouraging financial discipline among borrowers' (Devereux and Pares 1990: 57–58).

There are numerous other examples of constructing *homo oeconomicus* that have similar features.[17] They are designed to create the particular form of subjectivity necessary for the market economy to function. Among other things, these various projects and programmes are designed to teach people the basic tenets of micro-economics, to promote various forms of capitalist accounting techniques, to see the connection between products and costs, to employ recognisably modern management practices, and to use a 'systematic' approach to problem solving. The self which these projects are designed to create is disengaged and autonomous (freed from negative and dangerous social customs), innovative and reflexive (using a 'systematic approach to problem solving') and calculating (through functional numeracy and accounting techniques).

Transforming the state

In their attempts to construct economic rationality through institutional transformations and the inculcation of 'habits of industry', international organisations, such as the World Bank, are filling the role which Adam Smith gave to the state. Part of the activities of development organisations, particularly those of the World Bank, are directed towards creating the kind of state which can itself undertake these activities. Attempts are being made to enable the state to implement institutional reform programmes effectively and to govern its population in a detailed way. As the following examples show, these programmes have been targeted at both central and local government.

The Africa Technical Department of the World Bank has undertaken a region-wide Governance and Civil Service Reform Programme, with the objective of developing 'innovative ways to improve the effectiveness and efficiency of the civil service in the countries of Sub-Saharan Africa' (Pinto 1994: 10). In preparation for a Sectoral Adjustment Loan to support reform of the Gambian civil service, the World Bank undertook an Institutional Environmental Assessment (IEA) (Pinto 1994: 10). The assessment took the form of a questionnaire that was answered anonymously by civil service employees, as well as a sample of 'opinion leaders' in the community. There were 90 statements and questions, grouped around issues such as the legitimacy of the government, the rule of law, public service and the role of the state, and respondents had to indicate if they 'strongly agreed', 'agreed', 'disagreed', or 'strongly disagreed' (Pinto 1994: 64–70). The statements and questions included:

- the organisational structures of the government are not yet guided by values such as rule of law, accountability, and transparency;
- rules and regulations should be followed in order to get things done effectively;
- transparency and openness are necessary in order to maintain government legitimacy;
- revenue would increase if the accountability of government tax collection institutions, and individual staff were enhanced;

- the choice of the optimal-desirable size of government is arbitrary unless the Gambia defines the development objectives of its government and determines the systems and resources with which to perform effectively (Pinto 1994: 71–89).

The questionnaire was not designed as a normal statistical survey, but with the sole objective of presenting the results back to the respondents. It was to serve as a 'self-diagnostic mirror' (Pinto 1994: 36). This was done in a number of workshops that discussed the results and attempted to generate strategies for reform. In the Gambia, as in all civil services in sub-Saharan Africa, there are already existing norms and patterns of conduct. The IEA was an attempt to induce changes in these through forcing the respondents to measure these against the 'proper' standards of civil service conduct.

In the Philippines, the World Bank has designed and funded a Tax Computerization Project (World Bank 1993b). The project was designed to improve the capacity of the central government to raise tax revenue in order to finance much-needed infrastructural development. The problem was that only about 60 per cent of all the potential tax revenue was being collected (World Bank 1993b: 5). Under the World Bank project, the Bureau of Internal Revenue and the Bureau of Customs will receive new computer systems, and a new database of all taxpayers will be established. This database will utilise a tax identification number for each taxpayer, which will help create a 'national identification system' (World Bank 1993b: 2, 49–53). As part of this, the 'generalised use of nicknames' should be 'prevented by tax penalties and monitoring' (World Bank 1993b: 13). One of the expected benefits of the project is 'improved self-compliance'; the knowledge that tax returns are computerised and 'fully checked' will increase the number of taxpayers who volunteer to pay (World Bank 1993b: 28). In addition, the project will allow the integration of all tax records, and allow for cross-checking and auditing of tax information.

As a further example, the World Bank maintains that the District Assemblies in Ghana lack the necessary expertise, finance and information to carry out their administrative functions (the provision of health care, education and sanitation) effectively. The World Bank accordingly designed the Local Government Development Project as an attempt to overcome these problems (World Bank 1994c). Eleven cities were targeted in this project with the objectives of improving physical infrastructure and services, and strengthening the technical, managerial and financial capacity of the participating districts. As part of this process, Revenue Improvement Action Plans were drawn up to improve local resource mobilisation (World Bank 1994c: 79–84). The most obvious source for improved local revenue collection is property taxes: however, none of the eleven cities possessed an up-to-date register of ratable properties, and the District Assemblies did not possess the expertise or finance to develop one (World Bank 1994c: 65). The World Bank project provides for the development of up-to-date maps showing the existing properties (partly through the use of satellite mapping), and for the formalisation of house numbers and addresses to enable the development of automated production of tax bills and improved revenue collection operations (World Bank 1994c: 91, 97–102).

These projects can be understood as an attempt to transform government in developing countries. They are designed to give governments a new capacity to govern their populations through the collection and control of information, and through increased tax revenue, which can increase the autonomy of the state to pursue the regulatory, administrative and economic policy reforms necessary to produce a dynamic market economy.

Conclusion

It remains to be seen if all this activity will be successful. Most of the projects cited above have yet to run their course, and the assessment of the success or failure of these kinds of development interventions is notoriously difficult (Roemer and Stern 1981; Barnett 1981). Nonetheless, the attempt to construct 'economic rationality' and a new mode of government is a site of contestation. These organisations are attempting to transform existing institutions, attitudes, norms and patterns of conduct. Resistance to the reconstruction of persons and governments should not be seen as simple ignorance of the necessary conditions for people's material well-being; rather, resistance should be seen as arising out of pre-existing attitudes, norms and patterns of conduct.

There is an emerging body of literature on the activities of groups in developing countries who are protesting and attempting to resist the activities of the World Bank.[18] However, most of this literature focuses on global financial trends, such as debt flows, and not the construction of *homo oeconomicus*. We currently lack any very well-documented anthropological studies of the strategies and responses of 'recipient' groups (Hobart 1993; Long and Long 1992).

The analysis presented here has a number of important implications for the political economy of globalisation. Firstly, we need not accept those arguments that rely on a view that economic rationality is somehow natural. While the activities of the World Bank and other development organisations have been justified by such arguments, they are belied by the practices of these organisations, which attempt to create the economically rational agent upon which the economy is supposed to rest. Secondly, international organisations such as the World Bank are engaged in very intrusive interventions in the pursuit of the creation of rational subjectivity. This activity cannot be captured by thinking about the relationship between organisations such as the World Bank and developing countries simply in terms of the imposition of certain policies and programmes. We are seeing the pursuit of a very detailed programme of transformation targeted at governments, institutions and the habits, attitudes and mores of persons (Onuf 1998: Chapter 6).

Thirdly, we should be wary of how other social sciences might adopt the assumptions of economics. Rational choice theory is the clearest example, but there are other, perhaps less formalised accounts, which also rely on the view that the key to explaining social action is that persons pursue their interests. There is a good case for saying that this has become accepted as common sense within the social sciences generally (Mansbridge 1990). To the extent that persons do in fact behave in this way, economics, and indeed rational choice, may provide accurate descriptions of social action. There are reasons to think, though, that it is not an adequate description even of persons within highly developed capitalist economies (Blaug 1992). Regardless, there is a good case for saying that to the extent that persons are like this, they have to be made that way. Recognising this opens up an important area of investigation that is blocked off by assuming that the pursuit of self-interest is somehow natural.

Finally, the analysis presented here may at least enable us to gain a more accurate picture of how market-based economic arrangements are being spread around the world, and by so doing it begins to explore at least two of the issues raised by Fred Halliday: 'the forms of expansion of the capitalist system' and 'the manner in which agency operates transnationally' (1994: 242). Whatever the autonomous logic of capitalism, it also seems to require deliberate attempts to construct a rationality conducive to its development. It may be that the development of market-based economic arrangements is the best hope for material well-being in the modern world. However, even if this is the case it is important to be aware that this seems to require detailed transformations in the functioning of governments, institutions and persons. We should be aware of the fact that this might be a very difficult and potentially very messy thing to do.

Notes

1. This chapter draws on a paper presented to a round-table discussion, 'Forgetting Globalisation: Reclaiming Political Space' at the annual meeting of the International Studies Association, Toronto, 18–22 March 1997; and on papers presented to a seminar on non-governmental organisations in Africa at St Peter's College, Oxford University, January 1996; to a seminar at the department of politics at Lancaster University, May 1996; and to a seminar at the department of political studies, School of Oriental and African Studies (SOAS), University of London, November 1996. I am grateful to the participants at all these seminars for their comments. I am also very appreciative of the suggestions on a previous version of this chapter given by the anonymous referees of *Millennium*.
2. For some of this history see Clapham (1996).
3. Williams and Young (1994). A revisited version of this essay is Chapter Seven in this book.
4. Here I have drawn on Roy (1989: especially Chapter 10) and Blaug (1992: especially Chapter 6).
5. For an empirical demonstration of this, see Frey et al. (1984).
6. As Blaug (1992) has argued, many economists are not concerned first and foremost with the empirical accuracy of their models.
7. There are some parallels between this and Keynesian economics, and some of the original growth models designed for developing countries were derived from Keynes's work. For a discussion of this see Thirwall (1987). There remains some dispute within economics over whether Keynes's macroeconomic theory can be given neoclassical microeconomic foundation. See, for example, Leijonhufved (1968) and Negishi (1979). Whatever the importance of this dispute, orthodox development economists do seem to have thought that at least some macroeconomic problems could be understood using concepts drawn from microeconomics.
8. Lal worked in the World Bank's research division between 1984 and 1986.
9. In addition to the works cited below for this reading of Smith, I have benefited particularly from Fitzgibbons (1995); Meuret (1993); Bazerman (1993); and Shapiro (1993). I have also benefited from locating this reading of Smith in a line of commentary on other thinkers who can be read as having similarly transformative projects. For Hobbes, see Johnstone (1986); and for Locke, see Tully (1988).
10. Smith makes similar arguments about slavery (1976a: 387–90).
11. This self-reflexiveness is the key concept in Smith (1976b).
12. In fact, Smith never suggests this.
13. For an overview of these programmes, and case studies, see Mosley, Harrigan and Toye (1991).
14. For a graphic illustration of this, see Jeffries (1989).

15. Staff appraisal reports such as this one (World Bank 1996a), which are referenced in this chapter, are not formally published by the Bank, but are available to the public.
16. For a different perspective, see Fowler (1992).
17. See the case studies in the joint Oxfam/ACTIONAID pamphlet by Johnson and Rogaly (1997).
18. For one example, see Danaher (1994).

Chapter Four

The Developmental State is Dead
Long Live Social Capital?

Ben Fine[1]

THIS IS A SLIGHTLY EDITED VERSION OF THE 1999
ORIGINAL IN DEVELOPMENT AND CHANGE 30 (1): 1–21.
THE AUTHOR HAS ADDED AN AFTERWORD.

For those following the development literature, there surely can no longer be any doubt that some sort of intellectual and ideological upheaval is taking place within the World Bank. The signs have been there for some time, not least in the process leading from the *East Asian Miracle* (World Bank 1993a), through to the production of the *World Development Report* for 1997 and in the following years.[2] From anti-market, through market-conforming, to market-friendly, the state is now seen more positively, if cautiously so. The analytical agenda is shifting from one based on a simple dichotomy between market and state as respectively good and bad. Even more dramatically, the demise of the Washington Consensus was marked by the increasingly aggressive campaign of the World Bank's former senior vice-president and head of economic research, Joe Stiglitz. In early 1998, he made a speech heavily criticising the Washington Consensus and, more positively, proposing the alternative of a Post-Washington Consensus (Stiglitz 1998a).[3] Essentially, this acknowledges the prevalence of market imperfections and provides a rationale for micro and macro interventions on this basis.

In short, even before the old Washington Consensus has been decently buried, the pretender to its throne is already grabbing at the crown in a palace revolution. However welcome the demise of the old Consensus might be to those who have opposed it for almost two decades, the question of succession needs to be contested. It is also not simply a matter of posing alternatives to the new Consensus – should it be allowed to dominate the development agenda? – as did its predecessor by posing state versus market.

The first section of this chapter provides an outline of the economic analysis that supports the new Consensus. It leads to consideration in the second section of its counterpart in non-economic analysis and the rise to prominence of the notion of social capital. The third section suggests that these new initiatives together hold out the prospect of an even stronger stranglehold over the development debate than was held by the Washington Consensus. The concluding remarks call for a revival of political economy based on a rigorous conceptualisation of class and capital. If this does not happen, both in analysis and in policy making, a pale version of Keynesian/welfarism/modernisation will prevail on the basis of correcting micro-imperfections in economic and non-economic relations.

The microeconomic foundations
The intellectual origins of the new Consensus are readily identified. They arise out of the microfoundations of macroeconomics or the new Keynesian economics.[4] Essentially, the motivating idea is very old – that market imperfections justify state intervention to rectify them. The new twist, however, is to broaden the scope of what constitutes market imperfections. These are now organised around informational imperfections and asymmetries of various sorts, including the presence of transactions costs, so that market outcomes depend upon who has what information before, during and after the economy's passages in and out of exchange.

Stiglitz has been extremely active for almost two decades in this line of research, especially focusing on markets for finance.[5] But even though financial markets are an obvious area of application, given the respective roles and knowledges of borrowers and lenders, other markets are equally susceptible to the new microfoundations. Akerlof's pioneering contribution concerned the 'market for lemons' or second-hand cars, and the labour market is also prominent as an application – as is any market involving coordination failure, and monitoring of any sort including adverse selection and moral hazard.[6] When information is imperfect, even in equilibrium, markets may not operate at efficient levels, they may not clear (by bringing supply and demand into equality), and they may even fail to exist altogether.

It is crucial, however, to set these developments at the forefront of economics within a broader setting. Three aspects are significant. Firstly, as is apparent from the use of the term 'the microfoundations of macroeconomics' (as opposed to the alternative term, 'the new Keynesian macroeconomics'), relatively simple ideas at the *microeconomic* level are being translated into models of how the *macroeconomy* functions. This is transparent in the use of representative individuals or agents in macroeconomics models whose aggregate behaviour is more or less successfully coordinated through the market. Market imperfections at the microeconomic level, whether of the old or newer sort, become extrapolated to the economy as a whole and can give rise to results with a Keynesian flavour.

Secondly, the new microeconomics has spawned, or at least has been associated with, a blossoming of other new endeavours. The list is impressive: the new growth theory, the new trade theory, the new institutional economics, the new household economics, the new political economy, and so on. What these all tend to have in common is the extension of microeconomic principles to areas that have previously been unexamined or taken as exogenous in the light of standard assumptions within economics. Where do productivity increase, comparative advantage, economic policy, family decision making, and non-market institutions derive from?

In the work of economists such as Gary Becker, and those who follow him, the answer is primarily provided in terms of simply universalising the so-called 'economic approach' based on utility maximisation to all areas of life, including those that are traditionally perceived as lying outside the domain of economics.[7] This has allowed for considerable advance into some of the areas concerned, most notably in the general, and now uncritical, acceptance of the notion of human capital. It is also apparent in the new household economics and the new political economy or any analysis incorporating simplistic notions of rent seeking.

However, the new microeconomics has given rise to a most significant result as far as shifting the analytical boundaries of the scope of economic analysis is concerned. In what appears to be a squaring of the circle, it allows for the explanation of *social* structures and institutions even on the basis of *individual* optimisation. Faced with imperfect information, individuals can decide to create or engage in socially structured activity both within and between market and non-market forms of organisation. These forms become endogenous on a microeconomic basis, where previously they were taken as exogenous. Thirdly, then, and most novel from an intellectual point of view, mainstream neoclassical economics now has the power to offer an explanation of the social, without taking it as exogenous as previously. Ultimately, though, it always has to take something as exogenous, whether it be informational or initial conditions. Otherwise, individuals would have nothing over which to optimise.

The forward march of social capital

The significance of this last point will be taken up later. Before doing so, consider an equally rapid change that is evolving within and around World Bank thinking. It is the astonishing rise to prominence of the notion of 'social capital'. It had already made its way into the *World Development Report* for 1997 and, as Harriss and De Renzio (1997: 920) comment: 'Since 1993 "social capital" has become one of the key terms, of development lexicon, adopted enthusiastically by international organizations, national governments and NGOs alike.' They cite uses ranging from that of the Institute for Development Studies (IDS) at the University of Sussex as a theme for a research programme to the terms of reference of tenders for research on social policy formulated by the UK's department for international development (DfID). For the World Bank itself (World Bank 1997a), even though its use only seems to date back to 1994, it is already being heralded as the 'missing link' in development. It figured prominently in the draft programme for the *World Development Report* for 2000/1, with 'poverty and development' as its theme.

It is important, then, to deconstruct this conceptual wunderkind, a process that has already begun with a critical literature, including surveys such as that by Harriss and De Renzio (1997) and the even more comprehensive study by Woolcock (1998). The purpose here is to draw upon, and add to, these contributions in order to understand why the notion of 'social capital' should be so conducive to World Bank thinking even as it is itself establishing a new agenda.

Consider, first, problems surrounding the definition of 'social capital'. It is usually distinguished from physical, financial and human capital, with these generally being interpreted from within neoclassical orthodoxy. Although it can require the use of economic resources, it has to be something over and above other types of capital but, as such, it seems to be able to be *anything* ranging over public goods, networks, culture, etc. The only proviso is that social capital should be attached to the economy in a functionally positive way for economic performance, especially growth. As Harriss and De Renzio (1997: 921) observe in quoting Narayan and Pritchett (1996: 2) in what is probably an understatement: 'Social capital, while not all things to all people, is many things to many people.' In a three-page footnote of references, Woolcock (1998: 193–96) identifies seven different fields of application for social capital: (dys)functional families, schooling, community life, work and organisation, democracy and governance, collective action, and intangible assets.

The ambiguity and scope attached to social capital, however, are strikingly illustrated by the attempts to trace back its intellectual origins, a task that testifies to the speed and depth with which the notion has already been established (Harriss and De Renzio 1997: 921; Woolcock 1998). At one extreme, Hyden (1997) locates the concept within the different approaches to the relationship between the state and civil society as development proceeds, dating first explicit references to the mid-nineteenth century, albeit in Italian. In this context, social capital is concerned with grand theory and systemic analysis from whatever perspective.

At the other extreme, the more recent and more influential origins of 'social capital' are far more mundane. They derive from the work of James Coleman (especially 1987, 1988 and 1990). Coleman is a professor of sociology at the University of Chicago and is the counterpart and practising intellectual partner to Gary Becker. He is fundamentally committed to methodological individualism, although this is tempered by reference to social networks and the like (Fine 1998a). Coleman has inspired a range of empirical studies, mainly for the US, that seek to demonstrate how individual attainment is affected by family or other aspects of the microsocial environment, readily interpreted as (individual possession of) social capital. Whether parents are separated, mothers work or not, families belong to particular ethnic or cultural communities, are new or long-established migrants, move frequently, communicate with their children, watch television, and so on, are the variables that make up positive or negative social capital. These factors are used to interrogate success at school or college, including drop-outs, and correlation with criminality, delinquency and political extremism.[8]

It cannot be overemphasised how crude such studies are: they speculate about a few causal relations and then seek to demonstrate their validity through a statistical exercise. There is a striking parallel with mainstream econometrics but with the absence of the latter's reliance upon some underlying formal mathematical model. A further analogy applies where macrodata are substituted for microdata as if there were representative individuals – with crime rates, for example, explained by levels of unemployment, mobility and marriage as in MacMillan (1995). Such studies have the explicit aim of leaping from the individual to the social by the use of macrostructural indicators and statistics to avoid both conceptual issues and the causal mechanisms and processes by which the social is reproduced.

From a moment's reflection, it is apparent that such endeavours have nothing new to contribute through appeal to social capital that merely serves as a convenient peg on which to hang collections of dull and mechanistic empiricism. This is despite the unlimited scope of such studies in terms of variables that can be included and hypotheses putatively tested. But the notion of social capital is open to a richer qualitative interpretation that expands its compass even further, especially in the context of development. For Shetler (1995), as limited an object as a Kiroba text of popular history forms social capital in Tanzania since it depicts a constellation of networks and social relations that can inform and sustain those who draw upon it. Putterman (1995: 15), also addressing Tanzania, seeks to generalise social capital as culture beyond a set of individual ties 'to encompass the repertoires of entire material cultures'. Indeed, 'a society's division of labour with respect to the holding of its overall cultural capital stock can be regarded as a kind of collective memory algorithm'.

Such cultural interpretations of social capital have affinities with the work of Bourdieu, preceding by a decade or so the contributions of Coleman.[9] Bourdieu is concerned to demonstrate how class distinctions are constructed, created and reproduced by the interconnections between the different spheres of economic, political and cultural life. His approach involves deployment of various different types of social capital, such as the cultural and educational, the consideration of how these are converted into one another, and the attachment of such capitals to individuals as well as to socio-economic groupings. In short, the language and analogy of economic capital is embraced, and Bourdieu has engaged in case studies based on surveys. Consequently, his work has been referenced in support of other social capital studies.

Nonetheless, there is a major difference, even an analytical barrier, between Bourdieu and most of the subsequent literature.[10] Whilst critical of the excesses of postmodernism, and of Baudrillard in particular, Bourdieu is acutely aware that social capital has to be constructed in terms of its content as meaning. In contrast, current use of the notion of social capital relies almost entirely upon distinction by extrapolation from physical notions of capital. Whilst explicitly seeking to generalise beyond the physical, to distinguish social from economic and even human capital, the conceptual framework primarily remains tied to an understanding of the social as the informational or other cultural externalities between individuals. Accordingly, a network of whatever sort, for example, is the favoured non-individualistic example of social capital – although this begs the question within this perspective of how a network is created and how and why individuals participate within it. The result is to generate an abstract theory of social capital that focuses on the logistics of networks, at greater or lesser levels of formality, as for Burt (1992); Granovetter (1985, 1992); and Ostrom (1994).[11]

Consequently, the next major stage in the evolution of social capital is in the passage from Coleman to Putnam (1993a, 1993b, 1995). From a conceptual point of view, Putnam has added very little, and his study of differential Italian economic development according to local politics is open to question.[12] Most importantly, though, is the spread of the use of 'social capital' to politics and the state. Whilst his more recent work has focused on the revitalisation of US social capital, to the point of self-parody in seeking more ten-pin bowling clubs (Putnam 1995), the implications of his work for development have proved most attractive:

> Social capital is coming to be seen as a vital ingredient in economic development around the world. Scores of studies of rural development have shown that a vigorous network of indigenous grassroots associations can be as essential to growth as physical investment, appropriate technology, or (that nostrum of neoclassical economists) 'getting prices right' (Putnam 1993b: 38).

From one study of Italy (Putnam 1993a), in which the concept of social capital is only first introduced in a closing chapter, the floodgates are opened for that 'vital ingredient' to explain 'economic development around the world'.

In short, the notion of social capital is all-encompassing. As Woolcock (1998: 155) observes:

It now assumes a wide variety of meanings and has been cited in a rapidly increasing number of social, political, and economic studies, but – as so often happens with promising new terms in social science – with limited critical attention being given to its intellectual history or its conceptual and ontological status. These indiscriminate applications of social and 'other' capitals are part of what Baron and Hannan (1994: 1122–24) despairingly refer to as the recent emergence of a 'plethora of capitals'. Sociologists, they lament, 'have begun referring to virtually every feature of life as a form of capital'.

A second major feature, then, of social capital follows in that it is a totally chaotic concept, drawing its meanings from the more or less abstract studies or tidal wave of case studies on which it depends. This, in turn, has led to a critical literature along a number of lines which essentially reflect the imprecision with which the dual notions of 'social' and 'capital' have been used and combined. The social takes as its point of departure anything that is not reducible to individualistic exchange relations and, correspondingly, social capital is anything other than tangible assets. This immediately creates problems since it can never be clear where the capital ends and the social begins, once it is recognised that the impact of social capital depends upon its social context – unless any element of social capital is redefined holistically.

The point is illustrated by evidence of 'perverse' social capital. The term derives from the study by Rubio (1997) of Colombia where criminal activity is associated with strong networks.[13] The simplest economics, however, suffices to make the same point – as Adam Smith observed, producers meet and require trust to operate a cartel.[14] There is not necessarily anything positive or predetermined about the impact of social capital, until both its intrinsic and extrinsic content is examined. As Dezalay and Garth (1997) argue for the functioning of international law, large US law firms and law schools comprise legal and social capital (political connections) that lead to the Americanisation of laws to the advantage of US economic power.[15] The study by Beall (1997: 960) of waste collection services draws analogous conclusions:[16]

> Synergy across the public–private divide . . . between representatives of communities and governments were seen to reinforce and cement relationships founded on patronage and clientelism rather than to foster more inclusive forms of civic engagement . . . As with Bangalore so in Faisalabad, power relations and existing structures of inequality have to be understood because in both cases, investment in social capital in waste proved to be a solid investment, but for some far more than others.

This example illustrates that the chaotic and incoherent content of social capital as a concept does not, however, lead it to be without systematic content and influence. A third feature of the literature is that it tends to neglect power and conflict (no doubt reflecting the putative Pareto improvements that can be made with social capital), and to proceed from the micro to the macro (in conformity with its individualistic origins). It also spawns popularisation, as with Putnam but also Fukuyama (1995, 1996), for whom trust begins where history ends.[17]

These features of social capital – as catch-all, ambiguous if not incoherent, and yet analytically selective – have been the source, paradoxically, of a vibrant research programme around it rather than a cause of its demise. On the one hand, theory has sought to construct a range of intermediate concepts within which to accommodate the analytical and empirical anomalies that inevitably arise – from networks and trust to structural holes,[18] and from notions that social capital is free to its being slow to create and quick to dissipate.[19] By the same token, initial lines of causation posited from social capital to social outcomes can be reversed and refined. On the other hand, social capital can be taken for granted conceptually and incorporated into an ever-expanding collection of case studies or statistical exercises. These two different ways of proceeding feed upon one another, creating a web of eclecticism in which the notion of social capital floats freely from one meaning to another with little attention to conceptual depth or rigour.[20] As Woolcock (1998: 159) proposes:

Where do these criticisms of the idea of social capital ... leave us? Short of dismissing the term altogether, one possible resolution of these concerns may be that there are different types, levels or dimensions of social capital, different performance outcomes associated with different combinations of these dimensions, and different sets of conditions that support or weaken favourable combinations. Unravelling and resolving these issues requires a more dynamic than static understanding of social capital; it invites a more detailed examination of the intellectual history of social capital, and the search for lessons from empirical research that embrace a range of many such dimensions, levels, or conditions.

Neither Washington nor Post-Washington Consensus

It seems, then, that what has already happened with social capital as an organising concept is set to gather pace and momentum especially, if not exclusively, in development studies. For it is prospectively nothing other than the rewriting of social theory with some degree of economic content. But the question is why? In part, the answer is to be found in the shifting stance of the World Bank. The proposal for a Post-Washington Consensus from Stiglitz has social capital as its exact social and political counterpart. It builds up from the micro to the macro from notions of civil, as opposed to market, imperfections and with the potential for non-market improvements with impact upon the market.

It is one thing, however, to argue in principle that the economic analysis attached to the Post-Washington Consensus and the notions of social capital are mutually compatible. It is another to establish in practice that they are driving one another and are being integrated to form a new synthesis. At most, since these are early days, such a synthesis can only be suggested to be prospective. Stiglitz, for example, does not appear to use the term himself. However, this reflects the following factors that are of more general relevance.

Firstly, he does not need to do so. The new microfoundations, on which he has built his reputation and with which he is attacking the old neoliberal Consensus, have been around for at least two decades. The notion of market imperfections suffices as a proxy for social capital within the economist's vocabulary. Secondly, as an economist, Stiglitz has preferred to recognise the importance of the non-economic in the form of institutions, customs, etc., but without incorporating these as variables within his own analysis. Thirdly, economists tend to rely upon extremely formal mathematical models for which the vague notion of social capital is unhelpful. Rather than use the term, economists are liable to refer to its microeconomic specifics, such as infrastructure, networks, transparency, trust and monitoring.[21] Whether economists use the term, and whether they are happy with it, is less relevant than the way in which their new microeconomic understanding of market imperfections is being incorporated into the economic understanding of non-economists.

Nonetheless, Stiglitz comes as close to using the notion of social capital as his intellectual history allows. In the paper following his appointment to the World Bank, he asserts (1997: 19):

> Today, we recognise that development is more than the accretion of physical capital and even more than the accretion of human capital. It includes closing the knowledge gap between rich and poor economies. And it includes other transformations, such as those that result in lower population growth rates and changes in economic organisation.

However, irrespective of his personal stance, taken together, the new Consensus and social capital offer the World Bank the analytical opportunity to resolve what has been a glaring contradiction between its ideology and practice. Given the previous stance in favour of state minimalism, even if serving as a veil for considerable discretionary intervention in practice, there has been a problem in addressing what role the state should play given its continuing importance. We cannot argue that the state should do nothing but also debate what the state should do. The World Bank has been disarmed by its own ideology.

Now, rather than becoming genuinely more state-friendly, it is more appropriately interpreted as seeking to be more influential than before over what the state does – both in depth and scope.[22]

This new agenda explains why Putnam, for example, should prove to be so popular with the World Bank. Consider:

> *Social capital is not a substitute for effective public policy but rather a prerequisite for it and, in part, a consequence of it. Social capital . . . works through and within states and markets, not in place of them* . . . The social capital approach promises to uncover new ways of combining social infrastructure with public policies that work, and, in turn, of using wise public policies to revitalise America's stock of social capital (Putnam 1993b: 42).

And what is good enough for the US is good enough for the rest of the world. In short, as it is being deployed, social capital allows the World Bank to broaden its agenda whilst retaining continuity with most of its practices and prejudices, which include the benign neglect of macro-relations of power, preference for favoured NGOs and grassroots movements, and decentralised initiatives.[23]

The rapid rise to prominence of social capital has also had two crucial analytical effects, as will be seen shortly. Firstly, we should remember that, as Wade (1996b) has shown and is common knowledge, the shifting position of the World Bank has very little to do with consideration, let alone acceptance, of the overwhelming weight of scholarship that has long been turned critically upon its analytical posturing and the impact of its policies in practice. Nor is it a response to the new microfoundations orthodoxy, for Stiglitz and others have been active in this area for two decades. Rather, the increasing significance of Japan as donor, foreign investor and self-reflective case study has rendered the old Consensus increasingly unacceptable.[24]

Broadly, the criticisms that have been ignored by the old Consensus have been formulated, at times explicitly, around the notion of the case and conditions conducive to a developmental state. This is hardly surprising since to counter the old Consensus on its own terms is to posit the potential for a developmental state as opposed to relying as far as possible upon the supposedly free market. For the role of the state to be addressed more positively by the new Consensus, the issue arises of how it is to relate to the developmental state literature.

Firstly, then, the notion of social capital has provided the World Bank with the analytical capacity to propose its new agenda without having had to come to terms in any serious or substantive way with the critical literature of the old Consensus, especially that around the developmental state. And, I suspect, the new Consensus will be mild in reassessing the past practices of the old and how they were rationalised by those who will, presumably, continue to provide the rationale for the new agenda in the future. Whatever its merits, the literature on the developmental state will be ignored, as in the past, in pushing forward an agenda based on social capital and the need to enhance the market and relieve market imperfections.

Indeed, the way in which this is being done already has remarkable parallels with the way in which the developmental state literature itself developed. As Fine and Stoneman (1996) and Fine and Rustomjee (1997) suggest, there have been two broad approaches to the developmental state, denoted as the 'economic' and the 'political' schools. One identifies, for example from market imperfections, the case for state intervention without addressing why the state might have the capacity or the will to undertake the necessary policies. The other considers the (political) conditions under which the state is capable of, or can be induced to undertake, appropriate interventions without identifying what these are. The integration of these two schools has been quite limited but each has prospered by a widening circle of empirical case studies undermining more abstract theory and leading it to be refined by a proliferation of ideal types – most notable in the different theories of the sources of comparative advantage for the economic school and also the proliferating models of developmental or non-developmental states for the political school.

Corresponding to the economic school approach to the developmental state is the new microfoundational account of market imperfections. As Stiglitz emphasises repeatedly, such informationally based imperfections can rationalise state intervention. Yet, this depends upon applying a dramatic reductionism to the rationale for state intervention to a micro-level, around a single informational motif, in sharp contrast to the wealth of the theoretical and empirical factors that make up the economic school within the developmental state literature.

Social capital, following hard upon the new microeconomics, is the corresponding counterpart to the political school within the developmental state literature. It is about how the non-economic, or non-market, makes the economic work or work better. Again, a reductionism is involved, although it is less drastic than for the economic school, as it allows for notions such as custom, trust, culture and networks. Where it does correspond more closely with the new economic approach is in its capacity to set aside the broader methodological and theoretical agenda to be found within the critical developmental state literature emanating from the political school.

Secondly, then, the notion of social capital allows the new Consensus to be selective in where and how it addresses the role of non-economic factors in economic performance. In this light, social capital has had the analytical effect not only of perpetuating neglect of the critical contribution of the developmental state literature, but also of allowing that literature and its proponents to be incorporated on the terms set by the new Consensus. As Harriss and De Renzio (1997: 921) ask: 'does the fact that it means so many different things reflect the fact that it is an idea which serves as a convenient peg for different agendas?'

The answer is in the affirmative in that it opens up an agenda for those who opposed the old Consensus; but there is an admission price in terms of accepting the social as based on microfoundations and capital as based on market or non-market imperfections. Notably absent will be a political economy based on class and power, and capital interpreted as a social relation rather than as a non-physical, atomised resource. In short, where the developmental state literature previously stood as a critique of the old Consensus, it can now either be overlooked or be repackaged as new in terms of a much less radical content attached to market imperfections and social capital.

The prospect, then, is for the developmental state literature from the political school to be redigested within a social capital framework, just as the new microfoundations of macroeconomics have demonstrated the potential to incorporate much radical political economy based on institutions and macroeconomic structures. Consider, for example, the response to social capital of one of the leading proponents of the developmental state within political science. In a special section in *World Development* on social capital and the role of the state in the public/private sector divide, there is a remarkable and acknowledged synergy between the political and the sociological involved in networks and embeddedness (Evans 1996b: 1033): 'By labelling such norms and networks "social capital" contemporary theorists . . . project primary ties as potentially valuable economic assets . . . The language echoes Granovetter's classic work on the embeddedness of market relations.'[25]

In this way, the politics of bringing the state back in and the theory of the developmental state have become tied to the notion of social capital and more amenable to the tacit postulates of the mainstream economic theory associated with the Post-Washington Consensus. Of course, the location of such capital within the discipline of political science can lead to a more sophisticated account of, and focus upon, conflict which is perceived otherwise to be overlooked in addressing problems of collective action across the public–private divide – as Evans (1996a: 1127) unremarkably deduces in summarising the analytical conclusions of a number of case studies: 'If a community is riven by conflicting interests, the nature and meaning of social capital becomes more complicated.' The inevitable implication from this conclusion is that if conflict undermines the notion of social capital, then why not take conflict and its theoretical underpinnings as a starting point, rather than social capital, which is rendered both ambiguous and redundant? To proceed otherwise is to deploy social capital as a generalised proxy for the developmental state in ways such that conflict and its analytical prerequisites can be secondary, muffled or even be taken out.

Concluding remarks

Elsewhere, I have argued that conceptual initiatives around social capital are part and parcel of a more general, possibly revolutionary, shift taking place not so much within as around economics in its relationship with other social sciences (Fine 1997a, 1998c, 1998d). Economics is colonising other disciplines through universalising its methods, including those new microfoundations that now explain the social on the basis of the individual. The response from other social sciences has been mixed in depth and content. The promotion of social capital in the context of the Post-Washington Consensus is an example drawn from development studies. It promises to create economists out of social scientists who know no economics, just as it has been given life by economists as social scientists who know no social science. Even those Marxists most committed to base–superstructure models would be embarrassed by the reductionism of the economic approach to social science. By the same token, those wedded to some notion of autonomy, should shrink from the absence of the economic in many of the ways in which social capital is being deployed across the social sciences. For those genuinely committed to political economy, both the opportunity and the obligation have arisen to develop alternatives to, and to oppose, social capital and the new Consensus before they dominate the development agenda as did the old Consensus before them.

These observations are strikingly illustrated by the opposing conclusions drawn by the two recent surveys of the social capital literature. This is despite each of them making very similar critical commentary on the ambiguity and inconsistency of the notion. For Woolcock (1998: 188):

> Social capital provides sociologists in particular with a fruitful conceptual and policy device by which to get beyond exhausted modernization and world-systems theories ... In social capital, historians, political scientists, anthropologists, economists, sociologists, and policy makers ... may once again be able to find a common language ... that disciplinary provincialisms have largely suppressed over the last one-hundred-and-fifty years ... Theoretical claims and policy recommendations made on the basis of the incremental accumulation of evidence constitute the surest and most responsible agenda for future research.

Harriss and De Renzio (1997: 919) are considerably less sanguine: 'Policy arguments which pose civil society against the state, or which rest on the view that rich endowment in "social capital" is a precondition for "good government", are almost certainly misconceived.' They seem to seek a critical rethinking of social capital in which the traditional concerns of more radical social and economic theory are incorporated – whether it be conflict, class, globalisation or whatever.

In each of these surveys, despite its acknowledged conceptual weaknesses, social capital is accepted as a potential source for new research, although Woolcock is more upbeat in case of greater refinement in concrete details and Harriss and De Renzio for the incorporation of a radical content that could easily be omitted. As already suggested, the outcome is most likely to be a reworking of the developmental state debate, only on an analytical terrain that is less conducive to opponents of the new Washington Consensus, even though some advance is made, as intended, over the old. For the notion of social capital is fundamentally misconceived, especially in the context and sources from which it has evolved. For to deconstruct in the crudest way, term by term in reverse order, 'capital' has been defined negatively – by what it is not. It is not tangible, such as physical endowments or human capital. Rather, it is anything connecting individuals that contributes to the economy on the basis of their individual endowments of non-social capital. By the same token, the 'social' is the set of relations, market or non-market, connecting these individuals with a greater or lesser degree of imperfection. With these notions of social and capital, their genuine counterparts within political economy or within social theory – economic structures and tendencies, on the one hand, and power, stratification, conflict, on the other – can only be incorporated in bastardised or hopelessly eclectic forms.

It is imperative, then, that as and when the World Bank and the development agenda become potentially more progressive, that 'capital' and the 'social' be appropriately constructed on the basis of systematic understandings. As Marx and Marxists, for example, have long insisted, economic 'capital' is not a thing in the first place but is already social, global, exploitative and embedded, to coin a phrase, in broader relations of which the state forms a part. The social can only be added to capital if it has been illegitimately excluded in the first place. Such elementary insights need to be the starting point for developmental dissent to whatever Consensus the World Bank peddles.

Afterword

This chapter, in its original form, brought together a number of themes and, at the expense of some personal indulgence, I seek in this short Afterword to place them in the wider context of my continuing work in which fuller discussion and reference to the literature can be found. The first, and most obvious, theme to address is the account of social capital. In subsequent contributions, I have offered a more extensive critical charting of this concept's meteoric rise and spread across the social sciences (Fine 2001a, 2001b, 2002a, 2002b). In a nutshell, it has plundered and reduced existing social theory by viewing it through an analytical prism that has a strong attachment in practice, if not necessarily explicit and in principle, to rational choice theory. By focusing on civil society in its own fashion, it has suffered an absence of consideration of the contextual and the role of conflict, power, class, trade unions and the central state. In other words, the social capital of Bourdieu has been excised in favour of that of Coleman, and of Putnam who serves as its most ardent populariser. Whilst there are some signs of a move to bring Bourdieu and the contextual back into social capital, this is necessarily token and an afterthought, as with the re-introduction of other absences. It would in any case undermine the universalistic claims of social capital as a tool of social theory.

Secondly, social capital reflects the response to three intellectual trends across the social science at the turn of the millennium. One, highlighted in this chapter, is economics imperialism, also emphasised in Fine and Milonakis (2005) and Fine (2002a) in the context of development. Whilst social capital, as used by economists, does allow them to deploy a market imperfections approach to the economy and to incorporate non-economic factors (the social as everything that is not economic capital), social capital has figured more prominently as a form of imperialism across the social sciences other than economics. This itself reflects the two other trends: the dual retreat from postmodernism and neoliberalism, or an academic return to the 'real', and especially the attempt to understand the nature of contemporary capitalism. Social capital recognises both that there is a material world, and that it is not like a perfect market. But, unlike the globalisation literature that has also come to reflect these intellectual trends more critically in terms of systemic and global exercise of power, social capital has primarily been concerned with positive-sum outcomes. These are inappropriately perceived to be garnered out of cooperation at national or sub-national levels, with a tendency to disregard the economic other than as something that can be improved upon by the social (as if the economic form of capital is not social). In short, social capital is about raising self-help from the level of the individual to some collective level (Fine 2004a).

Thirdly are the developments within and around the World Bank. Since the chapter's first publication, its prognostications have been heavily borne out over the role that the new development economics plays in restoring the legitimacy of the World Bank. Yet the analysis can be taken further by emphasising the distinction between the rhetoric, scholarship and policy in practice of the Bank (and other IFIs). These are far from consistent with one another. Furthermore, they are mutually inconsistent in different ways according to the issue. This was forcibly illustrated by the sacking of Stiglitz, quickly followed by his award of the Nobel Prize; and yet the Bank continues to use Stiglitz-speak. As has been observed by many, the more state-friendly and humane rhetoric and scholarship of the Bank has been associated, in practice, with a very slight shift in policy. It is even associated with a strengthening and hardening of intervention across economic and social policy, as noted in Fine, Lapavitsas and Pincus (2003), Fine and Jomo (2005) and, for the apparent remarkable somersault on privatisation, Fine (2004b).

Meanwhile, fourthly, the World Bank's social capital juggernaut has gathered momentum. It has been excused for its legion of analytical and empirical fault lines because it is at least a more progressive way of proceeding than neoliberalism. And it offers the opportunity to convince (World Bank) economists of the virtues of taking the social into account. It is, however, a moot point whether it is possible to engage with such economists, even around the social, on terms other than their own. In any case, the issue is not so much to add the social to an otherwise unchanged economics as to challenge that economics itself (Fine 2003b).

Last is to confirm the extent to which the developmental state has been marginalised if not reduced to the point of death. Ironically, the World Bank's rethink offers a pale and reduced version of this literature without ever acknowledging it as such. More generally, though, the developmental state has been hard hit by the East Asian crisis. Even before this, however, it was in trouble because of its own weaknesses, despite its significant ideological and intellectual role in the era of neoliberalism. It tended either to focus on what would be appropriate economic policies for the state to adopt (without investigating the political conditions allowing it to do so). Or, conversely, it focused on the appropriate political conditions allowing for state autonomy without examining the economic interests and outcomes being served. This all reflected acceptance of the World Bank's Washington Consensus agenda of state versus market, although falling on the other side of the conflict than the Bank. Better analysis demands focus upon underlying economic and political interests and how they are represented and reformed through both state and market (Fine 2003a). To do otherwise is to accept the agenda, however critically, of good governance, structural adjustment and social capital that underpin World Bank rhetoric, but from which its practice so heavily departs in serving the interests of its own choosing.

Notes

1. Thanks to Costas Lapavitsas, John Sender and an anonymous referee for comments on earlier drafts of this chapter, which arose out of a programme of research at the School of Oriental and African Studies (SOAS) to assess the shifting positions of the World Bank and IMF. It has been slightly modified by David Moore, the editor of this book, to account for the fact that the World Bank essentially sacked Stiglitz. See Wade (2001b, 2002). For later critical analysis of the Post-Washington Consensus, see Fine, Lapavitsas and Pincus (2003).
2. See the special issue of the *IDS Bulletin* for April 1998, for a critical assessment of the *World Development Report* for 1997.
3. For a more tempered statement of his position in the context of the East Asian crisis, see Stiglitz (1998b). Nonetheless, possibly referring to the previous Consensus, he writes (1998b: 26): 'In any case, only an ideologue would claim that *but for their system of close government and business cooperation* they would have grown even faster.' For evidence of the rapid spread and ambition of the Post-Washington Consensus, consider the soon-to-be-published report on Latin America entitled, *Beyond the Washington Consensus: Institutions Matter* and also the interview with Grzegorz Kolodko in the June 1998 edition of *Transition*, the World Bank's in-house journal on eastern Europe.
4. For a fuller account, in the context of labour markets, see Fine (1998b: Chapter 2).
5. Stiglitz's early contribution (Stiglitz and Weiss 1981) is a classic. He has also been prominent in the new microeconomic approaches to rural institutions (see Hoff, Braverman and Stiglitz 1993).
6. More generally, see Akerlof (1984). On labour markets, see Fine (1998b: Chapters 2 and 4).
7. See Becker (1996) and Tommasi and Iurelli (1995). A critical assessment of Becker's work in the light of some of the themes explored in this chapter is provided by Fine (1995, 1997b, 1998d).
8. For a recent selection of such work, in order to give a feel for its scope, see Bianchi and Robinson (1997); Furstenberg and Hughes (1995); Hagan, Merkens and Boehnke (1995); Hagan, MacMillan and Wheaton (1996); Meyerson (1994); Parcel and Menaghan (1994); Sanders and Nee (1996); Schneider, Teske and Marschall (1997); Smith, Beaulieu and Seraphine (1995); Teachman, Paasch and Carver (1996); Valenzuela and Dornbusch (1994); White and Kaufman (1997); and Zhou and Bankston (1994).
9. See Fine (1998a) for a fuller critical account of Bourdieu's understanding of social capital and how it has been distortedly incorporated into more recent understandings.
10. For this reason it is unfortunate that Harriss and De Renzio (1997), in an otherwise highly perceptive review, simply perceive Bourdieu's use of social capital as similar to that of his followers.

11. Note that Burt (1997) appeals to the emerging network analysis to consider the content of flows within the network relations. But, significantly, this would imply that the substance of the network would be conflated with discursive content within the network, as if the two were interchangeable. By analogy, it would be necessary to distinguish between a grid and what flows along it. Social capital, in effect, is caught between being grid alone and both grid and flow. This reveals the ambiguity of the network notion of social capital, since identical networks can function positively or negatively for economic or other performance according to what is communicated. Also see the later discussion of perverse social capital.
12. See discussion and references provided in Harriss and De Renzio (1997). Most important are questions of causation between economic development and civic society and of differential development *within* as well as between regions.
13. See also Seron and Ferris (1995) who argue that men gain in professional occupations, over and above the networks in which they engage, because they enjoy the gendered social capital that requires that private lives are secondary and taken care of by others, presumed to be their wives. For a critique of Putnam from a perspective of the 'dark side' of social capital, see Putzel (1997).
14. Note also that the idea that the gaps between dense networks are a source of profitability, as opposed to networks themselves, is implicit in Hilferding's concept of finance capital.
15. By contrast, note that Arnold and Kay (1995) suggest that large law firms embody social capital since they are more liable to be self-monitoring in establishing legal and ethical standards.
16. See also Fox (1997). Stone (1995) draws similar conclusions for social capital concerning problems of definition and causation in commenting upon the account by Hinrich (1995) of inequality and redistribution in health provision in Germany.
17. To give him credit, Fukuyama does have the capacity to capture the intellectual mood, even if in the crudest forms:

> Over the past generation, economic thought has been dominated by neoclassical or free market economists, associated with names like Milton Friedman, Gary Becker, and George Stigler. The rise of the neoclassical perspective constitutes a vast improvement from earlier decades in this century, when Marxists and Keynesians held sway. We can think of neoclassical economics as being, say, eighty per cent correct: it has uncovered important truths about the nature of money and markets because its fundamental model of rational, self-interested human behavior is correct about eighty per cent of the time. But there is a missing twenty per cent of human behavior about which neoclassical economics can give only a poor account. As Adam Smith well understood, economic life is deeply embedded in social life, and it cannot be understood apart from the customs, morals, and habits of the society in which it occurs. In short, it cannot be divorced from culture (1996: 13).

For a critique of Fukuyama along the lines that it is the rule of law rather than custom that is important, see Fellmeth (1996: 169) who concludes, on the discovery that political culture matters to economic behaviour: 'Fukuyama has merely rediscovered the wheel, although he has used it as an impediment rather than a mode of transport.'

18. See Fedderke, De Kadt and Luiz (1998), who also emphasise that the ambiguities attached to social capital have their counterpart in the difficulties of operationalising the factors concerned empirically. Nonetheless, empirical studies proceed apace as in Knack and Keefer (1997), for example.

19. See Wilson (1997), for whom social capital is free, invisible but real, involving stakeholder participation, professional protocol, social learning, collaboration, trust, solutions to tragedies of the commons, collective responsibilities, etc. For Walker, Kogut and Shan (1997: 111), 'social capital is a means of enforcing norms of behaviour . . . and thus acts as a constraint as well as a resource'.

20. Most notable is the way that combinations of Bourdieu, Coleman, Putnam, Granovetter, Burt and, increasingly, Fukuyama are referenced for authority. See Nichols (1996), for example, for the idea that Russia lacks trust. See also Kolankiewicz (1996) for an appeal to Bourdieu and Putnam to explain who will become the new capitalists in eastern Europe. Pahl (1996) prefers to emphasise access to property over access to social capital. For various examples of the rounding up together of the founders of social capital, see Meyerson (1994) and Pieterse (1997), as well as Harriss and De Renzio (1997) and Woolcock (1998).

21. See the treatment by Konrad (1995), for example, of infrastructure as social capital. An older generation provides it for the younger, not out of altruism, but as an intertemporal optimising exercise in view of the later higher taxes it can take from the next generation's higher earnings for use as social security transfers to itself.

22. For a clear and perceptive account, see Hildyard (1998).

23. See Brown and Ashman (1996) for a selection of case studies tied to the notion of social capital.

24. See also Gyohten (1997), but especially the relevant articles collected in Ohno and Ohno (1998).

25. Granovetter is a sociologist who has inspired the notion of social capital as networks.

Chapter Five

The Bank's 'Greenspeak', the Power of Knowledge and 'Sustaindevelopment'

Thomas Wanner

THIS IS AN ORIGINAL CHAPTER FOR THIS BOOK.

There is a struggle, worldwide, to determine how 'sustainable development' or 'sustainable capitalism' will be defined and used in the discourse on the wealth of nations. This means that 'sustainability', in the first place, is an ideological and political, not an ecological and economic, question (O'Connor 1998: 153).

The World Bank, as the dominant global development agency, plays a critical role in the worldwide struggle over the meaning of 'sustainable development'. This chapter is about the Bank's power of language and knowledge in the creation and maintenance of a specific 'regime of truth' on 'sustainable development' legitimising and sustaining global capitalism's dominant power relations. It argues that the Bank, like the Ministry of Truth in George Orwell's novel *Nineteen Eighty-four*, produces and disseminates a certain 'truth' about 'sustainable development' through the manipulation and control of language and knowledge in order to meet the ideological needs of capitalist hegemony. One could label this as the World Bank's 'greenspeak', a contemporary version of the Orwellian 'newspeak'. It has the purpose not only to express and disseminate a certain ideology or worldview on 'sustainable development' but also 'to make all other modes of thought impossible' (Orwell 1970: 305). In 'greenspeak', the dominant ideology of 'sustainable development' can be translated to 'sustaindevelopment'.[1] It is strongly propounded and disseminated by the World Bank.

This chapter seeks to contribute to the deconstruction of the 'sustaindevelopment' ideology that makes claims to universal truth and subjugates, manipulates and dominates other less powerful forms of knowledge and ideologies on 'sustainable development'. The aim is to demonstrate *how* the Bank's 'greenspeak' and power of knowledge work to hide the conflicts and contradictions in 'sustaindevelopment'. The methodology is critical discourse analysis, strongly leaning on the work of Norman Fairclough in which Foucault's ideas about power, knowledge and discourse are placed within Gramsci's framework of hegemony (Fairclough 1995, 1996; Fairclough and Wodak 1997: 258–84). Fairclough views discourse as a social practice that constructs objects of knowledge, identities and representations of social reality. Critical discourse analysis is concerned with discourse as an instrument of power and control as well as an instrument of social construction and representation of reality. The aim is to show the dialectical relationships and interplay between language and social practice, ideology and discourse, text and context, structure and agency in the construction and contestation over the meaning of social reality. Critical discourse analysis is about how language use as a social practice is situated in social context, and about 'the ways discourse structures enact, confirm, legitimate, reproduce, or challenge relations of power and dominance in society' (Van Dijk 2001: 353).

Discourse and ideology work together in constructing and representing a certain meaning of the world, and in creating, sustaining or undermining the materialist structures and their relations of power and domination. The establishment and maintenance of hegemony is a complex process in which the dialectics of discourse and ideology play a vital part. The linked and mutually influential struggles within and between discourses and ideologies are major stakes in the struggle over hegemony. The struggle over language and knowledge is part and parcel of the struggles over discourses and over ideologies. For Gramsci, language contains 'a specific conception of the world' and is thus an absolutely vital component of the struggle over ideologies and hegemony (1971: 323, 325).

Language, ideology and power are closely interrelated. As Fairclough argues, 'the exercise of power, in modern society, is increasingly achieved through ideology, and more particularly through the ideological workings of language' (Fairclough 1989: 2; Wodak 1989). Ideologies shape text and language. They control what we speak and write about, and how we do it. This is especially the case for dominant ideologies that refer to ideologies of dominant groups or institutions for the reproduction of their dominance and the underlying interests. The use of language is a major instrument for domination, control and oppression, but also for resistance and opposition. Every ideological conflict, and every conflict over interests and power, therefore involves a conflict over language.

Texts (the spoken and written bodies of language use) are the reflection that power and social control are working discursively, and the struggle over power and hegemony is increasingly a struggle over the power to give meanings to social and political issues and events. This power to define is about what is to be 'normal' or 'natural' and presenting it as the universal 'truth'. It is part of creating consent in the Gramscian sense, in which the existing inequalities between the dominant and dominated classes and the former interests are represented as common and universal.[2] Texts are therefore important as they 'are often sites of struggle in that they show traces of differing discourses and ideologies contending and struggling for dominance' (Wodak 2001: 11). World Bank texts are utilised to discern meanings, ideological content, the effects of the Bank's 'greenspeak' and power of knowledge, and how they relate to capitalist hegemony.[3]

The World Bank and the economics of 'sustaindevelopment'

Marx argues that in capitalism, 'for the first time, nature becomes purely an object for humankind, purely a matter of utility' (Wood 2001: 280). The assets and services of global ecology are for capitalism a commodity, and a form of capital (termed 'natural capital') for continuous capitalist accumulation and profit maximisation, which requires continuous economic growth. Nature is not mobilised for human needs or the needs of ecology but for the imperative needs of the capitalist system. Capitalism inevitably creates ecological scarcity and ecological degradation through using nature as source and sink for economic production and consumption (Bellamy 1992).

The ecological crisis-generating tendencies of capitalism were highlighted in the 1960s and 1970s when the detrimental ecological effects of capitalist industrial development, such as air and water pollution, became increasingly apparent. Then, the counter-hegemonic ideology of *environmentalism* in advanced capitalist countries stressed the environmental *un*sustainability of the dominant 'development' ideology by pointing to limits of the global 'environment' as a constant source of natural resources and sink for the waste of economic development (Cotgrove 1982; Cotgrove and Duff 1980: 333–51; O'Riordan 1976). It was argued that there is a conflict between the sustainability of the global 'environment' and the sustainability of economic growth. This represented a threat to the dominant ideology of *developmentalism* based on the sustainability of economic growth, viewing the 'environment' as a free and limitless resource and sink to be exploited and controlled for capitalist production and consumption.[4] Sustainable economic growth needed to be rescued from its environmental critics and delinked from the global ecological limits discourse in order to sustain the existing capitalist hegemony and its dominant ideology of 'development'. In other words, a passive revolution was required through which the environmental concerns of the counter-ideology were incorporated into the dominant ideology so that the hegemony of the transnational capitalist class could be sustained.

It is within this context of 'growing ecological awareness, increasing ecological threats to capitalist accumulation, widening North–South disparities and agendas, the rise of global neoliberalism and the increasing opposition to economic growth in some advanced capitalist nations' that the international discourse of *sustainable development* originated in the 1980s (McManus 1996: 51). This discourse emerged from the intersection of the competing 'development' and 'environment' discourses. In 'sustainable development' discourse, the struggle over meanings centres around the issue of sustainability, and is in its most basic form about the interrelationship between ecology and economy.[5] It is about the problematic of the sustainability of global ecology (or ecological sustainability) versus the sustainability of economic growth and capitalist 'development' (or economic sustainability). There is an inverse relationship between weak or strong ecological sustainability and weak or strong economic sustainability. Weak ecological sustainability means strong economic sustainability, and vice versa.[6]

Two major worldviews about the ecology and economy interrelationship can be discerned in 'sustainable development' discourse: the dominant ideology 'sustaindevelopment'; and ecologism. 'Sustaindevelopment' emerged as a way to co-opt the threat that environmentalism posed to the dominant 'development' ideology. The counter-hegemonic ideology of environmentalism, stressing the conflict between the sustainability of the 'environment' and of 'development' because of inescapable ecological limits, was gradually diverted through 'sustaindevelopment' which emphasised complementarity, implying that sustainability for both the ecology and the hegemonic capitalist development model could be realised together. The World Bank is a strong proponent and disseminator of 'sustaindevelopment', in which economic sustainability is prioritised over ecological sustainability. The economic objective of sustainable economic growth comes before ecological objectives.

A passive revolution – the consolidation of consent – had gradually taken place enabling the maintenance of the existing international power structures and relations and their 'development' ideology.[7] 'Sustaindevelopment', as Sachs has put it, was a 'major rescue operation' of the dominant 'development' idea by shaping environmentalism to the requirements of developmentalism, and by assimilating the concerns, values and interests of environmentalism 'into the rhetoric, dynamics and power structures of developmentalism' (1999: x–xi).[8]

'Sustaindevelopment' could be called 'environmental developmentalism', also referred to as 'free market environmentalism' or 'green developmentalism'. Ecologism provides an alternative ideology of 'sustainable development' and understanding of the ecology–economy relationship based on ecological integrity, social and international justice, and prioritising ecological sustainability over economic sustainability.[9] It proposes radical reorientation of the present understanding and direction of development which needs to be done 'within the physical, thermodynamic and ecological limits of the biosphere' and the curtailing of the consumption levels of the North (Leis and Viola 1995: 42).

Neoliberalism's rise as the dominant development ideology in the 1980s coincided with the emergence of the international discourse of sustainable development.[10] The Bank, being part of the so-called Washington Consensus, has been a major promoter of neoliberal economic ideas to Third World countries through its structural adjustment programmes.[11] The new realities and impacts of globalisation and neoliberalism since the 1980s explain the increasing saliency of international organisations, such as the World Bank, vis-à-vis the state, in the global modernisation and development processes. These changes have resulted in the wider scale and reach of the World Bank's ideological power, and have cemented the logic and system of global capitalism (Gibbon 1993b). The Bank's role as a dominant agent of 'disciplinary neoliberalism' (Gill 1995; see also Cammack 2001b) was crucial in the linking and global dissemination of neoliberalism and 'sustaindevelopment' as one package. 'Sustaindevelopment' works for the promotion and legitimisation of neoliberalism through which global capitalism's relations and structures of power and domination are maintained. In 'sustaindevelopment', market liberalism and sustainable development are not two competing discourses, as claimed by Dryzek, but one package for realising both economic *and* ecological sustainability, in which neoliberalism is portrayed as the means to achieve sustainable development (Dryzek 1997: 7–8). For neoliberals, as Langhelle stresses, ecological problems and their risks for future generations 'arise not from exposure *to* capitalism but from exclusion *from* it' (Langhelle 1999: 131). Capitalist 'development', economic growth and the 'magic of the market' are seen more than ever as the solution, rather than the problem, for achieving ecological sustainability. Thus it is not that sustainable development 'took the initiative from neoliberalism', as McManus asserts, but that the dominant ideology of 'sustaindevelopment' took the initiative *for* neoliberalism (McManus 1996: 51).

'Sustaindevelopment' represents the weak ecological sustainability position which is 'a paradigm of resource optimism . . . deeply rooted within neo-classical economic thinking' (Neumayer 1999: 24–25).[12] It claims that through overcoming market and policy failures and 'better environmental management' both economic growth *and* the protection of the environment – economic sustainability *and* ecological sustainability – can be realised (World Bank 1992d: 10). In this view, the biggest market failure is that the ecologically destructive tendencies of capitalist production and consumption are not reflected in the market price of a good or service. 'Getting the prices right', so the belief goes, will adequately reflect environmental scarcity and costs. This will lead to the renewable substitution of non-renewable natural resources, such as fossil fuels or minerals. Market forces determine the substitution of human-made capital for natural capital, and market instruments, such as green taxes and tradable pollution permits, are seen as most effective for addressing environmental problems as long as property rights are clearly defined. This needs to be in combination with overcoming policy failures, such as subsidies for fuel or water that cause increased air pollution or water usage, and command-and-control policies of the state, such as the setting, monitoring and enforcement of emission standards and the requirement and enforcement of Environmental Impact Assessments (World Bank 1992d: 1–24). The 'big challenge', according to the *World Development Report 2003*, is 'finding the right balance between giving free play to market forces and monitoring and enforcement [by the state]' (World Bank 2002f: 33).

Finding this balance is difficult. Using economic instruments to address ecological concerns requires clear definition and allocation of property rights. This raises difficulties because 'many environmental assets do not have well-defined property rights, and operating in the market requires that property rights be assignable' (World Bank 2002f: 32). It is difficult to value and measure 'environmental assets', such as clean air or clean oceans. Even in the case of having defined property rights and prices attached to ecological assets, there is still the problem of institutions failing to implement economic and ecological policies. The World Bank has shifted its emphasis from 'getting the prices right' in *World Development Report 1992* to 'getting the institutions right' in *World Development Report 2003* (Gayatri and Dixon 2003).[13] This is an extension of the Bank's *good governance* approach to 'good institutions' for sustainable development. For the Bank, institutions are 'good' when they support the market and 'enable growth and sustainable development' (World Bank 2002f: 55). Good governance and 'good institutions' are part of promoting the neoliberal free market ideology. *World Development Report 2003* does not question whether the Bank itself is a 'good institution' or elaborate on its own role in global ecological governance to promote and enforce sustainable development.[14]

The globalisation of neoliberalism shifted the power to control capital from states to the world economy, and state and society were restructured in such a way as to facilitate the operation of the free market. The increasing dominance of economics over politics, the market over the state, and increasing imposition of the capitalist imperatives of capital accumulation, profit maximisation, and commodification on all aspects of social life, causes problems for democratic political control and accountability over economic processes and for effective environmental management (Wood 1997; Altvater and Mahnkopf 1997).[15] This has exacerbated finding the right balance between state and market interventions because, as Reed has shown, it weakened national institutions in government and civil society involved in managing the environment (1996).

The increasing marketisation of society is also detrimental to achieving equity with regard to who receives ecological costs and benefits. Markets fail to allocate ecological goods and services efficiently because there are problems with clearly defined property rights and prices. Neither national nor international levels of the market can be relied upon for a fair distribution of ecological benefits and costs, because the market operates under the principle of maximising efficiency, not equity. The 'efficiency first' principle of environmental economists requires, as stated earlier, a valuation of nature or putting a price on natural goods and services. As Daly has asked, who pays the price for that? 'From the point of view of efficiency it does not matter who receives the price, as long as it is charged to the users. But from the point of view of equity it matters a great deal who receives the price for nature's increasingly scarce services' (Daly 2002: 8).

For example, the elimination of water-use subsidies has ecological benefits, but the user-pays principle does not include differentials in ability to pay. This usually means the poor are more disadvantaged by the consequences of ecological degradation. Economic efficiency and ecological sustainability *might* be achieved in tandem, but to the detriment of equity. The economics of 'sustaindevelopment' hides issues of power and equity, and maintains the focus on the economy and on economic solutions to ecological concerns. The use of language is a crucial aspect to support these ideological functions of 'sustaindevelopment'.

The power of language: The Bank's 'greenspeak'

Language is a vital component of neoliberalism's restructuring of global and national economies and societies (Fairclough 2000). 'Greenspeak' augments the dominant 'sustaindevelopment' ideology and its emphasis on the sustainability of growth through (1) 'mainstreaming' the 'environment' and 'environmental sustainability' into economic sustainability; (2) concealing and downplaying the problems and contradictions of the weak sustainability position, and of Northern consumption issues; and (3) keeping the focus on economic sustainability and 'sustaindevelopment' by separating 'environment' from 'sustainable development'.

The language of 'mainstreaming' reflects the belief of 'sustain-development' that the economic system is not a subsystem of the ecological system, and that economic sustainability has priority over ecological sustainability. The World Bank's *Environment Strategy* 're-affirms the Bank's commitment to environmental sustainability', and is about the need to 'mainstream' it into all Bank operations (World Bank 2000e: xvii).[16] However, the integration or 'mainstreaming' of the 'environment' into the Bank's 'development' discourse remains on the rhetorical level of 'greenspeak'. According to the Operations Evaluation Department's 2001 Report on the Bank's environmental performance, 'the goal of environmental sustainability has not been integrated into the Bank's core objectives and country assistance strategies' (World Bank 2001b: 3).

World Bank documents often express a distinction between 'sustainable development' and the 'environment', further indicating that the 'environment' and 'environmental sustainability' have *not* been integrated into 'sustainable development', and that there is a difference between sustaining development and sustaining the environment. The following example highlights this: '[T]o discuss issues related to environmentally sustainable development *and* the environment . . . integrating environmental *and* sustainable development considerations into investment projects . . . there is a growing awareness [in the Bank] that sustainable development *and* environmental performance are linked' (World Bank 1995c: 51, 171, 193).

The 'environment' becomes separated from 'sustainable development', rather than being an inclusive part and major objective of it. This linguistic separation implies that the 'environment' and 'environmental sustainability' is *not* part of the discourse of 'sustainable development'. The focus shifts away from the 'environmental' dimension and thus emphasises 'sustainable development' as an economic objective. Another example of this linguistic separation is the Bank's claim that the 2002 World Summit on Sustainable Development in Johannesburg was '*no longer an environment summit* but . . . a platform to look at long-term sustainable development, particularly the linkages between sustainable growth and poverty reduction'.[17] We have come full circle from the focus on 'environment' and pollution in the North at the 1972 United Nations Conference on the Human Environment, in Stockholm, to poverty reduction and 'development' in the South in Johannesburg. In between there was the 1992 United Nations Conference on the Environment and Development in Rio de Janeiro, which concentrated, as the conference title reflects, on the integration of 'environment' *and* 'development'.[18]

The *World Development Report 1992* highlighted *poverty reduction* as the most important aspect to achieve global 'environmental benefits' (World Bank 1992d: 1). Although the *Report* acknowledges that 'high consumption levels in rich countries' cause some of the ecological problems in developing countries, such as global warming and ozone depletion, and that they therefore should bear the burden of fixing these problems, it does not cover what the role of the rich countries should be in global ecological governance (World Bank 1992d: 3). The shift towards poverty and the South is almost complete in the *World Development Report 2003*. The ecologically unsustainable levels of consumption in the rich North are not even mentioned in the main part of the *Report*. In 'greenspeak', the issue of 'overconsumption' has turned from a serious problem for achieving ecological sustainability to an 'open question' – When is consumption overconsumption? – which requires further dialogue. The role of Northern consumption levels in the global ecological crisis is talked away: 'the overall level of consumption is not the source of the problem' (World Bank 2002f: 196).[19]

This is not to deny that poverty can lead to ecological degradation, and that addressing poverty has ecological benefits. The point is that 'sustaindevelopment' diverts attention from the primary responsibility of the North for the ecological crisis and for its alleviation through changes in lifestyles, consumption and production levels. Linking ecological sustainability predominantly with poverty rather than with Northern consumption further legitimates the intervention and management of Northern development agencies in the South, and helps to justify the need for sustainable growth as panacea for all development problems. 'Sustaindevelopment' also masks the fact that global poverty is produced through unequal relations of power in the international political economy, and through the pursuit of economic growth (Saurin 1996: 670).[20]

The *World Development Report 2003* is still about protecting the sustainability of economic growth from ecological threats rather than the sustainability of global ecology. It emphasises that 'over the longer term prolonged neglect of environmental and social assets is likely to jeopardise the *durability of economic growth*' (World Bank 2002f: 13, emphasis added). The 'quite ambitious' goal of this *Report* on sustainable development was, as pointed out by its director, 'to bridge the gap and to address the sceptics on all sides of the debate revolving around the *perceived antagonism between growth and sustainable development* . . . We would *like to merge the concepts of sustainable development and growth*' (Shalizi 2003: 1, emphasis added).

This is 'greenspeak' at its best, given that 'sustaindevelopment' emerged to protect the sustainability of growth from its environmental critics, and that growth first and foremost is seen as needed for ecological sustainability. This kind of 'greenspeak' is intended to blur the lines in the war of position to critics, such as Herman Daly, who maintain the separation between sustainable growth and 'sustainable development'. For Daly the pursuit of sustainable economic growth within a finite global ecological system is impossible (1992: 267–75).

No-growth or limits-to-growth strategies are not among the options of 'sustaindevelopment'. The Bank's 'world without end' ethos allows for the growth of limits, not limits to growth: 'sustainable development is about development progress; it is certainly not a doctrine of "no-growth" environmental protectionism' (Serageldin and Steer 1994: 30) and is far from a 'steady-state concept' (World Bank 2002f: 14). The *World Development Report 2003* illustrates the strong economic, or weak ecological, sustainability focus: 'Limits-to-growth type arguments focus on strong sustainability, while arguments in favour of indefinite growth focus on weak sustainability. So far the former arguments have not been very convincing because the substitutability among assets has been high for most inputs used in production at a small scale' (World Bank 2002f: 14).

'Greenspeak' does not clarify what 'small-scale' economic production means, but makes sure that claiming strong substitutability among different forms of 'capital' discredits the argument for 'strong [ecological] sustainability'. The crucial question of the sustainability of substitution over time is not addressed. At some stage we will come to a point where the level of minimal natural assets or 'natural capital' needed for economic production, whether small- or large-scale, is reached.[21] As the same *Report* states: 'Thresholds are clearest when a renewable asset has been exploited beyond its capacity to regenerate or reproduce. When that threshold is reached, the productivity of other assets decreases – or if the degraded asset [for example, natural asset] is the main input, production may cease altogether' (World Bank 2002f: 22).

The *World Development Report 2003* acknowledges 'limits to substitutability among assets' and that for some ecological assets, such as the ozone layer or biodiversity, there are no substitutes or technological solutions (World Bank 2002f: 14). Although a shift from the strong technological optimism of *World Development Report 1992* can be detected, the belief of 'sustaindevelopment' in technological solutions 'to increase the potential substitutability among assets over time', and the marginalisation of physical ecological limits remain central (World Bank 2002f: 13–14).[22]

'Greenspeak' keeps the language about sustainability vague, often not making it plain as to which kind of sustainability – economic, ecological or social – it refers. As examples:

> We believe that the journey toward sustainability will bring many benefits to our clients (World Bank 2000e: 186).

> We have strived to integrate environment into the development agenda of the Bank because sustainability is at the heart of development (I. Johnson 2001).

What kind of sustainability is 'at the heart of development' is not specified, but linking it to 'development' ensures that it relates to economic sustainability. This becomes clear when 'environmental' references are included:

> The Environment Strategy . . . takes a long-term view of development and of the environmental factors that affect sustainability (World Bank 2000e: 45).

> Addressing environmental priorities that affect the long-term sustainability of development requires a proactive approach (World Bank 2000e: 56).

The *World Development Report 2003* even maintains that the definition of sustainability is still evolving, while at the same time asserting that it understands weak sustainability as weak constraints on growth which is more convincing than strong sustainability meaning strong constraints on growth (World Bank 2002e: 14). 'Managing Sustainability World Bank-Style' (Schatalek 2003) means managing and ensuring the sustainability of growth, and managing the conflicts and contradictions between economic and ecological sustainability to ensure 'sustaindevelopment'. In this 'greenspeak' is supported by the power of knowledge, to which we turn in the next section.

The power of knowledge: The Knowledge Bank and 'sustaindevelopment'

The Bank has been re-inventing itself as the 'Knowledge Bank' since 1996.[23] This was a reaction to the 'new realities' of capitalism and development, in which private capital flows are the major source of finance for developing countries, and in which 'knowledge' has become a commodity and form of capital.[24] In *knowledge capitalism*, knowledge itself has become a commodity to be produced and traded, and is seen as the most important form of capital for capitalist production and accumulation. As Alan Burton-Jones states, '[k]nowledge is fast becoming the most important form of global capital' (1999: vi).[25] The production and dissemination of knowledge has become a new profit-making opportunity in itself, not just a resource in the form of applying knowledge to economic production, as it had been since the Industrial Revolution. Knowledge is emerging as the main source of economic productivity, and the accumulation of knowledge capital is seen as being as important as the accumulation of finance capital. This does not mean that knowledge as capital is replacing finance capital, as claimed by Drucker, and that we have moved to a '*post*-capitalist society' (Drucker 1993, emphasis added). Both – finance and knowledge capital – work together within the logic of capital accumulation for economic production and economic growth. The capitalist logic and the need for constant capital accumulation, whether in the form of finance capital or knowledge capital, is still the driving force of the capitalist market economy. Through its new economic role, knowledge and information are even more tied to the logic of capital accumulation, and the production, dissemination and storage of knowledge is shaped by its economic value to capitalist production and accumulation. In the new knowledge economy the fundamental class relations between labour and capital remain the same but now also run along the lines of knowledge capital (Curry 1997; Nunn 2001/02). In knowledge capitalism, it is increasingly the knowledge and language of economics, and the *epistemic community* of economists that dominate all areas of social reality.

The Bank's re-invention as the Knowledge Bank is a strategic move to build on its comparative advantage about knowledge on development which arises from its vast accumulated knowledge and experience of the development process of the world's developing countries, and its position as global development agency interacting with many other stakeholders (Gilbert, Powell and Vines 2000: 55). Since the World Bank began operations in 1946, the transfer of money has always gone hand in hand with the transfer of ideas and knowledge. Finance is the channel for the dissemination of knowledge on development. It is debatable whether finance or technical assistance and development advice has been more important for the borrowing countries. Robert McNamara stressed in his last annual meeting speech in 1980: 'In the longer run . . . it is the non-financial assistance of the Bank that is of even greater value than its financial support' (quoted in Kapur, Lewis and Webb 1997: 272). The transfer of ideas and knowledge has been of greater value than financial lending for the Bank's role in promoting and establishing global consent to the dominant 'development' ideology.

'Knowledge for development' is the Bank's new resource for eradicating poverty and achieving 'sustainable development'. Wolfensohn emphasised in the foreword to the *World Development Report 1999* that the application of the *'power of knowledge'* will help with 'the great challenge of eradicating poverty and improving people's lives' (World Bank 1999d: iv, emphasis added). For the Bank, it is not just the lack of capital but also the lack of knowledge that causes poverty. The darkness of poverty has become a consequence of poor peoples' darkness of ignorance, which can be overcome by being enlightened through Northern knowledge.[26] This interpretation justifies intervention from the North and depends on Northern understanding and sources of knowledge. The modernisation paradigm continues in a new form – knowledge of the North is required for the ignorant poor in the South to overcome poverty (Schech 2002). The ideal of the modern, industrial 'knowledge' economies and societies can be achieved through the transfer of Northern knowledge to the South – the South can 'catch up' through knowledge:

> Developing countries have tremendous opportunities to grow faster *and possibly to catch up with the industrial countries.* To take advantage of these opportunities in a fast-moving global economy, developing countries cannot afford to limit themselves to accumulating physical capital and educating their people. They must also be open to new ideas and capture the benefits of technological progress. They must therefore extend the *power and reach of knowledge* to close the gap in living standards (World Bank 1999d: 25, emphasis added).

Further reflecting the tenets of modernisation theory and its current form of neoliberalism is the *Report*'s emphasis that it is the poor countries' fault that they are poor and experiencing a knowledge gap, and it is their responsibility to narrow it. According to the *Report*, the income gap between North and South is due to the knowledge gap, not to inequalities in the international economic system. The income gap can be reduced if the knowledge gap is overcome. Without taking inequities of power and wealth within and between nations into account, the proposed solution to overcome the income gap is overcoming the knowledge gap (World Bank 1999d: 26). This approach shifts the responsibility for the knowledge and income gaps to the South, and perpetuates the illusion of 'sustaindevelopment' 'catching up'.

The Bank's analysis also overlooks the creation of poverty and a widening gap of wealth between North and South through neoliberal economic reforms, as well as declining financial aid from the North through official development assistance and the exclusion of most of the South from private investment flows. The sharp increase in private capital flows since the 1980s has been restricted to a few countries showing the highest promise of economic returns on the investment. This means that the World Bank's importance as a 'lender of last resort' has increased as the very poor countries are not able to secure access to other finance.[27] The very poor countries are not only excluded from most private capital flows but, as Castells (1996) has argued, also from those of the global informational economy. Their marginalisation is based on exclusion from both capital and knowledge. The income gap and the knowledge gap are linked, and both tend to widen together.

The *World Development Report 1999* stresses that narrowing the knowledge gap requires three critical steps of developing countries: acquiring knowledge, absorbing knowledge, and communicating knowledge (World Bank 1999d: 2–3). The South needs to concentrate on acquiring and absorbing knowledge whereas the North concentrates on creating, transferring and managing knowledge. Most knowledge creation is done in Northern countries because knowledge is costly to create; and 'even greater than the knowledge gap is the gap in the capacity to create knowledge' (World Bank 1999d: 2). The *Report* does not address the critical questions of what kind of knowledge is created and disseminated by the North. It also neglects the creation of knowledge in the South, South–South exchanges about knowledge and South–North flows of knowledge (Mawdsley and Rigg 2002: 106). It assumes that Northern knowledge is superior and that the South is merely its recipient. This reinforces the global power relations and the dominance of the North and Northern knowledge in global knowledge management and sharing (Samoff and Stromquist 2001).

In contrast to business organisations more concerned with internal knowledge sharing, from the start in 1996 the Knowledge Bank had a strong external knowledge-sharing dimension in its knowledge management system. External knowledge sharing means that there is increased engagement with 'partners' in development. The 'power of partnerships' has become critical for 'sustaindevelopment'. The terminology of 'partnership' is another example of the power of language, as it conjures ideas of equity, empowerment, sharing and cooperation, hiding realities of domination, control and unequal power and knowledge relations. As King (2000) has argued, the Northern organisations' needs are first met in the knowledge-sharing process with 'partners' in the North; and the South – the intended recipients of knowledge sharing for development – is last. By the time the South receives knowledge from the North 'the knowledge priorities, lessons learned and best practices are sorted out', and knowledge for development has been shaped by Northern values and assumptions of what works (King 2000: 16). The notion of a 'global knowledge partnership' hides inequalities of power and knowledge, and Northern dominance in it (King and McGrath 2004).

In 2000 the Knowledge Bank shifted its emphasis from knowledge *management* to knowledge *sharing* (Wolfensohn, AGM address in 1996).[28] This is another example of the Bank using the power of language. The Bank either uses knowledge management and knowledge sharing interchangeably, or uses both together in sentences without clearly delineating their differences. The change in emphasis and language is due to the stronger association of knowledge sharing with partnership, equality and cooperation, whereas knowledge management is more associated with control and domination. Apparently Bank staff resisted the concept of knowledge management and preferred knowledge sharing.[29] The change in rhetoric does not hide the World Bank's approach to knowledge for development: it is still about knowledge management. As the Knowledge Bank states, the most critical question with regard to knowledge is not how it is created, adapted or utilised, but 'how to *manage* knowledge, for knowledge created or adapted is only as good as the system that keeps it organised, accessible, and dynamic' (World Bank 1999d: 131, emphasis added). It is the knowledge management system that counts, and that determines creation, transfer and application of knowledge. Knowledge sharing is an extension of knowledge management. Equating knowledge sharing with knowledge management is a rhetorical device that blurs this distinction. Knowledge managers decide whether to share or not, with whom, and what knowledge is shared. As the World Bank states: 'the most important decisions that an organisation must make in establishing its knowledge management system are the following: deciding with whom to share, deciding what to share, deciding how to share, and deciding *to* share' (1999d: 138, emphasis added).

The Bank's 'enormous power and global reach' is not based, as Goldman (2002) argued, on the World Bank's *production* of knowledge. Nor, as Mehta claims, is it the *ownership* of knowledge for development which drives the World Bank to become the Knowledge Bank so that its economic view of knowledge can be disseminated (2001: 192). Instead, the major source of its power lies in its ability to be involved in the global management of development knowledge and to be a major disseminator of such knowledge. The production of knowledge is certainly a prerequisite for having a product to disseminate to clients and partners, but the component of knowledge production in the Bank has declined compared to the increase in its involvement in dissemination and sharing.[30]

The Bank provides a narrow view of 'knowledge', confined to scientific, economic and technical knowledge, which is seen as neutral and universally applicable. To 'unleash the *power of knowledge*', the *World Development Report 1999* argues, governments need to recognise and respond to the two types of knowledge: knowledge about technology or technical know-how, and knowledge about attributes, such as the quality of products or the creditworthiness of a firm, required for the effective functioning of markets (World Bank 1999d: 2, emphasis added). The second type of knowledge is the classic economic problem of incomplete information causing market failure (Waud et al. 1992: 741–43). The *Report*, however, does not distinguish between information and knowledge. Equating knowledge with information is a general tendency in the Bank's approach to knowledge. Knowledge about how the market works and of its specific relations also facilitates better market functioning. The Bank's conception of knowledge is about the knowledge of the economy and the market. It is an economic approach to knowledge, in which knowledge is seen as another form of capital and as more valuable than capital in bringing about economic growth.[31]

This includes knowledge being seen as a commodity with economic value, sold and purchased on the market. As a commodity, knowledge is regulated through the property laws of capitalism. Through patents, copyrights and intellectual property rights (IPRs) this new commodity becomes owned by its producers or usurpers. IPRs become increasingly tight, and are dominated by the North. This can disadvantage the South in two ways, as stressed in the *World Development Report 1999*: 'by increasing the knowledge gap and by shifting bargaining power toward the producers of knowledge, most of whom reside in industrial countries' (World Bank 1999d: 35). It is thus apparent that knowledge is far from an international public good, meaning having the characteristics of 'non-rivalry' and 'non-excludability,' as the Bank claims.[32] Knowledge is very much contested and others can be excluded from it through patents and IPRs. Viewing knowledge as an international public good fits nicely with the Bank's depoliticised, neutral and economic approach to knowledge, supporting 'sustaindevelopment' and its role of promoting the neoliberal ideology.

Conclusion

The World Bank as the Knowledge Bank is deeply involved in the construction and dissemination of a specific meaning of 'sustainable development' linked to the imperatives of capitalism. The Knowledge Bank is ever more crucial for spreading 'sustaindevelopment' and maintaining capitalist hegemony. The dominant ideology of 'sustaindevelopment' stresses a technocratic, economic and managerialist approach through which the hegemonic neoliberal project is supported. 'Sustaindevelopment' prioritises economic sustainability over ecological sustainability, and hides the ecological contradictions of capitalism, which means it can at best achieve *weak* ecological sustainability. Conflicts and contradictions between economic and ecological sustainability are sidelined through the power of language and knowledge, which create the illusions (1) of a 'world without end' in which the sustainability of economic growth is not bound by ecological limits; (2) of the possibility of the South to 'catch up' to the North and the North to keep up its capitalist 'development' model of high ecological throughput; and (3) that 'sustainable development' is best achieved through free-market capitalism and 'sustaindevelopment'.

The Bank's 'greenspeak' diminishes the range of meanings of 'sustainable development', reducing the possibility of thinking, speaking and acting about the ecology–economy interrelationship in other ways than 'sustaindevelopment'. The World Bank is not the only agent in international political economy speaking 'greenspeak': it is also the language of international business and the governments of the world. It is the language of the transnational capitalist class that makes sure the power of 'greenspeak' remains strong and continues to eradicate any alternative, more radical ideologies of 'sustainable development' representing a threat to 'sustaindevelopment' and capitalist hegemony. We seem to be moving towards the final adoption of 'greenspeak'.[33] In 2050 there might only be 'greenspeak' and 'sustaindevelopment'. The recent World Summit on Sustainable Development in Johannesburg was not an 'environment summit', according to the World Bank. It was not primarily about ecological sustainability but about the sustainability of 'development' and economic growth. 'Sustaindevelopment' has completely absorbed and co-opted the environmentalist critique of the 1970s.

But the struggle over the meanings of 'sustainable development' is not over. Hegemony is never complete and stable. The global capitalist economy and the global ecology are in a dialectical relationship in which the workings and dynamics of both are mutually formative and transformative. The discourse of 'sustainable development' shapes and transforms global capitalism as much as the latter shapes and transforms the former. The increasing problems of ecological scarcity and destruction challenge and shape global capitalism. But it is impossible to make predictions about the future of capitalism and whether its adaptive capabilities can overcome the global ecological crisis, largely created by capitalism's ecological contradictions. Capitalism's internal contradictions, however, are the places of conflicts, struggles and resistance at which capitalism is challenged, and where it can be reinvigorated or transformed or overcome.

The possibility of radical new modes of thinking, new values and new ideas about 'sustainability' and 'development', and how they should be linked, requires the constant challenge of 'sustaindevelopment' and its powers of 'greenspeak' and knowledge. The creation of new meanings and realities of the society–economy–ecology linkage, in which ecological principles and interests rule over economic ones, necessitate a move from common (economic) sense to good (ecological) sense and 'detaching the power of truth from the forms of social, economic and political *hegemony* within which it operates at the present time' (Foucault 1980: 133, emphasis added).[34]

Notes

1. In Orwell's 'newspeak' there are compound words, two or more words put together, such as 'goodthink', which are specifically constructed for political and ideological purposes. They restrict meanings to what is desired by the Ministry of Truth.
2. Gramsci distinguishes between 'common sense' and 'good sense'. 'Common sense' refers to all views, beliefs and values common within society or, 'the ideological unity of the entire social bloc' (1971: 328). Gramsci's 'philosophy of praxis' requires the criticism of 'common sense' to supersede the dominant ideology, or this common thinking and understanding of the world (1971: 330). 'Good sense' refers to what is often called 'common sense' – the practical and empirical application of the intellect. 'Good sense' is the motivation for questioning 'common sense' and the search for new thinking and understandings: 'new truths' (1971: 341) or meanings of social reality.
3. The main texts used in this chapter are the *World Development Report 1992: Development and the Environment* (World Bank 1992d); the *World Development Report 1998/99: Knowledge for Development* (World Bank 1999d); the Bank's *Environment Strategy, Making Sustainable Commitments: An Environment Strategy for the World Bank* (World Bank 2000e); and the *World Development Report 2003: Sustainable Development in a Dynamic World – Transforming Institutions, Growth, and Quality of Life* (World Bank 2002f). For a similar analysis, see Mawdsley and Rigg (2002).
4. *Developmentalism* entails a linear, evolutionary, universally progressive and teleological process of transformation towards the modern, capitalist, industrialised, democratic – 'developed' – society. Deeply rooted in Western notions of rationality, scientific knowledge and emancipation, and the related development of industrial capitalism, it views nature as the 'environment' outside humanity, needing to be dominated, controlled and exploited for economic growth. I follow Andrew Dobson's (1990) distinction between *environmentalism*, a critique of industrialisation and 'development' because of the negative environmental consequences, and *ecologism* which rejects the ideology of *developmentalism* because environmental degradation is intrinsic to it. Thus the term 'environment' is inappropriate. It only perpetuates the Enlightenment understanding of nature as an object of domination. *Ecology* is a better term. It incorporates the complex interrelationship and interdependency between humans and nature, and reflects that humans are *part of* nature. Thus I talk about ecological, not environmental sustainability.
5. *Sustainability* means maintaining a specific kind of process indefinitely over time. This concept comes from the natural sciences of biology and ecology referring to the maintenance of specific biological or ecosystems over time despite natural changes.
6. The literature distinguishes between strong and weak sustainability. See Diesendorf (1997); Neumayer (1999); and Turner (1993).
7. The Brundtland Report (named after its chair, Gro Harlem Brundtland) played a crucial role in this passive revolution (World Commission for Environment and

Development 1987). It is not, as McManus (1996) argues, the beginning of the international discourse of 'sustainable development' before the term 'sustainable development' was co-opted, but a vital part of the co-optation process as it is more concerned with the sustainability of economic growth than the sustainability of ecology, and 'helped to reassert and rationalise Northern global ideological hegemony' (Graf 1992).

8. Sachs refers to the concept of 'sustainable development'.
9. See, for example, Engel and Engel (1990).
10. Neoliberalism is a form of modernisation theory, wherein the obstacles to development are seen to be *within* poor countries, without considerations of international political economy. Modernisation theory has helped to legitimise international inequalities – while purportedly providing solutions to them – and to spread late capitalism's logic. Some aspects of modernisation theory have changed: the 'magic of the market' replaced the state as the key development agent and its Western centrism has been weakened by the inclusion of other, particularly Asian, forms. Although 'development' remains a national project, the purely national level has expanded to include the global–national–local nexus.
11. The Washington Consensus refers to the concerted embrace and dissemination of neoliberalism by the Washington-based International Monetary Fund, the World Bank and the US Treasury. John Williamson argues that the term 'Washington Consensus' is falsely used as a synonym for neoliberalism or market fundamentalism, which was not his original intent when he first coined the term in 1989 (see Williamson 2000). There have been arguments that from the mid-1990s a move to a 'Post-Washington Consensus' has happened – see, for example, Gore (2000). Although neoliberalism has made some adjustments by giving the state and civil society more importance, the global economic structures and processes still run along neoliberal lines, and neoliberalism remains the dominant economic model and ideology of the global economic order.
12. The weak ecological sustainability position is promoted by *environmental economists*, viewing the 'environment' and the human economy as separate entities with the economy as the overarching system – thus the economic externality of the environment needs to be internalised into economic decision making. This approach needs to be seen as part and parcel of the co-optation of the environmentalist critique of industrialisation and economic growth as they perpetuate the myth of 'growth without limits' and a 'world without end' (Pearce and Warford 1993). In contrast, *ecological economists* view the economic system as a subsystem of the ecological system, which has limits to its carrying capacity.
13. Gayatri and Dixon stress that the *World Development Report 1992* did not anticipate or cover institutional failures in implementing market and state approaches to ecological problems.
14. The exclusion of the Bank's own role in development is a general trend in *World Development Reports* (Mawdsley and Rigg 2002: 104–06).

15. Capitalism has an inherent drive towards commodification, which means the transformation of all areas of social life and all social relationships, including the relationship to nature, into economic ones, dominated by economic values and commerce.
16. 'Mainstreaming' is used throughout the document, almost on every second page.
17. World Bank website on WSSD 2002; emphasis added, at http://lnweb18.worldbank.org/ESSD/essdext.nsf/43ByDocName/WorldSummitonSustainableDevelopment. Accessed 15 July 2004.
18. See also the Bank's *World Development Report 1992: Development and the Environment* (World Bank 1992d), prepared for the 1992 Summit.
19. A few 'open questions' for further debate are raised at the end of the *Report* (2002f: 196–97).
20. Lélé (1991) argues that the belief that economic growth achieves ecological sustainability through poverty alleviation is based on the wrong assumption that economic growth *does* lead directly to poverty reduction.
21. Bearing in mind that it is extremely difficult to set such minimum levels for maintaining ecological integrity needed for economic production and economic well-being, as acknowledged by the weak sustainability position.
22. *The World Development Report 1992* states that 'the positive forces of substitution, technical progress, and structural change ... [explain] why the environmental debate has rightly shifted away from concern about *physical limits* to growth' (World Bank 1992d: 10). Whether the limits of the earth as a source and sink 'will place bounds on the growth of human activity depend on the *scope for substitution, technical progress, and structural change*' (1992d: 9, emphasis added).
23. James Wolfensohn introduced his vision of a 'Knowledge Bank' at his first AGM speech as president in 1996. The theme continued in the 1997 AGM address, where he emphasised that 'the quality of *all* our work is being enhanced by the progress toward becoming a Knowledge Bank' and that his goal was 'to make the World Bank the first port of call when people need knowledge about development'. Wolfensohn was influenced by the trends around 'knowledge' and 'knowledge management' which emerged at that time in national and international business organisations.
24. For the importance of knowledge for late capitalism, see Bell (1973); Burton-Jones (1999); and Drucker (1989).
25. Many economists have theorised about the relationship of knowledge and economics and the productive value of knowledge before it became an economic end and commodity in itself. See, for example, Von Hayek (1937, 1945, 1948). See also Boulding (1971). (This article was first published in *American Economic Review* 56 [2] [1966]: 1–13.)
26. 'Knowledge is like light. Weightless and intangible, it can easily travel the world, enlightening the lives of people everywhere. Yet billions of people still live in the darkness of poverty – unnecessarily ... Poor countries – and poor people – differ from rich ones not only because they have less capital but also because they have less knowledge' (World Bank 1999d: 1).

27. However, as the 1999 Meltzer Report highlighted, the Bank itself favours the more economically viable countries, http://www.house.gov/jec/imf/meltzer.htm. Accessed 17 November 2006: 'The World Bank's rhetoric faults the private sector for concentrating 80 per cent of its loans in a dozen economies. It claims that its own lending provides resources to the entire developing world. In fact, official lending closely parallels private-sector choices.'
28. The Bank changed the orientation of its website from knowledge management to knowledge sharing, http://worldbank. org/ks/km.html.
29. Personal email communication with the editor of the knowledge-sharing website at the World Bank (2 May 2002).
30. This is supported by comments of Word Bank staff; see King (2000). See also the paper by Jo Ritzen (2000), vice-president for development policy. He argues that the balance between knowledge creation and dissemination has shifted to an overwhelming emphasis on dissemination, and that this balance needs to be remedied to ensure future Bank effectiveness.
31. The relationship between knowledge and economic growth is discussed in World Bank (1999d: 19–21).
32. Knowledge is '*non-rivalrous*', meaning the use of this commodity by one person does not preclude the use of the same by others. Knowledge is '*non-excludable*', meaning it is difficult for the creator of knowledge to prevent others from using it (World Bank 1999d: 16).
33. Orwell wrote that 'the final adoption of *Newspeak* ['greenspeak'] had been fixed for 2050' (Orwell 1970: 318). *The World Development Report 2003* takes a twenty to fifty year perspective to achieve the goal of 'sustainable development' (World Bank 2002f: 1–2).
34. I refer here to Gramsci's distinction between 'common' and 'good' sense (see Note 2 above).

Chapter Six

Governing through Participation?
The World Bank's New Approach to the Poor

Susanne Schech[1] and Sanjugta vas Dev

THIS IS AN ORIGINAL CHAPTER FOR THIS BOOK.

In the late 1990s a global consensus emerged that identifies the reduction (and eventual abolition) of absolute poverty as the world's greatest and most urgent challenge. The *World Development Report 2000/01: Attacking Poverty* is a powerful expression of this urgency (World Bank 2000/1d). At the same time, it marks an important point in the 'participatory turn in development' (Henkel and Stirrat 2001) which seeks to include the 'object of development'[2] – the world's poor, and, more broadly, civil society – in global policy making. Over the past decade the World Bank has increasingly used participatory research methodologies to improve its knowledge base about the target groups of its policies in developing countries. The global spread of new information technology networks, particularly the Internet, has raised hopes that the voices of marginalised groups will now reach the ears of global decision makers more swiftly and directly (World Bank 2000/1d: 187), and play a larger role in constructing 'innovative visions and practices' (Escobar 1995: 225). The new technologies can also assist in the endeavour to democratise the policy-making process because it facilitates the simultaneous discussion of policy documents by a large number of stakeholders located all around the world, if they have access to a computer, an Internet connection, and language skills in English, Spanish or French.

One of the broad issues raised in this chapter is whether we are witnessing, in the *Report*, a methodological shift at the World Bank underlining its claim to be the 'knowledge hub' capable of taking development policy into the informational era (World Bank 1999d). We focus on the question of how the World Bank has incorporated the voices of the main target group of its poverty policy – the world's poor – and global civil society, particularly those organisations claiming to be at the forefront of the fight against poverty on the ground. We explore this question through a textual analysis of key sections of the *Report*, a qualitative data analysis of the Electronic Discussion Forum (EDF) on the draft *Report*, and a critical reading of *Voices of the Poor*, which collects the World Bank's participatory research on the poor (Narayan, Patel et al. 2000; Narayan, Chambers et al. 2000; Narayan and Petesch 2000). While evaluating the effectiveness of the new approach to poverty outlined in the *Report* is beyond the scope of this chapter, it does raise some broader questions for interpreting two key aspects of development theory observed in recent years: firstly, the alleged shift towards participation and empowerment in mainstream development thinking (Pieterse 1998; Nelson and Wright 1995; Stiefel 1994; Woost 1997); and secondly, the serious fissures appearing to emerge in the Washington Consensus market approach to poverty reduction following the Asian economic crisis in 1997 (Mosley 2001).[3] On the one hand, there are those commentators who consider both developments to be a result of genuine institutional learning. They contend that the World Bank's earlier position on poverty, which combined a market approach with government human capital investments and a social safety net for those unable to compete in the market (World Bank 1990), has not met with widespread success, not least because it did not have adequate information about the conditions, experiences and views of the poor themselves. They say that the Bank has learned from its mistakes.[4] On the other hand, sceptics have been arguing that the World Bank is engaged in methodological window dressing designed to co-opt its critics, with its core message that capitalist development is the only pathway out of poverty still intact (Rich 2000; Øyen 2000).

In the remainder of this introduction, we briefly set out some of the parameters of this debate and suggest a third position that in our view captures more accurately the core issues. We argue that it is useful to look at the World Bank's work to increase its knowledge about the poor and to empower them in terms of its desire to refine its technologies of governance, and to strengthen its legitimacy as the world's largest development agency.

Contextualising *Attacking Poverty*
When the World Bank recast itself as a Knowledge Bank for the twenty-first century, it also increased the expectations of its *World Development Reports*. This transformation represented a further step away from its initial designation in 1954 as a primarily financial institution, with the added political task during the Cold War period of diverting developing countries from the clutches of communism through the power of capital. In the past two decades, the collapse of the communist Second World, accelerated economic globalisation and the associated international repercussions of local economic meltdowns, along with the information revolution, have radically changed the world stage on which the World Bank has to operate. On the positive side, these developments have created new policy spaces where different actors and discourses interact, which can become sites of genuine shifts in thinking and approaching development problems. As Brock, Cornwall and Gaventa (2001) point out, these new spaces are permeated with power relations and bounded by forms of discourse used within and about them. They can be opened up by discourse coalitions that produce alternatives to orthodoxy potentially reframing the policy debate. However, these alternatives can just as easily be incorporated by policy communities into superficial changes to orthodoxy.

The elimination of global poverty is the overarching mandate among the numerous missions that the World Bank has carved out in response to these changed conditions. To achieve such an enormous undertaking, many policies have been formulated to encourage or enforce action in such diverse areas as the protection of the environment, good governance, gender equality, human rights and democratisation (Einhorn 2001). While the elimination of poverty is the declared focus of the World Bank's work, the production, collection and dissemination of knowledge about development has become the main vehicle through which to convey the multifaceted, complex interactions between these areas, and between the various stakeholders in development policy.

Obtaining accurate knowledge about poverty and those who bear the brunt of it in developing countries has required the World Bank to find out from the 'horse's mouth' – in particular, the poor and those who work with them in one capacity or another. Under James Wolfensohn's presidency the World Bank frequently emphasised the important role of consultation with civil society in poverty alleviation strategies, so much so that one commentator claims 'the concept ... has become central to the repertoire with which the Bank has sought to remake its public face' (Francis 2001). Indeed, the organisation's own *Participation Sourcebook* spells out various tools for including the relevant stakeholders in development policies and strategies, such as Participatory Poverty Assessments and Participatory Action Research with groups of poor people (World Bank 1996c).[5] In relation to the *World Development Report 2000/1*, the World Bank's innovative 'consulting' approach involved using its website to display the various stages of report development, starting in 1998 with a description of the *World Development Report* team, and the likely themes it would cover. The process ended with an EDF similar to that introduced in preparing the *World Development Report 1999*. This promised a more transparent process that any interested party could not only follow, but also directly contribute to, albeit from a distance.

The great effort of consulting so widely was acknowledged by commentators and participants (Chambers 2001; H. Johnson 2001). By researching and publishing *Voices of the Poor*, the World Bank claims to have already begun to empower the poor, particularly vis-à-vis their respective governments. However, the final drafting of the *Report* indicated that much of the information gained through consultation and dialogue with the poor and their advocates was not utilised. The three substantive changes included, firstly, a new chapter on growth and poverty, signalling a downscaling of the emphasis on empowerment in the earlier drafts. Secondly, the chapter on free market reforms and unemployment no longer emphasised the need for the prior establishment of safety nets, but called for them to be implemented *simultaneously* with labour-shedding reforms. Thirdly, the long section on the need for capital controls was cut, and Malaysia's experience was dropped altogether (Wade 2001b: 134).[6]

Brock, Cornwall and Gaventa (2001: 18) have argued that this redrafting is due to the fact that '[t]he terms of engagement . . . remain very much in the realm of "invited participation" and "consultation", where more powerful actors frame the way that others are involved in the policy process'. The sudden departure in early 2000 of the *Report*'s team leader, Ravi Kanbur, indicates a power struggle among 'powerful actors', and has fuelled scepticism about the extent to which the World Bank is able to carry through its participatory aspirations in the face of mounting opposition from the US government to the dismantling of the Washington Consensus it involves.[7] Some critics claim that the participatory methodology, rather than being an open-ended process of policy making, actually seeks to bind the poor and their advocates into a predetermined policy approach making them easier to govern. According to Mick Moore's assessment (2001), this is an example of the broader process of absorbing alternative agendas of participation and empowerment into mainstream development discourse, with the effect of depoliticising them. James Ferguson (1990) has identified the same effect in his analysis of the World Bank's history with technocratic development projects in Lesotho. Has nothing changed? Are the participatory clothes of the World Bank so transparent that we can see the emperor's nakedness?

Based on our research, this chapter argues that the criticisms have some validity. The poor and other stakeholders are not evenly represented in the final *Report*. They are employed mainly to outline the experiences of poverty, rather than to formulate better strategies to combat it: this task remains in the hands of more powerful stakeholders. Serious doubts thus arise over the extent to which these strategies will be effective. If it makes such limited, and rather unpredictable, use of the information obtained, why did the World Bank invest such energy and resources in its participatory strategy? Unlike other commentators, whose critique focuses on the (mis)use of empowerment or on power struggles within the World Bank and among powerful vested interests, we argue here that the World Bank is only adopting aspects of democratic governance that have long been known and used in advanced industrialised countries to deal with poor citizens. The processes of participatory democracy, such as those employed by the World Bank, are not used to present answers to questions of power, inequality and political participation (Cruikshank 1999). Instead, they are modes of constituting and regulating citizens through social-scientific ways of knowing and democratic modes of governance. Before it is possible to wage a war on poverty, the social problems must be adequately understood. Participatory methods of collecting information are more effective in achieving this than abstract theories or expert opinions. This knowledge enables policy makers to formulate a set of possible actions – programmes, discourses, strategies – for democratic governance, which Cruikshank defines as 'forms of actions and relations of power that aim to guide and shape (rather than force, control or dominate) the actions of others' (1999: 4). The World Bank's new interest in empowering the poor serves as a case in point. Following Cruikshank's analysis of anti-poverty policies in the USA in the 1960s, we argue in the final section of this chapter that empowerment in the *Report* is established through expert knowledge and requires constant consultation, but remains unaccountable. As a technology of governance, the main purpose of empowerment is to increase poor people's capacity to reduce their poverty. In this sense empowerment enhances their freedom while at the same time turning them into governable subjects. In promoting empowerment in the context of poverty reduction, the World Bank is also seeking to increase its legitimacy as a global institution of economic governance, particularly in the eyes of international NGOs and the Bank's Southern-based target populations.

The World Bank's history with the poor

How has the World Bank's approach to poverty and the poor evolved? What is new about its current approach? To answer these questions we take a brief look at two earlier *World Development Reports*, in 1980 and 1990. This is not to deny Escobar's claim (1995: 44–47) that even before the 1970s the construction of poverty had played a key role in legitimising the professionalisation and institutionalisation of development. Our intention here is to argue, firstly, that despite the importance attributed to poverty, knowledge about this global problem was still rather scanty even in the 1980s, and the World Bank's understanding of the problem was driven more by ideology than by facts. Secondly, we want to show how these earlier reports construct the poor 'as universal, preconstituted subjects' (Escobar 1995: 53) without agency or power of their own, and that the *World Development Report 2000/1* breaks with this mould.

Perhaps the earliest indication of the World Bank recognising that to reduce global poverty requires more than just economic growth came under Robert McNamara's presidency. In his speech to the World Bank's Board of governors in 1972, he pointed out that economic growth had not improved living conditions of the 40 per cent poorest people in developing countries who 'remain trapped in conditions of deprivation which fall below any rational definition of human decency' (McNamara 1981: 217).

He described the poor as living in rural areas as subsistence farmers, 'menaced' by hunger and malnutrition, cut off from the rest of the world and 'beyond the reach of traditional market forces and present public services', their futures 'foreclosed' by illiteracy (1981: 217–18). The World Bank would assist developing countries in financing employment creation projects and better targeted public services, as well as encouraging them to undertake institutional reforms to redistribute economic power and adopt 'policies . . . to eliminate distortions in the prices of land, labour, and capital' (1981: 224–25). He pointed out that the 'growth first' position was morally untenable, as well as risking political rebellion: 'we know . . . that there is no rational alternative to moving towards policies of greater social equity' (1981: 223). The World Bank would also assist developing countries in gathering more and better quantitative data on employment and income distribution, because, McNamara admits, 'we are on the frontier of a new field of knowledge here' (1981: 224).

This approach to development, combining economic growth with increasingly wide-ranging poverty alleviation measures, became the stated policy of most countries during the 1970s (World Bank 1982), and was confirmed in the 1980 *World Development Report*. It defined the absolute poor as people whose incomes were too low to afford an adequate diet. While judging data on poverty as inadequate, the *Report* was nevertheless able to identify the poor as concentrated in rural areas, 'malnourished to the point where their ability to work hard is reduced', 'often sick', and also illiterate: 'Unable to read a road sign, let alone a newspaper, their knowledge and understanding remain severely circumscribed' (World Bank 1980: 33). The World Bank emphasised economic growth as the key to solving poverty in the first section of the *Report*, but pointed out in the second section that government should act to reduce absolute poverty through investing in human capital – education, health, nutrition and fertility control.

Ten years later – many developing countries having endured painful experiences with neoliberal structural adjustment programmes in the interval – the poverty theme was again taken up in the 1990 *World Development Report*. This time poverty was the *Report*'s sole topic. By then, the World Bank had some detailed household surveys at its disposal, which enabled it to sketch out the typical faces of poverty across the three developing continents. In 'the stories of three poor families living in three different countries' (World Bank 1990: 24), it emphasised the commonality of their experience of poverty. In representing the poor, the World Bank drew a homogenising picture of poor households composed of nuclear families where the husband's role as breadwinner is hampered by chronic underemployment. His wife 'typically spends her day cooking, caring for the children, husking rice, and fetching water from the well', but is 'always on the lookout for ways to earn a little extra' (World Bank 1990: 25). To assist governments in producing such 'snapshots of the poor' and facilitate 'consensus building on operational approaches to poverty reduction', the World Bank published a *Poverty Reduction Handbook* (World Bank 1993c: 1).

In outlining the 'new consensus on poverty' (Lipton 1997: 1003), the *World Development Report 1990* identified labour-intensive growth through market-friendly policies, state provision of health and education, and social safety nets to mitigate vulnerability and compensate those unable to work as the three key components in its new strategy against poverty (World Bank 1990: 3). In contrast to the previous policy statements (for example, World Bank 1980: 41), this *Report* downplayed redistributive measures, such as land reform, arguing that 'in most circumstances, political realities forbid reform to stray far from the status quo' (World Bank 1990: 64). Instead, emphasis is placed on giving the poor more opportunities to enter the market economy, for example, through microcredit schemes. Clearly, the shift towards economic liberalisation since the 1980s favoured rapid labour-intensive growth over radical redistribution of economic assets as a solution to poverty (Lipton 1997). Rather than the effect of persistent structural inequalities, poverty is portrayed as an individualised problem of not being able to or equipped to participate in the market economy. While the *Report* gives poverty a face, it tends to cast the poor person as a 'client' in the neoliberal language of the day. Their participation in poverty reduction programmes is justified in terms of ensuring the programmes' effectiveness (World Bank 1993c).

Whereas the *World Development Report 1990* viewed poverty in terms of low consumption and low achievement in education and health, the World Bank promised to adopt a more holistic approach in the *World Development Report 2000/1*, one that 'will have to go beyond standard economic analysis and reach out to the insights and contributions of other social sciences, if we are to better understand the design and implementation of successful institutions, mechanisms and policies'.[8] The two key inputs to make this difference were the 'voices of the poor', absent from all previous reports, and the conceptualisation of poverty as a deprivation of basic capabilities, rather than merely as excessively low income (World Bank 2000/1d: 15–16). Both of these inputs are inspired by Amartya Sen's work on poverty, starting in the 1970s (Kanbur 2002) and culminating in his lectures as a presidential fellow at the World Bank in 1996, which he elaborated in *Development as Freedom* (Sen 1999). As Sen has argued, '[P]olicy debates have ... been distorted by overemphasis on income poverty and income inequality, to the neglect of deprivations that relate to other variables, such as unemployment, ill health, lack of education, and social exclusion' (1999: 108). He advocates a shift away from the means (such as economic growth or income growth) to the ends of development, defining the latter as a person's ability to lead the kind of life she or he has reasons to value. Both identifying economic needs, and shaping an appropriate policy response to them requires, according to Sen (1999: 153), 'open discussion, debate, criticism, and dissent'; in other words, the 'exercise of basic political rights'.

Having identified the powerlessness of the poor as an important component of the problem of poverty, the World Bank moves to add 'empowerment' as a strategy in its attack on poverty. While the other two components of the strategy – increasing opportunity and security – are already foreshadowed in the 1990 Washington Consensus, empowerment is a new, and potentially rather radical, component revealing the influence of Sen's work on the *Report*:

> Empowerment means enhancing the capacity of poor people to influence the state institutions that affect their lives, by strengthening their participation in political processes and local decision making. And it means removing the barriers – political, legal, and social – that work against particular groups and building the assets of poor people to enable them to engage effectively in markets (World Bank 2000/1d: 39).

To its credit, the World Bank does not just use the *Report* to preach the new religion of participation to others but has also made an effort to practise it in the preparation of the *Report*. The first step that the World Bank took towards empowering the poor was to enlist their active participation in the construction of the *Report*. By drawing on their knowledge of poverty, the *Report* is not only able to portray a more complex and nuanced conceptualisation of poverty, but also reveals 'poor people as active agents in their lives' – dispelling earlier notions that the poor are ignorant and passive.

Participation in the World Bank

Back in the early 1990s the World Bank had started to use participatory research methods in its projects. The objective was to enable poor people to express and analyse their realities and priorities, so that these could be fed into the design of anti-poverty policies (IDS 1996; Brock, Cornwall and Gaventa 2001; Francis 2001). The World Bank's *Participation Sourcebook*, even though it falls short of identifying the Bank itself as the main culprit, suggests that the new approach promises to iron out some of the problems with the 'traditional' approach, which was less strong on participation:

> Bank-supported projects have in the past usually been prepared in a different manner. We call this more traditional approach the 'external expert stance' . . . Even when working in the external expert stance, Bank staff, their government colleagues, and the consultants they hire do consult with and listen to people in the local system. Admittedly, in the past, sponsors and designers may not have always listened to all the people or consulted poor and disadvantaged members of society, but this is changing (World Bank 1996c: 3–4).

The *Sourcebook* draws heavily on Participatory Rural Appraisal (PRA), a research methodology that Robert Chambers (1997) has developed and popularised since the early 1980s. 'PRA can be described as a family of approaches, methods and behaviours that enable people to express and analyse the realities of their lives and conditions, to plan themselves what action to take, and to monitor and evaluate the results' (IDS 1996). More recently, the World Bank has borrowed from these methods to develop its Participatory Poverty Assessments (Francis 2001: 85), which have been conducted in various countries since the early 1990s (Narayan, Patel et al. 2000: 15–16). They form the basis for the first and third volume of *Voices of the Poor* (Narayan, Patel et al. 2000; Narayan and Petesch 2000), discussed in the section below. Deepa Narayan of the World Bank's Poverty Group, team leader for the study, explained the importance of participation in the fight against poverty in the EDF (World Bank 2000/1a), in one of the handful of World Bank staff contributions: 'We undertook the study because we believe very strongly that poverty policies, whether at local, national or global levels, must be informed by poor women and men's priorities, experiences and realities.'

From the outset, the World Bank declared the preparation of the *Report* to be a process that 'will be highly consultative, establishing early and ongoing dialogue contact with the main constituencies outside the Bank' (World Bank 1998a). In contrast to the previous reports on poverty, which were designed behind closed doors by World Bank staff, this *Report* was to 'be capable of evolving and adapting as the consultation process progresses, and in fact be integrated into the consultation process' (World Bank 1998a). The Bank incorporated several constituencies in its participatory path: developing country governments, the United Nations, other multilateral and bilateral agencies, and different constituencies within the Bank itself. Above all, the poor themselves, and civil society in the broader sense of community organisations and NGOs, religious groups, the private sector, trade unions, journalists and academics from advanced and developing countries, were invited to 'consult' with the Bank through several mechanisms (discussed below). The poor, described by the Bank as the 'fundamental constituency' of the *Report*, would be included in the process of consultation, which 'will need to listen to their concerns, through their representatives but also directly, in their own words' (World Bank 1998a).

The strategies employed to capture this dialogue were both creative and exhaustive, including:

- direct and participative surveys of the poor;
- Internet-based international dialogues with civil society;
- consultations with academics targeted through a research programme comprising large conferences and smaller-scale workshops; and
- global level meetings with religious leaders, and with other civil society representatives (World Bank 1998a).

The rationale behind this participatory methodology was that the World Bank should draw on a wide range of experiences and expertise. However, there are clear limits set to stakeholders' ability to influence the final *Report*, as its then director, Ravi Kanbur, pointed out in his response to the EDF dialogue on the draft report in May 2000:

> the WDR [World Development Report] is an important vehicle for the Bank's dialogue with the international development community at large. He [World Bank President James Wolfensohn] said he would like WDRs to increasingly move away from pat answers to posing questions and issues which do not necessarily have easy answers. He also said that he would like the process of preparing WDRs to become more consultative, and we have tried to put that into practice this year. However, while the WDR is not a document of the Executive Board of the Bank and is thus not an official policy document, it is a document prepared by Bank staff and therefore represents the views of staff and management (Kanbur 2000).

From the beginning of the consultation process the World Bank left open what type of feedback it expected from its constituents on the *Report* draft, and whether and how such feedback was to be incorporated in its final version. Kanbur's comment sheds light on the reason why: after all the consultation, dialogue and participation, ultimately the *Report* represents the views of the World Bank. It cannot, and should not, be held accountable for including or excluding information, knowledge and viewpoints that might emerge from the consultative process.

The participation of the poor in the World Development Report process also raises some interesting issues. Wolfensohn justified the *Voices of the Poor* study in terms of the World Bank's need 'to know more about our clients as individuals' (quoted in Francis 2001: 85), suggesting that the need for information was the main motivator for employing participatory methodologies. The broadening of the World Bank's information base to include social, cultural and political factors can certainly be a powerful impetus for a more sophisticated understanding of poverty. As Sen has pointed out, 'the real "bite" of a theory of justice can, to a great extent, be understood from its informational base: what information is – or is not – taken to be directly relevant' (1999: 57). He forcefully argues for a broadening of the informational base for assessing poverty to take into account not only income and other resources, but also the social and personal circumstances which crucially affect a person's ability to convert income and resources into well-being (1999: 70–71). As these social and personal circumstances vary greatly, poverty theorists and policy makers must find out what lives poor people actually lead, and the choices and opportunities they have.

Local participation: The *Voices of the Poor* study
There is little doubt about the intensive effort that the World Bank has invested in finding out about the realities of the poor. The three substantial volumes, which together constitute the *Voices of the Poor,* contain a wealth of information on how the poor define their needs and interests, and what they consider to be the nature, causes and effects of poverty. In attempting to assess how this information has influenced the *World Development Report 2000/01,* we use the themes of 'participation' and 'empowerment' as the litmus test. Our focus will be on Volume 2 of *Voices* (*Voices 2*), which presents an analysis of poverty from the perspectives of poor people collected specifically for the *Report*

through 'open-ended participatory methods' (Narayan, Chambers et al. 2000: 2). Some 20 000 poor women and men from 23 countries in 4 continents participated in this study. We also draw on the first volume of the study (*Voices 1*), which was based on a review and analysis of Participatory Poverty Assessments (PPAs) involving 40 000 people, including decision makers at all levels of government, which had been conducted independently of the *Report*. Although local people involved in these processes usually have very limited ability to define the agenda of the PPAs, at least it ensures that NGO and grassroots actors are included in the process of inquiry (Brock, Cornwall and Gaventa 2001). The research team, headed by Deepa Narayan, defined the underlying principles of participatory research as engaging 'respondents actively in the research process' and aiming to 'empower participants', as well as leading to follow-up action (Narayan, Patel et al. 2000: 16).

One of the key philosophical premises of the participatory turn in development is that those most affected by interventions should participate in shaping the character of these interventions. In the present context, the poor should be involved in shaping poverty alleviation policies, not only because they are the targets, but also because they have first-hand experience of poverty. As Narayan, Chambers et al. state in their Introduction to *Voices 2*:

> There are 2.8 billion poverty experts, the poor themselves. Yet the development discourse about poverty has been dominated by the perspectives and expertise by those who are not poor – professionals, politicians and agency officials. This book seeks to reverse this imbalance by focusing directly on the perspectives and expertise of poor people (2000: 2).

The poor are presented as knowledge holders whose views are valuable and important, whose voices lend 'authenticity' (Narayan, Patel et al. 2000: ix) to the World Bank's poverty policy process. Despite their many 'lacks of capabilities', which include lack of information, education and skills (Narayan, Chambers et al. 2000: 237), the poor are portrayed as being rich in knowledge about their own lives, as well as having strong views about the economic and political institutions wielding power over them. The first assumption here is that the poor are in a position to provide accurate and truthful information on their condition, enabled by the participatory methods and 'non-dominating behaviours' of the researchers (Narayan, Chambers et al. 2000: 14). Secondly, the high value placed on poor people's authentic voices gives rise to the expectation that policy and decision makers will make better policies and decisions on the basis of the accurate information provided by their clients. However, as Spivak has pointed out, rhetoric in the service of 'truth' – 'where oppressed subjects speak, act, and know *for themselves'* – while seemingly transparent, 'leads to an essentialist, utopian politics that can . . . give unquestioning support to the financialisation of the globe' (1999: 259). In the context of this chapter, her point is that while researchers (and policy makers who use their research) seek to make themselves transparent by allowing poor people to speak for themselves, we should not be fooled into thinking that they no longer frame the poor within their own perspectives. The claim expressed in the above quotation, that providing a space for the voice of the poor contributes to a reversal of the power imbalance between development experts and the poor, suggests that the authors run the danger of conflating voice (portrayal) and power.

Both terms are often used in conjunction with each other. In *Voices 1*, for example, it is stated that '[l]ack of voice and power is experienced not only in interaction with the state, but also in poor people's interactions with the market, landlords, bankers, moneylenders, and employers' (Narayan, Patel et al. 2000: 40). While a close connection between voice and power is indicated, there is no clear theoretical framework provided through which this connection can be analysed and understood. The reader could be forgiven for thinking that in voicing their views the poor have experienced a boost in their power. However, elsewhere the book acknowledges that the voices of the poor only 'send powerful messages that point the way toward policy change' (Narayan, Patel et al. 2000: 3). Although still linked, the connection between 'voice' and 'power' is less direct. The policy change does not come through the agency of the poor, but is made by other parties. Whether it is made depends on 'those who have the power to affect decisions that affect poor people's lives' *listening*, and *responding* in particular ways (Narayan, Patel et al. 2000: 25). Towards the end of *Voices 2*, a distinction is made between voice and participation in decision making, both of which depend on transforming existing power relations:

> Poor people lack voice and power. They do exercise agency but in very limited spheres of influence... The voices that count most are those of the powerful and wealthy. It is they who make, influence and implement policy. To make a difference poor people must be able to make their voices heard in policy and have representation in decision-making forums. This implies changes in power relations and behavior... In today's 'wired' world the opportunities for sharing the realities of poor people's lives, for changing mind-sets and for ensuring that poor people's voices are heard have never been greater (Narayan, Chambers et al. 2000: 265).

At the end of this quotation, the authors fall back on the power of *information*. They express hope that poor people's accounts of their lives, spread through information technologies, will bring about changes in power relations and behaviour. While change is clearly the desired outcome, the authors also see the danger 'that development agencies will simply continue "business as usual"' (Narayan, Patel et al. 2000: 283). This danger, it seems, can be prevented only if the wealthy and powerful take the individual decision to change, decide to listen to the poor, and prioritise their interests (Narayan, Chambers et al. 2000: 288–89). The influence of Robert Chambers's work (1997) is evident in the absence of a theory of power from *Voices 2*. For Chambers, 'rectifying power relations lies in personal transformation', whereby the more powerful 'uppers' divest themselves of their power and hand it to the less powerful 'lowers' (Kapoor 2002: 111). Thus the agency for change lies with the powerful – the powerless can only hope and pray – and what would make them want to act is not clear. Chambers's 'challenge to change' and 'the primacy of the personal' are echoed in *Voices 2* but they rest on the terrain of moral challenges, rather than becoming policies with teeth.[9]

The state is often seen as the place where voice can influence policy. Sen has stated that 'the relevant freedoms include the liberty of acting as citizens who matter and whose voices count' (1999: 288). In stark contrast, *Voices 2* documents that poor people's voices do not count in most countries that were included in the study. They find state institutions to be 'either not accountable to anyone or accountable only to the rich and powerful', and view the rich as an 'obstacle to their struggles for a livelihood' (Narayan, Chambers et al. 2000: 203–04).

The *Report* picks up some of these comments in its treatment of empowerment when it focuses on ways in which the state can 'deliver more effectively' to poor people. The recipe includes familiar themes that hark back to the governance agenda the World Bank developed over the 1990s: improving the capacity of public administration to deliver services; making public administration more transparent and accessible; and subjecting the state to an appropriately reformed legal system (World Bank 2000/1d: 99–100). It is effectively a restatement of the World Bank's governance agenda which, as Paul Nelson (2000) has argued, is driven by its economic agenda, promoting good governance as a route to expanded investment and growth. The *Report*'s response to poor people's perception of rich people as obstacles (in other words, class conflict) involves a clever rhetorical move. It drops 'rich' from its discourse, replaces it with 'non-poor', and exhorts governments to persuade the latter that supporting public action against poverty is in their own interest: 'governments have to enhance the perception of common interests between the poor and the non-poor' (World Bank 2000/1d: 109). Poor people, it seems, play the role of beneficiary in these 'pro-poor coalitions' fostered by a seemingly neutral government.

The *Report* discusses participation, voice and empowerment mainly in the context of local politics and community organisations. About the latter, the *Report* claims that 'community-based, participatory grassroots organisations' are the most likely institutions to encourage active involvement of the poor, but they are 'limited in scope and depth' (World Bank 2000/1d: 110). On the former, the *Report* cautiously asserts that participating in local government 'helps increase the voice of poor people in local affairs' and 'can transform power relations over time' (World Bank 2000/1d: 108). While the *Report* acknowledges the role of external NGOs in extending the range and effectiveness of these organisations, it perceives the role of the state mainly in facilitating interactions between local administrations and communities, and in designing appropriate development policies for rapid local development (World Bank 2000/1d: 111, 125–26). The underlying message, that empowering the poor is best done at the local level, may be, as Mick Moore suspects, a deliberate ploy borrowed from neo-populist governments around the world, which is intended to appease Third World governments concerned with protecting established interests, as well as to garner support from development activists and NGOs (M. Moore 2001: 323). Chambers's criticism, that the *Report* fails to address power issues and explore the relationship between poverty and vested interest, indicates that the *Report* did not quite succeed in walking this tightrope. However, as we have pointed out above, *Voices of the Poor* and the broader literature on empowerment and participation can both be faulted in this respect. They share with the *Report* a tendency to view 'the local' as endowed with power awaiting activation through catalytic institutions.[10]

Global participation: The Electronic Discussion Forum

We now turn to the *World Development Report* EDF as the second illustration of the participatory methodology employed by the Bank and analysed in this chapter. The World Bank, in collaboration with the Bretton Woods Project and the New Policy Institute, set up the EDF to enable consultation with NGOs and other sectors of civil society on the first draft of the *Report*. While the *Voices of the Poor* study sought insights about poverty from local communities, the EDF set out to capture the feedback of a rather abstract 'global civil society' on the policy approach. In its invitation to participate, the World Bank indicated that the draft would be revised in light of comments received during the consultation (World Bank 2000/1c). The organisers asserted that they had strongly encouraged a diversity of input from researchers, civil society groups and others, especially from the South, on the basis of their views and experience on poverty, inequality and related issues. The discussion would be valuable as a forum in which the participants could exchange views on such a critical subject, and influential document, among themselves and with staff from the World Bank (World Bank 2000/1a).

This indicates that the EDF also was seen as a vehicle for generating a consensus on how to deal with poverty. Such 'public discussions to debate conventional wisdom on both practicalities and valuations can', as Sen notes, 'be central to the acknowledgment of injustice' (1999: 287). The decision to open up the *Report* draft to public scrutiny was welcomed by some participants. A representative of the UK-based NGO Catholic Action For Overseas Development (CAFOD) wrote approvingly that '[t]his step breaks new ground in terms of inclusive policy making, and sets the standard for other multilateral and government consultation processes' (World Bank 2000/1a).

The discussion forum took place over a six-week period between 21 February and 31 March 2000. While it generated hundreds of electronic responses from across the globe,[11] there were fewer contributions from the South than from the North (44 per cent and 56 per cent, respectively), and the rural South remained completely silent. Evidently, only the urban elites of the developed and developing world had access to the new technologies required to participate in the EDF, and the poor remained on the margins (Skuse 2000). Active participants introduced themselves as (among other categories) teachers, researchers, company managers, development bureaucrats, finance ministry officials and agitators (World Bank 2000/1b). Their hopes for an active debate with World Bank staff were, however, dashed by the low level of Bank workers' participation (World Bank 2000/1b), a fact that one staff member put down to 'a combination of too much work, [we've] already said too much, and unease about whether staff can speak in a personal capacity' (World Bank 2000/1a: Document 309)

Comments relayed through the EDF brought out a number of issues pertaining to the role of participation in the Bank's new strategy toward development. Several contributors expressed concern that most people, particularly in the South, had no opportunity to comment on the draft report, either because its language was difficult to understand or because they had no access to computer technology:

> ... the language is very technical rendering the report inaccessible to all but the very well educated. Furthermore, although efforts have been made to include French and Spanish speakers (summaries available and postings accepted in these languages), the fact remains that the report in its entirety as well as the vast majority of the postings, are in English (World Bank 2000/1a: Document 214).

> If we do not want the discussions to be exclusively for a small group which understands such words, then let us use words commonly found in dictionaries (World Bank 2000/1a: Document 195).

> I would like to ask the WDR moderators, or the authors of the *Report*, to describe what efforts have been made to solicit the comments of the poor on the draft report, in comparison with the unprecedented access that you have given to those of us who have a computer within easy reach (World Bank 2000/1a: Document 204).

The second major problem with the draft identified by EDF contributors concerns perceived contradictions in the policies and strategies offered by the Bank. Many participants acknowledged that some sections of the *Report* indicated that the World Bank was embracing a more holistic approach to poverty and genuinely advocating the empowerment of the poor. However, they pointed out that other parts of the *Report* either failed to provide appropriate policy recommendations, or simply echoed past World Bank policy approaches by reiterating that economic growth was the best weapon in the attack on poverty. The comments below illustrate this critical tenor:

> ... at many junctures too, reading the draft gives rise to a feeling of frustration because it comes near many times to reaching a strong policy conclusion, then ultimately draws back from making that appropriate logical recommendation (World Bank 2000/1a: Document 113).

> ... in so far as [the draft chapters] fight shy of explicitly and squarely acknowledging the fatal flaws of the 'Washington Consensus' and the adverse side-effects being visited on those least able to withstand the pains of 'structural adjustment', to that extent the draft WDR cannot escape the criticism of being 'willing to wound, yet unwilling to strike' (World Bank 2000/1a: Document 148).

> It is one thing to recognise that simplistic blueprinting doesn't work and apparently another to be willing to seek a new way forward that is not premised on the absolute virtues of the absolutely free market (World Bank 2000/1a: Document 226).

> Chapter 8 deals with the critical question of making markets work for the poor. Given the emphasis in earlier chapters on listening to the voice of the poor, one would have hoped that their voice might have penetrated through to this chapter but this does not appear to be the case (World Bank 2000/1a: Document 227).

Some EDF contributors took the opportunity to pull up the World Bank on its unwillingness to exercise self-critique, or at least to position itself in the *Report*. Pre-empting Chambers's criticism (2001: 306) that the World Bank should have included itself among the 'powerful vested interests' as a financial institution, contributors note in the draft:

> ... a curious but typical omission. Nowhere does it mention or observe the role of the financial élite i.e. the international bankers and financiers, the World Bank, the IMF, the Bank of International Settlements. To presuppose that these people and institutions are not involved in the persistence of poverty is at once laughable and lamentable (World Bank 2000/1a: Document 264).

> The draft WDR talks of the failure [of previous economic policies] in a detached way as if the Bank itself has not been involved. But of course it has. Also, whilst it admits the policies did not work, it does not admit the harm they did (World Bank 2000/1a: Document 162).

The question remains: to what extent did the *Report* take into account these criticisms? The redrafting process shifted the *Report* further towards the orthodox economic solutions, which many EDF contributors criticised but the US Treasury strongly advocated, as Wade has pointed out (2001b). There is no evidence of any EDF material having been directly used in the *Report*, indicating that the World Bank, whilst willing to engage with its constituents and its critics, intends to retain the power to decide which voices it will include in the end product, and to what effect.

Governing through participation

In the preceding sections we have found that the participatory methods used in the production of the *Report* have not brought new answers to questions of power, inequality and political participation. Their main purpose, it seems, has been to provide the World Bank with better information about the poor and their advocates. That 'knowledge is essential to decision making' (World Bank 2000/1d: 186) is an insight already present in the *World Development Report 1990* on poverty; what is new in this *Report* is that the likely target groups of these decisions are directly approached for information. Our analysis of two participatory methods employed by the World Bank to this purpose shows, however, that the decisions and policies at the end of the process do not radically diverge from those previously pursued.

In spite of this, the participatory strategy delivers an important advantage: it allows the World Bank to present its revised policy framework as a global project, supported by a harmonious coalition of a wide range of poor and non-poor, powerful and powerless actors (Øyen 2000). Secondly, by involving the poor in the policies that affect them, the World Bank is able to present its policy recommendations as something the poor themselves request, rendering its own interests, power and agency invisible in the process.

Why does the World Bank want a pro-poor coalition, and how does it set out to achieve it? As Øyen has observed, the *Report* confidently asserts that there is general agreement about the need to reduce poverty for the common good, and plays down the possibility that powerful groups could be adverse to pro-poor strategies which interfere with their interests (2000). One contributor to the EDF gives voice to the suspicion that the World Bank organised the on-line discussion 'to co-opt the willingness of the liberal intelligentsia across the world and to derive legitimacy from this exercise in formal democracy' (World Bank 2000/1a: Document 179), all the while continuing to push its familiar neoliberal agenda of economic reforms and trade liberalisation. Another email to the EDF opines that the World Bank's new-found interest in the poor as clients, though at one level welcome, reveals itself in later chapters of the *Report* as a tactic 'to deflect attention from the forces that are actually primarily responsible for producing the economic and social conditions that we all live in. And in the course of this, of co-opting the language of social action and social analysis' (World Bank 2000/1a: Document 291). Other more complimentary contributions indicate that terms such as 'participation', 'voice' and 'empowerment' certainly help in striking, as Moore observes, 'a positive chord with those "progressive" groups on whom the very existence of international aid agencies and programmes increasingly depends' (M. Moore 2001: 322). The World Bank must think about its own survival, having moved out of infrastructural finance and into a more low-income, country-oriented set of concerns including social protection, knowledge creation and global governance functions. In Mosley's view, 'it has moved down-market to countries where markets work less well or not at all' (2001: 312), and has to fine-tune its agenda accordingly to remain effective.

Hajer's concept of 'discourse coalition' (1996) is useful in explaining how the World Bank sets about achieving a pro-poor coalition.[12] He argues that in order for people from widely varying backgrounds to communicate, an overarching story line is needed which organises elements of various discourses – political, economic, scientific – into a more or less coherent whole. 'A discourse coalition is thus the ensemble of a set of story lines, the actors that utter these story lines, and the practices that conform to these story lines, all organized around a discourse' (Hajer 1996: 47). The assembling of such a discourse coalition requires access to a large, multidisciplinary information base, something not many actors would possess. The World Bank is one of the few institutions in this position, and has openly laid claim to 'providing leadership in the field of development knowledge' (Wilks 1998). Although the *Report* is not an official policy document of the World Bank,[13] it is the single most influential development report published by any institution, national and international, and important for defining 'what ideas the Bank projects' (Wade 2001b: 130). The *Report* may lack the coercion of other World Bank or government policies, but it is precisely such a policy without 'teeth', a broadly formulated plan of action, that Emily Martin argues has become 'the central means by which the new flexible, continuously changing, self-managed person is being constituted' even in the 'Third World' (1997).

Cruikshank's analysis of empowerment as a technology of citizenship is relevant to understanding the World Bank's participatory approach, although her reference point is anti-poverty programmes in the USA. She points out that the rhetoric of empowerment was first used by left-wing activists 'to generate political resistance', but by the 1980s it had also been adopted by neoliberal discourses on poverty that hoped 'to produce rational economic and entrepreneurial actors'. While neoliberals and leftists disagree on the nature of poor people's interests, they both use the same tactics, which is 'to act upon others by getting them to act in their own interest' (Cruikshank 1999: 68). The poor, instead of falling outside the reach of the state and other government institutions, or having to be governed through violence and coercion, are purportedly empowered through a range of programmes aimed to increase their capacity to act on their own behalf. This form of governance relies on social science knowledge, as well as participatory political processes, so the poor can be transformed into active, participatory, productive citizens. Cruikshank argues that Foucault's concept of 'bio-power' aptly describes how this type of governance exercises power not just over the body but also over the subjectivity of human beings, so that they come to identify their individual interests with the interests of society as a whole.

In the World Bank's poverty report (2000/1d), bio-power not only comes into the relationship between the poor and their national governments, but also pervades its own relations of governance. The *Report* argues that poverty must be tackled through empowerment and participation at the local, national and international level, pointing out that the main actors are the poor:

> National governments should be fully accountable to their citizenry for the development path they pursue. Participatory mechanisms can provide voice to women and men, especially those from poor and excluded segments of society... And international institutions should listen to – and promote – the interests of poor people. The poor are the main actors in the fight against poverty. And they must be brought centre stage in designing, implementing, and monitoring anti-poverty strategies (World Bank 2000/1d: 12).

As we have shown earlier, the *Report* reveals what the poor want from their governments is to be congruous with the World Bank's good governance agenda: accountability, transparency, efficiency and openness. It argues that governments in developing countries, by failing to undertake reforms to improve governance, actively contribute to the disempowerment of their poor citizens. The advantage of getting the poor to make these demands is that the World Bank can retreat into the role of a helper and facilitator in an empowering relationship with the poor, and with developing countries more generally. The relationship of empowerment is portrayed as one where power is not operating; 'it exhibits', as Cruikshank argues, 'the will to empower by displacing the will and the power of the organiser' (1999: 68). This is achieved by instrumentalising the voice of the poor, which comes to stand in for the will and the power of the World Bank. The knowledge that the World Bank unleashed through participatory social research methods has strengthened its authority to proclaim a shift in poverty reduction strategies (World Bank 2000/1d: 32–33), and, as Cruikshank reminds us, '[a]ny claim to know what is best for poor people, to know what it takes to get out of poverty and what needs must be met in order to be fully human, is also a claim to power' (1999: 38).

Placing the poor 'centre stage' and labelling them 'main actors' in this broad-ranging poverty reduction agenda has the dual advantage of bestowing a moral superiority on the agenda – by involving its beneficiaries – and, at the same time, improving its effectiveness as a tool of governance. In their assessment of the 'participatory turn in development', Henkel and Stirrat (2001: 178) make a similar point in suggesting that 'what the new orthodoxy boldly calls "empowerment" might be in effect very similar to what Michel Foucault calls "subjection"'. Drawing a comparison with nineteenth-century Christian reformers' and missionaries' sometimes benevolent, but always active, role in helping to integrate populations into the fold of the nation-state and colonial rule, they argue that contemporary participatory development interventions seek 'to integrate the beneficiaries of their projects into national and international political, economic and ideological structures – incidentally, structures about which the people concerned generally have very little control' (Henkel and Stirrat 2001: 183). While the poor have little control over these broader structures, their active participation in local development projects has the effect of reshaping their personhood in ways that facilitate their integration into the process of modernisation (Henkel and Stirrat 2001: 182).

Conclusion

In this chapter we have focused on the *World Development Report 2000/1: Attacking Poverty*, to see whether a new global consensus is emerging on how to deal with widespread, systemic poverty in many parts of the world. Since this new consensus would have to be, according to critics of the 'old' Washington Consensus, much broader-based, it would have to allow for the participation not only of non-government organisations, but also the target groups of poverty alleviation: the poor themselves. Thus we asked how the World Bank has incorporated the voices of the world's poor and of global civil society, particularly those organisations that claim to be at the forefront of the fight against poverty on the ground. We explored this question through a textual analysis of key sections of the *Report*, a qualitative data analysis of the EDF on the draft *Report*, and a critical reading of *Voices of the Poor*, which collects the World Bank's participatory research on the poor.

We have shown that the findings of the *Voices of the Poor* study were incorporated in the *Report* in a very selective manner that left out many issues. However, the Bank's considerable investment in the study, and its act of publishing the study alongside the *Report*, testify to its claim to having adopted a more open, democratic and participatory approach to development policy making. Similarly, the EDF on the draft *Report* was not simply a hypocritical exercise of pretending to consult with civil society, as some participants in the forum allege. Rather, it indicates that the World Bank is willing to open itself to criticism and make the *World Development Report* process more transparent, at least in some respects. Not in others, because we have no way of knowing the comments of other stakeholders on the draft, especially the governments of the most powerful shareholders in the Bank, and those of the developing countries. The outcome of the process, and the struggles along the way that Robert Wade (2001b, 2002) documents so vividly, demonstrate that the 2000/1 *Report* is a political document that tries to create a new discourse coalition by organising elements of various discourses into a more or less coherent approach to poverty. It signals a change in methods of research and consultation, but retains the broad neoliberal economic credo underpinning the development thinking of the past three decades.

The reason why the World Bank is increasingly concerned with participatory research methods and consultation with broader and more diverse constituencies is to do with its status as the foremost international development agency. As Wade (2002) has argued, the World Bank is caught between a rock and a hard place: how to promote neoliberal reforms which are, according to the 'old' *and* the 'new' Washington Consensus, the only reliable path to development, while at the same time maintaining its legitimacy as a Knowledge Bank that relies on independent, scientific, 'best-practice' research processes. Participation and consultation processes in the *World Development Report* achieve the incorporation – some would argue, co-optation – of organisations and subjects into the policy-making process with a similar objective as the expansion of democratic processes had in European and North American societies up until the 1970s. Firstly, these processes permit the World Bank to establish more accurate and thus useful knowledge about the poor, which in turn permits the formulation of better-targeted programmes and policies, and, secondly, empowerment of the poor and their advocates increase these agents' ability to act on poverty, thus turning them into modernising, more easily governable subjects. There are, however, important differences between the World Bank's current democratising endeavours and those discussed by Cruikshank in the 1960s US context. One is that the latter are set within the context of a democratic welfare state, whereas the World Bank is neither a democratic nor a welfare institution, and therefore cannot be held accountable in the way a democratic state can be. Most poor people live in states that are not democracies, and the World Bank cannot serve as a substitute. The second difference lies in the realm of economics. While welfare is an effective mode of government that includes the poor and other marginal groups, by working upon the capacities of citizens to act on their own behalf, it assumes that the government has the economic resources to intervene. This is not the case with the majority of developing countries, which have experienced low or negative growth and have undergone, under IMF/World Bank instructions, an economic restructuring process that has diminished, not increased, governments' welfare functions. While we admit to some doubts whether the World Development Report will indeed improve the governance of poverty and the poor, further research is needed, particularly on the Poverty Reduction Strategy Papers and their impacts, in the coming years.

Notes

1. Susanne Schech gratefully acknowledges research funding under the Flinders University Small Grant Scheme in 2001 and 2002.
2. Escobar (1995: 24) has argued that after the Second World War, poverty became the organising concept of the Third World, and interventions for the eradication of poverty became central to the world order; see also Ferguson (1990: 70–73).
3. World Bank chief economist (1996–99) Joseph Stiglitz combined his critique of the IMF's response to the Asian economic crisis with a call for a new post-Washington paradigm; see Gore (2000).
4. One such voice of approval, albeit not without some reservations, is Chambers (2001).
5. The *World Bank Participation Sourcebook* is a procedural manual designed for World Bank staff to enable them to support participatory processes in economic and social development projects.
6. However, elsewhere Wade (2002: 215–16) acknowledges that 'In the end the report proceeded with the messages of the January 2000 version for the most part intact.' Wade claims that superficial changes to the Overview and the chapter introductions and conclusions – the most-read sections of the *Report* – were incorporated probably in a last-minute effort to assuage critics in the US Treasury.
7. Gore (2000: 789–90) discusses the emergence of the Washington Consensus in the 1980s as a paradigm shift in development thinking, propagated by the IMF, the World Bank (and US Treasury), from earlier state-led development policies towards market-oriented policies which prioritised macroeconomic stability, trade liberalisation, and market deregulation. For a discussion of the Post-, or 'New' Washington Consensus, see Martin (2000).
8. World Bank, http://www.worldbank.orgpoverty/wdrpoverty/plan598i.htm. Accessed 18 September 2000.
9. Compare Narayan, Chambers et al. (2000: Chapter 12) with Chambers (1997: Chapter 1) on 'the challenge to change'; and Chambers (1997: 231) with Narayan, Chambers et al. (2000: 289) on 'the primacy of the personal'.
10. Kapoor (2002) argues that this tendency is inherent in Participatory Rural Appraisal methodologies.
11. In all, 424 contributions were posted from 44 countries, but 1 523 people from 80 countries subscribed to the list (see Wade 2002: 210).
12. Brock, Cornwall and Gaventa (2001) invoke Hajer.
13. As Joseph Stiglitz confirmed in a letter to Alex Wilks of the Bretton Woods Project on 26 August 1998, http://www.brettonwoodsproject.org/topic/knowledgebank/wdrs/. Accessed 12 February 2005.

Chapter Seven

The World Bank and the Liberal Project

David Williams and Tom Young

THIS IS A COMPLETE 'REVISIT' OF THE AUTHORS' 1994 ARTICLE IN POLITICAL STUDIES 42 (1): 84–100.

In an earlier paper (Williams and Young 1994) we provided one of the first analyses of a fairly recent revival of a then rather archaic term – 'governance' – by the World Bank to signal its recognition of the severe limitations of structural adjustment programmes (SAPs) and the importance of non-economic factors in questions of 'development'. Unusually then (and still) we sought to make our observations on these shifts in the context of a rejection of the standard positions in the social sciences that relegate 'ideas' to the role of epiphenomena and to suggest systematic parallels or connections between familiar stances in liberal political theory (and by extension) economics and the practices of institutions such as the Bank.

The position we continue to take is perhaps better articulated in relation to a central curiosity of certain forms of liberal discourse that contain an apparent contradiction. There is one set of claims that ideas are unimportant because human beings and their practices are (appearances to the contrary) essentially of one uniform type, a view espoused by those imagining themselves to be 'scientific' (most economics, and much international relations and political science). There is another set of claims that ideas are important but only one set of them is 'true'; the rest being ideology; false consciousness; prejudice or whatever (this is the message of much contemporary philosophy, legal thought as well as the tag end of religious beliefs in so far as they are still influential). At a time when liberal violence is increasingly visited on supposed 'enemies of democracy' it is best to speak plainly and reject both these sets of claims as completely bogus. There are no such constants or truths in human affairs and these formulae are more properly seen as the theoretical expressions of the boundless arrogance and will to power of Western modernity.

Such a broad statement of principle of course demands refinement and applications. Thus while we make no claims to have 'resolved' the relationship between 'ideas' and 'action' (it may be irresolvable) we offer examples of such refinement and application drawn from our own work since the original paper, as well as that of others. In particular, we shall draw attention to: firstly, the trajectory of the governance agenda since the early 1990s, both within and beyond the Bank; secondly, some central shifts in international politics that have shaped the development of the good governance agenda; and, finally, we present some analysis of the ways in which that agenda has been implemented, emphasising how the juxtaposition of 'theory' and 'practice' can illuminate both.

Good governance and liberal theory

Some preliminary remarks are in order, however, on the degree to which our original account has stood the test of time. In our 1994 paper we noted firstly the relative novelty of the governance agenda, acknowledging its filiations with an older concern about 'good government' but stressing a new emphasis on factors not hitherto taken to be central to 'development'. We also hinted at the relative vacuity of governance as a slogan, both on the part of Western politicians and the Bank itself, the latter in part due to some residual coyness about involvement in 'politics'. This coyness now seems almost a world away. There is room here for some analysis of the role of slogans in liberal politics, but governance then seemed to involve two elements. The first was a technical stream concerned essentially (we need not share the

Bank's wariness) with the building blocks of a liberal capitalist state with an especial emphasis on law. The second was a civil society stream, an emphasis which encompassed both the conviction that it is vigorous civil society that holds states to account, but also enabled the Bank to emphasise certain political virtues without appearing to mandate liberal democracy in the formal sense.

The novelty of the governance agenda established, we turned then to what could only be a tentative analysis of the factors that might have brought about these changes. All the factors identified remain highly pertinent and we revisit them in the following section. In part, of course, governance emerged from the Bank's increasingly disappointing experience with structural adjustment lending. It was becoming clear that structural adjustment programmes were not producing the expected results in terms of sustained economic growth. This led to two developments, the first of which was noted in our original paper. The difficulties that the Bank was having in getting its policies enacted led it to consider the social and political barriers to economic reform. In this way the Bank was drawn into analysis of the impact of political processes and social formations on developmental success. We did not stress the second development enough. This was that the Bank increasingly came to see institutional development, both in terms of the overall economy (for example, the legal system) and in terms of specific sectors of the economy (in terms of regulation), as important determinants of development success.

This experience, in turn, undoubtedly had effects on the internal organisation of the Bank. In our original article we suggested a number of internal changes that contributed to the rise of good governance. At the time we did not have a very clear understanding of these internal changes. Today we have a better sense (in part because the Bank has become less secretive) and our account of these changes would be more complex. In particular, we would stress more the central role that reflection on the development experience in sub-Saharan Africa played in forming the core ideas of good governance. We would also emphasise the ways in which certain senior managers played a crucial role in supporting research into good governance issues.

These internal reorganisations, while no doubt in part driven by an internal logic, also provided considerable space for the co-option of academic opinion into the Bank's deliberations. There is interesting material here for reflection on the role of academia in the construction of the liberal project, ranging as it does from overt 'consultancy' (often little more than the mouthing of the platitudes the funder wants to hear) to serious intellectual reflection. In our original paper we were concerned to draw attention to the Bank's interest in two areas of academic discourse. The first was a burgeoning literature on civil society, particularly in Africa, which had a welcome stress both on indigeneity and the possibility of political virtue. The second, a more austerely formal, and by its own lights at least, more scientific 'public choice' approach to politics, was an approach whose debunking tendencies doubtless appealed to a climate of opinion increasingly hostile to the African state.

There remained finally the crucial international and great power context in which all of this was taking place. This was perhaps the least adequate section of our original paper. 'Flavour of the month' was not its most cognitively illuminating, analytical term though we did at least make the point that, 'the crucial questions are of course what flavour, and perhaps more importantly, whose flavour'.[1] Above all, we were concerned to emphasise that the Bank's governance discourse formed part of a chorus of similar sentiments emanating from the Western powers. This suggested that there was a genuine phenomenon here, but also that it would be, at the least, short-sighted to see the Bank as entirely the 'tool' of the USA or Western governments more generally. As the purpose of the original paper was to draw attention to certain developments concerning governance and to make a case for their analysis in terms of liberal social theory, our lack of attention to the international political environment does not seem a major shortcoming – but we do move to rectify it below.

Having done something to situate the governance agenda in a fairly conventional sense we went on to suggest a series of connections between that agenda and some familiar themes in liberal political (and economic) theory. Developments in the last decade have served to convince us further of the value of analysis drawing attention (here we merely followed the lead of MacIntyre, Sandel and others) to the degree to which the kinds of positions the World Bank was assuming were informed by deep-seated, recognisably liberal commitments reproducing the ambiguities and problems of those commitments, as it were, on the terrain of policy and action. As a 'working ideology' we identified three notions as central liberal concerns: firstly, the idea of the 'neutral' state, a framework within which competing conceptions of the good can be equally pursued; secondly, that of 'civil society' characterised as a realm of freedom in which individuals engage in formally uncoerced transactions; and, thirdly, a certain conception of the 'self', denoting a free-choosing individual who is the best, indeed the only, judge of his or her own interests. It does not detract from the general value of this analysis to concede this was a rather flat account of liberal theory (though certainly not a caricature), constructed for the purposes of our argument. That account can be refined to take account of liberal debates about the 'neutral' state (and the 'public sphere' more generally), and disputes about the nature of civil society and the self.[2]

Good governance rules OK?

Despite our own emphasis on the governance agenda it is worth noting that in the early 1990s there were still extensive debates within the Bank (and beyond) about whether it should be getting involved in good governance at all. These debates centred on a number of issues. Firstly, there was the question of whether the idea of good governance breached the World Bank's Articles of Agreement. These Articles state that '[t]he Bank and its officers shall not interfere in the political affairs of any member; nor shall they be influenced in their decisions by the political character of the member or members concerned' (Article IV [10]). Secondly, there were anxieties about the extent to which the World Bank was really equipped to deal with the issues raised by good governance. Thirdly, there were doubts in the Bank about the extent to which the importance of good governance for a country's development prospects had been adequately demonstrated.[3] Finally, there was a good deal of anxiety on the part of borrower country representatives about what good governance concerns might concretely mean for developing countries.

Some ten years later the situation has been transformed into one in which good governance is now very widely accepted as a legitimate and important concern of the World Bank and, indeed, all other donor agencies. Good governance has become part of the accepted development 'common sense'. For the Bank, good governance is now seen as an essential component of its work in all areas. In 1999 James Wolfensohn, then the World Bank president, argued that 'good and clean government' was a *prerequisite* for development (1999b). Two of the Bank's recent policy initiatives illustrate the central place of good governance. The 'Comprehensive Development Framework' has good governance as one of the key areas of reform in a 'long-term holistic vision' of the future for developing countries. This framework is the 'guiding approach' for the Bank's country assistance work (Wolfensohn 2001). Poverty Reduction Strategy Papers (PRSPs) fit within the Comprehensive Development Framework. They are designed as mechanisms whereby donors and recipient governments agree on an overall development strategy. A core component of the PRSP process is agreement on governance reforms. Underlying this is the new wisdom that the 'problems of poverty and governance are inextricably linked' and that 'strengthening governance is an essential precondition for improving the lives of the poor' (World Bank 2006). In addition to this, the preparation of a PRSP is supposed to improve governance by encouraging civil society groups to reflect on their country's governing institutions.[4] Even though the World Bank has certainly taken the lead role in this area, beyond it virtually all other donor agencies have come to accept governance as an almost unquestionable part of development 'common sense'.

How can we explain this shift? We look firstly at developments internal to the Bank itself (though we are mindful of the difficulties of the internal/external distinction). Then we seek to locate these in a wider international political context.

World Bank 'learning'

We suggest, firstly, that just as reflection on structural adjustment prompted the concern with governance, so, subsequently, the Bank has continued to reflect on and draw lessons from its experience with governance programmes. On the one hand, it is, of course, the case that the World Bank has a particular vision of development, and in that sense there are limits to the kinds of positions and policies it can adopt while remaining within that vision. On the other hand, we take it that the World Bank is serious about getting its vision enacted, and in that sense is quite open to learning from its past experiences, if it can be shown that these experiences have something to contribute to the efficacy of the Bank's work. We think this has been particularly important with good governance.

All through the 1990s the World Bank's Operations Evaluation Department (OED) was pushing for good governance issues to be taken more seriously in Bank lending. Its assessments showed that a key component of successful lending was the extent to which issues of institutional development were taken seriously in project design (World Bank 1995a: Chapter 3). The 'Wapenhams Report' on World Bank operating procedures reinforced these findings. This report argued that institutional and organisational arrangements in the Bank's borrower countries were a crucial determinant of project success (Portfolio Management Taskforce 1992). Both OED and the Wapenhams Report also stressed the importance of issues of 'participation' and 'ownership'. An OED study showed that there was a correlation between the levels of participation by project beneficiaries and project success (Johnston and Wasty 1993). The findings of the OED and the Wapenhams Report raised the profile of good governance within the World Bank because they showed that it was crucial for the Bank's lending. That is, good governance was not just another policy the Bank had adopted; rather, it had come to be seen as crucial for the success of discrete project lending in all policy areas (World Bank 1992a, 1995b, 1997b).

There was a further reinforcement of the good governance agenda within the Bank by the publication of *The East Asian Miracle* (World

Bank 1993a). This report was undertaken in response to Japanese pressure.[5] It subsequently generated a great deal of debate (Wade 1996b; Amsden 1994). Whatever the merits of the report as an account of the development process in East Asia, it had the effect of raising the profile of good governance issues because it drew attention to the role of the state, and, particularly, reputable and effective bureaucracies, as a crucial determinant of development success in the region.[6]

A final point to note is that the World Bank has become a much more open organisation than it was ten years ago. Under James Wolfensohn there has been a more systematic attempt to make the Bank responsive to its critics. Obviously this responsiveness has its limits, but it does represent, we think, a genuine attempt on the part of the Bank to learn from other agencies. We do not see this simply as the Bank co-opting its critics; rather, we see it as the Bank being more open to ideas that make its own efforts more successful. For example, the World Bank argues that consultation with 'civil society organisations' has 'improved the quality of policy making, positively influenced the direction of country programmes, strengthened national ownership of key reforms, and promoted public sector transparency and accountability' (World Bank 2000b).

Internal Bank factors

This shift in stance has been matched by a number of changes in the way the World Bank operates. The first of these concerned the objection that good governance issues were beyond the remit of the Bank because they breached its supposed 'non-political' nature. In 1990 the World Bank's General Legal Counsel ruled on the extent of Bank activities in the realm of good governance allowed by its Articles of Agreement. The ruling argued that 'technical considerations of economic efficiency' should guide the Bank's work at all times, but that 'economic considerations in their broad sense do extend to the manner in which the state manages its resources', and that 'political events . . . may have significant direct economic effects which . . . may properly be taken into consideration' (Shihata 1991: 70–71). Among the 'political' issues Shihata identified as being within the remit of the Bank were civil service reform, legal reform, accountability for public funds and budget discipline. This was a somewhat narrow conception of good governance. However, and importantly, it provided the crucial impetus for those within the Bank who wanted to push the Bank to take governance issues more seriously. Since the early 1990s the definition of non-political has been expanded even further. In 1995 the General Legal Counsel argued that it was 'appropriate' for the Bank to advocate to member governments that they use 'participatory approaches' in the selection, design, implementation, and evaluation of development projects because it 'enhanced development effectiveness', and that it was legitimate for the Bank to advise governments to allow and foster a strong civil society that can participate in public affairs.[7] Again, this was important for providing an internal legitimacy to good governance concerns.

In terms of the operational aspects of the Bank's work there have been a number of important changes. As noted above with regard to the Comprehensive Development Framework and the PRSP process, governance issues have been given a much higher priority in the day-to-day activities of the Bank in its dealings with borrower countries. This is reflected in increased lending for governance reforms. In 2001 lending for public sector reform accounted for 14.5 per cent of total Bank lending, up from 3.7 per cent in 1997 (World Bank 2000a). There has also been a higher priority given to governance issues in terms of the organisation of the Bank. In a major reorganisation in 1997 a 'Public Sector Group' was created to focus the Bank's work on governance issues such as anti-corruption, civil service reform, legal reform and decentralisation.[8] This led to the creation of a World Bank strategy for improving governance in its borrower countries. It also led to a more focused recruitment strategy designed to bring staff with expertise in governance issues into the Bank. Finally, we would also stress the significant role that the then president of the Bank, James Wolfensohn, played in promoting the governance agenda within the Bank.

Intellectual influences

The most significant intellectual or academic influence on the acceptance of good governance was what we can broadly label as 'institutional economics'. Put briefly, institutional economics argues that the crucial variable in development is the institutional structure of a society. It is this structure that establishes norms of behaviour, creates property rights, and enforces contracts (North 1990). This view became increasingly accepted within the Bank during the 1990s, and was a vital component of the triumph of good governance, because it supposedly provided a theoretical rationale for the Bank to take governance issues seriously (Picciotto 1995; Klitgaard 1995). In 1992, a World Bank report on good governance argued that 'without the institutions and supportive framework of the state to create and enforce the rules, to establish law and order, and to ensure property rights, production and investment will be deterred and development hindered' (World Bank 1992a: 6). The best-known exponent of institutional economics, Douglass North, spoke several times at the World Bank, and in one instance said to the Bank, 'we can never say we'll just let markets work, as if markets grew on their own'.[9] The recent concern with good governance in the PRSP process is based on the view that 'governance refers broadly to the exercise of power through a country's economic, social and political institutions in which institutions represent the organisational rules and routines, formal laws, and informal norms that together shape the incentives of public policy makers, overseers and providers of public services' (World Bank 2006).

The appointment of Joseph Stiglitz as the World Bank chief economist in 1997 further bolstered this shift towards institutional economics. One of Stiglitz's main theoretical contributions to economic theory was to show that under conditions of imperfect information, and hence imperfect markets, governments could undertake interventions that were welfare-enhancing. He argued that this analysis 'completely undermined the standard theoretical basis for relying on the market mechanisms' (Stiglitz 1996: 156; Greenwald and Stiglitz 1986). He earlier (1989) stated that there was always a critical catalytic role for the state in development. The practical challenge for the Bank, then, was to find ways to create the kind of state that could undertake these interventions effectively.

One part of this overall concern with institutions that deserves special note is the concern with 'culture'. Traditionally the World Bank had shied away from saying anything about its borrower countries' cultures. During the 1990s this changed, at least with regard to Africa. Between 1992 and 1994 the Bank spent US$1.25 million on a research programme on culture governance and 'indigenous' management practices in Africa. It also held several conferences and published a number of papers (Serageldin and Taboroff 1994). While there is still a certain amount of reticence on the part of the Bank about the idea of culture and its impact on development, the logic of this concern is clear. If institutions, in the broadest sense, shape norms of behaviour, then cultural norms might shape the possibilities for development. And, of course, the implication of this is that cultural institutions that the Bank deems to be standing in the way of development should be dismantled.

The global context
The unquestioning acceptance of good governance among development agencies is partly related to the dominant place that the World Bank itself has among these agencies in setting the terms of the development discourse (Williams 1993). But it is also related to broader shifts in international politics. There is a great deal that could be said here but we will limit ourselves to observations that seem particularly pertinent to making sense of the governance agenda.

It is generally agreed that the Cold War gave many countries some room for manoeuvre as between the two superpowers and their junior allies. It also legitimated some elements of global pluralism in the social systems of sovereign states, thereby making intervention in their internal affairs somewhat problematic (though of course it did sometimes occur). The dramatic shift in the correlation of forces since the end of the Cold War has allowed not only Western states but the 'intergovernmental' agencies they control (essentially, all of them) to begin the imposition of their own agendas on the rest of the world. Much of this is driven by processes of globalisation, the dynamic for which emanates almost entirely in the West. On this protean issue we will allow ourselves the summary assertion that globalisation itself is to be seen as a project, rather than as a set of naturally occurring processes (Young 2002). The key points are clear. The Great Powers, all sorts of squabbles notwithstanding, are prepared to subject themselves to a series of increasingly demanding regimes regulating their international transactions. It is not controversial to suggest that the formulation and imposition of these regimes requires states that are capable of imposing and managing the processes of social change that such regimes increasingly require. This in turn generates a class of states that cannot, will not, or are reluctant to comply: in Duffield's striking image, the 'borderlands' (2001b).

It is in this context that the sovereignty of poorer states is no longer seen by the major states as pragmatically useful in managing inter-state relations. But while sovereignty may be eroded, historically legitimate means of dealing with the borderlands, at least in the form of colonialism, are no longer ideologically available (though, of course, some liberals harbour a nostalgic fondness for them).[10] Thus emerging systems of global governance, increasing contempt for states outside these systems and the illegitimacy of forms of direct rule have enhanced the readiness of a variety of forces in the West to intervene in the internal affairs of such states.

Three forms of such intervention can be briefly identified. The first is an increasing willingness to impose all sorts of conditionalities, including political conditionalities, on states hitherto regarded as sovereign (Williams 2000). The European Union's (EU) relations with its associated African, Caribbean and Pacific (ACP) countries clearly exemplify such shifts. Whereas before 1990 the EU's relations with the ACP countries were shaped by trade and development considerations, the treaties from Lome IV onwards (1990) began to prescribe political conditions. These have been further formalised in the most recent

Cotonou Agreement, which builds in definitions of good governance. Under the trade and aid provisions of the new agreement, forms of aid such as price stabilisation mechanisms for exported commodities that had been disbursed unconditionally, have now been replaced by systems in which aid is allocated after an assessment of the degree of economic and political reform achieved by the recipient country.

A second essential shift in the contemporary era is the practice of 'humanitarian intervention'. The Great Powers have now used armed force or waged open war against states or political forces within states on a number of occasions in which 'humanitarian' motives have been claimed. It is common to dismiss these claims as bogus, as little more than a cover for other more traditional realpolitik motives, but this is a mistake.[11] The distinction between traditional state 'interests' (themselves never given and always subject to discursive construction) and ethical motives fails to capture the sense in which Western elites increasingly regard their interests as served by the forcible (when necessary) reconstruction of whole societies.[12] The shrill chorus of support for this amongst civil society, NGOs and 'progressive' forces gives the lie (as we suggested in our original article) to any notion of a deep disagreement between Western states' elites, multilateral agencies and self-proclaimed civil society groupings. This is clearly indicated by the widespread usage of post-conflict processes as the intervening forces face the dilemma of withdrawal or further involvement in the target states' internal affairs.

There are, however, political constraints on such violent incursions and political risks in participating in them. Their justification to domestic constituencies may involve large-scale mendacity (as in the ongoing war against Iraq) which comes to haunt its promoters (and their claques in academia and the media), and their legitimation in terms of human sympathies may run up against the notoriously fickle limitations (and ignorance) of Western public opinion. These difficulties have prompted a third form of intervention which may be called the construction of 'reform coalitions' or, if we want to recall the historical precedents, the reinvigoration of modernising elites. Western agencies have not hesitated, of course, and especially not since the Cold War, to engage in various ad hoc pressures on ruling elites, most usually requiring them to concede open elections, but this has been subject to various political hazards and lacked consistency and continuity (S. Gibson 1999; Brown 2001). These experiences have promoted a readiness to commit long-term support to elite groups within certain countries who are deemed to have internalised the liberal project agenda (Hanlon 2002a).[13] This support is aimed at certain sections of the bureaucracy, notably the ministry of finance and the political elite more generally. The latter have benefited from huge flows of resources not merely to keep their state afloat (Uganda relies on external finance for 50 per cent of its budget), but also to fuel their own accumulation strategies. It is a reasonable surmise that, for all the talk about transparency and accountability, this is regarded by the Western powers as a price that has to be paid, at least in certain cases, for the reconstitution of the domestic modernisers.[14]

Liberalism and the practice of good governance

All these shifts in the global political climate have brought to the fore policies and practices designed to effect social change within states but without direct political control. Governance may be taken now as a general slogan that stands for this raft of techniques. It remains, however, to look at these techniques more closely and, although there is room to deepen our account of liberal theory, we find it useful to continue this analysis by reference to the state, civil society and the self, and the links between these.

Reform of the state

Within that theory the problem of the state is that it must be both weak and strong. Weak because, on the one hand, the state is purely an enabler, little more than a neutral mechanism providing security to allow free, equal individuals to pursue their life projects unhindered by others. In this understanding a strong state is a potential threat to free persons. These threats are twofold. Firstly, the state may attempt to impose some particular social order, which will invariably embody some set of values, which constrains people's freedom. Secondly, incumbents of the state may abuse its offices (and the stronger the state the greater the possible abuses). The way to counter these threats is to institutionalise some form of accountability and historicity. As a general tendency, this has taken the form, firstly, of a universal legal code to which state officials are also subject, and, secondly, a complex of institutions now generally referred to as 'liberal democracy' and comprising universal suffrage, political parties, rights of political participation and so on.

But this is only half the story. The other half is a series of arguments requiring that the state be strong. The strong state must be disengaged to a certain extent from social interests and certainly not be overwhelmed by them. It must be capable of imposing and maintaining a certain kind of social order, essentially a liberal capitalist order. Far from being merely accountable to social interests, it must be capable of ensuring that only the right kind of interests are in play; indeed, in terms of the European experience it is not implausible to suggest that the state itself is committed to the constitution of social classes as a new form of social order. In this half of the story it is quite impossible for the liberal state to be neutral and indifferent to values; rather, it must actively interfere in what people believe and how they live, even to the extent of inculcating certain kinds of values and dispositions. Such elaborate processes of transformation of both 'structures' and 'values' require not a minimalist state, but a state constituted in the form of an immense bureaucratic apparatus with all the necessary capacity for fine-grained social surveillance and social control.

These endless ambiguities about the state, accountable but not captured, autonomous but not oppressive, neutral but interventionist, are well illustrated by the extensive literature on the 'Third World' state. Here it seems that the state is always either too strong (too oppressive, too corrupt, too brutal) or too weak (captured, penetrated). These ambiguities are not to be resolved at the purely theoretical level. Rather they can only be made sense of in terms of a political project. There is no a priori set of rules dictating how 'weak' or 'strong' the state must be; rather there are sets of developmental 'problems'. Some require that the state be 'stronger' and some that it be 'weaker'. For example, the state must be made capable of raising tax revenue in order to fund development, but the way that it spends this money must be open to public scrutiny.

The World Bank's attempts to reform the state in Ghana precisely illustrate these tensions. From the early 1990s onward the World Bank undertook a number of projects that directly targeted the functioning of the central state in Ghana (see World Bank 1996b). All of them were animated by the desire both to constrain the state and to make it a more effective instrument of government. Put schematically, there are four elements to the ongoing reform programmes: limiting the realm of state action; increasing the accountability and transparency of the state; clarifying and codifying the role of the state; and enhancing state capacity to govern.

In terms of limiting the realm of state action we see the familiar themes of privatisation and reducing the size of government. An ongoing 'capacity-building' project has as one of its objectives the privatisation and/or commercialisation of nearly 200 government-owned or government-controlled agencies, ranging from the Ghana University Press and the national theatre to the Ghana Tourist Board (World Bank 1999b: 73–77). The stated aim of the project is to create 'an efficient public sector' (World Bank 1999b: 8). In the realm of accountability and transparency the World Bank is pursuing a host of initiatives. In the project just mentioned there is specific provision for 'private sector' representation on the boards of public organisations (World Bank 1999b: 7). In a recent public financial management project there is funding to improve the participation of civil society and other 'stakeholders' in the area of economic management. The project also supports capacity-building activities for the media so that 'it can effectively play its watchdog role vis-à-vis the fiscal and economic activities of the government' (World Bank 1999b: 3–4).

The Bank is also engaged in attempting to clarify and codify the role of the state. According to the Bank, the state in Ghana suffers from a lack of clarity about the mandates of its agencies and their relationships with one another, and a lack of rules governing the use of human and financial resources (World Bank 1999b: 4). The project supports a programme designed to 'remove duplications and overlaps, develop new missions and roles, and realign functions' within the state. It will also attempt to introduce 'performance-based management principles' for some public services (World Bank 1999b: 7–8). Another project supports the implementation of a new institutional framework for Ghana's revenue-raising agencies (World Bank 2000d: 3). The final component of state reform is that targeted at making the state better able to govern its population. For example, a project in the late 1990s was focused on the development of a 'Tax Identification Number' system for all taxpayers. Along with the introduction of computerised tax records, this will enable the state to collect information and monitor the compliance of taxpayers (World Bank 1996b: 8–9).

Engineering 'civil society'
Structurally similar ambiguities plague liberal notions of civil society. Despite the ludicrous pretensions of much social science to identify 'civil society' as those forms of order between the state and the family, it is plain that (leaving aside the formidable difficulties about public and private) this notion is entirely enmeshed in liberal presumptions about the 'right kind' of civil society. One liberal story has a civil society of private interests, whether played out in 'the market' or the 'public space', as endlessly dynamic as the state is inert, and in which the pursuit of private interest is the public interest. But another liberal story tells quite a different tale. Far from being a cold realm of compulsions and 'laws' of self-interest, constantly threatened by a reversion to barbarism, it may be understood as a realm of freedom for organised groups, a zone of communal autonomy, a space where citizens may freely associate in pursuit of multiple and unselfish ends, including that most unselfish of ends, the interest of all. In fact, of course, both the 'interests' the market requires, and the dispositions to make a society of interests work, are the objects of ceaseless liberal craftings, which, while not invisible in the heartlands of liberal capitalism, are plain to see in the 'borderlands', at least those under Western hegemony.

There the groups that are to be encouraged are those that represent modern liberal modes of association, particularly in the economic arena. The forces that are to hold the state to account are those that demand liberal political and economic reforms. Thus in a review of civil society groups in Zimbabwe the Bank identifies those civil society organisations 'which play a critical role in representing citizens on social, political and economic issues'. These include trade unions, gender-based organisations, consumer organisations, ratepayers' associations, vendors' associations, and human rights' groups (World Bank 2002a). These are all liberal modes of association. They are groups bound together in terms of either their interests (trade unions, vendors, ratepayers) or their commitment to liberal ideas (human rights' groups).

Lending policies are also informed by the desire to construct liberal forms of associational life. A recent project in East Timor is designed to 'empower' local community groups (World Bank 2002e). It provides for capacity building at the local level and the development of local radio services. One of its aims is to develop principles such as 'accountability, transparency and inclusion' at the local level (the Bank argues that these principles are 'new to most communities' in East Timor) (World Bank 2002e: 4). As part of this, communities will be encouraged to debate and discuss local government structures. The local radio component will 'inform, educate and entertain', and empower the community by 'giving a strong public voice to the voiceless' which will encourage 'greater accountability in public affairs'. This will also have the added advantage of maintaining the independence of the media (World Bank 2002e: 7, 9). In addition to encouraging communities to recognise and act on principles such as good governance and 'inclusion', the project also directly targets the form and composition of these local groups. They will be encouraged to use money they can access through a trust fund 'efficiently and effectively'. To ensure financial probity local groups will be provided with bookkeeping training. To encourage public scrutiny a 'Bill of Rights' will be disseminated to villagers explaining their rights to information and access to details of projects to be funded. The 'existing village leaders' are to be 'treated with respect' but 'encouraged to refrain from intervening' in decisions. The participation of women is to be encouraged (World Bank 2002e: 19–22).

Remaking the self

A set of tensions about human nature is at the heart of the liberal project, the obsessive analysis of which informs much of modern European social and political thought.[15] From this immense body of reflection we can identify two recurrent themes. The first is a tension between nature and culture. Liberalism's ruthless dismissal of all other positions as less than universal commits it to the recurrent search for firm foundations, whether found in 'nature', agreement or reason. At their most deliriously optimistic liberals tell us that true morality, 'already dwells in natural sound understanding and needs not so much to be taught as only to be clarified' (Kant 1997: 10). But in their deepest despair the search for foundations is plagued by a constant fear that nature may not suffice, that nature or deliberation or contract may not produce the 'right' result. Liberal reason must forever stand guard against this possibility. The second is a tension in understandings of (universal) human freedom. As is so often the case, two tales are told. One tells of the person driven by insatiable desires, which only he or she can know, moderated only by his or her understanding that all others are the same, and that they must agree on some ground rules to avoid mutual destruction. This person wants nothing but to be liberated from 'oppression' and then be left alone in the glory of personal freedom. But a second tale doubts that 'a democratic society can flourish if its citizens merely pursue their own narrow interests' (Audi 1998: 149). The tellers of this story are not persuaded of the centrality of preferences partly because the assumed endogeneity of preferences seems sociologically implausible; because welfare and preference satisfaction can be seen as different things; and, most importantly, because for them the value of freedom is to be understood rather as an autonomy that 'requires both the possibility of satisfying my desires and the possibility of standing beyond them' (Fleischacker 1999: 77) This universal person cannot live on desires alone but needs social participation, virtues and reflexivity.[16]

Contemporary liberal social science has been understandably coy about the grim business of changing selves and not always very theoretically literate as to the ambiguities of the liberal self (for acute discussion of changing selves, see Kelsall 2003). For these reasons, as we noted in our original paper, tracing these connections remains a difficult task, but the indications are there. There are occasional general pronouncements that indicate some acknowledgement of issues of self-formation. As the then chief economist at the World Bank, Joseph Stiglitz, has remarked, 'in the end, the transformation of society entails a transformation in the way *individuals* think and act' (1998c). And there is confirmation in certain aspects of the project work that the Bank undertakes (see Williams, Chapter Three in this book). For example, a project in the Philippines supports 'capacity building' for rural communities (World Bank 1996a). The aim is to enable the project beneficiaries to become 'farmer entrepreneurs'. To enable this, local communities will be provided with credit and financial management training and made familiar with 'commercial practices'. Similarly, in Ghana the Bank funded a project designed to make people see the relationship between 'services rendered and tariffs charged' (World Bank 1994b). Again, in the Philippines, the Bank funded a project that aimed to develop the ability of cooperative organisations to understand the cooperative as 'an economic enterprise' and provide knowledge of marketing, credit provision and resource mobilisation (World Bank 1995d).

Conclusion

We may conclude by suggesting that the triumph of good governance within the World Bank, and the shifts in international politics that have contributed to this triumph, have made the kind of analysis we provided in our original article even more pertinent. Looking back over some twenty years, in which the Bank's actions have become more and more obtrusive, it is clear that there has been a twin-track attempt both to weaken states (in certain sorts of ways) and to strengthen them (in other sorts of ways). This approach must be seen as a *project* – though, of course, one shaped by many contingencies, the international political situation, and the policy shifts of Western states and elites being only the most obvious. Yet through all these exigencies, the trajectory of the Bank, and latterly those of other international institutions, illustrates how this project has expanded and diversified from a narrow focus on economic growth to a concern with structures of governance. The project now embraces programmes of social reconstruction that in their scale and aspirations (if not yet in the political will and the resources committed to them) are paralleled only by nineteenth-century colonialism and the post-war occupations of Germany and Japan. Despite the dismissal of these efforts in certain quarters little evidence is offered that they are going to recede. They are complemented, indeed, by a growing amount of private sector involvement in this new civilising mission that goes far beyond 'development' in any of the conventional senses and (let us use the robust language of the colonial era) whose 'ultimate object is moral improvement'.[17]

It is important to stress the flexible and adaptive nature of liberalism as a political project. As a recent World Bank document put it: 'We need to start with a thorough understanding of what exists on the ground and emphasize "good fit" rather than any one-size-fits-all notion of "best practice"' (2002c: 17). We take statements such as these seriously. They suggest that we should indeed understand the World Bank as engaged in a project. The Bank clearly has a particular vision for the future of developing countries; and we have argued that it is a liberal vision. But the Bank is also aware of the need to consider the specificities of particular countries in order to pursue this project successfully. The Bank has moved away from simply imposing reforms on states. It has done this because it does not think that this is a particularly effective way of getting the reforms it wants. Rather, the Bank has recognised that the successful pursuit of the liberal project requires paying attention to the particular challenges that particular countries pose.

But in this, of course, the Bank has done no more than rediscover, as liberals are fated to rediscover, what it always knew; that human actions are shaped by beliefs and customs and the endlessly variable ensembles of these inscribed in obligations to real communities of social relationships across many dimensions, and that the persistence of these necessitates that people must in fact be reshaped to fit a liberal order; that neither self-interest nor autonomy, much less 'the individual', exist in any simple sense, waiting to be liberated or otherwise, but rather must be inculcated and habituated. And finally, that the endlessly ingenious devices of liberal theory which strip out the concrete characteristics of actual people in actual societies are less a cunning of reason and more a programme of social and political transformation, their role not so much to instantiate impartiality as to preserve the fiction (as necessary to its protagonists as to its objects) that the appeal of liberalism is still an appeal to all, if only as they would be rather than as they are.

Notes

1. The original quote was from the then new Bank president, Lewis Preston, as quoted in the *Independent on Sunday* (London), 10 May 1992.
2. Charney (1998); Chambers and Kopstein (2001); and Goodin (1990) provide pointers to liberal debates and anxieties on these matters.
3. See Serageldin (1990) for a sense of these debates.
4. We should, of course, remain sceptical as to the extent and type of 'participation' that the Bank encourages. See Fraser (2003).
5. For a discussion of the report and its preparation see Wade (1996b), reproduced in this book as Chapter Nine.
6. The Bank still considers these to be important components of good governance, but after the 1997 crisis there seems to be less confidence that they were actually manifested in the East Asian case. See World Bank (1998b, 2000c).
7. 'Prohibition of Political Activities in the Bank's Work', legal opinion to the Bank's Board of executive directors, 12 July 1995.
8. See World Bank, http://www.worldbank.org/publicsector/index/cfm. Accessed 28 November 2004.
9. Douglass North, transcript of a speech given at the World Bank, February 1994.
10. Various forms of quasi-control of weaker states were common in the nineteenth century and are being rediscovered today, for example, NATO protectorates, not to mention contemporary American efforts in Iraq.
11. This is a common position on the Left, of course, because the Left largely shares the liberal agenda and is reduced to impotent complaints about the good faith of its implementation.
12. Were large chunks of the humanitarian intervention literature not more or less a cognitive void it would hardly be necessary to make this embarrassingly obvious point. But see Paris (2002) for a not dissimilar argument.
13. Our argument parallels, and draws on, that of Harrison in Chapter Twelve of this book. For fascinating detail on a particular case, see Kelsall (2002).
14. Hanlon overdoes the argument but provides excellent material for reflection.
15. We hope that readers will forgive the necessarily summary nature of our assertions here. We are in no doubt that for more than three centuries the formulation of liberalism has attracted some of the finest minds in Europe.
16. The World Bank's recognition of the importance of 'social capital' can be understood in this way. See, for example, Knack (1999).
17. Sir Charles Grant (speaking in 1832) quoted in Mehta (1999: 30, Note 52).

Chapter Eight

Sail on Ship of State
Neoliberalism, Globalisation and the Governance of Africa

David Moore

THIS IS A SLIGHTLY ALTERED VERSION OF AN ARTICLE PUBLISHED IN *1999 IN* JOURNAL OF PEASANT STUDIES *27 (1): 61–96.*

Sail on, sail on
O mighty Ship of State!
To the Shores of Need
Past the Reefs of Greed
Through the Squalls of Hate
Sail on, sail on, sail on, sail on.
Leonard Cohen, 'Democracy is coming to the USA'[1]

Contrary to many claims, the 1997 *World Development Report: The State in a Changing World* is no radical departure from neoliberal development principles. Rather, it marks the culmination of the World Bank's gradual move away from crude anti-statism to its 'good governance' discursive efforts to 'get the state right' in its quest for a solution to the post-1970s development crisis. This chapter examines *The State in a Changing World* from within the Bank's discourse on the role of the state and its managers, and current academic discussions of the Third World state and globalisation. It is difficult for these realms of discourse to construct a hegemonic vision of development in the current conjuncture – particularly while the Bank remains hostage to private capital markets. Perspectives on the role of the state with deeper than Hayekian neoliberal roots must go beyond the contradictory mélange of anti-statism and managerialism which make up the current discourse of 'neo-statism'. However, such alterations take place within much larger realms of transformation than analyses such as the 1997 *Report* consider.

The World Bank's annual development reports are marked with much media hoopla, but have no direct policy implications. As such, they can be judged as a combination of global propaganda, markers of ideological shifts and measurement within the multilayered international institution itself, and textbook-like primers for the implementers of World Bank and IMF policies around the world – be they technocrats employed by those institutions, the national politicians and bureaucrats implementing the conditionalities imposed in the name of structural adjustment, or university development studies students. In this context they can be judged as the World Bank's signals of public relations and intentions – of hegemonic construction and maintenance. Their analysis can serve as heuristic guides to the Bank's policy practice and, as Robert Wade has put it in his incisive study of the Bank's *The East Asian Miracle* (World Bank 1993a), its politics of 'paradigm maintenance' (Wade 1996b and Chapter Nine in this book).

Africa is probably the continent most under the influence of the World Bank, and is likely to be subjected even more increasingly to the World Bank's gaze and attempted control – as Wade quotes a senior bank official, 'now the East Asia study is completed, the research agenda lies more in Africa and other developing countries' (Wade 1996b: 30). This may be even more the case now, as during the Asian financial crisis the Bank seems to have been swept into the role of social welfare agency, political bell-wether and 'good cop' while the IMF took on the job of stern taskmaster in that region of the global political economy. *The State in a Changing World* looks very much like the culmination of the official's promise to concentrate on Africa. This alone would suggest that students of African political economy and development examine the *Report* closely.

Just as importantly, the 1997 *Report* admitted that some countries' 1980s efforts to create a minimalist state 'sometimes tended to overshoot the mark' (World Bank 1997b: 24). (Note that the World Bank accepts no blame for the 'radical shift in perspective' in the 1980s.) This might indicate a move away from fundamentalist neoliberalism and a serious rethinking of the (African) state. As Ray Bush (1997: 506) has put it, the publication of the 1997 report suggests that 'there may be a glimmer of hope in sight that at last the previous 20 years of World Bank fundamentalism is wavering'. If John Gray is right and in a decade no one will admit having been a neoliberal (1998b), the 1997 World Bank *Report* may indeed look prescient. *The State in a Changing World* just may be the latest step – following the 1989 *From Crisis to Sustainable Growth* document on Africa, which ushered in the 'good governance' discourse, and the 1993 report on the 'miracle' – in the World Bank's move away from the worship of the free market.

The 1993 study, marked by a mammoth struggle between its Japanese sponsors and teams of Anglo-American-trained technocratic writers on the Bank's staff, comes off as a defence of laissez-faire principles in the face of much evidence in favour of statism; but the evidence does lead us to see that the hegemonic mechanics of paradigm maintenance can add up to clear evidence of 'inconsistencies' (Wade 1996b: 33; Amsden 1994; Taylor 1997: 147). As Berger and Beeson (1998) suggest, the report on the 'miracle' was an attempt to 'assimilate' the NIC experience into the neoliberal worldview. However, Gramscians know that hegemonic attempts to neutralise ideological challenges do result in slight changes to paradigmatic fundamentals. The state-friendly incongruities remaining in the 1993 report even after many attempts to wipe them out could suggest that the terms of the debate had widened

> without generating a backlash that would (have caused) the report to be dismissed as incompetent or ideological, and the Bank to be accused of changing its mind. The pro-industrial

policy statements, though at odds with the rest of the report, may function as attractor points by enabling those wishing to put new questions on the agenda to claim legitimacy from the *Miracle* study. This, it could be argued, is the most likely way that big organisations change their minds; sharp changes are rare (Wade 1996b: 33).

Is an early admission in *The State in a Changing World*, that some countries – and by implication the World Bank itself – bent the anti-statist stick too far, another step in Wade's stairs toward paradigm shift? Has the World Bank finally 'changed its mind'? Does the 1997 *Report*, in combination with its then Senior Vice-President and Chief Economist Joseph Stiglitz's apparent avowal of a 'Post-Washington Consensus' (Stiglitz 1998a; Biersteker 1995), portend a new, potentially social democratic, welfarist, or at least 'state capitalist' hegemony? It will be argued in these pages that, contrary to some journalistic comment in the wake of its publication (Denny 1997), the 1997 *Report* is not a U-turn from neoliberalism towards 'common sense' (Kaplan 1997). Nor is it an equivocal dispensing of grist for either pro- or anti-statist mills (Moore 1998).[2] Rather, it is a more sophisticated and 'constitutionalising' (Gill 1998) variation of the 'market-friendly intervention' discourse espoused in the late 1980s and early 1990s (Kiely 1998). However, as the World Bank's thousands of economists and advisers struggle towards a re-recognition of the role of the state in African development – in particular as the lessons of unregulated finance capital in Asia ripple through the Bank's departments (Stiglitz 1998a, 1998b) and many African states stagger slowly from crisis to crisis (Reno 1997, 1998) – *The State in a Changing World* may be seen as marking the space for significant change and innovative policy making from Africans themselves, *à la* Pádraig Carmody's suggestions (1998: 34–40). On its own, though, the *Report* does not veer far from the orthodoxies of the last few decades. It hardly appears to go beyond the Bank's tirades that 'there is no alternative' to government policies that stay within the bounds of 'strengthening the enabling environment for private sector development' (Wade 1996b:

35). However, its constant reminders of the difficulties of this process, and its advice to 'wait until the capability is right' may be a very slight advance on the past's seemingly eternal condemnation of intervention.

It should also serve as evidence that the Bank is not nearly as infallible as it might pretend, and that the task of attempting to maintain a single neoliberal voice in its multi-authored and interdisciplinary reports is becoming increasingly difficult. Its very confusion may indicate crisis. As neoliberal hegemony wears thin there should be more room for alternatives: possibly even reform that does more than bolster the status quo and goes beyond Gramsci's 'passive revolution'.[3]

Rather than seeing the glossy 1997 *Report* as signifying a radical shift in World Bank policy, then, we should see it as a culmination of trends in the past decade or so within the Bank, its associated multilateral financial institutions, and the international development community in general, marking recognition that 'the market' does not come about naturally and thus needs a strong, 'lean and mean' state to push it on unwilling subjects – including, ironically, many within the state itself. If the era of structural adjustment of the 1980s and earlier 1990s meant attempts to 'get the prices right' and to hack away indiscriminately at the state, then we are now in the age of 'getting the state right' to implement the same goals as before. The neoliberal aspirations have not been jettisoned, but there has been a recognition, long in the making, that they require a state more closely tailored to the requirements of the multilateral economists than has been produced heretofore either by the market or the earlier generation of modernisers. *The State in a Changing World* is very much about creating a new 'state class' (Elsenhans 1983), or at least reconstructing the old one.

Furthermore, if this attempt to remould the African state is not the last gasp of the neoliberal doctrine it may be the last hope for its consensual implementation. As Peter Gibbon notes, the World Bank's 'political economy' is but a marginal addition to its neoliberal nostrums, 'the main purpose of which appeared to be to save the model itself', going no further than ritualised condemnation of the 'patrimonial state', 'urban bias' and parastatals standing in the way of a deregulated 'enabling environment' for a civil society virtuously combining voluntarism and business (Gibbon 1996: 758; Beckman 1993). *The State in a Changing World* may only differ from that perspective in that it contradictorily wants the state to wither itself away through increasing strength. Even more paradoxically – and unhelpfully – it wishes that increasing virility to come through leanness, but offers very little to stop a lanky health from turning to emaciation. Thus towards the *Report's* end the cool sagacity of its rational-choice political economy and public sector management discourse disappears, replaced by Wagnerian overtures for leaders with 'clear' and 'compelling' vision, strong enough to engineer the 'leap of faith' needed to reshape 'the values and norms of the state and the state's relationship to the economy' (World Bank 1997b: 155–56). Its analysis of the most opportune moments for such leaders to leap into action seems rather romantic, if not reckless. They are to be times of external threat or economic crisis – 'when the normal rules of the game are in flux' – or during a new regime's honeymoon (World Bank 1997b: 144). One wonders if the Bank's hopes are with the Foday Sankohs of this world (Richards 1996),[4] the technocrats created in the wings of the African Capacity Building Foundation (D. Moore 1997), or if it imagines a creative unity of these two seemingly opposite forces.

Capability, role and 'universal public goods': Getting to the basics of capitalist construction

Between its admissions of excessive anti-statism and its revolutionary utopias, *The State in a Changing World* waxes and wanes on the political economy of matching state capability with role. Its prime conceptual innovation is its recognition that, yes, states should do things that the market cannot, but only if they have the 'capability' to perform these 'roles'. Thus states must 'match' capability and role. This sleight of hand allows the Bank to caution weak states to do very little until, somehow, they gain the capability to regulate and, sometimes, even make industrial policy. Thus the *Report* can acknowledge the success of industrialisation policies in the NICs (in a seemingly stronger sense than in the 1993 *East Asian Miracle* report), but advise weak states hoping to follow their example to hold their horses.[5] The train of such analysis would, of course, have advised the now-industrialised (albeit shaken by the 1997 crisis induced by finance capital) Asian countries, back in the 1950s and 1960s, that their states did not have the capacity or capability (it is not certain that the Bank's substitution of the word 'capability' for the recently favoured term 'capacity' has any real consequence) to perform the tasks that we now know were relatively successfully accomplished, albeit under a heavy authoritarian hand.

In the meantime, however, the *Report* advises its readers to concentrate on the 'universal public goods' of property rights (that is, the creation of the market, or universalised private property relations – in other words, the commodification of everyday life). Thus the second component of the Bank's analysis is the stern admonition that the most basic task for the state is the establishment of the *'pure public good'* of property rights. It is as if that is the holy grail from which all blessings will flow. If the state can 'get the property rights right', its main task will be done: it will have blended its society in with the 'single world marketplace' that the *Report* sees as an 'international public good' of equal provenance with world peace, a sustainable environment and 'basic knowledge' (World Bank 1997b: 131). In the early days of neoliberalism, the goal was 'getting the prices right'. That did not perform the transformative trick, so now the task is the infinitely greater one of creating the legal and institutional bases of a fully capitalist society (Leys 1996a). The *Report* forgets that this process has been going on for centuries now, fails to mention the crippling debt regime, poor terms of trade and over-reliance on a few agricultural or primary commodity exports, and simply announces that nirvana will arrive with some legal and constitutional adjusting – and the necessary enforcement mechanisms of 'law and order'. The old 'cultural' lags to modernisation seem to be replaced by legal ones, although in one slip of the tongue 'traditional forms of governance' do get blamed for state failure (World Bank 1997b: 162) – but it is not clear if 'traditional' means pre-capitalist or pre-structural adjustment. The 'simple institutions . . . the most basic underpinnings of markets . . . ranging from land titling and the collateralisation of movable property to laws governing securities markets, the protection of intellectual property, and competition law' are listed as the priorities beside 'the protection of life and property from criminal acts' (World Bank 1997b: 45) to make a seamless web of commodification and authority, or the market and 'law and order'. Somehow, the elimination of crime and the implantation of capitalist legal structures have become one and the same, and all can be accomplished by a state that magically matches 'capability and role'. There is hardly a word about the complicated economic – let alone historical – sociology necessary to begin to analyse, let alone facilitate, such a fortuitous combination (M. Moore 1997). The unstated assumption is 'revolution from above'.

It is only after emphasising the priorities of property rights and a 'non-distortionary policy environment, including macroeconomic stability' (World Bank 1997b: 4, 27) that welfarist or infrastructural issues such as 'control of infectious diseases, safe water, roads . . . protection of the destitute' (1997b: 27) and the environment (1997b: 4, but not 27) are tacked on as 'pure public goods'. The *Report*'s assuredness of the primacy of legally enshrined property rights and orthodox macroeconomics is emphasised by its hesitation to include social goods in its first category of public goods. At times, for example, protection of the environment slips into an 'intermediate function' for the state (1997b: 27). The *Report* stumbles over the idea that schooling and health should be the domain of the state. In education, it recommends that where all-out privatisation is not feasible, 'vouchers, contracting, and similar mechanisms [can provide] the bridge between the public and the private sector' (1997b: 54). On health, it claims that 'curative health care is a (nearly) pure private good – if government does not foot the bill, all but the poorest will find ways to pay for care themselves' (1997a: 53). Ultimately, the World Bank's idea of the ideal public good is the unified world marketplace and all other goods must be incorporated within it. The way to get there now is by getting the law right, not just the price.

If *The State in a Changing World* is an admission that the state will not be moulded into shape simply by following the logic of the market as hammered into existence by structural adjustment's array of liberalised and devalued currencies, reduced health and education services, pared-down parastatals, slashed consumption subsidies, opened-up imports, dizzying debt repayments[6] and truncated tariffs, then it is more a reflection of the roots of Hayekian neoliberalism than a signal of new endeavours in statecraft and political economy. It is wrong to think that neoliberals oppose 'the state'. As Richard Cockett (1995: 113) reminds us, for Hayek the state was needed to *promote* and *enforce* the market, competition, and prices – primarily through the legal order. Besides inadvertently coming close to suggesting that it is not 'natural' for humans to be competitively oriented, this notion is much different from laissez-faire, which may be more akin to J.S. Mills's idea that 'the abandonment of all harmful or unnecessary state activity was the consummation of all political wisdom' (Cockett 1995: 113). It would seem as if Hayekian liberals were of the opinion that people had to be forced to be free. For them, an ever-vigilant state is necessary to create a market order (which in the Third World has affinities to the process of primitive capital accumulation), as well as for maintaining it by legislating means to stop such phenomena as oligopoly and monopoly – and keeping trade unions weak. As Peter Evans (1995: 23, 16–17) tells us, the root and branch anti-statism in development discourse came only with the 'neo-utilitarians' who opened up the 'black box' of the state to find out that it produced an environment in which it was 'illogical for incumbents to behave in ways that were consistent with the common good', because 'state involvement would produce an economically stagnant, politically stable symbiosis between officials with the capacity to create rents and private actors anxious to take advantage of them'.[7]

However, as Evans goes on, although this cynical mode of analysis 'wip(ed) out the possibility of naïve faith in a naturally competent and benevolent state with ... elegance and vitriol', it did not offer much in its stead. Its assumptions slip too quickly from the neoclassical economists' 'assertion . . . that competitive markets will result in short-run allocative efficiency to the much stronger assertion that (they) are sufficient to produce the kind of structural transformation that lies at the heart of development' (1995: 22). As if recognising this shortfall, people in the World Bank began looking for new ways out of its dilemma almost as soon as they began implementing structural adjustment policies assuming the demonic nature of the state. As early as 1985, one of the gurus of structural adjustment was telling his masters that life was a bit more complicated than the current nostrums had led them to believe: Elliot Berg advised that 'the whole ruling class or élite was at issue', invoking Frantz Fanon, Paul Baran and René Dumont in his cause and outlining a long-term strategy of change that went well beyond the bounds of 'economics' per se (Berg and Batchelder 1985: 24).[8] This was the germination of the 'good governance' discourse that crept into World Bank public praxis by 1989,[9] and has culminated in the 1997 *The State in a Changing World*.

Ideology as the solution to the neo-statist paradox

The *Report*, then, is the result of a paradox. Laissez-faire is no solution to the problems of underdevelopment, yet the state cannot be trusted as it once was – in spite of the fact that Peter Evans's Weberian-statist *Embedded Autonomy* and three other works are in the *Report*'s bibliography, and, as will be shown below, it has some affinities with his later work.[10] Yet once the state's utility is grudgingly admitted, neoliberals have to find a way to limit its activities to those of stimulating (or – to raise a problem out of the realm of neoliberal or even Weberian thought [Wood 1995] – inventing) the market and maintaining competitive order, "'supplement(ing competition) where, and only where, it cannot be made effective'" (Hayek, in Cockett 1995: 113). The state must be stopped from 'intervening' in what is assumed to be the separate realm of 'the economy' (Wood 1995) – unless it is absolutely necessary. Therein lies the rub. It is now admitted that the Third World state is necessary, but still it is not trusted. How can it be made to police itself? This intellectual cul-de-sac could be labelled 'neo-statism'. The only way out of it is through the very narrow, nearly hidden and perhaps even illusory, alley of ideology. This can, as all theorists of complex 'superstructures' know, be rather maze-like.

This contention can be bolstered by Hayek's invocation of Keynes's perhaps idealistic – and egotistical – invocation of the economist's role vis-à-vis the education of a governing class faithful to the needs of liberal capitalism:

> the ideas of economists and political philosophers, both when they are right and they are wrong, are more powerful than is commonly understood. Indeed the world is ruled by little else. Madmen in authority, who hear voices in the air, are distilling their frenzy from some academic scribbler of a few years back. I am sure that the power of vested interests is vastly exaggerated compared with the gradual encroachment of ideas. Not, indeed, immediately, but after a certain interval; for in the field of economic and political philosophy there are not many who are influenced by new theories after they are twenty-five or thirty years of age, so that the ideas which civil servants and politicians and even agitators apply are not likely to be the newest. But, soon or late, it is ideas, not vested interests, which are dangerous for good or evil (Hayek, in Cockett 1995: 112).[11]

Mechanical materialists may dismiss this notion as romantic, but Hayek and his apostles took it seriously. The resulting institutions did create enough of a 'hegemonic alternative' to Keynesianism to ensure that with Reaganism and Thatcherism the Right had an answer of sorts to the intellectual dead-end marking the end of the post-Second World War golden age of capitalism in the 1970s. *The State in a Changing World* can be analysed in the light of a similar long-term struggle for ideological hegemony on the role of the Third World state – of getting its managers to think right. The time may be propitious for a shift in tactics to that end. Perhaps the authors of this tract think that nearly two decades of anti-statist neoliberalism and structural adjustment policies have brought them into the realm of hegemonic 'common sense', so it is safe to re-introduce the subject of the state into polite conversation. Today 'the market' seems to be accepted by all except Marxist mastodons and Polanyist pretenders as the best way to organise social life, so the Bank can now appear to relent from its neoliberal push, while simultaneously being alert to its mission of 'educating the educators'. It can admit that states do a lot of things that markets cannot do, even allowing a grudging admission that some East Asian states might deserve a mite of credit for their developmental roles (although the next annual report may retract that, given the recent bursting of the bubble – it may be easier to blame state sloppiness than too much laxity at the level of international finance). The state can now be ushered back in, if we are very careful not to burden it excessively. But as opposed to the so-called 'planning state' of the 1950s and 1960s, this new state, matching capability and role, will be the market's 'partner, catalyst and facilitator' (World Bank 1997b: 1). If we are to believe the words of the 1997 *Report* the Bank has finally reached a happy compromise between the excessively statist days of early development economics and the mistaken enthusiasm of the laissez-faire-leaning structural adjusters of the 1980s.

As well as being rooted in the paradox of needing a state to guard against its own excesses, this slight shift may be propaganda based in the paltry changes in attitude reflecting political alterations in the Anglo-Saxon world from which the Bank takes most of its cues: in the mid-1990s our ideological leaders were Clinton and Blair, not Reagan and Thatcher, so as the kinder policies of New Labour and Demi-Democrats trickled down to the Third World Fukuyama's end of history seemed not so bad after all: his 'liberal democracy' was closer to that of the baby-boomers' 1960s than the Victorian style of the Thatcherites. We could feel warm and fuzzy about a post-neoliberal-postcolonial state, supposedly returned to the pleasant Keynesian mixed economy mode of policy making and ushering in a world in which civil(ised) society could thrive. World Bank President James Wolfensohn can appear to be more concerned with poverty alleviation and 'sustainable development' than his more iron-willed predecessors, and more the leader of an inclusive 'Knowledge Bank' than the single-minded economic taskmasters of the recent past. Perhaps he was attempting to recreate the halcyon days of Robert McNamara.[12]

Before going too far down this road, however, it must be remembered, as Richard Cockett tells us in his chronicle of Hayekian hegemony, that the policies of Clinton and Blair were firmly in the mould of the 'new (neoliberal) political economy . . . ruling orthodoxy' (1995: 6). Furthermore, there are few indications that the new generation of Anglo-Saxon rulers have made a substantial impact on the socio-economic inequalities marking their societies, let alone most of those in the purview of the World Bank's mandate. Perhaps, then, the state has to be re-invoked, if for no other reason than to have an institution upon which the misimplementation of otherwise praiseworthy policies can be blamed (George and Sabelli 1994: 142–61). The World Bank can now say that the economic policies it knows and loves can be successfully imposed when the 'Third World state' is in shape: it is girding itself for the Keynesian/Hayekian battle for the hearts and minds of a new political generation entrusted with the task of creating that perfect conglomeration of institutions and power relations.

For 'globalisation' (not to mention the extraction of raw material, cheap food and docile labour as usual) to proceed apace, the peripheral state must be a willing and competent 'partner'. International coercion is an inefficient means to that end, and the demise of the Cold War has eroded the moral certainties that accompanied that era's intervention in the name of defending market liberty (while often bolstering markedly less than libertarian politicians in the name of that larger public good which would, of course, lead to political freedom in time). If the Third World state cannot be coerced into the role of enforcing competition (although, ironically, it may have to implement a substantial amount of coercion over its own society to perform such a task [Bernstein 1990]), and if, contrary to the desires of the most fanatical of laissez-faire neoliberals, the job will not be done by the forces of global competition if the state withers away, some sophisticated political science must be employed for the task of policy persuasion.

This is what the 1997 *Report* signifies. At first glance, it might seem to mark little difference from the early days of capitalist modernisation ideology and practice, with some of the rhetorical flourishes about basic needs thrown in from the early 1970s. However, the difference between what could be called a 'neo-statist' version of the modernisation motif and its first, post-Second World War manifestation is marked by the rational-choice/neo-utilitarian notion of the state which has supplemented the older liberal one: it still rests, albeit more uncomfortably than in its original, full-blown phase in the late 1970s and early 1980s, on the basic assumption that most occupants of the state are rent-seeking hangers-on, as opposed to the earlier belief that most state actors were honest brokers capable of planning and managing the emergence of peripheral capitalism.[13] *The State in a Changing World* is the result of more than a decade of World Bank attempts to come to terms with the paradox that in neoliberal thinking the state is an entity on the verge of being a monster, but at the same time is necessary for the establishment of capitalist legal and perhaps even cultural norms at the root of the market – and *may*, in exceptional circumstances, even play a role in economic growth and industrial development (World Bank 1997b: 61 ff.). Thus, as if to remind the potentates of power of the eternal risk of Third World state corruption, the *Report* is peppered with lines such as:

> ... the difficult job for reformers will be not only devising the right kind of reforms but *combating the deep-seated opposition of those with a vested interest in the old ways*. Matching role to capability means shedding some roles, including some that benefit *powerful constituencies*. Proponents of a more capable state will quickly discover that *it is in many people's interests to keep it weak* (1997b: 28, emphases added).

> Policies that are bad from a development perspective are often highly effective at channelling benefits to politically influential groups. Many macroeconomic problems – inflation, exchange rate misalignment – are in fact *covert ways* of levying unexpected taxes on the private sector or of redistributing economic benefits (1997b: 49).

Civil servants in many countries view their pensions as an entitlement, rather than a form of savings: they make limited contributions to a retirement scheme but receive a full salary as pension after thirty to thirty-five years of service . . . Or, as in some African countries, public bureaucracies direct towards themselves resources intended for social insurance or for vulnerable groups (1997b: 58).

Since independence in 1971 the government of Bangladesh has effectively doubled in size . . . from 450 000 . . . to almost 1 million in 1992 – a compound rate of increase of 3.6 per cent a year, compared with population growth of 2.5 per cent (1997b: 86, Box 5.3).

. . . the state has often become a massive source of jobs, with recruitment based on connections rather than merit (1997b: 93).[14]

Given this entrenched suspicion of the state, the task for neoliberal policy makers who have to come to grips with the need for such an institution is to create a very small corps of committed managers who will be paid well enough to satisfy their always insatiable worldly desires, and to offload the rest of the public service to the private sector. Interestingly, this 'private sector' sometimes includes non-government organisations competing to perform services for the state and official development agencies – and, 'unlike public providers, NGOs are not obliged to cater to the general needs of the population; this makes it simpler for them to provide services of a particular type and quality to specific groups' (1997b: 114). In other words, NGOs are not accountable to states or the general citizenry, so they are available for hire by the Bank and its partner agencies (Nelson 1995). The discipline of the market will force the former public employees to realise their wants via the road of vigorous competition rather than bureaucratic lassitude. Former state workers, ranging from garbage collectors to teachers, will have to compete to offer their services for the reproduction of globalised capital and its new ruling classes (be they in the private or public realm). Their 'facilitators' who have managed to hang on to the state will be 'world-class', with globally competitive salaries – truly members of Robert Cox's 'transnational managerial class' (1987: 359–60, 367–68) or Leslie Sklair's 'globalising bureaucrats' within the transnational capitalist class (1997: 521, 527–28): 'competent and reputable technocrats' such as 'Chile's group of high-level advisers – the Chicago boys – and Indonesia's Berkeley mafia and Thailand's gang of four' are cited as examples worth their weight in the gold of high wages, 'recognition, appreciation, prestige and awards' as they implement structural reform (World Bank 1997b: 83, 91–96).[15]

This is a concept of the state that is markedly different from the one that was prevalent in the 1950s and 1960s. There are at least two factors in its expression in *The State in a Changing World* that should alert us to its neoliberal modalities. Firstly, as discussed above, Third World states should not take on roles for which they have no capability. States' roles must 'match' their capabilities. As these capabilities are very vaguely defined, it is easy for the World Bank advisers to prescribe (and proscribe) 'roles' of their choice. This is certainly not a prescription for the expansion of state activities, and in many cases it is a recipe for shedding many of them. Yet, beyond creating a new state class, the cookbook is not clear on how to build up the state's capability so it can perform even the roles outlined as necessary – aside from reliance on the market (which, paradoxically, has yet to be fully created, so the 'international community' has to help at times) or NGOs to produce the resources upon which the state may rely at some time in the future.

Secondly, if the state is to intervene it is only to establish the 'pure public good' of property rights: a capital-friendly legal and institutional framework will be the foundation of transformation. After the property rights are right, the state will wither away.

The State in a Changing World is nothing if not recognition that this job is a hard one for the state, and it is clear its tasks cannot be left to 'the market' when the market is apparently not yet there. To go back a few years in the history of international advice on state making, it could be said that Samuel Huntington's *Political Order in Changing Societies* has returned with a vengeance – but this 'new order' is much more economically precise than his, not one with institutionalisation as an end in itself, and not one encouraging corruption (Huntington 1968; Remmer 1997). Perhaps the Bank is harking back even further, to the glory days of a state which Ernest Gellner has eulogised: an 'absolute (state) which was not all that absolute' – one that

> respected law and property (due to) ... a service aristocracy whose loyalty was bought by the security of its property and privileges ... This was the baroque state's most significant feature ... In its shadow, an independent civil society emerged, not supine, ready in due course to take the state to account and able to do so (1994: 85–86).[16]

If the World Bank can make the state in this image, its job will be done. Not only will the state be perfect, but it will change the nature of civil society so that it too mirrors the desires of the American dream.[17] This is the essence of the primary 'role' of the state – to metamorphose itself with the help of the 'international community'.

Of course, *The State in a Changing World* is not so cavalier as to forget the state's roles other than narcissistic self-transformation, including macroeconomic stability (first among equals). But as noted above, once these essentials are covered the authors of the *Report* seem to have been unable to decide on the priorities of anything other than paying the top civil servants enough to bear the risks of paring the state down to the optimum match between capability and role. Human resources and infrastructural investment seem to have equal parity with defence, good roads, protection of the never-quite-defined poor (Felice 1997: 107) and 'vulnerable', and the environment (World Bank 1997b: 40). The ordering of the basics secondary to property rights changes from page to page (on pages 26–27, the 'pure public goods' include defence, law and order, macroeconomic stability, control of infectious diseases, safe water, roads, and protection of the again unclearly defined destitute). The reader is carefully disabused of the notion that the state should be the sole provider of many educational, health and welfare functions (1997b: 27, 51–60). These are no longer 'basic needs' as they might have been defined in the past. As for the functions that could be performed by states with more capability than the average Third World one, they range from the 'management of externalities' (pollution, for example) to monopoly regulation, social insurance and keeping an eye on the banks. Finally, states with 'strong capability' can do the East Asian type of thing – promote markets with industrial and financial policy (1997b: 27). To be sure, to take a benign perspective on the priorities listed in *The State in a Changing World*, many of the states under consideration might not be badly advised to concentrate on some of the old Bank concerns such as building roads and schools and making provision for safe water. However, when states borrow money for such things this spending is liable to signal profligacy rather than 'credibility' and 'commitment' to the reinforcement of 'weak' domestic institutions, which 'stabilisation programs with the IMF . . . can help' (1997b: 60; compare Hanlon 1996). Better, then, to leave these to the market or NGOs. The weak states are damned if they do and damned if they don't.

It is little wonder, then, that *The State in a Changing World* spends few pages deliberating on how to build more and better roads and waterworks. These 'basics' are left to the side to leave room for the political and ideological fundamentals of governmental restructuring and its 'sequencing'. (In any case, it is a myth that 'project lending' does not involve policy restructuring: electric power projects being conditional on massive restructuring of pricing and subsidies, for example [Cahn 1993].) After laying out its version of the 'essentials', the *Report* issues its advice for state renewal and capability enhancement, ranging from tips on how states can 'cultivate the best and the brightest' (1997b: 94) to balancing questions of the state's 'precise role in regulation and industrial policy' (1997b: 61) – with a bias towards 'competition, voice and self-regulation' instead of too many regulations in the sphere of state–market relations (1997b: 71). It quickly becomes apparent that aside from ensuring a solid core of these best and brightest in the state's divisions of macroeconomic policy – through, for example, the Africa Capacity Building Foundation (D. Moore 1997) – most of the advice in *The State in a Changing World* amounts to 'wait until you've got more "capability" – if indeed you *really* want to do anything at all'. With regard to regulating environmental hazards, we are told that relying on 'public information and citizen participation' can be more effective than 'formal rules' (1997b: 66). If the citizens are not informed, so be it. Along the way, the reader is reminded as often as possible that most things – ranging from education to health and social insurance – she or he has assumed that the state can do, the market can do better. In the realm of industrial planning, 'leapfrogging' comparative advantage with too much infant industry protection could be 'fatal to . . . chances of achieving sustainable industrial development' (1997b: 72). Even decentralisation, at first breath extolled as a fine way to spread responsibility and participation, is cautioned against because the bureaucrats at the top of the hierarchy might 'lose control over the macroeconomy as a result of uncoordinated local decisions' (1997b: 110). Local accountability is fine, as long as it does not challenge the 'order' of the newly trained ruling group. To be brief, just about every word of advice in the *Report* is against increasing the role of the state, except for the institutions within it that will get it and keep it on the road to a centralised capitalism compatible with the only slightly altered 'Washington Consensus'.

The very generalities of the 1997 *Development Report* make it hard for the reader to guess whether or not its authors really think the members of the societies of which they write are primitively pre-capitalist or merely already existing individualist entrepreneurs frustrated (or seduced) by the ever-creeping state. If the former, the task of transformation is a huge one. As such, it is widely skirted, looming only quietly in the background under the basic unstated assumption that humankind is naturally individualistic and capitalistic. This enables a big problem to be avoided: the ways in which non-capitalist societies articulate with colonial-capitalist state structures can be left alone by making them appear irrational (or 'rational' only for 'vested interests' and thus irrational from the point of view of the 'public interest') and beyond the Anglo-Saxon pale. As Gellner (1997: 91) indicated, these values may be peculiarly American. They proclaim the 'historically eccentric' libertarian variants of Enlightenment values as 'self-evident'. Other societal values, or the long and violent struggles to heave them aside, are 'not within the realm of the imaginable' for the heirs of settler colonialism. But they represent a particular view of history. If, as Gellner asserted (and to which much of the World Bank's development discourse alludes, but does not admit) the 'problem of politics . . . is how does one escape from such (non-liberal) societies?' such an overt worldview is singularly ill-equipped to tackle it. Neither better managerialism nor better markets will do the trick. Nor, probably, will more democracy – not that the report has much to say on that question, other than that the jury is still out on the relationship of democracy to economic growth (1997b: 149), and that even formal elections 'without the necessary safeguards' – needing a strong central state or lots of international election observers, we suppose – are fraught with 'political interference . . . electoral fraud' and often misrepresent minorities (1997b: 112; compare Abrahamsen 1997; Robinson 1996; Saul 1997).

In the recent past, the closest such ideologues came to the admission that entrepreneurial behaviour is not natural was to suggest that it might take an 'incentive' or two to encourage its blossoming. Presumably the World Bank now thinks that if 'getting the prices right' is insufficient for economic take-off, the right sort of state can now get the incentives to enter the market right. If it cannot, there are plenty of clauses in the *Report* allowing for intervention in the form of 'international cooperation': the imperial consultants from the Washington belt will still have an abundance of work to do. Making states strong is no easy task. Sometimes, the sovereignty of 'quasi-states' (Jackson 1990; compare Inayatullah 1996) must be quelled in order to do it, especially now that it is not states in general that are the problem, but only certain kinds of state.

Thus the idea that the Third World 'primitives' need to be remade remains underneath the ostensible assumption that they are really Anglo-Saxons at heart, needing only liberation from old traditions and only partially newer states. Tinkering with states may appear to offer a solution to a task overladen with a Conradian horror from which World Bank economists have to recoil – and so they do. If 'making capitalism' is little more than the devastating process of primitive accumulation, and development economics is about producing wealth without appearing to hurt people, then the producers of intellectual capital such as the annual 'development reports' are faced with an acute dilemma. It must be rather difficult to advocate the violent restructuring of society to politicians, bureaucrats and development workers devoted to peace, order and the quiet pursuit of the nexus of liberty and wealth.

Yet the alternative view of the question of 'how capitalist are the people of the Third World?' is even tougher. If the task of primitive accumulation is assumed to be largely accomplished, with most of the world's peoples proletarians or small commodity producers and most property 'private', then the fact that most people are poor and most countries are relatively (and some absolutely) poorer than they were at the beginning of the age of development (Arrighi 1991; Castells 1998: 70–128), exposes at last the flimsy basis of the myth of capitalism as an equitable system of producing and distributing wealth.[18] If this is so, the problem is that the capitalist global system of the production and distribution of life chances is not a universally beneficial one. That might be worse for the apostles of world capitalism than the possibility that the construction of capitalist societies involves the shedding of blood along with 'tradition'. However, both these problems are ignored in favour of technicist musings on the question of restructuring the institutions of the state.

Within the constraints of that focus, there is still the predicament about whether the World Bank thinks the Third World does not deserve the state because it is not 'ready' – that is, not capitalist enough, so that the normally benign state becomes corrupted with the patron–client politics of kinship and ethnicity – or if the democratic state in and of itself is dangerous even in a fully capitalist society[19] and the neo-utilitarians' perspective simply becomes aggravated in societies structured by scarcity. The *Report* vacillates between these views, just as it does between the larger ones of whether or not the state is good or bad for liberalism in general. These questions, too, are sidestepped by concentrating on the exigencies of determining how the lines should be drawn between role and capability. Having resigned itself to the intransigence of the state (and indeed its growth in the West, in spite of neoliberalism [1997b: 2, Figure 1]), the Bank has consigned its scribblers to the task of damage limitation – keeping the banking system relatively clean, clearing the decks for polite competition, silently fostering a liberal civil society from above, establishing better tax collection modalities so that the locals can pay for this new global servicing class, etc. – under the illusion that the state can shed the messy task of capital accumulation by paying its managers a sum worthy of developmental referees, umpires, and nightwatchmen.

Thus *The State in a Changing World*'s stolid if unenthusiastic efforts to maintain a rational and optimistic tone about the future of the Third World state leave it with a slight semblance of schizophrenia. Its technocratic veneer is often imbued with lyrical fancies. Lack of concrete strategies for creating a better state is belied by a seemingly bracing fresh wind of advice on how to create *esprit de corps* (1997b: 92) among state cadres as the Bank expounds the relative merits of 'mandarin versus meritocratic' models of recruitment and promotion (1997b: 94). Its sections on the problem of transforming the state from the benighted condition of low capability and taking on too much to the nirvana of high capacity – while doing very little – veer between dry advice and the romantic overtures about state managers with the 'right stuff' at the right time mentioned above (1997b: 5). Its vacillations between cool rationality and visions of revolution illustrate the difficulties inherent in taking Berg's advice about creating a new ruling class.

It may be charming to see global technocrats relying on the romanticism of 'political will', but it is not good political analysis. It certainly crumbles when it grapples with predatory and collapsed states

(Duffield 1998; Mbembe and Roitman 1995; Reno 1995, 1997). As for corruption (Chapter 6 in the *Report* and now a very public Bank–IMF concern [Szeftel 1998]), if stopping subsidies, getting rid of price controls and liberalising imports does not solve that problem, the white knights from Washington will clear it up, too – especially if it gets too unpredictable (the businesspeople surveyed to make up the basis of this *Report* were not averse to *predictable* corruption [1997b: 99, 101]). As with most of the rest of the *Report*, the sphere of corruption makes a good excuse for paving the road to recolonisation. In spite of calling for a strong domestic state, *The State in a Changing World* promises an increasingly dependent one. With its advice, most Third World states will tend to stay that way.

The state in a changing world and globalisation

Consistent with efforts at 'modernisation' since the end of the Second World War, the missionaries of global development are still trying to re-invent the European state on *terra nova*. The 1997 representation of this effort resembles Gellner's memories of the previously cited perfect transitional state in early Europe: the *not quite absolute* absolute state complete with its loyal and well-looked-after 'service aristocracy' (1994: 85–86). Gellner and the World Bank share a desire to have their states and eat them too: to have a state that somehow will create a civil society in the bourgeois image; a state that is, ironically enough, strong enough to evoke a society in its likeness, but ready and willing to be called to task by it (Beckman 1993). Gellner had the courtesy to refer to Perry Anderson's Marxist *Lineages of the Absolutist State* (1974) for this ideal type of transitional state, but even he neglects to add Anderson's qualifier that in many cases rather than the 'service aristocracy' being 'bought by the security of its property and privileges' it was actually the aristocracy qua aristocracy that bought its offices in the bureaucracy. Thus in many senses of the word this class's 'security' was already established in a feudal society, and rather than diminishing was being buttressed by the purchase of structured influence in the emerging capitalist state. This looks remarkably like the 'corruption' and the 'privatisation of the state' by ruling classes losing their moorings in the old modes of production and trying to gain them in new ones in the Third World (Bayart 1993).

It is not hard to conclude that 'corruption' has had a key role to play in the evolution of advanced capitalist states just about everywhere: in seventeenth- and eighteenth-century England, for example, in Tom Paine's birthplace of Thetford, the Dukes of Grafton 'dispensed a rich harvest of patronage in the form of salaried jobs, tenancies . . . licences, building contracts, and provisions for elections and charity dinners (and) elected themselves (b)y purchasing votes and distributing favours . . . the going rate for a Thetford vote was fifty guineas' (Keane 1995: 14).[20]

The State in a Changing World even admits to historical corruption in the USA, quoting Mark Twain to that effect (1997b: 102). I wonder if the supposedly aberrant behaviour of early state makers parallels capitalist development everywhere, and if the Bank's reluctance to admit its functions is similar to the queasiness about the violence of primitive accumulation. Why should we expect early forms of capitalist democracy in Zambia or India to be different from those expressed in other parts of, and at other times in, the world? Corruption in the West is generally considered to have had beneficial effects for national economies: the North American railroad barons who influenced politicians to lay down the tracks in their interests usually had their interests in the same country, and the industries they linked up added to the process of national capital accumulation. In much of Africa, though, a good proportion of the capital of corruption is invested a long way away. Capital flight, which in conservative reckonings accounts for about a third of African public and private wealth (Bond 2006a: 50), can be recognised by the World Bank because it can be attributed to wilful rent-seeking behaviour. Still within the Bank's *weltanschauung*, the US$165–200 billion which individual Third World investors placed in international financial markets from 1975–85 (Hoogvelt 1997: 84) can be seen as a rational response to less than propitious investment climates in their own countries: with more World Bank/IMF medicine, this logic goes, the trend could be reversed and the halcyon days of the beginning of this century could return.[21] Yet given the dependent dimensions of their situation in the global economy, the forms of corruption would be expected to be more extreme than in the West; and, worse, perhaps not 'productive' in the long term.[22] But dependency (Blaney 1996), or any other concept alluding to Africa's exclusion from the benefits of classical capitalist development, is not even alluded to in *The State in a Changing World*.

It is the notion of dependency that alerts the reader to structural issues of the historical insertion of African state-society complexes into the political economy of global capitalism, and thus to debates on the nature of the relation of African states to the current phase of globalisation and their possibilities of getting development off to a start in this era. Ankie Hoogvelt's theory that a whole new post-1970 'post-imperialist' phase of the Third World's exploitation can be conceptualised not as global *expansion*, but as the era of global *implosion* and debt peonage, in which the transfer of economic surplus from South to North through the repayment of debt and its interest is occurring instead of the late-nineteenth-century export of Northern capital in the form of the railways, port infrastructure and the like, is not amenable to the Bank's worldview (Hoogvelt 1997: 17, 50, 84).[23] If, as she says, at the end of the 1980s the totality of Third World debt was equivalent to one-third of its GDP, then this 'legitimate' transfer of capital is of devastation equal to the more corrupt and less official transfer from the least savoury peripheral regimes. Furthermore, if this is all part of a global trend in which the 'fictitious capital' with which only 800 million people have a chance to play is more important in macroeconomic terms than the real stuff of roads and railways (not to mention food) which the other 4.2 billion need (Hoogvelt 1997: 83) then global trends seem negative from the perspective of the popular classes of the Third World. Closer to the issue of the Bank's concern with the African *state*, if the only way the international financial community can guarantee the repayment of the international private liabilities of African elites is to 'nationalise' them, but public debt might increase the power of the state over that of the national/comprador bourgeoisie (Hoogvelt 1997: 52),[24] then it is no wonder that the international financial institutions want to get the state classes on the Hayekian side of hegemony. If the state can be made to look responsible for the whole mess in the first place, its delegitimation and subsequent redemption through 'good governance' can proceed apace (George and Sabelli 1994: 142–61).

It is in this context that discussion of the role of the World Bank and the implications of *The State in a Changing World* can proceed under the rubric of the debate on globalisation. Regardless of whether or not the world economy is more or less globalised now as opposed to the end of the nineteenth century and whether more or less 'stateness' accompanies global integration (Weiss 1997; Hout 1997; Mann 1997; Shaw 1997), most discussions on globalisation and development take for granted the benefits of export orientation and more trade. They wonder only if more or less, and what kind of, state activity facilitates a positive insertion in the global political economy (in other words, for foreign direct or portfolio investment, local capitalist activity which will fit into the global market, and/or simply more efficient resource extraction methods). As Gregory Albo (1997) (speaking more of advanced capitalist countries than of those on the periphery) summarises, most of the debates on globalisation assume that 'even if there is a margin of manoeuvrability for national economic policies . . . this is merely a question of further building "extra-market institutions" to manage the new conjuncture as capitalist markets have proven their greater inherent efficiency and dynamism'. Yet neoliberals are making huge efforts to reduce even that narrow margin: the rules of the World Trade Organization and the idea of the Multilateral Agreement on Investment (be it a stand-alone agreement or one melded into the statutes of the WTO) allow for little scope for Third World state action. Thus there is little but a managerial role left for the Third World state if it is to follow what seems to be universally proclaimed as the inevitable path.

Thus the 1997 *Report* leaves the World Bank in a public sector training/state-building role while the IMF administers fiscal discipline. What are the chances of this *slightly* interventionist stance broadening if the deregulated nature of the global financial markets creates further crises? If the IMF's bad press during the Asian crisis is indicative of more dissension in the future, at the most comic level an engaging 'good cop-bad cop' scenario could be pursued by the two Washington institutions.[25] If our fancy were allowed to speculate even further on such melodrama, the World Bank – or some of its sections – might even take on the biases of the domestic capitalists.[26] As Luiz Pereira (1995) has noted, the Bank seems to be in a perpetual 'identity crisis', lurching from cause to cause and ideology to ideology as it guards its institutional prerogatives, placating both the Keynesians and Hayekians in its ranks while simultaneously trying to keep up with the hegemonic shifts accompanying global accumulation strategies, peripheral class formation and the whims of American presidents. *The State in a Changing World* could be interpreted as a document produced with the purpose of allowing the World Bank some latitude if the boundaries of globalisation ideology change.

Theoretical perspectives on the state in a changing world

It is these extra-institutional parameters that have to be analysed if we are to come to terms with the World Bank's role in the global political economy and the function of its annual ideological barometers. To that end there are a number of theoretical perspectives on offer. The most overarching of them is that offered by the Foucauldians, who see the World Bank and similar institutions contributing to the eternal and depoliticised bureaucratisation of the modernist world as the power and knowledge nexus of regulation and discipline creep around the globe, regardless of ideology (Escobar 1995; Ferguson 1990; Kiely 1995; Mitchell 1988; Mohan 1997). This view shares similarities with a more populist/anarchist perspective which sometimes appears to have affinities with a deep laissez-faire tendency, as articulated by Gavin Williams's comments (1995: 291) that 'the World Bank is generally criticised for favouring "free markets" over "state direction"; in practice it should be criticised for compromising with, and even promoting, state bureaucracies' (but see his earlier [1994] comments for a more complex view). This perspective may denote a global 'social movement' of bureaucrats, both in institutions such as the Bank and in the internationalised apparatuses of national states, but it is a sterile and apolitical one not apparently linked to a process of capital accumulation; specifically the dispersal of transnational capitalist cadres (Sklair 1997). At their extreme such perspectives lead to a condemnation of all states as potentially 'high modernist' destroyers of all that is spontaneous and good, as seems to be the trajectory of James Scott's gently anarchist *Seeing Like a State* (1998) – an analysis that would be vastly improved if linked to the imperatives of uneven development in peripheral forms of capitalism (or turned, in the international arena, to institutions such as the Bank, the IMF, and other agencies portending to promote what Cowen and Shenton [1996] suggest are the processes of 'immanent development'). If there is a hegemonic process in these perspectives, it is the very broad one of a repressive Western modernity, going far beyond the mundane Gramscian variations of socialism or capitalism, let alone neoliberal or Keynesian, laissez-faire or state-capitalist, globalist or regionalist, or financial or industrial capital varieties.[27] Indeed, it hardly need worry if the process is productive of poverty, pollution, or prosperity so long as it is seen as conducive to self-regulating and technocratic governmentality.[28] Thus, as Frankel (1997) concludes, some 'Foucauldians are in danger of appearing as the indirect apologists for neoliberalism', because, aside from bureaucratisation and 'discipline', the material consequences of capitalism (or even 'Westernism') and its variations are as ethereal for them as the illusions of resistance and repression or coercion and consent (compare Janmohamed 1995).

The merit of such all-encompassing analyses rests on the fact that the World Bank seems more successful at facilitating global bureaucratisation than at being an agency conducive to the eradication of relative and absolute poverty or the creation of a productive form of capitalism. However, unless we are an 'anti-developmentalist' more concerned with preserving the (often romanticised) sanctity of pre-capitalist, non-Western, or 'autonomous' modes of life than the universal value of alleviating poverty and ensuring sustainability, we cannot condemn rational-bureaucratic means of organising such efforts in and of themselves. This is barely more defensible than criticising states and their bureaucracies on the grounds that they inevitably breed corrupt and rent-seeking behaviour. One view sees all states as stultifying products of the iron cages of enlightenment and the other sees them as paralysingly parasitic. However, neither the state nor its bureaucracies – nor the regimes of knowledge, truth and power they generate and are generated by – are inherently 'evil': their ethical qualities depend more on the social and economic forces working in and around them than on whether or not they are products of the enlightenment (Nussbaum 1995). To understand those forces, a materialist analysis of global processes seems better than the postmodernist ones. Perhaps it is ironic, however, that recent indications of World Bank directions indicate a Foucauldian move. If James Wolfensohn's memorandum (1999b) on the Bank's post-millennium project is indicative, it seems that in the wake of failed structural adjustment programmes and a 'second-fiddle' image in the Asian financial crisis, the 'Knowledge Bank' is attempting to control (or at least coordinate) the whole gamut of international development activities through the construction of a panopticon-like grid of surveillance available to all who have access to the World Wide Web. In the age of diminishing resources for 'social development' this may be the essence of leadership in that realm.

As Colin Leys puts it (1996a: 43, 195; 1996b), to get at the nub of development theory we must ascertain the workings of the global political economy. The Bank does not seem to be doing that, any more than it attempts to analyse the specificities of the African state–society complex. Instead it works in terms of eternal neoclassical truths and performs what Wade (1997: 9) has called the 'Gramsci effect (it builds up a constituency of sympathetic officials and politicians who believe in its development strategy, partly by training them in its Economic Development Institute)'. Thus it can be effectively analysed within Cox's (1987; 1996) 'neo-Gramscian' mode of analysis on the hegemonic variabilities within the world system. Given that the current hegemonic struggles as reflected and refracted in dominant academic and agency development discourse (Moore 1995) seem to revolve around statist and free-market dichotomies – List versus Smith; Sen versus Bhagwati; Japan versus the US – this is the best realm of contention within which the contradictions of the World Bank's public musings can be analysed.

As such, we should use Wade's (1996b) mode of analysis of the World Bank's 1993 report on the East Asian 'miracle' to study *The State in a Changing World*. Without the benefit of fieldwork in Washington, though, we can analyse some recent academic reconsiderations of the Third World state's role to see if state-friendly 'inconsistencies' are filling the cracks in academic thinking on the Third World state's future prospects, and to situate the 1997 *Report* within this academic discourse. The mainstream theoretical attention devoted to the developmental role of the Third World state in the context of its relations to the world economy veers between the sceptical and the optimistic. Perhaps it is suitable that summaries of these perspectives appear in the fiftieth anniversary edition of *World Politics*, a conventional journal which has included some influential American perspectives on development in the past, few of which would be antithetical to the World Bank's political ideology. For Karen Remmer (1997: 48, 51–52, 58) it is ironic that increasing theoretical attention is being paid to the Third World state at the same time as its ability to alter developmental trajectories is diminishing. As she puts it, the 'new institutionalism' in Third World studies encouraging us to look at the 'cohesion, autonomy, administrative capacity, and societal linkages of state actors' pretends that the international pressures and structures have disappeared as 'key factors' just as they are becoming more important than ever. The beleaguered Third World state is prevailed upon to get its act together 'precisely when economic constraints have drastically narrowed the range of feasible policy options'. For Remmer, such a 'formula is reminiscent of Huntington's managerial perspective on development and is anything but theoretically compelling'.

Peter Evans, though, contends that in spite of the globally dominant *ideology* of state eclipse, states are not disappearing. However, such an ideology can have negative effects on what states do, and thus in times of crisis make statelessness 'a potential institutional reality' by making

> responses to a genuine crisis of state unrelentingly negative and defensive. The danger is not that states will end up as marginal institutions but that meaner, more repressive ways of organising the state's role will be accepted as the only way of avoiding the collapse of public institutions. Preoccupation with eclipse cripples consideration of positive possibilities for working to increase states' capacity so that they can more effectively meet the new demands that confront them (Evans 1997: 64).

Thinking positively, Evans suggests, may be all that is needed. His concerns are similar to those of *The State in a Changing World*: they both seem to fear that the globalists' ideology of state redundancy is too 'untrammelled by anxieties over potential political instability' (Evans 1997: 71). By ignoring the usefulness of 'stateness' when it comes to the small matter of 'order',

> transnational capital could become an accomplice in the destruction of the infrastructure of public institutions on which its profits depend ... By the time state capacity is so reduced that the unpredictability of the business environment becomes intolerable ... reconstructing public authority could be a long and painful process, even an impossible one (Evans 1997: 73).[29]

Thus for Evans, as for the Bank's 1997 *Report*, if capitalism is to flourish the state must be made legitimate again: if so there could be a 'mutual empowerment' between the state and the good burghers of civil society. One fiscally frugal way to do this would be by

> engaging the energy and imagination of citizens and communities in the coproduction of services ... a way of enhancing the state's ability to deliver services without having to demand more scarce

material resources from society. The increased social approbation that comes with more effective, responsive service then becomes an important intangible reward for those who work within the state (Evans 1997: 86).

However, Evans notes, the 'scarce supply (of) the kind of capacity necessary to make the state a dependable partner in a strategy of state–society synergy' and the hegemony of neo-utilitarianism 'ha(ve) solidified into a domestic political climate that makes engaging with the state as an ally seem far-fetched' (1997: 86), so otherwise charitably inclined denizens refrain from volunteering their services to reinvigorate disenchanted bureaucrats and better their society. Thus if international institutions intend to assist in the revitalisation of the state they had better directly support the besieged state elites, a set of allies 'potentially much less ambivalent about the value of public institutions than are the business élites who constitute the principal pillar of the leaner, meaner state'. The NGOs, who according to Evans do not want a 'mean and lean state' (1997: 86–87), could possibly join these forces.

It is towards this end, we suppose, that we must interpret the incantations within *The State in a Changing World* for more material incentives and camaraderie for the top-rung state managers while they try to get services to some people without demanding resources from wealthier others (the Bank's solution to which is to privatise the provision of services). Imagine how their spirits would rise if they were granted a moratorium on the debts to which the Bank is ultimately bound.[30]

The similarities between Evans and the World Bank are stretched, however, when Evans alludes to a more complicated process of state regeneration than ideological alterations to be implemented from the World Bank offices. He notes that the 'private elites' (who have undoubtedly done quite well out of the last few decades of free-market praxis, and are bound to do even better when the wave of privatisation in Africa and Latin America *really* gets under way)[31] are likely to see 'any state–society synergy that involves subordinated social groups . . . as a threat' (Evans 1997: 86). Class analysis has thus arrived through Evans's rear door while the state was returning through the front. For the World Bank, the former portal stays shut (only rent seekers are allowed to have class consciousness) but the Hayekian fear of the plebeians getting something from the 'wealth creators' for nothing remains very loudly unspoken: the contention that 'unlimited democracy (becomes) agreement by the majority on sharing the booty gained by overwhelming a minority of fellow citizens, or deciding how much is to be taken from them' (Hayek, in Schwarzmantel 1995: 16) is a well-entrenched motif in *The State in a Changing World*. No doubt a strong state is needed to keep the hordes from opening the gates of power as well as from closing the gates of trade.[32]

It is here, then, that we must focus if analysis is to proceed on the relationships emerging among the processes of globalisation and state and class formation in Africa. In Zimbabwe, for example, to understand its current crisis we must tie these strands together to appreciate the impact upon the state's 'capability and role' of structural adjustment policies, ever-deepening currency devaluations and increasing inflation, private- and public-sector working-class action, a series of strident demonstrations and riots in the mid-1990s over issues of price and tax increases, the state's efforts to parley ex-combatants' demands for war pensions, intervention supporting the contemporary regime in the Democratic Republic of the Congo, the reinvigoration of almost-forgotten promises of land redistribution, an emerging black bourgeoisie demanding much in the way of state largesse, and a labour movement strong enough to start up a political party (Saunders 1997; *Mail & Guardian* 1997, 1998; Raftopoulos 1996; Bond 1998, 1999). In the midst of this economic and legitimation crisis, the Reserve Bank headquarters in downtown Harare – a potent symbol of the links between the local state and international finance – boasts an indoor shooting range. In the discourse of *The State in a Changing World* this could be considered an example of a spendthrift state class's riotous rent seeking. By contrast, we might imagine visiting World Bank or IMF officials (also rent seeking?) enjoying a shot or two while their local colleagues practise diligently, given that the results of their combined policies demand steely nerves, keen eyes and steady aims. In the end, this may be what the current discourse of the 'strong state' is all about.

If the World Bank's language about 'bringing the state closer to the people' (World Bank 1997b: Chapter 7) does not become more precise about the nature of these 'people' than to refer to them, on the one hand, as an undifferentiated public of the 'poor and the marginalised' and 'other groups', and, on the other hand, as more particularised but no less anonymous private 'individual users' and 'private sector organisations' (1997b: 110), it will not be of great assistance in restoring reciprocity to relations between states and citizens in peripheral countries. If it wishes to expand the notion of 'social capital' referred to so briefly (1997b: 114–16; compare Fine 1999)[33] and it concedes the need for Gellner's 'not so absolute state', it might go to the words of a liberal with a deeper pedigree than Hayek's. According to Tom Paine, the

> transition to republican democracy ... requires in particular the building up of welfare institutions catering to the social rights of citizens. The elderly, the widowed, women, newly married couples, the poor and the unemployed, disbanded soldiers, and children, who would be required to attend school, must all be provided with state transfer payments. These would be ... considered 'not of the nature of a charity, but of a right' (Paine, in Keane 1995: 303).

If the Bank would turn its attention to the conditions for the emergence of this alternative, based as it would be on a merging of state and popular civil society (Bond 1995) rather than the current alliance of state with transnational capital and its segments of global-capital-oriented civil society, we might see a more productive future on the world's horizons. A strong, transparent, accountable and generally honest state is more necessary for the enhancement and preservation of human rights than for the primitive accumulation of property rights.[34] It is harder to achieve, too, but until the World Bank and similar institutions are forced to admit that their articulation of universal interests is limited to the latter array of concerns, the path to a state in which capability matches (public) role will never open up – not even to invisible hands. In the last analysis, the definition of the state's role, and the interests it serves, has to change. Whether it can pass the reefs of greed to the shores of need depends upon the social forces changing those definitions and making them hegemonic.

On that score, it is quite clear on whose behalf the World Bank is attempting to construct consent. As James Wolfensohn himself said to the Lambeth Conference in August 1998 (Australian Broadcasting Corporation 1998), visibly shaken after viewing a video made by Christian Aid on the effects of structural adjustment policies introduced to obtain repayment of unpayable debts, it is very difficult to break out of the status quo when reliant on the private market for funds. In that case, is there any alliance of international institutions and African state formations willing to grasp the nettle and to '(superintend) the mass dislocation and conflict that would . . . (result) from a rapid programme of converting land and labour into commodities' – that is, the task that Leys says the colonial powers did not perform (1994: 44–45; compare MacWilliam, Desaubin and Timms 1995), a task that, given the current structure of the global economy in relation to Africa, can have no guarantee of success today (Bush and Szeftel 1998: 175–76)?

The most we can expect is small inconsistencies in the hegemonic strictures of global capital into which local alternatives may slip. In their absence, newly minted configurations take on the shape of the Sierra Leone–Liberia and Great Lakes–Congo metamorphoses at one end of the spectrum, and Zimbabwe and South Africa at another. Neither is well addressed by *The State in a Changing World*, which appears to be still trying valiantly to create an 'idealised liberal democratic state which cannot be observed in any real-life democracy . . . with a Promethean capacity for economic and social development' (Petiteville 1998: 116) like that of the 1950s and 1960s, but through lean neoliberalism and Hayekian neo-statism rather than Keynesian calculation: neither mode of analysis nor prescription are historical, sociological or political enough to be of much assistance to scholar or policy maker.

The World Bank: Development, Poverty, Hegemony

Notes

1. From *Stranger Music* by Leonard Cohen, © 1993. Published by McClelland & Stewart. Used with permission of the publisher.
2. The special *IDS Bulletin* on the *Report* (Evans and Moore 1998) containing this Epilogue is an incisive collection, ranging from radical NGO to centrist responses. Essential reading, it indicates that *The State in a Changing World* will play a large role in consulting and policy-making circles.
3. Joseph Stiglitz's Prebisch Lecture to UNCTAD (1998c: 3) may indicate that such a perspective allows intervention across more than just what he characterises as simply 'economic' dimensions: his 'new development strategy' advocates 'transforming *whole societies*' (his emphasis) in a classic modernisation perspective, embracing culture, psychology, political science and sociology rather than simply economics. For those fearful of a World Bank world state, such sentiments may be more worrisome than even structural adjustment programmes.
4. Lest this statement be misunderstood as to be supporting Kaplan's (1994) caricature of the Sierra Leonean Revolutionary United Front as the 'new barbarians', Richards's excellent study (1996) is recommended as an essential antidote: but see Abdullah and Muana (1998) for cautionary notes regarding Richards.
5. We should note, too, that exclusive focus on the states' roles in the NICs' industrialisation processes neglects the agrarian transformations that preceded and accompanied statist industrial plans (Shin 1998), not to mention the authoritarianism of most NIC states in their developmental phase.
6. It could well be argued that structural adjustment policies – the conditions imposed by the international financial institutions for the privilege of borrowing and renegotiating to repay the interest on debts – are merely means to ensure that revenue continues to flow from the Third World to the financial institutions of the First: it is an oft-repeated nostrum that more money flows from South to North in the form of interest on debt than from North to South in official development assistance and investment, and that the debt increases instead of diminishing. As Moody (1997: 70) puts it, Third World

    > debt to the banks of the North has been like a mortgage that never ends. As of 1994 ... debt stood at $2.5 trillion, compared with $906 billion in 1980, about the same time the Third World debt crisis first surfaced. This is an increase of over 250 per cent in spite of the fact that almost all new ... borrowing has been to pay off the initial debt, which in effect has been paid off many times over.

    This is even more devastating when we realise that the South's share of world trade is decreasing and that commodity prices have fallen by half since 1980, according to Wade (1996a: 67). Moody suggests that efforts of international trade unions to cooperate to cancel the debt and to ensure that the fruits of this endeavour would be 'constructively redistributed' would 'do much to bind the movements in these two parts of the world that capital has sought to play against one another'. The issues of the debt crisis and worsening conditions of trade are not mentioned in the 1997 *World Development Report.*

7. Note also Toye's (1993) oft-quoted recognition that the Left's criticism of the 'political classes' in the Third World in the 1960s and 1970s was paradoxically similar to this tarring process.
8. Berg was the author of the World Bank's 1981 guide to structural adjustment, *Accelerated Development in Sub-Saharan Africa,* commonly referred to as the Berg Report.
9. The 1989 *Sub-Saharan Africa: From Crisis to Sustainable Growth. A Long-term Perspective,* was the World Bank's first public recognition of this paradox, followed by a surge of 'good governance' publications such as the 1992 *Governance and Development* for the underlying political theory of which see Williams and Young (1994) and Chapter Seven of this book.
10. Interestingly, Wade's (1990) *Governing the Market: Economic Theory and the Role of Government in East Asian Industrial Reform,* is not in the bibliography, but a World Bank report he wrote on the organisation of irrigation canals is.
11. Such insights support and extend the arguments of Helleiner (1994) and Andrews and Willet (1997: 481, 491, 505) that the liberalisation of global finance is not at all 'beyond politics'. It should be noted that this quote was hung on the wall of the Institute for Economic Affairs, the think tank established in London to carry out Hayek's hegemonic battle against the Keynesians. For an excellent Gramscian analysis of this phenomenon – not cited by Cockett – see Desai (1994), and also George (1997) on American think tanks.
12. Wolfensohn was named 1997 Australian of the year by the national newspaper, *The Australian,* in a process involving an editorial committee selecting from a list of nominees sent by readers. *The Weekend Australian,* 24–25 January 1998, states on page 1 that his 'dedication to his task and his single-minded desire to improve economic conditions for millions of people around the world' convinced the committee to choose him. The article notes that his 'first trips to Africa saw him weep in shock at the poverty', that he is 'trying to reform the Bank to improve the lives of hundreds of millions of people', and that his efforts to make projects 'effective, not just have them approved . . . has generated tensions within the bank itself'. See George and Sabelli (1994: 27–58) on McNamara. For debate on similar lines comparing Wolfensohn and Wolfowitz's impact, see Chapters Fifteen and Sixteen in this book.
13. If Cockett's work is accurate, Hayek and company did not doubt the integrity of state actors, and thus shared this aspect of 'liberalism' with Keynes and his like. Perhaps the 'neo' in 'neoliberalism', then, is due to the added element of the fear of generalised

rent seeking. For a counter to the modernisation ethos that seemed to trust Third World bureaucrats, see Shils's (1960) culturally conservative equivocations on the capacity of Third World intellectuals to manage the state. More generally, for the global shift in perspectives on the qualities of state managers, see Du Guy (1996).

14. A very cursory search of the 1997 *Report* has found other subtle and unsubtle negative references to state actors on pages i, ii, 8–9, 13, 99, 103–05, 130, 144, and 155.

15. See Portes (1997: 241) for a view suggesting that the state autonomy developed in Chile under Frei and Allende allowed for the disastrous early phase of neoliberalism under Pinochet and the 'Chicago Boys' to proceed with relative immunity. On Thailand and Indonesia, the World Bank is already eating its words (albeit with delicate bites): James Wolfensohn admitted in February 1998 that in Indonesia 'we got it wrong' (Australian Broadcasting Corporation, Radio National News, 6 February 1998).

16. As Berman (1997, 1998) notes, colonial states (and some of their present-day historians, for example, Crawford Young) attempted to replicate European absolutism, but 'had striking limitations on their capacity to control and transform the African societies over which they ruled' (1998: 314). The World Bank is still trying to surmount those 'limitations'.

17. Of course, the task is not just to proselytise the consumerist aspect of the dream: there is plenty of evidence of the success of that, as reflected in O'Hanlon's quote from a man in the middle of the People's Republic of the Congo: 'every child knows – America is a land where you eat as much meat as you want, and you're given blue jeans, and no one goes to a sorcerer because every wish is granted. In America, no one dies' (1996: 234). The real job is persuading people that in order to reach this nirvana they have to sell their labour according to the terms of the global market.

18. Hoogvelt (1997: 48) argues that the post-1970 changes in North–South relations have led to debt repayment being the main form of South to North surplus extraction. This came about because there were no more 'fresh' pre-capitalist areas into which capitalism could expand.

19. In a report commissioned by the Trilateral Commission, Huntington et al. (Crozier, Huntington and Watanuki 1975) argued that the demands of too much democracy in the West were leading to a fiscal crisis of the state and thus ungovernability. The implied solution was to demobilise the marginal groups that were making too many demands on the state. As Albert Hirschman notes (1991) there is some irony in Huntington's solutions for the Third World coming home to the First.

20. Hoogvelt (1997: 176) sees merit in Huntington's earlier blessing of corruption as 'the only means of integrating marginal groups into a disjointed social system', citing the long history of corruption in seventeenth- and eighteenth-century England as a necessary step 'in the long haul towards the institutionalisation of a political structure and administration relatively independent from the competing demands of

economic agents. It is the tragedy of Africa that history has not given it time to catch up.' Bayart (1993) seems to see corruption as a part of a long history of inequality in Africa. This new postcolonial stage simply draws in the West to its elites' strategies: they manipulate World Bank ideology and policies now as effectively as they did those of the Soviets and the Americans during the Cold War and other European colonialists before that.

21. See Sachs and Warner (1995) for the classic argument that liberalisation will lead to 'convergence', which shares some of Hoogvelt's assertions about the high rates of globalisation and Third World incorporation in the last years of the nineteenth century compared to now, but differs on explanations for this and future prospects.

22. Szeftel (1998: 237) suggests that corruption can serve as a mechanism of primitive accumulation for members of the state class to become a 'proper' bourgeoisie. But if the particular positioning of most African states in the global political economy prevents 'classical' capitalism from developing, clientalism and corruption will be a more permanent condition than this perspective allows. Reno's Sierra Leone (1995, 1997), in which the state has become a means through which weak capital can pursue gains, will be the template.

23. For Hoogvelt 'implosion' is the recent 'intensification of trade and capital linkages within the core of the capitalist system, and a relative, selective, withdrawal of such linkages from the periphery'. For Sachs and Warner (1995), this implosion can be blamed on Third World states 'closing' their economies in the post-Second World War era, but Hoogvelt's data and analysis suggests more core involvement in the periphery in the pre-1970 phase of the global economy than after that, indicating a more complicated scenario. For the most part, Sachs and Warner ignore the details of the 1945 to 1970s period. For Hoogvelt, today's 'openness' serves the interests of the Third World elites and enables debt repayment at the expense of the rest of society, while for Sachs and Warner it benefits everybody.

24. In the 1970s state borrowing from private transnational financial institutions increased state power in the Third World. Now, however, the nationalisation of private Third World debt in addition to the state debts gone bad from the 1970s brings them together into an easily enforceable and 'legitimate' state amenable to World Bank/IMF packages (Hoogvelt 1997: 168–69). However, the economic means of paying back the debts are denationalised, thus upholding the sovereignty of the state for the purposes of paying off debt but dismantling it in all other realms.

25. Perhaps indicative of an emerging academic tendency to focus on the IMF as 'bad guy' instead of the World Bank is the usually critical Wade (1997) appearing to come to the Bank's defence in a review of the scathing *Masters of Illusion: The World Bank and the Poverty of Nations* (Caufield 1996), in which he notes that many governments (especially in Africa) continuously 'outfox' the Bank, that it is only a 'minnow' in terms of financial capital, that it cannot be all that powerful in its own right because it is actually beholden to the USA (surely a reassuring thought to Leftist critics) and

that it is hobbled by its NGO critics. No doubt Wade would be happier if the World Bank were warmer to the idea of industrial policies; however, he is probably correct to note that the Bank has 'rather more nobility of purpose than either the IMF or the World Trade Organization'.

26. James Currey's 1998 publications catalogue reports that James Wolfensohn has been impressed with Hanlon's (1996) findings on the mess created by the IMF in Mozambique. Another Hanlon tale (1997) of Mozambican cashew producers demanding US$15 million reimbursement from the World Bank could also be indicative of tensions in the Bank over a pro-domestic capital versus globalisation line. On Bank advice, the industry was privatised in 1994. In 1995 and 1996 the Bank forced Mozambique through aid conditionality to drastically reduce its export tax on raw cashews so India could process them (with subsidised family labour to crack the acidy shells by hand – in Mozambique the process is done by machine). Facing bankruptcy, the industry persuaded Wolfensohn to commission a new report, which found the initial advice faulty. The cashew processors are asking to be repaid the money lost in the past two years. The Bank's vice-president for Africa rejected the new report. The Mozambican parliament's 1999 plans to re-impose a 20 per cent export tax have been barred by conditions attached to HIPC debt reduction programmes (Hanlon 1999).

27. The permutations among which many of the neo-Gramscian international political economists veer, for example, Gill (1994) and Van der Pijl (1994).

28. To be fair, Escobar – much more grounded in radical social movement praxis than the logical abstractions of Foucauldian theory would allow – is more critical than this. It should be noted, too, that his variation on the Foucauldian schema is that the discourses of development have actually played a great part in the *production* of poverty rather than simply being addenda to the uneven processes of peripheral capitalism.

29. If, as Chossudovsky (1997) suggests, World Bank and coffee-pricing policies contributed inexorably to the crisis and genocide in Rwanda, will the Bank admit its consequential complicity?

30. See Wade (1996b: 32) on the pressure on the Bank 'not to upset capital markets'.

31. Cohen (1997) notes that in sub-Saharan Africa (excluding South Africa) the establishment of new stock exchanges (there were only two in 1992; by 1997 there were seventeen) and pressure from the IMF should raise the percentage of privatisations through public offerings from the contemporary 5.4 per cent.

32. Faux (1997: 121) queries the economists' assumptions that 'trade' always brings appreciable gains.

33. In one place the *Report* (1997b: 116, Box 7.3) refers to the widely publicised findings of Putnam (1993a).

34. States encouraging 'national' primitive accumulation will no doubt exhibit notably different qualities in comparison with those facilitating 'global' primitive accumulation: but the choice between these alternatives may be a Faustian one.

Chapter Nine

Japan, the World Bank, and the Art of Paradigm Maintenance
The East Asian Miracle in Political Perspective

Robert Wade

THIS WAS ORIGINALLY PUBLISHED IN *1996* IN NEW LEFT REVIEW *1 (217): 3–37.*

To what extent is the World Bank an actor, an 'autonomous variable' in the international system?[1] Or to what extent are its objectives and approaches the mere manifestations of competition and compromise among its member states? Several writers have argued that the Bank has a relatively large amount of autonomy – from the state interests of its overseers – and that its staff have some autonomy from the senior management. They have traced this autonomy to variables such as 'lack of clarity of the priorities of organisational objectives', 'the difficulty and complexity of accomplishing the organisation's mandate', 'bureaucratised structure' and 'professionalism of staff' (Krasner 1982; Ascher 1983). But there is something strangely bloodless about this approach. It manages to discuss autonomy without conveying anything of the political and economic substance of the field of forces in which the Bank operates. By focusing only on morphological variables such as 'professionalism' and the 'complexity of accomplishing the organisation's mandate', it misses other variables such as 'correspondence of organisational actions with the interests of the US state'. If the Bank is propelled by its budgetary, staffing and incentive structures to act in line with those interests, the US state need not intervene in ways that would provide evidence of 'lack of autonomy'; yet the Bank's autonomy is clearly questionable.

This chapter describes an episode in Japan's attempts over the 1980s and 1990s to assert itself on the world stage, to move beyond the constraints of dependency in a US-centred world economic system. The episode involves a Japanese challenge to the World Bank and its core ideas about the role of the state in the strategy for economic development. Over the 1980s Japan poured aid and investment into East and South-East Asia, using its strong domestic capacity to strengthen its external reach. In doing so, Japan endorsed a market-guiding role for the state in recipient countries, and justified this role by pointing to its success in the development of Japan, Taiwan and South Korea. The World Bank found Japan's prescriptions inconsistent with its own programmatic ideas about the role of the state, which emphasised the need for thoroughgoing liberalisation and privatisation. Since the Bank's ideas are themselves derived from largely American interests in and ideas about free markets, Japan's challenge to the Bank was also a challenge to the US state – the Bank being an important instrument by which the US state seeks to project a powerful external reach, while having a much weaker domestic capacity than Japan's.

In the early 1980s, when the Bank started to champion liberalisation and the private sector, the Bank and the Japanese government proceeded along independent paths. But growing tension reached a head in the late 1980s when the Bank criticised Japanese aid programmes for undermining the aims of the Bank and the International Monetary Fund. In response, the Japanese government set out to change the Bank's core ideas about the role of the state in development strategy. It did so by inducing the Bank to pay more attention to East Asian development experience, so perhaps the Bank would change its mind, see more validity in the Japanese principles, and enhance Japan's role as a leader in development thinking. Japan's influence inside and outside the Bank would then grow. Specifically, the Japanese government persuaded the Bank to make a special study of East and South-East Asia, focusing on why this region has become rich and what other countries should learn from the experience. The study was published in September 1993 as *The East Asian Miracle: Economic Growth and Public Policy* (World Bank 1993a).

In this chapter we examine, firstly, the build-up of tension between Japan and the Bank; secondly, the process by which the study was written inside the Bank; and, thirdly, the resulting text. We shall ask whether Japan's attempt to get the Bank to change its mind was successful. We shall see how the final document reflects an attempt at compromise between the well-established World Bank view and the newly powerful Japanese view. The result is heavily weighted towards the Bank's established position, and legitimises the Bank's continuing advice to low-income countries to follow the 'market-friendly' policies apparently vindicated by East Asia's success. But the document also contains enough pro-industrial policy statements to allow the Japanese to claim a measure of success. Taken together with other Bank studies prompted by Japan at the same time, it provides a number of 'attractor points' for research and prescriptions more in line with Japanese views. Although the Bank emerges with its traditional paradigm largely unscathed, this particular episode may even be looked back on as an early landmark in the intellectual ascendancy, in East and South-East Asia if not in the West, of Japanese views about the role of the state. Finally, we shall come back to the issue raised in the first paragraph – the autonomy of the World Bank, and the extent to which it can be regarded as an 'actor' with objectives and approaches that are not simply the vector of the interests of its member states.

The World Bank's position in the development debate

The World Bank enjoys a unique position as a generator of ideas about economic development. Around the world, debates on development issues tend to be framed in terms of 'pro or anti' World Bank positions. The Bank's ability to frame the debate rests on (1) its ability to influence the terms on which low-income countries gain access to international capital markets; (2) a research and policy-design budget far larger than that of any other development organisation; and (3) its ability to attract global media coverage of its major reports.

In the early 1980s the Bank swung into line with a US-led consensus about the needs of the world economy and appropriate economic policies for developing countries. Reflecting the demise of Keynesianism and the ascendancy of supply-side economics in the US and some parts of Europe, the consensus – the 'Washington Consensus', as it has been called – was based on the twin ideas of the state as the provider of a regulatory framework for private-sector exchanges (but not as a *director* of those exchanges), and of the world economy as open to movements of goods, services, and capital, if not labour. The Bank's new Structural Adjustment Loans applied conditions conforming to these ideas, such that borrowers had to shrink the state and open the economy to international transactions. Its annual *World Development Reports* have provided the conceptual framework and evidence to justify these conditions. In particular, the *World Development Report 1987*, entitled *Trade and Industrialisation,* articulated a strong 'free-market' or neoliberal argument about the appropriate development approach.[2]

The central problem of developing countries, in the Bank's view, is the weakness of their 'enabling environment' for private-sector growth. The enabling environment consists of infrastructure, a well-educated work force, macroeconomic stability, free trade and a regulatory framework favouring private-sector investment and competition. Policies to secure such an environment are collectively called 'market friendly'. On the one hand, the 'market-friendly' approach is not the same as laissez-faire, the Bank is at pains to say, for there are areas where the market fails, in infrastructure and education, and where the government should step in with public spending (World Bank 1991c). On the other hand, the approach warns against intervention beyond these limits, especially against sectoral industrial policies designed to promote growth in some industries more than others. Market-friendly policies – neither complete laissez-faire nor interventionism – are optimal for growth and income distribution, says the Bank. This set of ideas is broadly consistent with US demands that its trading partners – Japan in particular – change their domestic institutions in order to create a 'level playing field' for free and fair trade.

In the late 1980s the Bank paid particular attention to financial sector reform. A Bank task force on Financial Sector Operations met to formulate policy on financial system reform, later to be put in the form of a mandatory Operational Directive. The task force championed a policy of far-reaching financial deregulation for developing countries, urging removal of all interest rate controls and all directed credit programmes. *The World Development Report 1989*, entitled *Financial Systems and Development* took a somewhat less extreme view. Written by a team that worked at the same time as the task force on Financial Sector Operations, it emphasised that private financial markets do make mistakes, particularly because of information problems and externalities – although these mistakes last for a *shorter time* than those of public financial agents. Where supervision and monitoring is effective, directed credit can work. Governments should, however, deregulate, but gradually. In August 1989, one month after the *World Development Report 1989* was published, the Bank issued the report of the task force on Financial Sector Operations – known as the Levy Report, after its chief author, Fred Levy. As noted, it took a strong view against government intervention in financial markets. The later Bank policy directive on financial sector operations took this report, not the *World Development Report 1989*, as its foundation.

The Japanese challenge

Throughout the 1980s the Japanese state has hugely strengthened its external reach through aid programmes and foreign investment. By the early 1980s it was already the principal co-financier of World Bank loans, the number two shareholder in IDA – the Bank's soft loan facility – and the biggest source of bilateral aid for Asia. In 1984 it became the second biggest shareholder in the World Bank (IBRD) after the US. By 1989 it had the biggest bilateral aid programme in the world. In 1990 it became the second biggest shareholder in the IFC – the Bank's affiliate for private-sector lending. In 1992 it became the second biggest shareholder – equal to Germany – in the IMF. By the early 1990s Japan passed the US to become the world's biggest manufacturing economy; it accounted for half of the developed world's total net savings (US savings accounted for 5 per cent); and it became the world's biggest source of foreign investment. For all these reasons, Japan has come to matter for international financial institutions as never before – and also for the US state, whose deficits it has been financing.

The Japanese government has encouraged its recipient governments – the US aside – to think more strategically and in more interventionist terms than can be accommodated by World Bank ideas. In particular, it has sanctioned attempts by low-income states to go beyond the conventional neoclassical tasks of providing a property-rights framework and moderating market failures due to public goods, externalities and monopolies. It has encouraged aid recipients to articulate national objectives and policy choices, to catalyse market agents, and to assist some industries more than others. The Japanese government claims that the potential benefits of the state's directional thrust are illustrated by the actual benefits from the sectoral industrial policies of pre- and post-war Japan, and more recently, of Taiwan and South Korea. A regulated, non-liberalised financial system capable of delivering concessional credit to priority uses, according to the Japanese, was a vital part of the organisational infrastructure of these policies.

In line with this thinking, in 1987 the ministry of international trade and industry (MITI) published *The New Asian Industries Development Plan,* setting out a regional strategy of industrialisation for South-East Asian countries.[3] Responding to the appreciation of the Japanese yen in the mid-1980s and the resulting need to transfer more Japanese production offshore, the plan outlined the ways that Japanese firms making location decisions consistent with the plan would benefit from various kinds of aid for infrastructure, finance, market access, and so on. Officials were explicit that 'Japan will increasingly use its aid . . . as seed money to attract Japanese manufacturers or other industrial concerns with an attractive investment environment.'[4]

The dispute over directed credit

'Directed' credit – meaning subsidised and targeted or earmarked credit – was to be a key instrument of this strategy. In the late 1980s Japan's ministry of finance (MOF) established the ASEAN-Japan Development Fund, which offered directed credit to support private-sector development. The fund was administered by OECF, Japan's largest aid agency. Unhappy at these developments, Bank officials expressed their reservations to Japanese officials informally – to no effect.

In June 1989, a new executive director (ED) for Japan, Masaki Shiratori, arrived at the World Bank. As a senior MOF official, he had helped to steer Japan's relations with international financial organisations for many years. Between 1981 and 1984, he played a central role in the strategy to raise Japan's shareholding in the IBRD from number five to number two.[5] More persuasive in English than his predecessors, he was concerned to shift Japan's role from cheque-writer to leader – 'no taxation without representation', some Japanese comment wryly – and to make the Bank drop its blanket opposition to directed credit policies.

By this time, both the World Bank and the Japanese government had well-articulated development strategies in place, the Bank emphasising free markets, including nearly free financial markets, the Japanese government emphasising guided markets, including guided financial markets. Japan was by then the second ranking shareholder in the World Bank after the US. And it had a new, articulate and forceful ED, determined to make the Bank pay more attention to the East Asian experience and to rethink directed credit policies.

In September 1989 the dispute between the Bank and Japan's OECF over credit policies became explicit. Citing the case of the Philippines, a senior vice-president of the Bank wrote to the president of OECF – in charge of the ASEAN-Japan Development Fund – asking him to reconsider the policy of subsidised targeted loans: passing these funds to the banks and final beneficiaries at below market interest rates 'could have an adverse impact on development of the financial sector' and hence '*would create unnecessary distortions and set back the financial sector reforms*' (emphasis added), which had been supported by the IMF's Extended Fund Facility and the Bank's Financial Sector Adjustment Loan.[6] The dispute highlighted the underlying differences of view, the Japanese arguing that financial policies should be designed to advance a wider industrial strategy, the Bank insisting that credit should always and everywhere be at 'market' or non-subsidised rates.[7]

Japan's ED made strong protests to the Bank's senior management and to the Board of EDs from member governments (the representatives of member states who act as overseers). Many EDs from developing countries agreed with the Japanese position, but to no avail; Bank management refused to back down. Japan's MOF and its OECF began to fight back. A key figure was Isao Kubota, a senior MOF official then on loan to OECF as managing director of the pivotal Coordination Department.[8] He did two things. Firstly, he established a team to write a paper setting out the broad principles of the Japanese government's understanding of structural adjustment. Secondly, he had discussions with Shiratori about how to get the Bank to pay more attention to the Japanese and wider East Asian development experience. This was the genesis of the *Miracle* study.

Meanwhile, tensions were growing between Japan and the US as well. From May 1989 through to 1992, the two states were negotiating over market access – the Structural Impediments Initiative (SII). The US tried to make the Japanese undertake domestic reforms of such features as the retail distribution system and the cross-ownership of firms, so making it more like the 'free-market' or American system. The Japanese mostly resisted and in turn urged reform of US institutions. An American business executive in Tokyo later said about the wider relationship between Japan, on the one hand, and the US and Europe, on the other:

The tired old technique of US and European leaders is to beat the Japanese with a piece of two by four. Not surprisingly, they resent it. They may be less cocky now that the economy is in recession, but there is a deep and growing and potentially damaging distrust of the West in the Tokyo corridors of power (Rafferty 1994).[9]

Also during this period, Tokyo was flirting with membership in the Malaysian-sponsored East Asian Economic Caucus, from which the US was excluded, while remaining cool to the American-endorsed Asia-Pacific Economic Coordination forum (see Johnson 1993b).[10] This underlined Japan's new willingness to pursue a course apart from, and even opposed to, that of the US.

Back at the Bank, Lawrence Summers, a Harvard economist, joined as chief economist and vice-president in January 1991. Not known for tact, he openly held the view that Japanese economists are 'second rate'. From January to June 1991, drafts of the Bank's *World Development Report 1991: The Challenge of Development*, underwent discussion within the Bank and the Board. Written under the leadership of a Chicago-trained economist, the *Report* restated a largely free-market view of appropriate public policy for development, under the label 'market-friendly'. The term was coined by Summers, who exerted influence at this late stage of the *Report* to moderate the extreme free-market position of the earlier drafts, but in Japanese eyes it still remained extreme.

Blueprint for development

Then in October 1991 the OECF – whose main parent ministry is the ministry of finance – issued the paper initiated by Kubota, entitled 'Issues related to the World Bank's approach to a structural adjustment: Proposal from a major partner'.[11] Its main points are as follows:

1. For a developing country to attain sustainable growth, the government must adopt 'measures aiming "directly" at promoting investment'.

2. These measures should be part of an explicit industrial strategy to promote the leading industries of the future.
3. Directed and subsidised credit has a key role in promoting these industries because of extensive failures in developing countries' financial markets.
4. Decisions about ownership arrangements, including privatisation, should relate to actual economic, political and social conditions in the country concerned, not to the universal desirability of privatising public enterprises. For example, there may be legitimate national sentiments about the desirability of foreign ownership.
5. 'Japanese fiscal and monetary policies in the post-war era may be worthy of consideration. These were centred on preferential tax treatment and development finance institutions' lendings' (OECF 1991: 5–6).[12]

Also in October 1991, at the annual meeting of the Board of governors of the World Bank and the IMF, Yasushi Mieno, head of the Bank of Japan, the central bank,[13] said,

> Experience in Asia has shown that although development strategies require a healthy respect for market mechanisms, the role of the government cannot be forgotten. I would like to see the World Bank and the IMF take the lead in a wide-ranging study that would define the theoretical underpinnings of this approach and clarify the areas in which it can be successfully applied to other parts of the globe.[14]

The International Finance Bureau of the MOF prepared Mieno's statement. Isao Kubota – by now transferred back from OECF to a senior position in this same bureau, and drafter of Mieno's statement – later made the point more vividly to reporters: 'It's really incredible. They think their economic framework is perfect. I think they're wrong.'[15]

By late 1991 tension between Japan and both the Bank and the US was running high. Articles based on interviews with Japanese officials began appearing in the American and Japanese press with titles such as 'Japan–US clash looms on World Bank strategy'. The anonymous Japanese officials called the Bank's approach 'simple-minded', resting on 'outmoded Western concepts that fail to take account of the successful strategy pursued by Japan and some of its Asian neighbours in developing their economies'.[16]

Privately, those officials accused Bank economists of gross arrogance, of presuming to lecture them on why the Japanese government was doing the wrong things while at the same time asking for more Japanese money.

Another statement of Japanese principles came out in April 1992, in the form of MITI's blueprint for economic reconstruction and development in Russia. '*Western* industrial countries', it said, 'can make many suggestions to help Russia with its economic reform. This paper ... focuses on what Russia can learn from *Japan's* experience ...' It described its approach as being in 'stark contrast' to that of the IMF, presented in a report on Russia earlier the same year. 'Market mechanisms cannot be almighty', it claimed, expressing doubts about whether 'macroeconomic approaches', such as those advocated by the IMF, were sufficient to meet the chief need of revitalising production. Japan's post-war economic renaissance could be used to formulate appropriate policies in, for example, the design of emergency measures to halt the plunge in output, and of 'priority production programmes' to ensure the supply of essential industrial goods. 'The worst choice would be to diversify investment in an all-out manner, because ... what is now most needed is focus on specific sectors of particular importance as a way to increase overall production' (Ota, Tanikawa and Otani 1992, emphasis added).[17] In other words, Russia must as a matter of urgency have a *sector-specific* industrial policy.

Why the Japanese challenge?

As the Japanese government greatly increased its capital contribution to the Bank, it wished, not surprisingly, to see its views more fully reflected in Bank thinking. But why present itself as a champion of anti-paradigmatic views? As it becomes more powerful, why does it not endorse free trade and obscure the mercantilist elements in its own history?

There are at least four possible reasons. The first is ideological conviction. The senior officials in those parts of the government leading the challenge genuinely believe that interventionist policies can be more effective than the Bank's 'market-friendly' set of policies. They emphasise the role of interventionist policies in Japan's own development – the ways in which selective interventions can help Japanese aid be more effective. Being able to demonstrate aid effectiveness is especially important when official development assistance (ODA) has been largely exempt from the government's budget cuts. With many Japanese policy makers disgruntled about the amount of aid, the finance ministry is under constant pressure to show it being well used. Indeed, said MOF officials, they have been criticised by other government agencies for being too focused upon aid effectiveness, for not paying enough attention to Japan's national interest. Their reply is that making best use of aid money helps to stabilise the world economy, which is also in Japan's national interest. Ideological conviction is especially intense on financial issues. The phrases, the 'moneymaking culture' and the 'thing-making culture', are in common use in Japan, representing a widespread sense – as in Islamic condemnations of usury – that making goods and providing services is intrinsically a more worthy activity than making money by financial dealings, and that the financial sector should be industry's servant.

The second reason for the challenge is organisational interest. The Bank's criticism of Japan's concessional and directed aid schemes in South-East Asia were aimed at what the MOF considered its greatest post-war achievement. Directed credit was its principal industrial policy instrument in the post-war renaissance of Japan; effective use of directed credit is the foundation of its claim to have played a major role in the 'miracle'. The claim is reflected in the OECF's mandate to provide directed and concessional credit as part of the Japanese aid strategy. No wonder MOF – and when we speak of Japan–World Bank relations we mean MOF–World Bank relations, for MOF jealously guards its monopoly – resents hearing the Bank announce to the world that directed and concessional credit can never be effective, all the more so since the Bank's claim rests on near-total ignorance of directed credit in North-East Asia.

The third reason is national material interest. Building a powerful market position across East and South-East Asia is a top Japanese government objective. Interventionist policies can potentially help Japanese firms and the Japanese government to consolidate profits and influence in the region – enabling the Malaysian government, for example, to give special support to the Malaysian joint-venture partner of a Japanese firm, or to the Japanese firm directly through targeted loans and protection.[18] Getting the World Bank to admit the potential desirability of selective industrial promotion would help to advance this agenda. But why might the Japanese government, or a part of it, wish to *advertise* the fact that it was playing by different rules in its aid programme? The answer may lie in the fact that the Bank had already strongly criticised Japan for doing so. This put the burden on Japan to show that playing by different rules could yield development outcomes better than those of the Bank – or to get the Bank to rethink.

The fourth reason is nationalism, the desire to overcome a sense of being judged inferior by representatives of other states – or in this case, multilateral financial institutions. This sentiment is caught in the phrase often heard in and about Japan, 'economic superpower and political pygmy', or in Ichiro Ozawa's likening of Japan to a dinosaur with a huge body but a tiny brain.[19] In response to the perception of being judged inferior, Japan adopted a state strategy of channelling economic activities so as to achieve independence from, leverage over, and respect in the eyes of other states, rather than to achieve consumer utility, private wealth, or freedom of society from government. As it has become during the 1980s a 'mature' economy with a very large role in the international economy, it has also frequently been criticised for lacking the leadership on the world stage befitting its economic might. There is a growing urge among Japanese officials, politicians and the general public for Japan to set this right. But how?

Japan cannot constantly bow to foreign – that is, US – pressure. It needs to be seen asserting its own views on appropriate rules for the international economy. These cannot be free-trade rules, for the US already leads the free-trade ideology. It can differentiate its principles from those of the US by basing them on its own experience of economic nationalism, presenting them as general principles confirmed by other East Asian experience and as sources of meta-policies for developing countries today. On these grounds, it can present itself as the champion of developing countries in the governing councils of the international financial institutions. At the same time, its principles also stay away from the dangerous idea of Japanese uniqueness. No country has come to exercise a leadership role in the world system without claiming to represent a universalistic ideology. In short, the Japanese challenge to the World Bank can be seen as part of a wider attempt by the Japanese elite to develop an ideology that goes beyond Japanese uniqueness and yet remains distinct from free trade and orthodox liberalism.[20]

The Bank's resistance

Bank managers saw the Japanese ideas about the role of the state – the emphasis on directed credit and the more general argument linking the appropriate role of the state to the amount of state 'capacity'[21] – as a serious threat. Why? Firstly, because concessional credit from the Japanese aid budget makes World Bank credit less attractive. The Bank especially needs to find borrowers in East and South-East Asia, where Japanese aid is concentrated, to raise the average quality of its loan portfolio. Secondly, the Japanese emphasis on directed credit as an instrument of the industrial policy of recipient governments runs flatly contrary to the Bank's emphasis on financial system deregulation, a central thrust of its macroeconomic reform formula through the 1980s. Thirdly, if the Bank were to embrace the interventionist role of the state wanted by the Japanese government it would, in the eyes of its managers, risk its ability to borrow at the best rates on world money markets – and so face lower demand for its now more expensive funds. It would also risk its second most valuable asset after its government guarantees – its reputation as a country-rating agency, a kind of international Standard and Poors that signals to private investors where they should put their money.[22] Why would such dire consequences follow? Because the Bank's ability to borrow at the best rates and to act as a country-rating agency depends on its reputation among financial capitalists, which in turn depends on its manifest commitment to *their* version of 'sound' public policies. Their version is based on the premise that only one set of rules should apply to all participants in the international economy and that those rules should express a non-nationalistic role of the state.[23] If this premise constitutes an imperative from the Bank's point of view, it is because any change of mind could be very costly.

Fourthly, if the Bank were to embrace the Japanese view, it would run up against the strategic and diplomatic power of the US, which has used the Bank as an instrument of its own external infrastructural power to a greater degree than any other state. And the Bank would delegitimise itself in the eyes of American academic economics, with its belief in the overwhelming virtues of markets and its political agenda of deregulation – an agenda endorsed by those who do well out of free markets. The president of the Bank has always been an American; Americans are greatly overrepresented at professional levels in the Bank relative to the US's shareholding; some two-thirds of World Bank economists are certified by US universities – and 80 per cent by North American or British universities.[24]

Fifthly, the Bank's constitution requires it to be 'apolitical', and the single meta-policy, sanctioned as it claims to be by a transcendent and apolitical 'economic rationality', helps the Bank to preserve the claim of 'political impartiality'. One of the most important conceptual contributions of the Bretton Woods conference – which created the World Bank and the IMF – was the idea of equal treatment of all members of the new financial order. It was intended to avoid the politicisation of the 1920s international rescue operations. There would be no 'favourites', but a community of states supporting each other at times of difficulty by means of a universalistic set of rules. To now admit the potential efficacy of sector-specific industrial policies would require the Bank to discriminate between countries in terms of such factors as government capacity and corruption, on the quite reasonable grounds that industrial policies are unlikely to be effective in states whose governments are thoroughly corrupt. But doing so would expose it to the charge of being 'political', and open it to pressure from *borrowers* saying, 'You urged/allowed country X to do A; why can't we?'[25]

Sixthly, commitment to the Bank's meta-policy allows the organisation to act quickly and concertedly. The meta-policy is derived from neoclassical economics and receives the endorsement of most US- and UK-trained economists who took control of the Bank from top to bottom over the 1980s; technical specialists – engineers, agronomists, health specialists, and so forth – were removed from operational management positions or not replaced when they retired (Stern 1993; Markoff and Montecinos 1993). The common commitment to the neoclassical meta-policy by the Bank's management cadre helps senior management to overcome the 'agency' problem of subordinates exercising discretion in ways they do not like. It keeps the whole management spine in proper alignment. It also allows country departments to be efficient advice givers. Policies seen to be inconsistent with neoclassical normative theory are excluded from the start. Of course, the Bank's lending practices on the ground have often differed from what the recipe calls for. But the case-by-case modifications come from the need to adjust pragmatically to 'political realities', not from a belief that the *economics* of the meta-policy might be less than universal. (So China, with one of the most interventionist, price-distorting governments of all, was the Bank's fastest growing borrower over the 1980s. The Bank and China need each other – China to get finance and intellectual help, the Bank to lend to a big absorber with little debt.) At the level of principles, the neoclassical and largely free-market meta-policy is insulated from particular modifications.

Seventhly, the Bank sees the Japanese position as posing a threat not only to itself but to its borrowers. The Japanese position requires the low-income country state to play a *strategic* role in governing the integration with the world economy – maintaining the relative separation of the domestic and international spheres for policy making – not just the role of transmission belt from the 'realities' of the world economy to the national economy. Such a strategic role, says the Bank, generally *lowers* national welfare. Even if some evidence suggests that some governments some of the time have played this role effectively, 90 per cent of governments have been unable to. Notwithstanding this, the vested interests pushing governments to intervene in counter-productive ways are so powerful that governments will go on doing so unless hindered by some impartial and powerful agency – the World Bank and the IMF, for example. The Japanese views, says the Bank, give unwelcome legitimacy to such interventionist impulses.

Finally, even if such policies raise national welfare in a single case, they can do so only by 'free riding' on the restraint of others – promoting industries to compete in US markets while closing the domestic market to US exports, for example. So the Japanese principles cannot be practised by all at the same time, and in that sense pose a *systemic* threat.

These eight reasons radically overdetermine the Bank's reaction of alarm and denial to the pro-interventionist views of its second-biggest shareholder. But the danger could be diffused and confrontation contained as long as the Bank did not have to deal explicitly with the causes of East Asia's economic success; in dealing with other regions or with 'development-in-general', it could simply ignore Japanese ideas about development strategy. If, however, it did have to examine in depth the causes of this success, a more or less explicit statement about the validity of apparently very different views would have to be made. Given Japan's power, that resolution would have to make some concession to Japanese views, for otherwise the number-two shareholder would lose too much face and become less cooperative. The Japanese MOF decided to force the issue.

Making the miracle: Stage one

To recap: in 1989 the Bank made a strong criticism of the Japanese aid agency, OECF, for its credit policies in South-East Asia. In response, senior MOF officials considered how to get the Bank to be more 'pragmatic' and heed the experience of Japan and other East Asian economies.

In 1991, soon after the arrival of Lewis Preston as the new president of the World Bank, the Japanese MOF pressed the Bank to make a thorough study of East Asian development experience. The Bank's senior management was reluctant to permit the study, but agreed for two reasons. Firstly, the Japanese would pay for it, the Bank having to bear only the time cost of its own staff.[26] Secondly, in return for the Bank's concession, the Japanese agreed to drop their opposition to the draft Operational Directive on Financial Sector Operations, which urged full-scale financial deregulation.[27] In January 1992 the study got under way, with a budget of US$1.2 million from the Japanese trust fund. It was to be written over eighteen months for publication at the time of the annual meeting in September 1993.[28]

The core study, giving the overall analysis and conclusions, was to be based in the Bank's research complex under Lawrence Summers and Nancy Birdsall (the director of the research department, an American). They appointed John Page (D.Phil. in economics from Oxford, undergraduate in economics at Stanford, another American) to head the study. Page put together a team of six people, all with Ph.D.s in economics, all but one from American universities.[29] None had adult experience of living and working in Asia.

There were also to be a number of case studies of countries organised by the Bank's East Asia vice-presidency; some to be written by authors inside the Bank, others by outside consultants. The outsiders were offered US$10 000 per case study, and required to submit drafts in six months – so their research had to be largely off-the-shelf. In addition, several background papers on Japan were commissioned from Japanese scholars.

Although it got the country studies, the East Asia vice-presidency felt passed over. The vice-president for East Asia, Gautam Kaji, first heard of the study at a Board meeting. Asked by an executive director for his views about the proposed study, he confessed not to know about it. Summers bypassed the East Asia vice-presidency, aware that its senior managers and economists held views towards the free market extreme of the Bank's range. The rivalry between the core team in the research complex and the East Asia vice-presidency was to shape the arguments of the study.

At the same time, a parallel and complementary project was initiated, again with Japanese funding, to examine the effect of directed credit in Japan. This was undertaken on behalf of the Bank by the Japan Development Bank (JDB), reviewing its own programmes. Its conclusions were to feed into the *Miracle* study.[30] A third Japanese-funded study about Japan, 'The Evolution, Character and Structure of the Japanese Civil Service, and its Role in Shaping the Interrelationships between the Government and the Private-Sector', was undertaken by the Bank's educational arm, the Economic Development Institute (EDI), for use in World Bank teaching courses. Suddenly the Bank was paying a lot more research attention to Japan than ever before, thanks to Japanese initiative and Japanese money.[31]

From early 1992 to early 1993, the first drafts of the *Miracle* chapters were written and discussed within the core group. John Page was given a free hand by senior managers, with no hint of the expected conclusions. Lawrence Summers urged him to think in new ways, to listen carefully to the Japanese arguments. 'We were eager to find a story that would be new, all the more so because the Bank's standard "market-friendly" story had already been told in *World Development Report 1991*', said Page later. Indeed, Summers's reaction to Page's proposed names for the team was: 'Too neoclassical, you will be seen as trying to force East Asian data into a neoclassical strait-jacket'. Page responded that for the report to have an impact in the Bank, it had to use the language of neoclassical economics: the team stayed as he proposed.

The team members accepted that East Asian governments implemented policies at substantial variance from the Bank's orthodoxy, but they found it difficult to unearth clear evidence about the causal impact of these non-orthodox policies on economic growth. Wrestling with this issue for many months, they eventually concluded: 'It is possible that some of these non-orthodox policies helped some of the time, but, with some exceptions, we can't show it.'

Also at this time, this version of the 'institutional basis' chapter was restructured. This version had taken as its main question, 'What features of East Asian institutions enabled these economies to avoid the costs that befall equally interventionist and authoritarian states elsewhere; or why did their many strategic interventions not lead to massive rent seeking?' It presented government–business consultative councils, for example, as an institutional device that reduced the authoritarian character of East Asian political regimes by providing an institutionalised channel of feedback from the people directly affected by business policies. Birdsall and Page thought this might be interpreted as sanctioning authoritarianism and interventionism – as saying, 'If you have institutional features X, Y, and Z you can avoid the expected costs of authoritarianism and interventionism'. In the rewriting, this theme was much diluted. The chapter was brought into line with the report's larger argument that East Asian states are more successful because they are *less* interventionist, and the implication that some authoritarianisms are better than others was removed.

Making the miracle: Stage two

Around March 1993 the second stage of the production process began with rounds of discussion at successively higher levels of the approval hierarchy. A full-time editor, Lawrence MacDonald, was hired from the *Asia Wall St Journal*.[32] Over the next several months he and Page sent material back and forth, the editor revising the drafts in line with comments, Page commenting on the editor's revisions, the editor taking on board Page's comments and resubmitting to Page. The editor was the only person on the project with work experience in Asia. He attempted to inject some discussion of cultural propensities to save and educate, and of the role of the overseas Chinese. The team rejected these suggestions, the former for being too difficult to pin down with evidence, the second for being too liable to be taken as racist.

To discuss the drafts, many meetings were held with people from the East Asia vice-presidency, which had something close to a veto over the study being approved for sending to the Board – and thence for public release. The East Asia staff attacked the work for excessive emphasis on government intervention. 'Where is the *evidence* for what you are saying?' they demanded. The East Asia vice-presidency was well versed in demolishing arguments about the efficacy of industrial policy, its chief economist having just co-authored a book reiterating a largely free-market interpretation of East Asian economic success (Agarwala and Thomas 1995); its vice-president, still smarting from being excluded from the study's initiation, provided support for such challenges. Its representatives badgered the team about 'strategy' – as in the working subtitle, 'Strategies for Rapid Growth' and phrases such as 'a strategic approach to growth'. Such phrases could be misconstrued to mean that East Asian growth was due primarily to 'strategic' interventions in industrial policy, or even to sanction the idea of an alternative East Asian type of capitalism. The East Asia representatives also argued, more generally, that the Bank had an interest in getting the market-friendly approach, as set out in the *World Development Report 1991*, accepted as the correct approach to economic policy in all developing countries, and it would look odd if the study of East Asia, of all regions, did not embrace it too. Not coincidentally, the *World Development Report 1991* was written by a team headed by the man who was then chief economist for East Asia.

The spectacle of the East Asia vice-presidency evacuating upon the draft convinced Page and Birdsall of the need to make concessions if the draft was to proceed up the approval hierarchy. What could they concede? Firstly, they recognised that 'strategy' and 'strategic' implied – at least to the East Asia vice-presidency – a stronger argument about the efficacy of industrial policy than they wished to make, and were distracting attention from the substance of the argument about market failures. All references to strategy were therefore deleted, being replaced, where necessary, with the innocuous 'functional', as in 'a functional approach to growth' (World Bank 1993a: 88, Figure 2.1). Secondly, they praised the market-friendly approach in several places. Lewis Preston's Preface was made more explicit: 'The authors conclude that rapid growth in each economy was primarily due to the application of a set of common, market-friendly economic policies' (1993a: vi). At this late stage, the editor was asked to write a box summarising the ideas and evidence for the market-friendly approach (1993a: 85, Box 2.1). He wrote, 'In the past twenty years a consensus has emerged among economists on the best approach to economic development . . . These ideas have crystallised into what is now called the "market- friendly" approach.'

By making these concessions, Page and Birdsall hoped to protect two key ideas in what they had earlier called 'strategy'. One was that growth is a function of three sets of policies – those to foster accumulation, efficient allocation, and growth in productivity. Whereas the standard, market-friendly neoclassical argument stresses the need for good performance on all of four dimensions – macroeconomic stability, trade openness, human capital, and a rule-based system hospitable to the private sector – Page and Birdsall thought that there is some substitutability between the policies for accumulation, allocation, and productivity. Hence it is conceptually possible that costs in allocative efficiency (due to distorting industrial policies) are more than offset by gains in productivity (due to learning). The second idea is that markets – effective coordinating mechanisms for private agents in many contexts – may not work well for large and uneven investments in the early stages of development; for these, other mechanisms are needed, such as 'deliberative councils'. But how to stop deliberative councils from becoming cosy havens for sharing out rents? Through contests between selected firms competing within tight rules and under the watchful eye of the government as referee.[33]

Other parts of the report also came in for strong criticism from elsewhere in the Bank – all the more so now that Summers had left to be under-secretary to the treasury for international affairs in the new Clinton administration – but in the final version they appeared little changed. The section on directed credit and financial repression was attacked for making too many concessions to the view that these instruments could sometimes work. Page countered that the section did not, as the critics contended, repudiate the Bank line: it clearly stated that there is no *proof* that directed credit worked in Japan and Korea but also that the normal adverse effects of directed credit are *not* seen in those countries. Similarly, on the wider question of financial repression, Page countered trenchant internal criticism by urging the critics to read carefully what the text actually said. While admitting the fact of financial repression in Japan and Korea, the text's explanation for why the normal adverse effects on growth are not observed was not out of line with established Bank thinking: these effects are not apparent because the degree of repression has been *moderate* – thanks to macroeconomic balance and only slightly concessional interest rates for priority uses. This section of the report was of greatest interest to its Japanese sponsors. Its credibility was bolstered by the pre-eminent status in the American economics profession of its main author, Joseph Stiglitz, winner of the John Bates Clark medal for outstanding work by an economist under the age of 40. In the event, despite all the criticism, the section was left largely unchanged.

The 'institutional basis' chapter, though already diluted, was attacked as the document proceeded up the hierarchy of approval. Many critics called for references to authoritarianism to be dropped. Birdsall and Page defended the chapter successfully, managing to retain oblique references to authoritarianism (1993a: 188, for example).

As the deadline loomed, intense effort was made to present a consistent message.[34] The Bank's senior in-house editor was called in. He pasted each chapter page by page along the wall of a conference room. Together with several members of the team, he took a bird's-eye view, suggesting how to bring the messages up front. He paid special attention to the headings, on the presumption that many readers do not go beyond them. Headings should themselves give the argument, he urged. Parts of the draft were revised to emphasise the neoclassical 'fundamentals'. Results of the econometric tests of the effectiveness of selective industrial policy were rephrased to make them more clearly contra than in the original draft.

Page later explained his principle for responding to criticism: if he agreed that the evidence was not strong enough to support a certain proposition, he toned down the statement, regardless of whether it was Bank orthodoxy or not. At the same time, he had to recognise that this was a World Bank document with an 'anonymous' author that sets out a 'Bank' position. So it should steer between the extremes, never straying outside the range of views represented within the Bank. Yet the team members were also anxious not simply to repeat the Bank's standard line, and saw themselves as a vanguard pushing out the frontiers of debate. They were also well aware of the importance of Japan to the World Bank and of Japan's interest in the conclusions. A senior manager later remarked: 'Without the strong leadership of Larry Summers, Nancy Birdsall, and John Page, the report would not have moved anything like as far [from Bank orthodoxy] as it did.'

Argument and evidence

The final document bears traces of the three-way tussle between Japan, the research vice-presidency, and the East Asian vice-presidency. It concedes for the first time in a major Bank publication the *fact* of extensive government intervention in most of East Asia. It also grants the argument that some of these interventions, in the areas of exports and credit, *may* have fostered growth and equity in some parts of East Asia. Further, the report states that 'More selective interventions – forced savings, tax policies to promote (sometimes very specific) investments, sharing risk, restricting capital outflow, and repressing interest rates also *appear to have succeeded* in some HPAEs [High Performing Asian Economies], especially Japan, Korea, Singapore, and Taiwan, China' (1993a: 242, emphasis added). And again: 'Our evidence leads us to conclude that credit programmes directed at exports yielded high social returns and, in the cases of Japan and Korea, other directed-credit programmes also may *have increased investment and generated important spill-overs* (1993a: 356, emphasis added).

Lewis Preston's Preface is significant because it is the president who ultimately must keep the main shareholders happy, and in this case the number-two shareholder evidently needed to be made less unhappy. The Preface was written within the core team and did not have to fight its way past the East Asian vice-presidency. It says, for example:

This diversity of [East Asian] experience reinforces the view that economic policies and policy advice must be country-specific, if they are to be effective ... The report also breaks some new ground. It concludes that in some economies, mainly those in Northeast Asia, *some selective interventions contributed to growth,* and it advances our understanding of the conditions required for interventions to succeed ... These prerequisites suggest that the institutional context within which policies are implemented is as important to their success or failure as the policies themselves (1993a: vi, emphasis added).

These are Japanese-style statements. Despite all the pressures for the Bank not to admit it has been wrong, the president of the Bank here hints at just that. The Preface does not even use the normal protective cover; it says 'some selective interventions contributed to growth', without the 'may have'. A cynic might say that the 'some selective interventions contributed to growth' statement by Preston, plus the line in the text on page 356 ('other directed-credit programmes also may have increased investment and generated important spill-overs') are the nuggets for which the Japanese paid US$1.2 million.

The rest of the text takes a much stronger anti-industrial policy line. The flavour of the overall document is expressed in statements such as 'industrial policies were largely ineffective', and 'We conclude that promotion of specific industries generally did not work and therefore holds little promise for other developing economies' (1993a: 312, 354). It is not surprising that the bulk of the report gives a strong endorsement of established World Bank ideas. We saw earlier why the Japanese ideas constitute a serious threat. But the Bank cannot credibly reject ideas just because they are a threat. It has to claim to reject them on the evidence – of which the *Miracle* provides lots for its anti-industrial policy arguments.

The trouble, as several analysts have shown, is that most of the evidence does not survive serious scrutiny.[35] Here are three examples:

1. The key proposition that more open economies grow faster than closed ones is based on the finding that indicators of openness are positively correlated with growth in the basic growth regression. One indicator of openness is an index constructed by David Dollar. As Dani Rodrik argues, the index is really a measure of real exchange rate divergence, not of openness (1994b: 35–39). But if used as an index of openness, Dollar's own published results reveal that Japan and Taiwan were *less open* during 1976–85 than Argentina, Brazil, India, Mexico, the Philippines, and Turkey – a result ignored by the *Miracle* study. Rodrik concludes that the evidence presented for the proposition that more open economies grow faster is simply not relevant. To the extent that it is, it points the other way. And here as throughout, had China been included, the evidence would have pointed still more strongly the other way.[36] Since the early 1980s, China has been outperforming most developing countries, yet it has remained – while liberalising – much less liberal than most, with extensive controls on finance, trade and industry.
2. The report says that 'price distortions were mild', or that 'East Asia's relative prices of traded goods were closer on average to international prices than other developing areas' (World Bank 1993a: 24, 301). This generalisation is important for the argument that, while industrial policies existed in East Asia, their magnitude was slight. But the report also acknowledges that the relative prices of Japan, Korea and Taiwan deviated *more* from international prices than those of such notorious interventionists as India, Pakistan, Brazil, Mexico and Venezuela in 1976–85, another finding it does not comment upon (1993a: 301). How does it reach the vital conclusion about low average price distortions? By averaging the price distortion scores of all eight East Asian cases, including the Hong Kong and Singapore minnows.
3. One of the tests of the effectiveness or otherwise of sector-specific industrial promotion uses the correlation between growth in output or value added by different industries, and the level of wages or value added per worker in the

same industries (1993a: Table A6.2). If sectoral industrial policies made a difference, the argument goes, we expect a positive correlation, because industrial policies aim to favour capital- and technology-intensive industries and these factor intensities are proxied by high wages. So if industries that grow faster also have higher wages, this means that the more capital- or technology-intensive industries are growing faster, and industrial policies can be declared successful. Conversely, if the correlation is negative we have grounds for concluding that structural change is driven not by industrial policy but by market forces. It can be argued that the test is mis-specified (see Rodrik 1994b). But the problem is with what the report does with its own evidence. The results for several time periods yield mostly positive correlations (pro-industrial policy) for Hong Kong, and Japan, and mostly negative ones (pro-free-market forces) for Taiwan and Korea. But none of the results is statistically significant – except the negative correlations for Korea. The report still concludes that these results confirm the *ineffectiveness* of industrial policy in East Asia.

The middle road
Once such standards of inference are allowed to leak into what we call 'evidence', confirming results can be pumped out like bilge water.[37] It is a fine irony that when the one member of the team with work experience in Asia suggested some discussion of cultural propensities to save and educate, he was told the matter could not be discussed because of lack of evidence. The weakness of evidence notwithstanding, the argument sweeps to its paradigm-protecting conclusions on the strength of several rhetorical techniques. One is to structure an argument as a triptych with two extremes and a middle, our confidence in the middle being elevated by the foolishness of what flanks it. In the *Miracle* we are shown two cartoonish interpretations of East Asian success – laissez-faire and government intervention – and then the sensible market-friendly approach in between. This was, however, a late addition. Together with the removal of 'strategy' and 'strategic', it was part of the price of acquiescence from the East Asian vice-presidency,

and the means by which the chief economist of the East Asia region could propel the conclusions of his *World Development Report 1991* to the forefront of the Bank's thinking on development. The report also seeks to persuade by ignoring serious alternative explanations of East Asian economic success. The main alternatives to such ideas as 'market-friendly policies plus export-push policies yield export-led growth' are not 'laissez-faire' or 'government intervention'. Indeed, no serious scholar has argued that the difference between East Asia and elsewhere is to be explained mainly in terms of government intervention.

The main alternative, rather, is 'favourable initial conditions – especially human capital and infrastructure – plus investment-led growth'. The causality runs from higher investment to faster technical change and higher imports, and from these to higher exports – these exports being more a result than a cause.[38] Certainly, export growth helped to maintain the key driving force – high rates of return on accumulation (by permitting economies of scale), but so, too, did rising skill levels and an array of government policies designed to boost productivity and keep the lid on income inequality. Sectoral industrial policies enter the explanation as an important cause of high rates of *aggregate* investment as well as a cause of the structure of that investment, helping East Asia to move quickly from the 'factor-cost'-driven stage of competitiveness to the 'investment'-driven stage (Porter 1990: Chapter 10). Of course the report notes the fact of unusually high investment in East Asia, but sees it as more a *result* of market-friendly policies and export-push than as being itself the primary proximate driver – though without doing the econometric tests to examine the causality. As for the fast growth of South-East Asia – Thailand, Malaysia, Indonesia – the report assumes the causes to lie in domestic factors, and fails to examine the extent to which their growth can be explained in terms of spillover effects from the fast growth of the more nationally focused, governed-market economies of East Asia.

Furthermore, the report tries to persuade by employing asymmetrical standards of evidence. As the drafts progressed, the many critics who asked 'what exactly is your evidence?' were concerned only with the pro-intervention propositions. They took for granted that if the evidence was not compelling it should be discounted, but did not apply the same scrutiny to propositions in favour of the free market. The market is innocent until proven guilty, the government is guilty until proven innocent.

Finally, the report fails to make explicit some key distinctions, with the effect of allowing readers more scope for interpreting the results in line with their preconceptions. The striking case in point concerns credit. The Japanese were especially interested in getting the Bank to admit that directed credit – targeted at particular sectors – had worked in Japan and elsewhere in East Asia. But the Bank is deeply committed to the view that selective industrial promotion cannot raise national welfare, and so needs to conclude that it did not do so in East Asia. Since directed credit is, it would seem, simply one instrument of selective industrial policy, the two propositions – Japan's directed credit, the Bank's selective industrial policy – cannot both be true at the same time. Yet the report manages to imply that they are. It does so by classifying interventions into three ostensibly non-overlapping categories: selective industrial policies, directed credit policies, and export-push policies. It concludes that the first failed, the third worked, and as for the second – the focus of Japanese interest – it states, as we have seen, 'that credit programmes directed at exports yielded high social returns, and, in the cases of Japan and Korea, other directed credit programmes also may have increased investment and generated important spill-overs' (World Bank 1993a: 356). On the face of it, this says that for Japan and Korea directed credit may have been *effective* as an instrument of sectoral industrial policy, though the report also claims that sectoral industrial policy did *not* work. Dani Rodrik writes that 'It is difficult to fathom how [such a logical inconsistency] found its way into the report (and as a major conclusion, to boot)' (1994b: 28).

Part of the reason was an editorial failure to make a clear distinction between two types of 'directed' or 'selective' policies: 'functional' and 'sectoral', where 'functional' refers to a non-sector-specific function, like R&D (research and development) or exports, and 'sectoral' refers to specific sectors – chemicals or machine tools, for example. When the text talks of 'selective' industrial policy it means 'sectoral' or 'sector-specific'; when it talks of 'selective' or 'directed' credit policy, however, it means 'functional'. Its only evidence on directed credit other than for exports comes from a study of the effects of subsidised R&D credit in Japan – that is, a study of a functionally directed, not sectorally directed credit policy. On the basis of this study, the report says that (functionally) directed credit worked in Japan in the sense that it had higher social returns than private returns, made a net addition to R&D investment rather than substituting for more expensive commercial credit, and was cut off when no longer needed. So the Bank's conclusion about directed or selective credit applies to functionally selective policy, while its conclusion about selective industrial policy applies to sectorally selective policy. Why was such an obvious source of confusion allowed to persist? The effect of fudging the distinction between functional and sectoral was to allow those sympathetic to the Japanese position on credit to infer a greater agreement with that position than was actually the case.

Responses
In August 1993 the World Bank EDs considered the final draft. Their reactions showed nothing like consensus. The US ED gave a glowing endorsement of what he took to be the free-market message of the report. (Some of the core team were disturbed to hear how he spindoctored all their qualifications away.) The newly arrived Japanese ED was cautiously complimentary. The Argentinean ED said, angrily, that the whole report was an apologia for interventionism. The Indian ED came close to saying that the report's anti-interventionist conclusions were fixed in advance and the evidence tailored to fit. Few changes were made in response to the Board's comments. If you are being attacked from all sides, Page later explained, the argument must be about right. Indeed, unknown to the EDs, the document had already been typeset by the time of the Board discussion to ensure readiness for the annual meetings. It could not have been changed even if the EDs

agreed on changes.[39] The incident illustrates the independence of the Bank staff from the Board, despite the Board's status as the supervisory body representing member countries.

On 26 September 1993, exactly on time, *The East Asian Miracle: Economic Growth and Public Policy* was launched at the annual meetings of the World Bank and IMF. There was a press conference, a press release, and a seminar for annual meeting participants. The report 'sells itself', because of outside interest. The diversity of views among the EDs was a microcosm of reactions outside the Bank. In the press, for example, some journalists (mainly Japanese) said that the study confirmed the effectiveness and replicability of East Asia's government interventions. Others (mainly American and British) said that it confirmed their ineffectiveness and unreplicability. The London *Financial Times* led its review of the report with, '*Industrial policies to promote particular sectors or companies have been a failure in East Asia* and do not explain the region's rapid growth in recent decades, according to a World Bank study' (27 September 1993: 16, emphasis added). The *Nihon Keizai Shimbun*, Japan's leading business paper, said 'the report cites the accumulation of high-grade human and physical capital as a motivating force and *highly evaluates the effects of government intervention*' (26 September 1993: 7, emphasis added).[40]

MOF officials celebrated the fact that the Bank had at last admitted that state intervention could be useful, but were also critical of some of the conclusions. In December 1993 former executive director Masaki Shiratori, now posted to the OECF, delivered a hard-hitting critique at a seminar in Tokyo. He argued that

> comparative advantage should be regarded as a dynamic notion rather a static one . . . It is theoretically right to pick and nurture specific promising industries which do not have comparative advantage now. Many developing countries desperately need to get rid of the monoculture in such commodities as coffee, cocoa, copper and tin, which resulted from static comparative advantage . . . A latecomer to industrialisation cannot afford to

leave everything to the market mechanism. The trial and error inherent in market-driven industrialisation is too risky and expensive considering the scarcity of resources (Shiratori 1993).

He went on to make a number of theoretical and technical points against the Total Factor Productivity test of the effectiveness of selective industrial policy, concluding, 'In view of these theoretical and technical problems in the Report's analysis of industrial policy, I hope further studies will be made within and outside the World Bank. In the meantime, I sincerely wish that the Bank will adopt "pragmatic flexibility" in prescribing policy advice to developing countries' (Shiratori 1993). Isao Kubota concluded his remarks at the same seminar, saying: 'Perhaps the best lesson could be that policy makers and policy advisers, including those in the World Bank, should not be dogmatic but be pragmatic. For that purpose *modesty, not arrogance, and a sincere attitude* toward finding the right policy measures, are essential' (Kubota 1993b).[41]

A senior MOF official close to the *Miracle* study characterised MOF and MITI reactions as follows:

MOF people consider this a good step forward, although they are not fully satisfied with the study's negative assessment on industrial policy. The reaction of the MITI people is mixed: they share the MOF view, on the one hand, but they are afraid to be accused of excessive intervention *now* in the course of negotiations with the US and the EC.

He referred to MITI concerns as expressed by, for example, Makoto Kuroda, MITI's best known hard-line negotiator with the US: 'We must not provide a dangerous basis for the argument that says Japan conducts itself by a different set of rules and must be treated differently. For some time I have repeatedly stated that we should avoid expressions such as "Japanese-style practices"' (Johnson 1993b: 59).

Opinion about the *Miracle* study within MITI differed between the two key bureaux, the International Trade Bureau and the Industrial

Policy Bureau. The former is preoccupied with maintaining access to the *American* market, for which avowed commitment to 'free-market' and 'level playing field' symbols is important. People from this bureau tended to be enthusiastic about the study's conclusion that selective industrial policy has, by and large, been ineffective in East Asia. The Industrial Policy Bureau, by contrast, is committed to boosting the idea of MITI's successful steerage of the Japanese economy, and people from this bureau tended to be more critical of the study. MOF's critical stance may reflect its concerns to maintain a strategic aid programme using directed credit and other infant industry incentives. The two agendas – that of the International Trade Bureau of MITI and that of MOF – may reflect a single higher-level strategy: to maintain access to the American market over the five-year middle-run, while building up a dense presence in the South-East Asian and China markets for the ten-year longer run, at the end of which these markets are expected to be more important than the American.[42]

Within the Board of the Bank, Shiratori's successor as Japan's ED was less active. He did not push the concerns that lay behind Japan's promotion of the *Miracle* study. This may reflect a high-level decision in Tokyo to calm relations with the World Bank in order to avoid causing even more turbulence in Japan's relations with the US. As part of this calming strategy, the Japanese government agreed with the Bank that Japan's directed credit programmes, though they continue, will not use *narrow* earmarking (will not define beneficiaries narrowly) and will not have a *big* subsidy element (not more than one or two percentage points below the market rate).

As for the Bank's response, a top manager said:

> We simply cannot afford to take a more custom-tailored approach to lending conditions, as the Japanese have been urging. If we were to say to the Philippines, "It is OK for Malaysia to do this but not for you", we could be accused of violating the political impartiality condition of our charter.[43]

No follow-up research has been planned. The director of the research department explained that 'the real issue is the relevance of the East Asian experience for other developing countries... *Now the East Asian study is completed, the research agenda lies more in Africa and other developing countries than it does in East Asia*' (Squire 1993, emphasis added).[44] He took for granted that 'the East Asian experience' is the experience as interpreted in the *East Asian Miracle*.

The art of paradigm maintenance – and change

Our story raises a more general question. How does the World Bank – a large institution, with some 4 000 professional staff drawn from many countries,[45] producing dozens of public reports a year – manage to deliver what the outside world hears as a single central message? The art of paradigm maintenance begins with the choice of staff. As noted, about 80 per cent of Bank economists were trained in North America or Britain, and all but a few share the preconceptions of mainstream Anglo-American economics (Frey et al. 1984). If they were to show sympathy for other ideas – if they were to argue that sectoral industrial policies could in some circumstances be effective, for example – they would be unlikely to be selected for the Bank, on grounds of incompetence. The organisation's few non-economist social scientists are employed on marginal issues such as resettlement and participation, like anthropologists by colonial administrations before them.

But within the staff there remains a range of views that command some following. The second technique of paradigm maintenance is the internal review process. A document goes through rounds of discussions at successively higher levels of the hierarchy, each level being a filter that narrows the range of views espoused by 'the Bank'. It is not just that higher levels are more concerned with the Bank's and the system's integrity than with the integrity of the research. It is also that promotion criteria select people for the higher levels who make decisions quickly and with closure, using 'facts' selectively to support preconceived patterns and convictions. Such people tend to be intolerant of those who do not share the conclusions to which they leap.[46]

Thirdly, the legions of Bank editors, some in-house, some employed as consultants, are a part of the maintenance mechanism. Their continued employment depends not only upon their ability to write clear English but also on their ability to write copy that, being in line with 'Bank thinking', will not attract criticism.

This is the review and editing mechanism. The criteria applied are partly formal and partly substantive. The formal criteria relate particularly to the need for a clear 'message'. Great emphasis is placed on having a clear message, on minimising 'on the one hand, on the other hand' statements which are thought to be confusing to the intended audience of policy makers. (Indeed, the early meetings of the writing team are often taken up with discussion of 'What are going to be the key messages of this report?', before the research is done.) The message is to consist not of a setting out of possible alternatives and conditions in which they make more or less sense, and still less of acknowledgement that the evidence is mixed or insufficient, but is to consist of the best policy for the 'typical' developing country. This makes for 'clarity'.

The need for a clear and consistent message for policy makers has implications for the content of the message. The members of the team, partly propelled by professional norms, may be concerned to speak the truth as they see it. But at the higher levels reviewers are sensitive to the more 'systemic' pressures for paradigm maintenance discussed earlier – the need not to upset capital markets, and the self-perception of the Bank as a bulwark against the vested interests that push governments to intervene in socially counter-productive ways. Their comments page by page are unlikely to allude directly to these systemic pressures. Rather, they insist that everything should fit the overall message.

This is the mechanism for conformity. All prominent Bank documents go through it. But what issues get onto the Bank's agenda in the first place? On the whole, the Bank has been a reactive rather than pro-active organisation, taking its lead from outside. The Bank ensures its own expansion and centrality by launching bids for expert status on some of the issues at the top of the current agenda of development debate, proposing market solutions with compensatory or mitigating elements, creating a consensus around its position, and marginalising more radical alternatives (Gibbon 1993b). Outside the Bank, the debate then tends to configure itself into 'pro- or anti-' Bank positions. This might be called, tongue-in-cheek, a strategy for the sustainable development of the World Bank.

The East Asian Miracle can be read as the latest expression of this strategy. East Asia and industrial policy came to centre stage in the late 1980s, as the US and European economies continued to limp and East Asian economies continued to soar. The new element in the situation – compared to, say, a report on Africa or the Bank's poverty work in the late 1980s – was that the number-two shareholder was putting pressure on the Bank to endorse, or at least make some concession to, its non-orthodox views about development principles. The mere centrality of the issue in the development debate would not have been sufficient to prompt the Bank to make a special study, for the issue was at once too indirectly tied to lending and too likely to annoy the Japanese or to complicate the Bank's policy formula.[47] But when Japan agreed to pay for the study and to drop its opposition to the operational directive on financial sector reform the Bank could not say no.

These initiating circumstances made it important for the team leader to be someone known to be solidly in the mainstream of Bank thinking, not a doctrinaire free marketeer. John Page met this condition; his pedigree, as a student of Ian Little's and protégé of Anne Krueger's,[48] was conservative, but he had subsequently espoused more pragmatic views. Likely candidates from the East Asia vice-presidency were either free marketeers or too much under their hierarchical command. Even so, the universalistic and non-institutional ethos of neoclassical economics meant that no premium was given to selecting people for the core team who had expertise in East Asia – whether Bank staff or consultants. Any Bank economist is expected to be an expert on a country or region within a matter of months.

As we have seen, the East Asia vice-presidency was excluded. True, it got the country studies, but the core team largely ignored these. Yet the East Asia vice-presidency could not be prevented from being the major reviewer, because in the higher-level review committees the East Asia vice-president met the Research vice-president on equal terms – and with much more personal influence in the Bank where he had spent his whole career. If the East Asia vice-president decided to do so, he could effectively prevent or at least delay the report in its path to the Board, and so hinder its publication. The cross-pressures among the Japanese sponsors, the core team, and the East Asian vice-presidency help to explain the report's inconsistencies.

Inconsistency as a register for change

The inconsistencies should not be seen simply as 'mistakes'. The authors may have left them in – to the extent that they were aware of them[49] – in an attempt to *widen* the grounds of debate without generating a backlash that would cause the report to be dismissed as incompetent or ideological, and the Bank to be accused of changing its mind. The pro-industrial policy statements, though at odds with the rest of the report, may function as attractor points by enabling those wishing to put new questions on the agenda to claim legitimacy from the *Miracle* study. This, it could be argued, is the most likely way that big organisations change their minds; sharp changes are rare.

The Japanese have influenced the Bank enough to provide attractor points beyond those in the *Miracle* study itself. The several studies of Japanese economic policy and civil service organisation sponsored by the Bank at about the same time – and also paid for by the Japanese – provide a set of policy ideas that can legitimise further work in these domains, outside and inside the Bank. In particular, the Bank's imprimatur can help legitimise the idea of 'Japan as model' *for Japan's* use in its own more dirigist Asian aid strategy, further strengthening the constituency for these ideas. It may also be argued that the Bank's softening of its stand against directed credit, as of 1995, owes something to the wider Japanese pressure on the Bank. Compared to the 1980s, the Bank is now less likely to insist that directed credit and interest rate subsidies should always be avoided. It is more likely to insist simply that the onus must be on the proposer to explain the special circumstances justifying directed credit in a given case.[50] The shift is small but not trivial, and gives the Bank more flexibility in responding to Japan's continued use of directed credit.

Although the Japanese government has ceased pressuring the Bank, it has not stopped promulgating its ideas in developing countries. Seeing 'the Japanese approach to industrial policy' as a new export product, it is building up an enormous capacity for teaching Asian bureaucrats, industrialists and scholars about the Japanese approach to industrial policy. One of the leading figures in this campaign recently declared,

> Free market theory has failed in many areas like Russia, Eastern Europe, and sub-Saharan Africa because it is too short-sighted and too market-oriented. Not enough attention was paid to these countries' own economic and social structures ... Japan started from a planned economy post-war, to become gradually liberalised over the years. I would say we are now 80 per cent of the way to being a free-market economy. In developing countries it should be more like 50 per cent. We are not saying that developing countries should imitate Japan. But they do need to study an alternative to neoclassical economic theory.

To supply them with such an alternative, in 1995 between 500 and 600 foreign government officials attended courses in economic development run by MITI and the ministries of finance, foreign affairs, and the Bank of Japan. Scores of Japanese officials will also leave Tokyo on secondment to governments in developing countries, or to swell the small ranks of Japanese officials in multilateral development agencies. Most of the countries targeted for receiving this attention are also lucrative markets for Japanese goods.[51]

The argument raises two wider points. The first is about the Bank's research function. The Bank's legitimacy depends upon the authority of its views; like the Vatican, and for similar reasons, it cannot afford to admit fallibility. At the same time, many of the Bank's research publications, especially the high visibility ones like the *World Development Reports*, are really *advocacy* statements, steered by the bedrock perception that the Bank must act as a counterweight to all the gravitational pulls towards excessive government intervention – which justifies erring on the side of markets. Hence for good organisational and political reasons the Bank's research is biased towards the conclusion that 'there is no alternative' to government policies that stay within the bounds of 'strengthening the enabling environment for private sector development'. The Bank's endorsement of this tenet is important for its authoritative image in the eyes of the interlocking social groups who embrace the 'Washington Consensus'. The research must also be largely quantitative, for numbers and econometric technique themselves confer authority. Research that meets these criteria thus helps to maximise staff commitment internally and authoritative reputation externally, and in turn colours the 'reality' against which those leaders of economic opinion check their expectations of the future. But its conclusions are not necessarily those that are most consistent with the evidence.

The second point concerns the Bank's autonomy. Our case study shows the Bank fending off a challenge to its way of seeing from its second-largest shareholder. On the face of it, this looks like autonomy. It seems consistent with William Ascher's argument that

> the viability of a development objective or strategy to be implemented through the World Bank depends not only on the acquiescence of the obvious international actors – the nation states through their formal institutional representation and their various pressures – but also on its congruence with the professional role models of the relevant staff. If the staff perceives the strategy or objectives as a 'decline in standards', as requiring them to become more 'political' vis-à-vis the borrower governments... its viability is doubtful unless altered role models can be quickly inculcated, new incentives provided, or rapid staff turnover undertaken (1983: 436).

The problem is not that this argument is wrong, as far as it goes, but that it stops short of asking about the structure of power in which the Bank operates, and how that structure affects the Bank's response to new development approaches. The story of *The East Asian Miracle* shows the determining importance of essentially American values and interests in the functioning of the Bank.[52] But the influence is exerted not mainly from the American government to the senior management of the Bank – if we look just at this relationship we see considerable autonomy, though the president has always been American. The influence comes partly through the Bank's dependence on world financial markets, and the self-reinforcing congruence between the values of the owners and managers of financial capital and those of the US state. It also comes through the Bank's staffing and professional norms. Not only are Americans greatly overrepresented in the professional and managerial ranks but, at least as important since the beginning of the 1980s, is a second channel of influence – the conquest of managerial positions by economists, and the recruitment of economists, including some from the developing countries, predominantly from North American and British universities (virtually none from Japanese universities). This channel of influence is obscured by talking of 'professionalism' as a source of the Bank's autonomy, without also talking about the *content* of that professionalism and from which member state's intellectual culture it comes.

By examining such factors we can see how the Bank forms part of the external infrastructural power of the US state, even though it by no means bows to every demand of the US government. Whereas the Japanese state uses its strong *domestic* infrastructural power directly to leverage its external reach – especially in South-East Asia and China – the US state, with much weaker domestic infrastructural power, relies upon its dominance of international organisations such as the World Bank and the IMF to keep those organisations pursuing goals that augment its own external reach. The Bank's stance as honest broker allows it to insist on the acceptance of those goals more openly than the US could itself. The story of *The East Asian Miracle* shows how this process worked itself out in one particular case.

Notes

1. In addition to the cited sources, this chapter is based on interviews with officials in Tokyo and Washington, DC, who prefer anonymity, and on my own experience as a World Bank economist in 1984–88. I thank Ngaire Woods, Linda Weiss, Ronald Dore, Devesh Kapur, Chalmers Johnson, Thomas Biersteker, Manfred Bienefeld, Wendy Law-Yone and Torn Yanagihara for comments. The chapter can be read as a companion to Wade (1994). The theoretical ideas behind the critique are set out in Wade (1990).
2. Note that 'trade' comes before industrialisation in the title. Anglo-American economists see trade and free-trade policy as the motor of industrialisation; Japanese economists see trade and managed-trade policy as a subordinate part of industrialisation and industrial strategy. See further Wade (1993).
3. The plan has not been translated into English, but for a brief description in English, see Japan Economic Institute, Report No. 22A, 18 June 1993, p. 9. Over the 1970s and 1980s MITI economists and Japanese academics put the empirical and analytic underpinnings of the plan in place by studies of natural resources, trade and industrialisation in South-East Asian economies. The plan and its history illustrate the long-term nature of Japanese planning, and the coordination between government and firms. The contrast with the unstrategic nature of British and American aid and Foreign Direct Investment (FDI) policies is pronounced. We see the results of the plan in the simultaneous spurt of Japanese FDI and aid to Thailand in 1988. Much of the aid was for the construction of industrial estates reserved for Japanese companies. The companies were exiting from Japan to escape quota restrictions on Japanese imports to OECD countries and environmental standards for industrial production, and to tap cheap Thai labour.
4. Tadao Chino, then vice-minister, ministry of finance, in 1991, cited in Lincoln (1993: 124).
5. Masaki Shiratori was born in 1936, graduated from Tokyo University Law Faculty (1956–60), joined the ministry of finance in 1960, studied economics at Columbia University (1964–66), and was director of Coordination Division, International Finance Bureau (1984–85): after two more moves (1985–88), he became senior deputy director-general of International Finance Bureau, then executive director for Japan, World Bank (1989–92), after which vice-president of the OECF (1992–). As chief of the International Financial Institutions division of the International Finance Bureau in 1981–84, in addition to raising Japan's rank in the IBRD, his second main goal was to get China accepted as a member of the Asian Development Bank, also successfully accomplished.
6. Senior operational vice-president Moeen Qureshi signed the letter. The Bank's interpretation is as follows: the story began in 1986 when the Bank agreed to help the government of the Philippines restructure two major public-sector banks – including the Development Bank of the Philippines. The banks were both bankrupt, partly

because they had become patronage pots – with directed credit as the primary means of patronage. Their restructuring involved eliminating directed credit. Then along came the ASEAN-Japan Fund offering directed credit with a substantial subsidy element for narrowly earmarked purposes – the same instrument the banks had been using to dispense patronage. This was very difficult for the Bank to swallow. 'I remember many heated meetings in Tokyo and here in Washington', said a Bank official closely involved.

7. On the contrast between the Japanese and American approaches to these issues, see Okuda (1993). See also Kubota (1993a).
8. Isao Kubota graduated from the Tokyo University law faculty in 1966, joining MOF immediately. He undertook a B.Phil. in economics, Oxford University, 1967–69. In 1985 he became director of the International Organisation division of the International Finance Bureau of MOF. Seven years and four postings later, he became senior deputy director-general of MOF, the same job Shiratori had had before going as ED to the World Bank.
9. On the SII see Yanamura (1990).
10. And see Johnson (1994) for pungent views on a whole range of issues to do with Japan, South-East Asia, and the US.
11. This is the OECF's *first* Occasional Paper, 30 years after its formation in 1961.
12. Kubota was the chief promoter of the paper, supported by the president of the OECF, Mr Nishigaki. They aimed to have the paper circulated widely at the annual meeting of the World Bank and the IMF in October 1991. Preparation was entrusted to Yasutami Shimamura, director of the Economic Analysis Department of OECF. In addition to drawing on the ideas of OECF people (notably Kubota and Kazumi Goto, a division chief in the Coordination Department), Shimamura also assembled a team of outside academic economists. They included Professors Yanagihara (Hosei), Horittchi (Tokyo), Horiuchi (JDB), Okuda (Hitotsubashi), Utata (Waseda). This group met once a month for five months. They 'found it very difficult to make a consensus on the content of the Japanese critique', said a participant. Some of them saw little to criticise in the neoclassical paradigm, and others who were sceptical of it were hesitant to openly criticise the World Bank at this time. Eventually, with time before the annual meeting getting short, Shimamura wrote a draft, presented it to the research team, modified it to take account of reactions, and then presented it to the Board of OECF, even though some members of the research team were not happy with the result. The OECF Board approved release of the paper in time for it to be circulated at the annual meeting. The haste – and the overriding of the rule of consensus – came from the knowledge that if they missed the October deadline they would have to wait a year until the next annual meeting. The paper is very short (fourteen generously spaced pages in the English typescript) and the quality of the argumentation leaves much to be desired. It is published (in Japanese) in OECF *Research Quarterly* No. 73, 1991. Shimamura has a bachelor's degree in economics

from Keio University (1960–65), and an MBA from Colombia University (1968–70). He is currently a professor of economics at Saitama University. His father is Osamu Shimamura, the celebrated author of the *Income Doubling Plan* (and Ph.D. in economics from Tohoku University). Kubota has elaborated his views (1991a; 1991b; 1991c). The first two of these papers were read at a biannual meeting between the World Bank and the OECF/J-EXIM (Japanese Export and Import Bank), in May and November 1991, respectively. Shiratori (1992) sets out his views. Goto (1993) gives his opinion. See also the views of Horiuchi (1992).

13. He was deputising for the finance minister, who is the governor of the Board for Japan.
14. World Bank, Press Release No. 16, 15 October 1991, cited in Johnson (1993a).
15. Quoted in 'Japan wants strings on aid: At odds with US, Tokyo urges managed economics', *International Herald Tribune*, 2 March 1992. Around this time, another event illustrated the divergence between the US and the Japanese position, and the Japanese willingness to challenge Bank management. In November 1991 the top management of the Bank and some key Western EDs opposed publication of a study of World Bank support for industrialisation in a number of industrialising countries (World Bank 1992c). Sanjaya Lall, an Oxford economist, had made the study for the Operations Evaluation Department (OED) of the Bank. It concluded that the Bank had failed to draw lessons from successful government intervention in Asian economies for the benefit of its lending practices elsewhere. One of the main lessons was that:

> Industrial success at the national level depends on the interplay of three sets of factors: incentives, capabilities, and institutions . . . Just one set of factors by itself cannot lead to industrial development . . . Each of the three determinants of industrialization may suffer from market failure . . . Industrial strategy should address all these interrelated issues (World Bank 1992c: iv, v).

The Bank, it said, has unwarrantedly discounted the positive role of industrial strategy, relying too heavily on incentives while underplaying the building up of capabilities and institutions. And it 'has only partially fulfilled the function of correctly analysing Korea's experience with industrialisation' (1992c: vii). The report urged the Bank 'to help governments design industrial policies', and to 'adopt a more differentiated, nuanced approach to recommending policy packages to individual governments' (1992c: 54, 55). The top management called for the report not to be made available outside the Bank until its conclusions had been suitably revised, on the grounds that it gave 'too strong an endorsement of government intervention . . . even if the causes of government failure could be identified and minimized, the report calls for the impossible: fine-tuning an array of trade and industrial interventions to deal with real or perceived market failures is generally not feasible'. The report, says the Bank, offers an approach that 'is at variance with best practices as we know them, and would therefore be very counter-productive to the country dialogues'. It would open the way for governments 'to point out that the Bank's own evaluation department has concluded that the Bank's current approach is incorrect'. (This text is taken from a memorandum sent from a senior vice-president to the chairman of the Joint Audit Committee, who was also the American ED, 11 November 1991. The Joint Audit Committee, made up of representatives from the Board of directors of the Bank – none from management – is the body to which the OED reports, which is why the senior vice-president was unable to squash the report himself.) Several EDs, mostly from borrowing countries but including, crucially, Japan's, pressed the Bank to publish the study as is. They prevailed and the study was published.

16. The title and quote come from an article by Rich Miller in the *Journal of Commerce* II (December 1991): 1a. See also 'Free market theory not practical in Third World: Interview with Masaki Shiratori', *Executive Intelligence Review (EIR)*, 27 March 1992; 'Japan challenges World Bank orthodoxy', *Far Eastern Economic Review*, 12 March 1992: 49; 'Japan presses World Bank on lending: Nation begins asserting independent voice in global forum', *The Nikkei Weekly*, 12 March 1992: 3.

17. The plan was not formally a MITI document. It came out of the MITI Research Institute. For a summary, see Rowley (1992).

18. The *Economist* gives its own gloss on this point. Talking about foreign car makers coming into Asian countries it says, 'Once in, the foreigners have a nasty habit of becoming as protectionist as any local. Their aim is to persuade Asian governments not to open up their car markets or allow in new investors until their local operations have grown big enough to become competitive' (15 October 1994: 81).

19. Ichiro Ozawa, *Nihon Kaizo Keikaku*: 17, cited in C. Johnson, 'The foundations of Japan's wealth and power and why they baffle the United States', typescript, University of California (San Diego), 1993.

20. What of the relative importance of the four reasons? We might proceed by comparing what the Japanese want for the World Bank and what they do in the Asian Development Bank (ADB). From the beginning they have had much more influence in the ADB than in the World Bank – from which we can infer that the pattern of ADB lending gives a close reflection of their principles. Relations between the Japanese president and the US ED have been strained over the past several years, in connection with lending priorities and the need to raise the ADB's capital stock.

21. Max Weber, of course, would have agreed, and also Gunnar Myrdal.

22. Standard and Poors is one of the two main US investment rating agencies.

23. This, at least, is how Bank officials often state the matter. The truth is more complicated. The Bank's top-grade credit rating primarily depends upon its non-borrowing governments' guarantees and its first claimant status for borrowing governments – this status being enforced by knowledge that a non-repaying government will get no more aid from a World Bank-affiliated government. So the

Bank's top-grade credit rating does not depend on financial markets' evaluation of the quality of its loan portfolio. Rather, the link between its credit rating and its reputation for 'sound' lending conditions comes via the legislatures of the non-borrowing governments. The decision to honour the guarantees would not, in practice, be automatic. The US Congress, in particular, would have to authorise the expenditure, and has a long history of delaying authorisation of foreign appropriations. If it held a low opinion of the Bank, it might delay authorisation of the guarantee expenditures for a long time. Whether it holds the Bank in disrepute depends on the Bank's reputation in the eyes of financial markets. Much of what the Bank says in its flagship publications is vetted with this in mind; see especially the two recent *World Development Reports* that have provided a broad overview of development experience and theory, those for 1987 and 1991.

24. This is based on the staff of the research complex (PRE) in 1991. Of the total 465 higher-level staff, 290 had graduate degrees from US universities, 74 from the UK, 10 from Canada, and none from Japan. I thank Devesh Kapur for this information.

25. In fact, since the early 1990s, the Bank *has* begun to talk more overtly about politics, but warily and in the reassuringly technical language of governance – 'accountability', 'transparency', 'predictability', and so on. Even this has generated unease and opposition within the Bank and the Board, on the grounds that it risks being inconsistent with the charter. The issue came to a head in a Board discussion about a research department study, three years in the making, entitled 'Bureaucrats in business', in July 1995, when some EDs argued strongly that the Bank should not be talking about these issues – the French ED in particular, perhaps with governance in ex-French sub-Saharan African countries in mind.

26. The money came from Japan's amply endowed Policy and Human Resource Development trust fund for the World Bank. Many rich country members of the Bank have trust funds that are controlled jointly by the member country and the Bank to cover jointly agreed operational expenses of the Bank. Twenty per cent of the Bank's operational budget is now met from trust funds. The great advantage of this arrangement from the rich countries' view is that each government has a direct say in how 'its' money is used. If, at the same time, these countries squeeze the regular budget, they are able to gain pleasing *bilateral* influence over the Bank. In the late 1980s, the Bank had similarly got the governments which had been voicing concern about the impact of structural adjustment programmes on vulnerable groups – the 'soft' Northern governments – to finance much of the Bank's work on the design of anti-poverty programmes.

27. It emerged as Operational Directive 8.30, Financial Sector Operations, February 1992. It was largely the work of those who had earlier written the Levy Report. The Japanese were its main opponents on the Board.

28. The Bank's staff costs were about US$800 000 (US$150 000/year × 1.5 years × 3.5 persons). The Bank provided another US$200 000 for miscellaneous costs. This brought the total *Miracle* budget to US$2.2 million, about the same as a *World Development Report*.

29. Other Bank staff included Ed Campos (Filipino, US Ph.D. in the social sciences but de facto in economics, from Caltech, working on institutional issues); and Marylou Uy (Filipina, US Ph.D. in economics from UCLA, working on financial issues). Page, Campos and Uy worked full-time on the study; Birdsall worked half-time. The main consultants included Max Corden (Australian, trade economist, working on macroeconomics); Joseph Stiglitz (American, economic theorist, working on finance); Howard Pack (American, development economist, University of Pennsylvania, working on tests of the effectiveness of selective industrial policy); Richard Sabot (American, development economist, Williams College, working on human capital). Nancy Birdsall also worked with Sabot on human capital. A commentator on an earlier draft, who helped to manage the study, queried my presentation of the personnel: 'Why do you emphasise the fact of so many Americans? It seems you are implying that because we are Americans we had predetermined conclusions. In fact, we were eager to find a story that would be new. Anyway, you are misleading because the team's composition was about average for World Bank economists.' It is true that the Bank employs very few East Asian economists – but a lot of US- or UK-certified South Asian economists. Experience of employing Japanese economists has been disappointing, perhaps because the Bank is unwilling to hire in groups.
30. The JDB's data were also made available to two American economists for independent econometric assessment of the effectiveness of the credit policies.
31. There was also a comparative study of tax systems in Japan, Taiwan, Korea and India. The additional studies had a combined budget of US$1.8 million from the Japanese Trust Fund.
32. MacDonald, also an American, worked intensively on the drafts and redrafts from March to September 1995.
33. 'Government as referee' has a powerful resonance in neoclassical economics, and the link to contests takes it towards East Asian realities; but it obscures the point that the government sometimes acts as both referee and player at the same time.
34. The draft was also debated in a Singapore round-table discussion (including senior or ex-senior government officials from Singapore, Malaysia and Indonesia) and in Tokyo – three meetings with individual senior officials who gave detailed comments on the first draft: Kubota (MOF), Tsukuda (number two in the OECF), and Ogata (deputy governor, Bank of Japan). Individual chapters were presented by members of the Bank team to academic seminars in Singapore, Indonesia and Korea.
35. See the papers by Rodrik, Wade, and Haggard in Fishlow et al. (1994); Singh (1995); Amsden (1994); Lall (1995); and Cappelan and Fagerberg (1995). See further, Hirsh (1992), for which I was a prime source.
36. The set of HPAE includes Japan, Taiwan, South Korea, Hong Kong, Singapore, Thailand, Malaysia, and Indonesia; not China and not the Philippines.
37. There are many other examples of dubious evidence in the report; see the papers by Rodrik, Wade, and Haggard in Fishlow et al. (1994), and the references cited therein.

38. Indeed, Trella and Whalley (1992) go so far as to conclude, from their own quantitative analysis and that of others, that 'outward-oriented policies in Korea have little significance in driving growth'. See also Bradford (1992); Rodrik (1994a); UNCTAD (1994); and Wade (1990: 47–48, Chapters 6 and 9). Nor does the report examine what many analysts, though few economists, consider to be central to East Asia's economic success: the 'informal sector', the skeins of relational networks that operate behind the apparently formal institutions of finance, business and government across the region.
39. The version sent to the Board had been revised in the month between being sent to the Board and actually being discussed by it. Many of the revisions addressed issues that the Board had brought up, and were subsequently reported to the Board as being made *in response to* Board suggestions.
40. The *Far Eastern Economic Review* (owned by the American firm Dow Jones) concludes from the study that 'today the price of growth is eternal vigilance against sometimes well-intentioned efforts to "help" selected industries or otherwise substitute bureaucratic preferences for the millions of individual decisions that each day constitute the wisdom of the marketplace' (21 October 1993: 5). The *Daily Yomuri* begins its report, 'Economic policies that fuelled East Asia's dynamic economic growth over the past thirty years can also work in other developing regions of the world, according to a new World Bank study . . .' (27 September 1993: 7).
41. An American source close to the Bank, who has talked at length to senior MOF officials about the report, characterises their reaction as follows:

> We feel intellectually vindicated, because the report does recognise that selective credit has worked effectively in Japan and Korea. We are now beginning to find our intellectual voice on development issues, even if our voice does not yet match the size of our financial contribution. We regard the *Miracle* study as a start. We will now wait, regroup, and exert quiet pressure on the Bank to be more pragmatic in its policy advice.

42. Indeed, a watershed has already been reached in Japan's trade: for the first time, the surplus with Asia exceeded the surplus with the US in the fiscal year 1993–94.
43. This is from an American source close to senior levels of the Bank (and himself a former senior official), who asked the most senior manager for his view of the report.
44. The Bank may have continued to do a little more, on the research side, if any of the three main protagonists, Summers, Birdsall, and Page, had remained in or close to their positions; but they all moved far from where they could influence the follow up. Nancy Birdsall went on to be executive vice-president of the Inter-American Development Bank, John Page became chief economist for the Bank's Middle East region, and Lawrence Summers, as we have seen, joined the Clinton administration.

45. In Bank parlance, higher-level staff. Total staff, including temporaries, in the 1994 financial year was just over 8 000.
46. This is based on the Myers-Briggs personality inventory, administered to over 1 000 Bank managers in the early to mid-1990s. The results show that over two-thirds of Bank managers (directors, division chiefs, task managers) are 'TJs' ('thinking and judging') and that among directors (just below vice-presidents) 70 per cent process information in an 'Intuitive' (patterns, linkages) rather than 'Sensing' (detailed) kind of way, compared to 58 per cent of division chiefs.
47. I worked in the Bank's trade policy division in 1987–88, at the time when a team from the division was formulating a paper setting out the Bank's trade policy and its empirical and conceptual underpinnings. As a member of the same small division, I repeatedly urged the team to examine East Asia's import-control regime, and especially to consider whether the regime contained design features that enabled Japan, Korea, and Taiwan – all three having highly protected economies for long periods – to escape some of the expected neoclassical costs. I indicated possible mechanisms (Wade 1991, 1993) and offered to provide relevant literature. But the team was unwilling even to consider the possibility that protection East Asian-style might have brought benefits as well as costs, and the trade policy paper refers to the import-control regimes in East Asia *only* in terms of their liberalisation. See 'Strengthening trade policy reform', World Bank, Washington, DC, November 1989.
48. Ian Little was professor of economics at Oxford University; Anne Kreuger was World Bank vice-president for research, and both are well-known conservative economists. See, for example, Little (1982).
49. My argument does not imply that these techniques were deliberately deployed in an attempt to maintain the Bank's central beliefs. We do not need to embrace postmodernism to agree that people's commitment to a particular paradigm has a large subjective element – is underdetermined by the evidence – and that they are largely unaware of how the commitment is protected, by themselves and others, from contrary evidence or interpretations.
50. And it would point out that the question cannot be debated without making several distinctions: credit may be directed by region, by urban/rural, by small firm/large firm, by sector, by sub-sector; it may contain a larger or smaller element of subsidy; the amount of subsidy may be calculated in relation to the cost of lending or in relation to the price that the lender would otherwise charge; directed credit may comprise a larger or a smaller percentage of total credit, and so on.
51. The quoted official is Mt Katsuhisa Yamada, director of Japan's Institute of Developing Economies. See Dawkins (1995). The Japanese are also helping to keep the debate going in the OECD academic world. During 1994 OECF invited scholars in OECD countries to write short comments on the *Miracle* study. For the eight comments from UK-based respondents plus two Japanese commentaries on

the *Miracle* see *Journal of Development Assistance* (1995). OECF's country offices have also arranged meetings with academics in their respective countries to discuss papers such as the one presented by the Economic Planning Agency (1994).

52. American hegemony in the Bank is eclipsed or ceded in regions where other major countries have particular interests. France's ex-colonies in West Africa are a good case in point. There the Bank acts within narrow limits set by the Elysée's adviser on African Affairs, occultly coordinating with the Ministre de La Coopération and French military intelligence.

Chapter Ten

Miracles of Modernisation and Crises of Capitalism
The World Bank, East Asian Development and Liberal Hegemony

Mark T. Berger and Mark Beeson

This is a substantially revised version of a 1998 article in Third World Quarterly *19 (3): 487–504,* http://www.tandf.co.uk.

The financial crisis in East Asia raised important questions about both the way in which the East Asian development model has been understood and the relevance of the East Asian path, or paths, to modernisation for national development trajectories elsewhere in the world. Until the crisis in 1997–98 the World Bank played an important role in encouraging the perception that East Asia was the site of a veritable miracle of neoliberal development. More broadly, for many years the Bank has occupied a central international position in the production and dissemination of liberal and neoliberal development knowledge about East Asia and the rest of the world. In concert with a number of other key transnational regulatory agencies, such as the IMF, the Bank has also been instrumental in attempting to shape the overall contours of East Asia's political economy. Yet the World Bank's influence and its understanding of development should not be conceptualised in monolithic terms.[1] Over time the conception of development and vision of modernisation encouraged by the Bank has shifted, mirroring wider regional and global trends. This chapter begins with a brief discussion of the changes in the World Bank's understanding of development and its visions of modernisation over the past 30 or 40 years. This is followed by an examination of the Bank's efforts to accommodate the industrial rise of East Asia within the dominant neoliberal narrative on international development. It will be emphasised that the changes in the Bank's understanding of capitalist development in East Asia need to be located in the context of the overall transformation of the global political economy and the nation-state system since 1945. The World Bank has been an important site for the consolidation and revision of influential conceptions of modernisation. It has helped to sustain the hegemony of liberal ideas about development and it has been a major participant in the wider re-invention of liberalism in the Cold War and post-Cold War era.[2] An examination of the World Bank's historical and contemporary role in the rise of, and revisions to, the model of East Asian development tells us much about both the Bank and its contribution to the hegemonic position of liberal and neoliberal development ideas.

Liberalism, neoliberalism and the World Bank

Cold War liberalism

The World Bank (the International Bank for Reconstruction and Development) came into existence as part of the overall Bretton Woods system that emerged from the capitalist crisis, global war and reconstruction of the 1930s and 1940s. The Bank – along with the IMF – was envisioned by the victorious allied powers as an instrument that could be used to both consolidate and manage the post-war international political economy (Gilpin 1987). Not only was the Bank charged with providing the capital and expertise with which to kick-start post-1945 reconstruction, but it was also an important component in locking countries into a US-centred economic order – a critical consideration in the light of the emerging superpower rivalry between the US and the Soviet Union. Indeed, it is important to remember that, particularly in the immediate post-war period, the Soviet Union was widely seen as a serious alternative to the crisis-ridden capitalist system that had been mired in the Great Depression prior to the outbreak of the Second World War (Hobsbawm 1991: 115–25). From its inception, therefore, the Bank was grounded in the wider power relations of the Cold War. This period saw the establishment of an elite liberal consensus about both the appropriate model of economic development and the best approach to the management of international economic relations (Ikenberry 1993). As time passed this consensus shifted, moving from the Keynesian liberalism of the early Cold War era to the neoliberal order that began to emerge in the 1970s (Ruggie 1982: 379–415).

Prior to the 1970s the conception of and approach to development which emanated from the World Bank reflected the Keynesian consensus and the Cold War liberalism (liberal developmentalism or classic modernisation theory) of the US political and economic elite and their allies. Washington's overall strategy towards what became known after 1945 as the developing, or Third World built on the experience of anti-communist reconstruction in Europe in the late 1940s and 1950s. The 1947 effort to keep Greece and Turkey from succumbing to international communism relied on both military and economic aid. After the apparent success of the economic component of the containment strategy on the eastern fringe of Europe, the Marshall Plan was launched in 1948 with the aim of facilitating the rebuilding of Western Europe (Hogan 1987). The apparent success of anti-communist reconstruction in much of Europe, and latterly in North-East Asia, contributed to 'the full flowering of liberal developmentalism' in the 1960s, manifested most dramatically in the Alliance for Progress in Latin America and the US anti-communist crusade in Vietnam (Benjamin 1987: 107; Berger 1995b: 66–97; Latham 2000). These influences were readily apparent during Robert McNamara's presidency (1968–81) of the World Bank. McNamara had served as the secretary of defence in both the Kennedy and Johnson administrations, and was one of the key architects of the Vietnam War until his resignation in 1968, when he took up the presidency at the Bank (McNamara 1996).

The overall approach of McNamara, and other Cold War warriors of his generation, was conditioned by the idea that the poverty of nation-states in Asia, the Middle East, Africa and Latin America was the key to the spread of communism. Into the 1970s the presumption that there was a direct link between poverty and revolution and that the communist threat could be eliminated via the emulation of the approach to economic modernisation believed to have been followed in North America and Western Europe, was at the heart of the dominant international discourse on development (Packenham 1973: 52–53). Under McNamara the World Bank significantly expanded its lending at the same time as 'the alleviation of poverty' was promoted as a major focus of the organisation's activity.

The Bank in the McNamara era reflected some of the optimism characteristic of the wider Cold War liberalism (liberal developmentalism or classic modernisation theory) that had emerged after 1945. For example, in the mid-1970s Hollis Chenery, the World Bank's vice-president for development policy, initiated a study of the Bank's record on economic development since 1950 (Morawetz 1977; Leys 1996a: 17–19). The study was researched and written by an outside consultant (David Morawetz). However, the conclusions it drew still crystallised the official viewpoint of the Bank in the McNamara era. Overall the study, like the Bank in the 1970s, took the view that on a global scale economic growth had been rapid and dramatic; however, this growth continued to be very poorly distributed. The Morawetz Report was confident to the point of complacency that 'the eradication of poverty is not likely to be just another fad', that the 'problems of monoproduct economies' could be mitigated, that excessive concern about debt problems was misplaced, and that the dramatic growth in commercial lending in the 1970s was not a cause for concern. Only with the second oil crisis (1979–80) did the Bank express any public reservations about the international financial system's ability to recycle enough funds to maintain economic growth and systemic stability (World Bank 1980: 3). This, combined with anti-inflation policies of recently elected neoliberal governments, such as the Thatcher administration in Britain, and the anticipation that energy prices might continue to rise dramatically throughout the 1980s, convinced McNamara that the world economy had undergone a permanent change. Once the perception of permanent change in the world economy took hold of the Bank in 1980, various other policy conclusions followed. While financial assistance to governments of developing countries had been used in the past as 'a substitute for structural adjustment', it was increasingly used to 'support structural adjustment'.[3] Thus the changing international context allowed the Bank to use structural adjustment loans to lock recipient governments into a particular sort of politico-economic order, one that reflected both the interests and assumptions of its major sponsors.

The neoliberal ascendancy
In the early 1980s neoliberal governments (particularly the Reagan administration in the US and the Thatcher administration in Britain) were in the ascendant in North America and Western Europe. The neoliberal ascendancy, however, did not flow from the inherent rationality of neoliberal policies – it was grounded in part in the apparent intractability of the economic and social problems of the 1970s. The apparent inability of the various governments in power in North America and Western Europe (and beyond) to deal with rising inflation was a central component of the rise of neoliberalism during the late 1970s. Cold War revivalism played an equally important role in defence and foreign affairs; significantly, however, opposition to the new Cold War was more effective than opposition to neoliberal economics (Cronin 1996: 177, 185). More broadly, the emergence of neoliberalism as the dominant narrative on development was linked directly to the dramatic changes in the overall character of the international political economy in the 1980s. Neoliberalism seemed to offer simple solutions to the economic problems of the North American and Western European electorates, its programme meshing with the aims and assumptions of a complex array of transnational forces that were the motor and the main beneficiaries of the neoliberal (or the emergent globalisation) project (Leys 1996a: 19).

Significantly, these wider shifts were marked by the end of McNamara's tenure as president of the World Bank. During the presidency of his successor, Alden Winship (Tom) Clausen (1981–86), the conception of development that had predominated at the Bank during the McNamara era was more or less erased. Clausen, whose previous position had been at the head of the Bank of America – the biggest commercial bank in the world – made it clear to the World Bank's top executives at the outset that he had no intention of maintaining his predecessor's focus on poverty alleviation. Mahbub Ul Haq, a long-time Bank staffer and adviser to McNamara observed that Clausen, a proponent of supply-side economics, was adamant 'that the only constituency that mattered was the United States' (in Caufield 1996: 144, 178). During the 1980s poverty alleviation was 'demoted to priority zero' with so-called structural adjustment policies emerging to take its place (Mosley, Harrigan and Toye 1991: 22–23). The dramatic shift in development thinking at the Bank was clearly represented by the Berg Report that was published in 1981. The official title of the report written by Elliot Berg was *Accelerated Development in Sub-Saharan Africa: An Agenda for Action* (World Bank 1981). The report relied on insights drawn from rational choice theory to evaluate the developmental record of governments in sub-Saharan Africa. Its prescriptions centred on the need for a greatly reduced role for the state in the economy and much greater reliance on the market as a means of accelerating economic activity, particularly in the agricultural sector. However, it is misleading to view the Bank during Clausen's presidency as being united around the neoliberalism reflected in the Berg Report. Under Clausen the Bank experienced greater policy fragmentation and diversity than was the case during the McNamara era.

In this period, for example, the research department of the World Bank was characterised by a particularly devout commitment to neoliberalism and an intolerance of dissent, which was not necessarily shared by other sections of the Bank. After 1981 the research department's operations and activities were devoted increasingly to 'large projects designed to substantiate what everyone knew in their hearts already: that economic liberalisation was right' (Mosley, Harrigan and Toye 1991: 23–24). The head of the research department was Anne Krueger, who Clausen had hired to replace Hollis Chenery, the Bank's chief economic theorist in the McNamara era. According to one insider Krueger was not interested in debating economic policy and '(s)he cut off anybody who ever had any relationship with Hollis Chenery' (Caufield 1996: 144–45). Nevertheless, staff on the operational side maintained a degree of pragmatism in their overall approach and policy prescriptions. Even during the early to mid-1980s, which were by far the most doctrinaire, the World Bank did not become a neoliberal monolith, and '(f)or every research report vindicating the neo-liberal position, one could find another Bank publication which looked more soberly at the social and technological constraints on development' (Mosley, Harrigan and Toye 1991: 24). For example, the *World Development Report 1987*, which focused on trade and industrialisation, outlined an approach to economic development that was particularly adamant in its commitment to neoliberalism (Wade 1996b: 5, and Chapter Nine in this book). However, four years later, in the 1991 *World Development Report*, entitled *The Challenge of Development*, it was emphasised that 'market-friendly policies – neither complete laissez faire nor interventionism – are optimal for growth and income distribution' (World Bank 1991c).

The end of the high period of neoliberalism at the World Bank had been reached long before 1991, however, and was marked by the change of presidents from Clausen to Barber Conable in 1986. During Conable's tenure as president (1986–91) the Bank was reorganised in an effort to make it more effective and smaller. Conable sought to reduce the organisation's 6 000 employees by 10 per cent and break the influence of powerful long-time managers, particularly Ernest Stern, the economist who 'had been the de facto power in the Bank since McNamara's retirement'. The Bank certainly was shaken up in the months after Conable first took over, but even before Conable left the size of the staff had returned to 6 000 and most of the powerful and long-serving 'politically attuned bureaucrats' at the Bank remained in place. For example, Ernest Stern remained at the Bank long after Conable had retired (Caufield 1996: 178–80). Nevertheless, while Conable was at the helm, the organisation's public image was seen to be more consensual than under Clausen, while poverty alleviation and the mitigation of the social costs of structural adjustment were given greater prominence. The neoliberal ideologues in the research department departed and the department itself disappeared as a separate vice-presidency in the reorganisation of 1987. However, as we will see, the World Bank's understanding of development into the 1990s continued to be, or increasingly became, influenced by rational choice theory (the new institutionalism and the new political economy), resulting in a highly mechanistic approach to the dynamics of political and economic change in the various countries which the researchers at the Bank sought to understand (Mosley, Harrigan and Toye 1991: 24–25).

Despite the shifts in neoliberalism between the late 1970s and the early 1990s, the 1980s saw the institutional and discursive consolidation of market-centred ideas, something that the demise of the Soviet Union (1989–91) as the most serious challenger to the hegemony of liberal Anglo-American-style capitalism simply served to reinforce. 'Actually existing socialism' in the Soviet Union and around the world had attempted from the beginning to 'mimic the economic achievements of capitalism', laying down objectives which capitalism was 'obviously much better equipped than socialism to achieve' (Dirlik 1994: 44). However, the fall of state socialism by the end of the 1980s reinforced the process of neoliberal consolidation that drew considerable sustenance from the view that the collapse of the Soviet bloc was a victory for the particular type of capitalism that predominated in Britain and North America in the 1980s (Keegan 1993: 4). At the same time, by the end of the Cold War, the view that the rise of East Asia was a result of state-guided economic development and other less systemic challenges to neoliberalism meant there was still a need for concessions to (or at least gestures in the direction of) proponents of planning and the role of government, sustainable development issues and environmental concerns. This conjuncture was encapsulated in October 1991 in an opening address to the annual conference of the World Bank and IMF, appropriately meeting in Bangkok, the capital of one of the key nation-states in the wider 'East Asian Miracle', by Conable's successor as president, Lewis Preston. In his speech, the new president of the Bank asserted that the demise of the Soviet bloc had led to 'the broad convergence of development thinking which has replaced ideological conflict' and a consensus based on the free market, a balance between the private sector and government and sustainable economic growth was spreading around the globe (Preston 1991: 22–23). Ultimately the 1980s and early 1990s witnessed the entrenchment of what Stephen Gill has described as 'market civilization' – the transformative practices by which capitalist expansion has become bound up with a legitimating neoliberal discourse of progress and development (Gill 1995: 399–423). Importantly, although it is a movement which is reinforced by the application of the political power of key actors such as the US, at another level its most subtle quality has been the way in which ideas about the superiority of market-mediated social relations have become hegemonic because they have become integral to common sense understandings of development.

The international development debate

As declarations such as Lewis Preston's remind us, the World Bank has occupied a central position in the wider consolidation of neoliberalism. The Bank is significant both as the source of authoritative knowledge about economic development and because of its key role in setting the agenda in the international development debate. This flows from its possession of an unrivalled budget for research and policy-formulation capacity in comparison to any other development organisation. At the same time, the World Bank is able to attract a high degree of international media attention for its pronouncements and major reports. This 'intellectual' influence is directly reinforced by its economic leverage with governments around the world looking for investment, loans and foreign aid (see Wade 1996b: 5, and Chapter Nine in this book; Payer 1982: 15–21). The ideas that form much of the Bank's policy agenda are also produced and disseminated in part by its own think tank. Set up in 1956, using financial support from the Rockefeller and Ford Foundations, the Economic Development Institute (EDI) instructed people from a wide range of developing countries in the creation and management of projects commensurate with the Bank's overall conception of development. According to its first director, Sir Alexander Cairncross, the intention of the EDI was to ensure that by associating with and studying at the Bank, students 'would carry with them ideas that were more congenial to the Bank when they went back to their own country'. Certainly, a number of EDI graduates have achieved positions of prominence in their countries of origin. In the late 1970s Cairncross observed that EDI graduates 'more or less ran' South Korea, and in Pakistan there were 'a great many ex-EDI men who quite consciously were pulling together and having an influence on development' (in Caufield 1996: 62–63, 196–97).

The US remains the Bank's most powerful member, although its position as a Bank shareholder is greatly reduced. However, the US still chooses the head of the Bank and it is the only country with a veto over amendments to the Articles of Agreement. Furthermore, the US closely monitors Bank activities, and is the only Bank member to review all loan proposals in detail; officials of the Treasury Department are in daily contact not only with the US executive director, but other Bank officials as well (Caufield 1996: 197). By the 1950s Washington's geopolitical goals were consistently linked to the economic and financial reforms the World Bank and the IMF demanded of governments around the world. The US government has always been candid about this linkage. As one US official noted in the 1970s, the IMF and the World Bank 'use their loans as leverage to encourage positive economic performance and acceptance of market economy principles in recipient countries'. It is clear that the US has effectively dominated the World Bank, the IMF and their affiliates. As Kolko notes, over 40 per cent of the World Bank's top managers are US citizens and the president has always been a US citizen (Wolfensohn, who is Australian-born, was only a partial exception) (1988: 232–36).

US influence is also grounded in the Bank's dependence on world financial markets, the central position of the US as a global financial centre, and the closely aligned interests of key financial actors with those of US foreign policy. This influence is further entrenched in the Bank's institutionalised norms and culture. At least 80 per cent of the economists working for the World Bank are trained in Britain or North America. Their approach and outlook, and that of virtually all of the remaining 20 per cent, is based on the assumptions and methodologies of Anglo-American liberalism and neoclassical economic thought. Robert Wade argues that since the late 1970s economists who do not subscribe to the main precepts of neoclassical economics are unlikely to even be employed by the Bank, while the small number of social scientists from other disciplines who work for the Bank are involved in peripheral projects and have no influence over economic policy formulation (see Wade 1996b: 16, 30–31, 35–36, and Chapter Nine in this book). Interestingly, prior to the 1960s the operations and overall approach to development at the World Bank was driven in part by the preponderance of professional engineers within the institution and their vision of development as the funding and building of physical structures (Mosley, Harrigan and Toye 1991: 29).

Its internal review process reinforces the current dominance of neoclassical economists within the upper echelons of the Bank. Within the Bank, policy documents go through a process of review and evaluation moving upwards through the numerous echelons of the organisation. Each echelon works to narrow the overall perspective. It is not just that higher levels are more concerned with the Bank's and the system's integrity than with the integrity of the research. It is also that promotion criteria select people for the higher levels who make decisions quickly and with closure, using 'facts' selectively to support preconceived patterns and convictions. This process is complemented by a conformist culture in which the Bank's prevailing editorial line is rigidly followed (Wade 1996b: 31, and Chapter Nine in this book). This is especially significant given the sheer volume of the Bank's widely disseminated and authoritative research. Yet, despite the Bank's internal culture of conformity and the undoubted influence of mainstream economics on the literature that emerges from it, the Bank is not immune to external influences. The significance of external influences is readily apparent in the shifts in the Bank's understanding of the East Asian trajectory.

Liberalism, neoliberalism and East Asian development

The invention of the East Asian miracle

By the 1980s, the World Bank, more than any other institution, was playing a key role in interpreting what was increasingly being viewed as the miraculous industrialisation of East Asia. Significantly, this interpretation was refracted through a pervasive framework of neoliberal ideas. The central prescription that the World Bank increasingly offered to governments in the so-called developing world was that underdevelopment was caused by excessive state intervention in the economy. It argued that privatisation and liberalisation would encourage economic growth and economic efficiency. To support their argument they pointed to countries such as South Korea, Taiwan, Hong Kong and Singapore, which they characterised as exemplars of the success of the free-market model, while pointing to the apparent failure of the public-interventionist model adopted by governments in Africa and Latin America (Todaro 1989: 83–84).

The rise of the newly industrialising economies (NIEs) of East Asia was consequently interpreted as a natural outgrowth of capitalist expansion. This was linked to a wider effort by the World Bank to promote a normative vision of capitalist transformation as the unfolding of a natural and liberal process (see Williams, Chapter Three in this book). One of the best-known World Bank economists to consistently articulate a neoclassical interpretation of industrialisation in East Asia has been Bela Balassa. From Balassa's perspective, comparative advantage (or the idea that countries should specialise in what they naturally excel) was a key factor in economic development. From this point of view the natural unfolding of the world economy results in the movement of national economies from the production of low technology goods to the manufacture of higher technology goods, as a particular country's comparative advantage shifts from unskilled, labour-intensive manufacturing to skilled, capital-intensive production (Balassa 1981). In the late 1980s Balassa argued that with the exception of Hong Kong, the newly industrialising countries (NICs) had all gone through an initial stage of import-substitution industrialisation, but in contrast to late-industrialising nation-states in Latin America, the East Asian NICs had subsequently and successfully embraced export-oriented industrialisation. For Balassa, this external orientation was a central and dynamic element of the comparative advantage framework, in so far as an external orientation facilitated the overcoming of domestic constraints, undercutting monopolistic and protectionist economic arrangements, and encouraging competition and the pursuit of technological improvement (Balassa 1988: S280–81, S286–88). Fitting the rise of East Asia into an economic framework grounded in neoliberalism was not simply a theoretical challenge, but an inherently political exercise. Other prominent economists, operating within the ambit of Anglo-American liberalism, took pains to construct explanations that presented the success of even the most obviously state-led developmental trajectories, such as Japan, as primarily the result of market forces.[4]

The attempt to depict the East Asian experience as essentially a 'normal' part of capitalist development that was in accord with the precepts of neoclassical economics is significant for several reasons. Firstly, interpreting East Asian development as a lesson in neoclassical economics inevitably informed the policy initiatives of both regional governments and outside agencies and actors such as the Bank, the IMF and the US. Secondly, it is significant because it increasingly flew in the face of an overwhelming amount of evidence detailing the attempts by various governments in East Asia to shape the content and direction of economic activity directly, rather than waiting passively for market forces to determine key economic outcomes. There is no intention here to review in depth the contending positions in the East Asian development debate or the voluminous literature that accompanies it. Rather, it is sufficient to note that since the 1980s there have been an increasing number of 'revisionist' Anglo-American policy-oriented studies that have attempted to challenge the dominant neoliberal approach to economic development and foreground the role of the state in capitalist development.[5] This literature on the developmental state, and approaches to and perceptions of the East Asian experience which originate from within the region generally, bear little resemblance to the vision of East Asia conjured up by neoclassical economists and the avatars of Anglo-American liberalism. Not only does the lineage of 'Asian' economic ideas owe more to the formulations of Friedrich List than it does to Adam Smith, but there are highly distinctive regional views about the character and purpose of capitalist organisation, and the place of a more assertive East Asian region and its distinctive patterns of political and economic organisation more generally (Sakakibara 1993; Mohamad and Ishihara 1995).[6]

Even if the relative success of the state-led East Asian development trajectory is in question, states in the region clearly acted as if intervention was likely to be efficacious, effectively undermining both the normative and theoretical aspects of neoclassical economics. Furthermore, as we shall see, the Bank itself has reluctantly come to accept that state intervention has played a role in regional development. Thus, despite the continuity in basic assumptions, the Bank's views on East Asia, and on economic development more generally, have been influenced by the wider international situation of which it is a part. This is readily apparent in the case of the now famous 1993 World Bank report entitled *The East Asian Miracle* (World Bank 1993a). The 1993 report was funded by the Japanese ministry of finance (MOF) and carried out in the context of ongoing efforts by the Japanese government to get the World Bank to revise its commitment to a neoliberal model of development, and by implication, to take the Japanese alternative more seriously (Caufield 1996: 160). Thus, the *East Asian Miracle* report was a profoundly political document produced out of a complex struggle within the Bank and between the Bank and the Japanese government.

While the Japanese government was not happy with the final product, the 1993 report was significant in that, for the first time in a major Bank publication, it conceded that government intervention had played some role in economic development in most of East Asia (Wade 1996b: 23, and Chapter Nine in this book).

Pressure for such a concession, if not a more dramatic acknowledgment of the role of the state in economic development, had been building throughout the 1980s.[7] Despite the growing international influence of neoliberalism, the Japanese government continued to 'intervene' in economic activity in a manner that flouted the rising neoliberal narrative. This ensured that it was increasingly subject to criticism in the context of apparently interminable trade disputes with the US (Schoppa 1997). During the 1980s the Japanese government continued to direct or assist the expansion of Japanese corporations overseas (Hatch and Yamamura 1996). In 1987, for example, the ministry of international trade and industry (MITI) planned a regional industrialisation strategy for the governments of South-East Asia, a key element of which was the allocation of 'directed credit'. At the end of the 1980s, the Japanese MOF set up the ASEAN-Japan Development Fund, which was administered by Japan's main aid agency and sought to provide credit to the private sector. Officials at the World Bank conveyed their concern about this approach through informal channels, but this had no discernible effect. Meanwhile, in June 1989, Masaki Shiratori became the World Bank's new executive director for Japan. The Japanese government was the second-ranking shareholder in the World Bank (after the US) and Shiratori, a senior MOF official, was 'determined to make the Bank pay more attention to the East Asian experience' generally, rethink direct credit policies, and to take the Japanese and East Asian approaches to industrialisation and development seriously. The potential for increased conflict over competing visions of regional development was exacerbated by the appointment, in January 1991, of Lawrence Summers to the position of chief economist and vice-president at the Bank. Summers was well known for dismissing Japanese economists as 'second-rate'. At the same time, it was Summers who came up with the term 'market-friendly', which was used to soften the overall free-market approach of the final version of the *World Development Report 1991: The Challenge to Development* (Wade 1996b: 6–10, and Chapter Nine in this book).

Not surprisingly, the terminological change did little to mollify the concerns of the Japanese government and it continued to promote its own model of economic development, using its increasing power in the Bank and the IMF as leverage (Rapkin and Strand 1997). In an address at the World Bank and the IMF's Board of governors annual meeting in October 1991, Yasushi Mieno, then head of the Bank of Japan, argued that the East Asian experience demonstrated the significance of government intervention. In his speech, which had been drafted by the MOF's international finance bureau, he made an explicit appeal for the IMF and the World Bank to initiate a 'wide-ranging study that would define the theoretical underpinning of this approach and clarify the areas in which it can be successfully applied to other parts of the globe' (Wade 1996b: 10–11, and Chapter Nine in this book). At the same meeting Attila Karaosmanoglu, the World Bank's vice-president and managing director, suggested that the NIEs of East Asia 'and their successful emulators are a powerful argument that a more activist, positive governmental role can be a decisive factor in rapid industrial growth', concluding that '(w)hat is replicable and transferable must be brought to light and shared with others' (Evans 1995: 21).

However, many officials at the World Bank viewed the Japanese model as a threat for a number of reasons. In the first instance, the concessionary credit that was part of the Japanese approach to development aid undermined the attractiveness of credit provided by the World Bank. Secondly, the emphasis on the importance of directed credit as an instrument of industrial policy that was also characteristic of the Japanese approach was at odds with the Bank's overarching focus on financial liberalisation. The upper echelons of the Bank also feared that if they put their imprimatur on the developmental state model it would undermine the Bank's own credit rating (and therefore borrowing and lending capacity) with the international money markets and its authority in the international economic system more generally. For the

Bank to change its attitude towards the Japanese model would also represent a major challenge to the US, which has historically used the Bank in its overall projection of power and influence. From the point of view of the World Bank, the Japanese model also gives legitimacy to the 'interventionist impulses' that exist amongst the governments and elites of the various countries that are beholden to the World Bank. Ultimately, for those looking out on the world from the commanding heights of the World Bank, the Japanese model was a 'systemic threat' to the status quo (Wade 1996b: 14–17, and Chapter Nine in this book).

It is not surprising, then, that although the *East Asian Miracle* report acknowledged that the state had, and could, play a role in economic development, it continued to emphasise that the key to the miracle still involved 'getting the basics right'. Furthermore, it continued to treat economic development as a technical policy question, in which the role of the state (or government institutions) was not seen as particularly relevant to an overall understanding of successful capitalist development, even if it was important to particular economic activities at particular times. However, even as the role of the state was being acknowledged, but downplayed, by the World Bank – to the annoyance of the Japanese sponsors of the 1993 report – the way was being paved for greater accommodation of the state-centred perspective in the context of the wider and ongoing re-invention of liberalism.

The re-invention of liberalism
At the end of the 1980s, the Bank began to produce a series of reports in which the idea of 'good governance' was critical.[8] Again, the focus was increasingly on a search for supposedly optimal forms of economic management, rather than positing capitalism as a paradigmatic rival to a declining or defunct state-socialist alternative. Although, in the immediate aftermath of the Cold War, the World Bank's conception of development had broadened somewhat in the changed political context, it also began to take on an increasingly 'technical' aspect (World Bank 1991a). The concept of good governance that emerged in this period depicted the relationship between the political and the economic in

a way which clearly reflected the influence of predominantly Anglo-American political thought and the essentially liberal notion of state neutrality (Williams and Young 1994: 84–100; and Chapter Seven in this book). As critics have been quick to point out, the Bank's interest in governance issues and its apolitical conception of the state allowed it to promote market-oriented reforms without necessarily challenging established elites whose position and power might be threatened by more serious calls for political reform (Schmitz 1995). Nevertheless, the growing emphasis on good governance helped to pave the way for greater attention to the state. Significantly, the notion of good governance has been taken up by elites in many parts of the world, including East Asia. Tommy Koh, former Singaporean representative to the United Nations, head of the Asia–Europe Foundation and a well known advocate of Asian values, has argued that the development of a shared conception of, and commitment to, good governance would help ground wider East–West relations (Koh 1993; Berger 1998: 14).

The overall process of revising liberalism in a way which incorporated the technocratic and elitist notion of good governance, and which accommodated the state-led development trajectory of East Asia to neo-classical economics, was clearly apparent in *The Key to the Asian Miracle*, which was published in 1996. Although not a World Bank publication as such, the book was written by Jose E. Campos, a World Bank economist and co-author of the 1993 *Miracle* report, and Hilton L. Root, an economic historian based at the Hoover Institution at Stanford University. In their book, they attempted to outline 'concrete lessons for the rest of the developing world' by examining 'the rationality of the structure and performance' of key institutions in East Asia. From their point of view, although East Asian institutions are not necessarily 'directly transferable' to other nation-states, knowing how they operate could still provide a 'guide' for other governments facing similar economic problems (Campos and Root 1996: viii). Their analysis, which clearly reflected the influence of rational choice theory (the new institutionalism and/or the new political economy), represented the high-performing Asian economies, or HPAEs (Japan, South Korea,

Taiwan, Hong Kong, Singapore, Thailand, Malaysia and Indonesia) as variations of a generalised form of enlightened authoritarianism. They argued that the governments of the HPAEs were aware that successful economic development necessitated coordinating the 'expectations' of various groups. This led to the crafting of institutional arrangements that sought to distribute 'the benefits of growth-enhancing policies widely', while reassuring businesses and individuals 'that they would share the growth dividend'. In the prescriptive tone, which pervaded their study, they emphasised that '(s)haring gave the less fortunate a stake in the economy'. This worked to discourage 'disruptive activities' and reduced 'the risk of regime failure'. Importantly, it also allowed the various governments to focus 'on promoting rational economic policies by reducing the need to constantly contend with issues of redistribution' (Campos and Root 1996: 1–3).

The authors observed that the East Asian regimes that had presided over the successful economic growth of the past decades were regularly regarded 'as authoritarian, even dictatorial'. They argued that this perception was misleading and 'occurs largely because of the failure of Western observers to recognise in East Asia systems for ensuring accountability and consensus building that differ from Western-style institutions'. They emphasised that 'the mechanisms that Westerners expect to see – written constitutions, elected legislators, a formal system of checks and balances – are but one set of solutions to establishing regime legitimacy and guaranteeing limits on government action'. From their point of view they made clear that there are 'other ways' of mobilising 'public support' and 'restraining ruling cliques from overriding the economic rights of others'. Furthermore, although the different HPAEs vary significantly from each other, they 'share enough common elements to suggest a developmental model that differs from the trajectory of the Western democracies and from the autocracies of the past and present'. According to the authors, instead of behaving 'like roving bandits' the regimes of the HPAEs 'have considered the future output of society and have offered incentives to productive investment (physical and human) that are typically found only in the Western democracies'. They concluded that, while the future for the HPAEs was uncertain and the historical context (the Cold War in particular) had altered, the governments of 'developing' nations around the world could still benefit from an examination of the HPAEs as a way of finding 'their own best starting points' (Campos and Root 1996: 174–77). Ultimately their analysis of the HPAEs legitimated authoritarianism and endeavoured to accommodate the developmental state and ideas about Asian democracy and Asian values to the dominant neoliberal discourse on development. At the same time, Campos and Root produced a homogeneous image of East Asia (which lumped Indonesia with Japan), conflating historically distinct national trajectories and reinforcing a dubious distinction between East and West.

In the wider context of the discovery of the state in East Asia, which is apparent in works such as *The Key to the Asian Miracle,* the process of liberal revisionism begun in the Bank's original *Miracle* report was more completely realised in *The State in a Changing World,* published with much fanfare in 1997 (World Bank 1997b). *The State in a Changing World* was a product of the increasing economic significance, and therefore political influence of the governments of East Asia, par-ticularly Japan, by the first half of the 1990s. The 1997 *Report* exemplified the World Bank's shifting position on the role of the state. Indeed, the entire *Report* is premised on the idea that the state is not just a necessarily important determinant of national economic welfare, but that 'its capability – *defined as the ability to undertake and promote collective actions efficiently* – must be increased' (World Bank 1997b: 3). Although the *Report* was at pains to describe the actions of Japan and the East Asian states more generally as 'market enhancing', it also clearly conceded that the 'state' was fundamentally implicated in defining the structure of market-mediated economic relations.

In other words, intervention per se was not necessarily a problem. Indeed, 'development without an effective state is impossible' according to the *Report.* East Asia took on a particular significance in this regard as it demonstrated, in the words of the *Report,* 'how government and the private sector can cooperate to achieve rapid growth and shared development'. What this amounted to was a heavily qualified endorsement of the close relationships between government and business that characterised the nation-states of Asia. For the late-industrialising nations of East Asia, and by implication for their counterparts in the rest of the so-called developing world, the *Report* concluded that the state was capable of 'not merely laying the foundations of industrial development but actually accelerating it' (World Bank 1997b: 6, 24, 46, 61). At the same time, the World Bank's 1997 *Report* defined an 'effective state' in a way that bypassed the wider social context and the social impact of the developmental states in the region. Not surprisingly, as with the Campos and Root 1996 study, the conception of an effective state in East Asia presented in *The State in a Changing World* was grounded in an elite-centred approach to political and economic change that implicitly, if not explicitly, valorised authoritarianism (Asia Monitor Resource Centre 1997: 6, 24–26).

The East Asian crisis and its aftermath

The publication of the World Bank's 1997 *Report* coincided with the onset of the East Asian crisis and the discrediting of the very state-guided model that the World Bank had partially accommodated during the 1990s. The dominant interpretation of the East Asian crisis attributed the dramatic waning of the East Asia miracle to the types of relationships between government and business that the World Bank had reluctantly come to endorse over the previous ten years. Rather than being seen as a source of effective planning and economic development, the governments of East Asia in the wake of the 1997–98 financial crisis were routinely associated with cronyism, corruption and inefficiency. Nevertheless, the Bank's post-crisis position did not involve a reversion to the neoliberal model of development and the free trade understanding of the East Asian trajectory it had championed in the early 1980s. Significantly, during and after the crisis a marked divergence emerged between the approach taken by the Bank and that of the IMF (the latter taking a much more prominent role in the management of the Asian crisis). These differences should not be exaggerated, but the Bank's criticism of the IMF's handling of the crisis marked a noteworthy fracturing of the so-called 'Washington Consensus' of wholesale liberalisation that had previously underpinned policy toward the region.[9]

In the second half of 1997, the IMF embarked on major efforts to restore financial stability to the region via loan packages to the governments of Thailand, Indonesia and South Korea. Its overall approach was premised on the widespread neoliberal view that the crisis flowed from the distortions and inefficiencies that were characteristic of state-guided capitalism in East Asia (Wolf 1998: 14). In this context IMF loans were conditional on the implementation of a range of austerity measures and liberalising initiatives. However, by 1998, the IMF was increasingly seen to have failed and/or aggravated a worsening situation, at the same time as other parts of the world were catching the so-called 'Asian Flu' (Sachs 1998b; Feldstein 1998). By late 1997, Joseph Stiglitz, the chief economist at the World Bank, was challenging the IMF's approach, arguing that the East Asian crisis flowed from 'inadequate oversight, not over-regulation' and as a result 'our emphasis should not be on deregulation, but on finding the right regulatory regime' to regain 'stability and confidence' in the region (in Wade 1998b: 1538, 1552).[10] Stiglitz's continuing criticisms (2000b) were not well received at the IMF. The IMF's close institutional allies at the US Treasury were instrumental in pressuring World Bank head James Wolfensohn to 'rein in' Stiglitz. Significantly, Stiglitz's subsequent departure from the Bank was not an isolated incident. Another prominent Bank economist, Ravi Kanbur, also resigned when his iconoclastic report on the causes of poverty, which was critical of the impact of financial liberalisation in the developing world, was rejected following Treasury and IMF objections (Wade 2001b).

This critique of the IMF plan for the region by a senior official at the World Bank was soon followed by others also emanating from the World Bank, as well as elsewhere (Wade 1998a; Wade and Venereso 1998a, 1998b).[11] In fact, the World Bank was in good company as a growing number of influential policy makers and economists (including writers such as Jeffrey Sachs, who had played an important role in the spread of neoliberal ideas and policies, and Paul Krugman) increasingly argued that the crisis in East Asia was the result of a 'financial panic' that fuelled a dramatic and unnecessary shift in investor confidence and market expectation, which led to the rapid movement of capital out of the region and the resultant currency collapses (Sachs 1998a; Krugman 1998). In September 1998 the *Wall Street Journal* described the growing reaction against IMF prescriptions in Asia, and the drift towards capital controls, as 'the most serious challenge yet to the free-market orthodoxy that the globe has embraced since the end of the Cold War' (Wessell and Davis 1998).

At one level then, the president of the World Bank, James Wolfensohn – who eventually joined his former chief economist, Joseph Stiglitz, in what were less sustained and acerbic criticisms of the IMF and of the way the Bank itself had operated, particularly its alienation from those whom it supposedly intended to help – simply reflected the fact that by the late 1990s promoters of neoliberalism often sought to respond to criticisms and problems by acknowledging that mistakes had been made (Wolfensohn 1997). More broadly, by the end of the 1990s, the World Bank had ostensibly made a shift from structural adjustment to a focus on a 'comprehensive development framework' that again foregrounded poverty alleviation, the ostensible focus of the Bank's efforts up to the end of the 1970s (Pender 2001). This shift has been reinforced by a renewed emphasis on foreign aid and poverty alleviation in the wake of the terrorist bombings in New York and Washington on 11 September 2001.[12] In the lead-up to the UN conference on financing development, held in Monterrey, Mexico, in late March 2002, Wolfensohn reiterated his call for the US and other OECD nation-states to increase their foreign aid budgets by at least 50 per cent.[13] The Bush administration surprised most observers when it announced at Monterrey that US foreign aid spending would in fact be increased by 50 per cent within three years, with the additional funds going to a new 'Millennium Challenge Account'.[14] But this shift still represents a limited change and, in comparison to defence spending, remains insignificant. Furthermore, these reorientations do not represent a retreat from any of the core elements of the US-led globalisation project within which the World Bank plays a central role (Cammack 2002). The World Bank remains profoundly implicated in the dominant technocratic and ahistorical conception of development that is grounded in the naturalisation of both historically contingent national trajectories and the process of capitalist transformation itself.

Conclusion: Miracles of modernisation and crises of capitalism

The 1997 crisis in East Asia seriously undermined the region's credentials as the site of a miracle of modernisation, and impacted dramatically on the post-Cold War international political economy. As with the end of the Cold War, the end of the East Asian miracle precipitated important changes in the contours of the global capitalist order. The passing of the miracle has led to a great deal of revision on the part of those who previously had seen it as a potential key to universal economic development. Between the 1970s and the second half of the 1990s the debate about the causes of, and the lessons which could be extracted from, the successful industrialisation of a growing number of countries in North-East and South-East Asia increasingly occupied a key position in the wider international development debate. During this period some of the most influential interpretations of East Asian industrialisation were closely linked to the wider rise of neoliberalism. This was readily apparent in the interpretation of the East Asian miracle specifically, and capitalist development more generally, offered by the World Bank, arguably the most prestigious and one of the most powerful producers of international development knowledge. Taking the dramatic events of 1997–98 as a crucial turning point, this chapter has provided an overview of the relationship between Anglo-American liberalism and East Asian dynamism since the 1970s. Ultimately, it has been emphasised that, in the context of the shifting contours of the global political economy and the nation-state system, the World Bank played a crucial role in domesticating the East Asian miracle to the dominant liberal narrative of modernisation and in facilitating the wider re-invention of liberalism in the post-1945 period.

Notes

1. Critics have often used a relatively fixed conception of the type of development model being promoted by both the World Bank and the West more generally. For example, see Mehmet (1995); and Escobar (1995: 224). For a discussion of Escobar's book see Berger (1995a).
2. Central to the shifting liberal narrative of modernisation are assumptions about the sanctity of private property, the superiority and naturalness of gradual or evolutionary political, economic and social change, the equation of democracy with elections and parliamentary government, and the assumption that free-trade (laissez-faire) and the market economy is a natural mode of economic activity and organisation. Of course, the relative emphasis that has been placed on free trade, and the actual implementation of laissez-faire policies has fluctuated dramatically over time. As Wallerstein has noted '[n]ot only is the capitalist system not properly described as a system of free enterprise today, but there never was a moment in history when this was a reasonably descriptive label. The capitalist system is and always has been one of state interference with the "freedom" of the market in the interests of some and against those of others' (1979: 121, 149).
3. For a good analysis of the move to Structural Adjustment Loans (SALs) and Sectoral Adjustment Loans (SECALs) see Mosley, Harrigan and Toye (1991: Vol. 1, 21–23, 27–61; and Vol. 2).
4. See, for example, Patrick (1977: 239). For a similar, but more general market-centred explanation of East Asian development, see Chen (1979).
5. A pioneering text in the Anglo-American revisionist tradition is Johnson (1992). For an overview of the literature and the debate see Henderson and Appelbaum (1992); Choi (1998); and Woo-Cumings (1999).
6. For overviews of this literature and the 'Asian Way' debate, see Berger (1996), revised and reprinted as Berger (1997); Wright-Neville (1995); and Dupont (1996).
7. For an overview of Japan's relationship with the World Bank see Gyohten (1997).
8. One of the first and most influential was World Bank (1989). On the contentious character of 'good governance' more generally, see Beeson (2001).
9. On the rise and fall of the Washington Consensus, see Higgott (2001).
10. Stiglitz's critique of the IMF's approach to the Asian crisis was subsequently outlined in exhaustive detail in Stiglitz (2002).
11. For an overview of this trend see Wade (1998b). Also see Wade and Veneroso (1998a and 1998b); and Wade (1998a).
12. For example, former US President Bill Clinton has repeatedly pointed to the need to 'close the gap between rich and poor' in order to 'defeat global terrorism' (Clinton 2002).
13. 'Help in the Right Places', *Economist*, 16 March 2002: 91–92.

14. Although it garnered most of the publicity, the US announcement of a dramatic increase (from a very low base) in aid was actually exceeded by the EU's pledge to increase European government spending on foreign aid from 0.33 per cent on average to 0.39 per cent of GNP ('Foreign Aid: A Feast of Giving', *Economist*, 23 March 2002: 93). See Chapters Fifteen and Sixteen in this book for more consideration of the George W. Bush regime in the USA and Paul Wolfowitz's time in the World Bank.

Chapter Eleven

Structural Adjustment and African Agriculture
A Retrospect

Henry Bernstein

THIS IS A COMPLETE RECONSIDERATION OF THE AUTHOR'S 1990 ARTICLE IN JOURNAL OF PEASANT STUDIES *18 (1): 3–35.*

[T]he African 'crisis' is a crisis of capitalism, more precisely of the variants of 'actually existing capitalism' characteristic of Africa (Bernstein 1990: 4).

'African countries have characteristics that are not conducive to reform . . .' (World Bank pundits quoted by Sender 2002: 193).[1]

In 1990 I published an article entitled 'Agricultural "modernisation" and the era of structural adjustment: Observations on sub-Saharan Africa', following a visit the previous year to Sokoine Agricultural University. It had been a while since I had worked in sub-Saharan Africa or written anything on developments there but that visit, and its opportunities to engage with colleagues and with a range of other Tanzanians in Morogoro, Dar es Salaam and elsewhere, provided the spur to express myself in writing about the discourses and hegemonic claims of structural adjustment in Africa by which I had been provoked, intellectually and politically, through the 1980s.[2]

The rationale and agenda of structural adjustment, as initially announced in the landmark Berg Report (World Bank 1981), was perhaps somewhat less triumphalist by the end of the 1980s, but it still declared the conviction that its peculiar neoliberal conception of comprehensive social engineering (the Washington Consensus, as it came to be known) was the only way to develop, and thereby to *order*, the failing economies – and with them the failing states, and indeed failing societies? – of sub-Saharan Africa. Hence the World Bank way should command the support of all those of generous heart and sound mind; in effect, it claimed, with classically hegemonic presumption, to articulate the common sense of the conjuncture as both moral and intellectual reason.

In trying to provide some elements of criticism of structural adjustment – its discourse, rationale, practices, and likely effects – I suggested that reflex responses of a nationalist or populist kind, in defence of African states and African peasantries respectively, were inadequate, and that a more rigorous approach required problematising and confronting the contradictory social realities of Africa generated by its specific historical forms of 'actually existing capitalism'.

In this chapter, I first summarise the main themes of my 1990 article, and then revisit some of its arguments in the light of subsequent World Bank positions and the effects of structural adjustment, in conjunction with other factors, for the course of 'actually existing capitalism' in the countrysides of sub-Saharan Africa.

The view from 1990

There were several, connected, points of departure for the original article.[3] A first was the ways in which the vocabulary of 'crisis' had been generalised so rapidly in discourses about Africa, including that of the World Bank which had hitherto wrapped its policy diagnoses and prescriptions in suitably more technocratic, hence anodyne, language. A 'crisis' of what? Answers to this could encompass, and combine, the plane of the macroeconomic, for example, increasingly severe problems of economic growth, inflation, declining foreign exchange earnings, and (foreign) debt; with regard to agriculture an apparently looming, and in some instances overwhelming, decline in domestic food production matched by the need for increased imports of food staples; an ostensibly gathering, and accelerating, environmental 'crisis' (of soils, water, pasture and fuel); and, associated with all the above, widespread and deepening poverty and mounting pressures on livelihoods/reproduction.[4]

Secondly, the context of such 'crisis', and its various manifestations, was the unravelling of the project of 'national development' proclaimed with independence from colonial rule.[5] This process was registered materially, for example, in the deteriorating performance of state and parastatal economic enterprises (in infrastructure and utilities, manufacturing industry, agricultural development and marketing) and of social provision. A common observation was that of increasingly predatory states displaying an increasing gap between their commitment (and capacity) to deliver economic growth and public goods and their consumption of the social product. And this provided the link to the crucial discursive (ideological) manifestation of African 'crisis': that this was indeed a crisis of 'developmentalism', that is, of state-led development and, by extension, of the postcolonial state in sub-Saharan Africa more generally[6] – of special significance to the World Bank which had been so heavily implicated in the formation of 'developmentalism' and its instrumentalities of macroeconomic and project planning.

And thirdly, of course, was the new gospel of market-led development, announced initially (and crudely) by the admonition to 'get the prices right'. On the one hand, this served the World Bank as a means to distance itself from its own history as major donor to, and indeed often designer and strategic agency of, 'developmentalism' in sub-Saharan Africa, the failure of which was now attributed above all to the policies and practices of African states and the multiple market 'distortions' they generated. On the other hand, the World Bank's vision of market-led development, which entailed 'rolling back the state' in order to get the prices right, promised an encompassing path of rational 'reform' that, finally, would deliver to African economies and societies, governments and citizens, the mutually linked benefits of prosperity and order unique to bourgeois civilisation.[7]

From this departure point of the 'context of crisis', the article proceeded to suggest 'the logic of agricultural "modernisation"' as this has developed in contemporary capitalism, in which the 'agricultural sector' is increasingly organised, or even constituted by, the concentration of capital in agribusiness upstream and downstream of farming.[8] It sketched three historic paths (among others) through which agricultural 'modernisation' confronts peasant farming: by dispossessing/'smashing' peasantries (the 'classic' path of primitive accumulation); by 'bypassing', hence ultimately marginalising, peasant farming; and by 'locking in' peasants through agribusiness-style integration. It illustrated the second and third of these paths with examples from Tanzania since independence. The purpose of these reflections on agricultural 'modernisation' was to point to some of the contradictions it has encountered, and generated, in modern African history, with respect to the environmental conditions of agriculture; the social relations and labour processes of peasant farming; and the forms of integration in markets and social divisions of labour, including peasant–state relations. I suggested that it was the last of these sources of contradiction and constraint that seemed most amenable to 'reform' promoted by structural adjustment:

(i) In important ways, agrarian failure is the result of contradictions between the pursuit of 'modernisation' and the appropriation of nature through the variant social forms of peasant production in Africa (the effect of specific historical patterns of commoditisation).

(ii) African states and the World Bank have collaborated, albeit as sometimes uneasy partners, in the pursuit of agricultural 'modernisation'; moreover, the technical packages and detailed planning of agricultural projects have been supplied by the World Bank (as well as other agencies), which is thus heavily implicated in their failure.

(iii) Transforming African farming systems and African peasantries in the way it wants is largely beyond the capacity of the World Bank (other than destructively), but states, it appears, are much more available targets, accessible to direct pressure and coercion.

(iv) Blaming the state for Africa's crisis, the World Bank simultaneously obliterates the history of its own major responsibility for the failure of agricultural 'modernisation', and sublimates the frustration of its incapacity to transform nature and society in rural Africa in the discovery that the principal problem all along was that of *incentives*... (Bernstein 1990: 15).

These points connected the discussion of agricultural 'modernisation' with an examination of 'the ideological foundations of structural adjustment', as presented in the Berg Report of 1981, and a later report on *Sub-Saharan Africa: From Crisis to Sustainable Growth. A Long-term Perspective Study* (World Bank 1989). The revival of agricultural production was central to macroeconomic recovery in the Berg Report, which suggested it required producer price incentives via market liberalisation and 'the adoption of realistic exchange rates' (that is, devaluation), the *conditio sina qua non* of structural adjustment macroeconomics. There was much less about agriculture in the *Long-term Perspective Study* published eight years later, although it recommended privatising property rights in land (versus 'communal' tenure) as well as input supply and crop marketing, rural credit provision, and the construction and maintenance of rural infrastructure; it reiterated the belief of Berg in the prompt and effective supply response of African farmers to proper price signals (including changes in relative prices); it made the standard noises about the need to develop and deliver appropriate, environmentally sound technologies; less predictably, hence more interestingly, it indicated a special role for medium- and large-scale 'farmers'.

The 1989 *Study*, it seemed to me, was a nice example of velvet glove over iron fist, World Bank style. It made more reference than had Berg to such appealing tropes as community participation in managing social services, support channelled to the 'grassroots' via NGOs, special provision for women, 'empowering the poor', and (most cynically?) drawing on 'African traditions of sharing', while emphasising – in dawning recognition of the epic scale of its enterprise, perhaps – that 'policy lending' should 'become far more selective among countries' and with respect to reform measures already initiated rather than merely promised: in short, putting some serious bite into conditionality (World Bank 1989).

What of the likely modalities and outcomes of structural adjustment? My scepticism about modalities focused on obstacles confronting the World Bank in implementing structural adjustment: firstly, that 'while seeking to push back the state it has to act through the state . . . in the context of complex indigenous political processes that it is unable to penetrate'; secondly, that African states, on whose pathology the Bank's diagnosis had centred, seemed an unlikely vehicle of so encompassing a project of (bourgeois) social engineering; thirdly, the kind of state called for by structural adjustment has to be not only 'leaner' but at the same time more efficient both technically, for example, in macroeconomic management, *and* in terms of securing the stability and order required by market-led development: 'controlling the social and political tensions (of class, of gender, of rural–urban divisions, of regional and cultural divisions) generated by the history of capitalism in Africa, and likely to be exacerbated by the effects of structural adjustment' (Bernstein 1990: 22–23).

At the same time, and for reasons implied by the above, I questioned the extent to which, and ways in which, programmatic World Bank documents like those reviewed can be treated as coherent statements of the Bank's intentions or a reliable guide to its actions. On the former, perhaps the central importance of such documents 'is to articulate and establish a particular view of the African crisis and its solutions as hegemonic . . . (claiming) the virtues of "pragmatism", of identifying the "highest common ground" from which (virtually) all will benefit'.[9] On the latter, the key issue is the extent to which, in individual cases, attempts will be made to enforce conditionality in a consistent or systematic way, how these attempts might be mediated, deflected or otherwise altered by indigenous political processes, how effective they are in securing the policy and institutional 'reforms' desired, and what the effects of such reforms are in practice (Bernstein 1990: 24).

Scepticism about modalities was matched by scepticism about outcomes. The shift by structural adjustment, with the moment of Berg, from one dominant version of agricultural 'modernisation', that of the 'technical fix' to another, that of the 'market fix', seemed no more likely to comprehend, and transcend, the inherited complex and contradictory forms of commoditisation – the 'actually existing capitalism' of African countrysides (and their diverse urban links).[10] This does not mean that the 'liberation' of petty commodity producers ('peasants') from state controls might not 'release hitherto fettered processes of differentiation and rural accumulation, generating some spurts of agricultural output growth, and at the same time expanding an impoverished "allotment holding" proletariat (in Lenin's phrase)' (Bernstein 1990: 25). And indeed, this dynamic may be stimulated by an important *contingent* effect, namely injecting new capital and commodities into exhausted economies as a result of structural adjustment agreements and loans, without necessarily resulting from the pursuit of structural adjustment policies.[11]

My conclusions sought to draw together and comment on various aspects of 'banking on hegemony' towards the end of the first, and as yet uncertain, decade of structural adjustment in sub-Saharan Africa. Firstly, I was convinced of the encompassing ambition of structural adjustment as an hegemonic project (or fantasy), and equally convinced that it would not yield significant (let alone 'sustainable') benefits to African economies or the vast majority of African people. Secondly, however, I felt that this stance could be argued without denying the increasing problems of African economies and states evident before structural adjustment. Thirdly, then, it was inadequate to respond to the offensive of the World Bank and its allies by rallying to the defence of African regimes, *or* alternatively to attempt to differentiate what was 'bad' (for example, cutting public goods provision) and 'good' (for example, gender sensitive projects) in the ever-swelling checklist of World Bank prescriptions and promises. Fourthly, none of this meant that the pursuit of structural adjustment would not have real effects for socio-economic and political processes, including, for example, facilitating particular (if strongly circumscribed) spurts of economic growth, and perhaps opening spaces in which popular democratic politics might take hold. Finally, I wanted to emphasise the specifically anti-democratic and *imperialist* character of the World Bank and the project of structural adjustment with its transformational ambitions:

> Politically there is the simple and basic fact of the lack of any *accountability* to the people of Africa. However poor the record of accountability in any democratic sense on the part of most African states, they do have to confront the consequences of their actions – if only by the exercise of repression – in ways that the World Bank or IMF do not. African regimes have often been overthrown as a direct or indirect result of popular discontent and opposition. Structural adjustment may wreak havoc on the lives of many in Africa with no costs to the World Bank (Bernstein 1990: 28).

The early twenty-first century

In the last twelve years or so, it is as if the World Bank has ballooned to fill the entire landscape of development discourse, diagnosis and prescription, above all as viewed from sub-Saharan Africa.[12] Firstly, the radical project of engineering a path to bourgeois civilisation has become even more grandiose as what the Bank pronounces on, and claims to act on, has continued to expand. As anticipated in my earlier article, the objective of comprehensive market reform has had to confront similarly comprehensive state reform as a condition of the former; in turn, the pursuit of 'good governance' has extended to, and embraced, notions of 'civil society' and the institutional framework and dynamics of society more generally. In short, the hegemonic claim of the only way forward has been maintained, if hardly without strain (see below), while the terrain of its application has become ever more inclusive to encompass the reshaping, or transformation, of social and political (and, by implication, cultural)[13] as well as economic institutions and practices.[14]

Secondly, an aspect of this process and one of special interest to academics, are the intellectual claims of this expansionary dynamic, especially in terms of new developments in – modifications of? – neoclassical economics, for example, what we might call 'the institutional turn' and the promotion of social capital. These intellectual claims were one aspect of the Bank's efforts to re-invent itself in the late 1990s as a (the?) 'Knowledge Bank' (Pincus and Winters 2002a: 10–15; see also Wanner, Chapter Five in this book); they featured again, somewhat differently, in the contemporaneous attempts of Stiglitz (before he was ousted) to articulate, and generate support for, a 'Post-Washington Consensus'.[15]

This omnivorous appetite for reconstructing the world through structural adjustment, and all its offshoots, is in part explicable as the World Bank's response to the intrinsic contradictions of its project: as new tensions appear – and strain the plausibility of that project, empirically, intellectually and politically – they are addressed by adding on more to the Bank's agenda (at least rhetorically) rather than revising any of its basic premises and ambitions, let alone reducing the latter. While this expansionary dynamic has been called 'mission creep' (in the vocabulary of corporate management), the term hardly does justice to the logic of the functioning – and expanded reproduction – of a discourse of such imperialising scope.[16]

Simultaneously with this continuing growth path of World Bank ambition, so barely sketched here, there is a large and accumulating body of commentary on the Bank's ideas, policies and activities, of various kinds and much of it highly critical (not least the chapters collected in this volume, of course). Such commentary includes a range of analysis from empirical scrutiny and testing of the economic effects (and claims) of structural adjustment policies on countries, sectors and regions (an area of massive and sometimes technically complex contestation of evidence) through case studies of specific experiences of 'reform' to fundamental examination of the theoretical frameworks and methods of World Bank social science and of the politics of its project.[17] Nor is this literature produced only from some or other 'radical' position, as a provocative study by Van der Walle (2001) shows. A political scientist who has worked extensively for the World Bank and uses its analytical framework of (good) governance to highlight the failure of state reform in sub-Saharan Africa under structural adjustment, Van der Walle summarises his argument with commendable brevity: 'it is extremely hard to eliminate rent-seeking behavior simply by changing policy regimes' (2001: 286).[18] He insists on donor complicity in the reproduction of African political classes through what he calls 'the adjustment of neopatrimonialism' (while public goods expenditure and provision have plummeted), and at least tries to analyse the indigenous political dynamics of African states in contrast to the strongly 'externalist' perspective of some of the radical (or *soi-disant* radical) criticism of governance, civil society, and the like, which tends, by default, to imply defence of 'the African' against 'the outside'.

The latter touches on the problem of viewing the World Bank as '*diabolus ex machina*', as Toye (1989), a consistently social democratic critic of neoliberalism (and of some of the foibles of the Left), pointed out and defined as a combination of malevolence and autonomy. That it is not an autonomous, nor monolithic, 'devil from the machine' is shown by another growing, and informative, genre of literature on the World Bank that focuses on the organisation, politics and tensions of its internal governance; its relations with (more) powerful others, above all branches of the US government (the Treasury, Congress); how the internal and the external interact, and the effects of such interaction for the policies and practices (and personnel) of the Bank (see, for example, Gibbon 1993b; Kapur 2002; Pincus and Winters 2002a; and

Rich 2002). One manifestation of those effects is periodic attempts by the Bank to 're-invent' itself, to justify its existence – and continuing prominence – in changing global conditions, for example, global financial liberalisation which, the most aggressive wing of neoliberalism contends, renders obsolete the original *raison d'être* of the World Bank: public sector lending is no longer needed now that private capital markets can do the job (Pincus and Winters 2002a: 6–9).

In my original article I suggested that views of the World Bank as unity of malevolence and autonomy, as Toye defined it, might be more accurately rendered as unity of malevolence and *omnipotence* for those who demonise it thus, to continue Toye's metaphor (Bernstein 1990: 25, 32). The view of the Bank's omnipotence, if misleading (see further below), is nonetheless more plausible when held in sub-Saharan Africa than anywhere else. Not only has the World Bank 'established a hegemonic position as the dominant source of economic and policy analysis' there, but foreign aid finances a vastly greater share of gross domestic investment and of imports of goods and services than in any other region of the South (Sender 2002: 186–87). Sender documents the basic continuities in World Bank policies in sub-Saharan Africa since the moment of Berg in 1981 and the generally dismal-to-disastrous record of national economic performance in the era of structural adjustment.[19] To the extent that evidence of the latter becomes more difficult to dismiss, or wish away, even for the World Bank, then this raises the ante on the explanation of failure. In turn, for the Bank, this can only reinforce further its stance that Africa's failure to develop is due to African incapacities (Sender 2002; also Arrighi 2002): that African countries 'are not conducive to reform'.

As with macroeconomic policy, so too with agriculture: despite a number of criticisms of structural adjustment policies in agriculture, both specific and more general, throughout the course of the 1980s and 1990s (Friis-Hansen 2000: Chapter 2; Sender 2002), the principal thrust was maintained. 'Internal' criticism from Bank staff was more influential, as the results of Bank studies showed the inadequacies of a policy approach so obsessed with price determination and credulous about supply response to relative prices (properly determined). Such studies suggested, for example, that variations in cotton output in West Africa had less to do with net taxation levels than with differences in farmers' trade-offs between cotton and food crops, and in levels of input subsidies and efficiency of producer payments systems; and 'tests of supply responsiveness appeared to show that . . . factors such as public investment in rural areas (especially in roads and education) carried more weight than price' (Friis-Hansen 2000: 14).[20]

Nonetheless, 'the main policy agenda of those within the Bank who were critical of the "get prices right" emphasis was to intensify reform rather than slow it down' (Friis-Hansen 2000: 15). This intensification, as noted, can be traced in the steps of a discourse of modernisation, and the policies it justifies, from technical fix to market fix to institutional fix, a process in which each step complements or absorbs, rather than displaces, the previous one(s). And the World Bank succeeded in forcing through this intensification of 'reform'. My original article had suggested the likelihood of major variations in the intensity, sequence and pace of implementation of reform measures in different countries, and in how effectively they would be implemented given the (differential) capacity of African states – and their constituent elements, including levels of sub-national government – to resist or otherwise deflect or shape implementation. The politics of such uneven implementation, with a focus on local (district level) processes, is exemplified in Stefano Ponte's excellent monograph on Tanzania (2002b: Chapter 6), which nonetheless acknowledges the eventual completion of the 'reform' process by the mid-1990s in the districts that he studied. By the end of the 1990s virtually the whole package of reforms had been implemented in relation to both food and export crop sectors in most of sub-Saharan Africa, while still being completed for some strategic export crops in francophone West Africa and Ghana.

I may have overstated the ability of African states, and of indigenous political processes more generally, to resist or otherwise frustrate the implementation of structural adjustment policies, with special reference to agriculture. Perhaps the determination and capacity of states to resist declined in the 1990s as increasing macroeconomic pressures enhanced World Bank (and IMF) leverage, or African political classes learned to adjust their practices to the modalities of structural adjustment (as Van der Walle, cited above, and others suggest), or some combination of these (and other) factors. If the World Bank (and its allies) proved to have the force to impose virtually all the main planks of its agenda within less than two decades, and in a considerably shorter period in a number of African countries, to what extent has the implementation of structural adjustment generated the promised results?

My original article had expressed scepticism about outcomes, as well as about modalities (the process of implementation), and outcomes are the most important matter, of course, above all for those who experience the effects of structural adjustment. My view was that its claims would mostly be confounded by the social realities and contradictions of 'actually existing capitalism' in sub-Saharan Africa. This remains my view, even allowing for the great diversity of agrarian (and rural–urban) social relations and practices, hence the need to disaggregate specific circumstances before and after structural adjustment, to do analytical justice to what T.J. Byres (1996), in another context, termed 'substantive diversity'.

With this qualification in mind, the following observations from the final chapter of the Centre for Development Research (CDR) study edited by Friis-Hansen (2000) can be highlighted. One is that the World Bank 'paid insufficient attention to the effects of globalisation, liberalisation, privatisation (and structural adjustment itself) on the conditions within which adjustment has to be implemented' (Friis-Hansen 2000: 90). This refers *inter alia* to the overall decline in the international terms of trade for Africa's principal agricultural exports during the era of structural adjustment, and factors that compound this trend, such as the declining unit prices received for some export crops as the privatisation of their domestic marketing has resulted in lower quality.

Another observation is that 'while privatisation and liberalisation of state institutions . . . to some extent have increased cost effectiveness . . .

the private sector has failed to take over a number of productive services and functions from the abandoned state organisations'. Improved cost effectiveness – registered in lower producer and consumer prices for food staples – is claimed most plausibly for 'the food sector' in some countries, but 'the picture of the export-crop sector after liberalisation is much more contested' (Friis-Hansen 2000: 93; and see Note 20 of this chapter). One empirical generalisation that does seem to hold for most farming areas is that input use, notably of fertiliser, has declined following liberalisation. The CDR study notes too that donor aid to agriculture has declined by about half over the past twenty years. While much of that aid was previously deployed for subsidy-based (government) schemes now ruled out by structural adjustment, it has not been redirected to enable public institutions to carry out 'their "normal" (non-developmental) regulatory functions' (Friis-Hansen 2000: 93), nor to invest in such services as (selective) input provision to areas, and groups, not reached by private suppliers, and in vital rural transport, water, and production and storage infrastructure (Friis-Hansen 2000: 94–95).

The final observation is that 'the effects of structural adjustment have been socially and geographically skewed, favouring better-off farmers and farmers living in areas with good market access' (Friis-Hansen 2000: 95), on which I want to focus here by presenting, however schematically, several different kinds of considerations. A first is that processes of class differentiation are intrinsic to processes of commoditisation: they are the 'normal' dynamic of capitalism, and this applies to agrarian structure and change in sub-Saharan Africa as elsewhere. This is not to suggest that class differentiation takes the same forms everywhere at all times, nor that it leads to the same outcomes. In the historical conditions of 'actually existing capitalism' in sub-Saharan Africa rural class formation is inextricably linked with, and shaped by, specific forms of gender and other social relations of difference/division (generation, 'ethnicity'). Likewise, it is typically linked to combinations of own farming and other types of economic activity and sources of income, and is not in most places manifested in the emergence of clear-cut or 'stereotypical' (to adopt Lenin's term) classes of landed property, agrarian capital and rural wage labour. None of this, however, means that class dynamics do not permeate the conditions of existence, and reproduction, of agricultural petty commodity production ('peasant' farming).[21]

In the period of structural adjustment, it is most likely that social differentiation has increased in the midst of – and, indeed, as *part of* – general trends of growing rural (and urban) immiseration and insecurity. Deborah Bryceson (1999: 186) has summarised the increasing crisis of livelihoods/reproduction in the last twenty years or so as the combined result of a 'collapse of real wages in the formal sector . . . the meaninglessness of an informal sector without a formal sector contrast, and the shrinkage of the peasant sector'.[22]

Bryceson's own studies have focused on the last of these – what she also terms 'depeasantisation' (1999) or 'deagrarianisation' (1996) – manifested in the growing proportion of rural incomes derived from activities other than own farming, in conditions where (for most farmers) the risks of farming have increased and its returns have decreased due, in significant measure, to the effects of structural adjustment. Those effects include the end of pan-territorial pricing and input (and credit) subsidies, the liberalisation of input and output markets, and – we should add – the decline of public goods provision, both infrastructure construction and maintenance (for example, rural transport) and social services (for example, education and health care).[23] At the same time, there is greater pressure, of course, on sources of income from off-farm activity that have long contributed to the investment necessary to reproduce many farming enterprises in sub-Saharan Africa. Bryceson's case studies point to suggestive changes in gender, generational and familial relations and dynamics in processes of 'depeasantisation' (not least in her emphasis on the individualisation of economic activity), and she is alert to the avenues of class differentiation presented by shifting economic patterns of livelihood and reproduction in Africa's countrysides (for example, new localised markets for products and services, as well as a generalised 'scramble for cash', as she calls it).

Although patterns of agricultural production are highly uneven, and almost impossible to generalise about with any adequacy, there are likely to be systematic differences between crops and the markets they are destined for, not least food crops for domestic markets and export crops. For example, Friis-Hansen's second observation (above) was that liberalisation seems to have improved 'cost effectiveness' in food production and markets, manifested in lower producer and consumer prices together with increased growth in food production; and Wiggins (2000), among others, shows why and how the performance of food production has been more robust than is often assumed. At the same time, the removal of pan-territorial pricing regimes, together with other reforms, has certainly had negative effects for many food producers, including quite specialised commodity producers like the maize growers in more remote areas of Tanzania's Southern Highlands. Then again, many rural areas close(r) to centres of (growing) urban demand have seen shifts from export crops (with their typically annual harvests and one-off payments) to food crop production, stimulated in part by the attractions of what Ponte terms 'fast crops' that help meet 'the increasing need for larger amounts and more regular supplies of cash' (2002b: 122). He also shows that shifts to 'fast crops' lead to new forms of labour-hiring contracts and arrangements (Ponte 2000, 2002b: Chapter 7).

On export crops, Sender notes that

> no fewer than twenty-two sub-Saharan countries recorded a lower volume of agricultural exports in 1997 than they had in 1970 ... The growth rates of total agricultural production were much more impressive over this period ... suggesting that attempts to increase the relative farm-gate prices of export crops through exchange rate liberalization, devaluations, and minimization of the role of the state in output and input marketing failed to achieve the incentive effects anticipated by orthodox analysis (2002: 191).

While there is evidence that farm-gate prices as a proportion of export (f.o.b.) prices have increased for a number of crops, this has often been off-set (or more than off-set) by declining world market prices, thereby connecting with a strategic element of Bryceson's account of 'depeasantisation: the 'fundamental problem . . . (of) African peasant agriculture's inability to compete in today's global market' (1999: 185). This potent thesis needs disaggregating in at least two ways. One is through investigating global markets for particular products – their forms of specialisation, 'governance', competition, and regulation – as studies applying global commodity chain analysis to African agricultural exports show (Raikes and Gibbon 2000; Daviron and Gibbon 2002; Ponte 2002c). These studies integrate recent shifts in the downstream links of global commodity chains (through corporate reorganisation and concentration, transport and inventory logistics, food industry manufacturing technologies, branding and other marketing strategies) with their upstream ('domestic') links from production through some first-stage processing to export. With regard to the latter, there is no doubt that the liberalisation of input and output markets, removal of subsidies, and changes in market institutions, have had major but not uniform effects, as Larsen (2002) shows for cotton in Zimbabwe and Ponte (2002a) for coffee in Kenya, Tanzania and Uganda. At the same time, many of the findings concerning the upstream links of these commodity chains (including their contract farming arrangements, where these exist) suggest that entry is often restricted to better-off petty commodity producers, and indeed that branches of production of higher value 'non-traditional' exports (notably fresh fruit and vegetables) tend to be dominated by agrarian capital on a larger scale.

This connects with the second type of disaggregation, of more general import: observations about 'peasant agriculture' in sub-Saharan Africa, as elsewhere, require attention to class and other social differentiation. In conditions of generalised commodity production, where commodity relations and dynamics are internalised in the social functioning of even the most remote countrysides, processes that generate (increasing) immiseration and insecurity for the majority create opportunities for a minority. And, as suggested above, in African circumstances capacity to command the means of agricultural production, especially of labour, is so often affected by access to off-farm sources of income and assets, similarly subject to the general recession of African economies in the period of structural adjustment. The agricultural economist Steve Wiggins observes:

> if access to market were much or all of the story, then all farmers in any given locality should be able to benefit. But do they? Social differentiation among the peasantry is no longer a fashionable area of inquiry, so case studies published during the last decade tend to be weak on such differences. What is reported, though, confirms our worst fear: differences are substantial. When and where farm economies blossom, it seems that the great bulk of the marketed surplus comes from a small fraction of the farmers ... What does divide farmers is their differential access to capital and labour, and the associated ability to bear risk. Capital rarely comes from formal lending; so most farmers have to depend on informal financial systems, and, above all, on their savings. These in turn can often be traced back to non-farm earnings, the proceeds of a successful temporary stay in a city, or recruitment to a government job (2000: 638).[24]

Structural adjustment has not produced the benefits its architects claimed for agriculture in sub-Saharan Africa, or for the great majority of its farmers, whether assessed by conventional measures of sectoral performance – especially for export crops – or by the experiences of growing rural poverty and insecurity, which make their own contributions to 'depeasantisation' and to a growing mass of 'footloose labour' seeking any means of livelihood.

Conclusion

The enduring crisis of development throughout sub-Saharan Africa presents the most concentrated challenge to the claim of neoliberalism as ideology and to structural adjustment as its programme. That challenge is experienced with greatest unease by the World Bank which promises, in a uniquely high-profile hence exposed manner, to fashion 'pro-poor' outcomes from now orthodox 'market-friendly' policies – *and* indeed in circumstances not of its own choosing (if partly of its own creation), those of the highly contradictory social realities of 'actually existing capitalism' in sub-Saharan Africa.

In conclusion, I revisit some of the strategic conclusions of my original article. A first point, just signalled, is that tracing the extremely diverse and uneven patterns of agrarian change in sub-Saharan Africa in the era of structural adjustment, presents great challenges both empirically (as noted by Wiggins 2000 and Sender 2002 among others) and analytically. The latter includes identifying and understanding the effects for African economies and agricultures of changes in the world economy in recent decades with the advent of 'globalisation' or 'world systemic' shifts as Arrighi (2002) terms them in a consideration of their 'regional aspects' for sub-Saharan Africa; and differentiating these effects from those of implementation of the various components of structural adjustment.

Such intellectual challenges, of course, are especially acute for the World Bank, which generally champions 'globalisation' as the unrestricted movement of money and commodities. But what if the money (notably in the form of direct foreign investment) does not flow into Africa (in growing quantities), and the export commodities in which it is comparatively advantaged do not flow out (in growing quantities)? This links to a second issue, on which much has been written: how does the World Bank defend its policies and practices in the face of accumulating evidence of their lack of success, and of powerful arguments why this is the case?

At the level of general intellectual argument, it is pointed out, with increasing frequency, how little the World Bank's theorists and researchers engage with (or even acknowledge) the work of their critics. This is one element in the Bank's practice of 'the art of paradigm maintenance' as Robert Wade (in Chapter Nine of this volume) memorably called it.

At another level, the Bank remains addicted to projections, not least of world market conditions, to gain credence for its policy prescriptions. This was indicated above with respect to the Berg Report (and see Note 5 of this chapter); nearly two decades later Friis-Hansen (2000: 90–91) observes:

> it is remarkable how consistently predictions of future world market commodity prices from the IFIs have forecast rising (or at worst unchanging) commodity prices, in the face of uneven but continuing deterioration over the past twenty years, in both prices and other market conditions. By virtually any criteria, the international context within which adjustment has to be implemented has worsened significantly in the 1990s.

At a third and, significantly, operational level, World Bank country, sector and programme reports are notorious for their 'data politics', that is, the ways in which data are used selectively, and typically incomplete and/or ambiguous data are presented to make the best case for policies prescribed *and* for the (positive) effects of policies implemented.[25]

The effect of such practices, as indicated several times already, is to attribute the manifest failures of structural adjustment to the various inadequacies of sub-Saharan Africa, be they the shortcomings of its states and governments, of its civil societies and funds of social capital, or of its cultures and behaviours. And this is the crucial link to my third and final point, with which I concluded the original article: that of the lack of any accountability, and responsibility, of the World Bank to those on whom its policies are imposed. This, above all, is a political point. If it is not very illuminating to regard the World Bank simply as *diabolus ex machina*, as malevolence incarnate, neither is it helpful to deflect criticism of the Bank with the observation that 'it is not monolithic' or to seek to assess the motivations of those who work for it on some scale of good and bad intention. On the former, I remarked that the Bank would be unique if it did not contain its own divisions, tensions and contradictions: in this sense 'no social entity is monolithic, including individual human beings. The question is always what are the conditions of, and limits on such internal struggles? the limits on how differences are resolved?' The way to answer such questions is not to seek to assess the (relative) merits of individual Bank employees and consultants by their good or bad faith (or professional competence) nor individual Bank policies by their rhetoric: 'slogans championing small farmers, the poor or women are *objectively* opportunistic in the context of the strategic objectives of structural adjustment' (Bernstein 1990: 26). It seems to me that the record of the World Bank in sub-Saharan Africa since that was written in 1990 provides no reason to change the stance expressed. Answering the questions posed – of the contradictions of its discourse, policy and practice, and of the limits to their resolution – necessarily starts from understanding how the World Bank functions within the conditions of contemporary imperialism and its institutional order.[26]

Notes

1. The source cited by Sender is Dollar and Svensson (1998).
2. An initial draft of the article was written and presented in Morogoro. A first full version, published as a Working Paper of the Development Policy and Practice Research Group at the Open University (No. 16, 1989), also contained an account of economic change in Tanzania in the 1980s omitted from the subsequent article. As far as I know, the 1990 article was among the first to provide a critical account, of any materialist theoretical content, of structural adjustment and African agriculture, albeit soon significantly extended by Peter Gibbon and his collaborators in work that also drew on substantial empirical investigation (Gibbon 1992; Gibbon, Havnevik and Hermele 1993). The 1990 article was subsequently reprinted in a collection edited by Roberts, Cushing and Wood (1995). While flattered by David Moore's invitation to reproduce it again in this volume, it seemed more worthwhile to attempt the retrospect offered here. As will be clear, like the original article this chapter is primarily analytical and illustrative, and quite selectively so, and does not pretend to review the large literature on African agriculture in the era of structural adjustment, nor evaluate the extensive, and often contested as well as confusing data on recent and current agricultural trends: Wiggins (2000) provides summary Food and Agricultural Organisation (FAO) national data series and a discussion of village-level data; the study by the CDR in Copenhagen, edited by Friis-Hansen (2000) is a usefully differentiated overview; and Ponte (2002b: Chapters 2, 4) also provides valuable insights. The underlying theoretical approach is explicated in more general work on agrarian political economy (for example, Bernstein 2000, 2002, 2003a, 2005a; Bernstein and Byres 2001), and some of the specific analytical points and empirical suggestions draw on applications of that approach to African conditions (for example, Bernstein 2003a, 2004a, 2004b, 2005b; Bernstein and Woodhouse 2001).
3. It seems worthwhile to reiterate these, as there are now several generations in both South and North who have grown up with some or other version of neoliberalism naturalised as the common sense of the epoch.
4. Without denying the deteriorating conditions of life for many, probably most, Africans, there was considerable and effective criticism of the quality and interpretation of much of the data used to depict a generalised crisis as the basis for advocating a similarly comprehensive 'solution', namely that of structural adjustment. For example, on food production and consumption I cited Guyer (1983); Berry (1984); and Raikes (1988), the last of which – *Modernising Hunger* – was a major stimulus to my article of 1990. Phil Raikes's death in 2001 prevented him from completing an updated version of that book which he planned to call, in characteristically sardonic fashion, *Postmodernising Hunger*. Wiggins (2000: 631–33) is a useful summary of continuing problems of aggregated food production data; I return below to what Ponte (2002b) calls the 'data politics' of the World Bank.

5. Of course, this was also a crucial conjuncture in the world economy: the recession of the 1970s had ended the post-Second World War 'golden age' of expansion and accumulation and generated processes of change in the international dynamics of capital soon assimilated to notions of 'globalisation'. The Berg Report, notoriously, emphasised *both* the comparative advantage of, *and* favourable world market conditions for, sub-Saharan Africa's agricultural exports, further grist to the mill of its argument that the causes of African crisis were principally (exclusively?) self-inflicted. In fact, as critics were quick to point out, Berg was published at a moment of declining international terms of trade for tropical agricultural commodities.

6. Ironically, as this was taken up and elaborated by the World Bank, it was able to appropriate elements of a critique of African states advanced by more radical nationalists and socialists in sub-Saharan Africa, for whom the postcolonial was often the 'neocolonial' state and its predatory practices the effect of a basic lack of popular democracy – which, of course, they linked to what they saw as the subservience of African states to foreign/international capital (and indeed the World Bank); for agrarian populists any, including neoliberal, 'confirmation' that African states 'exploited' their peasantries was apparently welcome (see further Note 20 of this chapter).

7. This point is worth emphasis for two reasons. Firstly, and especially given the style of World Bank documents, it is easy to overlook the *epic* scale of the ambition to establish bourgeois civilisation in this, the poorest and most benighted zone of the South; the radicalism of contemporary development discourse, in the sense suggested here for structural adjustment, is well conveyed by Duffield (2001a) who relates it to constructions of global 'liberal peace' and its fear of disorder, hence preoccupation with 'governance'. The second reason is that so much debate of Africa's modern history is permeated by (idealised) notions of 'full' or 'proper' capitalism, the lack of which is held to account for its problems. This approach is not confined to the mainstream but has its own versions in analysis from the Left (Bernstein 2005a).

8. In effect, 'agriculture' or the 'agricultural sector' in capitalism today is hardly synonymous with, let alone exhausted by, 'farming' in any received sense; by the same token nor are 'farmers' the principal agents of the dynamics of 'agriculture', let alone the heroic figures portrayed by the various currents of agrarian populism.

9. The term 'highest common ground' was used in the 'long-term perspective study' cited (World Bank 1989: 14); the only losers from structural adjustment in Africa would be 'rentiers parasitic on the public sector and its distortions, redundant bureaucrats . . . and *wage workers*, above all in "organised" sectors where they were the beneficiaries of "urban bias" until plummeting real wages in the 1980s engineered "*a brutal but necessary adjustment*"' (Bernstein 1990: 19 – '*a brutal but necessary adjustment*' is from the World Bank 1989, with emphasis added).

10. I explicated the 'technical fix' of models and practices of 'modernisation' in relation to a long-standing, and much debated, issue confronting capitalist agriculture, namely the effects of the unpredictability of nature for the production and realisation of

surplus value: farming entails the direct appropriation of nature and is thereby subject to its vagaries, by contrast with industrial manufacturing which transforms materials already appropriated from nature. 'Modernisation' ('scientific farming') aims to address this issue by *standardising* as much as possible the conditions of agricultural production, a process now at the stage of developing organisms that are genetically modified to possess the qualities desired. Standardisation, on an administratively and commercially minimum viable scale, was a feature of 'green revolution' success stories, above all in South and South-East Asia, which it proved impossible to replicate in African conditions, as the World Bank (1989: 95) partly recognised: 'the continent's diverse patterns of rainfall, soil and slopes combine to produce a bewildering diversity of micro-environments'. The scale required by any such 'technical fix' has its demographic dimension too: the vast expanses of sub-Saharan Africa with their diverse micro-environments are inhabited by a population about half the size of that of India. This could be termed a 'Boserup effect' (after Boserup 1965), which features strongly in the comparative analysis by Karshenas (2001) of agriculture and economic development in sub-Saharan Africa and Asia.

11. Especially basic consumer goods (wage goods, in effect) in economies with consumer goods' 'famines', or high levels of 'excess demand' as the conventional jargon has it.

12. In 1995 I joined the staff of the School of Oriental and African Studies, an extraordinary locus of the political economy of development, which has produced probably a more concentrated, sustained and analytically effective body of criticism of structural adjustment (and of its economic theory more generally) than any other single intellectual centre, as reference here to the work of such colleagues (among others) as Ben Fine, Chris Cramer, Massoud Karshenas, Mushtaq Khan, Jonathan Pincus, and John Sender illustrates.

13. Sender (2002: 193, Note 11) quotes Stiglitz's observation in his 1998 Prebisch Lecture that one of the problems of development in Africa is that 'people are wedded to traditional ways of thinking': is this the product of sixty-plus years of World Bank intellectual endeavour?

14. To the extent that much recent critical response to the World Bank's agenda and activities in Africa seems to focus as much on their discourses of governance and civil society as on their economics (and its effects), or even more so; see, for example, Abrahamsen's Foucauldian account (2000). Moore's essay on the 1997 *World Development Report*, reprinted as Chapter Eight in this volume, demonstrates that sub-Saharan Africa remains the principal zone of the prevalence of 'bad' governance, hence principal target of the World Bank's prescriptive agenda of 'good' governance/ state reform.

15. On social capital see Fine (2001b) and Chapter Four in this volume, and Harriss (2002); on the Post-Washington Consensus, see Fine, Lapavitsas and Pincus (2003); all of these works subject to critical examination the broader claims by the World Bank to intellectual innovation and/or credibility. Harriss's title adapts a term of Ferguson's influential book on Lesotho (1990) to emphasise a key point about

current World Bank discourse: that its profoundly political thrust wraps itself in the cloak of 'depoliticising development', advocating an agenda of change from which relations of power, in all their manifestations and contestations, are conjured away (as Ferguson had also shown).

16. One important example is the merging of development with security, as Duffield (2001a) puts it and illustrates convincingly. And if poverty was somehow overlooked in the earlier ('bad cop') phases of structural adjustment, this had to be re-inserted at the centre of discourse (as 'good cop') in the 1990s – a mission accomplished (for the time being) by the 2000/1 *World Development Report*. What goes around, comes around.

17. Examples of the four genres or types of work indicated include, respectively: Mosley, Subasat and Weeks (1995); Ponte (2002b); Fine (2001b); and Moore (Chapter Eight in this volume).

18. The conceptual and explanatory framework of rent-seeking, corruption, and so on, in the World Bank's approach to governance has been subjected to thorough, and convincing, criticism by Mushtaq Khan in the course of his work on the political economy of state failure (see, for example, Khan 2001, 2002).

19. Fine (2001a: 16) notes that any 'post-Washington consensus might just as well not exist as far as adjustment in Africa and Eastern Europe is concerned'.

20. The issue of price distortion through direct or indirect taxation of agriculture is, of course, central to some notions of 'urban bias' (see notably for sub-Saharan Africa, Bates 1981); it was a central element more generally of the World Bank's research agenda in the 1980s and of its rationale for internal and external trade liberalisation and devaluation (to stimulate agricultural export production), as well as applied to Africa with particular force in the Berg Report and since. Karshenas (1997) is an exceptionally powerful critique – analytical, methodological and evidential – of this research and policy prescription concerning 'the political economy of agricultural pricing policy' (Schiff and Valdes 1992b) also known as 'the plundering of agriculture in developing countries' (Schiff and Valdes 1992a). The ways in which, and degrees to which, 'developmentalist' states in sub-Saharan Africa did tax agriculture, or more precisely farmers, are contentious (Gibbon, Havnevik and Hermele 1993), although there seems to be considerable agreement that certain export crops were taxed much more than food crops for domestic markets, production of which was more likely to be subsidised, and often extensively so (Friis-Hansen 2000; Karshenas 2001).

21. This contentious position is a persistent (not to say insistent) theme of my work; see, for example, Bernstein (2000, 2005a, 2005b), Bernstein and Woodhouse (2001).

22. As well as declining employment in the formal sector both public and private. I read her observation about the informal sector to mean that to the extent it has a part to play in processes of accumulation and economic growth, this is realised through its symbiotic links with the development of large-scale industry via subcontracting, service and repair, reducing the cost of wage goods, etc. – an insight that informs the incisive analysis of the forms and dynamics of the informal sector in sub-Saharan

Africa, and its contrast with, say, much of Latin America and parts of Asia, by Meagher (1995). It is also important to note that the crisis of livelihoods extends to large sections of the urban middle class, which contributes to the complexity as well as intensity of the politics of accessing resources, including (agricultural) land, of which Peters (2002) provides a good comprehensive review and analysis.

23. Bryceson (1999: 172) reports that while the proportion of off-farm income varies regionally and between households within regions, 'survey reviews converge on an estimate of roughly 40 per cent of African rural household income on average being derived from non-farm sources'. The village surveys conducted by Ponte (2002b: Chapter 8) in Tanzania in 1994/5 gave results of 52.4 per cent and 68.9 per cent of off-farm income in total rural household income in Songea and Morogoro Rural Districts respectively. Bryceson's general speculation that income diversification is likely to exacerbate inter-household economic differentiation (1999: 174) differs from Ponte's specific finding that in Songea and Morogoro 'off-farm activities with low capital barriers played a positive role in mitigating an increasingly unequal rural income distribution' (2002b: 154).

24. Wiggins continues: 'With no insurance on offer and difficult access to credit, risking pitifully small sums ($100 can buy enough fertilizer, seed or additional labor to make a substantial difference for a low-input smallholder) against not-so-bad odds is simply unacceptable for the majority of farm households', and adds in an endnote (2000: 640): 'But then again, the same $100 invested in cattle trading or stocking a street-corner store, entails less risk, possibly better returns, and fewer days sweating in the fields'. This telling observation may also cast a different light, in certain circumstances, on the explanatory thrust of Bryceson's thesis of 'depeasantisation'.

25. For example, in the case of agricultural policy reform in Tanzania, where the 'government and the IFIs knew that the basis on which agricultural figures were produced was extremely shaky, and yet they produced sparkling accounts of the success of the reforms in boosting agricultural growth' (Ponte 2002b: 72); and in the case of privatisation in Mozambique (Cramer 2001) and more generally: 'selective use of data, analytical sleight-of-hand and over-aggregation of the issues are among the typical analytical tools . . . At the end of the 1990s, there has been little shift in these dimensions of World Bank analysis of privatisation' (Bayliss and Cramer 2001: 65).

26. I have no competence to offer 'alternative' policies. Pincus and Winters (2002b: 23–24) make the case for 're-inventing' the World Bank by returning it to its original purpose – 'making public sector loans to promote economic development' – but are sceptical that the US government would tolerate this; Sender (2002: 201) wants such a re-invented Bank to enable 'substantial state support to and protection of a new class of domestic capitalists' in manufacturing industry in sub-Saharan Africa; Friis-Hansen (2000: Chapter 11) and Ponte (2002b: Chapter 9) propose a range of agricultural policy reform measures formulated, we suspect, in a manner sufficiently 'realistic' (that is, modest) to find some room for manoeuvre that the forms of neoliberal hegemony might allow.

Chapter Twelve

The World Bank and the Construction of Governance States in Africa

Graham Harrison

This is an original chapter for this book.

Good governance is now part of the standard World Bank vocabulary. It has also become part of the accepted range of issues for researchers interested in the Bank (Dia 1993; Gibbon 1993b; Gillies 1996; Williams and Young 1994 and Chapter Seven of this book). This chapter analyses governance as a project of state reconstruction that has been selectively applied to certain states with the aim of *embedding neoliberalism*. The states I am interested in I shall call governance states. They provide the Bank with a set of cases now approximating its ideals in engaging with Africa more generally. This chapter investigates the generative processes of governance states with particular attention to the relations between states and the World Bank. It ends by reflecting on the meaning of governance states for Bank–African relations more generally.

The key features of a governance state can be easily sketched. They are those states that have made formal progress in internalising the logics and structures of (good) governance as articulated by the Bank.[1] We can clarify the nature of this progress by considering the distinction made between First and Second Generation Reform (Ul-Haque and Aziz 1999). First Generation Reform (FGR) is concerned with the disciplining and delimiting of public action; it involves retrenchment, privatisation, contracting out, and the relinquishing of mechanisms of economic control (for example, concerning exchange rates and domestic price controls). These are often referred to as 'stroke of the pen' actions – executive decisions that can be taken by a small number of people regardless of the more general nature of state administration and bureaucracy. Second Generation Reform (SGR) involves mechanisms of institutional development: training, new information systems, the promotion of new agencies and departments, the development of anti-corruption programmes, and the implementation of administrative reform programmes. SGR aims to embed new forms of public action throughout the state. A good candidate for a governance state is one in which formal progress in SGR, supported by substantial amounts of external financing, can be identified.

Uganda, Tanzania and Mozambique are all examples of governance states. Other countries may well make claims of progress arguing for their inclusion in the list, but these three seem to be the strongest pretenders at present. Uganda, Tanzania, and Mozambique all have Poverty Reduction Strategy Papers (PRSPs) and Heavily Indebted Poor Country (HIPC) status. They receive regular plaudits from external agencies and have close and relatively harmonious relationships with the World Bank. All have experienced formal economic growth above the general African levels from the mid-1990s. The rest of this chapter will be based on these three examples.

It would, however, be an error to define governance states in some scientific fashion, based on indices of growth, economic adjustment and institutional reform. These aspects are important, but (as we shall see), these states gain their identity in important ways from their external image, produced discursively by ruling governments and donor spokespeople. The language of a 'good reformer', 'star pupil', 'success story', produced by the World Bank and others in Paris Club meetings and Country Reports, construct governance states in significant ways. The Bank notes Tanzania's determination 'to break with past weaknesses' and its adoption of the correct policies and 'vision' (World Bank

2001d: ix, xix). Uganda has received perhaps stronger accolades from the donor community more generally – Consultative Group (CG) meetings regularly commence with groups of donors acknowledging 'great strides' in Uganda's progress;[2] Clare Short, the former UK minister for international development stated that 'Uganda is a star and a role model' (*New Vision*, Kampala, 29 June 2000). In Mozambique, the IMF praises Mozambique's economic reform and projects a future of expanded growth and structural change.

Regional encounters: States and order

'The retreat [of interventionism] from Africa has been replaced by a selective international re-engagement with the continent, especially to support strong economic reformers and governments able to contribute to order and stability in their subregions' (Stiglitz 1999: 69–70).

What has motivated the World Bank and others to support the construction of governance states? The answer to this question requires brief contextualisation. The Bank has been involved in Africa since the 1950s. Its lending strategies and project preferences have varied as would be expected: political change in Africa (Campbell and Loxley 1989); the geopolitics of the Cold War (Caufield 1996); the changing of Bank presidencies (Ayres 1983; Finnemore 1997); and so on, have all pushed the Bank in different directions (Kapur, Lewis and Webb 1997). Nevertheless, something of a watershed can be dated from 1980 when the Bank clearly abandoned a certain kind of statist modernisation for neoliberal macroeconomic change as its guiding principle for development (Leys 1996a; Moore 1999; Moore and Schmitz 1995; World Bank 1981).

The 'neoliberal revolution' was not specific to Africa; it was a generic ideological shift, more or less uncontested by the 1990s (Gill 1995). It is important to bear in mind that the World Bank was not a passive recipient of the collapse of Keynesian social democracy in the West: under President Clausen (1981–86) it was an active champion of neoliberal economic reform. The Bank had rapidly developed a strong ideological affinity with the rolling back of the state. Its infusion to lending in all states can be clearly seen in the massive profusion of Structural Adjustment Programmes (SAPs) from the early 1980s, customarily coordinated with IMF Structural Adjustment Facilities. Neoliberal policy-based lending became the norm the world over.

However, the Bank's global neoliberalism filtered differently through specific regional and country cases. We can see a regional patterning to the Bank's involvement in the former Soviet bloc, which is different to Latin America, and different again from sub-Saharan Africa. How can we characterise the Bank's regional engagement with Africa?

The Bank itself gives the following answer: 'Fundamental in many [African] countries is the deteriorating quality of government, epitomised by bureaucratic obstruction, rent seeking, weak judicial systems, and arbitrary decision making' (World Bank 1989: 3). That these problems were seen as 'fundamental' reflects a concern underlying all of the points made by the Bank in its engagement with Africa: a lack of order of a kind more profound than in other regions because it relates to the problematic foundations of the state rather than other more second-order issues concerning institutional capacity and stability (Harrison 2004a).

Understanding political instability, civil conflict, pervasive informal activity and the development of 'shadow states' would require a general postcolonial history of Africa (see Reno 1998; Clapham 1996), but the impact of SAPs is a most relevant aspect of this enduring political pattern. Structural adjustment, in the first place zealously wedded to notions of concerted and radical economic change, proved deeply destabilising to the social and political fabric of African societies (Gibbon 1993b; Walton and Seddon 1994; Zack-Williams 2000). A rash of protests swept through the continent in the 1980s; sustainable economic recovery did not take place; and states and societies did not transform into the lean, mean neoliberal machines that were expected.

The Bank thus contributed to the 'destabilisation' of many indebted African states through structural adjustment. In the wake of a range of critical accounts of SAPs in the late 1980s and early 1990s, the Bank and others became more fundamentally concerned with *state order*.[3] The

Bank realised that the preconditions for effective public action could not be assumed present and may well have been undermined by the actions of the IFIs themselves. Rather (and ostensibly rather curiously), states had to be reconstructed and rolled back simultaneously: they had to be changed from weak rent seekers to strong nightwatchmen. Neoliberal discipline and a range of capacity-building projects produced parallel desires to reduce and rebuild public action.

SGR and governance can be understood as the Bank's response to the problematic of state order. Both of these terms relate to state reconstruction, not roll-back. As a result, governance states have undergone a significant infusion of resources into some aspects of public action. But governance reform is also ensnared within the generalised neoliberalism adhered to by the Bank and all other large international organisations. In essence, the Bank's governance agenda is a normatively charged attempt to promote state stability, reconstruction, and legitimisation in the context of an ongoing neoliberal 'push'. As such, it is a project to embed neoliberalism. Embedding neoliberalism means producing an effective remit of state action rendering a logic of economic management socially acceptable (perhaps even legitimate) to its citizens. John Ruggie (1982) develops the notion of embedding to explain how Keynesian domestic economic management in the West and a regime of controlled currency prices socially underpinned a liberal trading order. The remit of state action that has been evoked to embed neoliberalism is far more parsimonious. Embedding neoliberalism requires an *effective* neoliberal state. It requires proactive public action to promote the private economy (Cammack 2002), to base this activity in 'law and order', to survey the economy and collate statistics for economic planning (Williams 1999), and to provide the market economy with a legitimising discourse – of growth, transparency, dynamism and so on. All of these themes have been explicitly developed in the Bank's *World Development Reports* from the mid-1990s.

Uganda, Tanzania and Mozambique have all made significant progress in embedding neoliberalism. This process is ultimately what defines governance states as a group of countries the World Bank and others speak of in approving terms, as well as providing large amounts of soft finance, and involving themselves in many areas of governance. Let us take three key features of governance states and comment briefly on the nature of external involvement.

Post-conditionality

> While Government was, in some circumstances, driven by the requirements of conditionality... it has demonstrated that once it is persuaded by the merits of the proposed [adjustment] strategy, it is willing to implement the policy promptly and comprehensively. There is no reason why sound economic management should be driven by the conditionalities attached to donor assistance (Emmanuel Tumusiime-Mutebile, former permanent secretary and secretary to the treasury, ministry of finance planning and economic development, Uganda).

Governance states have developed a politics of post-conditionality (Harrison 2001a). By this, I mean a relationship between donors and the state that is not one of frequently evoked conditioning of credit/aid disbursement on policy reform. Rather, governance states have internalised the liberal economic reform agenda which, although still monitored and invigilated by the IMF and World Bank, does not involve the kind of direct external discipline that characterised the general relationship between the Bank and IMF and adjusting states throughout the 1980s (Mosley, Subasat and Weeks 1995).

Governance states have developed their own institutional features to ensure liberal economic conformity. This is most clearly the case in the transformation of ministries of finance. Ministries of finance in all three countries under consideration have received substantial institutional development – new computer systems, new or rehabilitated buildings, substantial training packages, an infusion of expatriate technical advisers, and powerful ministers. Major programmes of externally funded capacity building for financial management have been effected in all three cases. Furthermore, ministries of finance have become the conduits between donors and the government more generally, managing aid and macroeconomic reform. As the fundamentals of neoliberal economic policy (devaluation, budgetary austerity, the removal of state regulative institutions from the economy, and divestiture) were 'locked in' to each of the three countries, the Bank and others formed close relations with ministries of finance and perhaps specific personnel therein. Subsequently, ministries of finance have worked as the point of encounter for almost all aid to governance states, even if a programme involves a specific line ministry or agency. Recent budgetary techniques such as cash budgeting – but potentially more significantly, the running of medium-term economic frameworks, integrated financial management systems, output-oriented budgeting, and public expenditure reviews – all situate the ministry of finance as the central invigilator of new protocols of resource management within the state. Most advanced in Uganda (Adam and Gunning 2002; Bigsten and Kayizzi-Mugerwa 2001; Dijkstra and Van Donge 2001), the trend is towards the Bank and other donor-creditors providing budgetary support rather than programmatic support on the assumption that the ministry of finance (and specialised agencies therein) can ably manage and survey expenditure in a way that donor-imposed policy conditionalities never could. Ministries of finance have implemented systems of budget management, surveying and expenditure tracking that hold all ministries, departments and agencies (MDAs) accountable to the ministry of finance; this is an integral part of the PRSP reforms. Liberal economic policy has been championed by a ministry whose power within the state has increased significantly throughout the 1990s.

One result of this is that donors have become less concerned with aid as a mechanism to impose neoliberal discipline because this role has been taken on by the ministry of finance. Instead, they have become more interested in aid as a mechanism to promote the recovery and restabilisation of public action. This is, to use a metaphor, a switch from stick to carrot. World Bank aid policy is now more interested in promoting institutional development, administrative reform and in some sectors a comprehensive reconstruction of government. In the words of the Bank:

> Supporting good policies is important but it is not enough. We learned in the 1990s that process is as important as policy . . . The way donors and recipients interact strongly influences the effectiveness of development cooperation. Relationships have tended to follow the preferences of donor countries, leaving recipients with little sense of ownership . . . If development co-operation is to attack poverty effectively and efficiently, donors will need to . . . provide sustained support for policy and institutional environments . . . (World Bank 2000/1d: 191–92).

Examples of this approach are: Sector-wide Approaches (SWAPs) in 'social' ministries;[4] the funding of agencies such as anti-corruption and human rights agencies; and the funding of ambitious and medium-term administrative reform programmes. Tanzania and Uganda are well into their second administrative reform programmes with substantial Bank funding; Mozambique is just embarking on a similar process. None of these programmes could possibly be implemented without these levels of Bank funding (with other bilateral donors, notably the British DfID). The central agency within governance states that promotes administrative reform and capacity building is the ministry of public administration.[5] As such, this ministry has also received World Bank funding and general donor support and has seen its fortunes rise as the governance agenda has proceeded.

Changes to the ministry of public service do not evoke an affinity with the neoliberal project as easily as those within the ministry of finance. Nevertheless, the founding faith of administrative reform is the same in all three countries. This readily brings us into neoliberalism's remit of devising ways in which state policy and institutions more closely approximate the logic of the free market. Administrative reform programmes are concerned to render bureaucracies subject to market or market-like imperatives. Using the language of New Public Management and a principal-agent approach, reform is to be implemented by creating the proper incentives and disciplines to ensure efficiency. All of this is keyed into the over-arching normative tropes of governance by rendering administrators as service providers to a society conceived as an ensemble of citizen-clients and businesses. The ideal that drives administrative reform is the positive-sum results of the interactions of a marketising administration with an expanding market society (Harrison 2001a).

Thus, we can identify key aspects of the institutional changes of post-conditionality: a powerful Panopticon in the ministry of finance and a renewed ministry of public administration charged with the implementation of market-like processes within the state. Unsurprisingly, the Bank does not put it quite like this.

Liberal governance discourse

A discursive change is integrated with the changing donor–state relationship outlined above. This I shall call *liberal governance discourse*. This discourse creates a specific image of power that has two very important effects. Firstly, it represents political and economic processes as harmonious and complementary – a classical liberal premise. Politics is imagined as intrinsically positive-sum, progressive, and driven by checks and balances. This is not a politics of rolling back the state as much as a politics of harmonious public–private intercourse. Public administration theories of new public management and new institutionalism feed into administrative reform that constructs the state as 'midwife' to an emerging market economy.

Secondly, it represents donor–state relations as one of partnership. In Mozambique, the term most used is 'smart partnership' (Pitcher 2002). The World Bank evokes the metaphor of governance states being in the 'driver's seat' (Tibana 1995), with donor/creditors responding to initiatives that emerge domestically. Consultative Group (CG)[6] meetings are held in each country's capital city (not Paris), and the sometimes harsh comments on donor representatives are largely replaced by praise and statements of willingness to participate in the domestic reform agenda. In Mozambique, strong statements concerning corruption and reform were replaced by far warmer CG statements once the economy started to expand (on paper) at remarkably high rates (Harrison 1999). In Tanzania and Uganda, after hiccups in the mid-1990s, CG statements are almost ceremonial in praising the government before cordially raising aspects of reform that could be further developed.[7] What is striking about donor statements is the increasing emphasis on a need to support government initiatives and encourage 'ownership'. The image is of a state leading reform, with supportive donors in tow.

We can glean a core vocabulary of liberal governance discourse which fleshes out the two points made above. For the first point: citizenship, civil society, accountability, transparency and customer; for the second point: participation, ownership, partnership and stakeholder. Two stylised statements demonstrate the power and articulation of this vocabulary, routinely used by the Bank and all other donors. Citizens, civil society organisations and customers all interact as rational self-interested agencies in a generally harmonious way because of the free flow of information (transparency) and the generally accepted obligations each has to the other (accountability). Adjustment and governance programmes are generated through the participation of stakeholders who act as partners and thus gain ownership over reform.

Liberal governance discourse provides a political imagery to support the construction of governance states. In the first place, it depoliticises the profound and powerful interventions of external agencies. In this sense, liberal governance discourse is clearly only possible within a general global context of Western domination and radical peripheral vulnerability that has produced a modern history of international projects of intervention and control (Escobar 1995). More specifically, depoliticisation involves the representation of politically involved reform as 'technique', that is, as neutral or sufficiently uncontroversial as to require no explicit political argument. In a related argument, Harriss (2002; see also Abrahamsen 2000; P. Nelson 1995) has identified this tendency in the way that the Bank uses the politically charged concept of social capital. Perhaps the best example that derives from administrative reform is the operationalisation of the notion of participation. Participation can hardly be anything other than political, but for the Bank this immediately raises an awkwardness of articulation within its pervasively technical and liberal discourse. Thus, participation is rendered a technique to improve development or project efficiency, rather than as an end in itself. It is also a process which must ultimately be controlled by parameters set by the Bank and other 'experts': 'fostering popular participation is a deeply serious matter, but it is not rocket science . . . we development professionals sense intuitively that participation is a good thing, and we know how to foster it' (World Bank Discussion Paper, quoted in Schmitz 1995: 57).

The discourse of partnership allows the Bank and others to represent themselves in ways that take very little cognisance of their massive material preponderance. The fact that governance states are heavily indebted states with practically no independent material existence is silenced. So is the Bank's very close working relationship with the IMF: collectively, these two serve as 'gatekeepers' for a raft of other bilateral and multilateral organisations. Furthermore, the Bank functions as a powerful, prestigious and influential producer of knowledge (Fine, Lapavitsas and Pincus 2003; Stern and Ferreira 1997; Stone 2003) that works to produce ontologies of pluralism, networks and positive-sums. Partnership, ownership and participation allude to forms of relationship that elide the Bank's material preponderance.

Thus, liberal governance discourse makes a *political argument*. This is that the Bank only works as a more or less equal partner of governance states to forge a project that is by and large technical in nature or of such obvious good sense that only the most extreme forms of critique can render it 'political'. In contrast, the argument here has been that the Bank's interventions are profoundly political: governance states represent the outcome of a decade of Bank intervention – material and ideational – to embed neoliberalism in a world region which has been subjected to relatively high levels of political instability. This latter consideration brings to mind the fact that governance states do not only need to be constructed; they need to be policed.

Stability, order, and state construction

As mentioned earlier, the politics of donor intervention in Africa has often had to reconcile itself with the lack of a modern/Weberian state form. Assumptions about the capacity of the state to act are undermined by informal economies, civil conflict, complex emergencies and shadow states. In this respect, governance states represent states that have made *significant progress* towards statehood in the traditional sense, at least compared with many other states in sub-Saharan Africa. Governance states are not just states that have managed successful economic liberalisation and governance reform. They are also states that have carried out projects of stabilisation in a more profound sense – stabilisation as the assertion of state power and the exercise of that power in institutional and regulated forms. It is the coupling of these two processes that gives governance states their identity, and this allows us to see how governance states require forms and practices of discipline in order to ensure the stability of neoliberalism. As a result, key aspects of governance reform are components of state restabilisation and ordering. We can take the World Bank's own definition (1992a) of governance to see this.

1. *Transparency and accountability*: The central aim here is to render state processes routine and predictable. It is not to open up governance to potentially drastic reformulation at the hands of a citizenry, but to discipline the state (Williams 1996) into certain strictures of administration. For the IMF, transparency is about narrowing the 'predictability gap' in policy processes (Kapur, Lewis and Webb 1997: 3).
2. *The 'rule of law'*: The project here is to construct within the state the capacity to stabilise property relations. Judicial reform, police training, technical assistance for land registries and Bank advocacy of land reform all aim to make the sometimes fluid and informally ratified nature of property subject to the

'iron cage' of modern property relations. Governance as the rule of law is, in Moore's phrase, about 'getting the property rights right' (1999: 66).
3. *Participation*: The goal here is to ensure that state execution of policy is more predictable and stable. Many grand projects of social engineering have foundered on the shores of a complex and sometimes rebellious social tapestry. Participation – a strongly normative and progressive term – is instrumentalised as a form of corporatism – to 'bring people on board', to ensure a terrain that is conducive to state policy. In Riley and Parfitt's words (1994: 167):

> The Bretton Woods Institutions [previously] focused upon the mechanics of government rather than ... popular participation. What was needed was ... 'good governance': a mixture of less corruption, more open decision making, managerial efficiency, and some degree of political pluralism. These ... reforms would assist the neoliberal economic reforms. Popular participation could do the reverse.

Governance states have thus stabilised themselves partly through governance reform itself. They have carried out administrative reform programmes to make administrative processes predictable and based on commonly recognised bodies of information; they have devised forms of participation and accountability that make programmes more stable in their execution, and they have attempted to institutionalise property relations as the foundation for a stable market-based social order. But there is a broader and more sociological aspect to stabilisation. This is what I call the stabilisation of elites. It involves the World Bank and the three countries under scrutiny as well.

Uganda, Mozambique and Tanzania have relatively stable ruling elites. In Uganda and Mozambique, this stabilisation is all the more remarkable when we consider the extreme turbulence of their post-colonial histories. In Tanzania and Mozambique, the ruling party has managed to stay in power, weathering profound changes along the way. In Uganda and (again) Mozambique, elite stabilisation has been achieved through war, peace processes and the management of divisions between 'new' and 'old' or pro- and anti-liberalisation factions.

Ruling groups gain considerable political capital through this external naming as 'good reformers'. There are close relations with donors. Their effective funding by external agencies maintains governance states that would very likely collapse without external finance. External finance does not just maintain the state within governance states, it also provides largesse. Groups within each state have found ways to use donor money for their own private accumulation strategies. A drastic example is the pillaging of banks by the politically well connected (Hanlon 2002b). The construction of villas by those well placed in government in all three countries during the governance era, the paltry levels of public wages even at higher levels, and the arrival of multimillion-dollar donor projects have led to a popular knowledge in all three countries that the ruling elite feathers its own nests with external finance. My interviews in all three countries revealed that knowledge of specific examples of graft is widespread within the government and donor community. In general, the image of showcase, the level of external funding, and the opportunities this provides for the well-being and opulence of those in government have stabilised ruling elites in governance states. This is one reason why donors sometimes become equivocal concerning some of the more honestly political aspects of good governance – multiparty democracy (Hauser 1999) and corruption (Marquette 2001). External agencies have to play off desires for elite stability and effective neoliberal reform with the necessarily contested (and therefore unpredictable) nature of democratisation and anti-corruption reform; for the Bank the former take preference over the latter.[8]

Conclusion

Governance states are an explicitly *selective* categorisation. They are those cases frequently invoked by the OECD and the World Bank as successes, or countries where aid might be effective (Burnside and Dollar 2000). We have seen how these states are constructed by external agencies as much as they are the results of postcolonial domestic politics. These states have undergone post-conditionality reforms, reproduced liberal discourses, and stabilised government and elites – all under the custody of the World Bank, IMF and others. The argument throughout this chapter is that this represents a project to embed neoliberalism – to institutionalise, stabilise, and perhaps legitimise the neoliberal fundamentals of economic management and market-based growth.

Although governance states are a subset of African states, the notion of governance states has broader repercussions for Africa and its relations with the World Bank. Firstly, the categorisation of governance states is neither stable nor robust: there are no positivistic criteria for entry, and entry does not guarantee that 'exit' will not occur. Ghana's 'showcase' status has dwindled since the early 1990s for example; and 'stable' HIPC states have met with drastic unravellings, the obvious case being Côte d'Ivoire recently. In proximity to the three cases studied here, post-Moi Kenya is undergoing a gradual warming with the Bank and IMF. As such, governance states serve as an ideal posed by the Bank and others as a measure for other states.

Secondly, a related point, the categorisation of governance states – and the external construction of this category by referring to 'good' and 'bad' adjusters, SGR and so on – produces a powerful form of political moralisation. The issue here is culpability: if Uganda can make a success of its reforms and do this whilst being in the 'driver's seat', then the failures of, say, Zimbabwe are portrayed as a result solely of Zimbabwe's bad governance. African states are culpable for failed governance transitions. The crucial role of the Bank, IMF and others (not least in the Zimbabwe case) is effaced. In the 1980s, the Bank was on the back foot – trying to defend structural adjustment in the face of poor results; governance states provide a powerful referent for the Bank that allow it to stop worrying about defending adjustment, chalk up governance successes, and wring its hands about the shortfalls of other states. Consider the words of a creditor official regarding Uganda: 'If Uganda can do it, no other government has an excuse' (in Reno 2002: 430).

Of course, ultimately, the prospects for governance states and their significance for the continent more generally, will depend on their 'success'. Underpinning the notion of success in all three cases is economic growth. This is a fundamental concern for the Bank, as it always has been. It is economic growth that allows the Bank to represent its various interventions to promote capitalism as a form of 'development'. All three cases have experienced relatively high levels of growth during their time as governance states. But there are good reasons to be very cautious about the prospective meaning of GDP growth rates of 5 per cent or more.

Firstly, economic growth has not mollified issues of social equality. In all three cases regions, classes, ethnic groups and groups of women have felt little improvement. This is not to say that there has been no improvement – Uganda's universal primary education (UPE) has provided a genuine massive increase in access to education,[9] and generally agricultural output in Mozambique has increased. However, issues of inequality remain extremely pressing – especially as economic recovery tends to have been spatially extremely delimited to a small number of urban areas and regions (Harrison 2002).

Secondly, percentage increases represent extremely small absolute increments. Tanzania, Uganda and Mozambique all remain relatively poor by African standards. GNI per capita in 2000 for the three cases are: Uganda US$280, Tanzania US$270, and Mozambique US$210 (World Bank 2002f: Table 2). We can statistically infer that all three have yet to reach per capita income levels similar to those in the heyday of statist modernisation. The best that can be said for economic recovery is that a very small first step has been taken.

Successive steps will depend on the ability of liberal economic management to produce structural transformations in economies. Although market reform has produced increased output in each economy, we have to bear in mind that these reforms are partly about domestic liberalisation but also about global liberalisation. As such, they key into an international institutionalisation that is far from auspicious. Instead, protectionism, the dominance of the Bank and others by the US, and older but resilient global structures which used to be called the international division of labour put powerful dampeners on market-based recovery. Some 'big statistics' exemplify this: between 1992 and 1998, HIPC countries gave US$5.8 billion more in debt repayments than they received in new loans and credits; First World countries impose 50 per cent higher tariffs against imports from the Third World than they do amongst themselves; Africa's gross income fell by an estimated 2 per cent as a result of the finalisation of the Uruguay Round; Western ODA fell by half between 1990 and 1998. My speculative argument here is that liberalisation is more akin to a new global structuration – global market relations managed by Western governments in ways that permit little room for governance states to become 'developmental states'. Institutional reform needs to be global as well as local.

Notes

1. The Bank has generally steered away from the explicitly normative term 'good governance' in order ostensibly to respect its own Articles and render governance as a concern of policy technique for effective development. See Shihata (1991) for a detailed consideration.
2. Notes from various CG meetings in Uganda are in my possession.
3. This is evident generally in World Bank (1997b: 162 ff.), which speaks of sub-Saharan Africa as a region with a 'crisis of statehood'.
4. SWAPs involve a coordination of donor funding (the creation of an aid 'basket fund') and support for a general sector-wide programme. This approach should negate the pre-existing tendencies of donors to support their own small projects within a ministry, leading to problems of management, coordination and information sharing. On SWAP, see Brown et al. (2001).
5. This is a generic term to cover specific formal titles in each country: ministry of public service (Uganda); civil service department (Tanzania); ministério de administração estatal or ministry of public administration (Mozambique).
6. On the institutional mechanics of the CGs and other forms of debt management, see Martin (1994).
7. Generally, the turning point for Tanzania is the accession of Benjamin Mkapa in 1995; for Uganda it is 1987 when Museveni came to power or perhaps 1989 when the president's brief dalliance with *dirigiste* economic policy came to an inauspicious end. Donor narratives on Uganda have a particularly phoenix-like quality to them.
8. In the case of Uganda the maintenance of a stable and determined elite has met with a markedly lukewarm response from the World Bank and some bilateral donors to the establishing of 'commercial networks put in place by Ugandan army commanders' in the pillage of the Democratic Republic of Congo, as a UN Security Council Report (2002) into the illegal exploitation of resources puts it. See, for example, Clark (2001); and Reno (2002).
9. Uganda's Gini coefficient has fallen slightly (Mackinnon and Reinikka 2002: 274), although more specific and qualitative research generates complex integrated stories of progress and setbacks (Ellis and Bahiigwa 2003). Uganda is the best 'surveyed' of governance states, with regular Service Delivery Surveys, expenditure tracking, household surveys, and many foreign-funded researchers carrying out fieldwork.

Chapter Thirteen

Levelling the Playing Fields and Embedding Illusions
'Post-conflict' Discourse and Neoliberal 'Development' in War-torn Africa

David Moore

THIS IS A SLIGHTLY REVISED VERSION OF A 2000 ARTICLE IN
REVIEW OF AFRICAN POLITICAL ECONOMY 27 (83): 11–28.

The World Bank's booklet *Post-Conflict Reconstruction: The Role of the World Bank* suggests that in its eyes the ravages of war-torn Africa present international financial institutions with an opportunity to create 'market-friendly' opportunities on the levelled playing fields assumed by 'post-conflict' discourse. As well as downplaying the conflict-laden and complex aspects of post-war situations, the illusion of peace and ordered government encouraged by 'post-conflict' language allows the traditional humanitarian side of the 'relief' and (neoliberal) 'development' continuum in post war situations to be obliterated (Macrae 2001). Thus, the World Bank and similar agencies are able to enter the killing fields even *during* conflict to lay the seeds of – or 'embed', to use a reversal of Polanyian perspectives – individual property rights and other aspects of neoliberal economic, social and political good governance. Perspectives from 'social capital' discourse also buttress this view. Such ideologies coincide with and justify the diminishing material resources allocated to a more traditional humanitarian agenda for post-war reconstruction, as well as sidelining alternatives.

A decade and a half ago, at the end of the Cold War, with typical Eurocentric chutzpah many analysts predicted that with the burden of superpower rivalry lifted from its shoulders Africa would surge forward to peace, democracy and development. Now we know better: from Ethiopia and Eritrea on the horn, Somalia in the east, Sierra Leone in the west, Rwanda and the Congo(s) in the middle and Angola in the south, great swaths of the continent have been soaked in more blood than before. Yet amidst this carnage, the notion of 'post-conflict' has emerged and taken flight within humanitarian and development discourse, as if by linguistic fiat a 'sustainable' peace will ensue and the traditionally separate realms of Western Third World-aiding agencies can come together and reconstruct war-torn societies in their image. The humanitarian dispensers of 'relief' can, it seems, join with the long-term implementers of 'development' in the long march from conflict to peace if only they can cooperate to work out the division of labour which has separated them in the past. Agreeing on what constitutes the proper activities during a 'post-conflict' interregnum is the basis of such a *modus vivendi*: but before that, we are told, both parties should share their understanding of the notion of 'post-conflict' itself.

This chapter will argue that the notion of 'post-conflict' is fraught with tensions other than the most obvious one that conflict does not disappear as easily as development discourse leads us to believe. Even beyond differences between humanitarian 'relief' and 'developmental' ideas for reconstruction projects and programmes (although it may share apolitical tendencies with the humanitarian agenda – Cliffe and Luckham 1999: 29), the concept is caught up in tensions between neoliberal and more interventionist visions of development in general. It is also imbricated in contention over the resources allocated from the coffers of the advanced capitalist world to the rebuilding of war-torn societies on the periphery. More fundamentally, it is entangled in the complex nature of the causes of and cures for conflict in Africa.

The most obvious place to see the neoliberal side of these perspectives is in the World Bank's exposition of its interest in 'post-conflict' reconstruction, namely, in its booklet *Post-Conflict Reconstruction: The*

Role of the World Bank (1998c). The pamphlet is a good indicator of the Bank's worldview on 'post-conflict' after its first interventions into the realm of war and its after-effects, which had their genesis in 1993. As Catherine Caufield (1996: 308–09) has pointed out, the Bank has been mission creeping into 'post-conflict' since a 'president's retreat' paper in early 1993. It contemplated the Bank's place in 'the changing nature of national sovereignty' and foresaw it being 'pushed into a new role as a conservator for failed nation states . . . or small new states unable to shoulder the full burdens of statehood . . . this role could be the economic and social, post-nationhood counterpart of the political trusteeship of the postwar era'.

Failed and 'premature' nation-states are, of course, very often born of war. This advice foreshadowed President Wolfensohn's 1995 signalling of 'post-conflict' projects in Angola (not likely in 1995!), Bosnia-Herzegovina, Gaza and the West Bank, Haiti and Lebanon. It also led to the establishment of a Post-Conflict Unit (PCU) in April 1997, with a budget of US$8 million for 'analytical and related work' (Stremlau and Sagasti 1998: 28–30). Since then, the Bank has also announced special post-conflict projects in countries such as Rwanda, Kosovo, Afghanistan and Iraq (World Bank 2003a).[1]

In addition to the booklet, some of the Bank's perspectives on 'social capital' indicate aspects of its thinking on conflict and its aftermath. They too will be considered in this chapter, as will opposition to these neoliberal perspectives, including classical humanitarian analysis and radical political economy texts based on empirical analyses of African conflicts. On a more conceptual level, the chapter will also suggest that Gill's (1998) reasoning on efforts to 'constitutionalise' neoliberalism, based largely on Cox's Gramscian understanding of the global political economy and Polanyi's fears of neoliberalism's disembedding of the economy from other social and political activities, makes worthy advances towards the dissection of the World Bank's view of post-conflict reconstruction. The chapter will also suggest that efforts to embed neoliberalism in war-torn Africa may create more conflict than before, and thus rest on a dangerous illusion.

Theoretical signposts

Gill's notion of the constitutionalisation of global capital refers to the legal, juridical and otherwise institutional means by which states and international organisations 'lock in' or entrench various means of protection for globalised and 'neoliberalised' capital so that it is irreproachable and unchallengeable, yet also appears to be free and natural. Polanyian thinking (1957) alerts us to the utopian nature of such a project that, in fact, produces dystopian results. Neoliberal (and often state-led) efforts attempt to rip 'the market' out of all the social roots or 'constraints' which stop labour and land from becoming completely commodified in pre-capitalist or welfarist societies, or which hold back dysfunctional and violence-producing inequalities from reaching their apotheosis. They try to pull an individualised 'market' out of a substantive economy which is 'embedded' in other socio-political relations such as kinship obligation or collective rights won by labour oganisations and (sometimes) protected by states. Thus they are bound to lead either to fascist ruin or socially and politically constructed positive alternatives: these reactions form Polanyi's 'double movement', entailing right- and leftward responses to the travail of the push to autonomous markets.

Gill's affinities with Cox (1987, 1996, 1999), Gramsci (1971) and Marx take us further than Polanyi by being more attuned to the way the market, somewhat fetishised in Polanyi's notion (Lie 1991), is actually forced into being by (now) globalised class fractions who simultaneously build their hegemony – they make this coercive process appear consensual – through the apparatuses of state and ideology. Gill's and Cox's insights on how neoliberalism (for Cox, hyperliberalism) is being made ideologically hegemonic complement Polanyi's notion of embeddedness and its opposite by suggesting that neoliberalism may have a chance of surviving if enough people believe in its illusions, even as it tears society apart. Polanyi would say such a process could not be organic or last long. Global neoliberalism's 'organic' intellectuals would suggest otherwise, but the struggles over the terms of its institutionalisation (for example, over the entrails of the Asian financial crisis) indicate uncertainty between Keynesian and Hayekian variants on the project. Only time will tell if the inherently disembedded and unembeddable can be made hegemonic, but Polanyi's notion of the 'double movement' suggests that all attempts to make neoliberalism natural are doomed to fail while Gramscian notions may, ironically, be more open-ended.

The tensions within a Polanyian and Gramscian-Marxian marriage allow us to question just how much a 'social democratic' end to Polanyi's 'double movement' is indeed a solution to capitalism's endemic problems (Lacher 1999), but that – along with many other theoretical issues raised in this realm – is a question for another day. For now, we can note how Gill's perspective highlights the contradictions inherent in the need for global capital to use very 'interventionist' means to implement ends which we are told are the results of the entirely unconstrained actions of millions of otherwise asocial beings (Gamble 1996; Gray 1998a; Kukathas 1999). For the purposes of this chapter, Gill's standpoint enables us to see how the discourse of 'post-conflict' is a part of the effort of capital's globally situated organic intellectuals to embed their particular utopias into the soils left untilled in a proliferation of 'complex political emergencies' or CPEs (Duffield 1994, 1996, 1998, 1999; Cliffe and Luckham 1999; Goodhand and Hulme 1999).[2] The wake of war leaves the 'level playing field' so beloved by these neoliberal discourses.

The meaning of 'post-conflict'

Some analysts have interpreted the emergence of the concept of 'post-conflict' as an excuse for the main development agencies and international powers to devote fewer resources to the amelioration of complex political emergencies in the Third World. The notion allows structural adjustment policies to reign as usual, instead of the supposed dependency-inducing tendencies of welfarist humanitarian assistance. To label war as peace is not only Orwellian, but it also justifies implementing shock therapy to create the market cure for war. As Jeff Crisp (1998) has put it, if donor states want to spend less on humanitarian relief; if they want to disengage from crisis-affected countries; if they want to suggest that the situation in those countries has 'normalised;' and if they want to impose the rigours of structural adjustment on the world's poorest and most devastated countries, then what better way than to suggest that such states have entered a 'post-conflict' phase?

At first glance the 1997 *World Development Report: The State in a Changing World* (World Bank 1997b) has little relationship to such a view. (This *Report* was published to some acclaim as an indicator of the end of a minimalist view of the state and a revival of something approaching social democracy, but more closely resembles a call to arms for states and international organisations which will establish property rights more efficiently than in the past.) More acute examination, however, confirms affinities, especially those concerning structural adjustment programmes. Most of the 1997 *Report* proceeds with the usual combination of cheeriness and 'bureaucratese', suggesting that although the condition of the Third World is a gloomy one, the proper dose of Anglo-American policy wisdom and states with a good match of 'capability and roles' will soon set things right. But towards the *Report*'s conclusion its cool and sagacious rational choice political economy and public sector management discourse is replaced by Nietzschean calls for leaders with 'clear' and 'compelling' vision strong enough to lead with the 'leap of faith' necessary to re-engineer 'the values and norms of the state and the state's relationship to the economy' (World Bank 1997b: 155–56). Its romantic and reckless advice tells these leaders to take action in opportune moments such as times of external threat or economic crisis – 'when the normal rules of the game are in flux' – or during a new regime's honeymoon (World Bank 1997b: 144). The Bank may be hoping for a fortuitous alliance between the seemingly opposed Revolutionary United Fronts of the continent (Richards 1996) and the technocrats of the African Capacity Building Foundation (D. Moore 1997).

It is as if the World Bank political scientists' revolutionary fervour sees the terrain of 'post-conflict' situations as ripe for the implementation of their kind of state, economy and society. If they can find the right kind of 'strongmen' at the right time – in our case, the 'post-conflict' moment, which may be the next best thing to the bliss of a new marriage, if not a happy divorce – their visions of the perfect political economy can be implemented.

Although nothing new in authoritarian variants of modernisation theory, the ideas of strongmen and their strong states to create a capitalist – or 'market-friendly' – society must be anathema to those who seem to distrust state intervention instinctively. There is a conundrum here for those who like to think of themselves as libertarians. However, a quick look at the history of Western intervention in the Third World suggests that, even before Cold War theory, political authoritarianism and outright brutality have never been seen as contradictory to market-friendly policies (Hochschild 1998). At an even deeper level than that, however, is the probability that the tendency to search for strongmen has its roots in a belief that European history shows the need for an 'absolutist' state to break pre-capitalist bonds. Only then can the supposedly natural tendencies of *homo oeconomicus* emerge from the murky depths of feudal restrictions (Gellner 1997; Williams 1999; Wood 1999). Perhaps even Hayek would have condoned the use of the state for the erasure of pre-capitalist fetters to 'market freedom', contrary to the beliefs of those who espouse his thought as a bulwark for the preservation of spontaneous 'local knowledge' (Kukathas 1999; Scott 1998; Cockett 1995; Gamble 1996). Thus we should not be surprised that the World Bank intends to establish 'watching briefs' in war zones to monitor conflict in order 'to develop an understanding of context, dynamics and needs so that the Bank is well positioned to support an appropriate investment portfolio when conditions permit' (World Bank 1998c: 6).

If the humanitarian agencies want a piece of the decreasing aid pie, perhaps it is understandable that they are deigning to dine with the devil that brews up such investment-friendly concoctions. Humanitarian agencies, including the United Nations High Commissioner for Refugees (UNHCR), have negotiated with the World Bank as the latter has become interested in 'post-conflict' (Wolfensohn 1999a, 1999b) and as sources of funds other than the Bank dry up (Stremlau and Sagasti 1998). Members of the Bank's PCU participate in many humanitarian agenda-setting exercises anyway, thus having crucial impact on the tenor of the 'relief to development' continuum. It remains to be seen, while the Bank's allegiance to the US and its presidency's incumbents varies with a pragmatic realisation that markets do not emerge magically from the killing fields *and* that the US does not practise free trade itself, whether or not a clear neoliberal line will hold: a Brookings Institute paper by a PCU officer is somewhat more evenly weighted on the 'free-market/intervention' balancing pole than the usual Bank rhetoric, but even then it holds quite astounding assumptions about the ease with which a 'normal' state gets up and running in war-torn interregna (Holtzman 1999). In more media-attuned discursive forays, the Bank's language sounds almost as 'radical' as that of the advocates of participatory development (World Bank 1999d). If 'rebuilding' involves something other than neoliberalism, we might argue that the World Bank is moving in the humanitarian direction. As the saying goes, the proof will be in the pudding, but as yet there is no distinctive move away from neoliberal policies. In Mozambique, for example, even with the implementation of a modicum of 'debt relief', there are new conditions for the privatisation of rural water and a strict 'no' to tariffs to rebuild its cashew-processing industry (Hanlon 1999).

Needless to say, those who hold strongly to the 'humanitarian' viewpoints are worried about their agenda being watered down by the 'development' agenda of the World Bank. There is a fear of the World Bank's 'mission creep' and its economistic efforts to home in on societies which have yet to recover from war and its attendant political and social complexities. It is interesting to note in this regard that many people working in the humanitarian realm equate 'development' with 'neoliberalism' almost automatically: it takes some time for an outsider to the humanitarian community to realise that 'development' has lost any left-leaning connotations in this discursive arena. This may be one reason why the humanitarian agenda is progressing towards the development and reconstructive side of the relief–development continuum: it is some sort of a response to the neoliberalisation of development discourse. On the other side of the fence there is a feeling among some humanitarians that their mandate has crept too far into the development realm rather than the old standard of simply protecting the basic rights of refugees: perhaps they too, albeit for different reasons, have fears of too much cooperation with the World Bank.

Both sides must agree, however, on the fact that resources for humanitarian action are scarcer while the intensity and intractability of conflict in Africa increases. As Jeff Crisp (1998) notes from within the humanitarian tradition,

> there is now substantial evidence to suggest that the industrialised states are disengaging from conflict-affected areas, which play a marginal role in the global economy. Donors have already made sharp reductions to their humanitarian assistance budgets, and increasingly justify such action with the unsubstantiated argument that emergency relief does more harm than good to its intended beneficiaries.

The neoliberal justification for this is that lingering humanitarian assistance builds in a dependency syndrome at best, discouraging farmers from planting seeds, for example – as if in the midst of wars farmers would be able to sow and harvest as usual and in post-war situations seed stocks will be in good shape. At worst, this argument goes, humanitarian aid feeds warriors (Luttwak 1999; Maren 1997). Serious radical scholars of the political economy of war also bring this insight to bear – although their analyses of the interaction between war economies and humanitarian operations note that the resources feeding war go far beyond aid, including land, livestock, labour and minerals (Keen 1994, 1998a, 1998b; Edkins 1996). They also extend beyond the 'local', stretching across the globe to the drug trade, exile communities and, of course, the business of small arms.

Perhaps ironically, poststructuralist writing condemning humanitarians for failing to go beyond 'passive victim' perceptions of their charges may also fit in with a neoliberal perspective (Campbell 1998). If the victims of political crisis have 'agency' should they not pick themselves up by their own bootstraps? (Or, from a more 'progressive' position, given that these conflicts are inherently political, should not humanitarians simply choose the 'agents' with whom they feel 'solidarity'? Perhaps the latter should be armed?)

If carried to their logical ends, both of these modes of justification for decreasing (impartial) humanitarian aid lead to bizarre scenarios. If humanitarian aid stops, for whatever reason, and there is no political resolution to the conflict, soldiers may have to coerce farmers for food rather than stealing it from aid agencies. Perhaps farmers – being agents of their own fate, not passive victims – will fight the soldiers for the right to till their soil, gaining their weapons from local entrepreneurs plugged into the global market. Maybe, but much less likely, when the farmers and the soldiers have reached a military stand-off, the soldiers will establish relationships of consenting trade and the solidarity of 'the market' with the farmers in order to eat and there will be a true revolution from below, in a Mao meets the market scenario. Such unlikely utopias illustrate at best that in situations of war we cannot know in advance: therein, writes Edkins (1996), also in a poststructuralist vein, lies the radical undecidability of the issue and its essentially *political* nature – but also, contra Edkins, the need for humanitarian impartiality. With an overly political take on wars and their uneven cessation we arrive full circle with the World Bank's emphasis on monitoring (or intelligence) and 'development aid' starter kits even before wars end: the Bank can then choose its allies in its own mode of (neoliberal) solidarity. Does this spell the end of impartial humanitarian assistance and the beginning of ideologically partial development? Is neoliberalism now pitted against interventionist humanitarianism in the midst of pre-existing battles?

Whatever the logic, there is

> a growing tendency amongst the industrialised states to suggest that crisis situations have 'normalised' (and that emergency

operations can therefore be terminated) even in situations where the level of human suffering remains extraordinarily high . . . one result of this, as revealed by recent evaluations in West Africa and Sudan, has been the premature phasing out of relief rations before compensating development opportunities are provided. Another has been the introduction of unrealistic cost-recovery programmes in the health systems of countries experiencing civil wars (Crisp 1998).[3]

The Bank could counter this assertion by stating that by going into only barely resolved situations it is providing 'compensating development opportunities' and thus resolving the problem of artificial 'stages' (that is, a unilinear track from conflict to restoration to the resumption of 'development as usual') which are never demarcated clearly. But if this argument is to hold, humanitarian organisations could provide 'development opportunities' along with relief rations (and of course, they do). It is much harder, however, to justify cost-recovery programmes in the social services unless we have dispensed ideologically with humanitarian or welfarist approaches. The debate is not really about 'relief' or 'development,' but about *what kind* of development is best in war-torn societies and indeed in the rest of the periphery.

With the promulgation of 'social capital' theory (which will be addressed in more detail later in the chapter), there is an attempt to jettison welfarist and/or statist approaches to development in the name of countering excessive humanitarianism. Before investigating the migration of this perspective to 'post-conflict' discourse, though, we should turn to the wider causes and consequences of conflict in contemporary Africa and its intractability. Aside from the battles among UN agencies, it seems clear that the protracted nature of 'post-conflict' interregna – that is, the constant postponement of their promise and the subsequent inadequacy of the term – is the primary cause of the debate and manoeuvre between humanitarian and neoliberal protagonists. If the nature of 'post-conflict' periods was apparent and self-descriptive, there would be no need for humanitarian assistance. Then, the debate would return to that within the discourses of 'development' (in spite of the self-acclaimed hegemonic status of neoliberalism). In the meantime, given this intractability it would not be wise to overuse the phrase: the United Nations Research Institute for Social Development's notion of 'war-torn' societies (War-torn Societies Project 1998) is much better than 'post-conflict' situations. So are the analyses inspired by the idea of 'complex political emergencies', but neither has become dominant in the discourse. Given the hegemony of 'post-conflict', we can only chip away at its edges, hoping that it continues to signify something different than the 'normalcy' that serves as an excuse for reduced humanitarian action or insensitive political interventions. Perhaps, if we examine the reasons why waiting for 'post-conflict' is akin to looking out for Godot, the notion's neoliberal veneer can be removed.

Why then are the conflicts so protracted?

'Postmodern' conflict in Africa: Causes and consequences

Although he is by no means a postmodernist, for Mark Duffield (1998, 1999; see also Reno 1998) certain aspects of the concept can be applied to the current African situation. He describes a world in which state boundaries are falling down; structural adjustment policies have deprived state makers and nation builders of the means to forge coalitions and ameliorate threats from pretenders to power; warlords have better links with global corporations and more efficient tax collection agencies than have putative politicians; 'retraditionalisation' re-invents latent ethnic identities; armies are replaced by ostensibly clean mercenary organisations while other soldiers and rebels change identities daily (the Sierra Leonean term *sobel* captures the confusion of people terrorised by armed youths who may be soldiers by day and rebels by night); and NGOs do the jobs formerly performed by more formal organisations such as states and official international agencies. For Duffield, the term

> addresses the emergence within the last couple of decades of political projects in the South, including qualified state

systems, which no longer seek or even need to establish territorial, bureaucratic or consent-based political authority in the traditional sense. It reflects the re-emergence of globalised political economies no longer reliant on an inclusive nation-state competence (1998: 76).

Structural and world-historical analysis needs to be employed to begin to understand the emergence of such a postmodern (or 'neo-medieval') condition. The fragility with which so many African states were being constructed in the 1960s and 1970s was exposed with the oil and debt crises of the late 1970s and 1980s, compounded extraordinarily by the already well-entrenched downward drift of commodity prices. Neoliberal economic policies exacerbated the severity of these trends. The end of the Cold War removed most great power motivations for aiding and abetting the process of 'passive revolution' or the 'reciprocal assimilation of élites' discussed by Jean-François Bayart in *The Politics of the Belly* (1993), which augmented the ruling classes in a system maintained by co-option. Now that these modes of accommodation have evaporated, in many societies war is the mode of production (Behrend 1998).

This is a mode of production far removed from the massive job-creating exercises with which Westerners are familiar from the experience of the Second World War and the capital- and intellect-intensive efforts of US/NATO-led attacks from on high on Serbia or US/UN wars against Iraq (and Iraq Mach II's 'reconstruction' will employ a good number of Americans, or at least American construction firms such as Bechtel). Rather, the war mode of production in peripheral economies is 'characterised by high levels of unemployment, high levels of imports and weak and fragmented and decentralised administration. It could be said that the war economy represents a new type of dual economy, typical of peripheral regions exposed to globalisation' (Bojicic, Kaldor and Vejvoda 1995, in Duffield 1998: 98).

Furthermore, in Africa this 'war mode' is grafted onto and grows from the uneven articulation of more traditionally conceived modes of production, that is, the poorly mixed blend of non-capitalist and capitalist economic, political and social relations that have made African history so complex. Remember, the Marxist economic anthropologists who first discussed the 'articulation of modes of production' thesis were convinced that the contest between modes would only be decided after protracted periods of violent conflict (Foster-Carter 1978). Mahmood Mamdani's (1996) bifurcation of the rural 'subject' under colonially inspired 'traditional' rule versus the urban 'citizen', and the conflict-ridden transition from one condition to the other could be called a 'politicist' version of articulation of modes of production theory. His analysis of the Congo side of the Great Lakes crisis (Mamdani 1998) illustrates the contemporary value of this approach. Could a teleologist safely say that the current mode of conflict is but a stepping stone to an inevitable and prosperous capitalist peace? After all, such a perspective might continue, Europe went through equally vicious periods and emerged as the paragon of the Enlightenment. As Charles Tilly (1985; Skocpol 1998) might put it, strong states are only protection rackets made polite by the fact that they have to bow to democratic niceties in order to continue taxing their subjects.

Although predictable, the responses to such propositions are not trite: Africa's historical and global positioning allows it no imperial empire to help expand its economies and build its states, and its ruling classes (be they in states or on their edges) seem unable to establish productive accumulation strategies at the moment (for a 'new culturalist' elaboration of this thesis see Chabal and Daloz 1999). Besides, even with all those advantages the European experience took a very long time. Humanitarians and developmentalists alike have too much hubris to abide history taking its course in such brutal ways. They think, in common, that the establishment of a firm peace is the only way to build 'sustainable' economies: they differ, however, on what are the starting blocks for the establishment of a strong political economy in moments of fragile peace. That difference rests on a classical ideological and philosophical dichotomy: intervention or laissez-faire.

Westerners' immediate historical experience makes them familiar with a war that built strong, interventionist and welfarist state-society complexes. The type of 'globalisation' that emerged after the Second World War saw the Cold War force a continuation of such military-industrial complexes, and to some extent compelled the capitalist powers to moderate the inequalities of the 'liberal' capitalism which began breaking down around the end of the nineteenth century (and that was unnatural to Polanyi) with welfare policies (thus its 're-embeddedness' with elements of social reciprocity and international financial regulation). The Marshall Plan in Europe and the Dodge Plan in Japan were constituent parts of that Cold War-bounded rebuilding process. The state-capitalist booms in the East Asian 'miracles', too, reflect that era as it stretched to include the war in Vietnam and other aspects of Cold War geopolitics in that region. However, the wars now familiar to denizens of the 'Third World' – especially in Africa – promise no such end. As long as the structural features of the global economy blend with the modalities of war in the way they do, it seems unlikely that humanitarian stopgaps or development solutions based on micro-enterprise and cost recovery will be the catalysts to bring the 'post-conflict' moments to the fruition most of those living within them deserve. Yet, the moment upon the signing of peace accords does offer a unique opportunity for creative transitional interventions. Appropriate ones have yet to be derived.

As he entered his ninety-first year, John Kenneth Galbraith invoked a much-mooted solution, and managed to do so without sounding too much like a paternalist colonial master:

> Nothing so ensures hardship, poverty and suffering as the absence of a responsible, effective, honest polity. In a humane world order we must have a mechanism to suspend sovereignty when this is necessary to protect against human suffering and disaster. Let there be government by the United Nations to bring about an effective and humane independence. Economic aid is important, but without honest, competent government it is of little consequence. We have here one of the major unfinished tasks of the century (Galbraith 1999).

Aside from the fact that the current world superpower has no intention of allowing the UN to do any such thing (Urquhart 1999), or, contra David Rieff's hopes, is far from planning to do so single-handedly unless from 15 000 feet in the air (Rieff 1999; Ignatief 1999), or there is something like oil involved (Klare 2003), Galbraith's solution is a little too interfering on the side of politics and not interventionist enough on the economics side (this may be a trait held in common by all publicly active economists, while political scientists may fall prey to the opposite tendency): debt cancellation, decent commodity prices, open Western markets and protected basic industries might go some way to solving many of Africa's problems. But Galbraith's way of addressing the 'capacity-building' problem is genuinely humanitarian, and perhaps in post-war/war-torn situations his notion of trusteeship is not completely inappropriate, even for those who jealously guard fragile Third World sovereignties.

Of course we would be averse to such a solution for Africa, but in particular 'post-conflict' moments it might be appropriate. Colin Leys (1996a: 195) has suggested something not too far from Galbraith's prescription. He recognises the current '*de facto* recolonisation of Africa by aid consortia, World Bank structural adjustment teams, the UN High Commission for Refugees, the UN Food Programme and a host of other agencies' – although the humanitarian side of the equation may be reduced in relative terms – but foresees it being changed into a 'new long-term, open and accountable system of collaboration between domestic and supranational political leaders and public servants, based on principles of mutual interest in creating the economic and social preconditions for a new and more genuine sovereignty'. Leys recognises some of the 'valid contributions' made by 'the neoliberal critique of past policies and the new institutionalist analysis of old institutions', and agrees that in Africa the market should be given more scope in some sectors. However, just as importantly, he cautions that 'non-market institutions that are resistant to politicisation and corruption and yield socially efficient results' will have to be *constructed*. Noting the lessons of the successful late developers in East Asia, among others, he reminds us that 'national success in the global marketplace depends on coherent long-term strategic action by *states*, and the construction and maintenance of a dense web of "intermediate" institutions (banks, financial and technical services, training, and infrastructure of all kinds) that the market needs but does not itself provide' (Leys 1996a: 195, emphasis added).

Given the weakening of states in the age of structural adjustment, the most fundamental political choices to be made revolve around confronting these issues. To make sure that readers do not think he is a starry-eyed utopian, Leys projects this scenario 50 years into the future, when the world is not as enamoured of global laissez-faire and ensnared in the webs of the culture of contentment (Galbraith 1993) as it is now. If such notions were to be applied to particular 'post-conflict' situations instead of the continent as a whole they might not look quite so much like an African Marshall Plan, and thus may be operable within a shorter timeframe of less than 50 years.

At times the World Bank has looked as if it might contemplate such ideas – most recently, albeit hesitantly, in its 1997 *The State in a Changing World*. Within months of the publication of that glorified press release, however, the notion of 'social capital' appears to have usurped the tentative return of the state. That is possibly because, as Duffield (1999: 19, 2002) indicates, the dominant tendency in post-conflict discourse is to 'normalise' situations of protracted instability so that 'development' can ensue without a well-entrenched local state. Thus has come, as he puts it, the 'demand', that 'humanitarian assistance should be made developmental'. Humanitarian aid assumes that the transfer of responsibility to states, and whatever democratic dialectic ensues between it and its citizens, is on the horizon. The encroachment of 'developmental' aid in volatile situations implies that such a wait will be too long, so the IFIs and various private entities might as well go in as soon as possible. This chapter now turns to consider the idea of social capital and how it fits in with 'post-conflict' discourse.

Social capital and post-conflict interregna

Duffield (1998, 1999, 2001a), Reno (1998) and Keen (1994, 1998b) show that war in Africa is at least partly a consequence of neoliberal globalisation's 'disembedding' of 'economies' from their very fragile social and political combinations of pre-capitalist and developmental statist contexts: contexts all the more delicate because the emergence of capitalism in Africa is by its very nature uneven. (More precisely, the project is one of introducing capitalism to societies in which the social, political and cultural aspects of life are embedded within 'economic' forms distinctly different from those of capital; thus it is not so much a process of disembedding, but of introducing new systems of production and exchange and, in so doing, severing the old ones from their roots, dispensing with them, and – willy-nilly, if possible and cheap – creating new forms of embeddedness or hegemony.) To attempt to force these forms of capital on societies just emerging from the violent consequences of these sorts of processes seems the height of folly – or a return to the imperialist British discourse of the nineteenth century when we could read that 'brutality [was] the only truly humane course of action . . . "We became an Imperial race by dealing necessary pain to other men . . . A wiser humanitarianism would make it easy for the lower quality of life to die"' (Stevens, in Brantlinger 1988: 138–39).

As noted above, in 1997 the World Bank appeared to consider the possibility of inventing new states, or reinvigorating old ones, to perform such tasks with a minimum – but clearly recognised – level of severity. More recently, the concept of 'social capital' has been investigated to see if it can carry the weight of such transformations.

In a speech honouring the memory of Raul Prebisch (who on turning in his grave at some points, may have twisted back on hearing criticism of the Washington Consensus), then World Bank Chief Economist Joseph Stiglitz outlined his version of primitive accumulation in the Third World in words that any undergraduate familiar with the tried and tired words of modernisation theory would understand. There is, though, a slight twist.

> Traditional societies often have a high level of organisational and social capital, though this capital may not be of a form

that facilitates change. But in the process of development, this organisational and social capital is often destroyed. The transformation may weaken traditional authority relationships, and new patterns of migration may sever community ties. The problem is that this process of destruction may occur before new organisational and social capital is created, leaving the society bereft of the necessary structure with which to function well (Stiglitz 1998c: 20).

The spectre of social capital, which according to Stiglitz 'includes the institutions and relations that mediate transactions and resolve disputes' (Stiglitz 1998c: 20), is now haunting the World Bank. In the absence of the 'traditional' forms of social capital that have been at best weakened or at worst destroyed – and in any case were 'inefficient' – it and/or similar institutions are entrusted with the task of creating new 'organisational and social capital' before chaos reigns. Americans have a hard time dealing with the idea that conflict can be a normal state of affairs (Graff 1992), and they try to avoid the idea of states, too. The notion of 'social capital' can hide both. Social capital is, ambiguously, 'trust', and with trust conflict supposedly disappears (Fukuyama 1996). Social capital resides in 'civil society' – Robert Putnam's famous bowling clubs (1993b, 1995) of old, now replaced by individuals playing the game as solitary consumers instead of social groups – and thus the state, the resources it tends to consume, and its often uncomfortable monopoly on the 'legitimate' use of force can be wished away. It is not surprising that 'social capital' has become part of the illusory 'post-conflict' discourse.

Stiglitz brought the idea of conflict into the social capital discourse very quickly, stating that 'one of the obstacles to successful development has been the limited ability of some countries to resolve conflicts. The ability to resolve disputes is an important part of social and organisational capital' (1998c: 15). Thus, the causes of conflict do not have to be addressed – especially if they are seen as the inevitable result of 'modernisation'. What is of concern is 'the ability to resolve disputes'.

By sidestepping the idea of states and other formal institutions, the notion of social capital becomes ethereal: we talk of vague notions such as 'participation', the *perception* of 'effort' and 'a sense of' various concepts such as fairness. Unjust 'reforms' that lead to inequalities and then conflict are thus swept away as inevitable, but workable if they are *seen* to be just:

> reforms often bring advantage to some groups while disadvantaging others. There is likely to be greater acceptance of reforms – a greater *participation* in the transformation process – if there is a *sense* of equity, of fairness, about the development process, a sense of ownership derived from participation, and if there has been an effort at consensus formation (Stiglitz 1998c: 15, emphasis added).

As Ben Fine remarks in his scathing critique (see Chapter Four) of the social capital paradigm, its easy acceptance into development discourse signals the hegemony of the linguistic style of 'economics': with its use economists can claim expertise in areas traditionally out of their zone of speciality, and at the same time the 'softer' social scientists can utilise it to impress the grant and consultancy gatekeepers with their facility with the dominant speech acts. We could accept all this with equanimity if it was all a matter of games within ivory-tower epistemic communities, but the economistic hegemony signified by such easy transference is likely to mean the privatisation of means of establishing trust. In more concrete terms, under this discourse private security firms – mercenaries in old-fashioned language – are more likely to gain contracts for preserving the 'peace' in so-called post-conflict transitions than public collective agencies. As Duffield (1999: 33) notes, this thinking has profound consequences on the ultimate 'political' issue of sovereignty: issues of UN relations with non-state actors in the current era have not been clarified, but in the meantime there has been increasing involvement between multinational corporations and private security firms and warlords. If the World Bank's qualms about the inability of 'some countries' (and by implication the UN?) to solve conflict translate into the encouragement of private social capital producers, does this bring the Executive Outcomes of the world to mind, or simply American university psychologists/conflict-resolution experts – who are, lest we forget, publicly funded intellectuals?

Post-conflict reconstruction entails a lot; as Cohen and Pinstrup-Anderson recapitulate, people have to

> remove landmines; restore soil and water management infrastructure; locate tools, seeds, livestock, and fuel; and obtain investment capital. In town and countryside alike, they must form or renew communities; rebuild social infrastructure, especially labour organisation; and secure cooperation among disparate political and ethnic elements with varying wartime experiences (1999: 402).

If we agree (even while disagreeing about essential meanings) with Stiglitz when he says that social capital must be 'developed from within, even if knowledge from outside about key ingredients can facilitate [its] creation'; and if we note his caution that 'the pace of change and the pattern of reforms must be adapted to each country's ability to create social/organisational [*sic*] capital' – indeed, that 'this factor may . . . be the most important constraint on the speed of transformation' (Stiglitz 1998c: 20) – then why the haste to get liberal reform instilled in 'post-conflict' moments? Another question that arises is: is the best way to rebuild 'social capital' in these moments through principles of competition or cooperation? We suppose that the answer to the first question is related to that of the second: it depends on what kind of social capital is desired by those with the greatest opportunity to affect the construction of post-conflict order.

Stiglitz's address mentions the concept of social capital at least eleven times, many of which include the notion of the conflict between 'tradition and modernity'. In his conclusion he refers again to the possible 'destruction' of the former and notes that much of today's development discourse 'focuses on the preservation of cultural values, partly because these values serve as a cohesive force at a time when many other such forces are weakening' (1998c: 29). He then notes that 'maintaining social organisation and enhancing social capital' are important parts of development success. It is not clear whether he is referring to 'traditional' or 'modern' social capital; nor does his assertion that healthy babies, high education and increased opportunities are 'almost universally held values' indicate whether or not his purported cultural clash can be resolved. No matter: he would have been better looking at some of the empirical histories of actually existing conflict, and examining the issue of 'timing reform' in such cases more closely, rather than conjuring up the old standby of cultural conflict and then escaping into technical (albeit slightly Keynesian) economism.[4]

The World Bank's post-conflict perspective

The World Bank's booklet on post-conflict reconstruction, written before Stiglitz's speech, pays no heed to the idea of 'social capital', but this does not alter the symmetry between its content and the reflections of its former chief economist. Nor are its analyses of the causes and consequences of war particularly illuminating. Statements such as: 'conflict may be a consequence of economic change' but that 'growth, as well as contraction' causes it (World Bank 1998c: 17) are equally banal. So are balancing acts such as these:

> Trends such as powerful global information linkages [video violence?], the spread of democratisation across countries ['backward' countries can't cope?] and freedom of expression within national borders [so the African press should be censored even more?] can serve either to dampen or to stimulate conflict, depending on individual circumstances (World Bank 1998c: 17).

Despite the Bank's uncertainty about the causes of conflict, it seems assured that Third World societies do not have the 'social capital' (by any other name) to cope.

Many developing countries with a fragile resource base, growing populations, and weak mediating institutions are likely to be confronted with competing demands by different population groups for control of shrinking national resources. In the absence of inbuilt mechanisms to resolve these demands amicably [that is, social capital], there is a risk that conflict will result. The management of these conflicts is becoming an international collective responsibility . . . (World Bank, 1998c: 17).

If we did not remember the shirking of this duty in Rwanda by the state recognised as the most influential on the World Bank we might think that this was a call for global trusteeship, if not at least quick humanitarian intervention. Is it instead a call for international private responsibility? No matter, because the Bank's prime concern is not with the causes of conflict and the war itself, but in positioning itself for the 'concomitant phenomenon of countries attempting to traverse the path of a transition out of conflict . . . As a key actor in the international community [it] must position itself, within its development mandate, to be able to respond to the challenge of investing' in such societies (World Bank 1998c: 17).

The booklet makes it clear that the Bank will not be giving anything away. It states in a not atypical *reductio ad absurdum* manner that 'international assistance will never be sufficient to completely rebuild a country after conflict' (World Bank 1998c: 25), as if humanitarians might just be contemplating that. Rather, the Bank suggests tackling the more intangible and consultant-friendly task of 'recreating the *conditions* that will allow the private sector and institutions of civil society to *resume* commercial and productive activities' (1998c: 25, emphasis added). Besides making 'civil society' and the 'private sector' look remarkably alike and making us ask just what these 'conditions' are (the answer is: the entrenchment of universalised property rights) that statement makes the huge assumption that the business-like activities it likes so well can simply be 'recreated' and 'resumed' – people can pick up where they left off before the small inconvenience of a war interrupted their lives. The very next line, however, suggests larger tasks: macroeconomic stabilisation, financial institutions and legal frameworks, and transportation and communication reconstruction will have to be 'addressed *simultaneously*' (emphasis added). These seem like they might be jobs for the state, but it will be subject to 'frequent weaknesses in . . . implementing capacity', so it is suggested that the decentralisation of such activities would be a better idea. Civil society – especially women as the ubiquitous 'agents of change' in this sort of framework – is seen to be very resilient in these cases. But most African countries, even those not having been through a war, are deficient in all of the items listed above, to some degree because of state-unfriendly structural adjustment policies. Thus *local* 'civil society' can be assisted, if not replaced, by *international* civil society (or private sector, given its equivalence to civil society in the eyes of the Bank). Thus, the consultancy train pulls up to the station for financial restructuring and the international contractors line up to rebuild the roads – all to be paid through World Bank-negotiated loans. To be sure, if they are funded at the 'post-conflict' till they will be at good rates of interest: but could a 'relief' model with NGOs and humanitarian agencies not do the same job, with different social relations? Or would that model 'embed' the wrong modalities in blending new markets and old institutions?

Conclusion

The above words contemplate a neoliberal approach to post-conflict interregna with some scepticism. Gill's and Polanyi's notions of 'constitutionalisation' and 'embedding' alert us to the efforts – whether fully conscious and conspiratorial, merely through ideological myopia, or due to the contingencies of cost-cutting in an aid-withholding world – to entrench the tenets of possessive individualism (Macpherson 1964) in volatile and war-torn post-war societies. The analyses of the contemporary global political economy of war warn us of the implausibility of neoliberal solutions to the problems of war-torn societies, especially if the vague concept of 'social capital' serves to take our attention away from the need for state-oriented solutions, and also the state's imbrication in civil society and its 'social capital'. All of the intellectual tendencies in this niche of development discourse indicate the 'normalisation' of increasing barbarism in Africa and the rest of the world's 'periphery'. The alternatives to barbarity were better known, or at least more often articulated, in the not too distant past. Tautological conclusions are by their nature pessimistic.

Notes

1. Kostner (1999) is a good example of the allegedly apolitical nature of World Bank post-conflict analysis. He rather innocently suggests that contemporary moves towards decentralisation in the Democratic Republic of the Congo should be encouraged. See Cramer and Goodhand (2002) for an excellent critique of post-conflict discourse *á la* Afghanistan, and Duffield (2002) for an analysis of the 'radical' nature of post-conflict *intent*. In the absence of material resources, however, 'intent' remains only that. Not even the market is installed with any lasting embeddedness.
2. The notion of CPE was first developed to problematise what may have been a too-easy transfer of humanitarian analyses of and solutions to 'natural' crises to those with political roots. It also alerts us to the fact that there are many parties benefiting from war. Finally, some parties to its genesis used it to suggest that post-1989 wars were more complicated than those in the Cold War era were. Fiona Terry (1999) criticises the way the notion of CPE has been used for: a) suggesting that Cold War conflicts were any less complicated than contemporary ones; and b) masking the often not-so-complex political origins of much conflict, thus placing the onus on humanitarian solutions rather than political ones. But see Duffield (1994, 1998) for use of the term without subterfuge. Duffield (1999) notes that Mick Dillon coined the term 'emerging political complexes' in 1997 in opposition to CPE to suggest that they are still in their infancy and may represent something completely new on the horizon.
3. It could be ironic that in the wake of the Iraq war such benign neglect of 'post-conflict' societies may not be possible. The argument goes like this: if the US is rebuilding Iraq, it has a moral imperative to do the same for Liberia. The fact that the November 2003 US$87 billion bill for the reconstruction of Iraq had an add-on of approximately US$200 million for Liberia speaks the truth to that hope. Alternatively, in Sierra Leone the British intervention may illustrate a different modality: see Reno (2003) for discussion of the singularity of that case, however.
4. See Nussbaum (1995) and Schech (1998) for discussion of issues of universalism, 'tradition' and feminism.

Chapter Fourteen

Producing the Poor
The World Bank's New Discourse of Domination

Richard Pithouse

This is a moderately edited version of a 2003 article in African Sociological Review 7 (2): 118–44.

The object of lumping all Negroes together under the designation of 'Negro people' is to deprive them of any possibility of individual expression. What is attempted is to put them under the obligation of matching the idea one has of them (Fanon 1967b: 17).

This chapter investigates the World Bank's representation of the poor via a close reading of its *Voices of the Poor* (Narayan, Patel et al. 2000) and critically comparing it with Ashwin Desai's *We are the Poors* (2002b). It argues that *Voices* is an attempt to represent the majority of humanity as the Poor and that this othering produces them as a category of people who are politically inert, largely responsible for their own circumstances and whose suffering justifies the position and work of the Bank and other social forces with similar agendas. The chapter also suggests that there are familial connections between this project and colonial discourses that sought to dominate other people via a process of racialisation.

The World Bank's *Voices of the Poor* is the first volume in a three-part series. It was conceived, researched, written/edited, designed and published by the World Bank with the support of researchers at Cornell University, the University of British Columbia, the UK's DfID and various NGOs.[1] The chief editor, Deepa Narayan, was the senior adviser in Poverty Reduction and Economic Management at the Bank. This is a well-funded, multinational and multisector elite project based on a series of research projects that interviewed over 40 000 people in 50 countries for 81 Participatory Poverty Assessment (PPA) reports. The Bank carried out most of the research by itself but, where possible, local consultants were used. The South African research was conducted by a team led by Julian May, a professor in development studies at the then University of Natal in Durban. In their Foreword Clare Short, the secretary of state for international development in the UK, and James D. Wolfensohn, president of the World Bank, state that the aim of *Voices* is to extract and convey the 'recurrent themes' that emerged from the interviews in order to present 'very directly, through poor people's own voices, the realities of their lives'. Short and Wolfensohn commend the book for its 'authenticity' (Narayan, Patel et al. 2000: ix). Yet the findings are grouped around thematic nodes selected by the Bank, the authorial/editorial voice actively seeks to delegitimate much of what emerges from the interviews, and the book concludes with the Bank's recommendations for 'The Way Forward'. The publication of *Voices* is an important moment in the Bank's movement towards participation and empowerment as key ideas in its development rhetoric. Some commentators see this shift as a consequence of 'genuine institutional learning' while others see it as new ideological cover for the same old neoliberal[2] policies resulting from widespread opposition to them.[3] Many holding the latter view argue that the Bank's shift to rhetorical commitment to participation and empowerment matches the move in US foreign policy, also consequent to popular struggles, away from creating and supporting overtly authoritarian regimes towards sponsoring formally democratic governments and civil society organisations loyal to the substantively anti-democratic neoliberal project (Robinson 1996; Roy 2002).

Ashwin Desai's *We are the Poors* was written by a sociologist fired and banned from the premises of the University of Durban-Westville (UDW) in Durban, South Africa, for organising workers and students against the closure of unprofitable departments, retrenchment of workers and exclusion of poor students. These pressures on the university followed the African National Congress (ANC) government's adoption of a self-imposed structural adjustment programme[4] strongly influenced by the Bank (Bond 2005: 155–91) and resulting in a continuing assault on South African universities similar to that inflicted, often with the direct involvement of the Bank, on universities across the continent.[5] Desai's only budget was the granting of the decommodified time that inadvertently comes with the misfortune of unemployment and the good fortune of enough savings to eat, drive and type for a few months. The book began as a personal account of the militant opposition to neoliberalism in two poor neighbourhoods in the Durban township of Chatsworth. It was initially published in a community-funded edition from which the pages begin to fall after one reading. It was later expanded to include accounts of the growing and increasingly interwoven resistance in other communities in the city and the country. Its republication by Monthly Review Press in New York and Novita' Librarie in Bologna means it has ended up as part of an international counter-hegemonic project. The publication of *We are the Poors* is an important moment in both the presentation of militantly anti-neoliberal and anti-ANC movements of the poor to South African society and in the weaving of these South African movements into the global movement of movements against market fundamentalism and imperialism. Some commentators see these movements as having the potential to effect systemic change while others see them as fragmented and unsustainable, concluding that they have limited transformative potential. Joseph Stiglitz, formerly the chief economist at the World Bank, and Mamphele Ramphele, who was recently a managing director at the World Bank, have both conceded that the Bank has changed policies as a direct result of the pressures from these movements.[6]

History is not over. Social problems are not purely technical. On the contrary, material realities render ethics and politics urgent. In this regard William Robinson argues that the emerging transnational order is characterised by 'novel relations of inequality' resulting from 'the rise of truly transnational capital and the integration of every country into a new global production and financial system' that functions in the interests of 'a new transnational capitalist class' into which 'a portion of the national élite has become integrated . . . [i]n every country in the world'. This process has been driven by 'the rise of a transnational state, a loose but increasingly coherent network comprised of supranational political and economic institutions, and of national state apparatuses that have been penetrated by transnational forces' that serve 'the interests of global over national accumulation process' (Robinson 2003: 2–3). Robinson adds that:

> In most countries, the average number of people who have been integrated into the global marketplace and are becoming 'global consumers' has increased rapidly in recent decades. But the absolute number of the impoverished – of the destitute and the near destitute – has also increased rapidly and the gap between the rich and the poor in global society has been widening steadily, and sharply, since the 1970s (2003: 2–3).

For Robinson the emerging transnational order is best characterised as global apartheid. He notes that 'Ruling groups and their organic intellectuals tend to develop both universalist and particularist discourses to legitimate their power and privilege in conformity with their own cultural and historical realities' (2003: 7) and concludes that 'political confrontation is inevitable' (2003: 11).

The Bank and Desai are on opposite sides of the growing political confrontation[7] and have not written their books for the same audience. The Bank's book has an epigram from Wolfensohn asserting that 'These are strong voices, voices of dignity.' Its third sentence states that 'the poor are not lazy, stupid, or corrupt' (Narayan, Patel et al. 2000: 3). This theme is echoed in the blurbs on the back cover. *Voices* is presented piously, as if for the edification of elites who think that the poor are weak, undignified, lazy, stupid and corrupt.

By contrast, Desai's book is clearly for an international Left audience assumed to share his critique of neoliberalism, but which he can disabuse of any residual faith or hope in the ANC's desire or potential to oppose this ideology. Desai's book is thus primarily written against what Robinson calls 'particularist' ideological support for neoliberalism which, in the case of South Africa, includes the authoritarianism of both conservative nationalism and the claim of the ANC and its alliance partners to be the sole material incarnation of the hopes of the poor. In Desai's sometimes sarcastic and sometimes enraged analysis the party has been captured by reactionary nationalists who have made 'self-serving deals . . . with local white élites and international capital' (2002b: 10) resulting in catastrophic consequences for poor and working-class South Africans. Desai's not altogether unspoken implication is that the new social movements rising to oppose the ANC's embrace of neoliberalism must now take the place of the ANC within the global Left.

Voices has a more subtle agenda. It moves from the implicit assumption that poverty is ultimately an ontological condition that can be transcended via transformation at the level of being. It contains no criticisms of the transnational capitalist class or the transnational state. It is full of statements about the multifactorial origins of poverty and denunciations of the exploitation of the poor by the not quite so poor, the venality and inefficiency of local bureaucracies and law enforcement agencies, and local and national governments' failure to sufficiently deregulate the economic spaces in which the poor seek livelihoods. But at the core of all this is the conviction that 'we' must develop the nobility of spirit to have compassion for the poor, as Christians are supposed to love the lambs that have strayed from the flock, despite 'their' responsibility for their position in moral and social space.

We are the Poors moves from the explicit view that poverty is ultimately a historical condition. It is a consequence of relations of domination that can only be challenged via the capacity of the poor to constitute counter-power and thus generate a capacity to make history. Desai sees local feudal lords, contemptuous bureaucrats, and vicious police and security officers as agents of structural domination or as parasites able to feed off a social body weakened by the vampire-like extraction of resources at the hands of global capital allied with local elites.

And so the Bank's book begins, if books begin with their covers, with an ahistorical, de-individualised, childlike and pejoratively ontological drawing of 'happy natives' dancing around a fragile hut. It ends by observing that its (South African) subjects (natives?) sing well:

> It is really amazing how they used songs to express themselves . . . The words of the final song were: 'Here they are, yes we agree, here they are, our visitors who were sent by the World Bank, yes here they are, they are here to help us . . . and we hope they won't forget us' (Narayan, Patel et al. 2000: 283).

Desai's book begins with a picture of an insurgent step into history: a man, his children looking on, is confronting a policeman in an armoured car. It ends with the declaration that 'We will not make the mistakes of the past, when all too often we trusted leaders or parties or nations to save us. We now know that only the freedom and justice we the people build together, has the strength to resist oppression' (2002b: 153).

A reified mass. Individuals. They. We. Faith in the Bank. Tending the growth of our courage. These are two very different books. It is true that the Bank and Desai both know that poverty is as corrosive as children prostituting themselves in a hopeless attempt to keep their family in a damp hovel. The Bank and Desai do both conclude that the poor have another burden to take up. But for the Bank that burden is to transform the self with a view to becoming a winner in the system that turns citizens into consumers and spits out losers. For Desai that burden is the need to transform the self with a view to being able to beat back the system enough for everyone to survive and perhaps even prosper.

They must be represented

Both of Hegel's Marxist and neoliberal children have evidently failed. So too have technicist and postmodern overreactions to these varieties of historicism. These failures have given new urgency – most dramatically and popularly expressed in Hardt and Negri's *Empire* (2000) – to the phenomenological challenge that thought and lived experience be weaved together. But because both the Bank and Desai seek to achieve this for others their books raise old but still urgent questions about the ethics and politics of representation. *Voices* claims to be based on a programmatic commitment to 'start with poor people's realities' (Narayan, Patel et al. 2000: 274), ends by asserting this as the first principle of the way forward, and assures it readers 'the process did not start with a presumed set of answers – the patterns emerged through objective analysis of poor people's descriptions of their realities' (2000: 266). This anthropological attempt to develop an account of the experiential and ontological condition of the poor is presented as an ethical *and* strategic endeavour: ethical because it is seen as democratic and respectful; and strategic because the book is presented as part of a broader project of empowering the poor by creating and mediating access to elite spaces. Desai's project is very different. He does not claim the legitimacy of science or to be a neutral channel for the voices of the poor. He describes his book as 'an account from the frontlines of the establishment's undeclared war on the poor' (2002b: 14), has written his book in a style that makes it clear that he has been a witness to the events described, and makes no attempt to hide his subjectivities. Desai's book certainly has things to say about the experience of poverty. It does carry ontological ideas but they are about the broad human condition. *We are the Poors* is essentially a narrative, meaning that it has movement and change at its heart. Desai's story starts in Chatsworth. He shows that for many in the poorer of the township's neighbourhoods the new South Africa meant unemployment after 10 000 jobs in the clothing industry were sacrificed to the market when tariffs protecting the South African market from sweatshop imports were removed – four years ahead of the WTO schedule. Disconnections from electricity and water followed. Then came evictions as the city council began reorganising the provision of basic, life-sustaining services in accordance with the Bank's 'international norms' and under the cold logic of profit. Desai tells us how a movement of the poor was built in Chatsworth, how it spread to other Durban townships, drew in students and workers, made connections with similar movements developing in Johannesburg and Cape Town, put somewhere between 20 000 and 30 000 people on the streets outside the 2001 UN conference on racism in Durban, and became part of the global movement of movements against the subordination of society to the market.

Us and them

The Bank writes about 'us' and 'we' – who we assume to be people in the development industry, the academy, NGOs, the media and so on – and 'they' and 'them' – the Poor. The implications of the subject–object relation implied in this sentence are not addressed. We are given technical information about the sampling techniques and software packages used but almost nothing about the profound ethical and political issues regarding which questions were asked to the interviewees, in what manner and by whom, or how the answers were recorded, translated, selected, and edited. In the text itself there is a firm boundary between italicised direct quotes from anonymous interviewees, usually identified only by year, country and sometimes gender, and the general exposition of, and comments on, the ideas that emerged from the interviews in plain text. The poor emerge as the Poor – a deindividualised and othered category.

Desai also invokes the 'us'/'them' binary but his 'us' includes all people resisting neoliberalism and his 'them' are people and social forces complicit with it. His 'us' therefore speaks to, and of, a chosen community. Nevertheless, he is writing about movements of the poor and the standard critique of engaged intellectuals could be mobilised against Desai for inserting his authorial voice, with its Ph.D. and potential to return to academic employment, into a movement of the very poor, many of whom have no realistic potential of finding employment. One response is to cite Fanon's commitment to the dialectics of personal choice fleshed out most thoroughly in *A Dying Colonialism* (1965),[8] to argue that Desai has become part of the collectivities about which he writes because he makes the choice to put his body in harm's way; suffers arrest; has, on at least one occasion, run a serious risk of death at the hands of an enraged police officer;[9] is clearly seen as part of an 'us' constituted by these movements[10] and has, therefore, earned his 'we'. But there is a second critical difference between the representation in the Bank's 'they' and Desai's 'we'. In the Bank's book not one of the people represented as 'they' is given a name. Desai's book overflows with names and the dates and places of meetings, marches, and court hearings. Anyone questioning the accuracy of Desai's description of events can simply find and speak to the people included in Desai's 'we' – or for that matter his 'they', government officials, academic consultants, police officers, judges, and local feudal lords. Desai gives readers the means to look at the events he narrates from other perspectives. He is therefore telling his story with exemplary respect for subjectivity and thus sincerity of purpose.

In these ways Desai jumps into long-standing debates about the ways in which social science represents and reifies its analytical subject. For example, in *Orientalism* Edward Said writes that 'we note immediately that "the Arab" or "Arabs" have an aura of apartness, definiteness, and collective self-consistency such as to wipe out any traces of individual Arabs with narratable life histories' (1995: 129). John Holloway's thoughts are also notable here. He argues that mainstream social science assumes society is the object while the social scientist is the subject. Consequentially, the best scientist is furthest away from the object of his study. For Holloway this is not only problematic because it is impossible – we cannot 'express a thought that excludes the thinker' (2003: 60) – but it also carries an inherent contradiction in that:

> the subject is present, but as a viewer, as a passive rather than an active subject, as a de-subjectified subject, in short as an objectified subject... Society presents itself to me as a mass of particulars, a multitude of discrete phenomena. I proceed by trying to *define* the particular phenomena that I want to study and then seeking the connection between those defined

phenomena. Identity implies definition. Once the flow of doing is fractured, once social relations are fragmented into relations between discrete things, then a knowledge which takes that fragmentation for granted can only proceed through defining, delimiting each thing, each phenomenon, each person or group of people ... Definition fixes social relations in their static, fragmented reified is-ness (2003: 62).

There are ethical as well as epistemological problems attached to this mode of producing academic analysis. In Sartrean terms this way of working constitutes sadism: the attempt to evade judgement by seeking to make dialogical modes of interaction impossible by abstracting oneself into pure subjectivity and ossifying other human beings into pure objectivity. As Lewis Gordon argues, the sadist 'fancies himself a pure, disembodied anonymous subject – pure mastery, absolute negation of specificity. He fancies himself God. But since the human being is neither thing nor God, his fancy manifests an oblique reference to an eliminated humanity. The sadist is fundamentally misanthropic' (1995: 19–20).

Holloway makes the additional point that, while this way of working claims subjectivity for the objectifying researcher, in actual fact: 'The subject in capitalist society is not the capitalist ... It is capital ... the leading members of society are quite simply its most loyal servants, its most servile courtiers. This is true not only of capitalists themselves, but also of politicians, civil servants, professors and so on' (2003: 34).

This seems to be an accurate account of the nature of the work Deepa Narayan et al. have done with *Voices*. It is certainly the case that in their analysis 'the poor' emerge as a fixed ontological category, with no meaningful sense of multiplicity or movement.

While the Bank's researchers are objects above objects, Desai is, explicitly, a subject amongst subjects. This makes his book a radically more sincere but inevitably messier, and in equal proportion more useful, attempt to grope towards some truth. As with all openly subjective accounts, our assessment of the usefulness and validity of Desai's narrative has to be conducted through the prisms of the same ethical and epistemological questions that inform assessments of journalism or poetry. These are ultimately philosophical, not assessments about the work's conformity to research methods held to be scientific and therefore authoritative.

Nevertheless, it is important to note that Desai's book is permeated by an obvious elision: aside from a photograph[11] of the author addressing a meeting against water disconnections in a Mpumalanga township there is no formal acknowledgement that he has been an active and often crucial participant in the movements that his book describes. Desai's work cannot be understood in terms of the model that Edward Said recommends in *Representations of the Intellectual* (1996) – that the intellectual should preserve his or her autonomy in order to be able to speak truth to power. Desai is more fruitfully understood in terms of Frantz Fanon's recommendation that the intellectual take a side *with* the people. For Fanon, theory only has value as a tool in the service of action aimed at the creation and destruction necessary to create a more human world: 'To educate man to be actional, preserving in all his relations his respect for the basic values that constitute a human world, is the prime task of him, who having taken thought, prepares to act' (1967a: 222). Hence Desai's memorable remark elsewhere that it will sometimes be necessary to lie to power. Desai adds that, while Nietzsche recommended that we philosophise with a hammer, in neoliberal South Africa, where people, and even whole schools and clinics, are regularly disconnected from water by the state, and radical social movements 'illegally' reconnect people, it is necessary to 'philosophise with a pair of pliers' (2002a: 63).

Desai's omission of his roles in the movements discussed in his book does not disguise the extent to which they have arisen in what Fanon calls the 'zone of occult instability' (1961: 182) created when radical intellectuals join the people in 'that fluctuating movement which they are just giving a shape to, and which, as soon as it has started, will be the signal for everything to be called into question' (1961: 183). Desai does make some remarks about the role of activist intellectuals with access to lawyers, the media, photocopying machines, etc. But as Fanon notes, the occult zone is an unstable zone of creation and destruction. A more direct exploration of its dangers and promises would have added interest.

Pain and anger (open hands and fists)
The Bank's book begins with the pain of poverty. Its second sentence observes that

> poor people suffer physical pain that comes with too little food and long hours of work; emotional pain stemming from the daily humiliation of dependency and lack of power; and the moral pain from being forced to make choices – such as whether to use limited funds to save the life of an ill family member, or to use those same funds to feed their children (Narayan, Patel et al. 2000: 3).

Much of the rest of the book explores the immediate causes of this pain – unemployment, hunger, and exclusion from social services – as well as its immediate consequences such as depression, sickness, migration, and prostitution. The italicised quotes, representing the direct (but translated) comments of the interviewees, often speak of extreme horror. But they are all presented and sourced in a strangely dispassionate tone. Consider the following examples:

> If you don't have money today, your disease will lead you to your grave. – Ghana 1995a (Narayan, Patel et al. 2000: 52).[12]

> I am old and I can't work, and therefore I am poor. Even my land is old and tired, so whatever little I manage to work does not give me enough harvest for me and my children. – Togo 1996 (2000: 52).

At night you wake up because of a stomach ache and because of hunger. – Moldova 1997 (2000: 67).

After the death of my husband, I tried to make money in different ways, but prostitution was the most cost-effective. – Widow with two children, Macedonia 1998 (2000: 110).

Voices does not refer to the transcripts of the original interviews, so it is not possible to go beyond speculation about the translation and editing.[13] But the tone of resignation without anger or desire is a constant and striking feature of the presentation of 'voices of the poor' in this book. The first sentence of the book states, in the authorial/editorial voice, that 'Poverty is pain' (Narayan, Patel et al. 2000: 3). This beginning seems to be an echo of the impetus that led John Holloway to begin his recent book with a similar sentence: 'In the beginning is the scream' (2003: 1). But there is a critical difference. For Holloway

> Our scream is a scream of horror-and-hope. If the two sides of the scream are separated they become banal. The horror arises from the 'bitterness of history', but if there is no transcendence of that bitterness, the one-dimensional horror leads only to political depression and theoretical closure. Similarly, if the hope is not grounded firmly in that same bitterness of history, it becomes just a one-dimensional and silly expression of optimism (2003: 8).

Similarly, Foucault writes: 'Do not think that one has to be sad in order to be militant, even though the thing one is fighting is abominable. It is the connection of desire to reality (and not its retreat into the forms of representation) that poses revolutionary force' (2002: 109).

In *Voices*, though, traces of anger and consequent capacity for agency and counter-power only emerge – by implication – via an acknowledgement that the Bank's researchers encountered some hostility, and on the two occasions where it is acknowledged that people 'steal' services such as medicine (Narayan, Patel et al. 2000: 111) and electricity (2000: 156) from which they have been excluded. That these acts could be political is not considered in either case. The presentation of the poor as resigned to their fate is a presentation of the poor as defeated – without any possibility of marshalling the agency to issue any kind of local or systemic challenge. It is politically and aesthetically banal, and closes down the acknowledgement of the possibilities for movement and agency to the point where it appears that all that is left is a void to be filled, via the charitable agency and the superior values of the rich. This presentation is typical of what Hardt and Negri call the 'charitable campaigns and mendicant orders of Empire' which are 'some of the most powerful pacific weapons of the new world order' (2000: 36). It presents poverty and its overcoming as ontological rather than political problems. It implies that the poor are the problem, not the structures of domination with their exploitation and marginalisation. We would do well to remember Said's observation that colonial discourses produce an idea of the colonised as 'inviting [colonial] interest, penetration, insemination – in short colonisation' (1995: 229). Is it not the case that the pain present in *Voices* is a softness, an openness, while anger – only getting into the Bank's book by implication and mistake – is a hardness, a hardness that can be both a defensive closure and an offensive thrust?

Desai also gives us lots of direct quotes from the poor. In his book, though, the quotes vary radically in tone, form and content. They range from utter resignation to militant defiance and include humour, anger, grief and sarcasm. They show multiplicity and individuality. Desai does not fall into the old Left trap. He does not turn some group amongst the marginalised or exploited into the fetishised vessel of his hopes by projecting a dehumanising ontological priority or revolutionary purity on to it. Consider just these three quotes. The first quotes the failure of a man, evicted from his home, to speak. He just sits. The second is a direct quote from a rapper in Bayview, Chatsworth. The third is a quote, in its context, from an avuncular shopkeeper who became an activist when he noticed that children were beginning to steal beans instead of sweets and was then branded a 'counter-revolutionary' by the local ANC:

When the reporters arrived they found Harinarian on a pavement surrounded by the family possessions. He held onto a pet tortoise (Desai 2002b: 23).

Women of Chatsworth unite
Women lead the fight
Pick up the stones
Break Council's bones (2002b: 63).

Mlaba and Cele have been deemed worthy of personal attack, being branded 'counter-revolutionaries'. Cele laughs. 'Everybody in Mpumalanga can see, the real counter-revolutionaries are in this government' (2002b: 88).

Out of time

The Bank's production of the poor as inert and resigned is compounded by the presentation of their voices in a strange mixture of corporate-speak and the contrived archaism colonial writers consistently attributed to the colonised. As J.M. Coetzee notes in the context of Alan Paton's presentation of Zulu-speaking characters in English: 'the archaism of the English implies something else too: an archaic quality to the Zulu behind it, as if the Zulu language, the Zulu frame of mind belonged to a bygone and heroic age' (1988: 128). There is a similar implication here, compounded by the corporate-speak. The forcefulness of the contrast between both it and the archaic language, and the Bank's evident power and the speakers' visible disempowerment, leads us to infer that the speakers are bewildered and out of time, and therefore requiring help. As the quotes above show, Desai's book is radically different in this regard. The voices that he quotes are contemporary, individual and diverse in tone, content, context and mode of expression.

Ideology

Voices consistently and inappropriately imposes corporate and neoliberal jargon on what it reports. The bizarre use of argot begins in the epigram where Wolfensohn writes that 'in order to map our own course for the future, we needed to know about our clients as individuals'. The first claim may well have some truth to it. The last has none. There are no individuals in this book. There are just 'the Poor' and 'us'. The Poor are produced as a generic ontological category. Wolfensohn's claim that he aspires to know his billions of 'clients' as individuals, in the manner of a village grocer, is ludicrous: but it is just dishonest to suggest that the world's poor are the Bank's clients. Elsewhere Wolfensohn has fumed that 'I have a job to do and I don't want to be instructed by someone else, unless my shareholders ask me to' (Bretton Woods Project 2002: 5). Companies provide goods or services to clients in order to generate profit for shareholders. In the case of the World Bank the poor are actually the raw material from whom wealth is extracted via privatisation and cost-recovery policies. Its actual clients are multinational corporations, Western governments representing their interests, and national elites facilitating corporate access to their human and natural resources.

The Bank even tells us that 'the woman in a village who takes a stand on behalf of her neighbour being beaten up by her husband' is a 'development entrepreneur' (Narayan, Patel et al. 2000: 281). This crude attempt to associate social virtue with capitalism is as blatantly ideological as saying, under India's Bharatiya Janata Party that a woman who takes such a stand is being a good Hindu or saying, under Stalin, that she is a good communist. So it goes throughout the book. A family in Mali choosing to go hungry rather than sell a bicycle in the pre-harvest season is 'diversify[ing] investments' (2000: 52); while in Moldova 'women have increasingly broken into the formerly male domain of seasonal labour migration' (2000: 191). Then there is the radical ideological bias. Consider the following:

> Women who enter the labour force may find work in non-traditional or traditional occupations. Women are engaged in trade, migrant labour, and to some extent in the sex trade as well as in traditional occupations such as domestic worker and maid.

Trade: a growth opportunity for women
I was not brought up to be a smuggler, and in the former system such activity was punishable and rightfully ridiculed.
– Macedonia 1998 (Narayan, Patel et al. 2000: 188).

The subheadings for the following subsections in *Voices* are 'Domestic workers and maids', 'Female migrant labour' and 'Migration and sex work'. Tanzanian women working as maids are quoted as saying 'We are not living. We are just surviving' (Narayan, Patel et al. 2000: 189). It is obvious, and utterly so, that these survivalist strategies would not be chosen in the absence of social crisis. The interviewees confirm this. Yet the authors/editors breezily impose the description of 'growth opportunity' on this suffering. This is like describing the Gulag as a re-education camp.

To be sure, Leftist thought has often subordinated the complexity and movement of lived experience to its own fetishes – the Party, the Working Class, the Revolution, the Future, the (ontologically pure) Militant, and so on. The consequences of this have generally been disastrous. But Leftist thought and activism has been given new vitality, perhaps even a new youth, via writers such as Sub-commandante Insurgent Marcos, Arundhati Roy, Michael Hardt and Antonio Negri, and movements such as the Zapatistas, seeking to oppose transcendent categories. They attempt to cultivate, as Fanon puts it, a 'voracious taste for the concrete' and move from the view that 'the unemployed man, the starving native do not lay a claim to the truth; they do not say that they represent the truth, for they are the truth' (1961: 38). Desai's book is firmly and self-consciously part of this movement to subordinate theory to lived experience.

Thus Desai has the ethical certainty to avoid postmodern impotence in the face of evil – he approvingly quotes the militant humanism[14] of an activist shot by the police while resisting evictions: 'We are not animals, we are human beings' (2002b: 142). Yet his ethics also has an openness to movement and multiplicity (human beings differ and change) and includes a firm point from which to exercise leverage (human beings require the basic means to a viable life). Desai does not subscribe to any ontological fetishes or totalising meta-narratives. He is committed to an analysis that employs theory strictly for illumination, never seeking to make reality conform to theory. This is made most explicit when he writes that:

> If I was a traditional Leftist, I would have to spend all my time first engineering the content of the life of people in these communities so that it accorded with the insights of socialism. That would be the struggle! But this is not the way things are. There is a rich, complex, imperfect, and sensuous collectivity existing in these communities . . . the way certain of these needs are expressed and stubbornly held onto as the basis for action is not frowned upon by people in the DSF [Durban Social Forum] as it is, even if secretly, by many socialists (2002b: 145–46).

It is important to note that this anti-ideological approach refuses the subordination of lived experience to the fetish of the pure militant as much as to any other. This fetish is so common on the Left and is so seductive that even Hardt and Negri succumb to it in the final paragraph of their book where they celebrate the example of Saint Francis of Assisi. Desai understands that resistance is ordinary and ubiquitous. It is always partial and compromised. It must be seen as coming from within and be encouraged as such.

These voices of the poor were brought to you by the Bank
Perhaps the most serious problem with the World Bank's claim to represent the voices of the poor is that there are often no clear boundaries between views ascribed to the interviewees – and therefore imbued with the 'scientific' legitimacy of a massive social science research project commended for its 'authenticity' by Wolfensohn in the Introduction – and the editors'/authors' comments on them. The apparent legitimacy of the former leaks into the latter and is used, in a variety of contexts, to justify the view – often directly contrary to the interviewees' – that 'social norms and institutions are the key obstacles

faced by poor women and men' (Narayan, Patel et al. 2000: 266). Consider the following two paragraphs, both referring to the results of interviews in the former Soviet republic of Georgia:

[F]unerals take on important symbolic and social significance, serving as occasions in which families demonstrate social solidarity . . . It is a time to display a family's prestige, honour and prosperity. Friends of the deceased and the deceased's extended family are expected to attend the funeral and bring gifts. During the socialist period most elderly Georgians were able to save funeral money to offset the considerable costs, but now most have lost the bulk of their savings (Narayan, Patel et al. 2000: 69).

[P]eople may also compare themselves to those wealthier than they are, ascribing that wealth to corruption and dishonesty. Particularly for people over 40, the rules of the new market economy seem to violate the values by which they were raised. Because of the belief that in the former system 'business was "speculation", and speculation was a dishonest and even criminal way of making money,' they compare themselves with their neighbours who have overcome their own psychological barriers to get involved in street trade and commerce (that has come to symbolise the new market relations). They claim they would rather retain their self-respect and the respect of their peers by working for meagre salaries in the state sector or selling personal possessions (2000: 72–73).

The first paragraph contains declarative statements of fact. It is reasonably easy to believe that the editors/authors are giving us their best sense of the researchers' interviews. In contrast, the second paragraph is riddled with qualifying punctuation, words, and phrases such as 'may', 'ascribing', 'the belief that' and 'claim'. They establish a critical distance between the interviewees' statements and the authors'/editors' transmission of them. Moreover, there is also a direct assertion that the reported ideals of self and peer respect actually indicate failure to overcome psychological barriers. It is clear that the second paragraph is designed to persuade readers to reject the validity of the interviewees' comments. This pattern is consistently repeated wherever the interviewees' comments move against the consensus that neoliberalism is trying to create. This means that the poor are taken very seriously when they point to the slightly less poor or corrupt, and inefficient elites and national governments, as the cause of their problems. However, when they point to larger structural forces or neoliberal economic policies such as privatisation their voices are immediately delegitimated. The blame is shifted to the inefficiencies and corruption of local elites and governments.

Desai makes no attempt to claim scientific legitimacy for his project. On the contrary, he presents his project as an eyewitness account of particular movements of the poor in particular times and places. As always, a close examination of the particular yields insights that, with reflection and comparison, may develop universal value. However, Desai is creating the circumstances for this reflection and comparison to be possible, rather than attempting to legislate universally in the name of science.

Dangerous men, willing women
The Bank's book devotes a lot of space to the abuse of women by men. From around the world, male and female interviewees consistently assert – often with overt sympathy – that men are under particular social pressure as they have been brought up to identify manhood with a role, employment, that no longer exists. This is reflected in some of the overviews gleaned in the country reports:

> many men, unable to keep up the socially mandated role of breadwinner, find that 'their sense of emasculation and failure often leads to a host of physical ailments and sharply increasing mortality, alcoholism, physical abuse of wives and children, divorce and abandonment of families'. – Georgia 1997 (Narayan, Patel et al. 2000: 194).

There is just one editorial recognition that part of the solution to the problem of abuse must lie in creating viable lives for men. However, this acknowledgement is limited and subordinated to neoliberal orthodoxy. 'Both poor men and women need greater access to economic opportunities, especially for profitable self-employment. This is difficult in an environment of corruption, lack of organisations of the poor, lack of support to battered women, and the breakdown of law enforcement agencies' (Narayan, Patel et al. 2000: 205).

The creation or recreation of employment is never considered. Instead, the burden to create self-employment and survivalist solidarity organisations is shifted onto the poor, and the usual suspects – corrupt states and poor law enforcement – are, without evidence, deployed to explain why this is so difficult. But the overwhelming view of the book is that poor men are just bad and need both to be taught, via deliberate projects, that their norms *are* bad and to be better policed. Women are just good and need to be affirmed as such: 'Many men are collapsing, falling into domestic abuse and violence, turning to alcohol and drugs, or abandoning their families. Women, on the other hand, seem to swallow their pride and hit the streets to do demeaning jobs to bring food to the family table' (Narayan, Patel et al. 2000: 269).

The book's concluding recommendations for change inform us that ideas about gender have 'become such a deep part of the psyche that they are resistant to change and hard to overcome'. Thus 'innovative approaches are needed to assist men with their fears of "emasculation and social impotence" when women step outside of the house' (Narayan, Patel et al. 2000: 280). Not one of the interviewees is reported as having said that the problem was women 'stepping outside of the house'. They are consistently reported as having said that the problem is that men were raised to provide for their families and that now the only means to scrape a living together – street trading, migrant work, domestic work, prostitution – are the lot of women. Yet the authors/editors breezily assert that the task is simply to prepare men to cope with the reality that the world they were raised to inhabit no longer exists. The authorial/editorial voice refuses to allow the possibility of changing both the world and men.

Reading *Voices* reminds us of prescient comments in the established critiques of capitalism and colonialism. It is quite some time since Karl Marx observed that capitalism's development replaces 'skilled labourers by less skilled, mature labourers by immature, male by female' (Comaroff and Comaroff 2002: 784). Marx's observation leads to deep suspicion of the Bank's optimism that women's movement into areas of work such as migrant labour is driven by their desire to unshackle themselves from patriarchy. Again, it is instructive to return to Said's observation that in orientalising discourses the 'male was considered in isolation from the total community in which he lived' and 'viewed with something resembling contempt and fear'. Said goes on to note that these discourses view women as 'above all willing' (1995: 207). In the Bank's book, poor women do seem, above all, willing to step into domestic work, prostitution and the other options described. Women never appear as refusers or fighters. We are also reminded of Fanon's remarks about how the immobility to which colonialism condemns the native in a Manichean world initially results in the colonised man expressing the 'aggressiveness which has been deposited in his bones against his own people' (1961: 40) before turning it on the coloniser. The Bank's book does acknowledge, in a brief section on methodology, that, in Bangladesh, 'youths' and a Mr Munna and 'five or six others' were 'aggressive' (Narayan, Patel et al. 2000: 20) to the Bank's researchers in Aga Sadek Sweepers colony in Dhaka, and that the researchers were driven out of Chitabatoli village in Hathazari by 'men of the village' (2000: 21). In moments like this hope escapes the intentions of the authors/editors and dances across the page.

Desai's largeness of vision is a world away from the Bank's bad men/willing women dichotomy. In Desai's book some women are driven to prostitution, some women fight, and it is entirely possible that some inhabit both positions or move from one to the other. Some men beat their wives, some men put their bodies in harm's way when the men with guns and dogs and sunglasses come to effect an eviction, and it is entirely possible that some men do both or move from one to the other. Through struggle men and women grow and develop new solidarities in and across neighbourhoods. A gangster becomes a struggle plumber and reconnects a widow's water. A single mother, timid in the sweatshop, becomes a fighter leading a throng jamming her neighbour's stairs to stare down batons and teargas to keep out the evictors and disconnectors. What's more, and so very much more, Desai shows us (2002b: 144) that some women escape prostitution by wrestling resources from the state through a refusal to conform to the World Bank's injunction, backed up with the armed force of the state, to pay for services such as water. Desai's representation of men and women who are poor is as much about creating openings and instability in objectifying bourgeois projections as the Bank's is about creating closures and stability.

Crime

Then there is crime. Around the world social panics about crime legitimate increased surveillance, coercion and incarceration of poor people and forms of racism and xenophobia otherwise considered unacceptable. The Bank's interviewees consistently assert the structural relationships that editors/authors seek to rule out of consideration by making direct links between crime and poverty. 'In country after country – Ethiopia, Jamaica, Kenya, South Africa and Thailand – poor people draw strong links between crime and unemployment. This is most extreme in the countries of the former Soviet Union' (Narayan, Patel et al. 2000: 273). Interviewees are also quoted as considering neoliberal policies such as privatisation as crime. Yet, in the final chapter on 'The Way Forward' the only suggestions with regard to crime recommend strengthening law enforcement. Desai's book makes the same point as the interviewees in *Voices* but he does add, largely by implication, that there is a positive potential to turn violence and disrespect for the law away from the innocent and on to the iron fingers of the state's right hand.

The unsaid – history

The Bank's book inhabits the perpetual present against which Winston Smith struggles in George Orwell's *Nineteen Eighty-four* (1970). There is an astonishingly complete refusal to take history seriously. Interviewees consistently explain that historical events caused or exacerbated their poverty. A story may start with 'When my father was made a *jeune retraite* (forced early retirement, as part of structural adjustment policies) back in 1985 . . .' (Narayan, Patel et al. 2000: 120) or 'When we lost the fish to the big companies . . .' (2000: 222) The interviewees consistently assert that life was better under communism or before privatisation. This is acknowledged in the editorial/authorial voices:

> After decades of steady employment guaranteed by the state and subsidised food, housing, education, medicine, and standards of living that, if not lavish, were for most at least adequate, the collapse of communism has resulted in the rapid erosion of virtually all social support systems, and has bred mass insecurities among the people of this region as they have watched their savings and accumulated assets dwindle and disappear . . . The transitions to a market economy, to 'independence', and to 'democracy' have become equated in the minds of many poor people with unprecedented vulnerability and social injustice (Narayan, Patel et al. 2000: 66).

But these views are immediately pyschologised and delegitimated:

> People from Eastern Europe and the former Soviet Union tend to think about their current economic position by comparing it with both their earlier standard of living and the current situation of others. Both are ways of attempting not only to comprehend rationally the transformations of their social status, but also to mediate their experiences psychologically. This is one of the most consistent features of the reports from this region. Comparing the present situation with the past is a way for respondents to externalise responsibility for the current situation. By pointing to specific events that impoverished everybody . . . or the criminality and duplicity of the wealthy, respondents feel that, at

least to a certain extent, their impoverishment is not the result of personal failings, but of events utterly beyond their control, such as the transitions associated with independence (Narayan, Patel et al. 2000: 71).

The editorial/authorial voice never enquires into the social forces that produced the arrangements channelling millions of complex lives into its twin categories of 'us' – readers of World Bank books and actors with the potential to effect social change – and 'them' – 'the Poor', objects of our paternalistic sympathies. The gaze is locked into the present. With neoliberalism we are always at the beginning of year zero. And without history poverty is naturalised as is, by implication, wealth. You are poor because you are the Poor. Just as under colonialism 'the cause is the consequence; you are rich because you are white, you are white because you are rich' (Fanon 1961: 31).[15]

Desai's approach is very different. His first sentence is historical rather than ontological. He writes that 'Chatsworth came into being forty years ago with the passing of the Group Areas Act' (2002b: 15). He goes on to tell us how the community he is writing from came into being and how generations of people struggled to make their lives against the structural forces of colonialism, apartheid and the ANC-implemented post-apartheid structural adjustment programme. He gives us the larger stories of the neighbourhoods about which he writes and in each case splices the stories of a number of individuals into the larger story. We get an immediate sense that individuals, communities and movements make themselves within and against history and thus become history makers themselves.

Also unsaid – the role of the Bank

These two books handle the issue of the larger political and economic context very differently. The Bank's editorial/authorial voice ignores both the macroeconomic context in which the World Bank has such influence and the social movements that oppose the Bank, its policies and market fundamentalism in general. This reads very strangely for two reasons. The first is that the authorial/editorial voice takes a very firm line against micro-local elites who behave in the same ways that the Bank is often accused of behaving – such as trapping people in debt; water management strategies that result in salination; raising costs of medicine, water and housing; insisting proposals be rewritten until they fit the agenda of the powerful; encouraging corruption and so on – without ever acknowledging the fact that the Bank is accused of precisely these practices on a global scale. The second omission is that while the interviewees are allowed to say that job losses consequent to privatisation or exclusion from education or basic services as a result of cost-recovery policies have resulted in personal disaster, the authorial/editorial voice never once acknowledges any connection between these polices and the Bank or any other social forces that advocate or demand these policies. On the contrary, these policies are naturalised to the point where it seems that, like the weather, they happen without any human agency. For example the authorial/editorial voice is quite happy to detail the suffering consequent to exclusion from access to clean water and to observe that 'Access to clean drinking water and water for irrigation frequently emerges as a characteristic difference between the poor and the rich' (Narayan, Patel et al. 2000: 267). But there is no acknowledgement in any form that the Bank is a key player in water policy. It explicitly seeks to pressurise African governments to commoditise water, with a view to shifting the costs of water onto 'consumers', consequently excluding the poor from its provision. In South Africa this process has resulted in 10 million people being disconnected, often at gunpoint, from access to safe drinking water (McDonald and Pape 2002). In its *Sourcebook on Community Driven Development in the Africa Region*, published a few months after *Voices*, the Bank wrote that 'work is still needed with political leaders in some national governments to move away from the concept of free water for all . . . [and to] ensure 100 per cent recovery of operation and maintenance costs' (Results 2003: 43). In Ghana the Bank's 'support' in the area of water policy included a recommendation, a year before the publication of *Voices of the Poor*, that the cost of water be raised by 95 per cent. Moreover, in Uganda and Burkina Faso, where new Bank Poverty Reduction Support Credits (the new name for structural adjustment loans) have been approved, the 'reform agenda' that goes with the loans includes water privatisation (Results 2003; Public Citizen 2003). The Bank also advocates and closely supports the process of setting up 'tri-sector partnerships' of state, business and specially invented and funded organisations that are then called 'civil society' to win legitimacy for the commodification of water and the consequent disconnection of former citizens who cannot afford to become consumers (Lumsden and Loftus 2003). In South Africa, as in other countries where there have been mass exclusions from access to clean water, a cholera epidemic ensued (Mkhize 2001; Bond 2001b). The South Africa government, like India's (Sharma and Shiva 2003), has dutifully followed the Bank's 'initiative' and launched a campaign to persuade poor people to wash their hands more often. As Mandisa Mbali shows (2002), this is an initiative reaching back to enliven a set of very old prejudices against the poor.

Desai is in continuous critical conversation with the successes and failures of the movements discussed in his book, the liberation movements and the Left in general. We may disagree with his assessments but he does not hide the agency of the social forces of which he is part. There is an explicit recognition that his book is intended to be a contribution to an ongoing conversation. The sincerity of purpose that drives this commitment to dialogical examination of social issues is entirely lacking in the Bank's complete failure to acknowledge, let alone examine and invite discussion around, the consequence of its agency and of the agency of allied social forces.

The radical unsaid – the political agency of the poor

The only reference to social movements in *Voices* is brief – and on the third page from the end. The authors/editors opine that 'Social movements bring about realignments of power, change social norms, and create new opportunity structures.' Out of this will emerge a mindset that 'applies liberalisation not only for the rich but also the poor'

(Narayan, Patel et al. 2000: 281). There is one piece of evidence to support the startling conclusion that, against all the declared intentions of most major national and international social movements, the consequence of this mobilisation will be liberalisation for the poor. This is the observation, completely unconnected to social movements, that in Ethiopia 'poor people in some rural areas' report that regulations around firewood cutting, street-trading, and at the local market have 'made the search for a livelihood more difficult' (2000: 281).

Desai's approach to the power of the poor to constitute counter-power is exemplary. Radical thought usually takes the oppressive power of the state and the market as its focus. To be sure, explaining the nature of the structural violence in and against which the oppressed must make their lives is important work. But Desai, like Frantz Fanon and the Italian Autonomist School, does something different. He begins with the creative energies of the oppressed, thus giving us storms and tributaries and rivers of struggle. We discover the Hindu festival of light, Diwali, re-imagined with the electricity-disconnecting Durban city council cast as the villain of darkness. And we meet the University of Durban-Westville students – steeled by the murder of one of their number by the police while protesting the exclusion of poor students from their university – who defend fragile new-born spaces for critical thought and action from 'the goons from the ANC youth league'. Here too are mothers and grandmothers across the country, such as Mama Manqele in Chatsworth and Mevrou Samsodien in Tafelsig, who rebel because obedience can mean disaster and even death. All of this attention to micro-struggles is explicitly set into a broader account of the rise of community movements against evictions and disconnections within the context of both the global class project of neoliberalism and the growing global resistance to it.

The way forward
The Bank's book makes recommendations for change throughout the text and in a dedicated final chapter entitled 'The Way Forward'. Almost all of the suggestions in the general text can be included in

three broad themes – achieving good governance, changing social norms, and strengthening social capital. Good governance is about strengthening the coercive right arm of the state – law enforcement is the key focus – and learning to use the withered developmental/welfare left arm of the state more effectively. In this regard, reducing corruption and inefficiency are the key foci. No consideration is given to the possibility of strengthening the left arm. Changing social norms is about doing away with certain prejudices about and amongst the poor (and, in particular, prejudices against groups such as widows and people living with Aids), resulting in people having to make demands on, or become a problem for, the state. This project also seeks to persuade the poor to accept responsibility for their condition rather than blaming structural factors, and then to form survivalist solidarity organisations and to seek self-employment to improve their condition. This is where the Bank appears most optimistic. The authors/editors observe that 'Much can be learned from the market penetration strategies of the private sector'[16] and go on to note that 'changes in social norms about cigarette smoking in the United States' (Narayan, Patel et al. 2000: 278) indicate that this can be achieved in broader society.

Social capital is a key theme in *Voices*. It is clear that the Bank sees social capital as a means for achieving an anti-politics of co-option via 'conflict resolution, and management of relations with outsiders' (2000: 143), and for shifting the responsibility for undoing poverty onto the poor via '[h]arnessing the potential of local-level associations and networks for poverty reduction' (2000: 150). The authorial/editorial voice does accept the regular comments from interviewees to the effect that what the Bank refers to as social capital is corroded by poverty, and does acknowledge that '[t]he social fabric, poor people's only "insurance" is unravelling' (2000: 7) but still holds it out as a key strategy for poverty alleviation, recommending organising the poor into collectives to cope better with their poverty and to bureaucratise conflict. There is no attempt to resolve this contradiction. Four 'strategies for change' are identified in the final chapter. They are:

1. Start with poor people's realities.
2. Invest in the organizational capacity of the poor.
3. Change social norms.
4. Support development entrepreneurs (2000: 274).

No consideration is given to macroeconomic policy. All four of these 'strategies for change' shift the responsibility for poverty onto the poor without questioning the economic and political arrangements that have produced and exacerbated poverty. Poor people are being told to cope better with the current system, and the possibilities of structural reform or revolution are not considered at all.

Desai, like the Bank, is interested in changing social norms. But for Desai taking the ecology of the neighbourhood seriously is not just a way to survive the onslaught of neoliberalism. At the same time, it is also a way to develop what Fanon called a 'fighting culture'.[17] Consider Desai's account of the celebration of Diwali in Chatsworth:

> Diwali, the Hindu festival of lights was celebrated. The festival had a relevant bent. The slogan raised was 'lights for all' and the Satanic villain was cast as the city council, which was disconnecting lights. Old mythologies from India were being reinterpreted in neoliberal South Africa. All religious groups and races living in the mosaic of Chatsworth participated. Indeed, about 30 per cent of the area is African and strong bonds between neighbours were being forged in the context of the struggle against the city council. In this way, Diwali in South Africa was being rethought, politicised, and made accessible to all the community (2002b: 41).

Desai makes no suggestions for alternative policies. His politics is essentially a politics of refusal that he explicitly presents as a beginning with unknown outcomes. His suggestions do not go beyond recommending that the poor constitute themselves into movements of counterpower and join the movement of movements against neoliberalism globally. He seems to imply that the aspirations of these movements are not to seize political power but rather to diffuse it with the aim of creating viable neighbourhoods in which individuals and communities can flourish. His opposition to vanguardist politics is well captured in the words of Mpumalanga (township) activist Maxwell Cele: 'No one is in charge of the protests, except the anger and hunger in every person' (Desai 2002b: 88).

But Desai does brings his intelligence to bear much more explicitly on the question of what can be learned and copied from the neighbourhood struggles he discusses. He writes that 'there is much that would be fruitfully grafted onto the stout stems of struggle in other places. This book is for such graft' (2002b: 7). And he has many insights. He argues that attitude does more than ideology; that the powerful will rush to blame the victims for their suffering and so the struggle for a profusion of positive identities is essential; that there is a danger that religious dogmatism and cultural chauvinism can co-opt the energies that drive resistance and he implies, against Marxist orthodoxy and in the spirit of Fanon, that communities rather than unions are likely to lead any challenge to the tyranny of the market.

Conclusion

The Bank sets out to convey the universal pain of poverty. Anyone who knows anything about poverty anywhere will recognise that *Voices of the Poor* captures much of this pain well. There is some value in the Bank's universalism given that claims about the specific aspirations of national governments, and the particular pathologies of their critics, are usually advanced to provide ideological cover for the general nature of local elites' accommodation with international capital.[18] If poor Indians and South Africans and Ghanaians and Georgians suffer in the same ways it must be possible for counter-hegemonic international networks of the poor to oppose the rival networks of the transnational capitalist class and state. Of course, *Voices* does not recommend this or even mention it as a possibility. In fact, the Bank's naturalisation of poverty and exclusion of anger and desire excludes this possibility a priori. Nevertheless, the acknowledgement of generic forms of suffering does make the book a useful corrective to nationalisms that allow a networked elite to ghettoise 'their' poor via particularist valorisations and stigmatisations. The book is also a useful corrective to the tendency for national panics about the apparently particular moral failings of particular societies. For example, it emerges that almost every social panic about 'moral degeneration' in South Africa – street children, chronic teacher absenteeism, corruption and sexual abuse in schools, dangerous and corrupt police officers, endemic violence against women and so on – is linked to pathologies accompanying poverty everywhere. The book draws very different conclusions but, despite its intentions, the universal emergence of these pathologies in the context of acute poverty constitutes useful evidence that poverty, rather than the attitudes of the poor, is the problem.

It is not surprising that throughout the book the interviewees are allowed to describe how it is to be poor and to say that their poverty is worsening without any authorial/editorial attempts to delegitimate their views. After all, the Bank presents its mission as the achievement of 'a world free of poverty', as the back cover has it. Whether we see this claim as truly reflecting the Bank's aims or as ideological cover for another agenda, we must agree that an organisation seeking to win legitimacy and influence by claiming to oppose poverty has a direct interest in presenting it as a bad thing. Consequently, it is no surprise that this book is filled with unmediated accounts of poverty's horrors. Nor is it surprising that the interviewees are allowed to say that their suffering is getting worse. The Bank routinely admits this itself.[19]

Yet the Bank retains its commitment to increasing the scope and pace of the integration of more aspects of more societies into the global market. The voices of the poor in *Voices of the Poor* are not allowed to issue unmediated challenges to this project. When ethical or political ideas contrary to neoliberalism are expressed they are immediately, implicitly or explicitly, presented as illusory or pathological. This blatant and unacknowledged double standard means that this book is, in Noam Chomsky's terms, propaganda.[20] Wolfensohn's claim that this book is a channel for the 'authentic' expression of the views of the 40 000 people interviewed is a lie.[21]

If the social forces described by Robinson are pushing us towards something like Hardt and Negri's *Empire*, defining its others in vertical social space rather than horizontal geographic space, we should be mindful of Said's observations about the production of the Orient by European colonialism. There are crucial differences between the way in which European colonialism and Empire produce and discipline their subjects – one of which is that there was much more overt animus in colonialism's discourses on its Orientals, Africans and Indians than in Empire's discourses on its Poor. But this does not necessarily imply progress. Empire replaces colonialism's reliance on 'traditional' indirect rule with governmentality. Foucault has shown us that, with governmentality, sovereignty is legitimated not by territoriality but by the population that becomes the end of government 'and which refers and has resort to the instrumentality of economic knowledge, (that) would correspond to a society controlled by apparatuses of security' (2002: 221). We care for you therefore you should accept our discipline. However, one of the many continuities is that Empire, like colonialism, seeks to produce amongst its subjects

> an intellectual élite with which we can work . . . who would thus form a link between us and the mass of the natives . . . with a view towards preparing the way for agreements and treaties which would be the desirable form taken by our political future (Said 1995: 245).

A further continuity, to be taken equally seriously, is Said's observation that eventually 'the modern Orient, in short, participates in its own Orientalising' (1995: 235).[22] After all, the Bank's strategic moves towards becoming a 'Knowledge Bank' and to 'harmonising' and seeking further 'coherence' between its policies and those of the IMF, the WTO and donors means the seduction of massive funding and endless NGO-organised workshops and conferences (Bretton Woods Project 2002).

Their direct aim is to capture extant movements of the poor, creating others under the guise of supporting 'civil society'. For example, Julie Hearn cites convincing evidence to show that in Mozambique, 'Aid is being deliberately directed to assist in the construction of new social groups committed to the market economy' (2000: 19). Moreover, she quotes a United States Agency for International Development (USAID) report that openly states that in Ghana

> [P]olitical risks include growing polarisation within the Ghanaian polity and perhaps an associated risk that a legally sanctioned change of government could have totally opposing development views and reverse long-term policies. USAID assistance to civic organisations that develop and debate public policy, and US support for consultation on government policies have been useful in shaping a vision for Ghana's future which is developing broad, bipartisan support (Hearn 2000: 19, 20).

In Zimbabwe, Hopewell Gumbo writes that the Movement for Democratic Change (MDC) started out opposing both the Mugabe dictatorship and neoliberalism, but that 'Massive funding was poured into the civic movement, mainly from the West' with the result that

> the intellectuals now largely subscribe to the neoliberal agenda and grassroots activists, many of whom have suffered as a direct consequence of neoliberalism, are just brought in to toyi-toyi when numbers and credibility are needed. The middle class MDC leadership, together with the labour bureaucrats and big white bosses believe that giving actual power to grassroots activists would bring 'instability' in to the movement (Gumbo 2002).

Hence, while there are some important benefits in the Bank's recognition of some of the ways in which the pain of poverty is universal, there is a simultaneous attempt to produce an image of the poor seeking to turn the majority of humanity into the Poor. In the Bank's discourse the Poor's attitude is the primary casual factor in producing and sustaining their condition. We do well to recall that colonialism's discourses of domination asserted that 'ultimately, the problem with other races is the races themselves' (Gordon 1995: 29). The connections between colonialism's racialised discourses of domination and the Bank's non-racial othering [23] of poor people are clear. And the Poor, as produced by the Bank, are a resource to be exploited for profit, a potentially rebellious majority to be made safe and co-optable, and a source of fresh legitimacy to the increasingly questioned tyranny of capital under the fetish of the Market.

If existential and humanist thought is correct then the objectification of what should be subjective is always mutilating and dishonest. More of the unstable, diverse nature of human reality will emerge through a self-consciously subjective engagement with subjective realities than through delusional attempts at objectivity. Indeed, we see that while the Bank's book speaks of the Poor and produces a generic image of the Poor as other, passive, defeated, inert and lacking, Desai's book invokes the idea of the multitude producing its image as multiple and including – within its flesh – hope, anger, desire and the capacity for agency and change. The Poor wait to receive. The multitude produce.

Hardt and Negri's *Empire* delineates the notion of the multitude. They oppose the idea of the multitude to the 'People', defining the former as 'the universality of free and productive practices' and the People as 'an organised particularity that defends established principles and properties' (2000: 316). It is perhaps more useful to note that they speak of the multitude as a disordered collection of desiring subjectivities and the People in terms of an ordered collection of subjectivities disciplined in the name of some transcendent power above and beyond the individual desires in which creative powers are taken to inhere. That transcendent power may be anything from God to the Nation, the Party, or the Market. Hardt and Negri are resolutely opposed to any transcendence of a realm or agency outside the grasp – in time, space or capacity – of the multitude. They insist that 'immanence', the radical refusal of transcendent power, 'is defined as the absence of every external limit from the trajectories of the multitude, and immanence is tied only . . . to regimes of possibility' (2000: 373).

There is, clearly, a profound difference between the enabling and expansive approach of recognising and encouraging the fractious, anarchic energies of the multitude and the normalising and restricting approach of reifying particular images of objectified humanity. Not all of the poors (and the plural is important) in Desai's book are disciplined, corralled or resigned. They have not all subjected themselves to surveillance. Many refuse to know their place and accept their fate. They are a living, divergent, choosing, changing multitude. They know their desire. Instead of the Poor we have Psyches, the rapper who makes beautiful the heroes of the latest ugly clash with the police; Sifiso Sithole, a polite young man who usually reconnects a few people to the electricity grid before settling down to his homework in the afternoons; Prava Pillay, the street-fighting philosopher, and Thulisile Manqele, the unemployed guardian to seven children and litigant against water disconnections. *We are the Poors* is alive with the energies and desires of the multitude. It dissolves political platitudes, orthodoxies and abstractions in a flood of actually existing humanity.

Desai has a politics to go with his ontology. It is a politics of refusal. While conceding that this is only a beginning, we could connect this to the noble philosophical tradition that moves from the assertion that the rebel is the person 'who says no, but whose refusal does not imply a renunciation' (Camus 1984: 14). Even in the midst of neoliberalism's brutal assault on the poor,[24] defensive struggles are not inevitable. Various forms of what used to be called false consciousness can and do persuade people that they deserve to suffer, that there is no alternative to their steady dispossession or, as in the case of neo-fascism and xenophobia, that their suffering should be blamed on some 'other' rather than state policy. This is why every act of refusal matters and why negativity, sheer refusal, is such a generative act.

Struggle is constant. The world is constantly being remade, moment to moment. Every time counter-power strikes a blow, its language and concerns are appropriated so that they can be co-opted and their simulacra manufactured across the razor wire and velvet ropes separating the dominated from the dominators. *Voices* and *We are the Poors* speak to the leading edges of our time's two great movements. The World Bank's book is a response to the crisis of legitimacy confronted by the transnational capitalist class. It seeks to turn the fractious, suffering, angry, desiring, resisting, accepting, self-destructing, self-creating, border-crossing multitude into the Poor – lost lambs who need to be guided home by its shepherds. Desai's book is a response to the emergence of movements of the poor that refuse the shepherds, the tunes they whistle and the encouragements they murmur, their dogs and crooks, and their promise of eventually joining the flock that spends its days with the fenced-in sweet grass. Desai seeks to incite rebellion: to 'blast open the continuum of history' (Benjamin 1999: 254).

Criticism of the Bank's policies is usually met with the outrageous rejoinder that an alternative should be presented. It may well be a mistake to accept this logic and to take on the burden of showing alternatives to the barbarism of millennial capitalism. Should not the burden of proof rest with the people defending the arrangements from which they profit so extravagantly? Nevertheless, I hope that this chapter has shown that the Bank's representation of poor people in its *Voices of the Poor* is deeply inaccurate, unethical and self-serving. *We are the Poors* shows that there are other, much more accurate and simultaneously empathetic ways of writing about poor people.

Notes

1. Funding for this project came from the Bank itself, Cornell University, DfID, and other sources.
2. William Robinson defines neoliberalism, or the Washington Consensus, as a 'revolution from above' involving

    > twin dimensions rigorously pursued by global élites with the backing of a powerful and well-organised lobby of transnational corporations. One is worldwide market liberalisation and the construction of a new legal and regulatory superstructure for the global economy. The other is the internal restructuring and global integration of each national economy. The combination of the two is intended to break down all national barriers to the free movement of transnational capital across borders and the free operation of capital within borders, and, in this way, to open up all areas of society to the logic of profit making unhindered by the logic of social need (2003: 4).

3. This tension is discussed with insight and depth in Schech and Vas Dev's Chapter Six in this book.
4. For many years the ANC denied that this policy, referred to as the Growth, Employment and Redistribution (GEAR) policy, was a structural adjustment programme but Mamphele Ramphele, World Bank managing director at the time, agreed that GEAR was a structural adjustment programme at an Institute for Democracy in South Africa (IDASA) conference in Cape Town on 11 August 2003.
5. See Federici, Caffentzis and Alidou (2000) for an excellent account of the impacts of the World Bank's structural adjustment programmes on African universities.
6. Joseph Stiglitz acknowledged this in *Globalisation and its Discontents* (2002) and Mamphele Ramphele acknowledged it, far more forcibly, at the IDASA conference referred to in Note 4.
7. See Dwyer and Seddon (2002) for an international overview of growing resistance to neoliberalism, and Zeileg (2002) for an account of African resistance.
8. In *A Dying Colonialism* Fanon presents five case studies, including the famous examples of the changing role of the veil and the radio in Algerian society, each of which shows that there can be a shift from constraining Manicheanism to dialectical progress with, in Nigel Gibson's words, 'its opportunity for radically new behaviour in both public and private life, a chance for cultural regeneration and creation where positive concepts of self-determination, not contingent upon the colonial status quo, are generated' (1999: 421).
9. See my account of this in Pithouse (2001).
10. Over 400 people from anti-neoliberal movements celebrated the launch of this book in Durban.

11. There are no photographs in the Italian edition, *Noi Siamo i Poveri: Lotte Comunitarie Nel Nuovo Apartheid*.
12. This quote is repeated on page 110 in a slightly different form (If you don't have money today, your disease will lead you to your grave – Ghana 1995a) and again in the original form on page 267 (Narayan, Patel et al. 2000).
13. However, we are informed that 'some of the poor who contribute to the PPAs are verbally expressive. They use wonderful turns of phrase, and describe their world with freshness and simplicity' (Narayan, Patel et al. 2000: 23).
14. For an analysis of what this means see Pithouse (2003b).
15. Compare Holloway (2003: 34): 'The crystallisation of that-which-has-been-done into a "thing" shatters the flow of doing into a million fragments. Thing-ness denies the primacy of doing (and hence of humanity). Thing-ness is crystallised amnesia.'
16. Again, a comment as crass as this demands a return to Said's critique of colonial discourses: 'the space of the weaker or underdeveloped regions like the Orient was viewed as something inviting French interest, penetration, insemination – in short colonisation' (1995: 219).
17. See Gibson's *Fanon and the Postcolonial Imagination* (2003) for a superb account of this idea in Fanon's work.
18. These are substantially generic but allegedly particular – the good African and the good Hindu are both required to obey.
19. Although this book does not recognise any connection between worsening poverty and the Bank's policies some officials have acknowledged this connection. For example, Giovanni Arrighi has noted that World Bank economist William Easterly recently admitted that:

> a significant 'improvement in policy variables' among developing countries since 1980 – that is, greater adherence to the agenda of the Washington Consensus – has been associated, not with an improvement, but with a sharp deterioration where the Bank's policies have been followed most directly; median rate of growth of their per capita income falling from 2.5 per cent in 1960–79 to 0 per cent in 1980–98 (Arrighi 2002: 17).

In Arrighi's analysis recognitions of this sort have not led the Bank to rethink its policy prescriptions fundamentally or to abandon its claim to be acting against poverty. On the contrary, the Bank seeks more effective ways of implementing its central policy prescriptions by abandoning its demand for a minimalist state in favour of a demand for 'effective bureaucracies and activist states in the implementation of structural adjustment programmes' (Narayan, Patel et al. 2000: 4).

20. The model, which Chomsky develops in *Necessary Illusions: Thought Control in Democratic Societies* (1989) argues that when there is a systematic double standard, revealed by close analysis of the treatment of paired examples, we have a case of propaganda.

21. There is also evidence from outside the text strongly suggesting that the sudden departure of the project's initial leader, Ravi Kanbur, was a result of pressures from above to channel the voices from below in particular directions and that 'the final drafting of the report indicated that much of the information gained through consultation and dialogue with the poor and their advocates was not utilised' (see Schech and Vas Dev in Chapter Six of this volume). Moreover, while the South African PPA report, one of the reports on which *Voices* drew, is primarily framed within neoliberal orthodoxy (it advocates privatisation, cost-recovery policies for basic service provision etc.) and is obsequiously uncritical of the ANC, it does argue for some non-liberal measures such as welfare, effective and rapid land reform, cutting interest rates on the basis that an increase in inflation will be a price worth paying for increased employment, and so on. Not one of these recommendations appears in the Bank's book.

22. Most of the reports on African countries were conducted by the Bank itself. But the following Africans participated in this project: D. Nyamwaya in Kenya; S. Agi, S. Ogoh, H. Bin, A. Damarola, M. Uchenna, D. Nzewi and D. Shehu in Nigeria; H. Attwood, P. Ewang, F. Lund, J. May, A. Norton and W. Wentzel in South Africa.

23. Of course, all kinds of racisms are still being produced at the heart of Empire – consider the American discourses that legitimate the occupation of Palestine and the American prison system. However, it is necessary to acknowledge that there are very influential forces that are seeking to drive a shift from colonialism's domination premised on race to Empire's domination premised on class, and that the Bank's book is part of this project. It is equally necessary to acknowledge that this shift has been necessitated by struggles against racism; that while it seeks, in a conveniently ahistorical manner, to avoid racialising discourses it is not anti-racist because it does not seek to address the legacy of centuries of racism. The shift away from racialised discourses of domination does not mean that domination is threatened. On the contrary, as Marx argued, 'The more a dominant class is able to absorb the best people from the dominated classes, the more solid and dangerous is its rule' (Spivak 1999: 84).

24. This is no exaggeration. In South Africa research by McDonald and Pape (2002) has shown in the post-apartheid era that along with the disconnection of 10 million South Africans from water referred to in the text, the same number of people have been disconnected from electricity, 2 million people have been evicted from their homes and a further 1.5 million have had their property seized for failure to pay their water and electricity bills. This assault on the poor, which is a key focus of Desai's book and is completely ignored in the Bank's book, is hardly unique to South Africa – remember Arundhati Roy's (1999) conservative estimate is that in India 33 million people have been displaced by dams, often World Bank projects.

Chapter Fifteen

The King is Dead (Long Live the King?)
From Wolfensohn to Wolfowitz at the World Bank

Marcus Taylor and Susanne Soederberg

THIS IS AN ORIGINAL CHAPTER FOR THIS BOOK.

When George W. Bush announced in 2005 that he would be nominating the former US deputy defense secretary, Paul Wolfowitz, as the next president of the World Bank, a collective groan of anguish rang through much of the development community. The premier international development organisation appeared on the verge of colonisation by a leading proponent of an explicitly imperialist project ('The New American Century') promulgated by the White House. Wolfowitz's appointment, it was widely – and not unreasonably – assumed, was one further moment in a strategy that sought to subordinate international development concerns to the immediate geopolitical interests of the US. One of the ironies of such a move was to throw a kinder light, almost overnight, on the preceding presidency of James Wolfensohn, who had directed the Bank since 1995. After all, Wolfensohn was the president who promised not only to re-emphasise the Bank's commitment to poverty reduction and environmental sustainability, but also to introduce a pluralist approach to policy formation that might break with the 'one size fits all' policy dogma of the structural adjustment years. Notwithstanding ongoing debates over the nature of these reforms, and in particular whether they represent tangible changes to Bank practice rather than lip service, the spectre of Wolfowitz and his neo-conservative agenda induced a degree of nostalgia for Wolfensohn even before his term had formally ended.

Does such sentiment stand up to an analysis of the Wolfensohn reforms at the World Bank? Does the neo-conservative approach to development policy that is personified in Wolfowitz actually signify a large-scale break with existing Bank policy approaches? To begin to answer these questions this chapter surveys the major changes in the Bank's approach to development policies over the Wolfensohn decade. The intention is to position the Wolfensohn-era reforms within historical context of the crisis of neoliberal development strategies, and then highlight changes in both the substantive policy content and the form of World Bank relationships with client countries.[1] The *World Development Report 2005* closed the Wolfensohn period at the Bank, and in the first section of the chapter we assess how this document fits into the broader policy approach adopted in piecemeal fashion over the preceding decade, with close attention to the synergies between the concepts of investment climate, good governance and empowerment.

Secondly, the issue of the form of the World Bank's operations – how reform programmes are designed and implemented in client countries – has come under particular scrutiny. With an emphasis on country ownership and participatory development, Wolfensohn's Bank claimed to have resolved the failures of conditionality evident since the debt crisis of the early 1980s. The nature of these changes is analysed in the second section of the chapter. Subsequently, the final section offers an analysis of recent US proposals for foreign aid reform and, more specifically, the 'Millennium Challenge Account' put forward by George W. Bush and applauded by Wolfowitz.[2] In so doing, it suggests that – while the neo-conservative approach embraces a stronger disciplinary aspect that we term 'pre-emptive development' – there are many complementarities between Bank policy in the Wolfensohn era and that of the present US administration. These relate to underlying synergy between the Bank's re-invention of neoliberal development strategies during the Wolfensohn period and those of the US administration. As such, in the absence of a renewed outbreak of global economic turbulence, the accession of Wolfowitz to the Bank is unlikely to herald any rapid or dramatic changes in either the Bank's theoretical approach to development issues or in its policies.

The World Bank in a world of contradictions
Since the early 1980s, the World Bank's policy approach has been beset by a fundamental contradiction. On the one hand, it has attempted to instigate neoliberal-style capitalist development on a global level while, on the other, simultaneously responding to its inevitable tensions and failures. The immediate results of rapid and widespread social restructuring across the South disappointed the expectations of World Bank staff and client governments alike, many of which had imposed reforms through political authoritarianism and widespread repression of adversely affected interests. The destructive side of the experiment was apparent enough in the 'lost decade' of development in the 1980s and the enormous human costs of adjustment. Less evident in this period, however, was any stable or sustained improvement in economic or social indicators in most of the global South, a factor reluctantly conceded by the World Bank (World Bank 2001d). Despite the belief that global monetary discipline would secure an era of harmonious prosperity, the 1990s were marked by the spectre of intense financial volatility that brought drastic economic and social devastation to many of the Bank's most acclaimed success stories (Mexico in 1995, South-East Asia in 1997, Russia in 1998, Argentina in 2001). Elsewhere in the global South, the promised rewards of structural adjustment largely failed to materialise. In contrast to the world of prosperity under the tutelage of liberated market forces, as predicted by the ideologues of the Washington Consensus, two decades of neoliberal restructuring were widely recognised as being characterised by profoundly uneven development, including increased poverty and inequality at the global level. This included the socio-economic stagnation of Latin America

and regression of sub-Saharan Africa, two regions that most dramatically implemented neoliberal-style restructuring, on a wide spectrum of development indicators.[3]

Unsurprisingly, the failure of structural adjustment to realise generalised and sustained growth, alongside successive and devastating financial crises and increasing social polarisation in the 1990s, severely dented the legitimacy of the Washington-based institutions and the neoliberal paradigm of structural adjustment, with the former increasingly denigrated by a range of social actors. The latter includes former insiders and emergent global social movements, but also the forces of the political Right in the US, and led to repeated propositions to reform, downscale, disband or privatise the Bank.[4] In this respect, the ongoing process of reform within the World Bank during the 1990s is an attempt to adjust the World Bank's theoretical orientation, ideological positioning and (more slowly) policy frameworks in direct reaction to the failure of structural adjustment to deliver the promised results of stability, growth and poverty reduction on a global level.

These reforms – at their most rapid under the Wolfensohn tenure and manifest in the unveiling of the Comprehensive Development Framework (CDF) in 1999 – are best understood as driven by a combination of lost legitimacy and the tangible need to address the failure of development programmes in the South. Without doubt, the new development agenda incorporates a heavy degree of populist rhetoric, including catchwords such as 'empowerment' and 'country-ownership', which are aimed to disarm critique from local opposition in client countries, antagonistic global social movements and internal dissenters within the Bank. Likewise, a renewed emphasis on poverty reduction is clearly a central axis in the global legitimation of the World Bank and IMF at the turn of the millennium.[5] At one level, the promise of ridding the world of poverty is endowed with greater legitimising potential than the mission of promulgating an increasingly questioned array of neoliberal economic fundamentals, even if the prescription to achieve the former still involves a heavy dose of the latter. At another, the pledge to do so through participatory and country-owned procedures also seems to address a second criticism of combative international social movements that emphasised the externally imposed nature of 'one size fits all' structural adjustment programmes.

This process of change, however, represents far more than an instrumentally designed ideological offensive, as is often prioritised in theories of hegemony.[6] That the Bank is actively attempting to find ways to re-invent its practices is an indication of the degree to which alternative policy packages need to be developed in the face of growing contradictions in the global South and the political repercussions that these instil. Neoliberal restructuring brought a heightening of the conflictual tendencies inherent in capitalist social relations and, in contrast to the rhetorical demise of state intervention in the face of abstract market forces, has induced strong pressures upon national states to re-invent comprehensively their forms of intervention in the relations of social reproduction.[7] In this fashion, from the late 1980s governments across the global South have faced the recurrent necessity of re-inventing neoliberalism in order to address new contradictions in a period of escalating social polarisation. A major trend in Latin America, for example, has been to introduce various forms of 'neoliberalism with a human face', many of which foreshadow the World Bank's current discourse by almost a decade. The latter include, for example, the Chilean 'Growth with Equity' strategy; Salinas's 'social liberalism' in Mexico (Soederberg 2001b); and, more recently, the attempts of Brazilian President Luiz Inácio da Silva (Lula) to counter widespread social deprivation within the context of neoliberal style macroeconomic management.

Such strategies – which represent a global shift towards variants of 'Third Way' neoliberalism – have involved increasingly innovative attempts at modifying the institutional forms of governance and social policy in order to mediate the social struggles engendered in the conflict-ridden project of societal restructuring and manage social polarisation more effectively (Taylor 2006; Kiely 2005). Concurrently, it is in no small measure as a response to the struggle-driven course of policy change in the South that the Bank has been harried into a strategic realignment. This has involved a change in the operating practices of the Bank in order to project a renewed relevance of Bank doctrines to the concrete problems faced by governments in the South, a process that has led to the adoption of the principles of 'comprehensive development', the renewed emphasis on poverty reduction as the central aim of all Bank activities, and the production of guidelines on the restructuring and regulation of an ever-wider array of social relations. The following section charts the key aspects of the Bank's changing development prescription over the Wolfensohn period.

The content of Wolfensohn's Bank: Investment climate, good governance and empowerment

With the publication of the *World Development Report 2005: A Better Investment Climate for Everyone* (World Bank 2004) at the end of the Wolfensohn era, the World Bank attempted to consolidate the modified neoliberal approach that it had unevenly developed since the mid-1990s. After several years of emphasising the need to strengthen governance structures, improve service provision and empower the poor, the 2005 instalment of its annual best-practice manifesto returned to key issues of capitalist development, including private sector investment, profits and expansion. In so doing, the Bank attempted to build a more coherent statement regarding its best-practice prescription by tying together its recent, and rather fragmented, conceptual initiatives. By re-emphasising the importance and mechanisms of private sector expansion, a new formal coherence can be found between the Bank's three pillars of development policy: (1) an emphasis on neoliberal macroeconomic management; (2) a good-governance framework; and (3) the 'empowerment' of the poor. The following paragraphs briefly highlight the main prescriptions emanating from this *Report*, the theoretical foundations they are grounded on, and the way in which they link up to the concepts of 'good governance' and 'empowerment' that have been the major themes of recent World Bank literature.

The *World Development Report 2005* focuses resolutely on the political reforms required to create an institutional environment that is strongly conducive to private sector investment as a condition for creating new jobs, higher wages, cheaper commodities and, therein, reducing poverty. Investment climate, in the words of the Bank, is the 'set of location-specific factors that shape the opportunities and incentives for firms to invest productively, create jobs and expand' (World Bank 2004: 1–2). The concept of investment climate is employed by the Bank to help highlight and explain the dramatically uneven and often socially disastrous consequences of earlier restructuring projects, which repeatedly failed to live up to the expectations of their proponents. By highlighting the differences in political and institutional contexts in which reforms are implemented the Bank has been able to provide a potential explanation for the discrepancies between the predications of neoclassical thought and the diverse outcomes of 'actually existing neoliberalisms', without questioning the theoretical integrity of the former.[8] They also are able to identify further reforms necessary for successful development, concurrently justifying the Bank's own position as an international financial institution.

In its immediate outlook, therefore, the central thrust of the *Report* is an enquiry into how political institutions affect the development of the productive forces, and how these dynamics can lead to economic growth and poverty reduction. Ever-conscious of the politico-ideological context within which its *World Development Reports* are consumed, the Bank sets out its credentials as a pro-poor institution by emphasising that creating a good investment climate, far from pandering to the interests of existing firms, involves constructing the institutional framework for a level playing field in which public institutions are stripped of politically created biases that infringe primarily upon the ability of underprivileged individuals and firms to reap the rewards of their market activities. In the words of the Bank, it intends to set down 'what governments at all levels can do to create a better investment climate – an investment climate that benefits society as a whole, not just firms, and one that embraces all firms, not just large or politically connected firms' (World Bank 2004: 1).

The first and foremost aspect of the 2005 *Report* is the emphasis on stability and ensuring 'the rules of the game' in order to maximise investor certainties. Property rights are a linchpin of a good investment climate as they are understood as the nexus that links effort to return by enshrining the right of an individual to receive the full market reward for utilisation of whichever factor of production they own (World Bank 2004: 9, 79). Given the stability of due process, curbs on corruption and erratic government behaviour, and an institutional climate that ensures a basic level of economic security, investor confidence will rise as assessed risks decrease. Three aspects are particularly important. Firstly, the World Bank lauds the curtailment of corruption, viewed as the primary ailment in developing economies that skews the latent competitive market environment and therefore produces a serious drain on economic growth in general and pro-poor growth in particular.[9] Anti-corruption is then supplemented with an emphasis on the enforcement of contracts, which requires an efficient and impartial legal process.

The second important claim of the document is that corporate and societal interests are closely bound – in that the prosperity of the private sector is assumed to lead directly to increased employment and higher wages. However, the two are not synonymous and in various ways the public good can clash with the interests of a particular firm, as in the case of corruption leading to market-distorting favours, or lax environmental regulation creating negative externalities that impact on overall efficiency. This reinforces the need for impartial and technocratised governance structures that can enforce technocratic rationality over short-term gain. As such, the Bank calls for institutional measures that can 'align individual incentives with social incentives', although it emphasises the need for a cautious pragmatism in achieving such goals and sees no essential conflict in reconciling such interests (World Bank 2004: 25).

The third aspect emphasised in the *Report* is the need for states to counteract monopoly conditions that may emerge within the domestic ambit. Specifically, cartels are to be forbidden, mergers to be closely scrutinised, and dominant firms prohibited from engaging in price-setting activities (World Bank 2004: 105, 121, 183). The underlying goal is to keep markets competitive and free from distortions that could occur should the size and power of specific market actors allow them to override the disciplines asserted by competition, therein disturbing the natural tendency towards equilibrium and efficiency that is otherwise assumed to prevail.

These best-practice prescriptions emerging from the 2005 *Report* are consistent with the recent embrace of the major theoretical tenets and policy implications of information-theoretic economics within the World Bank. This shift is most evident in the influence of Joseph Stiglitz's contribution to Bank thought and the consequent emphasis on the need for effective institutional structures as an integral part of development policy (Fine 2001a). In contrast to the former doctrine of the minimalist state, the new doctrine professes that states need to intervene actively to facilitate and regulate the conditions for free economic exchange and to correct potential market failures caused by asymmetries of information. The latter are particularly prevalent within the developing world owing to the less well established nature of capitalist social relations, and therefore necessitate a much fuller role of the state in establishing institutions that channel information about market conditions, goods and participants than the anti-state bias of the initial restructuring models suggested (World Bank 2001d).

Subsequently, 'good governance', which in the World Bank's presentation entails the creation of transparent and accountable institutional forms leading to market-enabling policy content, has become a primary objective of Bank development initiatives in the twenty-first century. The 2005 *Report* provides two further steps towards expanding the realm of good governance: firstly, by further specifying the importance of depoliticised institutional forms to investment decisions (a process that began in *World Development Report 1997*); and, secondly, by consolidating the association between good governance and 'the common good' through revealing more explicitly the theoretical linkages between governance, accumulation and the material development of societies. In this respect, good governance is deemed necessary in order to allow individuals, and particularly the impoverished sections of society, to remove politically constructed barriers to market participation and take full advantage of the opportunities offered by the first generation of macroeconomic reforms.

Indeed, with respect to the overarching aim of poverty reduction, the new strategy rests upon the hypothesis that numerous social and institutional factors obstruct poor people from effectively exchanging assets in markets and thereby perpetuate their poverty. It is not the substantive irrationalities of marketised social relations that are causatively related to the failure of development goals and the reproduction of poverty; but rather the failure of poor people to adequately access and participate in markets owing to institutional and social impediments – such as lack of information, corruption, discrimination and political voicelessness. Poverty is therefore the result of contingent yet cumulative human, social and political failures, factors that are external to capitalist social relations and that can be remedied by correcting institutional forms through a 'good governance' strategy. For example, a poorly constructed investment climate that provides monopoly rents for large companies can reduce the potential rewards for microenterprise investment, therein curtailing profits and employment in those sectors that provide for the majority of jobs in the developing world.[10]

One of the innovations of the Wolfensohn period was not merely the advancement of the theory and prescription of good governance, but also its radicalisation through the notion of 'empowerment'. According to the World Bank, empowerment is a process whereby the poor are politically mobilised to aid the reform of institutions in order to reduce bureaucratic and social constraints on economic activity and upward mobility (World Bank 2000/1d). Pro-poor 'coalitions' are to be encouraged, which involves the government and development agents providing the conditions under which the interests of the poor and non-poor can be linked in the form of political associations or, in the World Bank's formulation, 'enhancing the perception of common interests between the poor and the non-poor' (World Bank 2000/1d: 109). The manner by which this is to be achieved is threefold: firstly, through promoting democracy and the rule of law; secondly, through reducing informational asymmetries via education and ensuring the transparency of government actions and decision making; and thirdly, through technical assistance to civil society groups that can help form 'pro-poor coalitions' (World Bank 2000/1d: 108).

In respect of the latter – and controversially so in the eyes of the US executive and more conservative elements within the Bank[11] – poor people are encouraged to form political pressure and self-help groups that can act as a countervailing power against state corruption and political rent seeking. As detailed above, corruption is seen as a particular problem as it can serve to restrain the development of capitalist social relations as special interests either extract rents or block social change that would enable the proliferation of free market exchanges. Collective action by the poor, according to the Bank, is therefore to be used for applying political pressure in order to guarantee the quality of state services and peer monitoring of their delivery, thereby mitigating the possibilities of development resource capture by elites. In an apparent reversal of power relations, the World Bank lauds the empowerment of poor people in order to 'monitor and discipline service providers' (World Bank 2003e: 1). Collective action beyond ensuring accountability and a superior quality of service delivery is, however, not welcome. Political movements that might threaten the status quo as enshrined by property rights and the primacy of free markets are symptomatic of poor people who do not recognise their own best interests.[12] Unionisation, as we might expect, is not encouraged as it can act as a barrier to the flexibility of labour markets and, in particular, the achievement of a market-clearing price for labour that will ensure optimal levels of employment and productivity.[13] The Bank's conceptualisation of empowerment, therefore, rests on the notion that empowerment is the removal of obstructions to participation in market relations. In short, and with no small degree of irony, poor people should act collectively to enforce free markets and good governance and therein create the conditions in which market individualism can reign supreme.

It is worth noting, therein, that the World Bank's theorisation is characterised by a notable political determinism. Investment climate is presented primarily as the result of the political creation of an institutional environment that shields market outcomes from extra-market disturbances and that facilitates social agents to participate in this seemingly separate and autonomous social sphere. Thus the solution to development goals is to be found in a relatively narrow range of government decisions and state activities, which are institutionalised to create a good governance framework. Even to the extent that human capital factors are incorporated into this assessment, the Bank sees this as a process of a forging a correct institutional balance between the public and private provision of healthcare, education, and basic services such as water, electricity, and sewage based on efficiency considerations (World Bank 2004). On the one hand, politics is essentially reduced to a technocratic science, a science of crafting the correct institutional environment within which development can flourish. To the extent that politics is to be a proactive process, this is strictly delineated within the World Bank's concept of empowerment – that is, collective action to create a good governance framework (and therein remove the necessity for collective action). On the other hand, processes and outcomes within the market sphere are endowed with a naturalness that belies the need to examine them theoretically or consider their social foundations. Development, it appears, is simply what occurs naturally through marketised social relations within a good governance framework.

By reconciling its conceptualisation of economic expansion with its notions of good governance and empowerment, the 2005 *Report* closes the Wolfensohn period by providing a more comprehensive rationalisation of the reforms begun in the Bank in the mid-1990s. In so doing, however, many of the weaknesses of the Bank's theorisation of capitalist development come to the fore. The original neoclassical arguments that seek to justify neoliberal restructuring posited that, so long as individuals submit to the play of market forces mediated through monetary relations, the optimal conditions for capital accumulation will predominate to the benefit of the individual and common good. The new development theory of the Bank – manifested in the conceptual triad of investment climate, good governance and empowerment – prescribes a much greater range of social and institutional engineering in order to harness the market utopia. However, it retains the overarching liberal tenets that inefficient social outcomes – in this case poverty and underdevelopment – result from the insufficient provision of the institutional preconditions for market activities and remains blind to the irrationalities of the process of capitalist accumulation that it promotes. As such, it does not recognise many of the most fundamental phenomena of capitalist development, including the conflictual relations between social classes in production, the systematic insecuritisation of social reproduction for a majority of individuals and households, and the inherent tendency toward destructive crises (Clarke 1991).

The form of Wolfensohn's Bank: Comprehensive development and ownership

For its second generation of reforms to be truly effective, the Bank argued, changes were also needed in the way that development policies are implemented. To this end, the Wolfensohn Bank took the lead in 1999 by announcing a shift to a 'Comprehensive Development Framework' through which it insists that the design and ownership of the reform programmes by the participating country is essential for success. According to Wolfensohn, and in contrast to former programmes that were crafted by the Bank and IMF, ownership entails that: 'Countries must be in the driving seat and set the course. They must determine the goals and the phasing, timing and sequencing of programmes' (Wolfensohn 1999b). Furthermore, ownership is suggested to mean that the policies formed within the framework of the Bank and IMF's Poverty Reduction Strategy Papers (PRSPs) must find their initiative in the country itself, through a partnership between elements of the government, civil society, private sector and international development community, and not solely in the World Bank. Reforms must not be centrally imposed, therefore, but require the support of all affected social groups.

Given the emergence of the CDF/PRSPs as part of an effort to re-address the effectiveness of conditionality agreements, the bold assertion that each participant country needs to 'own' its programme and the implications of autonomy that this connotes appear as particularly incongruous aspects of the Comprehensive Development Framework. The notion of 'ownership' is taken directly from business management, where it has been developed to improve the commitment of employees to their employers' projects (Cooke and Kothari 2001). As such, the practices associated with 'ownership' are constituted within complex power relationships, in this case between international finance provider and national governments. On the one hand, ownership explicitly aims at improving the viability and efficiency of programme designs through a specialisation of functions. The elaboration of a PRSP necessarily involves acceptance of the larger framework of economic liberalisation and good governance established by the Washington institutions. Beyond this, however, ownership provides the grounds for national governments to take the lead in establishing social and structural programmes with respect to local conditions and idiosyncrasies – including the trajectory of social struggles and the specific concrete tensions that restructuring had engendered – that they would be in a relatively privileged position to comprehend.

On the other hand, the concept of ownership also belies a transformation and, feasibly, an extension of conditionality. Since both the IMF and World Bank directorships must vet all development programmes before funding is approved, it is highly improbable that the broad trends of the development strategy will be allowed to diverge far from Bank and Fund orthodoxy. On the contrary, given the wide propagation of what the Bank considers to be 'best development practice', national governments are expected to internalise these lessons in order to receive funding. In this manner, ownership could be considered as a kind of 'Trojan horse' through which Bank-inspired doctrines are adopted by countries without need of direct tutelage and with a greater room for their creative adaptation to local circumstances. To overemphasise this aspect, however, is to miss how the Bank has recognised the imperative of giving national governments greater leeway in mediating the multiple contradictions that have beset the implementation of neoliberal-style reform across the developing world (Taylor 2005).

As such, behind the World Bank's overemphatic pronouncements of the virtues of ownership, participation and shared responsibilities, there is an essential and very real manner in which country ownership must be taken seriously. This is the manner by which governments are to proceed with implementation at a pace in accordance with the generation of compliance from and the effective participation of civil society and private sector groups. In effect, the national government has to ensure that the political conditions for implementation exist, and, as such, the onus of ownership falls upon the leadership role of the former. In the terminology of the Bank's OED, national governments must seize the 'locus of initiative' to ensure that key policy makers are intellectually convinced and that there is evident public support. Specifically, the World Bank suggests that policies formed within the ambit of the Comprehensive Development Framework must be subjected to a process of national dialogue between all relevant stakeholders. These not only include the World Bank, IMF and national government, but private sector and civil society organisations as well (World Bank 2005a).

A 'hands-off' approach to the implementation of programmes by the Bank presents national governments with the obligation to discipline both themselves and various component interest groups in order to receive development finance. While the Bank remains at arm's length, able to provide specific guidelines and the funds to carry out operations, this new division of labour places the functions of consensus generating in reaction to the idiosyncrasies of local socio-political environments in the hands of the domestic government. In this respect, ownership indeed provides the grounds for national governments to take the lead in establishing policies and programmes with respect to local conditions and idiosyncrasies – including the trajectory of social struggles and the specific concrete tensions that restructuring had engendered – that the

World Bank is singularly unable to address. As the Bank affirms: 'The whole framework rests on the premise that the Bank need not lead – or even be involved – as long as the process produces the desired results' (World Bank 2000/1d).

In the World Bank's vision of the PRSPs formation process, the private sector, civil society, NGOs, national and regional governments and the international lending agencies would all have an equal opportunity to put forward their particular views on different aspects of the system. The projected *raison d'être* for this participatory form of deliberation is one of efficiency, which relates to the division of expertise that, as noted above, frames the concept of ownership. A shift towards more participatory development projects had begun in the later 1980s in recognition that externally imposed and technocrat-orientated forms of research and implementation showed serious shortcomings (Cooke and Kothari 2001). Participatory development is based on the principle that recipient groups and poor communities are in a privileged position to know their own needs, allowing accurate information regarding the kind of micro-projects necessary to promote capitalist development to float upwards through the deliberation process. This is intended to lead to better-targeted projects that will have greater chances for success. Moreover, given their common role as equal participants in the programme design process, the Bank intends that recipient groups will view projects as having greater legitimacy and will also act in order to facilitate programme realisation.

Like many Bank conceptualisations, however, this vision is shrouded in a model of harmony that, as noted by Else Øyen (2000: 3), is 'seducing in all its goodwill and buzzwords of partnership, sharing of social capital, equality and acceptance'. The notion of participation masks the problematic nature of power relations that permeate the process. On the one hand, the assumed equality of voices ignores the vast inequalities in material and political power that enable privileged groups to exercise a profound influence over deliberations and implementation. Alongside its own power vis-à-vis client countries, the World Bank's discourse conveniently overlooks deeply embedded national power structures that profoundly condition the process of political decision making.

Secondly, even within these curtailed possibilities for political pluralism, as in all good management practices derived from business studies, the realm of influence of subordinate groups is delineated to particular micro levels. The modes in which subordinate groups can participate are shaped at the level of the World Bank and national policy elites, and they enter the 'national dialogues' that are intended to precede PRSP formation on these terms. Within the framework of the PRSPs, which separate the IMF's focus on macroeconomic policy from the World Bank's social and structural policies undertaken within the CDF, fundamental issues such as trade liberalisation, privatisation and other macro and structural policies are partitioned off from pluralist deliberation at a prior level. This follows the trend witnessed throughout the neoliberal period of removing key decisions (monetary policy aimed at price-stability is a prime example) from the ambit of politics and placing them in the realm of technocratic decision making, such as an independent central bank. At issue is the containment of inherently political issues behind a façade of neutrality grounded in technocratic rationality.

Emerging empirical case studies provide support for an interpretation of ownership and participation not as a mere smokescreen but as a contradictory attempt at incorporating diverse social groups into a constrained realm of decision making in order to promote both efficiency and legitimacy (Cavero et al. 2002; Craig and Porter 2003; Crawford 2003). The CDF presents not the Bank's resolution of the contradictions of managing neoliberal reform at a global level but merely an expression of them – a new institutional form through which struggles will take shape. Moreover, it is not simply an audacious attempt by the World Bank to become a pre-eminent hegemonic force, but an expression of the World Bank's rearguard reaction to the contradictions of uneven development manifested at a plethora of different levels. Far from a show of strength, the CDF recognises the failure of previous Bank approaches as well as the very real limits that constrain its operations. Most interestingly for a variety of popular movements, the Bank's actions have opened up new areas for struggle as different groups contest what it means to be 'included' and 'empowered'.

Wolfowitz's Bank: Towards 'pre-emptive development'?

As highlighted in the Introduction to this chapter, the appointment of Paul Wolfowitz – fresh from his leading role in the US occupation of Iraq – caused deep consternation amongst much of the development community, including within the World Bank itself. Nonetheless, to what extent would a fundamental overhaul of Bank philosophy be desired by the US administration? If Wolfowitz has been appointed to the World Bank in order to lead a neo-conservative revolution within the institution, it is pertinent to examine the basic tenets of the neo-conservative approach to development financing as lauded by the Bush administration. The latter's primary initiative has been the establishment of the Millennium Challenge Account (MCA) at the Financing for Development (FfD) Conference in Monterrey, Mexico, in March 2002.[14] The MCA initiative was self-consciously launched to act as a trend-setting mode of managing aid and was put in the charge of a new institution, the Millennium Challenge Corporation (MCC). The White House is trying to establish the MCC as an independent corporation, whose head is chosen by the president of the US.[15] The following four principles will guide the 'unique mission' of the MCC: (1) encourage policy reform and reward performance; (2) target growth; (3) operate in partnership; and (4) focus on results (www.mca.gov).

Unlike traditional forms of development assistance, the programme seeks to reward performance and measure results so as to create an operational action plan aimed at ensuring that the goals set by the national security strategy are reached. In the words of President George W. Bush:

> Countries that live by these three broad standards – ruling justly, investing in their people, and encouraging economic freedom – will receive more aid from America. And, more importantly, over time, they will really no longer need it, because nations with sound laws and policies will attract more foreign investment. They will earn more trade revenues. And they will find that all these sources of capital will be invested more effectively and

productively to create more jobs for their people . . . I challenge other nations, and the development banks, to adopt this approach as well (Bush 2002).

The funds released by the US government through the MCA are intended to provide aid to those countries which have successfully demonstrated that they meet acceptable levels on sixteen indicators spanning the 'three broad standards' mentioned in the president's 'challenge'. Success in these areas is judged primarily through quantifiable scores measured according to indices, the majority of which have already been established by the World Bank (see the table below), covering each of the sixteen criteria. Those countries that have demonstrated success in these areas are then eligible for grants from the MCA. In this fashion the polarity of conditionality is reversed. Countries now have to enact reforms prior to receiving funds. To coin a term in the Bush administration's mould, this is a strategy of 'pre-emptive development'.[16]

Eligibility criteria for the MCA[17]

INDICATOR	SOURCE
I. Ruling justly	
1. Control of corruption	World Bank Institute
2. Rule of law	World Bank Institute
3. Voice and accountability	World Bank Institute
4. Government effectiveness	World Bank Institute
5. Civil liberties	Freedom House
6. Political rights	Freedom House
II. Investing in people	
7. Immunisation rate: DPT and measles	WHO/World Bank
8. Primary education completion rate	World Bank

9. Public primary education spending/ GDP	World Bank
10. Public expenditure on health/GDP	World Bank
III. Economic freedom	
11. Country credit rating	Institutional Investor
12. Inflation	IMF
13. Regulatory quality	World Bank Institute
14. Budget deficit/GDP	IMF/World Bank
15. Trade policy	Heritage Foundation
16. Days to start a business	World Bank

While these conditions reflect the concerns of the official development discourse – reproducing the imperative of world market integration through open current and capital accounts, sound macroeconomic fundamentals, good governance, and democratic values – the 'empowering features' seem to be overshadowed by the pre-emptive nature of the MCA, not to mention the complementary scheme of pre-emptive conditionality imposed by the International Development Association (IDA). Although the MCA is wrapped in the same discourse of empowering development found in the Post-Washington Consensus (emphasising ownership and social inclusion, for example), the Bush administration's 'new global compact' is embedded within an array of disciplinary measures over client countries. Indeed, the concern for 'empowering' individuals is limited to ensuring that the reform, along the lines of the above sixteen criteria, is home-grown in a similar manner to the Bank's notion of 'ownership'. As Wolfensohn emphasised when he launched the Comprehensive Development Framework, the architects of the MCA stress the necessity of a strong domestic momentum for change. Yet, as the following quote indicates, this domestic momentum is to be given a strong push through management-style forms of discipline and surveillance. In the words of the US State Department, partnership between the MCA and recipient countries is to be established in the following manner:

The MCA will use time-limited, business-like contracts that represent a commitment between the United States and the developing country to meet agreed performance benchmarks. Developing countries will set their own priorities and identify their own greatest hurdles to development. They will do so by engaging their citizens, businesses and government in an open debate, which will result in a proposal for MCA funding. This proposal will include objectives, a plan and timetable for achieving them, benchmarks for assessing progress and how results will be sustained at the end of the contract, delineation of the responsibilities of the MCA and the MCA country, the role of civil society, business and other donors, and a plan for ensuring financial accountability for funds used. The MCA will review the proposal, consulting with the MCA country. The Board will approve all contracts (Larson 2003).

In this manner, the MCA employs an extremely similar discourse to Wolfensohn's Comprehensive Development Framework, therein emphasising significant continuities between the US neo-conservative approach and that of the Bank in the Wolfensohn period. Certainly, the emphasis on grants over loans, and the pre-emptive qualities of the MCA indicate the intention to tighten the mechanisms of conditionality. Indeed, pre-emptive development seeks to surmount all aspects of non-compliance by client countries by making aid conditional on accomplished, rather than future, reforms. The latter is a strategy that the US has repeatedly promoted within the IDA wing of the World Bank.

Conclusions

How can we summarise this story of two 'Wolves' at the World Bank and the general malaise within the development community that marked the passing of Wolfensohn? On the one hand, James Wolfensohn's period at the Bank corresponded to an era in which neoliberal development strategies underwent notable revision in an attempt to counter the contradictions in them and the political struggles that they had unleashed. Wolfensohn had been brought into the Bank specifically to reinvigorate the institution and he placed all of his widely noted passion and energy into this process, resulting in: (1) a shift in theoretical orientation towards the neo-institutionalist-influenced triad of investment climate, good governance and empowerment; and (2) a re-invention of Bank–client relations within the aegis of the Comprehensive Development Framework, a management device that posited an active role for civil societies, NGOs and private sectors within the formation of domestic policy.

The accession of Wolfowitz is unlikely to disrupt these now established parameters for several key reasons. Firstly, the World Bank is a complex organisation with multiple structures of authority and a strongly embedded research department that has gained consistency over the Wolfensohn period. Moreover, the level of opposition within the Bank to the appointment of Wolfowitz was substantial, and may suggest an added level of institutional inertia should major reforms be attempted. Secondly, major reforms to development strategy are unlikely given the underlying consistency between the neo-conservative emphasis on good governance and free markets and the Bank's approach. This is indicated through both the substantive content of the Bush administration's Millennium Challenge Account – with its explicit borrowing of World Bank indices for governance and other measures of 'good policy' – and the operational form of the MCA, which is situated in a similar discourse of ownership, partnership and consensus while armed with notable disciplinary mechanisms.

Where, then, does potential for divergence exist? Perhaps the foremost area in which the US Right has looked to make an impact is the refocusing of development assistance upon the least-developed countries or 'failed states'. This has become increasingly prominent since the architects of the 'War on Terror' have explicitly linked failed states with the production of 'extremism'. That the World Bank continues to make large loans to 'middle-income' states such as India and, particularly, China has been derided in the US senate despite the presence of vast poverty in these countries, owing to the belief that private investment (foreign direct investment of portfolio investment) can cover all credit needs. As analysed above, the Bush administration's MCA model that it hopes will be widely emulated focuses on giving grants solely to 'heavily indebted poor countries' (HIPCs) based on these countries implementing reforms prior to receiving aid. This process is ongoing with the IMF's 'Multilateral Debt Relief Initiative' that requires at least a six-month track record of 'sound economic policies' before being eligible for debt relief (IMF 2006). Similarly, the US Right has an oft-noted propensity for critiquing institutional overreach, evident in the Meltzer Commission's and others' suggestions that the Bank needs to focus on its core areas of expertise – governance issues and economic reform.

Wolfowitz might indeed seek to cut back gradually on the Bank's lending to middle-income countries and to curb its recent sorties into myriad development issues, including gender and environment. Nonetheless, it will be interesting to see whether such a perspective would find resonance within the wider international development community or in the Bank itself, not least because issues of gender equity and environmental sustainability have become so firmly embedded in the practices of NGOs and international development organisations worldwide. Even if desired, to re-invent the World Bank in the image of the MCA, for example, would require a process of institutional transformation that, to be successful, would necessitate more than the presence of a leading neo-conservative at its helm. Such a strategy would incur opposition from other core capitalist states and a majority of developing world governments, with the outcomes of such struggles formed through institutionally embedded mediations between Bank and states, as well as between internal Bank factions. What is most notable, however, is that periods of sustained change at the World Bank habitually coincide with periods of crisis in the accumulation of capital at a global level. Another round of crises in conjunction with unprecedented social movements against neoliberal globalisation would also offer opportunities for the demise of the moral and intellectual leadership of the Bank.

The World Bank: Development, Poverty, Hegemony

Notes

1. A fuller elaboration of the theoretical framework and policy analysis underlying this perspective of World Bank policy shifts can be found in Taylor (2004b, 2005).
2. A more complete synopsis of these dynamics can be found in Soederberg (2006).
3. See Milanovic's (2003) critique of poverty and inequality indices from within the Bank. Indeed, such studies demonstrate that the absolute number of people in the world living in conditions of extreme poverty rose considerably in the 1980s and continued a more moderate upward trend in the 1990s. The relative proportion of the population in extreme poverty also rose during the 1980s, but fell moderately in the 1990s, largely due to the influence of China and India. Inequality between North and South and within Southern countries has escalated dramatically, thereby undermining the neoclassical prediction of a general convergence of wages and wealth amongst national states in conditions of open trade. For further discussion, see Weeks (2001); World Bank (2001d); Wade (2004); and Kiely (2005).
4. Such discussions were given tangible form by the Meltzer Commission at the close of the 1990s. For an examination of different notions to reform the Bank, see Pincus and Winters (2002b). In this respect, the Bush administration's creation of the 'Millennium Challenge Account' and its reformulation of lending to heavily indebted poor countries are of importance, as discussed further below.
5. The degree to which the discourse of poverty reduction has pervaded the day-to-day operations of the leading international financial institutions is aptly captured by one World Bank researcher who suggested that: 'The poverty issue is so red-hot that IMF and World Bank staff began to feel that every action inside these organisations, from reviewing public expenditure to vacuuming the office carpet, should be justified by its effect on poverty reduction' (Easterly 2001: 2).
6. For two divergent applications of hegemony applied to the World Bank, compare Cammack (2003) and Wade (2002). For critique, see Taylor (2005).
7. Petras, Veltmeyer and Vieux (1997) present a range of struggles raised by structural adjustment in Latin America, and Kiely (2005) provides further examples at a global level.
8. We borrow the term 'actually existing neoliberalism' from Neil Brenner and Nik Theodore who wished to emphasise the great variance in policy regimes and social outcomes of restructuring projects owing to the specific socio-economic contexts in which they are embedded. See Brenner and Theodore (2002).
9. For a critique of the Bank's perspective on corruption, see Khan (2002).
10. The influence of Peruvian economist De Soto (2003), who emphasises the ability of the poor to become microcapitalists within the correct institutional setting, is notable.
11. The issue of empowerment has provoked serious conflicts within the Bank, and between the Bank and the US, and the resulting discourse represents a compromise reached after several rounds of negotiations; compare Wade (2001b).

12. In the words of the Genoa report produced by officials from the eight richest countries in the world yet speaking on behalf of the global poor: 'From the perspective of the poor, there are risks that justified concerns about their interests are manipulated to support a return to protectionism' (Group of Eight 2001).
13. On the World Bank's prescription vis-à-vis labour flexibilisation, see Taylor (2004a).
14. For a more detailed analysis of the FfD Conference and the 'Monterrey Consensus' see Soederberg (2004).
15. US Congress, by contrast, would like to see the MCC fall under the jurisdiction of the State Department, thereby curbing some of its independence.
16. For further analysis of this term and the MCA see Soederberg (2006).
17. For more information, see the Millennium Challenge Corporation's website at http://www.mca.gov/about_us/overview/index.shtml. Accessed 20 June 2006.

Chapter Sixteen

Civil Society and Wolfowitz's World Bank
Reform or Rejection?

Patrick Bond[1]

THIS IS AN ORIGINAL CHAPTER FOR THIS BOOK.

Can the World Bank and the International Monetary Fund (IMF) be reformed? Or should they be rejected outright – and closed? What kinds of analysis, strategies, tactics and alliances allow us to even pose the question in the stark terms of 'fixing' or 'nixing' (that is, defunding and decommissioning) the Bretton Woods Institutions (BWIs)? Does the advent of neo-conservative control of the World Bank, along with 'anti-corruption' posturing in 2006, make any difference?

James Wolfensohn's presidential reign (1995–2005) muddied these debates, dividing advocacy movements over matters of legitimacy, accountability and militancy. At his retirement, some NGOs even gave him a fond farewell party. With Paul Wolfowitz running the Bank at least until 2009 these questions are being raised in a new and different way. At last there is the possibility of uniting global justice movements to the broader anti-imperialism struggle via a focused campaign against an institutional enemy.

But matters are not so simple. Firstly, consider the terrain upon which campaigners have been working over the past decade. When Bill Clinton anointed Wolfensohn as Bank president, several opportunities arose for organisational change, based upon internal processes and external pressures (Mallaby 2005). Some followed directly on the sudden legitimacy crisis of the Bretton Woods twins in 1997–99, combining the institutions' global-governance 'democratic deficit', their continued reliance upon the 'Washington Consensus' approach to public policy, the Bank's ongoing orientation to controversial mega-projects, both agencies' failure to relieve Third World debt and international financial speculation born of liberalised capital markets, and the tenure of Joseph Stiglitz as chief economist during a period of middle-income meltdowns. Other catalysts included international, intersectoral commissions – emerging from public campaigning – on structural adjustment, dams and extractive industry.

We begin by considering these factors, then take stock of the first year of the Wolfowitz regime, and end with critical arguments about global justice movement capacities and priorities.

Wolfensohn's 'reform' era

The internal procedural changes, rhetorical shifts, individual initiatives and multi-stakeholder forum exercises introduced under Wolfensohn occurred at a time (the millennium decade 1995–2005) of legitimacy crisis for neoliberal ideology. Free-market economic principles were applied widely to macroeconomic and micro-development policy in the Third World (including South Africa, Brazil, Korea and India under mass-popular governments), and also in many Northern 'Third Way' regimes. In spite of declarations at the March 2002 United Nations Financing for Development (FfD) Conference in Monterrey, Mexico, that 'a shift from the Washington Consensus to a new Monterrey Consensus' (Gabriel 2002) had emerged, the 'Post-Washington Consensus' challenge by Stiglitz, starting with his famed January 1998 speech in Helsinki, made no dent. Issues posed by reformers – debt relief, citizen 'participation' in neoliberal programme design, democratic governance, transparency, global financial regulation, and commissions dealing with structural adjustment, dams and energy – were all rebuffed.

The FfD conference was one site to pose and begin answering such questions. It occurred auspiciously, just after South Africa's dramatic

2001 currency crash, in the wake of similar declines in Argentina, Turkey, Brazil, Russia, Korea, Malaysia, Indonesia and Thailand in a four-year arc of destruction that also included a US$7 trillion meltdown in New York stock markets.[2] However, rather than seriously addressing the structural challenges of Third World debt and financial speculation, the FfD meeting's leadership[3] merely reiterated UN Millennium Development Goals' rhetoric while relying upon orthodox strategies and policies. It correctly observed 'dramatic shortfalls in resources required to achieve the internationally agreed development goals' (United Nations 2002), but endorsed the Heavily Indebted Poor Countries (HIPC) debt relief initiative as 'an opportunity to strengthen the economic prospects and poverty reduction efforts of beneficiary countries'. The limits of the institutions' capacity to change become evident on examination of HIPC, followed by subsequent attempts to draw in civil society through 'participatory' structural adjustment design and governance reform.

Notwithstanding its support for the HIPC debt scheme at Monterrey, the Bank conceded long-standing criticisms that its staff 'had been too optimistic' about the ability of countries to repay under HIPC, and that projections of export earnings were extremely inaccurate. Thus half the HIPC countries failed to reach their completion points (*Financial Times*, 27 February 2003).[4] The once pro-HIPC London lobby group Jubilee Plus admitted, 'According to the original HIPC schedule, 21 countries should have fully passed through the HIPC initiative and received total debt cancellation of approximately $34.7 billion in net present value terms. In fact, only eight countries have passed Completion Point, between them receiving debt cancellation of $11.8 billion' (Jubilee Plus 2003). Add a few other countries' partial relief via the Paris Club (US$14 billion) and it appears that the grand total of the 1996–2003 debt relief exercise was just US$26.13 billion. (The 1998 G8 – France, USA, UK, Germany, Japan, Italy, Canada and Russia – summit in Cologne, Germany, had promised US$100 billion.) More than US$2 trillion of Third World debt that should be cancelled remains, including not just HIPCs but also Nigeria, Argentina, Brazil, South Africa and other major debtors not considered by global elites to be highly indebted or poor. The more radical Jubilee South network, with leading members in Argentina, Nicaragua, the Philippines and South Africa, rejects Jubilee Plus ideas about how much debt is 'sustainable' and 'repayable', arguing for full cancellation, repudiation and G8-country reparations.

In 1999, HIPC was accompanied by a renamed structural adjustment philosophy: Poverty Reduction Strategy Papers (PRSPs). As the World Development Movement put it, the new version did not fool the victims: 'PRSPs have failed to deviate from the IMF's free market orthodoxy' (Ellis-Jones 2003). In the same spirit, a May 2001 Jubilee South conference of the main African social movements concluded in Kampala:

- The PRSPs are not based on real people's participation and ownership, or decision making. There is no intention of taking civil society perspectives seriously, but participation is kept to public relations legitimisation.
- The lack of commitment to participation is further manifested in the failure to provide full and timeous access to all necessary information, limiting civil society's capacity to contribute meaningfully.
- The PRSPs are introduced according to pre-set external schedules, resulting in inadequate time for effective participatory processes in most countries.
- In addition to the constraints placed on governments and civil society organisations in formulating PRSPs, the World Bank and IMF may veto the final programmes. This mocks the claim that the PRSPs are based on 'national ownership'.
- Another concern is how PRSPs co-opt NGOs to 'monitor' their own governments for the Bank and IMF, directly and indirectly (Jubilee South 2001).

This last gambit was failing when the FfD convened in Monterrey. For example, Ugandan civil society organisations expressed concern that their own 'participation in the endeavour has amounted to little more than a way for the World Bank and IMF to co-opt the activist community and civil society in Uganda into supporting the same traditional policies' (Nyamugasira and Rowden 2002) Other NGO, funding agency and academic studies of PRSPs were highly critical (Bond 2006b). It was, hence, not surprising that subsequent debt relief concessions in 2005 were also unsatisfying; the G7 (the G8 without Russia) finance ministries provided merely US$2 billion per year in relief affecting fewer than twenty countries, whose debts were not completely written off, contrary to the advertised promise. The Bank and IMF periodically attempted to sabotage even that partial debt relief by limiting the countries eligible and delaying implementation.

Lack of internal democracy is partly to blame. Barely acknowledging the global system's power imbalances, the Monterrey Consensus offered only timid suggestions for governance reforms. Just two directors represent the BWIs' nearly fifty sub-Saharan African member countries, while eight rich countries enjoy a director each and the US maintains veto power with more than 15 per cent of the votes. (There is no transparency as to which Board members take what positions on key votes.) The leaders of the Bank and IMF are chosen from, respectively, the US and EU, with the US Treasury secretary holding the power of hiring or firing.[5] Although reformist gestures were needed for the sake of appearances,[6] the Development Committee's 2003 Bank/Fund strategy offered only minor amendments, such as adding *one* additional representative from the South to the 24-member Board. In mid-2003 a leaked World Bank paper proposed raising developing country voting power from 39 to 44 per cent and adding one new African executive director, but the June 2003 proposals neglected IMF governance, Bank/IMF Board transparency and Bank/IMF senior management selection (World Bank 2003b). Even those milquetoast reforms were too much for the US, and the Bush regime's executive director to the Bank, Carol Brooking, opposed reforms, suggesting an extra research capacity fund instead (http://www.brettonwoodsproject.org).

Reforms from the outside?
Under the prevailing balance of power, the top-down reform processes discussed above could not have worked. What of other efforts at reform

from the outside (ostensibly from below) – particularly via international commissions in which the World Bank played a crucial hosting and financing role? Well-meaning civil society advocates recently went inside the Bank in three major processes: the World Commission on Dams (WCD), the Structural Adjustment Participatory Review Initiative (SAPRI) and the Extractive Industry Review (EIR). In the first, Bank water expert John Briscoe actively lobbied Southern governments to reject the findings of a vast, multi-stakeholder research team in 2001 (*Mail & Guardian*, 27 April 2001). According to Patrick McCully of International Rivers Network, 'The World Bank's singularly negative and non-committal response to the WCD Report means that the Bank will no longer be accepted as an honest broker in any further multi-stakeholder dialogues' (McCully 2002: 40).[7]

As for SAPRI, hundreds of organisations and scholars became involved in nine countries: Bangladesh, Ecuador, El Salvador, Ghana, Hungary, Mexico, the Philippines, Uganda and Zimbabwe. From 1997–2002 they engaged in detailed analysis, often alongside local Bank and IMF officials. Bank staff withdrew from the process in August 2001. In April 2002, when civil society groups tabled the 188-page report on *The Policy Roots of Economic Crisis and Poverty*, Washington ignored them (Peet 2003: Chapter 4).

The EIR also nearly went off the rails when, despite environmental, human rights and social justice communities' objections, the Bank approved loans for two pipelines in Chad–Cameroon and the Caspian. By late 2003, civil society pressure against the Bank was sufficient to move the EIR leader, former Indonesian environment minister Emil Salim, to include radical recommendations in the draft report: an end to World Bank coal lending by 2008 (worth billions in countries such as India and China); mandatory revenue sharing with local communities; extensive environmental and social impact assessments; 'no go' zones excluding mining or drilling in environmentally sensitive areas; no new mining projects dumping tailings in rivers; obligatory environmental restructuring and increased renewable energy investments. Few were surprised when the lead Bank energy staffer Rashad Kaldany immediately and publicly disagreed with the Salim recommendations (World Bank 2003e). Several major environmental NGOs remarked upon the institution's poor track record:

> One of the Bank's most important environmental reforms of the 1990s was its more cautious approach to high-risk infrastructure and forestry projects. This policy is now being reversed. The World Bank recently announced that it would re-engage in contentious water projects such as large dams in what it refers to as a 'high risk/high reward' strategy. In 2002, the Bank dismissed its 'risk-averse' approach to the forest sector when it approved a new forest policy (Environmental Defence, Friends of the Earth and International Rivers Network 2003).

In August 2004, the institution's Board rejected the main EIR recommendations. According to Samuel Nguiffo of Friends of the Earth Cameroon, 'The Bank's response is a deep insult for those affected by its projects.' His Amsterdam colleague Janneke Bruil added: 'Billions of misspent public dollars and sixty years of outcries by people around the world have not been enough. What more does it take?' (Friends of the Earth International 2004).

Much more protest will be needed to tackle the primary environmental challenge, namely to urgently reduce carbon and other greenhouse gas emissions from levels already responsible for severe climate change. Instead of reducing, the Bank promotes a dubious mitigation strategy through its Prototype Carbon Fund (PCF), which manages monies from seventeen corporations and several carbon-intensive Western governments. Thanks to the Bank's propensity to invest in projects such as methane extraction from toxic waste dumps (of which Durban's Bisaser Road is notorious, given the government's 1996 pledge to close it) or destructive timber plantations (such as Brazil's controversial Plantar), the Northern polluters who support the PCF face greatly reduced official pressure to cut emissions (Bond and Dada 2005). In opposition, international environmental and social activists signed a 'Durban Declaration' in

October 2004. Signatories suggested numerous alternatives once governments and international agencies become serious about global warming: regulation, taxation, support for existing low-fossil-carbon economies, energy efficiencies, development of renewables and non-fossil-fuelled technologies, responsible tree planting, and other strategies not involving commerce and not presupposing that big business already owns the world's carbon-cycling capacity (http://www.carbontradewatch.org).

Far from seeking such alternatives, by April 2006 the Bank was endorsing nuclear power and mega-dam hydropower as potential 'clean energy' sources, and promoting the dubious science of carbon sequestration, in a paper before its Development Committee. Renewable energy funding remains an extremely low priority, even though a group of ecological economists within the Bank had tentatively begun to value depleted natural resources as a corrective to standard wealth/income/savings accounts. As Michael Goldman demonstrates in his book *Imperial Nature*, the Bank's 'green neoliberal project' fuses '*neocolonial* conservationist ideas of enclosure and preservation and *neoliberal* notions of market value and optimal resource allocation' in order to make 'particular natures and natural resource-dependent communities legible, accountable and available to foreign investors . . . by introducing new cultural and scientific logics for interpreting qualities of the state's territory' (2005: 184).

Hence the April 2005 merger of the Washington Consensus neoliberal agenda and the Pentagon-White House neo-conservative programme was no shock. The Board meeting where Wolfowitz was confirmed as James Wolfensohn's replacement may represent the peak moment for the big oil and energy companies.

Enter Paul Wolfowitz
The Bank's leadership transition from Wolfensohn – the long-time Democrat and neoliberal financier – to the neo-conservative Wolfowitz, based in the petro-military complex, was revealing. George W. Bush needed some very strong allies to appoint a man responsible for mass

destruction in Iraq and Afghanistan. Along with the presidents of France, Germany, Japan and Italy, South Africa's Thabo Mbeki was the other world leader whom Bush phoned to vet the appointment. A year earlier, Mbeki had expressed 'the urgent need for radical reform' of Bank and IMF governance (2004). Yet the same month, South African Finance Minister Trevor Manuel wrote a letter – as chair of the BWI's Development Committee – conceding that reforms on 'voting rights' were 'likely to be postponed for some time'. In the meantime, said Manuel, the committee should address 'those situations where countries' quotas/capital shares were egregiously out of line with their economic strength' (Manuel 2004). That strategy, endorsed by IMF leadership in 2006, will further empower wealthier countries, especially Japan. The IMF will receive greater voting rights alongside increasing IMF quotas and World Bank capital investment. The result will be much more money for the two institutions, in the process strengthening the systemic inequality by which rich countries exert control. Tellingly, Manuel's letter did not refer to the highly controversial question of who will run the IMF.

This was either a glaring oversight or a reflection of political cowardice, because a revolt was then brewing – supported by some IMF/Bank executive directors – against a 'Europeans Only' sign on the IMF managing director's office door. The sign was obviously in place when Horst Köhler resigned to become president of Germany in early 2004. From Spain's outgoing conservative regime, Finance Minister Rodrigo Rato got the job, thanks to support from British Chancellor of the Exchequer Gordon Brown, chair of the other crucial IMF/Bank Board committee. Rato's austerity-oriented role in Spain, according to University of Barcelona professor Vincente Navarro, should have generated a massive protest from Africa and the rest of the Third World. Rato, Navarro put it, 'is of the ultra-right'. As minister he encouraged the compulsory study of religion in schools, with more hours spent on the subject than on mathematics, worked against progressive taxation policies, funded a Francoist foundation, and refused to condemn the former fascist dictatorship. He reduced public social expenditures dramatically to eliminate the public deficit, resulting in 'the most austere social budget of all the governments of the European Community' (Navarro 2004).

Notwithstanding four years of lobbying by Manuel, Mbeki and other Third World politicians for BWI reform, the succession of IMF leadership was less amenable to Africa in 2004 than in 2000. In the earlier struggle over the managing director's post, Africa's finance ministers adopted what *Time* described as a 'clever' strategy: nominating Stanley Fischer, the Zambian-born, South African-raised acting managing director of the IMF. But Fischer's 'fatal flaw' was his US citizenship, so Köhler got the job instead, in view of the unwritten rule that divides such spoils between the US and Europe (Hillenbrand 2000). There was no such clever attempt in 2004, and Africa's finance ministers expressed hope, instead, merely for a few more advisers to Rato and more resources for the two African executive directors (Seria 2004).

From such experience, Bush could reasonably expect Mbeki, other Third World elites and even the Europeans to accede to his appointment. At a press conference in March 2005 to announce Wolfowitz's qualifications, Bush ad libbed with typical depth:

> He helped manage a large organisation. The World Bank is a large organisation; the Pentagon is a large organisation – he's been involved in the management of that organisation. He's a skilled diplomat, worked at the State Department in high positions. He was Ambassador to Indonesia where he did a very good job representing our country (White House 2005).

Indeed, during his stint in Jakarta as Ronald Reagan's ambassador in the late 1980s Wolfowitz shored up Suharto's dictatorship. He regularly bragged about the strong role of US oil companies there, but never went on record against Suharto's myriad abuses, which in 1998 led to intense street riots and a forced resignation (Vallette 2005).

Wolfowitz demonstrated similar diplomatic skills when he justified choosing to invade Baghdad, instead of Pyongyang, which really *did* control weapons of mass destruction: 'The most important difference between North Korea and Iraq is that economically, we just had no choice in Iraq. The country swims on a sea of oil' (*Guardian*, 4 June 2003). Wolfowitz also told *Vanity Fair* that the rationale for the invasion of Iraq was one of political convenience, not honesty: 'For reasons that have a lot to do with the US government bureaucracy, we settled on the one issue that everyone could agree on which was weapons of mass destruction as the core reason' (Westphal 2005).

This was not his only lapse of judgement. US political commentator Arianna Huffington noted that during preparations for the war,

> Wolfowitz mocked Gen. Shinseki as 'wildly off the mark' for saying the US would need at least 200,000 troops on the ground in Iraq. 'It's hard to conceive,' Wolfowitz told Congress three weeks before the invasion, 'that it would take more forces to provide stability in post-Saddam Iraq than it would take to conduct the war itself and to secure the surrender of Saddam's security forces and his army. Hard to imagine.' That failure of imagination has led to the death and mutilation of thousands of Americans and tens of thousands of Iraqis (2005).

Wolfowitz stated that the US would not have to pay for Iraq's occupation and reconstruction, thanks to '$10 to $20 billion in frozen assets from the Gulf War', and '$15 billion to $20 billion a year in oil exports'. In fact, reported Huffington, the taxpayer tab for Iraq exceeded US$250 billion within three years (2005).

Colin Powell's former chief of staff in the State Department, Lawrence Wilkerson, explained how he and his boss helped to advance Wolfowitz's agenda: 'I participated in a hoax on the American people, the international community, and the United Nations Security Council' (PR Newswire 2006). In the journal *Foreign Affairs*, former senior CIA analyst Paul Pillar claims that the hoax required Bush, Cheney, Rumsfeld and Wolfowitz to simply ignore their own spy agency: 'If the entire body of official intelligence analysis on Iraq had a policy implication, it was to avoid war – or, if war was going to be launched, to prepare for a messy aftermath' (Pillar 2006).

In view of Wolfowitz's central role in the US–Iraq catastrophe, former IMF chief economist Kenneth Rogoff advised him 'to put himself in the hands of the professionals who run the World Bank's external relations department'. With an 'extreme makeover' at their hands 'he'll be a star on his own in no time' (World Bank Press Clips 2005). The *Los Angeles Times* (28 September 2005) confirmed that he took this counsel quickly: 'Wolfowitz's most valuable contribution to date may simply be his role as a cheerleader.' As Huffington observed, the 'Extreme Political Makeover' had 'Wolfie' moving 'from war hawk to ... Mother Teresa – all without having to make any kind of redemptive pit stop in political purgatory or having to apologise for being so wrong about Iraq' (Huffington 2005). *Washington Post* journalist Dana Milbank addressed the same theme:

> Being Wolfie means not having to say you're sorry ... Since taking the World Bank job six months ago he has found a second act. He has toured sub-Saharan Africa, danced with the natives in a poor Indian village, badgered the United States to make firmer foreign aid commitments and cuddled up to the likes of Bono and George Clooney (2005).

For balance, other people Wolfowitz was close to within his president's suite included Robin Cleveland, Kevin Kellums and Suzanne Rich Folsom, high-profile Republicans from the military-industrial complex and Bush regime. While an official in the White House Office of Management and Budget, Cleveland had been entangled in a Boeing/Pentagon scandal resulting in Air Force Secretary Jim Roche losing his job, and in nepotism charges. Ironically, a January 2006 brouhaha emerged over Wolfowitz's displacement of several Bank officials amid an anti-corruption drive led by his Republican cronies. Cleveland and Kellems were accused of receiving 'excessive pay and open-ended contracts' by Bank staff who filed a complaint to the Department of Institutional Integrity's whistleblower hotline, and the Bank Staff Association complained that standard hiring procedures were ignored for the Kellems and Folsom appointments (Harkavy 2006).

Still, after March 2005, Wolfowitz talked 'left' about unfair trade subsidies, meagre US aid, and corruption. The test to see if this was merely newly learned rhetoric, veiling the petro-military complex agenda, would be in August 2005 in Ecuador. There, the centrist government employed a Keynesian finance minister, Rafael Correa, who renewed Ecuador's long-standing US$75 million tax-avoidance complaint against Occidental Petroleum. Wolfowitz opposed not only this, but also a new law which would redirect 20 per cent of an oil fund towards social needs and 10 per cent for national development in science and technology, instead of putting the surplus into debt servicing to foreign lenders. (The oil price rise windfall from US$18/barrel when the fund was set up, to US$70/barrel in 2005, was being directed to creditors.) Correa aimed to rescind Occidental's control of the oilfields, as the original contract allowed under conditions of non-performance.

Just two days after Ecuador decided to cancel Occidental's contract, Wolfowitz shelved the country's loan assistance, claiming it was financially unstable. This created a governmental crisis, and President Alfredo Palacio persuaded Correa to resign, also firing the head of the national petroleum company. Its new head had previously assisted Occidental and favoured more privatisation (Anonymous 2005; Weitzman 2005). Wolfowitz had ridden to the rescue of the oil company before. In Colombia, he had helped Occidental to defend one of the most productive oil fields in the world, Cano Limon, whose pipeline runs through jungle adjacent to guerrilla-controlled territory. The US Defence Department established a Colombian 'Pipeline Brigade' with a US$150 million grant that Wolfowitz arranged when he was the second-ranking Pentagon official.

A seemingly opposite case arose a few months later in Africa. There, the controversial Chad–Cameroon oil pipeline's funds were redirected from poverty alleviation to the military. In spite of Wolfowitz's warnings, Chad's authoritarian president Edriss Déby and the country's parliament amended a 1999 petroleum revenue management law during December 2005. (According to Transparency International, Chad is tied with Bangladesh as the most corrupt country in the world.) The case was important because Bank co-financing of the US$3.7 billion pipeline was targeted by community, human rights and environmental groups in a long-running international campaign on grounds that it would simply empower the Chad regime without supporting health, education and rural development, or providing for future generations. In 1999, the Bank responded with the revenue legislation to mitigate these concerns. Hence Déby's 2005 amendment triggered Wolfowitz to withhold new funds, and halt disbursement already under way of US$124 million in International Development Association monies. A local group, the Chadian Association for the Promotion and Defence of Human Rights, endorsed the sanctions because 'new money would mainly be used for military purposes and increasing repression of the Chadian people. But we regret that the Bank did not listen to the warnings of civil society organisations earlier.'

Indeed, the Bretton Woods Project records that 'poverty, public health, human rights abuses and environmental problems continue to increase as the Exxon-Mobil-led consortium running the project expands drilling activities in both existing and new oilfields'. The Bank's International Advisory Group monitoring the project's implementation, reports 'that the oil consortium is taking land from poor subsistence farmers without ensuring... compensation payments' adequate to replace lost livelihoods. Local and military authorities 'extort money from villagers when they receive cash compensation from the oil companies' and the local human rights organisations defending people's rights are often threatened with death. The poorest people's health and crops are suffering the effects of pollution, and no studies are made on these matters (Bretton Woods Project 2006).

Perhaps surprisingly, in this case the World Bank acted against the interests of its allies among the repressive regimes and multinational corporations. Wolfowitz apparently required a dose of public credibility in Africa's highest-profile oil-related financing dispute. Cynics could add, however, that the clampdown also functioned to impose Bank discipline on an errant country, thus sending a tough lesson to others to obey Washington's orders.

The same conflict of objectives arose in Ethiopia and Kenya in late 2005. In the former, Africa's second most populous country and the world's seventh poorest, donors suspended US$375 million in budget support following severe state repression, including a massacre of opposition political protesters and mass arrests. Although this threatened to wipe out a third of the country's budget, and although President Meles Zenawi – an ex-Marxist ex-guerrilla – was a neoliberal favourite, the Bank complied with the wishes of the donors.

In Kenya, a corruption scandal debilitated Mwai Kibaki's government. By January 2006 Wolfowitz again suspended financing, in this case US$265 million, over half of which had been approved by the Bank's Board a few days earlier. The motive here was the need to save face, given that the main Kenyan corruption investigator, John Githongo, had fled to Oxford. As Michela Wrong reported, the Kenyan press began to 'drip-feed' Githongo's 36-page compilation of charges just as the Bank's loan was announced. His report accused key ministers, including finance, of establishing fraudulent contracts and misappropriating hundreds of millions of dollars in public funds. Worse, even though Githongo had informed Kibaki, no action was taken (Wrong 2006).

Former British ambassador Edward Clay accused Wolfowitz of 'blind and offensive blundering' for initially providing the loan to Nairobi, yet the UK's DfID Minister Hillary Benn granted Kibaki £55 million at the same time, essentially turning a blind eye to Nairobi's corruption. As Wrong explains, these paradoxes can be explained because Britain, 'having pushed for a doubling of aid and less conditionality for "progressive" African governments . . . is finding it embarrassingly difficult to disburse'. Moreover, Nairobi was a solid ally of the UK and US against Islam. Thus the temporary retraction of Bank funds earmarked for Kenya (loans resumed in April) reflected the embarrassment of the Bank's collaboration in corruption, just as Wolfowitz was shaking out the Bank staff of officials implicated in various other scandals.

By early 2006 at least one such scandal appeared as too challenging for Wolfowitz. The Bank's Multilateral Investment Guarantee Agency had made a US$13.3 million political risk insurance investment in the Democratic Republic of the Congo's Katanga province just before an October 2004 massacre. The Dikulushi Copper-Silver Mining Project, run by the Australian firm Anvil Mining, gained support in spite of the country's intense social unrest. Indeed, DRC armed forces killed 100 people during the suppression of a rebellion by the Mayi-Mayi militia in Kilwa. The Australian Broadcasting Corporation reported that Dikulushi trucks moved troops to the massacre's site and then moved corpses out. Although company headquarters denied knowledge of an Anvil role in the massacre, critics in the DRC and watchdog agencies assumed that a subsequent Bank investigation would reveal corporate connivance. With Wolfowitz still reluctant to disclose the facts five months after receiving the document, Nikki Reisch of the Bank Information Centre remarked: 'Stalling the release of the report only gives the impression that the Bank Group has something to hide. It seems strange that an audit of such a high-profile and controversial project would be kept secret' (Meckay 2006).

Meanwhile in Iraq, which Wolfowitz knew far better, resistance to Bank and IMF dictates began shortly after he took office. The Bank agreed to co-administer the International Reconstruction Fund Facility for Iraq and World Bank Iraq Trust Fund in 2003, thus coordinating much international aid funding. The Pentagon and State Department, meanwhile, were short-changing the reconstruction programme notwithstanding the immense damage done by US/UK bombing (with laser range finders supplied by South Africa), pulling back financing for hundreds of promised projects. This gave the Bank the opportunity, in July 2005, to prepare paperwork for US$500 million in International Development Association loans, to begin in November.

But strings were attached. For example, the Bank and IMF argued to the new government in late 2004 that the world's second-largest oil reserves be exploited by multinational companies through a very unusual arrangement: production-sharing agreements amounting to a privatisation process. According to the international NGOs producing the report *Crude Designs*, Iraq would suffer more than US$74 billion in losses for 40 years, because Baghdad would be prevented from controlling the country's oil sector, responsible for 90 per cent of Iraq's GDP.

Other IMF conditionalities began biting in December 2005, as a US$685 million stand-by credit was advanced to Baghdad on four conditions: cutting public subsidies, especially on fuel (the cheapest in the world); restructuring Iraq's external debt; strengthening administrative capacity, including statistical reporting; and restructuring Iraq's two state-owned banks. Riots ensued when the Baghdad government raised petrol and diesel prices by up to 200 per cent, and the oil minister, Ibrahim Bahr al-Uloum, resigned in protest. Five Iraqi trade unions criticised IMF and World Bank policies and demanded:

- complete Iraqi sovereignty over its petroleum and natural resources;
- increased transparency and additional Iraqi representation in IFI decision-making structures;
- cancellation of the former regime's debt and an end to conditionality;
- rejection of the privatisation of publicly owned entities; and
- rejection of petroleum product price increases.

There are many other cases of Bank corruption that Wolfowitz has avoided and will avoid, according to Washington watchdog NGOs Food and Water Watch, 50 Years is Enough!, Jubilee USA Network and the Development Group for Alternative Policy. For instance, Bank-financed Lesotho Highlands Water Project dams, which supply Johannesburg, were rife with bribery by a dozen multinational corporations. Although the Maseru government prosecuted several of the firms, 'foot-dragging on the part of the World Bank to debar the convicted companies has softened the impact of this high-profile case'. In particular, the German firm Lahmeyer International was indicted in 2001 and convicted two years later, but, by April 2006, the Bank had taken no action. In Ghana and Peru, the Bank's International Finance Corporation (IFC) financed

Newmont Mining in spite of citizens' protests over corruption and environmental destruction. In Uganda, AES Corporation was forced to pull out of a major World Bank project, the Bujagali dam, 'after corruption associated with one of its subcontractors was found. The Ugandan government and the US Justice Department investigated the deal. The IFC has invested $800 million in AES projects since 1995.' The Bank also made US$15 million in investments in Shell oil operations in the Niger Delta, in spite of the firm's role in 'human rights abuses, including its collusion with the Nigerian authorities for the mass murder of community people impoverished as a result of the devastation of their natural environment and the destruction of community sources of livelihood by Shell' (www.foodandwaterwatch.org, accessed on 15 June 2006). Major firms that the Bank has supported in recent decades include Exxon-Mobil, Enron and others with histories of corruption and destruction, which Wolfowitz has made no effort to prosecute.

What can we conclude about the state of international development finance under the leadership of Wolfowitz, Rato and the like? In spite of rhetoric about 'good governance' under neo-conservative rule, genuine democratisation has simply not happened, as Manuel conceded during a Development Committee press conference in April 2005: 'Both Rodrigo here and Paul Wolfowitz are wonderful individuals, perfectly capable. But unfortunately, the process hasn't helped. It's not their fault. It is a governance issue' (World Bank 2005b). At the September 2005 annual meetings, Manuel blithely remarked that the undemocratic system was impervious to change: 'Part of the difficulty in the present milieu is that it is more comfortable for too many countries to live with what we have, because there's a comfort zone around this, and that, I think, is a challenge' (World Bank and IMF 2005). If the elites are not interested in *fixing* the system, the challenge posed to civil society is whether the financial agencies should be *nixed*. That, and how to do it.

Civil, civilised and uncivil society reactions

In the face of systemic elite failure, two responses from civil society forces have emerged: accommodation and activism. As South African activist

Virginia Setshedi – one of roughly 200 000 protesters in Washington on 24 September 2005 demanding US withdrawal from Iraq – put it: 'It is not just about war. It is about how many people die around the world because of unfair policies and actions – a large part of which are economic. So it is not just the military injustice that we are facing. We need to connect the dots together.' Anti-war organisers attacked BWI policies for placing 'corporate profits ahead of basic human needs worldwide. We will speak out against the corporate theft of Iraq's resources and the decimation of the Iraqi economy through privatisation and "free trade"' (Shirin 2005).[8] According to Reuters, protesters grieved for 'the rights of the poor in Louisiana displaced by Hurricane Katrina, the poor in Iraq who are being hurt by war and those that protesters say are forced into poverty by IMF policies' (Lambert 2005). A mock wedding was held outside the Bank on 22 September by the Mobilisation for Global Justice (MGJ), uniting the Pentagon with the Bank under Wolfowitz's leadership.

Two high-profile leaders of, respectively, the US global justice network 50 Years is Enough! and the anti-war movement, Njoki Njoroge Njehu and Leslie Cagan, wrote that the Bank's new president 'makes the link between US military and economic policy clear':

> It will do what is necessary to control whatever resources it considers essential, and it will use the available political, military, and economic tools to ensure that its dominance is never threatened, and in fact extended however possible ... The culmination of any intervention by the United States and its allies ... whether economic or military, is the re-structuring of their economies to serve foreign and corporate interests. Sometimes that means preserving unsavoury regimes; occasionally it means overthrowing them. Most often it requires less violent means – the enforcement of economic contracts by international institutions like the World Bank (Njehu and Cagan 2005).

Hundreds of activists from both Jubilee South Africa and the Anti-Privatisation Forum protesting Wolfowitz's mid-2005 visit to Johannesburg seemed to agree. So did the Congress of South African Trade Unions (COSATU). Although formally allied to the ruling African National Congress – whose head, Mbeki, had invited Wolfowitz – COSATU voiced this condemnation:

> Mr Wolfowitz embodies all the worst features of the international financial institutions ... Like them, he has been dedicated to entrenching the power of big business and multinational corporations, at the expense of the workers and the poor ... Cosatu endorses the view of Joseph Stiglitz, former chief economist of the World Bank, that Wolfowitz's appointment is 'an act of provocation' that could 'bring street protests and violence across the developing world' (COSATU 2005).

But we must also consider World Bank resilience, as reflected in September 2005 both in Wolfowitz's successful meetings with civil(ised) society organisations inside the Bank, and in the release of the *World Development Report 2006: Equity and Development*, whose cover notably borrowed the Leftist Mexican muralist Diego Rivera's incendiary 'Dream of a Sunday afternoon in Alameda Park' (1947–48). Rivera once worked for the Rockefellers, who destroyed his great Rockefeller Center mural because he would not remove Lenin's face. We could assess the Mexican National Museum's licensing of the artwork to the World Bank as either a blasphemous mistake or a logical result of Bank austerity policies leading to Mexican state fiscal shrinkage, especially in the arts, requiring the museum to shill its art collection even to Wolfowitz's World Bank. The use of the mural on the Bank's flagship report may also be a signal about how badly the institution requires legitimacy, given its new president's record. The 2006 *Report* may be covering the Banks' slipping intellectual credentials too. According to Sanjay Reddy, it

> often relies on questionable indicators and analytical tools. For example, more secure property rights, as judged by foreign

investors, are used as a proxy for the 'quality of institutions' . . . Its intellectual basis is weak, its contents are not adequately complete and its prescriptions are often either questionable or of limited practical value (2005).

As for the co-option of 'civilised society', a transcript of the meeting with Civicus and Wolfowitz, just after the mock wedding in Washington's streets, is indicative. The meeting's chair, Civicus Board President Aruna Rao, opened the meeting by joking to Wolfowitz: 'We hope that despite the recent marriage you will be open to a liaison with civil society organisations.' She closed with praise for Wolfowitz's 'openness to dialogue with civil society organisations on a range of issues. So I will go back to how I started. I think this liaison, despite the marriage, is something that can continue.' An alternative approach for *un*civil society groups, in contrast, is to acknowledge frankly the marriage of neoliberalism and militarism – and then to nix any further liaisons.[9]

Starting from scratch

What, then, is to be done about the BWIs: fix them or nix them? The debate continues amongst the intelligentsia and activists. From a vantagepoint in the chief economist's office, however, David Ellerman finally threw up his hands and declared them 'now almost entirely motivated by big power politics and their own internal organisational imperatives . . . Intellectual and political energies spent trying to "reform" these agencies are largely a waste of time and a misdirection of energies' (2004). Even Stiglitz contemplates abolishing the IMF (though he is quiet about the Bank), citing its abuse of power and dogmatic ideology: 'Is the institution so resistant to learning to change, to becoming a more democratic institution, that maybe it is time to think about creating some new institutions that really reflect today's reality, today's greater sense of democracy?' (*Financial Times*, 21 August 2002).[10]

Ready to answer in the affirmative was Cape Town's Anglican Archbishop Njongonkulu Ndungane:

[If] we must release ourselves from debt peonage – by demanding the repudiation and cancellation of debt – we will campaign to that end. And if the World Bank and IMF continue to stand in the way of social progress, movements like Jubilee South Africa will have no regrets about calling for their abolition (2003: 31).

According to Walden Bello, director of Focus on the Global South in Bangkok and a key strategist in the global justice movement, the Bank's 'own evaluation of its projects shows an outstanding 55–60 per cent failure rate'. It is even higher – ranging from 65 to 70 per cent – in the poorest countries, supposedly the targets of the Bank's 'anti-poverty approach'. Bello argues that 'it would be better to abolish an institution that has made a big business out of "ending poverty"' than to expect extraordinarily well-paid technocrats 'to do the impossible – designing anti-poverty programmes for folks from another planet'. Local, national and regional institutions would be 'better equipped to attack the causes of poverty' (Bello 2000a).

By the early 2000s three universal reasons emerged for nixing the Bretton Woods twins:

- virtually all core value reforms in key areas of eco-socio-economic advocacy have been explored, and the profound limitations unveiled;
- restoring national state sovereignty, mainly through lifting IMF/Bank pressure, is of greater urgency than there is time to convince tens of thousands of Washington economists to reverse the policy advice defining their worldview since graduate school; and
- the hard-currency component of IMF and Bank lending should not be required once appropriate conditions are achieved.

This last argument deserves justification, for if local, national and regional development finance is appropriate, then the technical (not political, moral, environmental) reasons to have an IMF and Bank evaporate. Such was the viewpoint of the ANC in its 1994 *Reconstruction and Development Programme (RDP)*, in a sentence won only after much left-wing lobbying:

'The *RDP* must use foreign debt financing only for those elements of the programme that can potentially increase our capacity for earning foreign exchange' (African National Congress 1994). (The ANC broke more than one such promise, but the principle here merits careful reflection.)

The motivation for rejecting hard-currency loans for 'development' are the fear of the rising cost of repayment on foreign debt, once the currency declines, and the record of hard-currency utilisation in most African economies. Foreign currency inflows via new Bank or IMF loans typically do *not* finance basic needs projects (with their low import intensity) but instead are used to repay illegitimate foreign debt, import luxury goods for the rich, and replace local workers with inappropriate, job-killing, dependency-inducing, capital-intensive technology from abroad. In sum, why take a US dollar-denominated loan for – to take an example – building and staffing a small rural school that has virtually no foreign input costs?

If most basic-needs development can be drawn from local resources, and if the hard currency needed to import petroleum or other vital inputs can be readily supplied by export credit agencies (competing against each other, in contrast to centralised financial power and coordination in Washington), the basic rationales for the World Bank fall away. To be sure, financing local development by issuing local securities – or even 'printing money' – certainly adds a risk of generating inflation, but that risk is smaller than the problems of repaying hard-currency loans for the same projects, given the need for greater export orientation and the rising cost of repayment once a local currency depreciates against hard currencies. And instead of relying upon the IMF to maintain a positive balance of payments when fickle international financial inflows dry up or run away frightened, Third World countries that climb out (in future) from under the heel of the IMF and Bank could realistically impose exchange controls and tax unnecessary imports. They would also have more freedom to default on illegitimate debt.

Argentina's experience is telling. In 2002, when a US$140 billion debt payment moratorium was imposed, the government ran out of money to repay. This was ultimately resolved in 2004 when the foreign lenders were granted as little as 30 per cent of the original debt. The IMF's standard power of blacklisting did not work, because Argentina's trade surplus permitted easy access to trade finance. In 2005, Argentina announced it would repay IMF commitments early so as not to face subsequent pressure and neoliberal conditionalities. Brazil and Indonesia did the same. Several other countries with foreign currency reserves – Russia, Thailand and Bolivia – were expected to follow in 2006, leaving some observers wondering if the IMF would have any relevance for emerging market economies, and IMF staff worried that financial models based on interest drawn from such economies would now break down, leaving their institution in the red (Engler 2006).

In sum, the South ultimately should not need a dollar-denominated IMF and Bank for development. Indeed, it is probable that only when Washington's institutional power fades that local-level, national and perhaps regional development finance officials can re-acquire the ability they once enjoyed, a few decades ago, to tame their own financial markets. (Such 'financial repression' entailed state interest rate subsidies, directed credit, prescribed asset requirements on institutional investors, community reinvestment mandates and other means of socialising financial capital.)

Thus the case for nixing (not fixing) the Bank and IMF reflects their:

- inappropriateness as institutions for basic-needs development finance;
- role as global neoliberalism's 'brains' *and* policemen;
- reliance upon unreformed neoliberal logic, ranging from macroeconomics to micro-development policy;
- responsibility for even project-level conditionality;
- support for commodification of even the most vital public services (as well as of air, in the case of carbon trading); and
- severe legitimacy crises, as reflected in periodic IMF riots and other activism.

Popular campaigning has become quite surgical:

- Several international lobbies aim to force the WB/IMF and WTO to stop commodifying water, health, education and

other services, and to remove the institutions from destructive roles in mega-projects, such as large dams or energy financing (they achieved partial success, as the US Congress now prohibits health and education user-fee requirements on Bank/IMF financing).
- Global justice movement components in particular Third World cities, towns and villages directly confront BWI-imposed neoliberalism or specific Bank projects.
- Jubilee and other anti-debt movements continue fighting for debt repudiation and reparations (including for the vast ecological debt that the North owes the South).

The most intriguing tactic is the World Bank Bonds Boycott.[11] US groups such as the Center for Economic Justice and Global Exchange continue working with Jubilee South Africa and Brazil's Movement of the Landless, among others, to ask of their Northern allies: is it ethical for socially conscious people to invest in the World Bank by buying its bonds (responsible for 80 per cent of the Bank's resources), hence drawing out dividends representing the fruits of enormous suffering? The Boycott impressed a London *Evening Standard* financial markets commentator during the IMF/Bank spring 2002 meetings: 'The growing sophistication of radical activists increases the likelihood that once-accepted fixed-income investment practices can no longer be taken as off-limits from the threat of moral suasion' (*Evening Standard*, 17 April 2002).

In the short term, the Boycott campaign sends a clear signal to the Bank: end anti-social, environmentally destructive activities, and cancel the debt. When enough investors endorse the campaign, the Bank will suffer a declining bond rating, making it fiduciarily irresponsible to invest. This could lay the basis for a 'run on the Bank', defunding the institution entirely. This will happen initially through a collapsed bond market and then through Northern taxpayer revolt, as the campaign gathers momentum and publicity.

The World Bank Bonds Boycott is only one of a variety of campaigns that could become more explicitly anti-capitalist, or that could rest at a comfortable populist, moral level. The anti-capitalist component of the global justice movements understands that the World Bank and IMF may have changed their rhetoric but not their structural adjustment programmes. The rhetoric of 'pro-poor' development does not conceal that the BWIs maintain their commitment to accumulation by appropriation and dispossession. The institutions' legitimacy is the only target that Third World social movements can aim at. They have done so in recent years with an increasingly militant perspective that worries *not* about the World Bank's 'failure to consult' or 'lack of transparency' or 'undemocratic governance' – all easy populist critiques. Rather, leading activists' attention to the Washington Consensus ideology is directed to the core content: *commodification*, whether in relation to water, electricity, housing, land, health services, education, basic income grant support or other social services, ideally all at once and in cross-sectoral combinations.

Although this is not the place to elaborate one, a feasible alternative strategy can be found in the efforts of grassroots movements to decommodify the goods and services which the World Bank and IMF increasingly put out of reach. If the Bonds Boycott and subsequent taxpayer revolts against the institutions can galvanise a popular 'run on the Bank' from the North, and if ongoing IMF Riots and occasional defaults by Third World governments continue, then talk of reforming the operations of the Bank and IMF, especially during the Wolfowitz presidency, will become just as irrelevant as the reforms have been in practice.

Postscript (April 2007)
It turns out that Wolfowitz is not a 'wonderful individual, perfectly capable', as South Africa's Finance Minister Trevor Manuel supposed. In 2007, his job looked highly vulnerable as a strange scandal/ emerged: he paid his Bank-employed girlfriend more than Secretary of State Condoleezza Rice, to work for Rice. If he in the process crippled the Bank's credibility, that's a shame, for bigger questions badly need asking.

Notes

1. Various aspects of the arguments below are expanded upon in Bond (2000b, 2001a, 2004, 2005, 2006a, 2006b).
2. For more background to contemporary international financial power relations, see Armijo (2001); Lee (2002); Gowan (1999); and Soederberg (2006).
3. Part of the problem was the choice of FfD managers. Civil society critics argued that the FfD Conference was tainted from the outset, in 2000, given that Mexico's ex-president Ernesto Zedillo managed the process. The neoliberal economist's five-year term was notable for repression, failed economic crisis management and the end of the 85-year rule by his corrupt Party for the Institutionalisation of the Revolution. Controversially, Zedillo appointed as his main adviser (and official document author) John Williamson of the Institute for International Finance, a Washington think tank primarily funded by the world's largest commercial banks. Williamson is considered to be one of the establishment's most vigorous neoliberal ideologues, taking credit, indeed, for the term 'Washington Consensus'. South African Finance Minister Trevor Manuel and former IMF Managing Director Michel Camdessus were the UN Secretary-General's special representatives.
4. This possibility, stated at the outset by civil society critics, was only hinted at in Monterrey's official information source: the International Monetary Fund and International Development Association (2001). The Bank, paradoxically, blamed failure upon 'political pressure' to cut debt further as the key reason repayments were still not 'sustainable'.
5. A reformed IMF International Monetary and Financial Committee opens the door for greater Third World inputs, but this has not changed power relations.
6. Weak governance reform proposals can be found in Pincus and Winters (2002a); UNDP (2002); United Nations University – World Institute for Development Economics Research (2002); Varma (2002); and Griffith-Jones (2002).
7. For more on the background and South African politics associated with the Commission (headed by local Water Minister Kader Asmal), see Bond (2002c: Chapters 3 and 7).
8. The links continued to be made, into even the World Bank's host city, according to a statement issued by the Mobilisation for Global Justice (2005):

> These policies extend even into the US: as residents of Washington DC, we are the reluctant hosts of the World Bank, the IMF, and other institutions of empire. With our only public hospital closed, a deteriorating public school system, and a private baseball stadium being built with public funds, we see that the same policies of private gain at public expense imposed on borrowing countries by the World Bank and IMF are also at work in Washington. The World Bank and IMF make billions a year in profits, use services provided by the city, and sit on valuable property downtown, yet they pay no property taxes or corporate revenue taxes.

> This is an injustice in a city with a majority low-income population and is a cruel hypocrisy on the part of the institutions, which state 'poverty reduction' and 'economic development' as part of their goals.

9. http://www.imf.org/external/np/tr/2005/tr050922a.htm.
10. Stiglitz was interviewed by Doug Henwood on WBAI radio in New York.
11. http://www.worldbankboycott.org. Organisations that endorsed the World Bank Bonds Boycott included major religious orders, the most important social responsibility funds (including Calvert Group), universities (including an Oxford college), US cities (including San Francisco), and major trade union pension/investment funds. During late 2003, the American teachers' – and the world's largest pension fund – TIAA-CREF, sold its World Bank bonds as campaigners made it a special target.

Contributors

MARK BEESON is a senior lecturer in the Department of Politics at the University of York, England. He was editor of *Reconfiguring East Asia: Regional Institutions and Organisations after the Crisis* (ed., 2002); and his latest book is *Regionalism and Globalization in East Asia: Politics, Security and Economic Development* (2007).

MARK T. BERGER of the University of New South Wales in Sydney is visiting professor in the Department of Defense Analysis at the Naval Postgraduate School (Monterey, California). He is the author of *The Battle for Asia: From Decolonization to Globalization* (2004), when he also guest-edited the twenty-fifth anniversary edition of *Third World Quarterly*. He is editor of *From Nation-Building to State-Building* (2007); and co-author of *Rethinking the Third World: International Development and World Politics* (with Heloise Weber, 2007).

HENRY BERNSTEIN is professor of Development Studies at the University of London. He has long-standing research interests in social theory and agrarian political economy, and has done studies of peasant farming in Tanzania in the 1970s and of the maize industry and its politics in South Africa in the 1990s. He was co-editor of the *Journal of Peasant Studies* (with T.J. Byres), and is founding co-editor of the *Journal of Agrarian Change*. Recent publications include 'Rural land and land conflicts in sub-Saharan Africa' in *Reclaiming the Land: The Resurgence of Rural Movements in Africa, Asia and Latin America* (eds. Sam Moyo and Paris Yeros, 2005), and 'Development Studies and the Marxists' in *A Radical History of Development Studies: Individuals, Institutions and Ideologies* (ed. Uma Kothari, 2005).

PATRICK BOND is professor of Development Studies and director of the University of KwaZulu-Natal's Centre for Civil Society, in Durban, South Africa. His most recent book is *Looting Africa: The Economics of Exploitation* (2006). He has also published *Elite Transition: From*

Apartheid to Neo-Liberalism in South Africa (2005 [2000]); *Talk Left, Walk Right: South Africa's Frustrated Global Reforms* (2006 [2004]); *Zimbabwe's Plunge: Exhausted Nationalism, Neoliberalism and the Search for Social Justice* (with Masimba Manyanya, 2003); and *Uneven Zimbabwe: A Study of Finance, Development and Underdevelopment* (2000).

BEN FINE is professor of Economics in the School of Oriental and African Studies at the University of London. His books include *The World of Consumption: The Material and Cultural Revisited* (2002); *Social Capital versus Social Theory: Political Economy and Social Science at the Turn of the Millennium* (2001); and *South Africa's Political Economy: From Minerals-Energy Complex to Industrialisation* (with Zavareh Rustomjee, 1996). In 2001 he co-edited *Neither Washington Nor Post-Washington Consensus: Challenging Development Policy in the Twenty-first Century* (with Costas Lapavitsas and Jonathan Pincus); and in 2006 he co-edited *The New Development Economics: After the Washington Consensus* (with K.S. Jomo).

GRAHAM HARRISON teaches International Politics and is co-director of the Political Economy Research Centre at the University of Sheffield, England. He has published *The World Bank and Africa: The Construction of Governance States* (2004); *Global Encounters: International Political Economy, Development and Globalization* (2004); and *Issues in the Contemporary Politics of Sub-Saharan Africa: The Dynamics of Struggle and Resistance* (2002). He is currently researching local government reform in Tanzania. He is an editor of *New Political Economy*; *Review of African Political Economy*; and *African Review*.

SCOTT MACWILLIAM teaches Development Studies at the Crawford School of Economics and Government, Australian National University, in Canberra. He co-authored *Indigenous Capital in Kenya: The 'Indian' Dimension of Debate* (with Michael Cowen, 1996), and has published widely on poverty and governance in Fiji, including in the *Journal of Pacific Studies* (2001); and *Pacific Economic Bulletin* (2002).

Contributors

DAVID MOORE teachers in the Economic History and Development Studies Programme at the University of KwaZulu-Natal in Durban, South Africa. In 1995 he co-edited *Debating Development Discourse: Institutional and Popular Perspectives* (with Gerald Schmitz). Since then he has published on Zimbabwe, the Democratic Republic of the Congo and development theory in journals such as *Journal of Contemporary African Studies; Review of African Political Economy; Third World Quarterly; Rethinking Marxism; African Studies;* and *Historical Materialism.*

RICHARD PITHOUSE is working on his doctorate in the Philosophy Department at the University of KwaZulu-Natal in Durban, South Africa, after having been a research fellow at the Centre for Civil Society at the same university. Before joining the Centre he taught Philosophy at the University of Durban-Westville, South Africa, for eight years and Politics and Economics at The Workers' College, also in Durban. Among many publications, he has edited *Asinamali: University Struggles in Post-Apartheid South Africa* (2006).

SUSANNE SCHECH is associate professor of Geography and heads the Development Studies Programme at Flinders University in Adelaide, Australia. She is co-author of *Culture and Development: A Critical Introduction* (with Jane Haggis, 2000); and co-editor of *Development: A Cultural Studies Reader* (with Jane Haggis, 2002). She has written on 'whiteness' and migration to Australia, the Internet and development, and the cross-cultural aspects of feminism and development, in journals including *Society and Space; Australian Feminist Studies; Canadian Journal of Development Studies;* and the *Journal of International Development.*

SUSANNE SOEDERBERG holds a Canada research chair in Global Political Economy and is associate professor in the Department of Development Studies at Queen's University, Canada. She is the author of *The Politics of the New International Financial Architecture: Reimposing Neoliberal Domination in the Global South* (2004); and *Global Governance in*

Question: Empire, Class, and the New Common Sense in Managing North-South Relations (2006). She is currently working on *The Global Reproduction of American Corporate Power: Governance, Activism, and Imperialism.*

MARCUS TAYLOR is assistant professor in the Department of Development Studies at Queen's University, Canada. He has written *From Pinochet to the Third Way: Neoliberalism and Social Transformation in Chile* (2006). He has researched in the areas of development studies and Latin American studies, publishing recently in *Third World Quarterly*; *Latin American Perspectives*; *Historical Materialism*; and *Global Social Policy*.

SANJUGTA VAS DEV is a doctoral candidate in the Department of Politics and International Studies at the Flinders University of South Australia, for which she is comparing the role of non-governmental organisations engaged in advocacy for asylum seekers in Australia and Malaysia. Sanjugta has consulted with the Asian Development Bank on gender and youth budgeting in the Pacific and has been involved in delivering training courses on gender analysis and gender mainstreaming in Indonesia. She has published 'The reluctant host: The socio-cultural impact of refugees on developing communities', in *Mots Pluriels* (2002).

ROBERT WADE is professor of Political Economy and Development at the Development Studies Institute, London School of Economics. He has authored *Irrigation and Politics in South Korea* (1982); *Village Republics: The Economic Conditions of Collective Action in India* (1994 [1988]); *Governing the Market: Economic Theory and the Role of Government in East Asia's Industrialization* (2003 [1990]), which won the American Political Science Association's Best Book in Political Economy Award; and *The Gift of Capital* (1999). More recently, he has published 'Escaping the squeeze: Lessons from East Asia on how middle-income countries can grow faster' in *For John Kenneth Galbraith and the Future of Economics* (ed., Blandine Laperche, 2005).

Contributors

THOMAS WANNER is a lecturer in the School of Geography, Population and Environmental Management and the Centre for Development Studies at Flinders University in Adelaide, Australia. He specialises in sustainable development issues in international political economy, and gender and ecology in developing countries.

DAVID WILLIAMS lectures at the Centre for International Politics at City University, in London. Previously he lectured for a number of years in the Department of Politics and International Relations at the University of Oxford. His research focuses on the World Bank, and the international relations of developing countries, particularly sub-Saharan Africa. He has published in journals such as *Review of International Studies*; *Africa*; *Political Studies*; and *World Development*. His book on the World Bank and sovereignty has just been completed.

TOM YOUNG teaches politics at the School of Oriental and African Studies at the University of London. He has edited *Readings in African Politics: A Critical and Theoretical Sourcebook for African Politics* (2003); and has co-authored *Confronting Leviathan: Mozambique since Independence* (with Marion Hall, 1997).

Select Bibliography

Abdullah, I. and P. Muana. 1998. 'The Revolutionary United Front of Sierra Leone: A revolt of the lumpenproletariat', in C. Clapham (ed.), *African Guerrillas*. Oxford: James Currey, 172–93.

Abrahamsen, R. 1997. 'The victory of popular forces or passive revolution? A neo-Gramscian perspective on democratisation', *Journal of Modern African Studies* 35 (1): 129–52.

———. 2000. *Disciplining Democracy: Development Discourse and Good Government in Africa*. London: Zed Books.

Achebe, C. 1958. *Things Fall Apart*. London: Heinemann.

———. 1969. *A Man of the People*. London: Heinemann.

———. 1987. *Anthills of the Savannah*. London: Heinemann.

Adam, C. and J. Gunning. 2002. 'Redesigning the aid contract: Donors' use of performance indicators in Uganda', *World Development* 30 (12): 2045–56.

Adams, S. 2001. *Comrade Minister*. New York: Nova Science Publishers.

Africa Action. 2003. 'Africa's debt: Fueling the fire of AIDS'. Washington, DC, http://www.africaaction.org/action/debt2003.pdf. Accessed 20 April 2006.

African National Congress. 1994. *Reconstruction and Development Programme*. Johannesburg: Umanyano Publications.

Agarwala, R. and V. Thomas. 1995. *Sustaining Rapid Growth in East Asia and the Pacific*. Washington, DC: World Bank.

Aguiton, C. 2003. *The World Belongs to Us!* London: Verso.

Akerlof, G. 1984. *An Economic Theorist's Book of Tales*. Cambridge: Cambridge University Press.

Albo, G. 1997. 'A world market of opportunities? Capitalist obstacles and Left economic policy', in L. Panitch (ed.), *Socialist Register 1997: Ruthless Criticism of All That Exists*. London: The Merlin Press, 119–32.

Alcock, P. 1997. *Understanding Poverty*. London: Macmillan.

Alexander, N. 2002. *An Ordinary Country: Issues in the Transition from Apartheid to Democracy in South Africa*. Pietermaritzburg: University of Natal Press.

Alidou, O., G. Caffentzis and S. Federici (eds.). 2001. *A Thousand Flowers: Social Struggles against Structural Adjustment in African Universities*. Trenton, NJ: African World Press.

Altvater, E. 2001. 'The growth obsession', in L. Panitch and C. Leys (eds.), *Socialist Register 2002: A World of Contradictions*. London: The Merlin Press, 73–92.

Altvater, E. and B. Mahnkopf. 1997. 'The world market unbound', *Review of International Political Economy* 4 (3): 449–50.

Alves, J. 1999. 'Privatizing the state enterprise sector', in B. Ferraz and B. Munslow (eds.), *Sustainable Development in Mozambique*. Oxford and Trenton, NJ: Ministry for the Coordination of Environmental Action in association with James Currey and Africa World Press, 58–63.

Amin, S. 1985. *Delinking: Towards a Polycentric World*. London: Zed Books.

Amin, S. and F. Houtart (eds.). 2003. *The Globalisation of Resistance: The State of the Struggles*. London: Zed Books.

Amsden, A. 1989. *Asia's Next Giant: South Korea and Late Industrialization*. New York: Oxford University Press.

———. 1990. 'Third World industrialization: "Global Fordism" or a new model?', *New Left Review* 1 (182): 5–32.

———. 1994. 'Why isn't the whole world experimenting with the East Asian model to develop? A comment on the World Bank *East Asian Miracle* report', *World Development* 22 (4): 627–33.

Anand, A., A. Escobar, J. Sen and P. Waterman (eds.). 2003. *Are Other Worlds Possible? The Past, Present, and Futures of the World Social Forum*. New Delhi: Viveka.

Anderson, D. and V. Broch-Due (eds.). 1999. *The Poor are not Us: Poverty and Pastoralism in Eastern Africa*. Oxford, Nairobi and Athens, Ohio: James Currey, East African Educational Publishers and Ohio University Press.

Anderson, P. 1974. *Lineages of the Absolute State*. London: Verso.

———. 2002. 'Force and consent', *New Left Review* 2 (17): 5–30.

Andrews, D. and T. Willet. 1997. 'Financial interdependence and the state: International monetary relations at century's end', *International Organization* 51 (3): 479–511.

Anonymous. 2001. 'Angolan civil society debates way forward', *World Bank Watch SA? SA Watch WB!* (December).

Anonymous. 2005. 'Wolfowitz at the World Bank: A new leaf?', *Mrzine*, 25 August, http://mrzine.monthlyreview.org/anonymous25085.html. Accessed 3 July 2006.

Apollis, J. 2002. 'The political significance of August 31', *Khanya* 2.

Armijo, L. 2001. 'The political geography of financial reform: Who wants what and why?', *Global Governance* 7 (4): 379–96.

Arnold, B. and F. Kay. 1995. 'Social capital, violations of trust and the vulnerability of isolates: The social organization of law practice and professional self-regulation', *International Journal of the Sociology of Law* 23 (4): 321–46.

Aronson, D. 1998. 'Mobutu Redux?', *Dissent* (Spring): 20–24.

Arrighi, G. 1991. 'World income inequalities and the future of socialism', *New Left Review* 1 (189): 39–66.

———. 2002. 'The African crisis: World systemic and regional aspects', *New Left Review* 2 (15): 5–36.

Arrighi, G. and B.J. Silver. 2001. 'Capitalism and world (dis)order', *Review of International Studies* 27 (5): 257–79.

Ascher, W. 1983. 'New development approaches and the adaptability of international agencies: The case of the World Bank', *International Organization* 37 (Summer): 415–39.

Select Bibliography

Asia Monitor Resource Centre. 1997. *Everyone's State? Redefining an 'Effective State' in East Asia*. Hong Kong: Asia Monitor Resource Centre.

Asian Development Bank. 2001. *Fighting Poverty in Asia and the Pacific: The Poverty Reduction Strategy*. Manila: Asian Development Bank.

Audi, R. 1998. 'A liberal theory of civic virtue', *Social Philosophy and Policy* 15 (1): 149–70.

Australian Broadcasting Corporation. 1998. 'Report on Religion', 12 August.

Ayres, R. 1983. *Banking on the Poor: The World Bank and World Poverty*. Cambridge, MS: MIT Press.

Badiane, O., D. Ghura, L. Goreuz and P. Masson. 2002. 'Cotton sector strategies in West and Central Africa'. Policy Research Working Paper No. 2867. Washington, DC: World Bank, July.

Balassa, B. 1981. *The Newly Industrializing Countries in the World Economy*. New York: Pergamon Press.

———. 1988. 'The lessons of East Asian development: An overview', *Economic Development and Cultural Change* 36 (3) (Supplement): 273–90.

Barnett, T. 1981. 'Evaluating the Gezira Scheme: Black box or Pandora's Box?', in J. Heyer, P. Roberts and G. Williams (eds.), *Rural Development in Tropical Africa*. London: Macmillan, 306–24.

Baron, J. and M. Hannan. 1994. 'The impact of economics on contemporary sociology', in R. Swedberg (ed.), *Economic Sociology*. Cheltenham: Edward Elgar, 1–26.

Barry, T. 2004. 'Pax Americana: What's the alternative?', *The Brussels Tribunal*, 14–17 April, http://www.brusselstribunal.org. Accessed 14 May 2006.

Baskin, M. 2003. 'Review article: Post-conflict administration and reconstruction', *International Affairs* 79 (1): 161–70.

Bates, R. 1981. *Markets and States in Africa*. Berkeley: University of California Press.

Battersby, J. 2003. 'G3 heads the assault on Old World Order', *Sunday Independent*, 21 September.

Bayart, J-F. 1993 [1989]. *The State in Africa: The Politics of the Belly*. London and New York: Longman.

Bayart, J-F., S. Ellis and B. Hibou. 1998. *The Criminalization of the State in Africa*. London and Bloomington: International African Institute in association with James Currey and Indiana University Press.

Bayliss, C. and C. Cramer. 2001. 'Privatisation and the Post-Washington Consensus: Between the lab and the real world?', in B. Fine, C. Lapavitsas and J. Pincus (eds.), *Development Policy in the Twenty-first Century: Beyond the Post-Washington Consensus*. London: Routledge, 52–79.

Bazerman, C. 1993. 'Money talks: The rhetorical project of *The Wealth of Nations*', in W. Henderson, A. Dudley-Evans, and R. Blackhouse (eds.), *Economics and Language*. London: Routledge, 173–98.

Beall, J. 1997. 'Social capital in waste: A solid investment', *Journal of International Development* 9 (7): 951–61.

Beattie, A. 2002. 'Debt relief scheme missing targets, says IMF', *Financial Times*, 5 September.

Becker, E. 2003. 'Poorer countries pull out of talks over world trade', *New York Times*, 15 September.
Becker, G. 1996. *Accounting for Tastes*. Cambridge: Harvard University Press.
Beckman, B. 1993. 'The liberation of civil society: Neo-liberal ideology and political theory', *Review of African Political Economy* 20 (58): 20–34.
Beeson, M. 2001. 'Globalisation, governance, and the political-economy of public policy reform in East Asia', *Governance: An International Journal of Policy, Administration and Institutions* 14 (4): 481–502.
Behrend, H. 1998. 'War in Northern Uganda: The Holy Spirit Movements of Alice Lakwena, Severino Lukoyo and Joseph Kony (1986–1997)', in C. Clapham (ed.), *African Guerrillas*. Oxford: James Currey, 107–18.
Bell, D. 1973. *The Coming of Post-industrial Society*. New York: Penguin Books.
Bell, T. and D. Ntsebeza. 2001. *Unfinished Business*. Cape Town: RedWorks.
Bellamy, J.F. 1992. 'The absolute general law of environmental degradation under capitalism', *Capitalism, Nature, Socialism* 3 (3): 77–82.
Bello, W. 2000a. 'Meltzer report on Bretton Woods twins builds case for abolition but hesitates', *Focus on Trade* 48 (April).
———. 2000b. 'UNCTAD X: Pies, preachers and poets', *Focus on Trade* 46 (February).
———. 2002. *Deglobalization: Ideas for a New World Economy*. London: Zed Books.
Bendaña, A. 2002. 'Byebye Poverty Reduction Strategy Papers, and hello good governance'. Unpublished paper, Managua: Cafod, Oxfam and Christian Aid.
Benjamin, J. 1987. 'The framework of US relations with Latin America in the twentieth century: An interpretive essay', *Diplomatic History* 11 (2): 91–112.
Benjamin, W. 1999. *Illuminations*. London: Pimlico.
Berg, E. and A. Batchelder. 1985. *Structural Adjustment Lending: A Critical View*. Alexandria, VA: Elliot Berg Associates for the World Bank Country Policy Department.
Berger, M.T. 1995a. 'Post-Cold War capitalism: Modernisation and modes of resistance after the fall', *Third World Quarterly* 16 (4): 717–28.
———. 1995b. *Under Northern Eyes: Latin American Studies and US Hegemony in the Americas*. Bloomington: Indiana University Press.
———. 1996. 'Yellow mythologies: The East Asian miracle and post-Cold War capitalism', *Positions: East Asia Cultures Critique* 4 (1): 90–126.
———. 1997. 'The triumph of the East? The East Asian Miracle and post-Cold War capitalism', in M.T. Berger and D.A. Borer (eds.), *The Rise of East Asia: Critical Visions of the Pacific Century*. London: Routledge, 260–87.
———. 1998. 'A new East–West synthesis? APEC and competing narratives of regional integration in the post-Cold War Asia–Pacific', *Alternatives* (23) 1: 1–28.
———. 2004. *The Battle for Asia: From Decolonization to Globalization*. London: Routledge Curzon.
Berger, M.T. and M. Beeson. 1998. 'Lineages of liberalism and miracles of modernisation: The World Bank, the East Asian trajectory and the international development debate', *Third World Quarterly* 19 (3): 487–504.

Select Bibliography

Berman, B. 1997. 'The perils of *Bula Matari*: Hegemony and the colonial state in Africa', *Canadian Journal of African Studies* 31 (3): 556–70.

———. 1998. 'Ethnicity, patronage and the African state: The politics of uncivil nationalism', *African Affairs* 97 (388): 305–41.

Berman, M. 1999. 'Freedom and fetishism', in M. Berman, *Adventures in Marxism*. London and New York: Verso, 37–56.

Bernstein, H. 1990. 'Agricultural "modernisation" and the era of structural adjustment: Observations on sub-Saharan Africa', *Journal of Peasant Studies* 18 (1): 3–35.

———. (ed.). 1996. *The Agrarian Question in South Africa*. London: Frank Cass.

———. 2000. '"The peasantry" in global capitalism: Who, where and why?', in L. Panitch and C. Leys (eds.), *The Socialist Register 2001*. London: The Merlin Press, 25–51.

———. 2002. 'Land reform: Taking a long(er) view', *Journal of Agrarian Change* 2 (4): 433–63.

———. 2003a. 'Farewells to the peasantry', *Transformation: Critical Perspectives on Southern Africa* 52: 1–19.

———. 2003b. 'Land reform in southern Africa in world-historical perspective', *Review of African Political Economy* 96: 203–26.

———. 2004a. '"Changing before our very eyes": Agrarian questions and the politics of land in capitalism today,' *Journal of Agrarian Change* 4 (1 & 2): 190–225.

———. 2004b. 'Considering Africa's agrarian questions', *Historical Materialism* 12 (4): 114–44.

———. 2005a. 'Development studies and the Marxists', in U. Kothari (ed.), *A Radical History of Development Studies: Individuals, Institutions and Ideologies*. London: Zed Books, 111–37.

———. 2005b. 'Rural land and land conflicts in sub-Saharan Africa', in S. Moyo and P. Yeros (eds.), *Reclaiming the Land: The Resurgence of Rural Movements in Africa, Asia and Latin America*. London: Zed Books, 67–101.

Bernstein, H. and T. Byres. 2001. 'From peasant studies to agrarian change', *Journal of Agrarian Change* 1(1): 1–56.

Bernstein, H. and P. Woodhouse. 2001. 'Telling environmental change like it is? Reflections on a study in sub-Saharan Africa', *Journal of Agrarian Change* 1 (2): 283–324.

Berry, S. 1984. 'The food crisis and agrarian change in Africa: A review essay', *African Studies Review* 27 (2): 59–112.

Bhatnagar, B. and A. Williams. 1992. 'Participatory development and the World Bank: Potential directions for change'. World Bank Discussion Paper No. 183: Washington, DC.

Bianchi, S. and J. Robinson 1997. 'What did you do today? Children's use of time, family composition, and the acquisition of social capital', *Journal of Marriage and the Family* 59 (2): 332–44.

Biersteker, T. 1995. 'The "triumph" of liberal economic ideas in the developing world', in B. Stallings (ed.), *Global Change, Global Response: The New International Context of Development*. New York: Cambridge University Press, 174–96.

Bigsten, A. and S. Kayizzi-Mugerwa. 2001. 'Is Uganda an emerging economy?' Nordiska Afrikainstitutet Research, Report No. 118.

Bircham, E. and J. Charlton (eds.). 2002. *Anti-Capitalism: A Guide to the Movement*. London: Bookmarks.

Black, E. 1963. *The Diplomacy of Economic Development*. New York: Atheneum.

Blaney, D. 1996. 'Reconceptualizing autonomy: The difference dependency theory makes', *Review of International Political Economy* 3 (3): 459–97.

Blaug, M. 1992. *The Methodology of Economics: Or How Economists Explain*. Cambridge: Cambridge University Press.

Block, F. 2001. 'Using social theory to leap over historical contingencies: A comment on Robinson', *Theory and Society* 30 (2): 215–21.

Bojicic, V., M. Kaldor and I. Vejvoda. 1995. 'Post-war reconstruction in the Balkans: A background report prepared for the European Commission'. Sussex European Institute, Working Paper No. 14.

Bond, P. 1991. *Commanding Heights and Community Control: New Economics for a New South Africa*. Johannesburg: Ravan Press.

———. 1995. 'Urban social movements, the housing question and development discourse in South Africa', in D. Moore and G. Schmitz, *Debating Development Discourse: Institutional and Popular Perspectives*. London: Macmillan, 149–77.

———. 1998. *Uneven Zimbabwe: A Study of Finance, Development and Underdevelopment*. Trenton, NJ: Africa World Press.

———. 1999. 'Zimbabwe: A post neoliberal politics', *Southern Africa Report* 14 (3): 23–26.

———. 2000a. *Cities of Gold, Townships of Coal*. Trenton, NJ: Africa World Press.

———. 2000b. 'Defunding the Fund, running on the Bank', *Monthly Review* 52 (1): 127–40.

———. 2001a. *Against Global Apartheid: South Africa Meets the World Bank, IMF and International Finance*. Cape Town: University of Cape Town Press.

———. 2001b. 'The World Bank in the Time of Cholera'. http://www.nu.ac.za/ccs. Accessed 5 April 2006.

———. (ed.). 2002a. *Fanon's Warning: A Civil Society Reader on the New Partnership for Africa's Development*. Trenton and Cape Town: Africa World Press and AIDC.

———. 2002b. 'Globalisation hits the poor', *City Press*, 8 September.

———. 2002c. *Unsustainable South Africa: Environment, Development and Social Protest*. London and Pietermaritzburg: The Merlin Press and University of Natal Press.

———. 2003. 'Labour, social movements and South African foreign economic policy', in P. Nel and J. van der Westhuizen (eds.), *Democratising South African Foreign Policy*. New York and Cape Town: Lexington Books and University of Cape Town Press, 97–122.

———. 2004. 'Should the World Bank be "fixed" or "nixed"? Reformist posturing and popular resistance', *Capitalism, Nature, Socialism* 15 (2): 85–105.

———. 2005. *Elite Transition: From Apartheid to Neo-liberalism in South Africa*. London and Pietermaritzburg: Pluto Press and University of KwaZulu-Natal Press.

———. 2006a. *Looting Africa: The Economics of Exploitation*. London and Pietermaritzburg: Zed Books and University of KwaZulu-Natal Press.
———. 2006b. *Talk Left, Walk Right: South Africa's Frustrated Global Reforms*. Pietermaritzburg and Trenton: University of KwaZulu-Natal Press and Africa World Press.
———. forthcoming. 'Embryonic African anti-capitalism', in R. Neumann and A. Hsiao (eds.), *Anti-Capitalism: A Field Guide to the Global Justice Movement*. New York: New Press.
Bond, P. and R. Dada (eds.). 2005. *Trouble in the Air: Global Warming and the Privatised Atmosphere*. Durban and Amsterdam: UKZN Centre for Civil Society and Transnational Institute.
Bond, P. and M. Manyanya. 2003. *Zimbabwe's Plunge: Exhausted Nationalism, Neoliberalism and the Search for Social Justice*. London, Pietermaritzburg, Trenton and Harare: The Merlin Press, University of KwaZulu-Natal Press, Africa World Press and Weaver Press.
Booker, S. and W. Minter. 2001. 'AIDS is a consequence of global apartheid', *The Nation*, 2 July.
Boserup, E. 1965. *The Conditions of Agricultural Growth: The Economics of Agrarian Change under Population Pressure*. London: Allen and Unwin.
Boulding, K.E. 1971. 'The economics of knowledge and the knowledge of economics', in D.M. Lamberton (ed.), *Economics of Information and Knowledge*. Harmondsworth: Penguin, 60–72.
Bradford, C. 1992. 'From trade-driven growth to growth-driven trade: Reappraising the East Asian development experience'. Paris: OECD Development Centre.
Brantlinger, P. 1988. *Rule of Darkness: British Literature and Imperialism, 1830–1914*. Ithaca: Cornell University Press.
Brenner, N. and N. Theodore. 2002. 'Cities and the geographies of "actually existing neoliberalism"', *Antipode* 34 (3): 349–77.
Brenner, R. 1998. 'The economics of global turbulence: A special report on the world economy, 1950–98', *New Left Review* 1 (229): 1–265.
———. 2000. 'The boom and the bubble', *New Left Review* 2 (6): 5–43.
Bretton Woods Project. 2002. 'Harmonisation and coherence: White knights or Trojan horses?', http//:www.brettonwoodsproject.org/topic/knowledgebank/coherence.pdf. Accessed 25 October 2006.
———. 2006. 'Bank freezes pipeline funds to Chad', http://www.brettonwoodsproject.org/art.shtml?x=507557. Accessed 15 April 2006.
Brock, K., A. Cornwall and J. Gaventa. 2001. 'Power, knowledge and political spaces in the framing of poverty policy'. Institute of Development Studies Working Paper No. 147, Brighton, Sussex.
Brown, A., M. Foster, A. Norton and F. Naschold. 2001. 'The status of sector wide approaches'. London: ODI Working Paper No. 142.
Brown, L. and D. Ashman. 1996. 'Participation, social capital, and intersectoral problem solving: African and Asian cases', *World Development* 24 (9): 1467–80.

Brown, S. 2001. 'Authoritarian leaders and multiparty elections in Africa: How foreign donors help to keep Kenya's Daniel Arap Moi in power', *Third World Quarterly* 22 (5): 725–39.
Brown, W. 2002. 'Africa, the donors and anti-capitalism: A comment'. Paper presented to the conference 'Towards a new political economy of development: Globalisation and governance', Political Economy Research Centre, Sheffield University, 4–6 July.
Bryceson, D.F. 1996. 'Deagrarianization and rural employment in sub-Saharan Africa: A sectoral perspective', *World Development* 24 (1): 97–111.
———. 1999. 'African rural labour, income diversification and livelihood approaches: A long-term development perspective', *Review of African Political Economy* 26 (80): 171–89.
Burawoy, M. 2003. 'For a sociological Marxism: The complementary convergence of Antonio Gramsci and Karl Polanyi', *Politics and Society* 31 (2): 193–261.
Burnside, C. and D. Dollar. 2000. 'Aid, growth, the incentive regime and poverty reduction', in C. Gilbert and D. Vines (eds.), *The World Bank: Structures and Policies*. Cambridge: Cambridge University Press, 210–27.
Burt, R. 1992. *Structural Holes*. Cambridge, MA: Harvard University Press.
———. 1997. 'A note on social capital and network content', *Social Networks* 19 (4): 355–74.
Burton-Jones, A. 1999. *Knowledge Capitalism*. Oxford: Oxford University Press.
Bush, G.W. 2002. 'Remarks by the president on global development, inter-American development bank', http://www.whitehouse.gov/news/releases/2002/03/20020314-7.html. Accessed 16 January 2006.
Bush, R. 1997. 'Africa's environmental crisis: Challenging the orthodoxies', *Review of African Political Economy* 24 (74): 503–13.
Bush, R. and M. Szeftel. 1998. 'Commentary: "Globalization" and the regulation of Africa', *Review of African Political Economy* 25 (76): 173–77.
Byres, T.J. 1996. *Capitalism from above and Capitalism from below: An Essay in Comparative Political Economy*. London: Macmillan.
Cahn, J. 1993. 'Challenging the new imperial authority: The World Bank and the democratization of development', *Harvard Journal of Human Rights* 6: 159–94.
Callaghy, T.M. 2001. 'Networks and governance in Africa: Innovation in the debt régime', in T.M. Callaghy, R. Kassimir and R. Latham (eds.), *Intervention and Transnationalism in Africa: Global–Local Networks of Power*. Cambridge: Cambridge University Press, 115–48.
Callinicos, A. 1992. *South Africa between Apartheid and Capitalism*. London: Bookmarks.
———. 2003. *An Anti-capitalist Manifesto*. Cambridge: Polity Press.
Cammack, P. 2001a. 'Making poverty work', in L. Panitch and C. Leys (eds.), *Socialist Register 2002: A World of Contradictions*. London: The Merlin Press, 193–210.
———. 2001b. 'Neo-liberalism, the World Bank, and the new politics of development', in U. Kothari and M. Minogue (eds.), *Development Theory and Practice: Critical Perspectives*. London: Palgrave, 215–30.

Select Bibliography

———. 2002. 'Attacking the global poor', *New Left Review* 2 (13): 125–32.
———. 2003. 'The governance of global capitalism: A new materialist perspective', *Historical Materialism* 11 (2): 37–59.
Campbell, B.K. and J. Loxley. 1989. *Structural Adjustment in Africa*. Basingstoke: Macmillan.
Campbell, D. 1998. 'Why fight: Humanitarianism, principles, and post-structuralism', *Millennium* 27 (3): 497–521.
Campos, J. and H. Root. 1996. *The Key to the Asian Miracle: Making Shared Growth Credible*. Washington, DC: Brookings Institution Press.
Camus, A. 1984. *The Rebel*. New York: Vintage.
Cappelan, A. and J. Fagerberg. 1995. 'East Asian growth: A critical assessment', *Forum for Development Studies* 5 (2): 175–95.
Carmody, P. 1998. 'Constructing alternatives to structural adjustment in Africa', *Review of African Political Economy* 25 (75): 25–46.
Carrier, J. and D. Miller (eds.). 1998. *Virtualism: The New Political Economy*. Oxford: Berg.
Carroll, R. 2002. 'More blacks believe apartheid country ran better', *Mail & Guardian*, 13 December.
Castells, M. 1996. *The Information Age: Economy, Society, and Culture, Volume 1: The Rise of the Network Society*. Oxford: Basil Blackwell.
———. 1998. *The End of Millennium*. Oxford: Basil Blackwell.
Caufield, C. 1996. *Masters of Illusion: The World Bank and the Poverty of Nations*. London: Pan.
Cavero, R.J.C., J.C. Requeña, R. Nuñez, R. Eyben and W. Lewis. 2002. 'Crafting Bolivia's PRSP: Five points of view', *Finance and Development* 39 (2): 13–16.
Center of Concern, International Gender and Trade Network and Institute for Agriculture and Trade Policy. 2003. 'IMF-World Bank-WTO close ranks around flawed economic policies', http://www.coc.org/resources/articles/display.html?ID=484. Accessed 8 September 2003.
Chabal, P. and J-P. Daloz. 1999. *Africa Works: The Political Instrumentalisation of Disorder*. Oxford: James Currey.
Chambers, R. 1997. *Whose Reality Counts?* London: Intermediate Technology Publications.
———. 2001. 'The *World Development Report*: Concepts, content and a Chapter 12', *Journal of International Development* 13 (3): 299–306.
Chambers S. and J. Kopstein. 2001. 'Bad civil society', *Political Theory* 29 (6): 837–65.
Chang, H-J. 2003. 'Unfree global markets', *Le Monde Diplomatique* (August).
Charney, E. 1998. 'Political liberalism, deliberative democracy and the public sphere', *American Political Science Review* 92 (1): 97–110.
Chen, E.K.Y. 1979. *Hyper-growth in Asian Economies: A Comparative Study of Hong Kong, Japan, Korea, Singapore and Taiwan*. London: Macmillan.

Cheru, F. 2001. *The Highly Indebted Poor Countries Initiative: A Human Rights Assessment of the Poverty Reduction Strategy Papers*. Report submitted to the United Nations Economic and Social Council, New York, January.

Choi, A.H. 1998. 'Statism and Asian political economy: Is there a new paradigm?', *Bulletin of Concerned Asian Scholars* 30 (3): 50–60.

Chomsky, N. 1989. *Necessary Illusions*. London: Pluto Press.

Chossudovsky, M. 1997. *The Globalization of Poverty: Impacts of the IMF and World Bank Reforms*. London: Zed Books.

Clapham, C. 1996. *Africa and the International System*. Cambridge: Cambridge University Press.

Clark, J. 1991. *Democratizing Development: The Role of Voluntary Organizations*. London: Earthscan.

———. 2001. 'Explaining Ugandan intervention in Congo: Evidence and interpretations', *Journal of Modern African Studies* 39 (2): 261–87.

Clarke, S. 1991. *Marx, Marginalism and Modern Sociology*. London: Macmillan.

Cliffe, L. and R. Luckham. 1999. 'Complex political emergencies and the state: Failure and the fate of the state', *Third World Quarterly* 20 (1): 27–50.

Clinton, B. 2002. 'World without walls: How do we defeat global terrorism?', *Guardian*, 26 January.

Cockett, R. 1995. *Thinking the Unthinkable: Think-Tanks and the Counter-Revolution, 1931–1983*. London: Fontana.

Coetzee, J.M. 1988. *White Writing: On the Culture of Letters in South Africa*. New Haven: Yale University Press.

Cohen, L. 1994. 'Democracy is coming to the USA', in L. Cohen, *Stranger Music: Selected Poems and Songs*. Toronto: McClelland and Stewart.

Cohen, M. and P. Pinstrup-Anderson. 1999. 'Food security and conflict', *Social Research* 66 (1): 377–416.

Cohen, T. 1997. '1998 set to be year of privatisations in Africa', Neoludd@Earthlink.Net, 17 December.

Cole, S. 1989. 'World Bank forecasts and planning in the Third World', *Environment and Planning* 21 (1): 175–96.

Coleman, J. 1987. 'Norms as social capital', in G. Radnitzky and P. Bernholz (eds.), *Economic Imperialism: The Economic Method Applied Outside the Field of Economics*. New York: Paragon House Publishers, 133–56.

———. 1988. 'Social capital in the creation of human capital', *American Journal of Sociology* 94 (Supplement): 95–120.

———. 1990. *Foundations of Social Theory*. Cambridge: Harvard University Press.

Collier, P and D. Dollar. 2002. *Globalization, Growth and Poverty: Building an Inclusive World Economy*. Washington, DC and New York: World Bank and Oxford University Press.

Collier, P., A. Hoeffler and C. Pattillo. 2001. 'Flight capital as a portfolio choice', *World Bank Economic Review* 15 (1): 55–88.

Comaroff, J. and J. Comaroff. 2002. 'Alien-nation: Zombies, immigrants, and millennial capitalism', *South Atlantic Quarterly* 101 (4): 779–807.

Consultative Group Meeting for Vietnam. 1999. *Vietnam Development Report 2000 Attacking Poverty*. Joint Report of the Government-Donor-NGO Working Group, 14–15 December.

Cooke, B. and U. Kothari. 2001. *Participation: The New Tyranny?* London and New York: Zed Books.

Cooper, F. 2001. 'Networks, moral discourse, and history', in T.M. Callaghy, R. Kassimir and R. Latham (eds.), *Intervention and Transnationalism in Africa: Global–Local Networks of Power*. Cambridge: Cambridge University Press, 23–46.

COSATU (Congress of South African Trade Unions). 2005. 'Statement on the visit of Paul Wolfowitz', Johannesburg, 17 June.

Costello, A., F. Watson and D. Woodward. 1995. *Human Face or Human Façade? Adjustment and the Health of Mothers and Children*. London: Centre for International Child Health.

Cotgrove, S. 1982. *Catastrophe or Cornucopia: The Environment, Politics and the Future*. Chichester: Wiley.

Cotgrove, S. and A. Duff. 1980. 'Environmentalism, middle class radicalism and politics', *Sociological Review* 28 (2): 333–51.

Cowen, M. 1986. 'Change in state power, international conditions and peasant producers: The case of Kenya', *Journal of Peasant Studies* 22 (2): 355–84.

Cowen, M. and S. MacWilliam. 1996. *Indigenous Capital in Kenya: The 'Indian' Dimension of Debate*. Interkont Books, No. 8. Helsinki: Institute of Development Studies, University of Helsinki.

Cowen, M. and R. Shenton. 1996. *Doctrines of Development*. London: Routledge.

———. 1999. *Community between Europe and Africa: A Historical Lexicon*. Political Science Series No. 64. Vienna: Institute for Advanced Studies.

Cox, M. 2005. 'Empire by denial: The strange case of the United States', *International Affairs* 81 (1): 15–30.

Cox, R. 1979. 'Ideologies and the new international economic order: Reflections on some recent literature', *International Organization* 33, 2 (Spring): 257–302.

———. 1987. *Production, Power and World Order: Social Forces and the Making of History*. New York: Columbia University Press.

———. 1996 [1981]. 'Social forces, states, and world orders: Beyond international relations theory', in R. Cox and T. Sinclair, *Approaches to World Order*. Cambridge: Cambridge University Press, 85–123.

———. 1999. 'Civil society at the turn of the millennium: Prospects for an alternative world order', *Review of International Studies* 25 (3): 3–28.

Craig, D. and D. Porter. 2003. 'Poverty Reduction Strategy Papers: A new convergence', *World Development* 31 (1): 53–69.

Cramer, C. 2001. 'Privatisation and adjustment in Mozambique: A "hospital pass"?', *Journal of Southern African Studies* 27 (1): 79–103.

———. 2002. '*Homo economicus* goes to war: Methodological individualism, rational choice and the political economy of war', *World Development* 39 (11): 1845–64.

———. 2006. *Civil War is Not a Stupid Thing: Accounting for Violence in Developing Countries*. London: Hurst.

Cramer, C. and J. Goodhand. 2002. 'Try again, fail again, fail again better? War, the state and the "post-conflict" challenge in Afghanistan', *Development and Change* 33 (5): 885–909.

Crawford, G. 2003. 'Partnership or power? Deconstructing the "Partnership for Governance" programme in Indonesia', *Third World Quarterly* 24 (1): 139–59.

Crisp, J. 1998. 'The "post-conflict" concept: Some critical observations'. Geneva: United Nations High Commission for Refugees, mimeo.

Cronin, J. 1996. *The World the Cold War Made: Order, Chaos and the Return of History*. London: Routledge.

Crozier, M., S. Huntington and J. Watanuki. 1975. *The Crisis of Democracy*. New York: New York University Press.

Cruikshank, B. 1999. *The Will to Empower: Democratic Citizens and Other Subjects*. Ithaca: Cornell University Press.

Cumings, B. 1998. 'The Korean crisis and the end of "Late Development"', *New Left Review* 1 (231): 43–72.

Curry, J. 1997. 'The dialectic of knowledge-in-production: Value creation in late capitalism and the rise of knowledge-centered production', *Electronic Journal of Sociology* 2 (3), http://www.sociology.org/archive.html. Accessed 25 October 2006.

Dagnino, E. and A. Escobar (eds.). 1998. *Cultures of Politics; Politics of Cultures: Revisioning Latin American Social Movements*. Boulder, CO: Westview.

Dallaire, R. 2003. *Shake Hands with the Devil: The Failure of Humanity in Rwanda*. Toronto: Random House.

Daly, H. 1992. 'Sustainable growth: An impossibility theorem', in H. Daly and K. Townsend (eds.), *Valuing the Earth: Economics, Ecology, Ethics*. Cambridge, MS: Massachusetts Institute of Technology Press, 267–73.

———. 2002. 'Sustainable development: Definitions, principles, policies'. Invited address, World Bank, 30 April 2002, Washington, DC, http://www.brettonwoodsproject.org/topic/knowledgebank/wdrs/Dalyonwdr03.doc. Accessed 25 October 2006.

Danaher, K. (ed.). 1994. *50 Years is Enough: The Case against the World Bank and the International Monetary Fund*. Boston, MA: South End Press.

Darrow, M. 2003. *Between Light and Shadow: The World Bank, International Monetary Fund and International Human Rights Law*. Portland: Hart.

Dauvergne, P. (ed.). 1998. *Weak and Strong States in Asia–Pacific Societies*. Sydney: Allen and Unwin.

Davies, J. 1992. *Exchange*. Buckingham: Open University Press.

Daviron, B. and P. Gibbon (eds.). 2002. *Global Commodity Chains and African Export Agriculture*, special issue of *Journal of Agrarian Change* 2 (2).

Davis, M. 2001. *Late Victorian Holocausts: El Niño Famines and the Making of the Third World*. London: Verso.

Dawkins, W. 1995. 'Pedlars of the Japanese Model to Developing World', *Financial Times*, 7 February.
Dawson, J. and A. Jeans. 1997. *Looking beyond Credit: Business Development Services and the Promotion of Innovation among Small Producers*. London: Intermediate Technology.
De Soto, H. 2003. *The Mystery of Capital: Why Capitalism Triumphs in the West and Fails Everywhere Else*. New York: Basic Books.
De Waal, A. 1997. *Famine Crimes: Politics and the Disaster Relief Industry in Africa*. Oxford: James Currey.
Deininger, K. 2003. *Land Policies for Growth and Poverty Reduction*. Oxford: World Bank and Oxford University Press.
Denny, C. 1997. 'World Bank in surprise policy U-turn', *Guardian Weekly*, 1 July.
———. 2000. 'Don't Bank on it: Factions at the World Bank argue', *Guardian*, 4 July.
Desai, A. 1999. *South Africa Still Revolting*. Durban: Natal Newspapers.
———. 2002a. 'Neo-liberalism and its discontents', http://www.nu.ac.za/ccs. Accessed 8 November 2002.
———. 2002b. *We are the Poors*. New York: Monthly Review Press.
———. 2003. *Noi Siamo i Poveri: Lotte Comunitarie Nel Nuovo Apartheid*. Bologna: Novita' Librarie.
Desai, R. 1994. 'Second-hand dealers in ideas: Think-tanks and Thatcherite hegemony', *New Left Review* 1 (203): 27–54.
Devereux, S. and H. Pares. 1990. *Credit and Savings for Development*. Oxford: Oxfam.
Dezalay, Y. and B. Garth. 1997. 'Law, lawyers and social capital: "Rule of law" versus relational capitalism', *Social and Legal Studies* 6 (1): 109–41.
Dia, M. 1993. *A Governance Approach to Civil Service Reform in Sub-Saharan Africa*. Washington, DC: World Bank.
Diesendorf, M. 1997. 'Principles of ecological sustainability', in M. Diesendorf and C. Hamilton (eds.), *Human Ecology, Human Economy: Ideas for an Ecologically Sustainable Future*. Sydney: Allen and Unwin, 64–97.
Dijkstra, A.G. and K. van Donge. 2001. 'What does the "show case" show? Evidence of and lessons from adjustment in Uganda', *World Development* 29 (5): 841–63.
Dinnen, S. 2001. *Law and Order in a Weak State: Crime and Politics in Papua New Guinea*. Adelaide: Crawford House.
Dirlik, A. 1994. *After the Revolution: Waking to Global Capitalism*. Hanover: Wesleyan University Press.
Dobson, A. 1990. *Green Political Thought*. London: Harper Collins.
Dollar, D. and J. Svensson. 1998. *What Explains the Success or Failure of Structural Adjustment Programs?* Washington, DC: World Bank, Macroeconomics and Growth Group.
Drucker, P. 1989. *The New Realities*. New York: Harper and Row.
———. 1993. *Post-capitalist Society*. New York: Harper Collins.
Dryzek, J. 1997. *The Politics of the Earth: Environmental Discourses*. Oxford: Oxford University Press.

Du Guy, P. 1996. 'Organizing identity: Entrepreneurial governance and public management', in S. Hall and P. du Guy (eds.), *Questions of Cultural Identity*. London: Sage, 151–69.

Duffield, M. 1994. 'The political economy of internal war: Asset transfer, complex political emergencies and international aid', in J. Macrae and A. Zwi (eds.), *War and Hunger: Rethinking International Responses to Political Emergencies*. London: Zed Books, 50–89.

———. 1996. 'The symphony of the damned: Racial discourse, complex political emergencies and humanitarian aid', *Disasters* 20 (3): 173–93.

———. 1998. 'Post-modern conflict: Warlords, post-adjustment states and private protection', *Civil Wars* 1 (1): 65–102.

———. 1999. 'Globalisation and war economies: Promoting order or the return of history?', *Fletcher Forum of World Affairs* 23 (2): 19–36.

———. 2001a. *Global Governance and the New Wars: The Merger of Development and Security*. London: Zed Books.

———. 2001b. 'Governing the borderlands decoding the power of aid', *Disasters* 25 (4): 308–24.

———. 2002. 'Social reconstruction and the radicalisation of development: Aid as a relation of global liberal governance', *Development and Change* 33 (5): 1049–71.

Duncan, J. 2002. *Broadcasting and the National Question*. Johannesburg: Freedom of Expression Institute.

Dunn, J. 2005. *Setting the People Free: The Story of Democracy*. London: Atlantic Books.

Dupont, A. 1996. 'Is there an "Asian way"?', *Survival* 38 (2): 13–33.

Dwyer, P. and D. Seddon. 2002. 'The new wave: A global perspective on popular protest'. Paper presented at the Eighth International Conference on Alternative Futures and Popular Protest, Manchester, 2–4 July.

Eagleton, T. 2003. *After Theory*. New York: Basic Books.

Easterly, W. 2001. *The Effect of International Monetary Fund and World Bank Programs on Poverty*. Washington, DC: World Bank.

Economic Planning Agency. 1994. 'Possibility of the application of Japanese experience from the standpoint of the developing countries'. Agency paper, November.

Edkins, J. 1996. 'Legality with a vengeance: Famines and humanitarian relief in "complex emergencies"', *Millennium* 25 (3): 547–75.

Einhorn, J. 2001. 'The World Bank's mission creep', *Foreign Affairs* 80 (5): 22–35.

Ellerman, D. 2004. *Helping People Help Themselves: From the World Bank to an Alternative Philosophy of Development*. Ann Arbor: University of Michigan Press.

Elliott, L. and C. Denny. 2003. 'EU waters down concessions', *Mail & Guardian*, 12–18 September.

Ellis, F. and G. Bahiigwa. 2003. 'Livelihoods and rural poverty reduction in Uganda', *World Development* 31 (6): 997–1013.

Ellis-Jones, M. 2003. *States of Unrest III: Resistance to IMF and World Bank Policies in Poor Countries*. London: World Development Movement.

Select Bibliography

Elsenhans, H. 1983. 'Rising mass incomes as a condition of capitalist growth: Implications for the world economy', *International Organization* 37 (1): 1–41.

Engel J.R. and J. Gibb Engel. (eds.). 1990. *Ethics of Environment and Development: Global Challenge, International Response*. London: Belhaven Press.

Engels, F. 1887 [1845]. Translated by F. Kelley Wischnewetzky. *The Condition of the Working Class in England*. New York: W. Lovell Company.

Engler, M. 2006. 'Latin America unchained', *Foreign Policy in Focus*, 16 March.

Environmental Defence, Friends of the Earth and International Rivers Network. 2003. *Gambling With People's Lives*. Washington, DC and Berkeley, 19 September.

Epprecht, M. 1997. 'Investing in amnesia, or fancy and forgetfulness in the World Bank's approach to healthcare reform in sub-Saharan Africa', *Journal of Developing Areas* 31 (3): 337–56.

Escobar, A. 1995. *Encountering Development: The Making and Unmaking of the Third World*. Princeton, NJ: Princeton University Press.

Evans, A. and M. Moore (eds.). 1998. *The Bank, the State and Development: Dissecting the 1997 World Development Report*, special edition of *IDS Bulletin* 29 (2).

Evans, P. 1995. *Embedded Autonomy: States and Industrial Transformation*. Princeton, NJ: Princeton University Press.

———. 1996a. 'Government action, social capital and development: Reviewing the evidence on synergy', *World Development* 24 (6): 1119–32.

———. 1996b. 'Introduction: Development strategies across the public–private divide', *World Development* 24 (6): 1033–37.

———. 1997. 'The eclipse of the state? Reflections on stateness in an era of globalization', *World Politics* 50 (1): 62–87.

Fairclough, N. 1989. *Language and Power*. London: Longman.

———. 1995. *Critical Discourse Analysis: The Critical Study of Language*. London: Longman.

———. 1996. *Discourse and Social Change*. Cambridge: Cambridge University Press.

———. 2000. 'Language in the new capitalism', http://www.uoc.es/humfil/nlc/LNC-ENG/lnc-eng.html. Accessed 3 July 2004.

Fairclough N. and R. Wodak. 1997. 'Critical discourse analysis', in T.A. van Dijk (ed.), *Discourse Studies. A Multidisciplinary Introduction. Volume 2: Discourse as Social Interaction*. London: Sage, 258–84.

Fanon, F. 1961. *The Wretched of the Earth*. New York: Grove Press.

———. 1965. *A Dying Colonialism*. New York: Grove Press.

———. 1967a. *Black Skin White Masks*. New York: Grove Press.

———. 1967b. *Towards the African Revolution*. New York: Grove Press.

Faux, J. 1997. 'Hedging the neoliberal bet', *Dissent* (Autumn): 118–22.

Fedderke, J., R. de Kadt and J. Luiz. 1998. 'Growth and social capital: A critical reflection', mimeo.

Federici, S., G. Caffentzis and O. Alidou (eds.). 2000. *A Thousand Flowers: Social Struggles against Structural Adjustment in African Universities*. Trenton, NJ: Africa World Press.

Feldstein, M. 1998. 'Refocusing the IMF', *Foreign Affairs* 77 (2): 20–33.
Felice, W. 1997. 'The Copenhagen Summit: A victory for the World Bank?', *Social Justice* 24 (1): 107–19.
Fellmeth, A. 1996. 'Social capital in the United States and Taiwan: Trust or rule of law?', *Development Policy Review* 14 (2): 151–72.
Femia, J. 1981. *Gramsci's Political Thought: Hegemony, Consciousness and the Revolutionary Process*. Oxford: Clarendon Press.
Ferguson, J. 1990. *The Anti-politics Machine: 'Development', Depoliticization, and Bureaucratic Power in Lesotho*. Cape Town: David Philip.
Financial Stability Forum. 2001. *International Standards and Codes to Strengthen Financial Systems*. Basle, www.fsforum.org/Standards/Reiscfs.html. Accessed 23 February 2004.
Fine, B. 1995. 'From political economy to consumption', in D. Miller (ed.), *Acknowledging Consumption*. London: Routledge, 127–63.
———. 1996. *The Political Economy of South Africa*. London and Johannesburg: Christopher Hurst and University of Witswatersrand Press.
———. 1997a. 'The new revolution in economics', *Capital and Class* 61 (Spring): 143–48.
———. 1997b. 'Playing the consumption game', *Consumption, Markets, Culture* 1 (1): 7–29.
———. 1998a. 'From Bourdieu to Becker: Barbarism confronts the social sciences', mimeo.
———. 1998b. *Labour Market Theory: A Constructive Reassessment*. London: Routledge.
———. 1998c. 'A question of economics: Is it colonising the social sciences?', mimeo.
———. 1998d. 'The triumph of economics: Or "rationality" can be dangerous to your reasoning', in J. Carrier and D. Miller (eds.), *Virtualism: The New Political Economy*. London: Berg, 49–73.
———. 1999. 'The developmental state is dead: Long live social capital?', *Development and Change* 30 (1): 1–19.
———. 2001a. 'Neither the Washington nor the Post-Washington Consensus: An Introduction', in B. Fine, C. Lapavitsas and J. Pincus (eds.), *Development Policy in the Twenty-first Century: Beyond the Post-Washington Consensus*. London: Routledge, 1–27.
———. 2001b. *Social Capital versus Social Theory: Political Economy and Social Science at the Turn of the Millennium*. London: Routledge.
———. 2002a. 'Economics imperialism and the new development economics as Kuhnian paradigm shift', *World Development* 30 (12): 2057–70.
———. 2002b. 'The World Bank's speculation on social capital', in J. Pincus and J. Winters (eds.), *Reinventing the World Bank*. Ithaca: Cornell University Press, 203–21.
———. 2003a. 'Beyond the developmental state: Towards a political economy of development', in H. Hirakawa, M. Noguchi and M. Sano (eds.), *Beyond Market-driven Development: A New Stream of Political Economy of Development*. Tokyo: Nihon Hyoron Sha, 21–43.

———. 2003b. 'Social capital: The World Bank's fungible friend', *Journal of Agrarian Change* 3 (4): 586–603.

———. 2004a. 'Examining the idea of globalisation and development critically: What role for political economy?', *New Political Economy* 9 (2): 213–31.

———. 2004b. 'Public service provision and poverty alleviation in Africa: Departing the road to privatisation'. United Nations Development Programme, mimeo.

Fine, B. and K.S. Jomo (eds.). 2005. *The New Development Economics: A Critical Introduction*. Delhi and London: Tulika and Zed Books.

Fine, B. and D. Milonakis. 2005. *Economic Theory and History: From Classical Political Economy to Economics Imperialism*. London: Routledge.

Fine, B. and Z. Rustomjee. 1997. *South Africa's Political Economy: From Minerals-Energy Complex to Industrialisation*. Johannesburg: Witwatersrand University Press.

Fine, B. and C. Stoneman. 1996. 'Introduction: State and development', *Journal of Southern African Studies* 22 (1): 5–26.

Fine, B., C. Lapavitsas and J. Pincus (eds.). 2003 [2001]. *Development Policy in the Twenty-first Century: Beyond the Post-Washington Consensus*. London: Routledge.

Fine, R. and D. Davies. 1991. *Beyond Apartheid*. London: Pluto Press.

Finnemore, M. 1997. 'Redefining development at the World Bank', in F. Cooper and R. Packard (eds.), *International Development and the Social Sciences*. Berkeley: California University Press, 203–27.

Fisher, W. and T. Ponniah (eds.). 2003. *Another World is Possible: Popular Alternatives to Globalization at the World Social Forum*. London: Zed Books.

Fishlow, A., C. Gwin and S. Haggard (eds.). 1994. *Miracle or Design? Lessons from the East Asian Experience*. Washington, DC: Overseas Development Council.

Fitzgibbons, A. 1995. *Adam Smith's System of Liberty, Wealth and Virtue: The Moral and Political Foundations of* The Wealth of Nations. Oxford: Clarendon.

Fleischacker, S. 1999. *A Third Concept of Liberty: Judgment and Freedom in Kant and Adam Smith*. Princeton, NJ: Princeton University Press.

Food and Water Watch. 2006. 'World Bank Finances Corporate Corruption', http://www.foodandwaterwatch.org/water/WBWatch/world-bank-finances-corporate-corruption. Assessed 20 April 2006.

Foster-Carter, A. 1978. 'The modes of production controversy', *New Left Review* 1 (107): 47–77.

Foucault, M. 1980. 'Truth and power', in C. Gordon (ed.), *Power/Knowledge: Selected Interviews and Other Writings, 1972–1977*. Brighton: Harvester Press, 109–33.

———. 1994. *The Order of Things: An Archaeology of the Human Sciences*. New York: Vintage.

———. 2002. 'Preface to *Anti-Oedipus*' and 'Governmentality', in J. Faubion (ed.), *Power*. London: Penguin, 106–10, 201–22.

Fowler, A. 1992. 'Distant obligations: Speculations on NGO funding and the global market', *Review of African Political Economy* 55: 9–29.

Fox, J. 1997. 'The World Bank and social capital: Contesting the concept in practice', *Journal of International Development* 9 (7): 963–71.

———. 2002. 'The World Bank Inspection Panel and the limits of accountability', in J. Pincus and J. Winters (eds.), *Reinventing the World Bank*. Ithaca and London: Cornell University Press, 131–63.
Francis, P. 2001. 'Participatory development at the World Bank: The primacy of process', in B. Cooke and U. Kothari (eds.), *Participation: The New Tyranny?* London: Zed Books, 72–87.
Frankel, B. 1997. 'Confronting neoliberal regimes: The post-Marxist embrace of populism and realpolitik', *New Left Review* (1) 226: 57–92.
Fraser, A. 2003. 'Poverty Reduction Strategy Papers: Now who calls the shots?' Paper presented at the *Review of African Political Economy* conference, Birmingham, September 2003.
Freeden, M. 1996. *Ideologies and Political Theory: A Conceptual Approach*. Oxford: Oxford University Press.
Frey, B.P., F. Schneider, W. Pommierhene and G. Gilbert. 1984. 'Consensus and dissension among economists: An empirical inquiry', *American Economic Review* 74 (5): 986–94.
Friedman, B. 2002. 'Globalization: Stiglitz's case', *New York Review of Books* 49 (13): 48–53.
Friends of the Earth and Halifax Initiative. 2002. *Marketing the Earth: The World Bank and Sustainable Development*. Washington, DC and Ottawa, August.
Friends of the Earth International. 2004. 'Media Advisory: World Bank misses historic opportunity', Washington, DC, 3 August.
Friis-Hansen, E. (ed.). 2000. 'Agricultural policy in Africa after adjustment'. CDR Policy Paper, Copenhagen: Centre for Development Research.
Fukuyama, F. 1995. 'Social capital and the global economy', *Foreign Affairs* 74 (5): 89–103.
———. 1996. *Trust: The Social Virtues and the Creation of Prosperity*. New York: Free Press.
———. 2002. 'Has history restarted since September 11?' 19th Annual John Bonython Lecture, Melbourne, Centre for Independent Studies Occasional Paper 81, October.
———. 2004. *State-building: Governance and World Order in the 21st Century*. Ithaca: Cornell University Press.
———. 2006. *America at the Crossroads: Democracy, Power, and the Neoconservative Legacy*. New Haven: Yale University Press.
Furstenberg, F. and M. Hughes. 1995. 'Social capital and successful development among at-risk youth', *Journal of Marriage and the Family* 57 (3): 580–92.
Gabriel, N. 2002. 'Monterrey: Spinning the Washington Consensus all the way to Johannesburg'. Pretoria: Southern African Catholic Bishops' Conference.
Galbraith, J.K. 1993. *The Culture of Contentment*. London: Penguin.
———. 1999. 'For richer, for poorer', *Guardian*, 29 June.
Gamble, A. 1996. *Hayek: The Iron Cage of Liberty*. Cambridge: Polity Press.

Gayatri, A. and J. Dixon. 2003. 'No one said it was going to be easy!: An analysis of the recommendations made by the 1992 *WDR* and the experience in the last decade'. *World Development Report 2003*, background paper, http://econ.worldbank.org/ dr/wdr2003/library. Accessed 28 November 2003.

Gellner, E. 1994. *Conditions of Liberty: Civil Society and its Rivals*. London: Penguin.

——. 1997. 'Reply to critics', *New Left Review* 1 (221): 81–118.

George, S. 1997. 'How to win the war of ideas: Lessons from the Gramscian Right', *Dissent* (Summer): 47–53.

George, S. and E. Sabelli. 1994. *Faith and Credit: The World Bank's Secular Empire*. London: Penguin.

Gibbon, P. 1992. 'A failed agenda? African agriculture under structural adjustment with special reference to Kenya and Ghana', *Journal of Peasant Studies* 20 (1): 50–96.

——. (ed.). 1993a. *Social Change and Economic Reform in Africa*. Uppsala: Scandinavian Institute for African Studies.

——. 1993b. 'The World Bank and the new politics of aid', *European Journal of Development Research* 5 (1): 35–62.

——. 1996. 'Structural adjustment and structural change in sub-Saharan Africa: Some provisional conclusions', *Development and Change* 27 (4): 751–82.

Gibbon, P., K.J. Havnevik and K. Hermele. 1993. *A Blighted Harvest: The World Bank and African Agriculture in the 1980s*. London and Trenton, NJ: James Currey and Africa World Press.

Gibson, N. 1999. 'Radical mutations: Fanon's untidy dialectic of history', in N. Gibson (ed.), *Rethinking Fanon*. New York: Humanity Books, 408–46.

——. 2003. *Fanon and the Postcolonial Imagination*. Cambridge: Polity Press.

Gibson, S. 1999. 'Aid and politics in Malawi and Kenya: Political conditionality and donor support to the "human rights, democracy and governance" sector', in L. Wohlgemuth, S. Gibson, S. Klasen and E. Rothschild (eds.), *Common Security and Civil Society in Africa*. Uppsala: Nordiska Afrikainstitutet, 163–79.

Gilbert, C.L., A. Powell and D. Vines. 2000. 'Positioning the World Bank', in C.L. Gilbert and D. Vines (eds.), *The World Bank: Structure and Policies*. Cambridge: Cambridge University Press, 39–86.

Gill, S. 1994. 'Structural change and global political economy: Globalizing elites and the emerging world order', in Y. Sakamoto (ed.), *Global Transformation: Challenges to the State System*. Tokyo: United Nations University Press, 169–99.

——. 1995. 'Globalisation, market civilisation, and disciplinary neoliberalism', *Millennium: Journal of International Studies* 24 (3): 399–423.

——. 1998. 'New constitutionalism, democratisation and global political economy', *Pacifica Review* 10 (1): 23–38.

Gillies, D. 1996. 'Human rights, democracy, and good governance: Stretching the World Bank's policy frontiers', in J. Griesgraber and B. Gunter (eds.), *The World Bank: Lending on a Global Scale*. London: Pluto Press, 101–41.

Gilpin, R. 1987. *The Political Economy of International Relations*. Princeton, NJ: Princeton University Press.

Goldin, I., H. Rogers and N. Stern. 2002. 'The role and effectiveness of development assistance: Lessons from World Bank experience', in World Bank, *A Case for Aid: Building a Consensus for Development Assistance*. Washington, DC: World Bank.

Goldman, M. 2002. 'The power of World Bank knowledge', http://www.realworldbank.org/knowledge_power_of_wb.htm. Accessed 26 November 2003.

———. 2005. *Imperial Nature*. New Haven: Yale University Press.

Gomes, R.P., S. Lakhani and J. Woodman. 2002. 'PRSP – politics, power and poverty: A civil society perspective', *Economic Policy Empowerment Programme*. Brussels: Eurodad.

Gondal, G. and C. Madavo. 2002. 'New swipe at fighting poverty', in P. Bond (ed.), *Fanon's Warning: A Civil Society Reader on the New Partnership for Africa's Development*. Trenton, NJ: Africa World Press, 74–77.

Goodhand, J. and D. Hulme. 1999. 'From wars to complex political emergencies: Understanding conflict and peace-building in the new world disorder', *Third World Quarterly* 20 (1): 13–26.

Goodin, R.E. 1990. 'Liberalism and the best-judge principle', *Political Studies* 38: 181–95.

———. 1995. *Utilitarianism as a Public Philosophy*. Cambridge: Cambridge University Press.

Gopinath, D. 2003. 'Doubt of Africa', *Institutional Investor* (May).

Gordon, L. 1995. *Fanon and the Crisis of European Man*. New York: Routledge.

Gore, C. 2000. 'The rise and fall of the Washington Consensus as a paradigm for developing countries', *World Development* 28 (5): 789–804.

Goto, K. 1993. 'Japan loan aid in perspective: Alice's adventures in OECF-land'. OECF, London Office, 3 December.

Gourevitch, P. 1998. *We Wish to Inform You that Tomorrow We Will Be Killed with Our Families: Stories from Rwanda*. New York: Farrar Straus and Giroux.

Gowan, P. 1999. *The Global Gamble: Washington's Faustian Bid for Global Dominance*. London: Verso.

Graf, W.S. 1992. 'Sustainable ideologies and interests: Beyond Brundtland', *Third World Quarterly* 13 (3): 557–58.

Graff, G. 1992. *Beyond the Culture Wars: How Teaching the Conflicts can Revitalize American Education*. New York: Norton.

Gramsci, A. 1971. *Selections from Prison Notebooks*, edited by Q. Hoare and G. Nowell-Smith. New York: International Publishers.

———. 1996. *Prison Notebooks: Volume II*, edited and translated by J. Buttigieg. New York: Columbia University Press.

Granovetter, M. 1985. 'Economic action and social structure: The problem of embeddedness', *American Journal of Sociology* 91(3): 481–510.

———. 1992. 'Economic institutions as social constructions: A framework for analysis', *Acta Sociologica* 35(1): 3–11.

Select Bibliography

Gray, J. 1998a. *False Dawn: The Delusions of Global Capitalism*. London: Granta.

———. 1998b. Interview in 'Moving to a Global Depression?', *Background Briefing*, Australian Broadcasting Corporation, 26 July.

Greene, G. 1948. *The Heart of the Matter*. London: Heinemann.

———. 1955. *The Quiet American*. London: Heinemann.

Greenwald, B. and J. Stiglitz. 1986. 'Externalties in economies with imperfect information and incomplete markets', *Quarterly Journal of Economics* 101 (2): 229–64.

Greenwood, N.O. *The Republican Legacy in International Thought*. Cambridge: Cambridge University Press.

Greider, W. 2002. 'The end of Empire', *The Nation*, 23 September, www.globalpolicy.org/globaliz/econ/2002/0923empire.html. Accessed 16 November 2002.

Gresh, A. 2005. 'Lebanon: An illusion of unity', *Le Monde Diplomatique*, 5 June.

Griffith-Jones, S. 2002. 'Suggestions on reforming the governance of the World Bank'. University of Sussex, Institute of Development Studies, http://www.gapresearch.org. Accessed 8 November 2002.

Group of Eight (G8). 2001. *Global Poverty Report 2001: A Globalized Market – Opportunities and Risks for the Poor*. Genoa.

Gumbo, H. 2002. 'Zimbabwean Civil Society: A Report from the Front Lines', www.nu.ac.za/ccs/default.asp?3,28. Accessed 12 February 2003.

Guyer, J. 1983. 'World Bank (The Berg Report): Accelerated development in sub-Saharan Africa', *Review of African Political Economy* 10 (27): 186–92.

Gyohten, T. 1997. 'Japan and the World Bank', in D. Kapur, J. Lewis and R. Webb (eds.), *The World Bank: Its First Half Century, Volume II: Perspectives*. Washington, DC: Brookings Institution Press, 275–316.

Haas, E. 1990. *When Knowledge is Power: Three Models of Change in International Organizations*. Berkeley: University of California Press.

Hagan, J., R. MacMillan and B. Wheaton. 1996. 'New kid in town: Social capital and the life course effects of family migration on children', *American Sociological Review* 61 (3): 368–85.

Hagan, J., H. Merkens and K. Boehnke. 1995. 'Delinquency and disdain: Social capital and the control of right-wing extremism among East and West Berlin youth', *American Journal of Sociology* 100 (4): 1028–52.

Haggard, S. 1994. 'Politics and institutions in the World Bank's East Asia', in A. Fishlow, C. Gwin and S. Haggard (eds.), *Miracle or Design? Lessons from the East Asian Experience*. Washington, DC: Overseas Development Council, 81–109.

Hajer, M.A. 1996. 'Discourse coalitions and the institutionalization of practice: The case of acid rain in Britain', in F. Fischer and J. Forester (eds.), *The Argumentative Turn in Policy Analysis and Planning*. Durham: Duke University Press, 43–76.

Halliday, F. 1994. *Rethinking International Relations*. London: Macmillan.

Hamilton, L. 1999. 'A theory of true interests in the work of Amartya Sen', *Government and Opposition* 14 (4) (December): 516–46.

Hanlon, J. 1996. *Peace Without Profit: How the IMF Blocks Rebuilding in Mozambique*. Oxford: James Currey.

———. 1997. 'Can Mozambique make the World Bank pay for its mistakes?', *Around Africa*. African Faith and Justice Network, Afjn@Igc.Apc.Org.

———. 1999. 'Mozambique gains an extra $28 mn per year from HIPC debt relief but IMF imposes new conditions on cashews and rural water', 50-years@igc.org.

———. 2002a. 'Are donors to Mozambique promoting corruption?' Paper presented to the 'Towards a new political economy of development' conference, Sheffield, July.

———. 2002b. 'Bank corruption becomes site of struggle in Mozambique', *Review of African Political Economy* 29 (91): 53–72.

Hardt, M. and A. Negri. 2000. *Empire*. Cambridge, MA: Harvard University Press.

Harkavy, W. 2006. 'Wolfie at the door: Preaching against corruption at World Bank, he practises it – and staff rebels', http://www.villagevoice.com/blogs/bushbeat/. Accessed 24 January 2006.

Harriman, E. 2005. 'Where has all the money gone?', *London Review of Books* 27 (13): 7 July.

Harrison, G. 1999. 'Clean-ups, conditionality, and adjustment: Why institutions matter in Mozambique', *Review of African Political Economy* 26 (81): 323–33.

———. 2001a. 'Administering market-friendly growth? Liberal populism and the World Bank's involvement in administrative reform in sub-Saharan Africa', *Review of International Political Economy* 8 (3): 528–47.

———. 2001b. 'Post-conditionality politics and administrative reform: Reflections on the cases of Uganda and Tanzania', *Development and Change* 32 (4): 634–65.

———. 2002. 'Mozambique: Development, inequality, and the new market geography', in A. Lemon and C. Rogerson (eds.), *Geography and Economy in South Africa and its Neighbours*. Aldershot: Ashgate, 252–72.

———. 2004a. 'Sub-Saharan Africa', in A. Payne (ed.), *The New Regional Politics of Development*. Basingstoke: Palgrave, 355–75.

———. 2004b. *The World Bank and Africa: The Construction of Governance States*. London: Routledge.

Harriss, J. 2002. *Depoliticizing Development: The World Bank and Social Capital*. London: Anthem Press.

Harriss, J. and P. de Renzio. 1997. '"Missing link" or analytically missing? The concept of social capital: An introductory bibliographic essay', *Journal of International Development* 9 (7): 919–37.

Harriss, J., J. Hunter and C. Lewis (eds.). 1995. *The New Institutional Economics and Third World Development*. London: Routledge.

Harsanyi, J. 1983. 'Morality and the theory of rational behaviour', in A. Sen and B. Williams (eds.), *Utilitarianism and Beyond*. Cambridge: Cambridge University Press, 39–53.

Hart, G. 2002. *Disabling Globalization: Places of Power in Post-apartheid South Africa*. Pietermaritzburg and Berkeley: University of Natal Press and University of California Press.

Select Bibliography

Hartwell, R.M. 1988. *The Long Debate on Poverty*. Sydney: Centre for Independent Studies.

Hatch, W. and K. Yamamura. 1996. *Asia in Japan's Embrace: Building a Regional Production Alliance*. Cambridge: Cambridge University Press.

Hauser, E. 1999. 'Ugandan relations with Western donors in the 1990s: What impact on democratisation?', *Journal of Modern African Studies* 37 (4): 621–43.

Hearn, J. 2000. 'Foreign aid, democratisation and civil society in Africa: A study of South Africa, Ghana and Uganda'. Discussion Paper No. 368, Institute for Development Studies: Brighton.

Heertje, A. (ed.). 1989. *The Economic Role of the State*. Oxford: Blackwell.

Helleiner, E. 1994. *States and the Reemergence of Global Finance: From Bretton Woods to the 1990s*. Ithaca: Cornell University Press.

Henderson, J. and R.P. Appelbaum. 1992. 'Situating the state in the East Asian development process', in R.P. Appelbaum and J. Henderson (eds.), *State and Development in the Asian Pacific Rim*. Newbury Park: Sage, 1–26.

Henkel, H. and R. Stirrat. 2001. 'Participation as spiritual duty: Empowerment as secular subjection', in B. Cooke and U. Kothari (eds.), *Participation: The New Tyranny?* London: Zed Books, 168–84.

Higgott, R. 2001. 'Contested globalization: The changing context and normative challenges', *Review of International Studies* 26: 131–53.

Hildyard, N. 1998. *The World Bank and the State: A Recipe for Change?* London: Bretton Woods Project.

Hillenbrand, B. 2000. 'Economic upheaval', *Time Europe* 155 (10), 13 March.

Hinrich, K. 1995. 'The impact of German health insurance reforms on redistribution and the culture of solidarity', *Journal of Health Politics, Policy and Law* 20 (3): 653–87.

Hirschman, A. 1958. *The Strategy of Economic Development*. New Haven: Yale University Press.

———. 1991. *The Rhetoric of Reaction: Perversity, Futility, Jeopardy*. Cambridge, MA: Belknap.

———. 1997. *The Passions and the Interests: Political Arguments for Capitalism before its Triumph*. Princeton, NJ: Princeton University Press.

Hirsh, M. 1992. 'The state strikes back', *Institutional Investor* (September): 82–92.

Historical Materialism. 1999. Symposia Nos. 4 and 5.

Hobart, M. (ed.). 1993. *An Anthropological Critique of Development*. London: Routledge.

Hobsbawm, E. 1991. 'Goodbye to all that', in R. Blackburn (ed.), *After the Fall: The Failure of Communism and the Future of Socialism*. London: Verso, 115–25.

———. 1995. *Age of Extremes: The Short Twentieth Century 1914–1991*. London: Abacus.

Hochschild, A. 1998. *King Leopold's Ghost: A Story of Greed, Terror, and Heroism in Central Africa*. Boston: Houghton Mifflin.

———. 2004. *Bury the Chains: Prophets and Rebels in the Fight to Free an Empire's Slaves*. Boston: Houghton Mifflin.

Hoff, K., A. Braverman and J. Stiglitz (eds.). 1993. *The Economics of Rural Organisation: Theory, Practice, and Policy*. New York: Oxford University Press.

Hoffman, J. 1984. *The Gramscian Challenge: Coercion and Consent in Marxist Political Theory*. Oxford: Basil Blackwell.

Hogan, M.J. 1987. *The Marshall Plan: America, Britain, and the Reconstruction of Western Europe, 1947–1952*. Cambridge: Cambridge University Press.

Holloway, J. 2003. *Change the World Without Taking Power*. London: Pluto Press.

Holman, M. 2005. *Last Orders at Harrods*. Edinburgh: Birlinn.

Holtzman, S. 1999. 'Rethinking "relief" and "development" in transitions from conflict'. Occasional Paper, Brookings Institution Project on Internal Displacement, Washington, DC, January.

Hoogvelt, A. 1997. *Globalisation and the Postcolonial World: The New Political Economy of Development*. London: Macmillan.

Horiuchi, A. 1992. 'Comments on OECF occasional paper No. 1', *OECP Research Quarterly* 74 (in Japanese).

Hout, W. 1997. 'Globalisation and the quest for governance', *Mershon International Studies Review* 41 (1): 99–106.

Howell, J. 2002. 'Manufacturing civil society from the outside: Donor interventions', in J. Howell and J. Pearce, *Civil Society and Development: A Critical Exploration*. Boulder, CO and London: Lynne Rienner, 89–121.

Huffington, A. 2005. 'When did the World Bank become the home for wayward architects of war?', *The Huffington Post*, 29 November.

Huntington, S. 1968. *Political Order in Changing Societies*. New Haven: Yale University Press.

Hyden, G. 1997. 'Civil society, social capital, and development: Dissection of a complex discourse', *Studies in Comparative International Development* 32 (1): 3–30.

IDS (Institute of Development Studies). 1996. 'The power of participation: PRA and policy', *IDS Policy Briefing* 7.

Ignatieff, M. 1998. *Soldiers' Honour: Ethnic War and the Modern Conscience*. New York: Metropolitan.

———. 1999. 'Human rights: The midlife crisis', *New York Review of Books*, 22 May.

Ikenberry, G.J. 1993. 'Creating yesterday's new world order: Keynesian "new thinking" and the Anglo-American postwar settlement', in J. Goldstein and R.O. Keohane (eds.), *Ideas and Foreign Policy: Beliefs, Institutions and Political Change*. Ithaca: Cornell University Press.

IMF (International Monetary Fund). 2006. 'IMF provides debt relief for 19 countries', *IMF Survey* 35 (1): 3–8.

IMF and International Development Association. 2001. 'The impact of debt reduction under the HIPC initiative on external debt service and social expenditures'. Washington, DC, 16 November.

Inayatullah, N. 1996. 'Beyond the sovereignty dilemma: Quasi-states as a social construct', in T.J. Biersteker and C. Weber (eds.), *State Sovereignty as Social Construct*. Cambridge: Cambridge University Press, 1–21.

———. 2002. 'A foresight and policy study of multilateral development banks'. Prepared for the Swedish ministry of foreign affairs, Stockholm, November.

Jackson, R. 1990. *Quasi-states: Sovereignty, International Relations and the Third World*. Cambridge: Cambridge University Press.

Jacobs, S. and R. Calland (eds.). 2002. *Thabo Mbeki's World: The Politics and Ideology of the South African President*. London and Pietermaritzburg: Zed Books and University of Natal Press.

Janmohamed, A. 1995. 'Refiguring values, power, knowledge: Of Foucault's disavowal of Marx', in B. Magnus and S. Cullenberg (eds.), *Whither Marxism? Global Crises in International Perspective*. New York: Routledge, 31–64.

Jayarajah, C. and W. Branson. 1995. *Structural and Sectoral Adjustment: World Bank Experience, 1980–92*. Washington, DC: World Bank.

Jeffries, R. 1989. 'Ghana: The political economy of personal rule', in D. Cruise O'Brien, J. Dunn and R. Rathbone (eds.), *Contemporary West African States*. Cambridge: Cambridge University Press, 75–98.

Johnson, C. 1992. *MITI and the Japanese Miracle: The Growth of Industry Policy 1925–1975*. Stanford: Stanford University Press.

———. 1993a. 'Comparative capitalism: The Japanese difference', *California Management Review* (Summer): 51–67.

———. 1993b. 'History restarted: Japanese–American relations at the end of the century', in R. Higgot, R. Leaver and J. Ravenhill (eds.), *Pacific Economic Relations in the 1990s: Conflict or Cooperation?* Boulder, CO: Lynne Rienner, 39–61.

———. 1994. 'Wake up America!', *Critical Intelligence* 2 (8).

Johnson, H. 2001. 'Book review: *Voices of the Poor. Can Anyone Hear Us?*', *Journal of International Development* 13: 377–79.

Johnson, I. 2001. 'World Bank's environmentally and socially sustainable development network', quoted in 'World Bank incorporates environmental concerns into lending programs', http://ens-news-com/ens/jul2001/2001L-07-19-05.html. Accessed 28 September 2004.

Johnson, S. 1996. *Education and Training of Accountants in Sub-Saharan Anglophone Africa*. Washington, DC: World Bank.

Johnson, S. and B. Rogaly. 1997. *Microfinance and Poverty Reduction*. Oxford: Oxfam.

Johnston, J. and S. Wasty. 1993. 'Borrower ownership of adjustment programs and the political economy of reform'. World Bank Discussion Paper, Washington, DC.

Johnstone, D. 1986. *The Rhetoric of Leviathan: Thomas Hobbes and the Politics of Cultural Transformation*. Princeton, NJ: Princeton University Press.

Jubilee Debt Campaign. 2003. 'Did the G8 drop the debt?', http://www.jubileeresearch.org/analysis/reports/G8final.pdf. Accessed 8 April 2006.

Jubilee Plus. 2003. 'Real progress report on HIPC'. London, September.

Jubilee South. 2001. 'Pan-African declaration on PRSPs'. Kampala, 12 May.

Jung, D. 2003. *Shadow Globalization, Ethnic Conflicts and New Wars: A Political Economy of Intra-state War*. London: Routledge.

Kahn, J. 2001. 'World Bank presses inquiry on economist who dissents', *New York Times*, 7 September.
Kanbur, R. 2000. 'Electronic discussion on draft *World Development Report On Poverty 2000/01*: Response to final summary'. Electronic Discussion Forum, World Bank.
———. 2002. 'Conceptual challenges in poverty and inequality: One development economist's perspective', www.arts.cornell.edu/poverty/kanbur/CCPI.pdf. Accessed 26 October 2006.
Kant, I. 1997. *Groundwork of the Metaphysics of Morals*. Cambridge: Cambridge University Press.
Kaplan, R. 1994. 'The coming anarchy', *Atlantic Monthly* (February).
———. 1997. 'Review of *The State in a Changing World*', *Foreign Policy* 108: 167–68.
Kapoor, I. 2002. 'The devil's in the theory: A critical assessment of Robert Chambers' work on participatory development', *Third World Quarterly* 23 (1): 101–17.
Kapur, D. 2002. 'The changing anatomy of governance of the World Bank', in J. Pincus and J. Winters (eds.), *Reinventing the World Bank*. Ithaca and London: Cornell University Press, 54–75.
Kapur, D., J. Lewis and R. Webb (eds.). 1997. *The World Bank: Its First Half Century. Volume 1: History*. Washington, DC: Brookings Institution Press.
Karshenas, M. 1997. 'Dynamic economies and the critique of urban bias', in H. Bernstein and T. Brass (eds.), *Agrarian Questions: Essays in Appreciation of T.J. Byres*, special issue of *Journal of Peasant Studies* 24 (1/2): 60–102.
———. 2001. 'Agriculture and economic development in sub-Saharan Africa and Asia', *Cambridge Journal of Economics* 25 (3): 315–42.
Kay, G. 1976. *Development and Underdevelopment: A Marxist Analysis*. London: Macmillan.
Keane, J. 1995. *Tom Paine: A Political Life*. London: Bloomsbury.
Keegan, W. 1993 [1992]. *The Spectre of Capitalism: The Future of the World Economy after the Fall of Communism*. London: Vintage.
Keen, D. 1994. *The Benefits of Famine: A Political Economy of Famine and Relief in Southwestern Sudan, 1983–1989*. Princeton, NJ: Princeton University Press.
———. 1998a. 'Aid and violence, with special reference to Sierra Leone', *Disasters* 22 (4): 318–27.
———. 1998b. 'The economic functions of violence in civil wars'. Adelphi Paper 320. London: International Institute for Strategic Studies.
Kelsall, T. 2002. 'Shop windows and smoke-filled rooms: Governance and the repoliticisation of Tanzania', *Journal of Modern African Studies* 40 (4): 597–620.
———. 2003. 'Democracy, de-agrarianisation and the African self'. Occasional Paper, Centre of African Studies, University of Copenhagen.
Khan, M.H. 2001. 'The new political economy of corruption', in B. Fine, C. Lapavitsas and J. Pincus (eds.), *Development Policy in the Twenty-first Century: Beyond the Post-Washington Consensus*. London: Routledge, 112–35.

―――. 2002. 'Corruption and governance in early capitalism: World Bank strategies and their limitations', in J. Pincus and J. Winters (eds.), *Reinventing the World Bank*. Ithaca and London: Cornell University Press, 164–84.

Kiely, R. 1995. 'Third Worldist relativism: A new form of imperialism', *Journal of Contemporary Asia* 25 (2): 159–78.

―――. 1998. 'Neoliberalism revised? A critical account of World Bank concepts of good governance and market-friendly intervention', *Capital and Class* 64: 63–89.

―――. 2005. *The Clash of Globalisations: Neoliberalism, the Third Way, and Anti-globalisation*. Leiden: Brill.

Kimani, S. (ed.). 2003. *The Right to Dissent: Freedom of Expression, Assembly and Demonstration in the New South Africa*. Johannesburg: Freedom of Expression Institute.

King, K. 2000. 'Towards knowledge-based aid: A new way of working or a new North–South divide?', *Journal of International Cooperation in Education* 3, 2 (2000): 23–48.

King, K. and S. McGrath. 2004. *Knowledge for development? Comparing British, Japanese, Swedish and World Bank Aid*. London: Zed Books.

Kitching, G. 1980. *Class and Economic Change in Kenya: The Making of an African Petit Bourgeoisie 1905–1970*. New Haven: Yale University Press.

Klare, M. 2003. 'For oil and empire? Rethinking war with Iraq', *Current History* 102: 129–35.

Klein, N. 2000. *No Logo*. London: Picador.

Klitgaard, R. 1995. 'Institutional adjustment and adjusting to institutions'. World Bank Discussion Paper. Washington, DC: World Bank.

Knack, S. 1999. 'Social capital, growth and poverty: A survey of cross-country evidence'. Social Capital Initiative Working Paper (7 May).

Knack, S. and P. Keefer. 1997. 'Does social capital have an economic payoff? A cross-country investigation', *Quarterly Journal of Economics* 62 (4): 1251–88.

Koh, T. 1993. 'The ten values that undergird East Asian strength and success', *International Herald Tribune*, 11 December.

Köhler, G. 1999. 'Global Keynesianism and beyond', *Journal of World Systems Research* 5, http://jwsr.ucr.edu/archive/vol5/number2/v5n2_split/jwsr_v5n2_köhler.pdf. Accessed 26 October 2006.

Köhler, G. and A. Tausch. 2002. *Global Keynesianism: Unequal Exchange and Global Exploitation*. Huntington, NY: Nova.

Kolankiewicz, G. 1996. 'Social capital and social change', *British Journal of Sociology* 47 (3): 427–41.

Kolko, G. 1988. *Confronting the Third World: United States Foreign Policy 1945–1980*. New York: Pantheon.

Konrad, K. 1995. 'Social security and strategic inter-vivos transfers of social capital', *Journal of Population Economics* 8 (3): 315–26.

Kostner, M. 1999. 'Toward inclusive and sustainable development in the Democratic Republic of the Congo'. World Bank Post-Conflict Unit, Africa Region, Working Paper Series, 2 (March).

Krasner, S. 1982. 'Regimes and the limits of realism: Regimes as autonomous variables', *International Organization* 36 (2): 497–510.

Krugman, P. 1998. 'Saving Asia: It's time to get radical', *Fortune* (7 September): 32–37.

Kubota, I. 1991a. 'The case for two-step loans'. Paper read at biannual meeting between the World Bank and the OECF /J-EXIM, May.

———. 1991b. 'Reflections on recent trends in development aid policy'. Paper read at biannual meeting between the World Bank and the OECF /J-EXIM, November.

———. 1991c. 'The role of domestic saving and macroeconomic stability in the development process', Economic Society of Australia, *Economic Papers* 2 (2): 34–42.

———. 1993a. 'The East Asian miracle: Major arguments on recent economic development policy', *Finance* (Japanese ministry of finance monthly journal) (December) (in Japanese).

———. 1993b.'On the "Asian Miracle"', Japanese ministry of finance, mimeo.

Kukathas, C. 1999. 'The "Asian way" and modern liberalism: A Hayekian perspective', *Policy* 15 (2): 3–9.

Kymlicka, W. and W. Norman (eds.). 2000. *Citizenship in Diverse Societies*. Oxford: Oxford University Press.

Lacher, H. 1999. 'The politics of the market: Re-reading Karl Polanyi', *Global Society* 13 (3): 313–26.

Ladd, P. 2003. 'Options for democratising the World Bank and the IMF'. London: Christian Aid.

Lal, D. 1983. *The Poverty of 'Development Economics'*. London: Institute of Economic Affairs.

Lall, S. 1995. 'The *East Asian Miracle*: Does the bell toll for industrial strategy?', *World Development* 22 (4): 645–54.

Lambert, L. 2005. 'Thousands in US protest Iraq war, globalisation', Reuters, 25 September.

Langhelle, O. 1999. 'Nature, market and ignorance: Can development be managed?', in W.M. Lafferty and O. Langhelle (eds.), *Towards Sustainable Development: On the Goals of Development – and the Conditions of Sustainability*. London: Macmillan, 140–62.

Lanning, G. (producer). 1998. *The Bank, the President and the Pearl of Africa*. London and Paris: Channel 4 and La Sept Channel.

Larsen, M.N. 2002. 'Is oligopoly a condition of successful privatization? The case of cotton in Zimbabwe', *Journal of Agrarian Change* 2 (2): 185–205.

Larson, A. 2003. 'The Millennium Challenge Account: Statement before the senate foreign relations committee', Washington, DC (4 March).

Latham, M.E. 2000. *Modernization as Ideology: American Social Science and 'Nation Building' in the Kennedy Era*. Chapel Hill: University of North Carolina Press.

Lee, S. 2002. 'Global monitor: The International Monetary Fund', *New Political Economy* 7 (2): 283–98.

Select Bibliography

Leftwich, A. 1993. 'Governance, democracy, and development in the Third World', *Third World Quarterly* 14 (3): 605–24.

Legassick, M. (forthcoming). *Towards Socialist Democracy*. Pietermaritzburg: University of KwaZulu-Natal Press.

Legum, M. 2002. *It Doesn't Have to Be Like This! A New Economy for South Africa and the World.* Cape Town: Ampersand Press.

Leijonhufved, A. 1968. *On Keynesian Economics and the Economics of Keynes*. Oxford: Oxford University Press.

Leis, H.R. and E.J. Viola. 1995. 'Towards a sustainable future: The organizing role of ecology in the North–South relationship', in F. Fischer and M. Black (eds.), *Greening Environmental Policy: Politics of a Sustainable Future*. London: Paul Chapman, 33–50.

Lélé, S. 1991. 'Sustainable development: A critical review', *World Development* 19 (6): 607–21.

Leonard, D.K. 1991. *African Successes: Four Public Managers of Kenyan Rural Development*. Berkeley: University of California Press.

Levin, R. and D. Weiner (eds.). 1997. *No More Tears*. Trenton, NJ: Africa World Press.

Leys, C. 1971. 'Politics in Kenya: The development of peasant society', *British Journal of Political Science* 1 (3): 307–37.

———. 1975. *Underdevelopment in Kenya: The Political Economy of Neo-colonialism*. London: Heinemann.

———. 1978. 'Capital accumulation, class formation and dependency: The significance of the Kenyan case', in R. Miliband and J. Saville (eds.), *The Socialist Register 1978*. London: The Merlin Press, 241–66.

———. 1987. 'The state and the crisis of simple commodity production in Africa', *IDS Bulletin* 18 (3): 45–48.

———. 1994. 'Confronting the African tragedy', *New Left Review* 1 (204): 44–45.

———. 1996a. *The Rise and Fall of Development Theory*. London, Bloomington, and Nairobi: James Currey, Indiana University Press and East African Educational Publishers.

———. 1996b. 'The world, society and the individual', *Southern Africa Report* 11 (3): 17–21.

Lie, J. 1991. 'Embedding Polanyi's market society', *Sociological Perspectives* 34 (2): 219–35.

Lincoln, E. 1993. *Japan's New Global Role*. Washington, DC: Brookings Institution Press.

Lind, M. 2004. 'A tragedy of errors', *The Nation*, 23 February.

Lipton, M. 1997. 'Editorial: Poverty – are there holes in the consensus?', *World Development* 25 (7): 1003–07.

Little, I. 1982. *Economic Development: Theory, Policy and International Relations*. New York: Basic Books.

Long, N. and A. Long. (eds.). 1992. *Battlefields of Knowledge: The Interlocking of Theory and Practice in Social Research and Development*. London: Routledge.

Lumsden, F. and A. Loftus. 2003. 'Inanda's struggle for water through pipes and tunnels'. University of KwaZulu-Natal, Centre for Civil Society, Research Report No. 6, http://www.nu.ac.za/ccs.
Luttwak, E. 1999. 'Give war a chance', *Foreign Affairs* 78 (4): 36–44.
Luxemburg, R. 2003 [1913]. *The Accumulation of Capital*. London: Routledge.
Mackinnon, J. and R. Reinikka. 2002. 'How research can assist policy: The case of economic reforms in Uganda', *World Bank Research Observer* 17 (2): 267–92.
MacMillan, R. 1995. 'Changes in the structure of life courses and the decline of social capital in Canadian society: A time series analysis of property crime rates', *Canadian Journal of Sociology* 20 (1): 51–79.
Macpherson, C. 1964. *The Political Theory of Possessive Individualism: Hobbes to Locke*. Oxford: Clarendon.
Macrae, J. 2001. *Aiding Recovery? The Crisis of Aid in Chronic Political Emergencies*. London: Zed Books.
MacWilliam, S. 1986. 'International capital, indigenous accumulation and the state in Papua New Guinea: The case of the Development Bank', *Capital and Class* 29: 150–81.
———. 1987. 'International companies and nationalist politics in Papua New Guinea', *Journal of Contemporary Asia* 17 (1): 19–41.
———. 1988. 'Smallholdings, land law and the politics of land tenure in Papua New Guinea', *Journal of Peasant Studies* 16 (1): 77–109.
———. 1996. '"Just like working for the dole": Rural households, export crops and state subsidies in Papua New Guinea', *Journal of Peasant Studies* 23 (4): 40–78.
———. 1999. 'Back to back they faced each other: Indigenous capital in Fiji, 1984–1999'. Paper presented at a seminar, National Centre for Development Studies, Australian National University, Canberra, December.
———. 2002. 'Poverty, governance and corruption in Fiji', *Pacific Economic Bulletin* 17 (1): 138–45.
———. 2003 'The poverty of plenty: Review article', *Historical Materialism* 11 (1): 199–221.
MacWilliam, S. and V.M. Daveta. 2000. 'Electoral democracy, coups and indigenous commerce: The case of tourism in Fiji, 1987–1999'. Paper presented at the Finnish Society for Development Studies annual conference, Helsinki, 4–5 February.
MacWilliam, S., F. Desaubin and W. Timms. 1995. *Domestic Food Production and Political Conflict in Kenya*. Monograph No. 10. Nedlands: Indian Ocean Centre for Peace Studies, University of Western Australia.
Mail & Guardian. 1997. 'Zimbabwe: Protestors and government', 12 December.
———.1998. 'People power pays off in Zimbabwe', 23 January.
Makhaye, D. 2002. 'Left factionalism and the NDR: The ANC must respond to professionals of the "Left"', *ANC Today*, http://www.anc.org.za/ancdocs/anctoday/2002/text/a48.txt. Accessed 26 October 2006.
Malherbe, P. 2003. 'The danger of high interest rates', *Sane Views* 3 (20) (June).

Mallaby, S. 2005. *The World's Banker: A Story of Failed States, Financial Crises and the Wealth and Poverty of Nations*. New Haven: Yale University Press.

Mamdani, M. 1996. *Citizen and Subject: Decentralized Despotism and the Legacy of Late Colonialism*. Princeton, NJ: Princeton University Press.

——. 1998. 'Understanding the crisis in Kivu: Report of the CODESRIA mission to the Democratic Republic of Congo'. Dakar: Council for the Development of Social Research in Africa.

Mandeville, B. 1970. *The Fable of the Bees*. Harmondsworth: Penguin.

Manji, M. 1995. *Madatally Manji: Memoirs of a Biscuit Baron*. Nairobi: East African Educational Publishers and Kenway Publications.

Mann, M. 1997. 'Has globalization ended the rise and rise of the nation-state?', *Review of International Political Economy* 4 (3): 472–96.

Mansbridge, J. 1990. 'Self-interest in political life', *Political Theory* 18 (1): 132–253.

Manuel, T. 2000. 'Address to the seminar on South Africa's relations and creation of national wealth and social welfare', Rand Afrikaans University, Centre for European Studies, Johannesburg, 20 October.

——. 2002a. 'Mobilizing international investment flows: The new global outlook'. Speech to the Commonwealth Business Council, 24 September.

——. 2002b. 'Remarks at the finance minister's retreat', International Conference on Financing for Development, Monterrey, Mexico, 19 March.

——. 2002c. 'Remarks to the international business forum at the International Conference on Financing for Development', Monterrey, Mexico, 18 March.

——. 2002d. 'Remarks to the International Conference on Financing for Development', Monterrey, Mexico, 18 March.

——. 2003. 'Input to the HSRC conference', Kleinmond, 4 May.

——. 2004. 'Dear Colleague' letter to members of the joint ministerial committee of the Boards of governors of the Bank and the Fund on the transfer of real resources to developing countries. Pretoria, 29 March.

Marais, H. 2000. *South Africa: Limits to Change*. London and Cape Town: Zed Books and University of Cape Town Press.

Maren, M. 1997. *The Road to Hell: The Ravaging Effects of Foreign Aid and International Charity*. New York: Free Press.

Markoff, J. and V. Montecinos. 1993. 'The ubiquitous rise of economists', *Journal of Public Policy* 13 (1): 37–68.

Marquette, H. 2001. 'Corruption, democracy, and the World Bank', *Crime Law and Social Change* 36: 395–407.

Marsden, K. 1990. 'African entrepreneurs: Pioneers of development'. Discussion Paper No. 9. Washington, DC: International Finance Corporation, World Bank.

Marshall, A. 1962. *Principles of Economics*. London: Macmillan.

Martin, B. 2000. *New Leaf or Fig Leaf? The Challenge of the New Washington Consensus*. London: Bretton Woods Project and Public Services International.

Martin, E. 1997. 'Managing Americans: Policy and changes in the meanings of work and the self', in C. Shore and S. Wright (eds.), *Anthropology of Policy: Critical Perspectives on Governance and Power*. London: Routledge, 239–57.

Martin, M. 1994. 'The bargaining process of policy-based lending', in W. van der Geest (ed.), *Negotiating Structural Adjustment*. Oxford: James Currey, 197–223.

Marx, K. 1930 [1867]. 'Primary accumulation', in *Capital: In Two Vols.*, London: Everyman's Library.

———. 1974 [1875]. 'Critique of the Gotha Programme', in D. Fernbach (ed.), *The First International and After: Political Writings*, Volume 3. London: Penguin, 340–55.

———. 1976. *Capital*, Volume 1. London: Penguin.

Mason, E. and R. Asher. 1973. *The World Bank since Bretton Woods*. Washington, DC: Brookings Institution Press.

Mawdsley, E. and J. Rigg. 2002. 'A survey of the *World Development Reports*, I: Discursive strategies', *Progress in Development Studies* 2 (2): 93–111.

May, J. (ed.). 1998. 'Poverty and inequality in South Africa'. Report prepared for the office of the executive deputy president and the inter-ministerial committee for poverty and inequality.

———. 2000. *Poverty and Inequality in South Africa: Meeting the Challenge*. Cape Town: David Philip.

Mayekiso, M. 1996. *Township Politics: Civic Struggles for a New South Africa*. New York: Monthly Review Press.

Mbali, M. 2002. '"A bit of soap and water, and some Jik": Historical and feminist critiques of an exclusively individualising understanding of cholera prevention in discourse around neoliberal water policy'. Paper delivered at the Services for All? Conference, Municipal Services Project, Johannesburg, May.

Mbeki, T. 2002a. 'Address by President Mbeki at the welcome ceremony of the World Summit on Sustainable Development', Johannesburg, 25 August.

———. 2002b. 'Statement of the president of the African National Congress, Thabo Mbeki, at the ANC policy conference', Kempton Park, 27 September.

———. 2004. 'Remarks at the consultative meeting of African governors on voice and participation of developing and transition countries in the Bretton Woods institutions', Johannesburg, 12 March.

Mbembe, A. and J. Roitman. 1995. 'Figures of the subject in times of crisis', *Public Culture* 7 (2): 323–52.

Mboweni, T. and T. Manuel. 2001. 'Joint press statement', Reserve Bank and ministry of finance, Pretoria, 21 December.

McCandless, E. and E. Pajibo. 2003. 'Can participation advance poverty reduction? PRSP process and content in four countries'. Paper in Afrodad PRSP Series, Harare, January.

McCully, P. 2002. 'Avoiding solutions, worsening problems: A critique of the World Bank Water Resources Sector Strategy', www.irn.org/new/0205.wrsscritiquea.pdf, 27 May. Accessed 18 January 2007.

McDonald, D. (ed.). 2002a. *Environmental Justice in South Africa*. Cape Town: University of Cape Town Press.

Select Bibliography

———. 2002b. 'The bell tolls for thee: Cost recovery, cutoffs, and affordability of municipal services in South Africa', in D. McDonald and J. Pape (eds.), *Cost Recovery and the Crisis of Service Delivery in South Africa*. London and Pretoria: Zed Books and HSRC Publications, 169–79.

McDonald, D. and J. Pape (eds.). 2002. *Cost Recovery and the Crisis of Service Delivery in South Africa*. London and Pretoria: Zed Books and HSRC Publications.

McGee, R. 2002. 'Assessing participation in Poverty Reduction Strategy Papers: A desk-based synthesis of experience in sub-Saharan Africa'. University of Sussex, Institute for Development Studies.

McKendrick, N. 1961. 'Josiah Wedgwood and factory discipline', *Historical Journal* 4 (1): 30–55.

McKibbin, W. and M. Will. 1999. 'The East Asian crisis: Investigating causes and policy responses'. Policy Research Working Paper No. 2172. Washington, DC: World Bank, August.

McKinley, D. 1997. *The ANC and the Liberation Struggle: A Critical Political Biography*. London: Pluto Press.

McManus, P. 1996. 'Contested terrains: Politics, stories and discourses of sustainability', *Environmental Politics* 5 (1): 48–73.

McMichael, P. 2001. 'Revisiting the question of the transnational state: A comment on William Robinson's "Social theory and globalization"', *Theory and Society* 30 (2): 201–10.

McNamara, R.S. 1981. *The McNamara Years at the World Bank: Major Policy Addresses of Robert S. McNamara, 1968–1981*. Baltimore: Johns Hopkins University Press.

———. 1996. *In Retrospect: The Tragedy and Lessons of Vietnam*. New York: Vintage.

Meagher, K. 1995. 'Crisis, informalization and the urban informal economy in sub-Saharan Africa', *Development and Change* 26 (2): 259–84.

Meckay, E. 2006. 'Groups question World Bank's role in troubled mine', Inter Press Service, 1 February.

Mehmet, O. 1995. *Westernizing the Third World: The Eurocentricity of Economic Development Theories*. London: Routledge.

Mehta, L. 2001. 'The World Bank and its emerging knowledge empire', *Human Organization* 60 (2): 189–96.

Mehta, U. 1999. *Liberalism and Empire: Essays on Nineteenth-century British Liberal Thought*. Chicago: University of Chicago Press.

Melvern, L. 2000. *A People Betrayed: The Role of the West in Rwanda's Genocide*. London: Zed Books.

———. 2004. *Conspiracy to Murder: The Rwanda Genocide and the International Community*. London: Verso.

Meuret, D. 1993. 'A political genealogy of political economy', in G. Mike and T. Johnson (eds.), *Foucault's New Domains*. London: Routledge, 49–74.

Meyerson, E. 1994. 'Human capital, social capital and compensation: The relative contribution of social contacts to managers' incomes', *Acta Sociologica* 37 (4): 383–99.

Migdal, J. 1988. *Strong Societies and Weak States: State–Society Relations and State Capabilities in the Third World*. Princeton, NJ: Princeton University Press.

Milanovic, B. 2002. 'The two faces of globalization: Against globalization as we know it'. Second draft. Washington: World Bank Research Department, May.

———. 2003. 'The two faces of globalization: Against globalization as we know it', *World Development* 31 (4): 667–83.

Milbank, D. 2005. 'Ex-neocon hawk Paul Wolfowitz now touts peace: World Bank chief tries to distance himself from Bush', *Washington Post*, 8 December.

Millard, E. 1987. *Financial Management of a Small Handicraft Business*. Oxford: Oxfam.

Miller, P. 1992. 'Accounting and objectivity: The invention of calculating selves and calculable spaces', *Annals of Scholarship* 9 (1/2): 61–86.

Miller, P. and E. Cleary. 1987. 'Accounting and the construction of the governable person', *Accounting, Organisations and Society* 12 (3): 235–65.

Mitchell, T. 1988. *Colonising Egypt*. Berkeley: University of California Press.

Mkhize, T. 2001. 'Cholera and the water business', *Debate* 5: 17–24.

Mobilisation for Global Justice. 2005. 'Block the Bank! Fight the Fund! Reclaim our communities! Confront economic violence and corporate capitalism during the World Bank and IMF annual meetings'. Pamphlet distributed in Washington, DC, 21 July.

Mohamad, M. and S. Ishihara. 1995. *The Voice of Asia: Two Leaders Discuss the Coming Century*. Tokyo: Kodansha International.

Mohan, G. 1997. 'Developing differences: Post-structuralism and political economy in contemporary development studies', *Review of African Political Economy* 24 (73): 311–28.

Mokonyane, D. 1995. *The Big Sell Out*. London: Nakong ya Rena.

Moleketi, J. and J. Jele. 2002. 'Two strategies of the National Liberation Movement in the struggle for the victory of the national democratic revolution'. Discussion document distributed by the African National Congress, Johannesburg, October.

Monbiot, G. 2003a. 'How to stop America: The Chartist movement of the 21st century', *New Statesman*, 9 June.

———. 2003b. 'The worst of times', *Mail & Guardian*, 5–11 September.

Moody, K. 1997. 'Towards an international social-movement unionism', *New Left Review* 1 (225): 52–72.

Moore, D. 1995. 'Development discourse as hegemony: Towards an ideological history – 1945–1995', in D. Moore and G. Schmitz (eds.), *Debating Development Discourse: Institutional and Popular Perspectives*. London: Macmillan, 1–53.

———. 1997. 'Issuing a new ruling class: "Good governance" and the African Capacity Building Foundation', in P. Ahluwalia and P. Nursey-Bray (eds.), *The Post-colonial Condition: Contemporary Politics in Africa*. New York: Nova, 178–88.

———. 1999. '"Sail on o ship of state": Neoliberalism, globalisation, and the governance of Africa', *Journal of Peasant Studies* 27 (1): 61–96.

———. 2000a. 'Humanitarian agendas, state reconstruction, and democratisation processes in wartorn societies'. United Nations High Commission for Refugees Policy and Evaluation Unit, Working Paper 24, June.

———. 2000b. 'Levelling the playing fields and embedding illusions: "Post-conflict" discourse and neo-liberal "development" in war-torn Africa', *Review of African Political Economy* 27 (83): 11–28.

———. 2001. 'Africa: The black hole at the middle of *Empire?*', *Rethinking Marxism* 13 (3/4): 100–18.

———. 2003a. 'Hardt and Negri's *Empire*, real Empire and the "Third World" after 9/11', *Acme*, 2 (2): 112–31.

———. 2003b. 'The political economy of the DRC war', in G. Le Pere and S. Naidoo (eds.), *The War Economy in the Democratic Republic of the Congo*. Johannesburg: Institute for Global Dialogue, 16–39.

———. 2004a. 'The Second Age of the Third World: From primitive accumulation to public goods?', *Third World Quarterly* 25 (1): 87–109.

———. 2004b. 'War in the DRC', *New Agenda* 14: 90–92.

Moore, D. and C. Kukathas. 1999/2000. 'Hayekian interpretations: A debate over the "Asian Way" and modern liberalism', *Policy* 15 (4): 30–32.

Moore, D. and G. Schmitz (eds.). 1995. *Debating Development Discourse: Popular and Institutional Perspectives*. Basingstoke: Macmillan.

Moore, M. 1997. 'Societies, politics and capitalists in developing countries: A literature survey', *Journal of Development Studies* 33 (3): 287–363.

———. 1998. 'Epilogue: Is the state back in fashion?', in A. Evans and M. Moore (eds.), *The Bank, the State and Development: Dissecting the 1997* World Development Report, *IDS Bulletin* 29 (2): 45–47.

———. 2001. 'Empowerment at last?', *Journal of International Development* 13 (3): 321–29.

Moran, D. 2000. *Introduction to Phenomenology*. London: Routledge.

Morawetz, D. 1977. *Twenty-five Years of Economic Development 1950–1975*. Baltimore: Johns Hopkins University Press for the World Bank.

Mosley, P. 1997. 'The World Bank, "global Keynesianism" and the distribution of the gains from growth', *World Development* 25 (11): 1949–56.

———. 2001. '*Attacking Poverty* and the "Post-Washington Consensus"', *Journal of International Development* 13: 307–13.

———. 2002. 'The African green revolution as a pro-poor policy instrument', *Journal of International Development* 14 (6): 695–724.

Mosley, P., J. Harrigan and J. Toye. 1991. *Aid and Power: The World Bank and Policy-based Lending, Volume 1, Analysis and Policy Proposals*. London: Routledge.

———. 1995. *Aid and Power: The World Bank and Policy-based Lending*. London: Routledge.

Mosley, P., T. Subasat and J. Weeks. 1995. 'Assessing adjustment in Africa', *World Development* 23 (9): 1459–73.

Murray, M. 1995. *Revolution Deferred*. London: Verso.

Mutasa, C. 2003. 'Cancelling Africa's debt: A critical appraisal of the HIPC process', *Pambazuka News* 109, 10 May.

Myburgh Commission. 2002. *Commission of Inquiry into the Rapid Depreciation of the Exchange Rate of the Rand and Related Matters.* Pretoria, 30 June.

Nairn, T. 2005. 'Make for the Boondocks', *London Review of Books* 27 (9) 5 May.

Narayan, D., R. Chambers, M.K. Shah and P. Petesch. 2000. *Voices of the Poor. Volume 2. Crying out for Change.* New York: Oxford University Press.

Narayan, D., R. Patel, K. Schafft, A. Rademacher and S. Koch-Schulte. 2000. *Voices of the Poor. Volume 1. Can Anyone Hear Us?* New York: Oxford University Press.

Narayan, D. and P. Petesch. 2000. *Voices of the Poor. Volume 3. From Many Lands.* New York: Oxford University Press.

Narayan, D. and L. Pritchett. 1996. 'Cents and sociability: Household income and social capital in rural Tanzania'. Policy Research Department, Washington: World Bank, DC, mimeo.

Navarro, V. 2004. 'Meet the new head of the IMF', *Counterpunch*, http://www.counterpunch.org, 19 June.

Ndungane, N. 2003. *A World with a Human Face: A Voice from Africa.* Cape Town: David Philip.

Neeson, J.M. 1993. *Commoners: Common Right, Enclosure and Social Change in England 1700–1820.* Cambridge: Cambridge University Press.

Negishi, T. 1979. *Microeconomic Foundations of Keynesian Macroeconomics.* Amsterdam: Elsevier.

Nelson, N. and S. Wright (eds.). 1995. *Power and Participatory Development: Theory and Practice.* London: Intermediate Technology Publications.

Nelson, P. 1995. *The World Bank and Non-governmental Organisations: The Limits of Apolitical Development.* Basingstoke: Macmillan.

———. 2000. 'Whose civil society? Whose governance? Decision making and practice in the new agenda at the Inter-American Development Bank and the World Bank', *Global Governance* 6 (4): 405–31.

Neumayer, E. 1999. *Weak versus Strong Sustainability: Exploring the Limits of Two Opposing Paradigms.* Cheltenham: Edward Elgar.

Nichols, T. 1996. 'Russian democracy and social capital', *Social Science Information* 35 (4): 629–42.

Njehu, N. and L. Cagan. 2005. 'Wolfowitz's move to the World Bank presidency and the sharpening of economic policy as a weapon of mass impoverishment', http://www.commondreams.org/views05/0531-33.htm. Accessed 13 February 2006.

North, D. 1990. *Institutions, Institutional Change and Economic Performance.* Cambridge: Cambridge University Press.

Ntsebeza, L. 2001. 'Traditional authorities and rural development in post-apartheid South Africa: The case of the Transkei region of the Eastern Cape', in J. Coetzee, J. Graaff, F. Hendricks and G. Wood (eds.), *Development: Theory, Policy, and Practice.* Cape Town: Oxford University Press, 317–30.

Nunn, A. 2001/02. 'Interpreting the "knowledge economy" cacophony: The extension of commodification to information production, dissemination and storage', http://libr.org/isc/articles/14-Nunn.html. Accessed 16 March 2003.

Select Bibliography

Nurkse, R. 1953. *Problems of Capital Formation in Underdeveloped Countries.* Oxford: Oxford University Press.

Nussbaum, M. 1995. 'Human capabilities, female human beings', in M. Nussbaum and J. Glover (eds.), *Women, Culture and Development: A Study of Human Capabilities.* Oxford: Clarendon Press, 61–104.

Nussbaum, M. and J. Glover (eds.). 1995. *Women, Culture and Development: A Study of Human Capabilities.* Oxford: Clarendon Press.

Nyamugasira, W. and R. Rowden. 2002. 'New strategies, old loan conditions: Do the IMF and World Bank loans support countries' Poverty Reduction Strategies? The case of Uganda'. Kampala: Uganda National NGO Forum and RESULTS Educational Fund, April.

O'Connor, J. 1998. 'Is sustainable capitalism possible?', in M. O'Connor (ed.), *Is Capitalism Sustainable? Political Economy and the Politics of Ecology.* New York: Guildford Press, 152–75.

O'Hanlon, R. 1996. *Congo Journey.* London: Penguin.

O'Meara, D. 1996. *Forty Lost Years: The Apartheid State and the Politics of the National Party, 1948–1994.* Johannesburg and Athens: Raven Press and Ohio University Press.

O'Riordan, T. 1976. *Environmentalism.* London: Pion.

OECF (Overseas Economic Cooperation Fund). 1991. 'Issues related to the World Bank's approach to a structural adjustment: Proposal from a major partner'. OECF Occasional Papers No. 1, October.

Ohno, K. and I. Ohno (eds.). 1998. *Japanese Views on Economic Development: Diverse Paths to the Market.* London: Routledge.

Okuda, H. 1993. 'Japanese two step loans: The Japanese approach to development finance', *Hitototsubashi Journal of Economics* 34: 67–85.

Ong'wen, 'O. 2001. 'The PRSP in Kenya', *World Bank Watch SA? SA Watch WB!* (December).

Onuf, N.G. 1998. *The Republican Legacy in International Thought.* Cambridge: Cambridge University Press.

Operations Evaluation Department. 2001. *Review of the Bank's Performance on the Environment.* Washington, DC: World Bank.

Orwell, G. *Nineteen Eighty-four.* 1970 [1949]. London: Martin Secker and Warburg.

Ostrom, E. 1994. 'Constituting social capital and collective action', *Journal of Theoretical Politics* 6 (4): 527–62.

Ota, F., H. Tanikawa and T. Otani. 1992. 'Russia's economic reform and Japan's industrial policy'. MITI Research Institute, typescript (April).

Oxfam. 1995. *A Case for Reform: Fifty Years of the IMF and World Bank.* Oxford: Oxfam.

Øyen, E. 2000. 'Six questions to the World Bank on the *World Development Report 2000/01: Attacking Poverty*'. International Social Science Council, Comparative Research Programme on Poverty, http://www.crop.org/wdroyen1.htm. Accessed 21 June 2003.

Packenham, R.A. 1973. *Liberal America and the Third World: Political Development Ideas in Foreign Aid and Social Science.* Princeton, NJ: Princeton University Press.
Pahl, R. 1996. 'Comment on Kolankiewicz', *British Journal of Sociology* 47 (3): 443–46.
Panos. 2002. *Reducing Poverty: Is the World Bank's Strategy Working?* London: Panos.
Parcel, T. and E. Menaghan. 1994. 'Early parental work, family social capital, and early childhood outcomes', *American Journal of Sociology* 99 (4): 972–1009.
Paris, R. 2002. 'International peacebuilding and the "mission civilisatrice"', *Review of International Studies* 28: 637–56.
Patrick, H. 1977. 'The future of the Japanese economy: Output and labor productivity', *Journal of Japanese Studies* 3 (2): 219–49.
Payer, C. 1982. *The World Bank: A Critical Analysis.* New York: Monthly Review Press.
Pearce, D.W. and J.J. Warford. 1993. *World Without End: Economics, Environment and Sustainable Development.* New York: Oxford University Press.
Peet, R. 2003. *The World Bank, IMF and WTO.* London: Zed Books.
Pender, J. 2001. 'From "structural adjustment" to "comprehensive development framework": Conditionality transformed?', *Third World Quarterly* 22 (3): 397–411.
Pereira, L. 1995. 'Development economics and the World Bank's identity crisis', *Review of International Political Economy* 2 (2): 211–47.
Peters, P. 2002. 'The limits of negotiability: Security, equity and class formation in Africa's land systems', in K. Juul and C. Lund (eds.), *Negotiating Property in Africa.* Portsmouth, NH: Heinemann, 45–66.
Petiteville, F. 1998. 'Three mythical representations of the state in development theory', *International Social Science Journal* 50 (1): 115–24.
Petras, J., H. Veltmeyer and S. Vieux. 1997. *Neoliberal Restructuring and Class Conflict in Latin America.* London: Macmillan.
Picciotto, R. 1995. 'Putting institutional economics to work: From participation to governance'. World Bank Discussion Paper. Washington, DC: World Bank.
Pieterse, J. 1997. 'Equity and growth revisited: A supply-side approach to social development', *European Journal of Development Research* 9 (1): 128–49.
Pieterse, N. 1998. 'My paradigm or yours? Alternative development, post-development, reflexive development', *Development and Change* 29 (2): 343–73.
Pillar, P. 2006. 'Intelligence, policy and the war in Iraq', *Foreign Affairs* 85 (2): 15–27.
Pincus, J. 2001. 'The Post-Washington Consensus and lending operations in agriculture: New rhetoric and old operational realities', in B. Fine, C. Lapavitsas and J. Pincus, *Development Policy in the Twenty-first Century: Beyond the Post-Washington Consensus.* London: Routledge, 182–218.
Pincus, J. and J. Winters. (eds.). 2002a. *Reinventing the World Bank.* Ithaca and London: Cornell University Press.
Pincus, J. and J. Winters. 2002b. 'Reinventing the World Bank', in J. Pincus and J. Winters (eds.), *Reinventing the World Bank.* Ithaca and London: Cornell University Press, 1–25.

Pinto, R. 1994. 'Projectizing the governance approach to civil service reform: An institutional environmental assessment for sectoral adjustment loans in the Gambia'. Washington DC: World Bank.

Pitcher, A. 2002. *Transforming Mozambique*. Cambridge: Cambridge University Press.

Pithouse, R. 2001. 'The aunties' revolt', *Sunday Tribune*, 4 February.

———. 2003a. 'Producing the poor: The World Bank's new discourse of domination', *African Sociological Review* 7 (2): 118–44.

———. 2003b. 'That the tool never possess the man: Taking Fanon's humanism seriously', *Politikon* 30 (2): 107–32.

Polanyi. 1957 [1944]. *The Great Transformation: The Political and Economic Origins of our Time*. Boston: Beacon.

Ponte, S. 2000. 'From social negotiation to contract: Shifting strategies of farm labor recruitment in Tanzania under market liberalization', *World Development* 28 (6): 1017–30.

———. 2002a. 'Brewing a bitter cup? Deregulation, quality, and the re-organization of coffee marketing in East Africa', in B. Daviron and P. Gibbon (eds.), *Global Commodity Chains and African Export Agriculture*, special issue of *Journal of Agrarian Change* 2 (2): 248–72.

———. 2002b. *Farmers and Markets in Tanzania: How Policy Reforms Affect Rural Livelihoods in Africa*. Oxford: James Currey.

———. 2002c. 'The "latte revolution"? Regulation, markets and consumption in the global coffee chain', *World Development* 30 (7): 1099–122.

Porter, M.E. 1990. *The Competitive Advantage of Nations*. New York: Free Press.

Portes, A. 1997. 'Neoliberalism and the sociology of development: Emerging trends and unanticipated facts', *Population and Development Review* 23 (2): 229–59.

Portfolio Management Taskforce. 1992. 'Effective implementation: Key to development impact'. Washington, DC: World Bank, September.

PR Newswire. 2006. 'Powell's former chief of staff Lawrence Wilkerson calls pre-war intelligence a "hoax on the American people". Tonight on PBS Program NOW', http://tinyurl.com/7qgou. Accessed 26 October 2006.

Prasad, E., K. Rogoff, S.J. Wei and M. Ayhan Kose. 2003. 'Effects of financial globalization on developing countries: Some empirical evidence'. Washington, DC: International Monetary Fund, 17 March.

Preston, L.T. 1991. World Bank press release, 15 October, cited in B. Rich, *Mortgaging the Earth: The World Bank, Environmental Impoverishment and the Crisis of Development*. Boston: Beacon Press, 1994, 22–23.

Public Citizen. 2003. 'Bearing the Burden of IMF and World Bank Policies', http://www.citizen.org/cmep/water/cmep_water/wbimf/articles.cfm?ID=7802. Accessed 26 October 2006.

Putnam, R. 1993a. *Making Democracy Work: Civic Traditions in Modern Italy*. Princeton, NJ: Princeton University Press.

———. 1993b. 'The prosperous community: Social capital and public life', *The American Prospect* (13): 35–42.

———. 1995. 'Bowling alone: America's declining social capital', *Journal of Democracy* 6 (1): 65–78.
Putterman, L. 1995. 'Social capital and development capacity: The example of rural Tanzania', *Development Policy Review* 13 (1): 5–22.
Putzel, J. 1997. 'Accounting for the "dark side" of social capital: Reading Robert Putnam on democracy', *Journal of International Development* 9 (7): 939–49.
Rafferty, K. 1994. 'Sun sets upon Japanese miracle', *Guardian*, 15 January.
Raftopoulos, B. 1996. 'Fighting for control: The indigenization debate in Zimbabwe', *Southern Africa Report* 11 (4): 3–7.
Raikes, P. 1988. *Modernising Hunger: Famine, Food Surplus and Farm Policy in the EEC and Africa*. London: James Currey.
Raikes, P. and P. Gibbon. 2000. '"Globalisation" and African export crop agriculture', *Journal of Peasant Studies* 27 (2): 50–93.
Rapkin, D.P. and J.R. Strand. 1997. 'The US and Japan in the Bretton Woods Institutions: Sharing or contesting leadership?', *International Journal* 52 (2): 265–96.
Reddy, S. 2005. 'The *World Development Report 2006*: A brief review'. Unpublished paper, Columbia University, New York.
Reed, D. (ed.). 1996. *Structural Adjustment, the Environment, and Sustainable Development*. London: Earthscan.
Remmer, K. 1997. 'Theoretical decay and theoretical development: The resurgence of institutional analysis', *World Politics* 50 (1): 34–61.
Reno, W. 1995. *Corruption and State Politics in Sierra Leone*. Cambridge: Cambridge University Press.
———. 1997. 'War, markets and the reconfiguration of West Africa's weak states', *Comparative Politics* 29 (4): 493–510.
———. 1998. *Warlord Politics and African States*. Boulder, CO: Lynne Rienner.
———. 2002. 'Uganda's politics of war and debt relief', *Review of International Political Economy* 9 (3): 415–35.
———. 2003. 'African conflicts, colonialism, and contemporary intervention'. Paper presented at African Studies Association of Australasia and the Pacific Conference, Flinders University, Adelaide, 1–4 October 2003.
Results. 2003. 'World Bank Water Policies Undermine Public Health', http://www.results.usa.org. Accessed 28 July 2004.
'Retort' (I. Boal, T.J. Clark, J. Matthews and M. Watts). 2005. *Afflicted Powers: Capital and Spectacle in a New Age of War*. London: Verso.
Rich, B. 2000. 'Still waiting: The failure of reform at the World Bank', *Ecologist Report* (September): 8–16.
———. 2002. 'The World Bank under James Wolfensohn', in J. Pincus and J. Winters (eds.), *Reinventing the World Bank*. Ithaca and London: Cornell University Press, 26–53.
Richards, P. 1996. *Fighting for the Rain Forest: War, Youth and Resources in Sierra Leone*. Oxford: James Currey.

Select Bibliography

Rieff, D. 1999. 'A new age of liberal imperialism?', *World Policy Journal* 16 (2): 1–10.

Riley, S. and T. Parfitt. 1994. 'Economic adjustment and democratisation in Africa', in J. Walton and J. Seddon (eds.), *Free Markets and Food Riots*. Oxford: Blackwell, 135–70.

Ritzen, J. 2000. 'Where the World Bank stands: Issues in knowledge creation and management', http://www.worldbank.org/knowledge/conference/kcmg/papers/ritzen.htm.

Roberts, B.R., R.G. Cushing and C. Wood (eds.). 1995. *The Sociology of Development*, Volume 2. Aldershot: Edward Elgar.

Robertson, G. 1999. *Crimes against Humanity: The Struggle for Global Justice*. London: Allen Lane.

Robinson, M. 1993. 'Aid, democracy and political conditionality in sub-Saharan Africa', *European Journal of Development Research* 5 (1): 85–99.

Robinson, W. 1996. *Promoting Polyarchy: Globalization, US Intervention and Hegemony*. Cambridge: Cambridge University Press.

———. 2001a. 'Response to McMichael, Block, and Goldfrank', *Theory and Society* 30 (2): 223–36.

———. 2001b. 'Social theory and globalization: The rise of a transnational state', *Theory and Society* 30 (2): 157–200.

———. 2002. 'Remapping development in light of globalisation: From a territorial to a social cartography', *Third World Quarterly* 23 (6): 1047–71.

———. 2003. 'Social activism and democracy in South Africa: A globalization perspective'. Paper presented at the IDASA conference on 'Social activism and socio-economic rights: Deepening democracy in South Africa', Cape Town, 11–13 August 2003.

———. 2005. 'Gramsci and globalisation: From nation-state to transnational hegemony', *Critical Review of International Social and Political Philosophy* 8 (4): 1–16.

Rodrik, D. 1994a. 'Getting interventions right: How South Korea and Taiwan grew rich', Economics Department, Columbia University, mimeo.

———. 1994b. 'King Kong meets Godzilla: The World Bank and the East Asian Miracle', in A. Fishlow, C. Gwin and S. Haggard (eds.), *Miracle or Design? Lessons from the East Asian Experience*. Washington, DC: Overseas Development Council, 35–39.

———. 2001. *The Global Governance of Trade as if Development Really Mattered*. New York: United Nations Development Program, October.

———. 2002. 'Is the World Bank starting to understand growth?', *The Straits Times*, 12 February.

Roemer, M. and J. Stern. 1981. *Cases in Economic Development: Projects, Policies and Strategies*. London: Butterworths.

Rosenberg, N. 1960. 'Some institutional aspects of *The Wealth of Nations*', *Journal of Political Economy* 68 (6): 557–70.

Rothschild, E. 2004. 'Real, pretended or imaginary dangers', *New York Review of Books* 51 (5), 25 March.

Rowley, A. 1992. 'To Russia with pride: Japan offers economic model', *Far Eastern Economic Review* (13 August 1992): 59–60.

Roy, A. 1999. 'The greater common good', in A. Roy, *The Cost of Living*. London: Flamingo, 6–102.

———. 2002. 'Democracy: Who's she when she's not at home?', http://www.nu.ac.za/ccs.

Roy, S. 1989. *Philosophy of Economics: On the Scope of Reason in Economic Inquiry*. London: Routledge.

Rubio, M. 1997. 'Perverse social capital: Some evidence from Colombia', *Journal of Economic Issues* 31 (3): 805–16.

Ruggie, J.G. 1982. 'International regimes, transactions, and change: Embedded liberalism in the postwar economic order', *International Organization* 36 (2): 379–415.

Sachs, J. 1997. 'Power unto itself', *Financial Times*, 11 December.

———. 1998a. 'Global capitalism: Making it work', *Economist* (12 September): 19–23.

———. 1998b. 'The IMF and the Asian Flu', *The American Prospect* 37: 16–21.

Sachs, J. and A. Warner. 1995. 'Economic reform and the process of global integration', *Brookings Papers on Economic Activity*, 1: 1–118.

Sachs, M. 2003. 'Interview', in P. Kingsnorth, *One No, Many Yeses: A Journey to the Heart of the Global Resistance Movement*. London: Free Press, 115–24.

Sachs, W. 1999. *Planet Dialectics: Explorations in Environment and Development*. London: Zed Books.

Said, E. 1995 [1978]. *Orientalism*. London: Penguin.

———. 1996. *Representations of the Intellectual*. New York: Vintage.

———. 2003. 'Preface 2003', in *Orientalism*. London: Penguin.

Sakakibara, E. 1993. *Beyond Capitalism: The Japanese Model of Market Economics*. Lanham: University Press.

Samoff, J. and N. Stromquist. 2001. 'Managing knowledge and storing wisdom? New forms of foreign aid?', *Development and Change* 32 (4): 639–42.

Sanders, J. and V. Nee. 1996. 'Immigrant self-employment: The family as social capital and the value of human capital', *American Sociological Review* 61 (2): 231–49.

Saul, J.S. 1993. *Recolonization and Resistance in Southern Africa*. Trenton, NJ: Africa World Press.

———. 1997. '"For fear of being condemned as old fashioned": Liberal democracy vs. popular democracy in sub-Saharan Africa', *Review of African Political Economy* 24 (73): 339–53.

———. 2005. *The Next Liberation Struggle: Capitalism, Socialism and Democracy in Southern Africa*. London, New York and Pietermaritzburg: The Merlin Press, Monthly Review Press and University of KwaZulu-Natal Press.

Saul, J.S. and C. Leys. 1999. 'Sub-Saharan Africa in global capitalism', *Monthly Review* 51 (3): 13–30.

Saunders, R. 1997. 'Striking back: Worker militancy in Zimbabwe', *Southern Africa Report* 13 (1): 18–21.

Select Bibliography

Saurin, J. 1996. 'Globalisation, poverty, and the promises of modernity', *Millennium* 25 (3): 657–80.

Schalatek, L. (ed.). 2003. 'Managing sustainability World Bank-style: An evaluation of the *World Development Report 2003*'. World Summit Paper No. 19, Heinrich Böll Foundation.

Schech, S. 1998. 'Between tradition and post-coloniality: The location of gender in Australian development policy', *Australian Geographer* 29 (3): 389–404.

———. 2002. 'Wired for change: The links between ICTs and development discourses', *Journal of International Development* 14: 13–23.

Schiff, M. and A. Valdes. 1992a. *The Plundering of Agriculture in Developing Countries*. Washington, DC: World Bank.

———. 1992b. *The Political Economy of Agricultural Pricing Policy*. Baltimore: John Hopkins University Press.

Schmitz, G.J. 1995. 'Democratization and demystification: Deconstructing "governance" as development paradigm', in D. Moore and G. Schmitz (eds.), *Debating Development Discourse: Institutional and Popular Perspectives*. Basingstoke: Macmillan, 54–91.

Schneider, M., P. Teske and M. Marschall. 1997. 'Institutional arrangements and the creation of social capital: The effects of public school choice', *American Political Science Review* 91 (1): 82–93.

Schoppa, L.J. 1997. *Bargaining with Japan: What American Pressure Can and Cannot Do*. New York: Columbia University Press.

Schwarzmantel, J. 1995. 'Capitalist democracy revisited', in L. Panitch (ed.), *Socialist Register 1995: Why not Capitalism?* London: The Merlin Press, 207–24.

Scott, J. 1998. *Seeing Like a State: How Certain Schemes to Improve the Human Condition Have Failed*. New Haven: Yale University Press.

Sen, A. 1999. *Development as Freedom*. Oxford: Oxford University Press.

Sen, A. and S. Ogata. 2003. *Human Security Now*. New York: United Nations Commission on Human Security.

Sender, J. 1999. 'Africa's economic performance: Limitations of the current consensus', *Journal of Economic Perspectives* 13 (3): 89–114.

———. 2002. 'Reassessing the role of the World Bank in sub-Saharan Africa', in J. Pincus and J. Winters (eds.), *Reinventing the World Bank*. Ithaca and London: Cornell University Press, 185–202.

Serageldin, I. 1990. 'Governance, democracy and the World Bank in Africa'. Discussion paper presented at a World Bank Legal Department Staff Meeting, 30 November.

Serageldin, I. and A. Steer. 1994. 'Making development sustainable: From concepts to action'. Environmentally Sustainable Development Occasional Paper Series No. 2. Washington, DC: World Bank.

Serageldin, I. and J. Taboroff (eds.). 1994. *Culture and Development in Africa*. Washington, DC: World Bank.

Seria, N. 2004. 'African states call for more say in IMF', *Business Day*, 15 March.

Seron, C. and K. Ferris. 1995. 'Negotiating professionalism: The gendered social capital of flexible time', *Work and Occupations* 22 (1): 22–47.

Shah, A. 2006. 'The US and foreign aid assistance', *Sustainable Development*, http://www.globalissues.org/trade related/debt/USAid.asp. Accessed 26 October 2006.

Shalizi, S. 2003. 'The *WDR 2003* on sustainable development with a dynamic economy'. Presentation to the European Sustainable Development Forum, Paris, 29 May, http://econ.worldbank.org/wdr/wdr2003/library/doc?id=3237.

Shapiro, M. 1993. *Reading Adam Smith: Desire, History and Value*. London: Sage.

Sharma, S. and V. Shiva. 2003. '*Of World Bank, Toilet Paper and Washing Soap*', http://www.mindfully.org.WTO/World-Bank-Toilet_paper23sep02.htm. Accessed 3 October 2003.

Shaw, M. 1997. 'The state of globalization: Towards a theory of state transformation', *Review of International Political Economy* 4 (3): 497–513.

Shenton, R. 2000. 'Obituary: Mike Cowen (1945–2000)', *Journal of Peasant Studies* 27 (4): 160–67.

Shetler, J. 1995. 'A gift for generations to come: A Kiroba popular history from Tanzania and identity as social capital in the 1980s', *International Journal of African Historical Studies* 28 (1): 69–112.

Shihata, I. 1991. 'The World Bank and "governance" considerations in its borrower countries', in I. Shihata (ed.), *The World Bank in a Changing World: Selected Essays*. Dordrecht: Martinus Nijhoff, 82–93.

Shils, E. 1960. 'The intellectuals in the political development of the new states', *World Politics* 12 (3): 328–68.

Shin, G. 1998. 'Agrarian conflict and the origins of Korean capitalism', *American Journal of Sociology* 103 (5): 1309–51.

Shiratori, M. 1992. 'Development assistance to developing countries: Japanese model more relevant than simple marketism', *Nihon Keizai Shimbun*, 20 May (in Japanese).

———. 1993. 'The role of government in economic development: Comments on the "East Asian Miracle" study'. Paper presented to OECF seminar on the *East Asian Miracle*, Tokyo, 3 December.

Shirin, S. 2005. 'Thousands rally against "economic apartheid"', InterPress Services, Washington, DC, 24 September.

Silver, B. and G. Arrighi. 2003. 'Polanyi's "double movement": The *belles époques* of British and US hegemony compared', *Politics and Society* 31 (20) (January): 325–55.

Singh, A. 1995. 'How did East Asia grow so fast? Slow progress towards an analytical consensus'. UNCTAD Discussion Paper No. 97.

Sklair, L. 1997. 'Social movements for global capitalism: The transnational capitalist class in action', *Review of International Political Economy* 4 (3) (October): 514–38.

Skocpol, T. (ed.). 1998. *Democracy, Revolution and History*. Ithaca: Cornell University Press.

Skuse, A. 2000. 'Information communication technologies, poverty and empowerment'. DfID Background paper, June.

Smith, A. 1976a. *An Inquiry into the Nature and Causes of the Wealth of Nations*, Glasgow edition. Oxford: Oxford University Press.

———. 1976b. *Theory of Moral Sentiments*, Glasgow edition. Oxford: Oxford University Press.

Smith, J. and H. Johnston (eds.). 2002. *Globalization and Resistance: Transnational Dimensions of Social Movements*. Lanham: Rowman and Littlefield.

Smith, M., L. Beaulieu and A. Seraphine. 1995. 'Social capital, place of residence, and college attendance', *Rural Sociology* 60 (3): 363–80.

Soederberg, S. 2001a. 'The emperor's new suit: The new international financial architecture as a reinvention of the Washington Consensus', *Global Governance* 7 (4): 453–67.

———. 2001b. 'From neoliberalism to social liberalism', *Latin American Perspectives* 28 (3): 104–20.

———. 2001c. 'The new international financial architecture: Imposed leadership and emerging markets', in L. Panitch and C. Leys (eds.), *Socialist Register 2002*. London: The Merlin Press, 175–92.

———. 2004. *The Politics of the New International Financial Architecture: Reimposing Neoliberal Domination in the Global South*. London: Zed Books.

———. 2006. *Global Governance in Question: Empire, Class and the New Common Sense in Managing North–South Relations*. London: Pluto Press.

Somberg, B. 2005. 'The world's most generous misers'. FAIR (Fairness and Accuracy in Reporting), September/October, http://www.fair.org/index-php?page=2676. Accessed 26 October 2006.

Southgate, C. and D. Hulme. 2000. 'Uncommon property: The scramble for wetland in southern Kenya', in P. Woodhouse, H. Bernstein and D. Hulme (eds.), *African Enclosures? The Social Dynamics of Wetlands in Drylands*. Oxford, Trenton, NJ, Cape Town and Nairobi: James Currey, Africa World Press, David Philip and East African Educational Publishers, 73–118.

Spivak, G.C. 1999. *A Critique of Postcolonial Reason: Towards the Vanishing Present*. Cambridge, MA: Harvard.

Spoor, M. 2002. 'Policy regimes and performance of the agricultural sector in Latin America and the Caribbean during the last three decades', *Journal of Agrarian Change* 2 (3) (July): 381–400.

Squire, L. 1993. *Proceedings of the Symposium on the East Asian Miracle*. Tokyo: World Bank and OECD.

Starr, A. 2000. *Naming the Enemy: Anti-corporate Movements Confront Globalisation*. London: Zed Books.

Stern, N. 1993. 'The Bank as an intellectual actor'. Paper for World Bank History project, London School of Economics.

Stern, N. and F. Ferreira. 1997. 'The World Bank as "Intellectual Actor"', in D. Kapur, J. Lewis and R. Webb (eds.), *The World Bank: Its First Half Century*. Washington, DC: Brookings Institution Press, Volume 2, 523–609.

Stiefel, M. 1994. *A Voice for the Excluded: Popular Participation in Development: Utopia or Necessity?* London: Zed Books.

Stiglitz, J. 1989. 'Market, market imperfections, and development', *American Economic Review* 79 (2): 197–303.

———. 1996. 'Some lessons from the East Asian miracle', *The World Bank Research Observer* 11 (2): 155–77.

———. 1997. 'An agenda for development for the twenty-first century'. World Bank Ninth Annual Conference on Development Economics, 30 April–1 May.

———. 1998a. 'More instruments and broader goals: Moving toward the Post-Washington Consensus'. WIDER Annual Lectures, No. 2, Helsinki, 7 January.

———. 1998b. 'Sound finance and sustainable development in Asia'. Keynote address to the Asia Development Forum, Manila, 12 March.

———. 1998c. 'Towards a new paradigm for development: Strategies, policies, and processes'. Annual Prebisch Lecture, UNCTAD, Geneva, 19 October.

———. 1999. 'Whither reform? Ten years of the transition'. Paper presented at Annual Bank Conference on Development Economics.

———. 2000a. 'Democratic development as the fruits of labor'. Keynote address, Industrial Relations Research Association, Boston, January.

———. 2000b. 'The insider', *New Republic*, 17 April.

———. 2002. *Globalisation and its Discontents*. London: Penguin.

———. 2003. 'Democratising the International Monetary Fund and the World Bank: Governance and accountability', *Governance: An International Journal of Policy, Administration, and Institutions* 16 (1): 111–39.

Stiglitz, J. and Y. Shahid (eds.). 2001. *Rethinking the East Asia Miracle*. New York: Oxford University Press.

Stiglitz, J. and A. Weiss. 1981. 'Credit rationing in markets with imperfect information', *American Economic Review* 71 (3): 393–410.

Stone, D. 1995. 'Commentary: The durability of social capital', *Journal of Health Politics, Policy and Law* 20 (3): 689–94.

———. 2003. 'The "Knowledge Bank" and the global development network', *Global Governance* 9 (1): 43–63.

Stremlau, J. and F. Sagasti. 1998. *Preventing Deadly Conflict: Does the World Bank Have A Role?* Washington, DC: Carnegie Commission on Preventing Deadly Conflict.

Swainson, N. 1980. *The Development of Corporate Capitalism in Kenya 1918–1977*. London, Ibadan and Nairobi: Heinemann.

Swedberg, R. (ed.). 1996. *Economic Sociology*. Cheltenham: Edward Elgar.

Szeftel, M. 1998. 'Misunderstanding African politics: Corruption and the governance agenda', *Review of African Political Economy* 25 (76): 221–40.

Tanzanian Feminist Activism Coalition. 2001. 'Position Paper'. Dar es Salaam, 6 September.

Taylor, L. 1997. 'Editorial. The revival of the liberal creed: The IMF and the World Bank in a globalized economy', *World Development* 25 (2): 145–52.

Taylor, M. 2004a.'Interrogating the paradigm of "labour flexibilisation": Neoclassical prescriptions and the Chilean experience', *Labour, Capital and Society* 35 (2): 222–51.
———. 2004b. 'Responding to neoliberalism in crisis: Discipline and empowerment in the World Bank's new development agenda', *Research in Political Economy* 21: 3–30.
———. 2005. 'Opening the World Bank: International organisations and the contradictions of global capitalism', in *Historical Materialism* 15 (1): 153–70.
———. 2006. *From Pinochet to the Third Way? Neoliberalism and Social Transformation in Chile, 1973–2003*. London: Pluto Press.
Teachman, J., K. Paasch and K. Carver. 1996. 'Social capital and dropping out of school early', *Journal of Marriage and the Family* 58 (3): 773–83.
Terry, F. 1999. 'Reconstituting whose social order? NGOs in disrupted states'. Paper presented at conference on 'From civil strife to civil society: Civil–military cooperation in disrupted states', Canberra, Australia, 6–7 July.
Therborn, G. 1996. 'Critical theory and the legacy of twentieth-century Marxism', in B.S. Turner (ed.), *The Blackwell Companion to Social Theory*. Oxford: Blackwell, 53–82.
Thiong'o, Ngugi wa. 2006. *Wizard of the Crow*. London: Harvill Secker.
Third Community Empowerment and Local Government Project. 2002. World Bank Report No. 24119 TP, June.
Thirwall, A.P. (ed.). 1987. *Keynes and Economic Development*. Basingstoke: Macmillan.
Thompson, H. and S. MacWilliam. 1992. *The Political Economy of Papua New Guinea: Critical Essays*. Wollongong and Manila: Journal of Contemporary Asia Press.
Tibana, R. 1995. 'Stabilization and structural adjustment in a dual transition: Mozambique in the 1990s'. Paper presented at the seminar on 'Mozambique: Post-electoral challenges', London School of Economics.
Tilly, C. 1985. 'War making and state making as organized crime', in P. Evans, D. Rueschemeyer and T. Skocpol (eds.), *Bringing the State Back In*. New York: Cambridge University Press, 169–91.
Todaro, M.P. 1989. *Economic Development in the Third World*. New York: Longman.
Tommasi, M. and K. Iurelli (eds.). 1995. *The New Economics of Human Behaviour*. Cambridge: Cambridge University Press.
Toye, J. 1989. 'Can the World Bank resolve the crisis of developing countries?', *Journal of International Development* 1 (2): 261–72.
———. 1993. *Dilemmas of Development: Reflections on the Counter-Revolution in Development Theory and Policy*. Oxford: Basil Blackwell.
Trella, I. and J. Whalley. 1992. 'The role of tax policy in Korea's economic growth', in T. Ito and A. Krueger (eds.), *The Political Economy of Tax Reform*. Chicago: University of Chicago Press.
Tully, J. 1988. 'Governing conduct', in E. Leites (ed.), *Conscience and Casuistry in Early Modern Europe*. Cambridge: Cambridge University Press, 12–71.
———. 1995. *Strange Multiplicity: Constitutionalism in an Age of Diversity*. Cambridge: Cambridge University Press.

Turner, R.K. 1993. 'Sustainability: Principles and practice', in R.K. Turner (ed.), *Sustainable Environmental Economics and Management: Principles and Practice*. London: Belhaven Press, 3–36.

UK Department for International Development. 1997. 'Eliminating world poverty: A challenge for the 21st century'. White Paper on International Development. London: The Stationery Office.

———. 2000. 'Eliminating world poverty: Making globalisation work for the poor'. White Paper on International Development. London: The Stationery Office.

Ul-Haque, N. and H. Aziz. 1999. 'The quality of governance: "Second generation" civil service reform in Africa', *Journal of African Economies* 8: 68–107.

UNCTAD (United Nations Conference on Trade and Development). 1994. 'The visible hand and the industrialization of East Asia'. *Trade and Development Report*, 1994.

———. 1999. *African Development in a Comparative Perspective*. Geneva, Oxford and Trenton, NJ: UNCTAD, James Currey and Africa World Press.

———. 2002. *The Least Developed Countries Report 2002: Escaping the Poverty Trap*. New York and Geneva: UNCTAD.

UNDP (United Nations Development Programme). 2002. *Deepening Democracy in a Fragmented World*. New York: UNDP.

United Nations. 2002. 'Report of the international conference on financing for development'. A/CONF.198/11, Monterrey, Mexico, 22 March.

———. 2005. *Report of the Fact-finding Mission to Zimbabwe to Assess the Scope and Impact of Operation Murambatsvina by the UN Special Envoy on Human Settlements Issues in Zimbabwe, Mrs Anna Kajumulo Tibaijuka*. New York: United Nations, 18 July.

United Nations Security Council. 2002. 'Final report of the panel of experts on the illegal exploitation of natural resources and other forms of wealth of the Democratic Republic of the Congo'. S/2002/1146 (16 October).

United Nations University – World Institute for Development Economics Research. 2002. *Governing Globalisation: Issues and Institutions*. Helsinki: UNU–WIDER.

Urquhart, B. 1999. 'The making of a scapegoat', *New York Review of Books*, 12 August.

Valenzuela, A. and S. Dornbusch. 1994. 'Familism and social capital in the academic achievement of Mexican origin and Anglo adolescents', *Social Science Quarterly* 75 (1): 18–36.

Vallette, J. 2005. 'The Wolfowitz chronology', Institute for Policy Studies, Sustainable Energy and Economy Network, http://www.ips-dc.org/wolfowitz/tl_intro.htm. Accessed 18 February 2006.

Van der Gheest, W. and R. van der Hoeven (eds.). 1999. *Adjusting Employment and Missing Institutions in Africa: The Experience in Eastern and Southern Africa*. Geneva and Oxford: International Labor Office in association with James Currey.

Van der Pijl, K. 1994. 'The cadre class and public multilateralism', in Y. Sakamoto (ed.), *Global Transformation: Challenges to the State System*. Tokyo: United Nations University Press, 82–106.

———. 1998. *Transnational Classes and International Relations*. London: Routledge.

Van der Walle, N. 2001. *African Economies and the Politics of Permanent Crisis*. Cambridge: Cambridge University Press.
Van Dijk, T.A. 2001. 'Critical discourse analysis', in D. Schiffrin, D. Tannen, and H.E. Hamilton (eds.), *The Handbook of Discourse Analysis*. London: Blackwell, 352–71.
Varma, S. 2002. 'Improving global economic governance'. Occasional Paper No. 8. Geneva: South Centre.
Veblen, T. 1948. 'The preconceptions of the classical economists', in M. Lerner (ed.), *The Portable Veblen*. New York: Viking.
Verheul, E. and G. Cooper. 2001. 'Poverty Reduction Strategy Papers (PRSP): What is at stake for health?'. Amsterdam: Wemos, September.
Verlet, M. 2000. 'Growing up in Ghana: Deregulation and the employment of children', in B. Schlemmer (ed.), *The Exploited Child*. London and New York: Zed Books, 67–82.
Vogel, U. 1988. 'When the land belonged to all: The land question in eighteenth-century justifications of private property', *Political Studies* 36 (1): 102–22.
Von Hayek, F. 1937. 'Economics and knowledge', *Economica* 4: 33–54.
——. 1945. 'The use of knowledge in society', *American Economic Review* 35 (4): 519–30.
——. 1948. *Individualism and Economic Order*. Chicago: University of Chicago Press.
Vriend, N. 1996. 'Rational behaviour and economics theory', *Journal of Economic Behaviour and Organisation* 29 (2): 263–85.
Wade, R. 1990. *Governing the Market: Economic Theory and the Role of Government in East Asian Industrial Reform*. Princeton, NJ: Princeton University Press.
——. 1991. 'How to protect exports from protection: Taiwan's duty drawback scheme', *The World Economy* 14 (3): 299–310.
——. 1993. 'Managing trade: Taiwan and South Korea as challenges to economics and political science', *Comparative Politics* 25 (2): 147–67.
——. 1994. 'Selective industrial policies in East Asia: Is *The East Asian Miracle* right?', in A. Fishlow, C. Gwin and S. Haggard (eds.), *Miracle or Design? Lessons from the East Asian Experience*. Washington, DC: Overseas Development Council, 55–79.
——. 1996a. 'Globalisation and its limits: Reports of the death of the national economy are greatly exaggerated', in S. Berger and R. Dore (eds.), *National Diversity and Global Capitalism*. Ithaca: Cornell University Press, 60–88.
——. 1996b. 'Japan, the World Bank, and the art of paradigm maintenance: *The East Asian Miracle* in political perspective', *New Left Review* 1 (217): 3–37.
——. 1997. 'Success or mess?', *Times Literary Supplement*, 12 December.
——. 1998a. 'The Asian crisis and the global economy: Causes, consequences, and cure', *Current History* 97 (622): 361–73.
——. 1998b. 'The Asian debt-and-development crisis of 1997–? Causes and consequences', *World Development* 26 (8): 1538–52.
——. 2001a. 'Capital and revenge: The IMF and Ethiopia', *Challenge* (September/October): 67–75.

———. 2001b. 'Showdown at the World Bank', *New Left Review* 2 (7): 24–37.
———. 2002. 'US hegemony and the World Bank: The fight over people and ideas', *Review of International Political Economy* 9 (2): 201–29.
———. 2003. 'The invisible hand of the American empire', *Open Democracy* 13 (3), www.opendemocracy.net/globalisation/article_1038.jsp. Accessed 10 December 2003.
———. 2004. 'Is globalization reducing poverty and inequality?', *World Development* 32 (4): 567–89.
Wade, R. and F. Veneroso. 1998a. 'The gathering world slump and the battle over capital controls', *New Left Review* 1 (231): 13–42.
———. 1998b. 'The resources lie within', *Economist*, 7 November: 19–21.
Walker, G., B. Kogut and W. Shan. 1997. 'Social capital, structural holes and the formation of an industry network', *Organization Science* 8 (2): 109–25.
Wallerstein, I. 1979. *The Capitalist World Economy*. London: Cambridge University Press.
Walton, J. and D. Seddon (eds.). 1994. *Free Markets and Food Riots: The Politics of Global Adjustment*. Oxford: Basil Blackwell.
Warren, B. 1973. 'Imperialism and capitalist industrialization', *New Left Review* 1 (81): 3–44.
———. 1980. *Imperialism: Pioneer of Capitalism*. London: Verso.
War-torn Societies Project. 1998. Booklets on Projects in Eritrea, Guatemala, Mozambique and Somalia. Geneva: United Nations Research Institute for Social Development, http://www.unrisd.org/wsp/pop2/toc.htm. Accessed 27 November 1999.
Waterman, P. 2001. *Globalization, Social Movements and the New Internationalisms*. London: Continuum.
———. 2002. 'What's left internationally? Reflections on the Second World Forum on Porto Alegre'. Working Paper Series No. 362, Institute of Social Studies, The Hague.
Waud, R., A. Hocking, P. Maxwell and J. Bonnich. 1992. *Economics*. New York: HarperCollins.
Weeks, J. 2001. 'The expansion of capital and uneven development on a world scale', *Capital and Class* 74: 9–31.
Weiss, L. 1997. 'Globalization and the myth of the powerless state', *New Left Review* 225: 3–27.
Weitzman, H. 2005. 'Ecuador finance minister quits over loan dispute', *Financial Times*, 6 August.
Werner, D. and D. Sanders. 1997. *Questioning the Solution: The Politics of Primary Health Care and Child Survival*. Palo Alto: Healthwrights.
Wessell, D. and B. Davis. 1998. 'Currency controls gain a hearing as crisis in Asia takes its toll', *Wall Street Journal*, 4 September.
Westphal, D. 2005. 'Behind Iraq prewar debate', *Sacramento Bee*, 27 November.
White, M. and G. Kaufman. 1997. 'Language usage, social capital, and school completion among immigrants and native-born ethnic groups', *Social Science Quarterly* 32 (1): 3–30.
White House. 2005. 'President's press conference'. White House transcript, 16 March.

Wiggins, S. 2000. 'Interpreting changes from the 1970s to the 1990s in African agriculture through village studies', *World Development* 28 (4): 631–62.

Wilks, A. 1998. '*World Development Reports*: The preparation process'. Bretton Woods Project, http://www.brettonwoodsproject.org/topic/knowledgebank/wdrproc.html. Accessed 4 September 2004.

Wilks, A. and F. Lefrançois. 2002. 'Blinding with science or encouraging debate?: How World Bank analysis determines PRSP policies'. London: Bretton Woods Project.

Williams, D. 1993. 'Liberalism and the development discourse', *Africa* 63 (3): 419–29.

———. 1996. 'Governance and the discipline of development', *European Journal of Development Research* 8 (2): 157–77.

———. 1997. 'The emergence and implementation of the World Bank's "good governance" agenda'. Ph.D. thesis, University of London.

———. 1999. 'Constructing the economic space: The World Bank and the making of *Homo Oeconomicus*', *Millennium* 28 (1): 79–99.

———. 2000. 'Aid and sovereignty: Quasi-states and the international financial institutions', *Review of International Studies* 26 (4): 557–73.

Williams, D. and T. Young. 1994. 'Governance, the World Bank and liberal theory', *Political Studies* 42 (1): 84–100.

Williams, G. 1987. 'Primitive accumulation: The way to progress?', *Development and Change* 18 (4): 637–59.

———. 1994. 'Why structural adjustment is necessary and why it doesn't work', *Review of African Political Economy* 21 (60): 214–25.

———. 1995. 'Review of P. Gibbon, K. Havnevik and K. Hermele, *A Blighted Harvest: The World Bank and African Agriculture in the 1980s*', in *Journal of Contemporary African Studies* 13 (2): 287–91.

Williamson, J. 2000. 'What should the World Bank think about the Washington Consensus?', *World Bank Research Observer* 15 (2): 251–64.

Wilson, P. 1997. 'Building social capital: A learning agenda for the twenty-first century', *Urban Studies* 34 (5–6): 745–60.

Winch, D. 1983. 'Adam Smith's "enduring particular result": A political and cosmopolitan perspective', in I. Hont and M. Ignatieff (eds.), *Wealth and Virtue: The Shaping of Political Economy in the Scottish Enlightenment*. Cambridge: Cambridge University Press, 250–60.

Wodak, R. (ed.). 1989. *Language, Power and Ideology: Studies in Political Discourse*. London: Benjamins Publishing Company.

———. 2001. 'What CDA [Critical Discourse Analysis] is about: A summary of its history, important concepts and its development', in R. Wodak and M. Meyer (eds.), *Methods of Critical Discourse Analysis*. London: Sage, 1–13.

Wolf, C. 1998. 'Blame government for the Asian meltdown', *Asian Wall Street Journal*, 5 February 1998.

Wolfensohn, J. 1997. 'People first'. Paul Hoffman Lecture, New York, 29 May, http://www.worldbank.org.

———. 1999a. 'Press conference: April 22'. World Bank website, http://www.worldbank. org. Accessed 1 April 2003.

———. 1999b. 'A proposal for a comprehensive development framework (a discussion draft)', 29 January, mimeo.

———. 2000/1. 'Foreword', in *World Development Report 2000/1: Attacking Poverty*. Oxford: Oxford University Press.

———. 2001. 'A proposal for a comprehensive development framework', in World Bank, 'Comprehensive development framework: Meeting the promise? Early experience and emerging issues', 17 September.

———. 2002. 'A partnership for development and peace', in World Bank, *A Case for Aid: Building a Consensus for Development Assistance*. Washington, DC: World Bank, 1–14.

Wolfgang, S. 1999. *Planet Dialectics: Explorations in Environment and Development*. London: Zed Books.

Woo-Cumings, M. 1999. 'Introduction: Chalmers Johnson and the politics of nationalism and development', in M. Woo-Cumings (ed.), *The Developmental State*. Ithaca: Cornell University Press, 1–31.

Wood, E. 1995. 'The separation of the "economic" from the "political" in capitalism' and 'History or teleology? Marx versus Weber', in E. Wood, *Democracy against Capitalism: Renewing Historical Materialism*. Cambridge: Cambridge University Press, 19–48, 146–80.

———. 1997. 'Modernity, postmodernity or capitalism?', *Review of International Political Economy* 4 (3): 539–60.

———. 1999. *The Origin of Capitalism*. New York: Monthly Review Press.

———. 2001. 'Contradiction: Only in capitalism?', in L. Panitch and C. Leys (eds.), *Socialist Register 2002: A World of Contradictions*. London: The Merlin Press, 275–93.

Woodhouse, P., P. Trench and M. Tessougue. 2000. 'A very decentralized development: Exploiting a wetland in the Sourou Valley, Mali', in P. Woodhouse, H. Bernstein and D. Hulme (eds.), *African Enclosures? The Social Dynamics of Wetlands in Drylands*. Oxford, Trenton, NJ, Cape Town and Nairobi: James Currey, Africa World Press, David Philip and East African Educational Publishers, 29–72.

Woolcock, M. 1998. 'Social capital and economic development: Toward a theoretical synthesis and policy framework', *Theory and Society* 27 (2): 151–208.

Woost, M.D. 1997. 'Alternative vocabularies of development? "Community" and "participation" in development discourse in Sri Lanka', in R.D. Grillo and R.L. Stirrat (eds.), *Discourses of Development: Anthropological Perspectives*. Oxford: Berg, 229–54.

World Bank. 1980. *World Development Report 1980*. New York: Oxford University Press.

———. 1981. *Accelerated Development in Sub-Saharan Africa: An Agenda for Action*. (The Berg Report.) Washington, DC: World Bank.

Select Bibliography

———. 1982. *Focus on Poverty: A Report of a Task Force of the World Bank.* Washington, DC: World Bank.

———. 1989. *Sub-Saharan Africa: From Crisis to Sustainable Growth. A Long-term Perspective Study.* Washington, DC: World Bank.

———. 1990. *World Development Report 1990: Poverty.* New York: Oxford University Press.

———. 1991a. *Managing Development: The Governance Dimension.* Washington, DC: World Bank.

———. 1991b. Press release no. 16, 15 October.

———. 1991c. *World Development Report 1991: The Challenge of Development.* Washington, DC: World Bank.

———. 1992a. *Governance and Development.* Washington, DC: World Bank.

———. 1992b. 'Republic of Ghana: Literacy and functional skills project'. Staff appraisal report, number 10164-GH, 28 February.

———. 1992c. 'Support for industrialisation in Korea, India, and Indonesia'. Washington, DC: World Bank.

———. 1992d. *World Development Report 1992: Development and the Environment.* New York: Oxford University Press.

———. 1993a. *The East Asian Miracle: Economic Growth and Public Policy. A World Bank Policy Research Report.* Oxford: Oxford University Press.

———. 1993b. 'Philippines: Tax computerization project'. Staff appraisal report, number 11355PH, 31 March.

———. 1993c. *Poverty Reduction Handbook.* New York: Oxford University Press.

———. 1994a. *Adjustment in Africa: Reforms, Results and the Road Ahead.* New York: Oxford University Press.

———. 1994b. 'Ghana: Community water and sanitation project'. Staff appraisal report, number 12406-GH, 21 March.

———. 1994c. 'Republic of Ghana: Local government development project'. Staff appraisal report, number 12332GH, 18 January.

———. 1995a. *Evaluation Results 1993.* Washington, DC: World Bank, Operations Evaluation Department.

———. 1995b. *Governance: The World Bank's Experience.* Washington, DC: World Bank.

———. 1995c. *Mainstreaming the Environment: The World Bank Group and the Environment since the Rio Earth Summit.* Washington, DC: World Bank.

———. 1995d. 'Philippines: Second rural finance project'. Report number 13116-PH, August 1995.

———. 1996a. 'Philippines: Agrarian reform communities development project'. Staff appraisal report, number 15624-PH, 24 October.

———. 1996b. 'Technical annex: Republic of Ghana: Public financial management technical assistance project'. Report No. -6977-GH, West Central Africa Department, 10 October.

———. 1996c. *The World Bank Participation Sourcebook*. Washington, DC: World Bank.

———. 1997a. 'Social capital: The missing link?', in *Monitoring Environmental Progress: Expanding the Measure of Wealth*, draft, Washington DC: World Bank, Environment Department.

———. 1997b. *World Development Report 1997: The State in a Changing World*. New York: Oxford University Press.

———. 1998a. Draft work programme on *World Development Report 2000/1: Attacking Poverty*. May.

———. 1998b. *East Asia: The Road to Recovery*. Washington, DC: World Bank.

———. 1998c. *Post-conflict Reconstruction: The Role of the World Bank*. Washington, DC: World Bank.

———. 1999a. 'Building trust to rebuild Rwanda: World Bank supports community reintegration and development', in *World Bank Supports Community Reintegration and Development*. News Release No. 99/2003/AFR.

———. 1999b. 'Public sector management reform project'. Capacity Building Unit, Project Appraisal Document, report number 19004-GH, Africa Region, 6 April.

———. 1999c. *World Bank Annual Report, 1999*, http://www.worldbank.org/html/extpb/annrep99/over.htm. Accessed 18 October 2003.

———. 1999d. *World Development Report 1999: Knowledge for Development*. New York: Oxford University Press.

———. 2000a. *Annual Report 2000*. Washington, DC: World Bank.

———. 2000b. 'Consultations with civil society organizations: General guidelines for World Bank staff', June 2000.

———. 2000c. *East Asia: Recovery and Beyond*. Washington, DC: World Bank.

———. 2000d. 'Ghana: Financial management reform project II, Africa regional office'. Report number PID9535, 29 September.

———. 2000e. *Making Sustainable Commitments: An Environment Strategy for the World Bank*. Washington, DC: World Bank.

———. 2000/1a. 'Attacking poverty: A public discussion of *World Development Report 2000/1*'. Washington, DC: World Bank, Bretton Woods Project and New Policy Institute, http://www.worldbank.org/devforum/forum_poverty.html. Accessed 10 May 2003.

———. 2000/1b. 'Electronic discussion on draft *World Development Report* on poverty 2000/1'. Final summary.

———. 2000/1c. 'Public electronic discussion on *World Development Report 2000/1*'.

———. 2000/1d. *World Development Report 2000/1: Attacking Poverty*. Oxford: Oxford University Press.

———. 2001a. *Globalization, Growth and Poverty: Building an Inclusive World Economy*. Washington, DC and New York: World Bank and Oxford University Press.

———. 2001b. *Review of the Bank's Performance on the Environment*. Operations Evaluation Department. Washington, DC: World Bank.

Select Bibliography

———. 2001c. *Tanzania at the Turn of the Century*. World Bank Country Study, Washington, DC: World Bank.

———. 2001d. *World Development Report 2002: Building Institutions for Markets*. Washington, DC and New York: World Bank and Oxford University Press.

———. 2002a. 'Africa and decentralization: Enter the citizens'. World Bank, Africa Region, July.

———. 2002b. *A Case for Aid: Building a Consensus for Development Assistance*. Washington, DC: World Bank.

———. 2002c. 'Reforming public institutions and strengthening governance: A World Bank strategy: implementation update'. April.

———. 2002d. 'Subsidies hurt cotton producers: World Bank and International Cotton Advisory Committee collaborate on cotton's role in the world economy'. DevNews Media Center, www.worldbank.org, 23 July.

———. 2002e. 'Third community empowerment and local government project'. Report number 24119 TP, June.

———. 2002f. *World Development Report 2003: Sustainable Development in a Dynamic World – Transforming Institutions, Growth, and Quality of Life*. New York: Oxford University Press.

———. 2002g. *World Development Report 2004*, Draft 24. September.

———. 2003a. 'Iraq watching brief: Building knowledge and partnerships'. Washington, DC: World Bank, June.

———. 2003b. 'Issues note: Enhancing the voice of developing and transition countries at the World Bank'. Washington, DC: World Bank, 9 June, http://www.brettonwoodsproject.org/ topic/governance/WBgovissuesnote.pdf. Accessed 12 February 2005.

———. 2003c. *Land Policies for Growth and Poverty Reduction*. Oxford: World Bank and Oxford University Press.

———. 2003d. World Bank Press Review, 10 December.

———. 2003e. *World Development Report 2004: Making Services Work for Poor People*. Oxford: Oxford University Press.

———. 2004. *World Development Report 2005: A Better Investment Climate for Everyone*. Washington, DC: World Bank.

———. 2005a. 'Comprehensive development framework questions and answers', http://web.worldbank.org/website/external/projects/strategies/cdf/. Accessed 7 February 2006.

———. 2005b. 'Proceedings of press conference'. Washington, DC, April, http://www.worldbank.org.

———. 2005c. *World Development Report 2006: Equity and Development*. Washington, DC: World Bank.

———. 2006. 'Poverty reduction strategy sourcebook', http://web.worldbank.org/wbsite/external/topics/extpoverty/extprs. Accessed 10 February 2006.

World Bank and IMF. 2005. 'Transcript of a joint IMF/World Bank town hall with civil society organisations'. Washington, DC, 22 September, http://www.imf.org/external/np/tr/2005/tr050922a.htm. Accessed 6 February 2006.

World Bank Press Clips. 2005. 'Wolfowitz tries to reassure World Bank staff', 13 May.
World Commission for Environment and Development. 1987. *Our Common Future*. Oxford: Oxford University Press.
World Health Organisation. 2001. 'Health in PRSPs: WHO submission to World Bank/IMF review of PRSPs'. Geneva: WHO Department of Health and Development, December.
Wright-Neville, D. 1995. 'The politics of Pan Asianism: Culture, capitalism and diplomacy in East Asia', *Pacifica Review* 7 (1): 1–26.
Wrong, M. 2006. 'Kenyans want to know why we're feeding corruption', *Guardian*, 30 January.
Yanamura, K. (ed.). 1990. *Japan's Economic Structure: Should it Change?* Seattle: Society for Japanese Studies.
Young, T. 1995. '"A project to be realized": Global liberalism and contemporary Africa', *Millennium* 24 (3): 527–46.
———. 2002. '"A project to be realized": Global liberalism and a new world order', in E. Hovden and E. Keene (eds.), *The Globalisation of Liberalism*. Basingstoke: Palgrave, 173–90.
Zack-Williams, A. 2000. 'Social consequences of structural adjustment', in G. Mohan, E. Brown, B. Milward and A. Zack-Williams (eds.), *Structural Adjustment: Theory Practice, and Impacts*. London: Routledge, 61–80.
Zeileg, L. (ed.). 2002. *Class Struggle and Resistance in Africa*. Cheltenham: New Clarion Press.
Zhou, M. and C. Bankston. 1994. 'Social capital and the adaptation of the second generation: The case of Vietnamese youth in New Orleans', *International Migration Review* 28 (4): 821–45.

Index

accountancy, training   110–13, 220
activists   426, 429, 446
adjustment, structural   *see* structural adjustment
affirmative action   13
Afghanistan   22, 389, 487
Africa   300, 328
   agriculture   343–63
   aid, Japan   268, 271–72, 278–80, 283
   and China   21
   conflict   387–98, 405–11
   culture   213
   development   3–4, 7, 228–32, 259, 261, 345, 387–411
   post-conflict   387–411
   environment   49
   governance   369–86
Africa Capacity Building Foundation   245, 392
Africa, sub-Saharan   372, 456
   agriculture   343–63, 456
   development   205, 344–63
   exports   355
   post-colonial state   345
   structural adjustment   346, 348–63
African National Congress (ANC)   415, 417, 426, 437, 440, 498, 500–01
agriculture, African   343–63
   modernisation   346
aid   402
   humanitarian   403
   reform   454
Aids   441
Al Queda   29
Albo, Gregory   252
Anderson, Perry   58 n.18, 249

Anglo-American policy   300, 330, 334, 392
Angola   388–89
anti-globalisation   23
Anti-Privatisation Forum (South Africa)   497
apartheid   437
   global   416
apprentice system   103–05
Arabs   421
Argentina   292, 296, 455, 481–82, 501–02
arms trade   395–96
Arrighi, Giovanni   361
Articles of Agreement   326
ASEAN-Japan Development Fund   331
Asian crisis, 1997   75, 172, 253, 294, 317
Asia-Pacific Economic Co-ordination Forum   275
authoritarianism   289, 335–37, 393, 417
autonomy   99–100, 107–08, 110

Balassa, Bela   328–29
Bangladesh   241, 434, 484, 491
Bank of International Settlements   193
Bank Poverty Reduction Support Credits   439
Baran, Paul   236
barbarity   411
Baudrillard, Jean   127
Bayart, Jean-François   399
Beall, J.   129
Becker, Gary   123, 126
Beeson, Mark   17, 23, 53, 229
Bello, Walden   500

Benn, Hillary 493
Berg, Elliot 236, 248, 322
Berg Report, 1981 322, 344, 347–49, 353, 362, 365 n.5
Bernstein, Henry 7, 17–18, 21, 28, 52
Bhagwati, Jagdish 256
Birdsall, Nancy 284, 286–90
Blair, Tony 238–39
Block, Fred 36
Bolivia 31, 502
Bond, Patrick 17–18, 23, 45, 56
Bosnia-Herzegovina 389
Bourdieu, Pierre 127, 139
bourgeoisie 71, 259
  national 28
  transnational 45, 56, 345, 350, *see also* transnational, class
Brazil 292, 457, 480–81, 502, 503
Bretton Woods Institutions (BWI) 189, 281, 318, 381, 479–80, 492, 499–500
Brown, Gordon 487
bureaucrats 29
Burkina Faso 439
Bush, George W. 10, 29, 37, 453–54, 470–71, 486–90

Cairncross, Alexander 326
calculating ability 100, 107, 110
Callaghy, Thomas 24
Canada, provincial organisation 38–40
Cancun (WTO meeting) 11, 29, 37, 57 n.5
capital
  African 355
  knowledge 158–59
  social 124–41, 403–11, 441
  transnational 36, 257, 260, 416, 450, *see also* capitalism, transnational
capitalism 4, 6, 8, 10–11, 13–14, 19, 22, 27, 30, 32–33, 37–38, 45, 51, 58 n.16, 64, 68, 70–71, 118, 140, 145, 148, 151, 158–59, 165, 247–48, 250–51, 254, 384, 434
  Africa, sub-Saharan 344
  African 404
  East Asian 287, 324, 328, 333, 338, 356, 361
  free market 165
  global 1, 11, 19, 58 n.16, 150, 166, 251, 261
  liberal 219, 237
  state 230
  transnational 257, 260, 416, 450 n.2, *see also* capital, transnational
carbon, trading 485–86
Castells, M. 161, 247
Catholic Action for Overseas Development (CAFOD) 190
Caufield, Catherine 389
Chad 491–92
Chad–Cameroon pipeline 484, 491
Chambers, Robert 181, 185, 187–89, 192
Chenery, Hollis 320, 323
Cheney, Dick 489
Chile 242, 457
China 9, 14, 21, 56, 79–80, 282, 286, 290, 292, 299, 474, 484
  power 50
cholera 439
Chomsky, Noam 444
Christian Aid 261
Christianity 417
class
  conflict 188
  formation, Africa 356–57, 359–60
  transnational *see* transnational, class
Clausen, Alden Winship 322–23, 371
Clay, Edward 493
Clinton, Bill 10, 238–39, 479

clothing industry 419
coal 484
Coetzee, J.M. 427
coffee 83–84, 359
Cold War 29, 173, 213, 216, 239, 318–21, 333, 371, 388, 393, 399, 401
Coleman, James 126–28, 139
colonialism 5, 214, 223, 345, 434, 437, 445, 447
Columbia, oil 491
commodification 233–34, 261, 502, 504
communism 173, 319–20, 436
Comprehensive Agrarian Reform Programme (CARP) 109
Comprehensive Development Framework (CDF) 208, 211, 456, 465–69, 472–74
Conable, Barber 323–24
conflict, Africa 387–98, 405–11
Congo(s) 24, 261, 388, 400
Congress of South African Trade Unions (COSATU) 498
consumption 69–74, 79, 155
copper 494
corporations (and/or companies) 41, 49, 118, 148, 165, 242, 254, 450
corruption 4, 8, 23, 102, 249–50, 264 n.20, 265 n.22, 282, 337, 381–82, 432–33, 438, 441, 444, 460, 463, 471, 491, 493
Côte d'Ivoire 383
Cotonou Agreement 215
cotton 359
Cowen, Mike 78, 254
Cox, Robert 34, 242, 255, 389–90
credit, 'directed' 273, 288–90, 295–96, 299, 303–04, 331–32
 rating 310 n.23
crime 435
culture 213, 293

Daly, Herman 156
debt 258, 261, 399, 402, 438
 cancellation 481, 500, 504
 foreign 345
 international 24
 relief 475, 482–83
 repayments 251–52, 385, 501
Déby, Edriss 491–92
democracy 55, 176, 194, 199, 259, 436, 463
 Asian 23, 336
 liberal 217, 238, 261
 social 391–92
Democratic Republic of Congo (DRC) 22, 30, 31, 40, 259, 412 n.1, 494
democratisation 66, 174, 408, 496
department for international development (DfID) 125, 376, 414, 493
development 73–76, 91 n.7, 158–60, 177–78, 180, 195–96, 204–05, 208, 218, 238, 255–56
 human 69
 Japanese policy 275–77, 335–36
 participatory 467–69
 sustainable 145–66, 238
Dezalay, Y. 129
DfID see department for international development (DfID)
Diwali 440, 442
Dodge Plan 401
Doha 11, 29
Dollar, David 292
DRC see Democratic Republic of Congo (DRC)
Drucker, Peter 159
drugs trade 395
Dryzek, John 150
Duffield, Mark 41, 214, 398, 403, 406
Dumont, René 236
Durban Declaration 485–86

Eagleton, Terry   15–16
East Asia   121, 141, 210, 238, 244, 268–69, 274, 279, 283–87, 290, 292–95, 300, 303, 328–40, 401, 402
   dynamism   340
   financial crisis   317–18, 337–40
   neoliberalism   324, 327–41
   'strategy'   287–88
East Asian Miracle, The   209–10, 228–29, 233, 256, 267–306, 330–31, 333–35
East Timor   41, 220
Economic Development Institute (EDI)   326
Economics, New Institutional   101–02
economy
   Keynesian   *see* Keynes
   neoclassical   101, 329–30, 334
   open   292
Ecuador   484, 491
education   34, 46–50, 69, 85, 101, 106, 109–13, 234, 384, 463, 471–72, 502–03
El Salvador   484
elections   246
Electronic Discussion Forum (EDF – World Bank)   172, 174, 183, 189–93, 195, 198
Empire   445–47
empowerment   456
   local communities   220
empowerment of the poor   88, 176, 180–81, 188–89, 191–92, 196–99, 348, 414, 419, 458, 462–65, 474
energy, renewable   486
environment   48–50, 54, 145–66, 245, 484–85, 496
   enabling   270
Environmental Impact Assessment   151

environmentalism   149
equality, social   384
Eritrea   35, 388
Escobar, A.   177
Estonia   49
Ethiopia   388, 435, 493
ethnic groups   38
Evans, Peter   136, 235–36, 256–59
exchange rates   347, 358
exports   83–84, 290, 294–96, 329, 355
   Less Developed Countries   82
Extractive Industry Review   484

Fanon, Frantz   236, 420, 423–24, 429, 434, 440, 442, 443
farming, peasant   346, 357, 359–60
fascism   28, 44, 48
Ferguson, James   52, 175
finance   159–60, 271
Financial Sector Operations   271
Fine, Ben   17, 19, 35, 53, 134, 139, 140, 406
Fischer, Stanley   488
food crops   358
   export   358–59
   prices   84, 358–59
   production   73, 76, 79, 82–84, 345, 395
Ford Foundation   326
forests   485
Foucault, Michel   20, 99, 146, 196, 197, 253–55, 425, 445
France   487
free market   89, 152, 175, 192, 229, 256, 258, 268, 270, 273–75, 281–82, 287, 295–96, 299, 304, 325, 328, 377, 463, 482
free trade   29, 32, 39, 270, 278
freedom   221
Fukuyama, Francis   130, 143 n.17, 238

G7 483
G8 481–82
Galbraith, John Kenneth 401–02
Gambia, civil service 114–15
Gaza 389
Gellner, Ernest 243, 246, 249, 260
gender equality 13, 174, 384, 433
Georgia (Soviet) 431–32
Germany 223, 487
Ghana 111, 115, 222, 354, 424, 438, 484, 495
  state reform 218–19, 383, 446
Gill, Stephen 325, 389–91, 410
global warming 486
globalisation 29, 31, 116, 140, 150, 173, 214, 239, 249–53, 259, 355, 361, 399, 401, 404
good governance 204–24, 227, 229, 236, 252, 333–34, 350–52, 369–86, 441, 458, 461–65, 471–72, 474, 496
governance, good *see* good governance
governance reform, finance 211
governance states 370–83
  finance 374–75
Gramsci, Antonio 2, 16–17, 19, 28, 30, 42, 48, 55, 146–47, 167 n.2, 231, 390
Gray, John 229
Great Depression 76, 319
Greece 319
Greene, Graham 2
greenhouse gases 485
'greenspeak' 145–66
Group Areas Act 437
growth, sustainable economic 156–58
Gulf War assets 489

Haiti 389
Halliday, Fred 118

Hardt, Michael 419, 426, 429–30, 445, 447
Hayekian dilemma 53, 228, 235, 237, 239, 252–53, 259–61, 391, 393
health 63–64, 69, 85, 234, 397, 471, 502
Heavily Indebted Poor Countries (HIPC) 43–44, 82, 370, 383, 475, 481–82
hegemony 2, 5, 9, 13, 16–19, 22, 41, 55, 166
  American 36, 64
  capitalist 145–49, 165, 228–30
  economic 24, 255–56, 318, 351, 406
  global 27–56
  neoliberal 231
  transnational 36
HIPC *see* Heavily Indebted Poor Countries (HIPC)
Hirschman, Albert 100
Hobsbawm, Eric 78
Holloway, John 421–22, 425
homo oeconomicus 19–20, 22, 31, 53, 97–118, 393
Hong Kong 292–93, 328–29, 335
Human Development Index 8
human rights 12, 44, 174, 215, 220
humanitarianism 41, 389, 393–97, 402, 404
Hungary 484
Huntington, Samuel 243, 256

IBRD *see* International Bank for Reconstruction and Development (IBRD)
illiteracy 178
IMF *see* International Monetary Fund (IMF)

imperialism 40, 140
imports 294, 399
 tariffs 385
income
 gross national 384
 rural 69, 78–79, 357, 368 n.23
 see also wages
India 250, 292, 296, 439, 442, 474, 480, 484
Indonesia 31, 50, 242, 294, 335–36, 338, 481, 488, 502
industrialisation 272, 276, 291–93, 295, 297–99, 303, 323, 328–29, 331–32, 337, 340
inefficiency 337
inflation 321
information, power 187
infrastructure 109, 244, 251, 347, 354, 356–57, 410
institutions, transformation 107–10, 114
interest rates 290, 403, 410
Intermediate Technology 112–13
International Bank for Reconstruction and Development (IBRD) 65, 88, *see also* World Bank
International Development Association 492
International Finance Corporation 49, 65, 87
International Monetary Fund (IMF) 23, 36, 44, 47, 193, 244, 268, 281, 297, 317, 329, 332, 383, 479
 Asian crisis 337–39
 closure? 499–504
 fiscal discipline 252–53
 free-market 482
 globalisation 51
 Japanese contribution 272
 Multilateral Debt Relief Initiative 475

policies 228, 277, 326, 497
 staff selection 482–83, 487–88
 Structural Adjustment Facilities 372
 welfare 200
 World Bank relations 374, 379, 445, 466
International Trade Bureau 298–99
investment 100–01, 250, 252, 275, 458–60, 465, 470, 474–75
 foreign 85, 161, 272, 290, 294, 361
Iraq 2, 9, 12, 13, 19, 22, 28–30, 36–37, 40, 215, 389, 399, 470, 487–89, 494–97
Islamism 20

Jamaica 435
Japan 16, 22, 133, 210, 223, 229, 256, 267–306, 329–33, 401, 487
 aid programmes 271–72, 299, 303, 330–32
 direct credit 331
 East Asian Miracle, The 267–306
 economy 299
 industrial policy 304
 industrialisation 293, 331, 336–37
 US, conflict with 274, 276–77, 280–81, 296, 299, 309 n.15, 331
 World Bank, dispute with 273–84, 289–91, 295–96, 299, 330–33
 yen 272
Japan Development Bank 285
Jubilee Plus 481–82
Jubilee South Africa 482, 497, 500, 503

Kanbur, Ravi 175, 183, 338, 452 n.21
Kant, Immanuel 221
Kenya 78, 359, 383, 435, 493

Index

Keynes, John Maynard   9, 18, 24, 32, 43, 45, 51, 122–23, 237–39, 253–54, 261, 270, 319, 371, 373, 391, 408
Kibaki, Mwai   493
knowledge   158–66, 186
  capital   159
  development   162–63, 195
Knowledge Bank   158–59, 162–63, 165, 169 n.23, 173–74, 199, 238, 255, 351, 445
knowledge gap (North/South)   161, 164
Köhler, Horst   487, 488
Korea   289, 290, 293, 295, 480–81
Kosovo   41, 389
Krueger, Anne   302, 323

labour   77–79, 88, 103, 179, 434, 463
  migrant   428
  rights   75
  skilled   86, 434
  underutilised   100
laissez-faire   20, 54, 229, 235–36, 238–39, 253–54, 270, 293, 400, 403
Lal, Deepak   101
land redistribution, Zimbabwe   13, 259
  reform   380, 452 n.21
  tenure   38, 79, 104–05, 109–10, 179, 234, 347
language power   146–47, 153–58, 162
Lassalle, Ferdinand   71–72
Latin America   319, 328–29, 372, 455, 503
law
  enforcement   441
  rule of   463, 471
Lebanon   389
leftism   426, 429, 430, 439
Lesotho   175, 495

less-developed countries (LDCs)   80–82
Leys, Colin   33, 255, 261, 402–03
liberalisation   268, 355, 358, 385, 439–40
liberalism   53, 203–07, 216–24, 248, 318–20, 326–37
liberation movement (South Africa)   439
Liberia   40, 261
libertarianism   393
List, Friedrich   256, 330
literacy, Ghana   111–12
living standards   64, 68, 71, 74, 76–77, 79, 82–83, 160, 177, 436
local government   116, 189, 220
Lome IV   214

Macedonia   425, 429
macroeconomics   122–23, 244–45, 277, 280, 288, 347, 410
Malaysia   275, 279, 294, 299, 335, 481
Mali   65, 428
Mamdani, Mahmood   400
Mandeville, B.   99
Manuel, Trevor   487–88, 496
Maoism   396
market economy   48–49, 95–110, 113, 116–18, 121–23, 135–36, 141, 151, 159, 179, 234, 238, 294, 322, 326, 347, 373, 436, 446
market-friendly policy   269–70, 278, 285, 287–88, 293–94, 331–32, 361, 387, 393
marketing   109
  authorities, privatisation   83, 108
markets
  free   253
  reform   384
Marshall, Alfred   98

Marshall Plan 319, 401, 403
Marx, Karl 30, 69–73, 390, 434
Marxism 5, 21, 71, 137–38, 238, 249, 391, 400, 418, 443
Mbeki, Thabo 487–88, 498
MCA *see* Millennium Challenge Account (MCA)
McNamara, Robert 51, 160, 177–78, 239, 319–23
McNamara Fellowships 48
Meltzer Commission 475
Merck Pharmaceuticals 49
Mexico 292, 455, 457, 484, 498
microeconomics 122–23
Mieno, Yasushi 276, 332
Milbank, Dana 490
Millennium Challenge Account (MCA) 470–75
Mills, J.S. 235
mining 494, 496
modernisation 318–19, 346–47, 349, 354, 393, 404–05
Moldova 425, 428
Monterrey Consensus 480–83
Morawetz Report 320
Movement for Democratic Change 446
Mozambique 55, 65, 384, 394, 446
governance state 370–71, 373, 376–78, 381–82, 384
Mugabe, Robert 446
Multilateral Agreement on Investment 252
Multilateral Debt Relief Initiative 475
Museveni, Yoweri 12

Narayan, Deepa 125, 182, 185, 414, 422
nationalism 89
Ndungane, *Archbishop* Njongonkulu 499–500

Negri, Antonio 426, 429–30, 445, 447
neoconservativism 23, 77
neoliberalism 10, 17, 22, 36–37, 42–45, 50–51, 54, 77, 140–41, 149–51, 161, 164, 196, 227, 229–31, 240–41, 248, 254, 261, 318–33, 260, 369, 371–75, 380, 383, 389–91, 394–98, 415–17, 432, 437, 442, 457–58, 480, 499
definition 450 n.2
neo-statism 228, 261
New Asian Industries Development Plan 272
Newly Industrialised Countries (NICs) 79
Nicaragua 482
Nietzsche, F.W. 392, 423
Niger Delta, oil 496
Nigeria
banking scam 4
debt 481
oil 496
North American Free Trade Agreement 39
North, Douglass 102, 212
North-East Asia 279, 291, 319
nuts, cashew, Mozambique 394

oil 12, 41, 59 n.22, 320, 399, 402, 486, 488–89, 492
Ecuador 491
Iraq 494–95
pipelines 484, 491
price 491
Orwell, George 145–46, 435
Oxfam 51, 113
ozone layer 155, 157

pain of poverty   424–25, 443, 446
Paine, Tom   250, 260
Pakistan   292, 326
Papua New Guinea   63, 79
paradigm maintenance   300–03
participation, global   189–98
Participatory Poverty Assessments
   (PPAs)   185
Participatory Rural Appraisal
   (PRA)   181–83
Paton, Alan   427
Peru   495
Philippines   115, 222, 273, 292, 299,
   482, 484
Polanyi, Karl   40, 44, 238, 389–91,
   410
police   421, 429, 433, 435, 440, 444,
   448
political economy   135–38
pollution   148, 492
population   80
Post-Conflict Reconstruction   387–88
postmodernism   140, 398–99
post-structuralism   396
poverty   18, 19, 39, 50–51, 54, 63–90,
   100, 109, 155, 161, 320, 322,
   345, 384, 413–52, 455, 462,
   465, 500
  absolute   70, 72, 74, 178
  reduction   155, 160, 171–200, 254,
   339, 441, 456, 458–59, 462,
   481
  relative   67–71
  statistics   81
Poverty Reduction Handbook   179
Poverty Reduction Strategy Papers
   (PRSP)   43, 82, 200, 208,
   211–12, 370, 375, 465–69,
   482–83
Powell, Colin   14, 489
power   16
  knowledge   164
  nuclear   486

  people's   16
  political   156, 443
  of the poor   440
  social   146
  state   217–18, 222, 441
Prebisch, Raul   404
press censorship   408
Preston, Lewis   284, 287, 290–91, 325
price, 'right'   151–53, 234–35, 246,
   345, 347, 353–54
price stabilisation   84, 128, 215
prices   292
  commodities   362, 402
  food   358–59
privatisation   108, 140, 218, 258, 268,
   276, 328, 355, 409, 432, 435–
   36, 438, 491, 494, 497
production   31, 77, 113, 148, 157,
   272, 277, 400, 460, 465
  agricultural   85, 108–09, 347
  capital intensive   329
  commodity   21, 64, 70
  forces of   9, 14, 18, 71, 76, 84, 87
  global   416
  labour extensive   65
  labour intensive   88
  means of   65, 67
  modes of   13, 30–32, 37–38, 40,
   51, 56, 250, 399–400
  peasant   346
  small-holder   54, 66–67, 73, 76–79,
   83, 157, 359–60
productivity   64, 74, 77, 101, 108–10,
   288, 294, 298, 463
proletarianisation   88
property
  registration   116
  rights   152–53, 233, 242–43, 260,
   387, 392, 409, 460, 498–99
prostitution   425, 433–35
Prototype Carbon Fund   485
Putnam, R.   128, 130, 133, 139, 405

racialisation 413
racism 420, 452 n.23
Ramphele, Mamphele 415
rationality, economic 98–105, 107, 112, 114, 116, 118
Rato, Rodrigo 487–88, 496
Reagan, Ronald 321, 488
Reaganism 76, 237–38
reconstruction (states) 40–41, 53, 318, 369–86, 388, 456
   financial 410
   post-conflict 388–411
reflexivity 100, 108, 110
refugees 395
relief, humanitarian 391–95
Reno, W. 403
repression, financial 288–89
revolution, passive 399
Revolutionary United Fronts 392
rice 65, 73
Rivera, Diego 498
Robinson, William 36–39, 53, 415–17, 445
Rockefeller Foundation 326
Rodrik, Dani 292, 295
Rogoff, Kenneth 490
Roy, Arundhati 429
Rumsfeld, Donald 14, 489
Russia 277, 304, 455, 481, 502
Rwanda 12, 40, 388–89, 409

Sachs, Jeffrey 149, 339
Said, Edward 19–20, 421, 423, 426, 434, 445
Saint Francis of Assisi 430
SAPs *see* Structural Adjustment Programmes (SAPs)
Scott, James 254
Seattle (WTO), 1999 37
security firms 406
Sen, Amartya 56, 68–69, 180, 184, 188, 190, 256

services, provision to the poor 258, 419, 464
Shenton, Robert 254
Short, Clare 371, 414
Sierra Leone 22, 31, 40, 65, 261, 388, 398
Singapore 290, 292, 328, 335
slavery 5, 24
smallholdings 76, 78–79, 82–84, 101
Smith, Adam 97–100, 102–07, 110, 113, 129, 256, 330
smoking, United States 441
social capital 124–41, 143 n.11, n.13, 389, 397
social services 86, 397, 424–26
   sub-Saharan Africa 357
socialism 324, 430
Somalia 388
South Africa 38–40, 59 n.23, 261, 435, 439, 480, 487
   debt 481–82
   rand value 481
South-East Asia 278–79, 283, 299, 455
South Korea 268, 272, 326, 328, 334, 338
Southern African Development Community 39
Soviet Union 86, 318–19, 323–25, 372, 435–36
Spain 487
Spivak, Gayatri Chakravorty 186
Stalinists 31
state
   African 206, 229, 231, 251, 255, 261
   development or developmental 12, 23, 133, 135, 138
   and economy 102–03, 114, 238, 253, 328, 330–34, 336–37, 392–93

intervention (in the economy) 286–87, 293–97, 331–33, 401–02
national 39, 66–67, 73, 83–84, 89, 103, 124, 152, 416, 500
reform, Africa 227–32, 251, 259–61, 348–50, 369–85
transnational or global ix, 9, 19, 29, 34, 37, 41, 56, *see also* transnational, state
State in a Changing World, The 227–61, 336–37, 329, 403
states
governance 369–85
reform 369–86, 404, 456
sub-Saharan Africa 343–63
Third World 256–57
Stern, Ernest 323–24
Stiglitz, Joseph 11, 23, 51, 121–22, 131–33, 140, 212, 222, 230, 289, 338–39, 351, 404–05, 407, 408, 415, 461, 480, 498, 499
structural adjustment 270, 343, 346, 348–57, 361–63, 364 n.4, 392, 398, 403, 410, 415, 437, 439, 450 n.4, 454–57, 482, 504
loans 270
Structural Adjustment Participatory Review Initiative (SAPRI) 484
Structural Adjustment Programmes (SAPs) 43, 203, 205, 346–63, 372, 383
Structural Impediments Initiative 274
sub-Saharan Africa 322
development 345–63
labour 85
subsidies 11, 34, 64–65, 93 n.28, 151, 153, 274, 276, 299, 304, 354, 356, 436, 491
First World 11

Sudan, relief 397
Suharto 9, 488
Summers, Lawrence 11, 22, 275, 284–85, 288, 290, 331
sustainability 111, 145–66, 254, 347, 400
'sustaindevelopment' 148–58, 161–62, 164–66

Taiwan 268, 272, 290, 292–93, 328, 335
Tanzania 18, 55, 65, 127, 346, 354, 358, 384
governance state 370, 373–76, 378, 381
women 429
taxation 116
agriculture 354, 367 n.20
Ghana 219
Philippines 115
taxes 248
collection 398
terrorism 398
Thailand 36, 242, 294, 335, 338, 435, 481, 502
Thatcher, Margaret 320–21
Thatcherism 76, 237–38
Third World 2, 37, 39, 42, 51, 217, 237, 319
capitalism 14, 240
corruption 12, 240–41
debt 11, 250, 480–81
development 391, 404, 408, 480
industry 52
state 256
transformation 11, 14, 239–40, 247–48, 256, 407
Tilly, Charles 400
Togo 424
Toye, J. 352, 353
trade unions 220, 235, 463
transformation of the state 114–17, 406

transnational
  capital   *see* capital, transnational
  class   27–30, 32, 37, 45, 50, 52, 57 n.10
  hegemony   *see* hegemony, transnational
  institutions   265 n.24, 317
  intelligentsia   46
  order   415
  state   ix, 5, 9, 24, 25 n.6, 27–28, 32, 36, 38, 39, 40–42, 53, 62 n.43, 416–17, 443, *see also* state, transnational or global
transnationalism   417
Turkey   292, 319, 481
Twain, Mark   250

Uganda   18, 40, 55, 216, 359, 370–71, 373, 384, 439, 482–84, 496
  governance state   370, 373, 375–76, 378, 381–84
Ul Haq, Mahbub   322
United Nations (UN)   401–02, 406
UN Conference on Environment and Development, Rio de Janeiro, 1992   155
UN Conference on the Human Environment, Stockholm, 1972   155
UN Conference on Trade and Development (UNCTAD)   80–81
UN Food Programme   402
UN High Commissioner for Refugees (UNHCR)   41, 394, 402
UN Millennium Development Goals   481
UN Security Council   37, 41
unemployed/unemployment   64–65, 72–77, 79, 84, 87, 174, 399, 419, 424, 435

United States (US)   56, 256, 268, 270–72, 296, 298, 319, 326–27, 329, 453, 473
  9/11   29, 339
  capital   36
  economy   302
  foreign aid   339, 491
  power   50, 281, 318, 325, 333
  Right   474–75
  Treasury   36, 44, 326, 338, 352, 483
US Agency for International Development (USAID)   446
University of Durban-Westville   440
urbanisation   25 n.13
Uruguay Round   11, 385
US   *see* United States (US)

Van der Walle, N.   352, 355
Venezuela   292
Vietnam   37, 80, 319, 401
Voices of the Poor   174, 184–89, 198, 413–14, 417–49

Wa Thiong'o, Ngugi   2
Wade, Robert   16–18, 27, 34, 44, 46, 52, 133, 193, 199, 228–30, 255–56, 326, 361
wages   70–73, 79, 106, 242–43, 292–93, 357, 382, 431, 459
Wapenhams Report   209
war
  Africa   398–403, 409
  economy   395–96, 399–401
  Iraq   489, 497
warlords   398, 406
warming, global   155
Washington Consensus   32, 58 n.13, 121–22, 131–38, 150, 168 n.11, 172, 175, 180, 192, 198–99, 201 n.7, 230, 245, 270, 305, 338, 344, 351, 404, 455, 472, 480, 486, 504

Index

waste, toxic   485
water   65, 109, 111, 153, 394, 423, 438–39, 452 n.24, 484–85, 495, 502–03
  privatisation   439
weapons of mass destruction   488–89
West Africa
  Onchoceriasis Control Programme   64
  relief   397
Wolfensohn, James   2, 9–12, 14, 17–18, 51, 63, 68, 160, 174, 183–84, 208, 210–11, 238, 255, 261, 263 n.12, 326, 338–39, 389, 414, 416, 428, 430, 444, 453–54, 456–69, 472–74, 479–80, 486–99
Wolfowitz, Paul   2, 9–10, 14, 18, 23, 453–55, 470–71, 474–75, 479, 486, 488–98, 504
women
  abuse   432–34, 444
  labour, migrant   428–29, 434
  protests   440
  status   221, 410, 428, 433–34, 441
World Bank
  accountability   362
  Africa policy   3–4, 10, 114, 228–32, 255, 346–63
  Articles of Agreement   207, 210
  autonomy   269, 305–06
  Bonds Boycott   503–04
  development plans   3, 6–8, 12–15, 44, 52, 64, 107, 109, 115–16, 121–41, 209, 227–61, 318–21, 325–27, 339–40, 345–63
  development strategy   268–79, 302, 442, 453–55, 473
  expenditure   58 n.20
  financial sector   61 n.41, 91 n.3, 271
  General Legal Counsel   211
  Groups   91 n.2
  hegemony   353
  Knowledge Bank   50, 158–66, 172
  omnipotence   353
  Operations Evaluation Department (OED)   209
  policies   3–4, 8, 140, 281–83, 327, 465
  Post-Conflict Unit (PCU)   389, 394
  Public Sector Group   211
  reform   499–504
  staff   46–47, 281–82, 297, 300, 306, 314 n.45, 323, 326–27, 453–75, 483–84
World Bank Day   6
World Bank Participation Sourcebook, The   174, 181, 201 n.5
World Commission on Dams   484
World Development Movement   482
World Development Report 1987   270, 323
World Development Report 1991   275, 285, 287, 293, 323, 332
World Development Report 1997   227–61, 336–37, 392
World Development Report 2000/1   63–90, 184, 188, 192–200
World Development Report 2005   454, 458–61
World Development Report 2006   498
World Summit on Sustainable Development, Johannesburg, 2002   154–55, 165
World Trade Organisation (WTO)   29, 37, 39, 43, 252, 419, 445, 502

Zambia   250
Zenawi, Meles   493
Zimbabwe   13, 25 n.4, 220, 259–61, 359, 383, 446, 484